JAMES T. &
KARLA L. MURRAY

Vinyl NYC

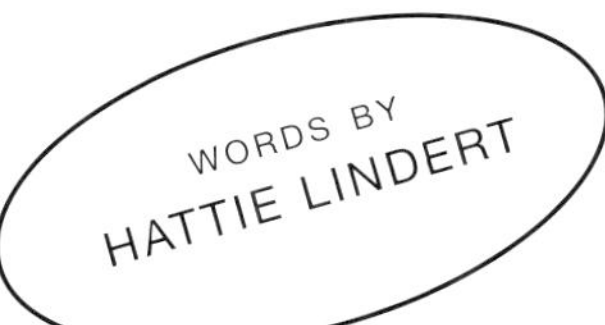

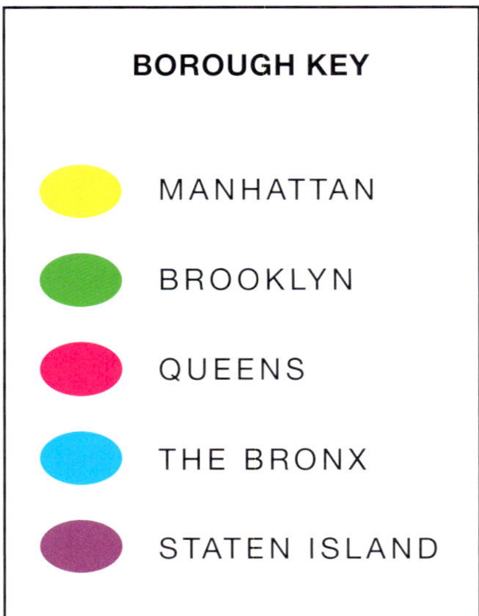
BOROUGH KEY
MANHATTAN
BROOKLYN
QUEENS
THE BRONX
STATEN ISLAND

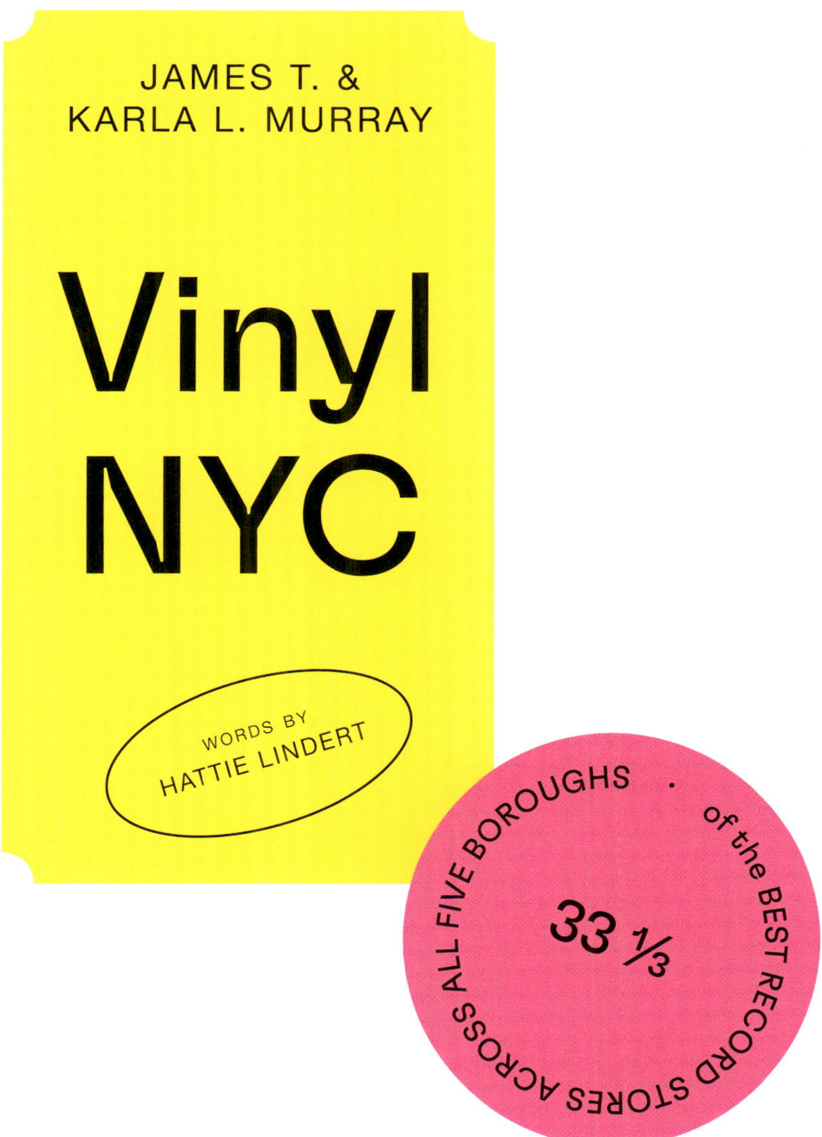

PRESTEL

MUNICH · LONDON · NEW YORK

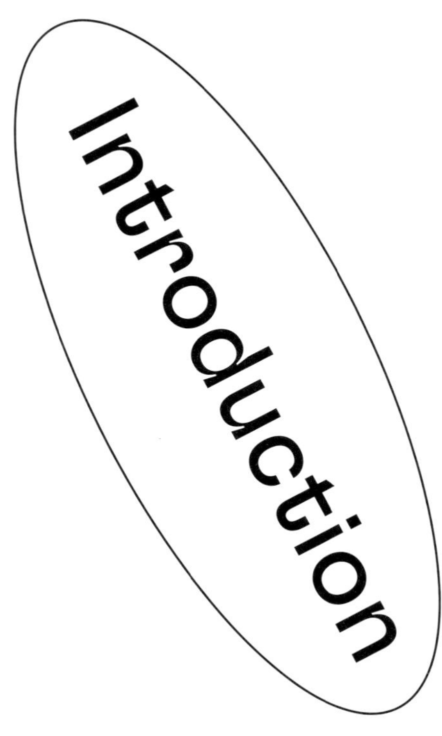

WE'VE BEEN DOCUMENTING NEW YORK CITY'S culture and beloved small neighborhood businesses for decades and have shared this work in our critically acclaimed books, including *Store Front NYC: Photographs of the City's Independent Shops, Past and Present*. Most recently, we concentrated on the city's bars with our publication *Great Bars of New York City: 30 of Manhattan's Favorite Storied Drinking Establishments*. However, our mutual love for independently owned vinyl record stores goes back much further, to our childhoods. We both remember eagerly awaiting the opportunity to go shopping for vinyl at our local mom-and-pop record shops, most often searching the racks of 45s, as an entire album was too extravagant a purchase at the time. Throughout the 1990s as a married couple, we continued to search for vinyl, concentrating our collection on 12-inch singles, as LPs were still a luxury item for us.

Although we witnessed firsthand the closing of many of our favorite record stores in New York City in the early 2000s (due to vinyl's waning popularity at the time, coupled with ever-increasing rents), we've been excited to see a more recent resurgence of these shops. Not only have we noticed that older stores, which have endured through the changing tides of musical artists, genres, and formats, have broadened and increased their inventory, but many new shops devoted to vinyl have opened in the past few years, especially in Manhattan and Brooklyn.

Similar to the spots we featured in our *Great Bars of New York City* book, the Big Apple's record stores provide a sense of community and are true melting pots, places where people from all backgrounds and musical tastes can mingle and share stories and recommendations. The person digging next to you could be discovering the joy of vinyl for the first time or may even be a legendary musician, producer, or DJ searching for inspiration and new beats or grooves. Entering a vinyl shop always offers an escape from the hustle and relentless pressures of life. Here, problems are left behind and the sole focus is on listening to music, possibly finding something new being spun on the in-store decks or discovering an exciting label or artist among the racks and bins.

Crate diggers (ourselves included) are always on the never-ending search to find that "black gold." They are driven by the thrill of the hunt and the hope of finding a long-forgotten musical treasure that perhaps accompanied them during a certain phase or time in life that they can now return to. Or else, they're looking to discover a new album, leading to further exploration and even more sonic enjoyment. Record Store Day, the annual event celebrating the culture of the independently owned record shop, with its special limited edition vinyl pressings, also keeps collectors on the lookout. Whether it's rock, hip-hop, electronic, punk, jazz, pop, house, funk, or reggae, they are all at your fingertips in these shops.

The number of record stores we feature in this book is a nod to 33⅓ revolutions per minute (RPM), the standard playing speed for long play (LP) vinyl records. When selecting the locations, we decided to showcase stores in all five boroughs, including both long-standing historic establishments and newer shops. In these pages you'll find well-known neighborhood destinations like A-1 Record Shop, which we consider to be one of the best spots in Manhattan for used vinyl; Casa Amadeo, the longest-running Latin music store in New York City, located in the Bronx; and VP Records, the iconic reggae, dancehall, and soca music shop and distributor in Queens. We've also included many newer businesses that have opened since 2021, including Paradise of Replica, a hidden second-floor gem on Manhattan's Lower East

Side named after a Japanese avant-garde album, and Billy's Record Salon in East Williamsburg, Brooklyn, with its living room-like feel, which has quickly become known for its preloved selection of jazz, funk, and soul.

Other stores we feature have found unique niche markets in which to set themselves apart and thrive. This includes Jazz Record Center in Manhattan's Chelsea neighborhood, which, despite being located on the eighth floor of a commercial building with no exterior signage, has managed to survive since 1983. There's also Face Records in Williamsburg, Brooklyn, which sells a highly curated selection of titles by Japanese artists, as well as Manhattan45, the only shop in New York City that exclusively sells new vinyl records, with a focus on electronic dance music.

We've additionally included shops which have thoughtfully diversified their offerings to further attract customers and entice them to spend more time inside. A couple examples of this are Black Star Vinyl in Brooklyn's Bed-Stuy, where you can go crate-digging with a side of coffee and pastries plus purchase candles and incense, and Black Gold Records in Carroll Gardens, also in Brooklyn, which, in addition to selling coffee alongside its vinyl, offers up antiques, oddities, and vintage clothing.

All of the photography included in this book was completed in 2024, as we wanted to focus on shops that are currently in business. However, there are many more noteworthy vinyl record stores in the five boroughs to visit, particularly in lower Manhattan and in a wide array of neighborhoods in Brooklyn.

We spent hours in the stores featured on these pages, making our own musical selections before heading home to partake in what we refer to as our "Japanese tea ceremony." First, we give reverence and time to examining and admiring a record's jacket (sometimes we choose unfamiliar vinyl solely based on its artwork). We then slowly pull out the inner sleeve to read the lyrics and study the liner notes, and then gently clean the vinyl, being careful not to leave any fingerprints. Next, we place it on the turntable and softly drop the needle on the record to finally listen, only stopping to flip from side A to B.

We hope this book encourages you to go out and explore the city's many independent vinyl record shops, letting the music, memories, and new discoveries move you so that these stores can stay in business for generations to come. And next time you contemplate whether or not to purchase some vinyl at your local shop, try to remember the motto at Human Head Records in Bushwick, Brooklyn: "Records before rent."

JAMES T. & KARLA L. MURRAY

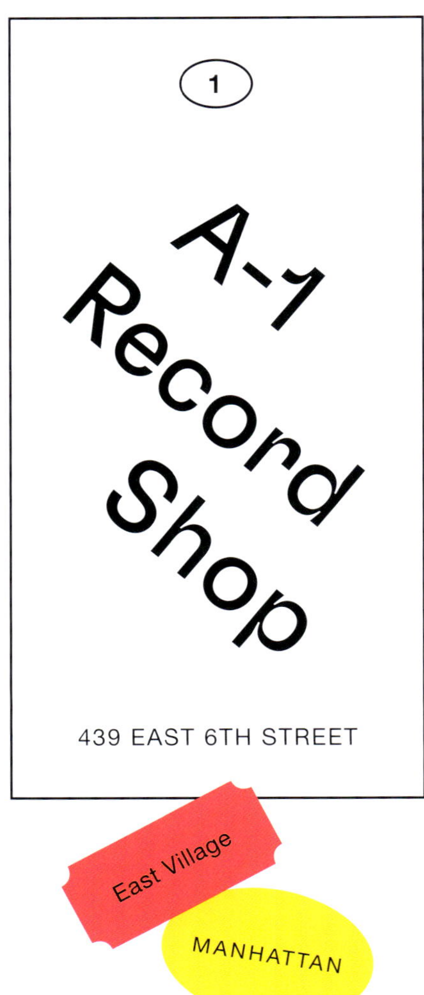

EVERY NEW YORK CRATE-DIGGING EXPEDITION starts somewhere, and you'll be hard-pressed to find a better spot to begin than A-1 Record Shop. Established in 1996 by veteran collector Isaac Kosman, A-1 welcomes first-time shoppers and legendary selectors alike to engage in the two words painted over its doors: "seek" and "find."

Born and raised in the Philadelphia suburbs, Kosman began his vinyl career at Bard College, hawking records and literature outside the dining hall with a group he called Books Brothers. When he moved to New York in 1983, he brought the hustle with him, tabling outside Columbia before graduating to a regular spot at the Chelsea Flea Market through the '80s—then a by-appointment, rented space for bulk deals in an old sewing factory—to a first real storefront on 17th Street. By the time he opened A-1 at 439 East 6th Street, he had a robust collection and a client list to match: college kids, European dealers, and flea market regulars all hip to his taste for jazz, soul, and funk. "The day we opened," Kosman recalls, "people flooded in."

This happened to be during the halcyon days of vaunted local producers like DJ Premier and Pete Rock. Soon, the sounds of A-1 became the sounds of New York hip-hop, transforming the modest insiders-only store into a genre lynchpin, influencing everyone from Grandmaster Melle Mel to the Alchemist. On any given day at the shop, which only stocks used vinyl and select reissues, it's also no surprise to brush elbows with one of the many pioneers it counts among its customers: RZA, Questlove, LL Cool J, Mobb Deep, Grandmaster Caz. But Kosman holds a special place in his heart for one regular: DJ Danny Krivit, who has been giving A-1 his business since the Chelsea Flea Market days, when he'd buy up to three hundred pieces at a time. "He was the first obsessive collector I encountered who made it seem like, 'Hey, I could actually make a business out of this!'" Kosman recalls. "He was the embodiment of records before rent."

A-1's hip-hop collection may rival any in the city, but the decades-old shop hasn't thrived in just one lane. "I think we try to have something for everyone," Kosman shares. "We're not a pricey boutique with only fancy records." For many international DJs only in New York for a brief stay, A-1 is the logical first stop to nail down some heat ahead of a big set, knowing that somewhere among its roughly twenty-thousand-record floor stock is the fuel needed to please virtually any crowd. Look up while perusing the bins inside, and you'll even find records plastered to the ceiling.

"A-1 is special because they're experts in all the genres they stock," Justin Carter, a DJ and promoter who co-founded the beloved Ridgewood club Nowadays, told music site *XLR8R* in 2019. "It's rare to go into a shop and find well-curated selections in so many different directions." Even A-1's overflow merits its own annex—with the help of his daughter, Kosman founded a Paris location, A-One Paris, in 2023.

These days, the flagship A-1 runs thanks to a vibrant employee roster of vinyl heads, including Jeremie Delon, who refers to his role as "senior guy." The staff's hobbyist devotion shines through in the store's omnivorous selection, as attentive to $2 classics and an all-weather outdoor table as the limited-edition gems featured along the wall. In one of the most expensive cities in the world, Kosman knows the worth of carrying "a great Aretha [Franklin] record for $20, which hardly buys you a burger today."

Great records, Kosman and his team know well, beget great artists. Any ascendant producer needs the right raw material for their technique to shine—and there's a reason most of New York's brightest start their search behind the sticker-laden windows on 6th Street. Per Kosman, the shop's rap canon "approaches comprehensiveness." But after decades of discovery, he can count himself among the city's greatest wellsprings of information. As veteran crate-digger and owner of reissue label 180 Proof DJ Amir told *XLR8R*, "Hip-hop owes a lot to A-1 Records."

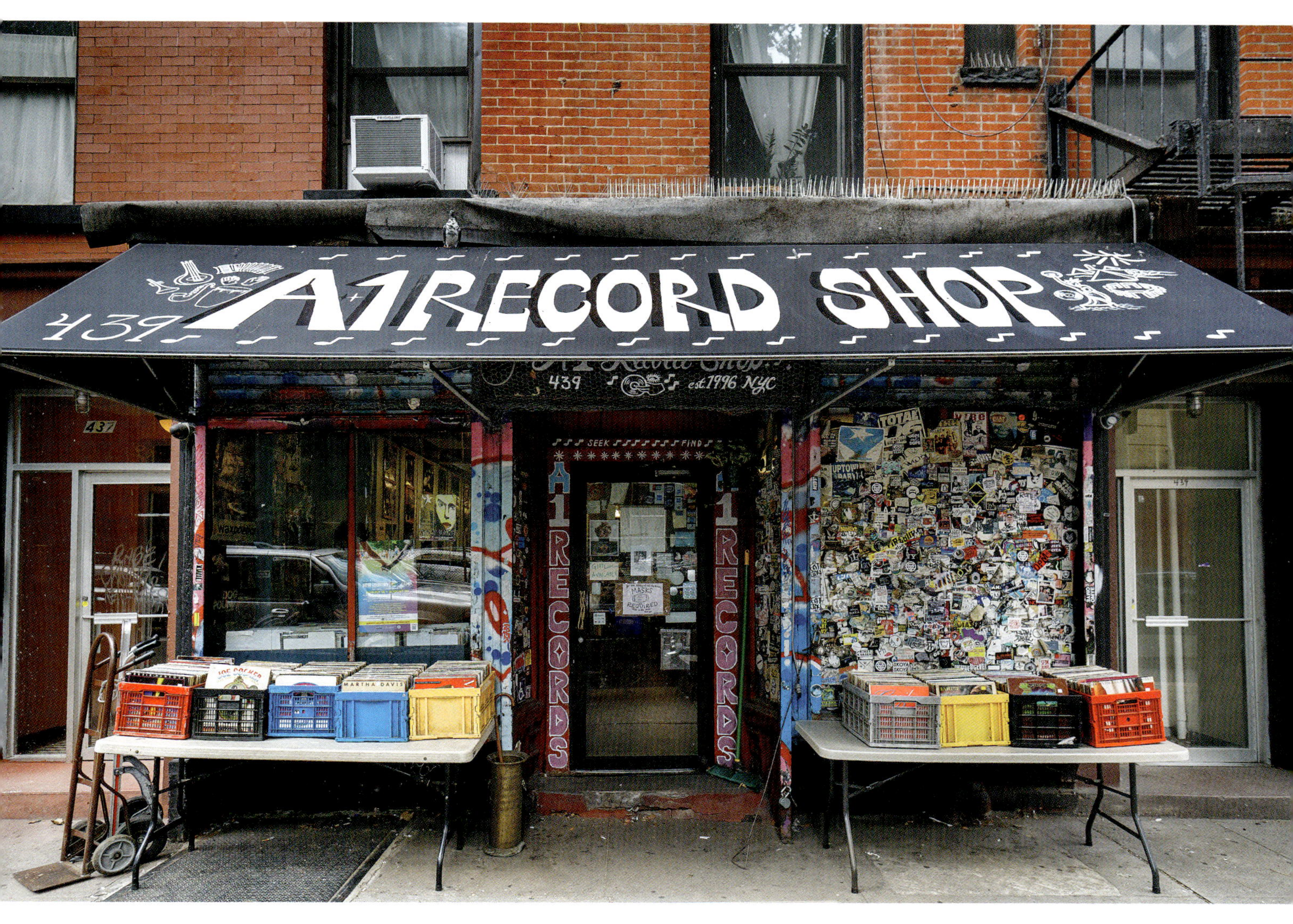

ABOVE A-1 Record Shop was founded in 1996 by Isaac Kosman and is well-known among DJs, producers, and collectors as one of the best spots for crate-digging. Tables are set up daily outside the shop, selling LPs for $2 and up.

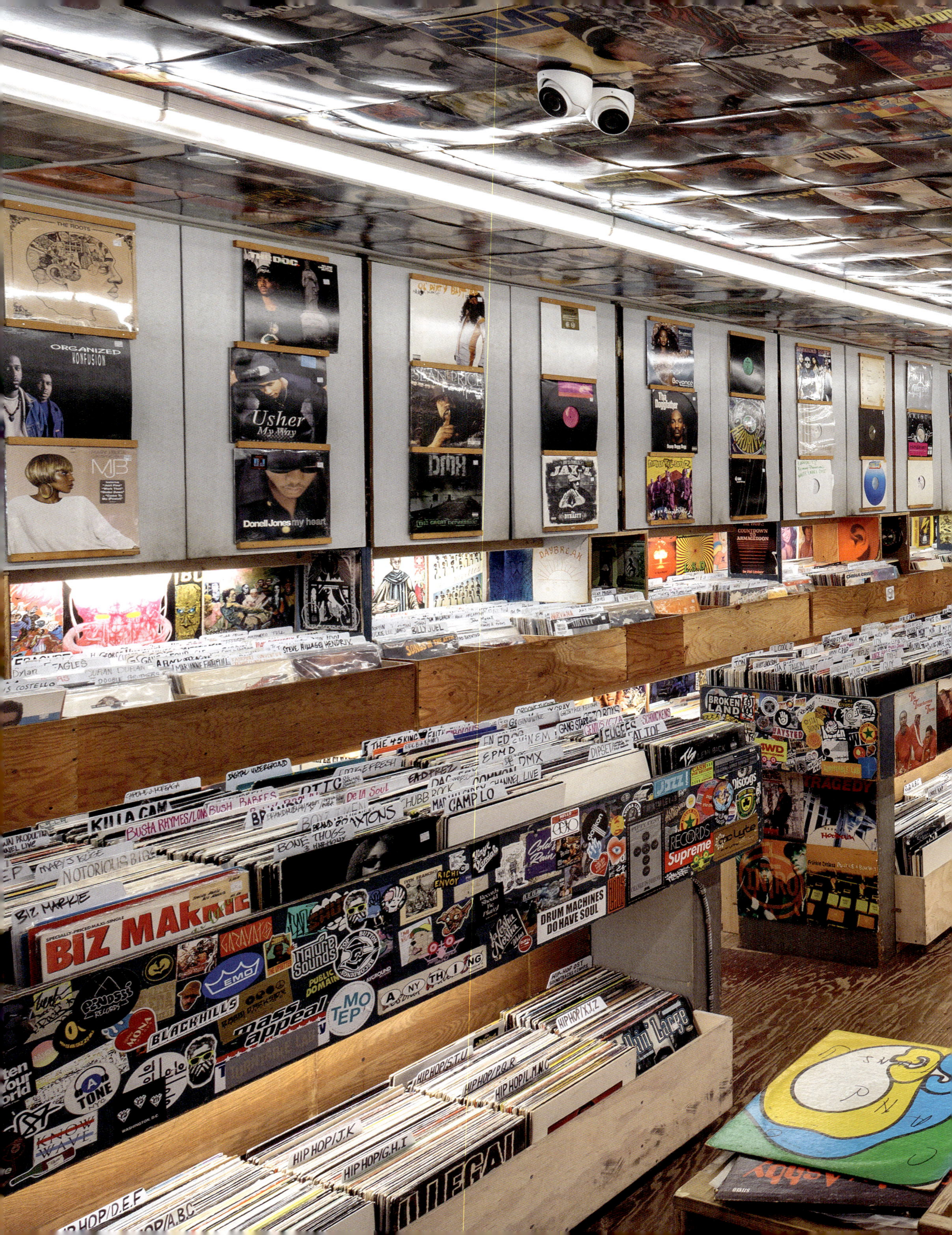

THE ROOTS
ORGANIZED KONFUSION
Usher
My Way
Donell Jones my heart
DMX
Beyoncé
JAY-Z
BILLY JOEL
STEVE HILLAGE
HENDRIX
EAGLES
DOUBLE
COSTELLO
KILLA CAM
BUSTA RHYMES/LONE
NOTORIOUS BIG
BIZ MARKIE
BIZ MARKIE
EPMD
CAMP LO
DMX
COMMON
DIPSET
FUGEES
De La Soul
BONE THUGS
TRAGEDY
Supreme
RECORDS
DRUM MACHINES
DO HAVE SOUL
EMD
Nature Sounds
PUBLIC DOMAIN
MO TEP
mass appeal
BLACKHILL'S
HIP HOP/X.Y.Z
HIP HOP/S.T.U
HIP HOP/P.Q.R
HIP HOP/L.M.N
HIP HOP/J.K
HIP HOP/G.H.I
HOP/D.E.F
ILLEGAL

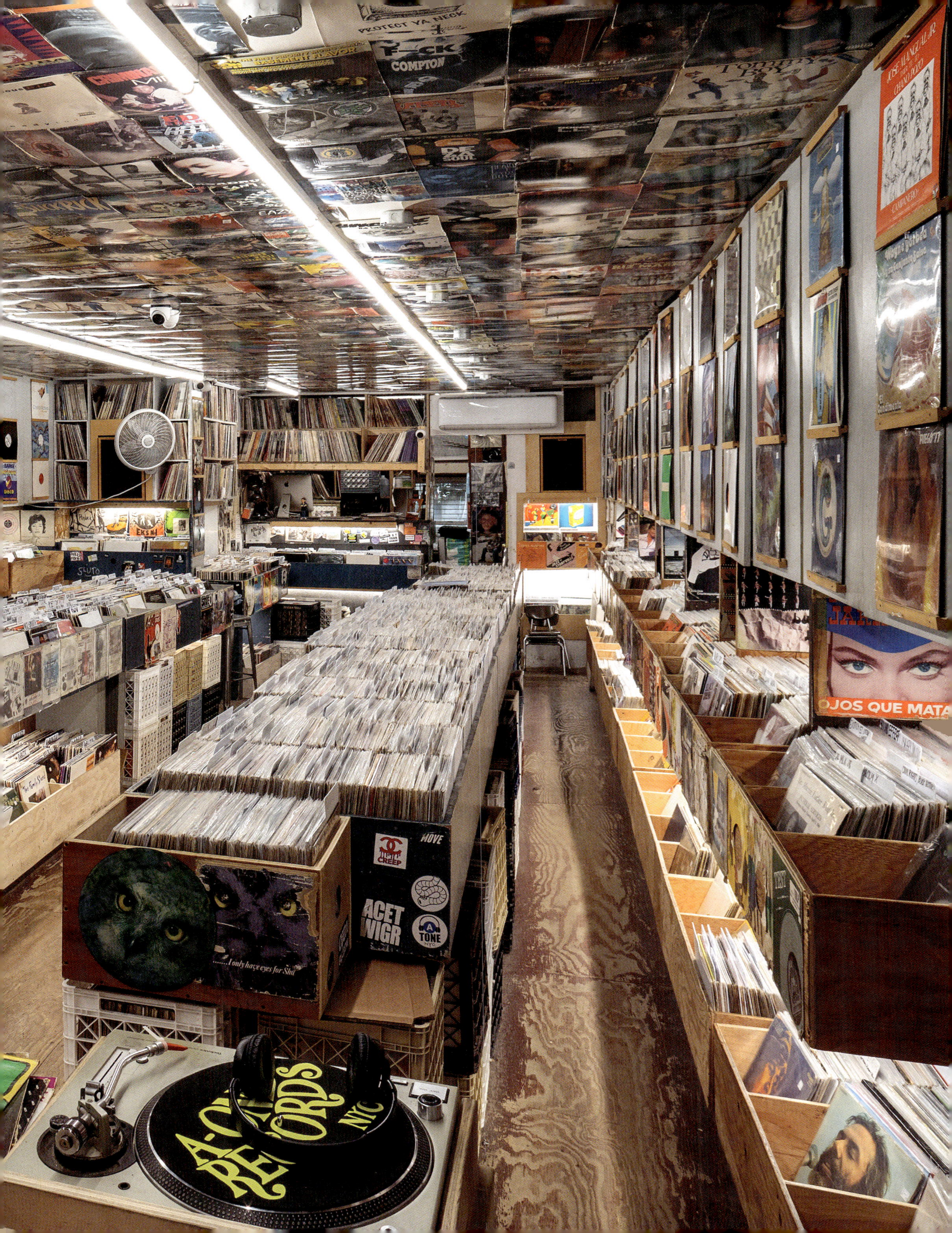
PROTECT YA NECK
COMPTON
OJOS QUE MATA
CREEP
TONE
NYC

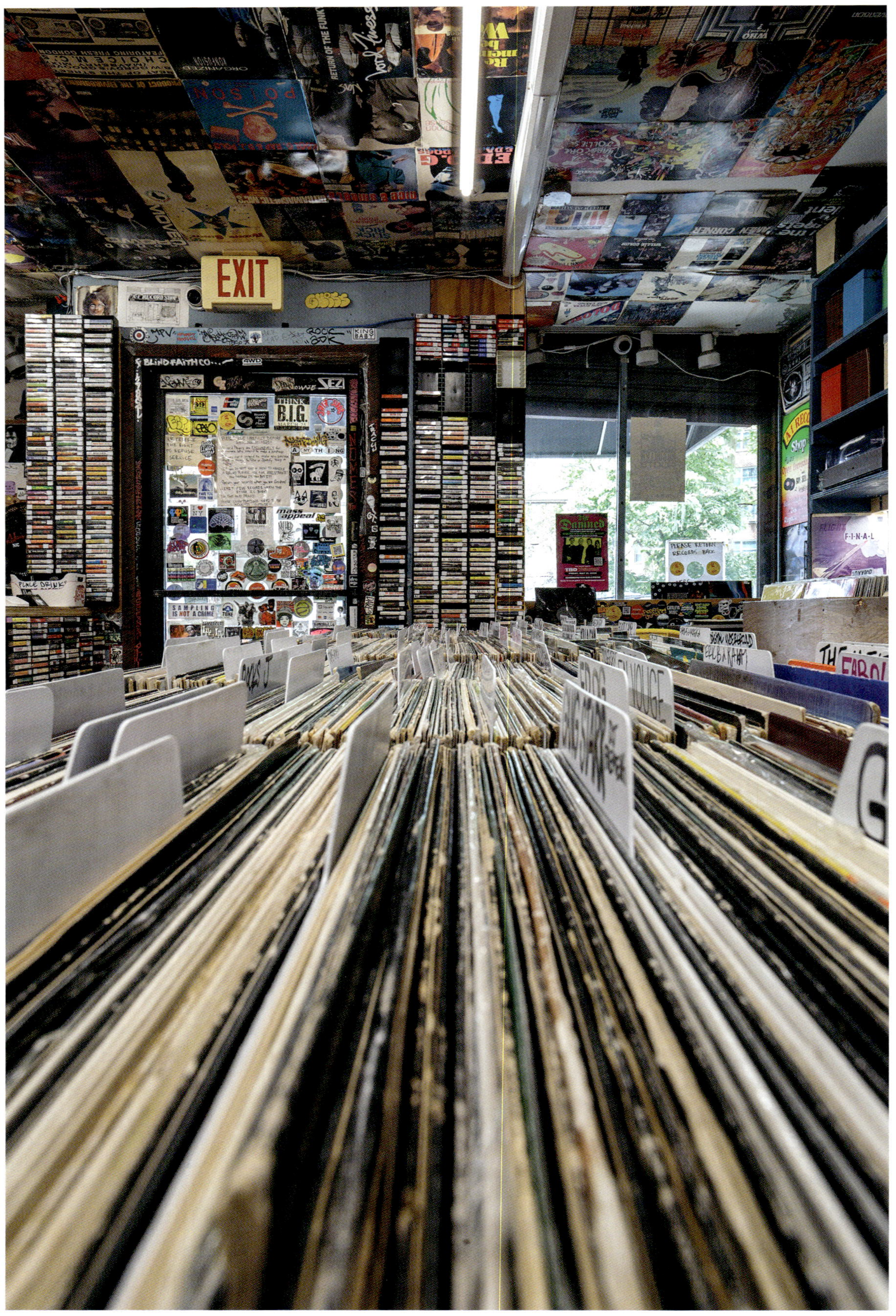
EXIT
B.I.G.
mass appeal
SAMPLING IS NOT A CRIME
Damned
PLEASE RETURN RECORDS BACK
F·I·N·A·L

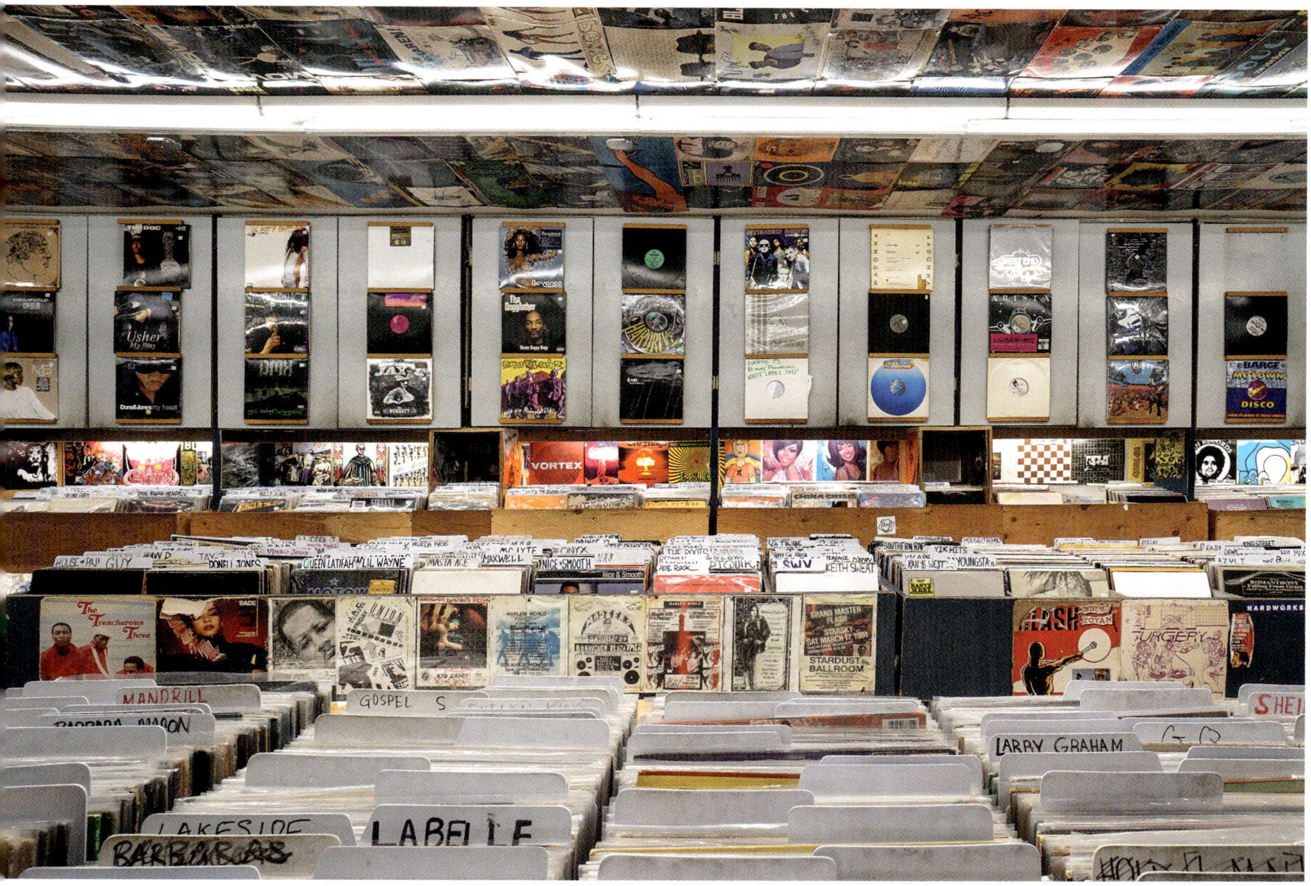

PREVIOUS SPREAD A-1 sells only secondhand and reissued records and has one of the broadest and largest selections in the city, including hip-hop, soul, funk, jazz, reggae, disco, and house.

RIGHT Seth "Shef" Yamasaki has been working at A-1 since 2004. He can usually be found sorting the inventory, which is organized with handwritten dividers into genres, artists, and record labels.

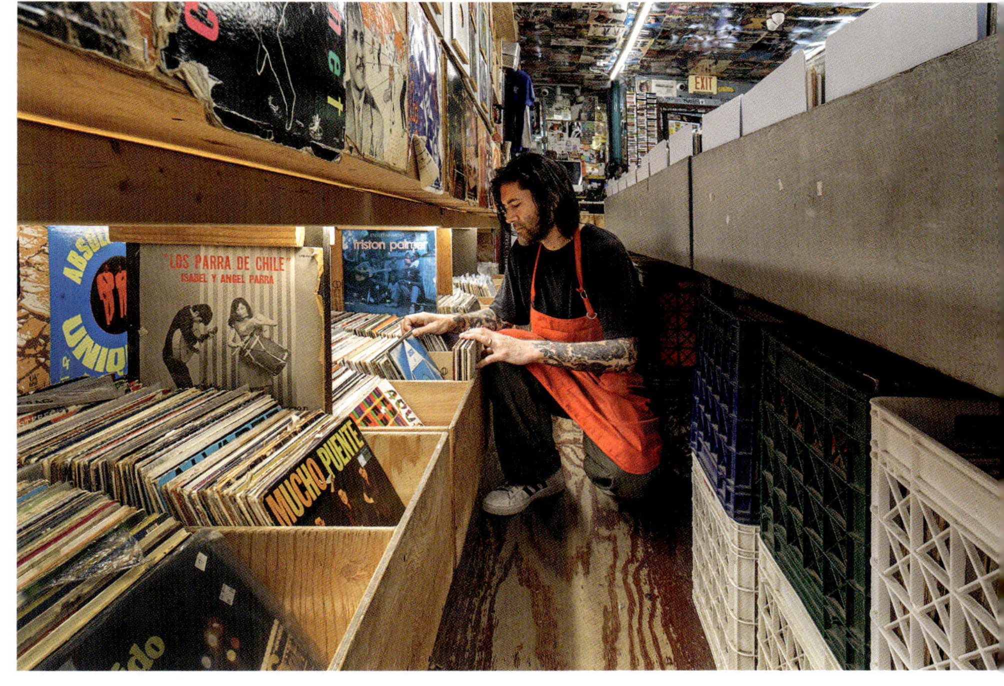

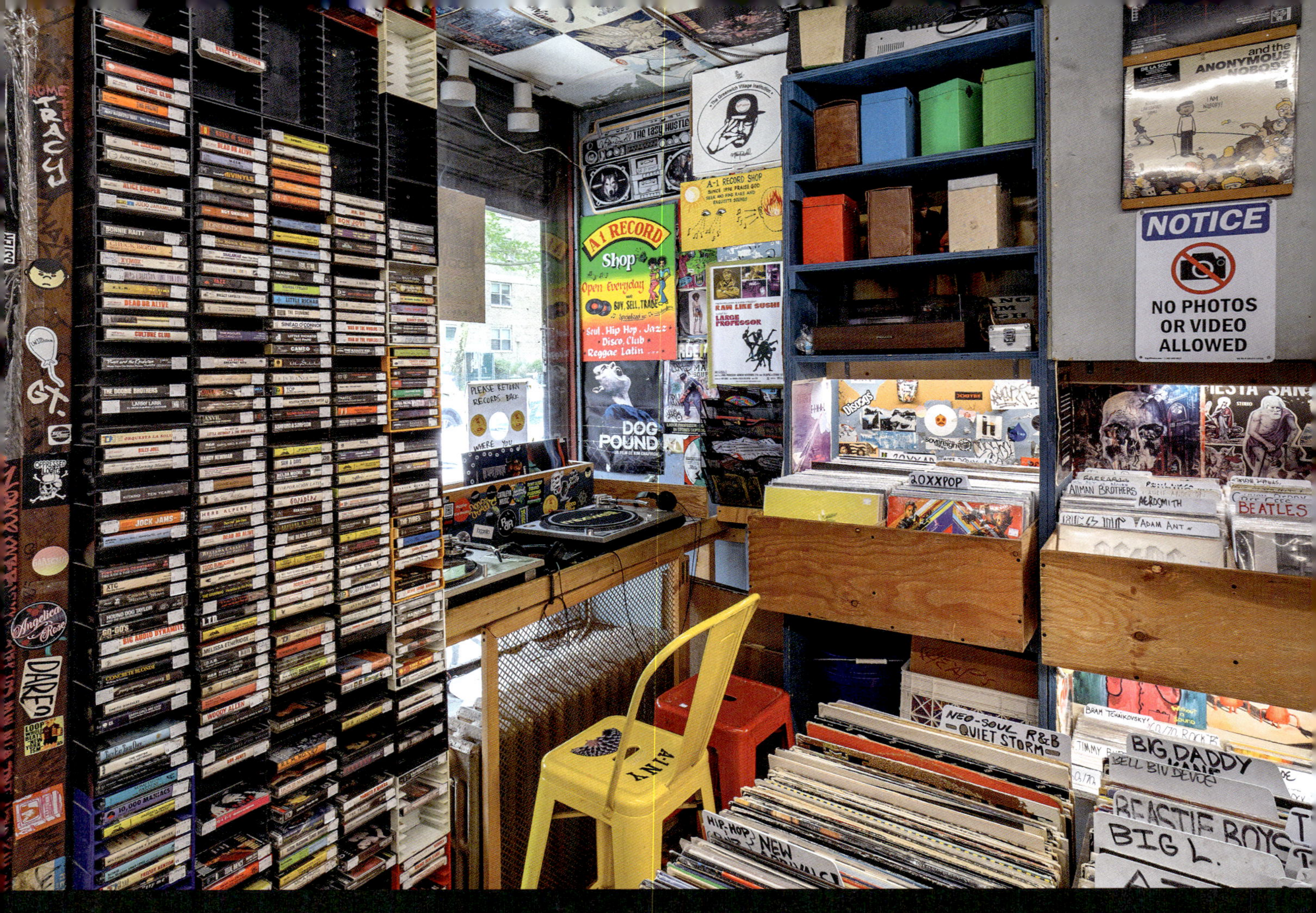

"I like being surrounded by art, that environment and that feeling—when you go to a museum or something, and in the section that you love, there's a kind of peace. In our apartment, my kids are growing up with records surrounding them everywhere they look."

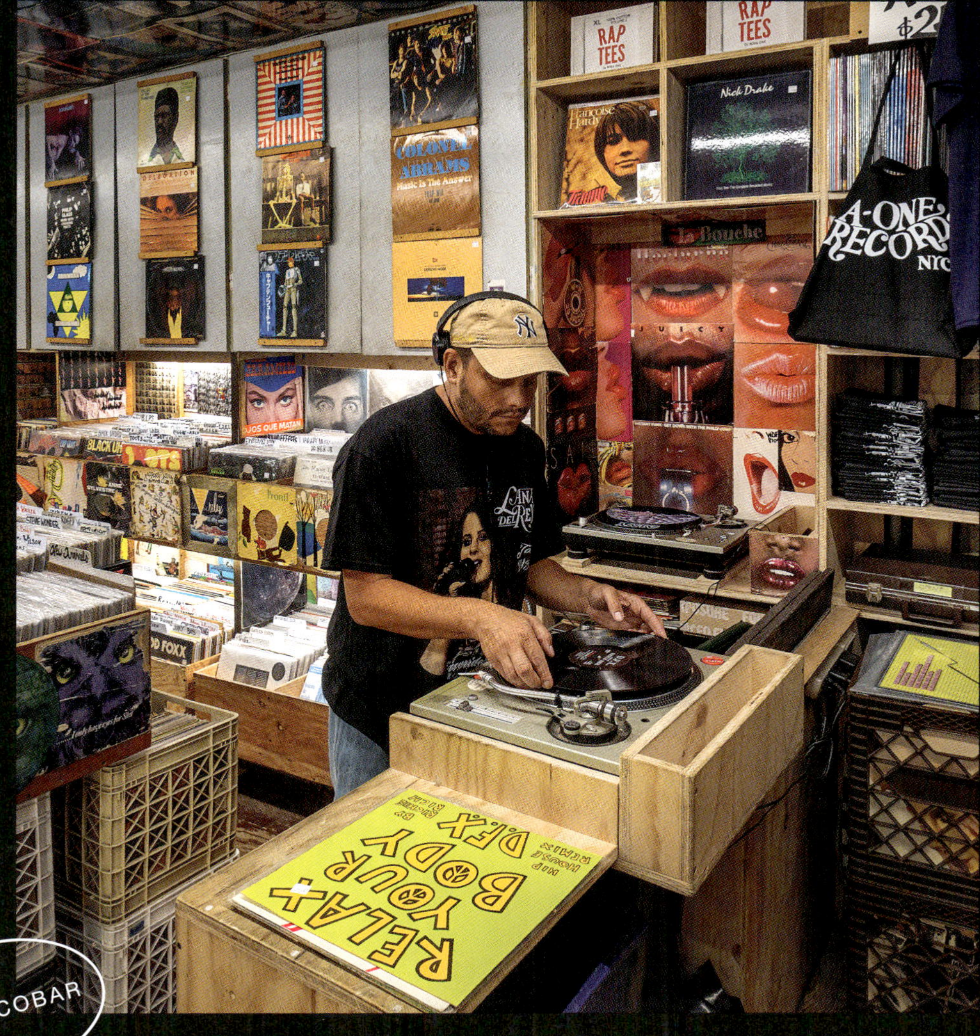

ELI ESCOBAR

DJ, PRODUCER, AND CO-OWNER OF GABRIELA NIGHTCLUB

Eli Escobar may have been born in the Bronx, but his childhood belonged to Manhattan, where he was raised. It was as a preteen that he discovered his penchant for record collecting through a passion for hip-hop, gathering West Coast radio classics—and eventually, the soul and disco cuts they sampled—the way his peers collected baseball cards. By the time he inherited his first DJing equipment as a high school senior, he'd already spent years studying the seamless mixes of his heroes on the independent radio station WFMU.

Over the years, Escobar has amassed a serious enough collection to withstand a decades-long career in dance music, in part by making a pilgrimage to A-1 every week since it first opened. He now leads Saturday services at the city's top-tier clubs like Le Bain, Good Room, and House of Yes. Known for roiling house and disco sets that can fill the dance floor all day, all night, or both, he also co-hosts the beloved party Tiki Disco, which has run at various venues across Brooklyn since 2009. He's released solo work with labels like Nervous and Strictly Rhythm, and in 2014 put out an acclaimed LP, *Up All Night*, through his club-night-turned-label imprint Night People. In late 2023 he even co-founded his own club in Williamsburg called Gabriela. The way Escobar sees it, his career might not look the same without the crop of curated secondhand record stores that emerged in New York in the late '90s. He recalls: "For DJs, it was like a godsend."

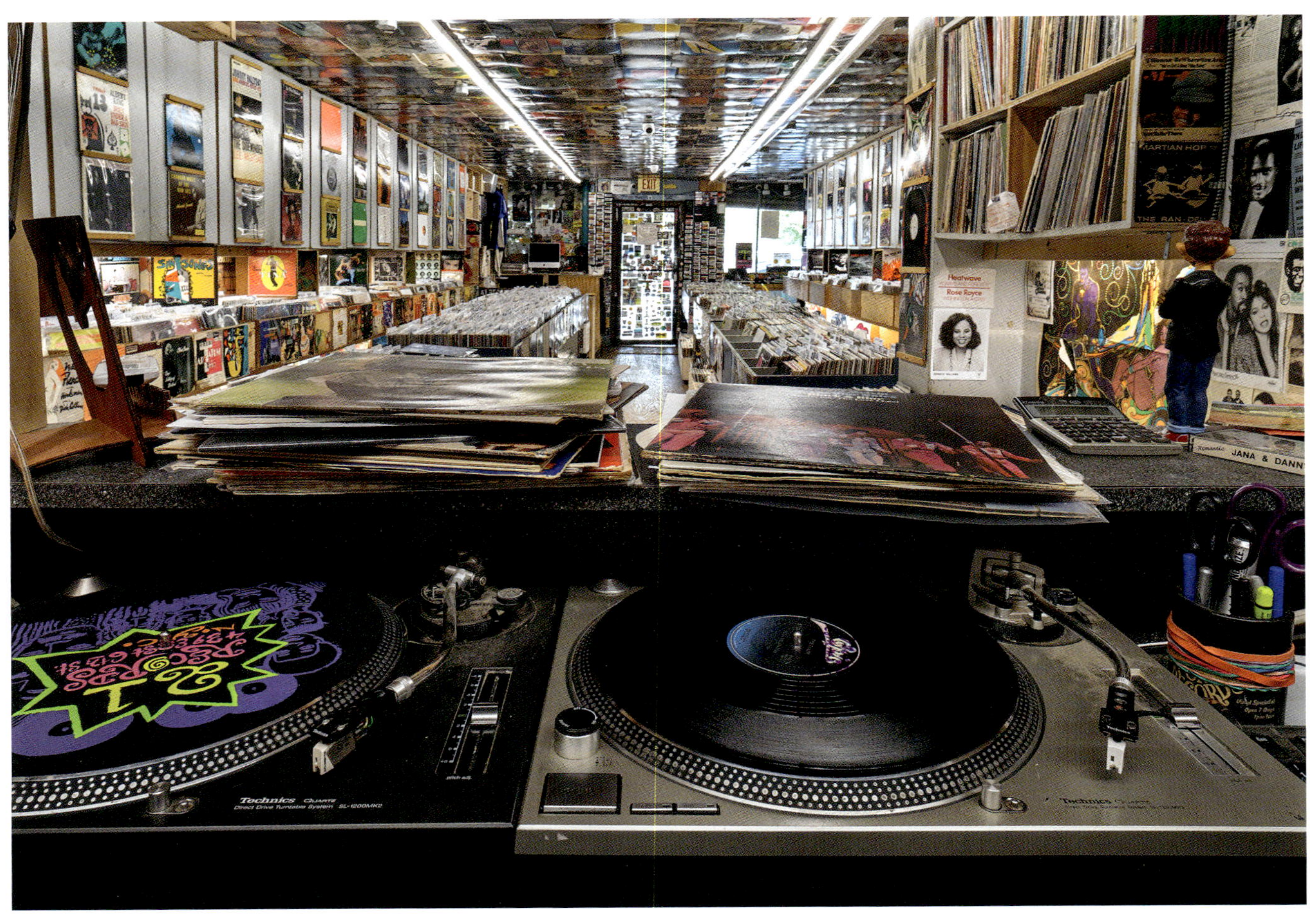

ABOVE Records are always playing from the decks at the back of the shop, which can encourage the discovery of new music.

OPPOSITE BOTTOM Almost every surface of A-1 is covered with music-related items, including stickers, photos, and memorabilia of many of the famous artists who have shopped there over the years. There are even album covers on the ceiling.

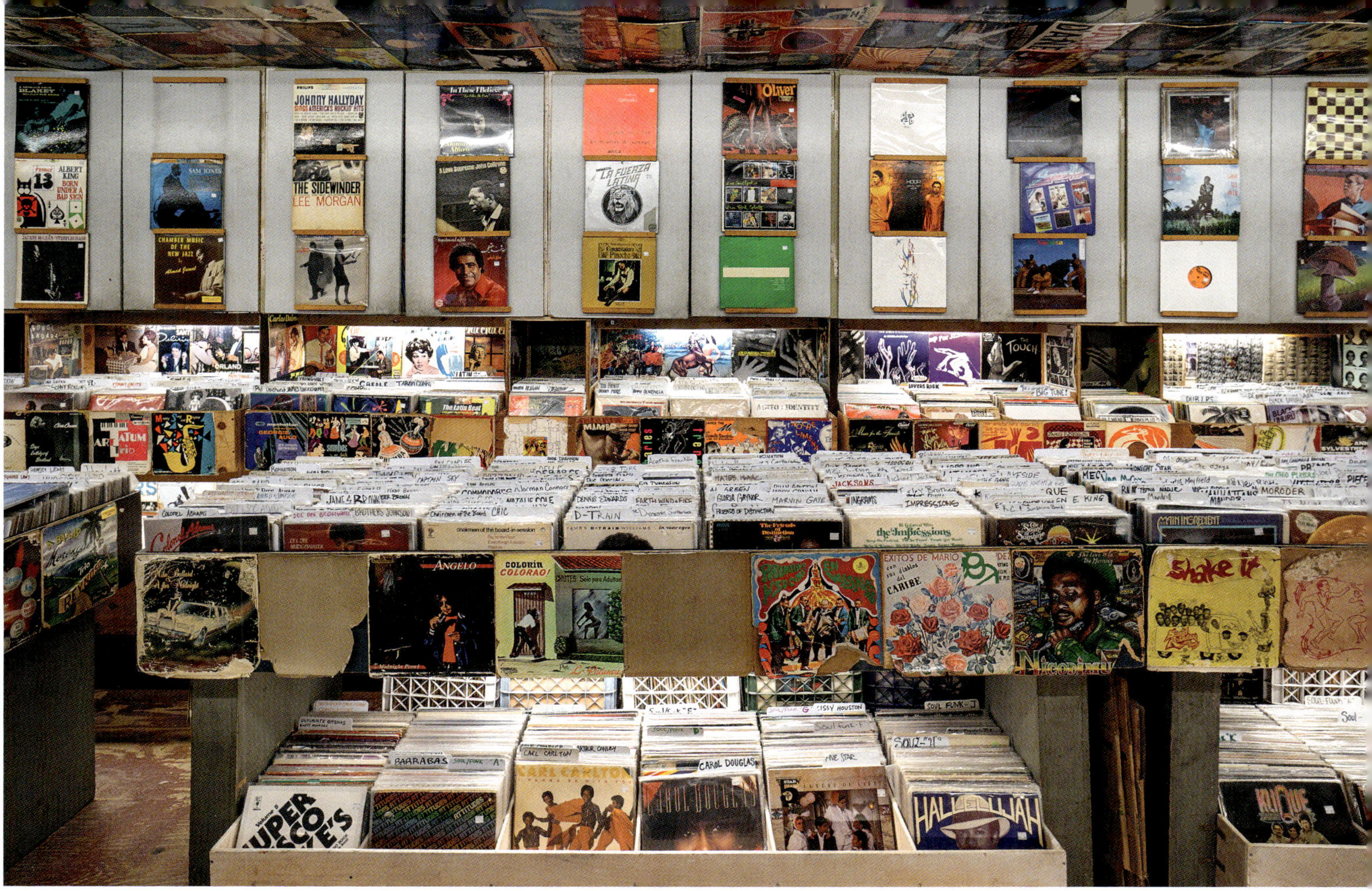
JOHNNY HALLYDAY
THE SIDEWINDER
LEE MORGAN
ANGELO
Shake it
HALLELUJAH
CARL CARLTON
CAROL DOUGLAS

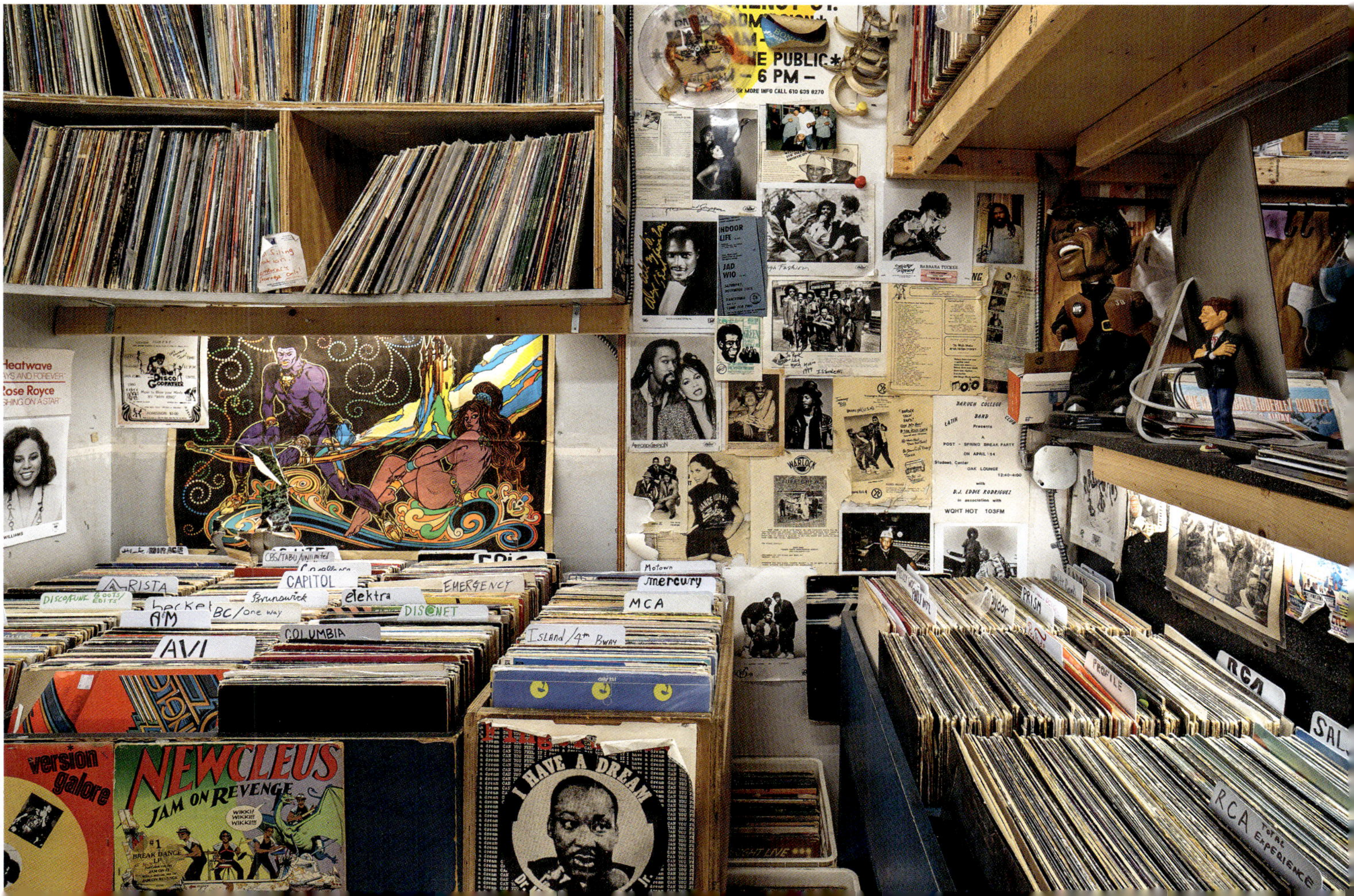
Heatwave
Rose Royce
ARISTA
CAPITOL
elektra
EMERGENCY
AVI
COLUMBIA
MCA
Motown
Mercury
RCA
NEWCLEUS
JAM ON REVENGE
version galore
I HAVE A DREAM

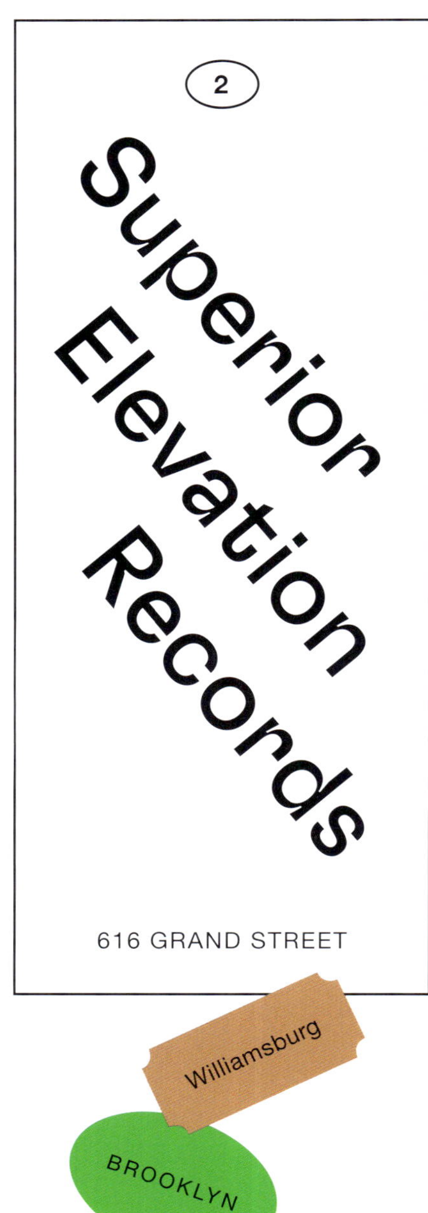

THE LOUISIANA FUNK BAND SILK GREEN—which was initially named Superior Elevation—has a special legacy in the vinyl community. The group's 1985 song "Giving You Love," once a hard-to-access slice of prime '80s boogie funk, popped up at shops across the country in 2024 after a Record Store Day exclusive reissue 12-inch vinyl. But only one of those shops operates under the group's original name, with their official blessing.

Superior Elevation evolved from Lotus Land, a record store that Milwaukee native Tom Noble co-founded in 2000. He credits his ex-wife Ellen Kanamori with encouraging him to expand the business, first into a record label in 2010 and then to a Bushwick storefront in 2015. Damage dealt by Hurricane Ida brought the shop to its present location in Williamsburg in 2021, where a beguiling decal of a brunette woman in a trench coat beckons passersby from the yellow awning. Inside, the shop houses a prized collection of undersung Jamaican soul and Venezuelan pressings—but don't mistake this for a rule. As Noble puts it, "We specialize in every genre."

He sees his role as that of a "professional shopper," explaining: "I get to drive around the entire tri-state area looking for wax. And I know a lot about areas outside of Hipsterville New York and Brooklyn…I probably wouldn't have gone to any of these places had I not been in pursuit of records." Noble doesn't always have to chase down these outside-the-margins experiences, though: once, he recalls, a couple hundred bags of mystery cocaine tumbled from the confines of an Italo disco collection the store received.

Beyond its bustling record exchange, Superior Elevation also functions as a pop-up music classroom. The shop's internal DJ school, which thrives primarily off donations, runs classes and free workshops throughout the year, including eight-week courses for students of all levels. Interested parties can also book private lessons or plain old practice time. A DJ and producer himself currently signed to the Razor-N-Tape imprint, Noble knows well that, in a market as competitive as New York, a clear point of view is just the first step to success for aspiring selectors. And in a rapidly changing borough with little to no longevity guaranteed, why not help out the neighborhood by making his small business a community center, as long as the doors are still swinging? "We are just one chair in a never-ending game of musical chairs which makes up Brooklyn," he explains.

Noble estimates the Superior Elevation team receives about twenty-five thousand titles a week. The importance of courting a thriftier clientele by pricing these records affordably rings true to him as both owner and patron—after all, he might not have the same love affair with vinyl he has today had he not spent a few years in the '90s living across from a record store that never hiked prices above $10. (A cardboard crate of "$5 Latin" nestled by Superior Elevation's floor-to-ceiling windows seems to pay homage to those humble beginnings.) To an unemployed then-twenty-something like Noble, a store that could promise funk, soul, and Latin music at a generous price point was the difference between a pastime and a pursuit. Access, even if he had to dig for it, meant just as much as ownership. "They want something to hold on to," he notes of his younger customers. "Maybe they realized that streaming isn't the way to understand what they are listening to."

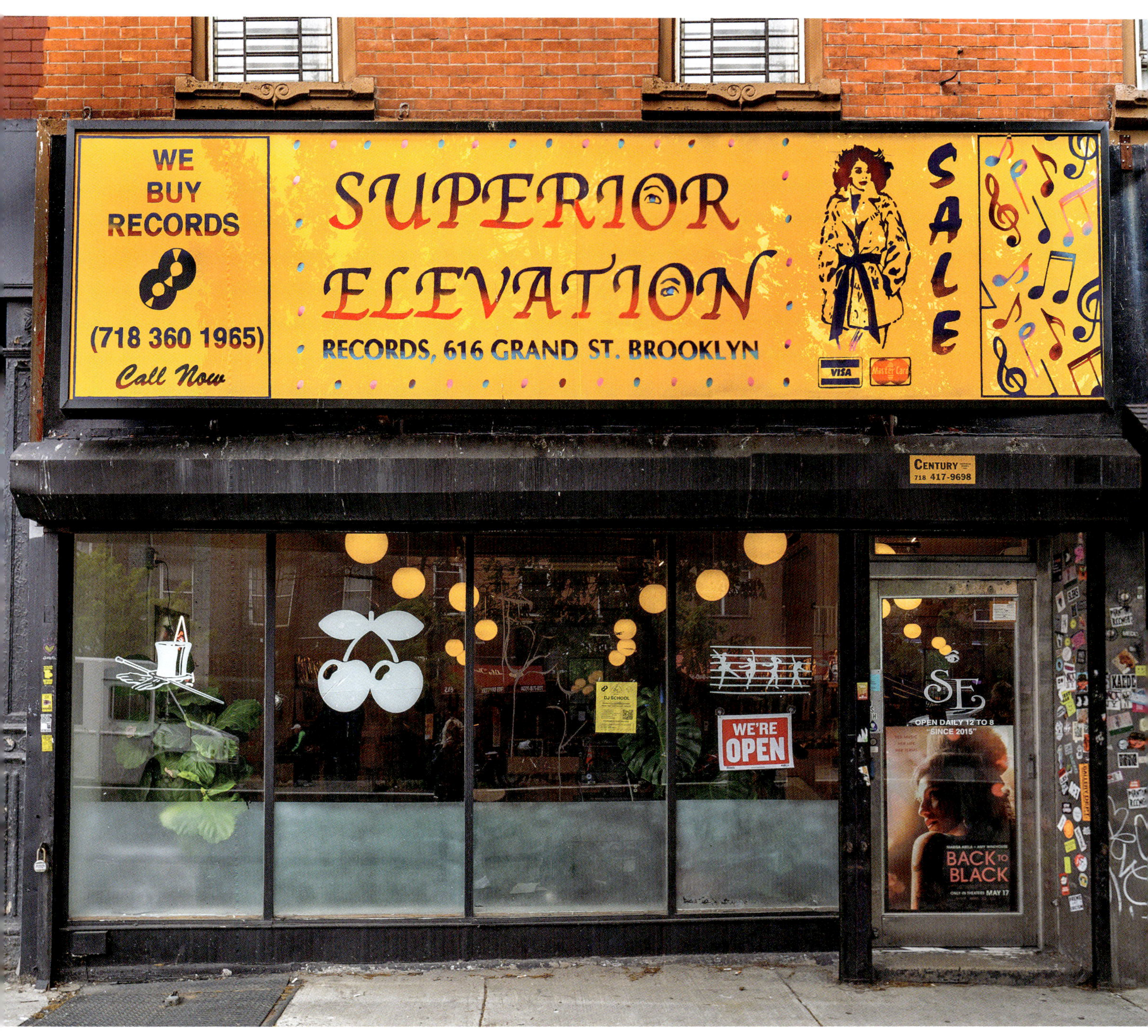

ABOVE Superior Elevation was founded by DJ/producer and veteran record collector Tom Noble. It carries a wide variety of mostly used vinyl, including sought-after hip-hop, R&B, soul, funk, reggae, house, and disco, as well as a selection of new arrivals.

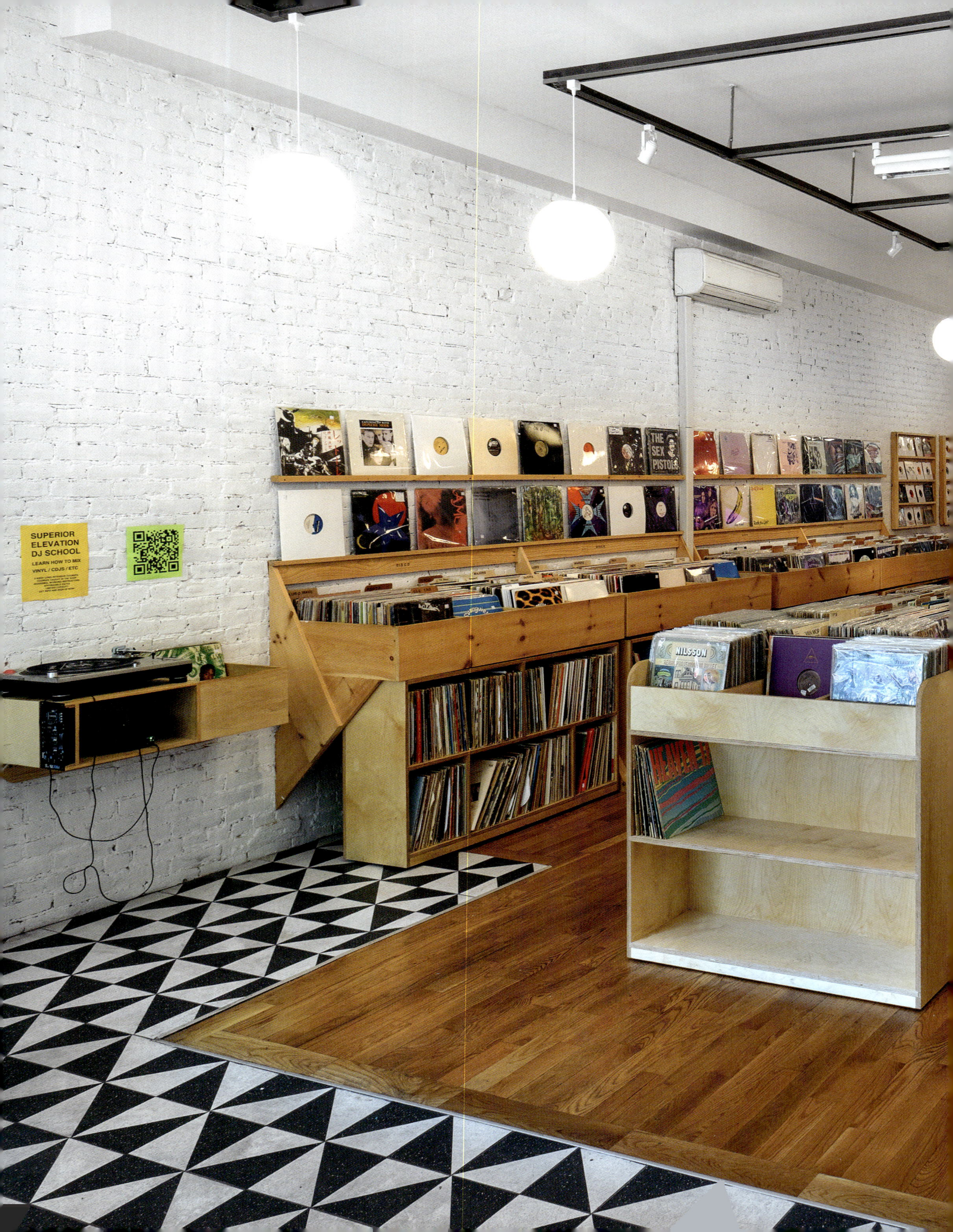
SUPERIOR
ELEVATION
DJ SCHOOL
LEARN HOW TO MIX
VINYL / CDJS / ETC
NILSSON

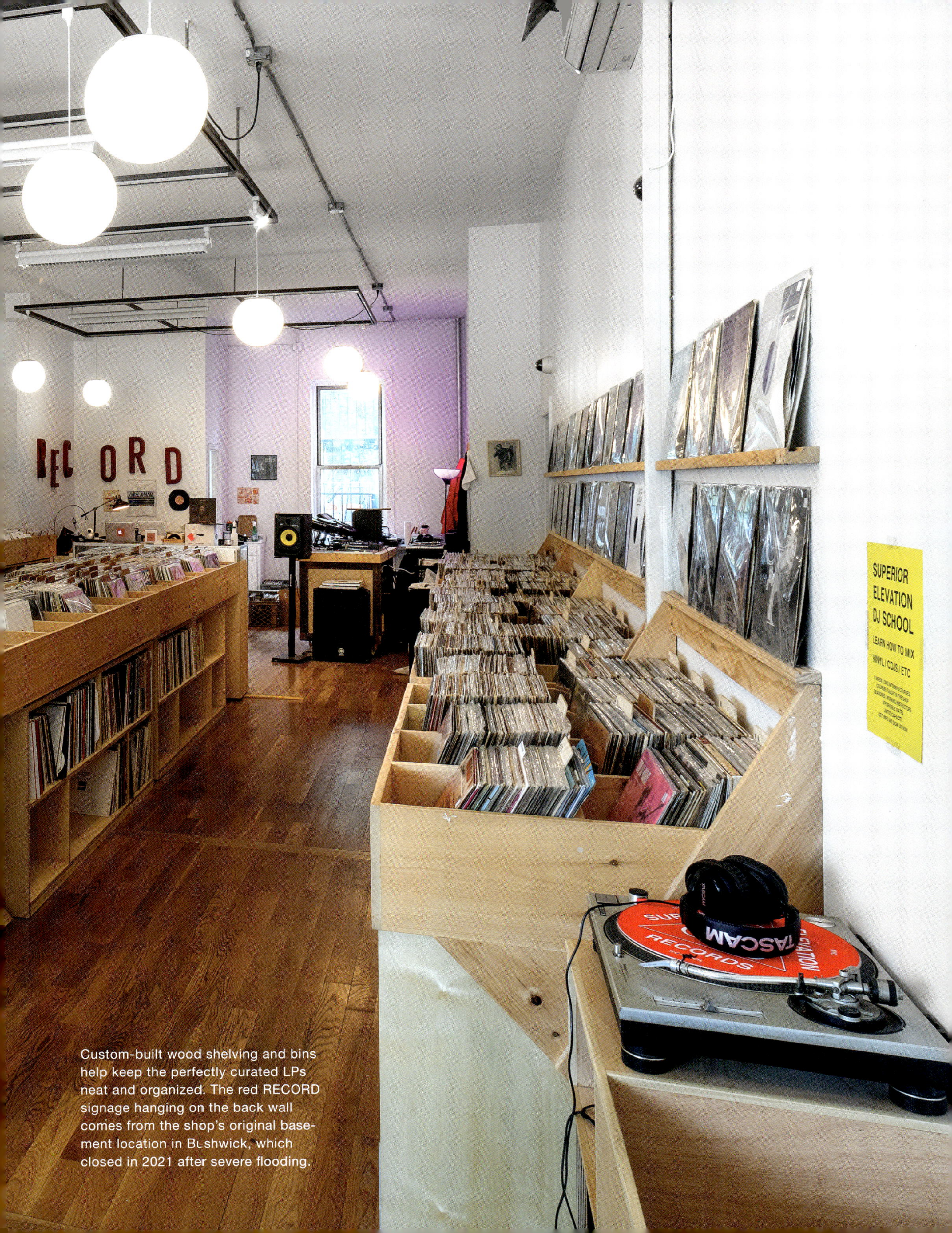

Custom-built wood shelving and bins help keep the perfectly curated LPs neat and organized. The red RECORD signage hanging on the back wall comes from the shop's original basement location in Bushwick, which closed in 2021 after severe flooding.

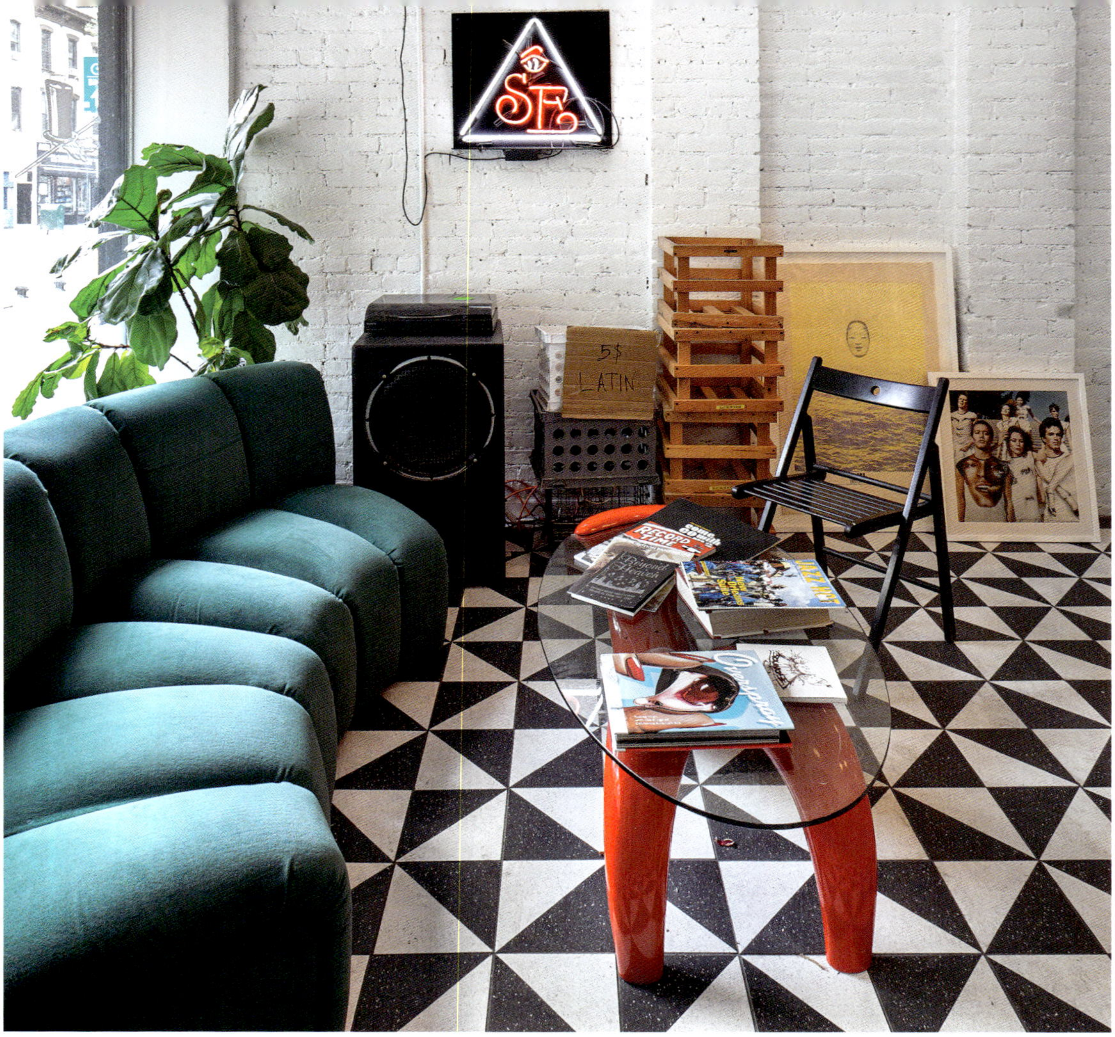

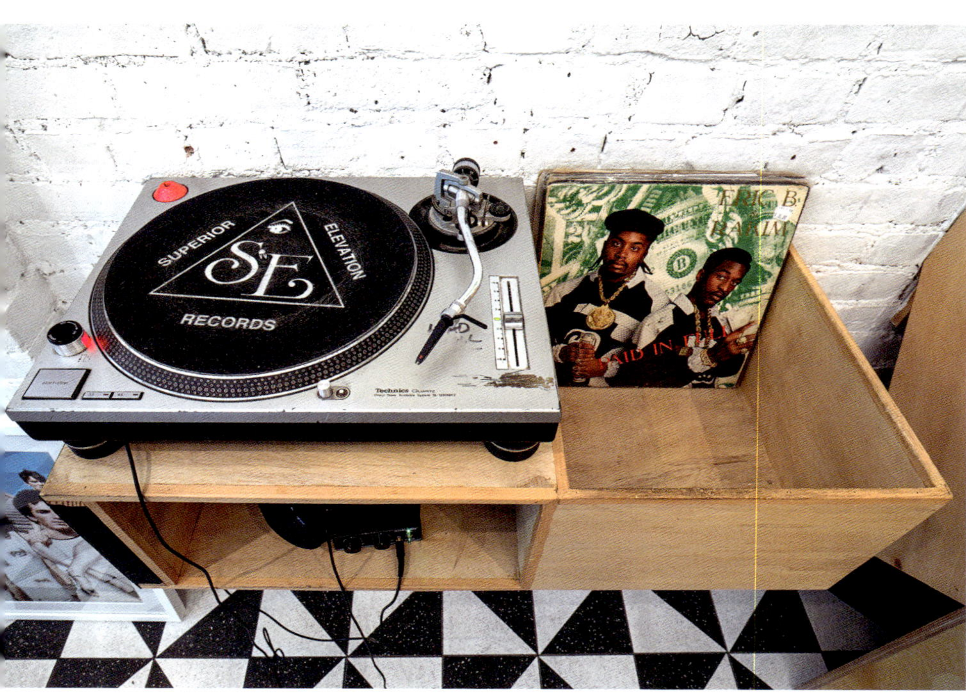

LEFT The two listening stations at the front of the shop have bins adjacent to them so customers can easily stack and view their selection.

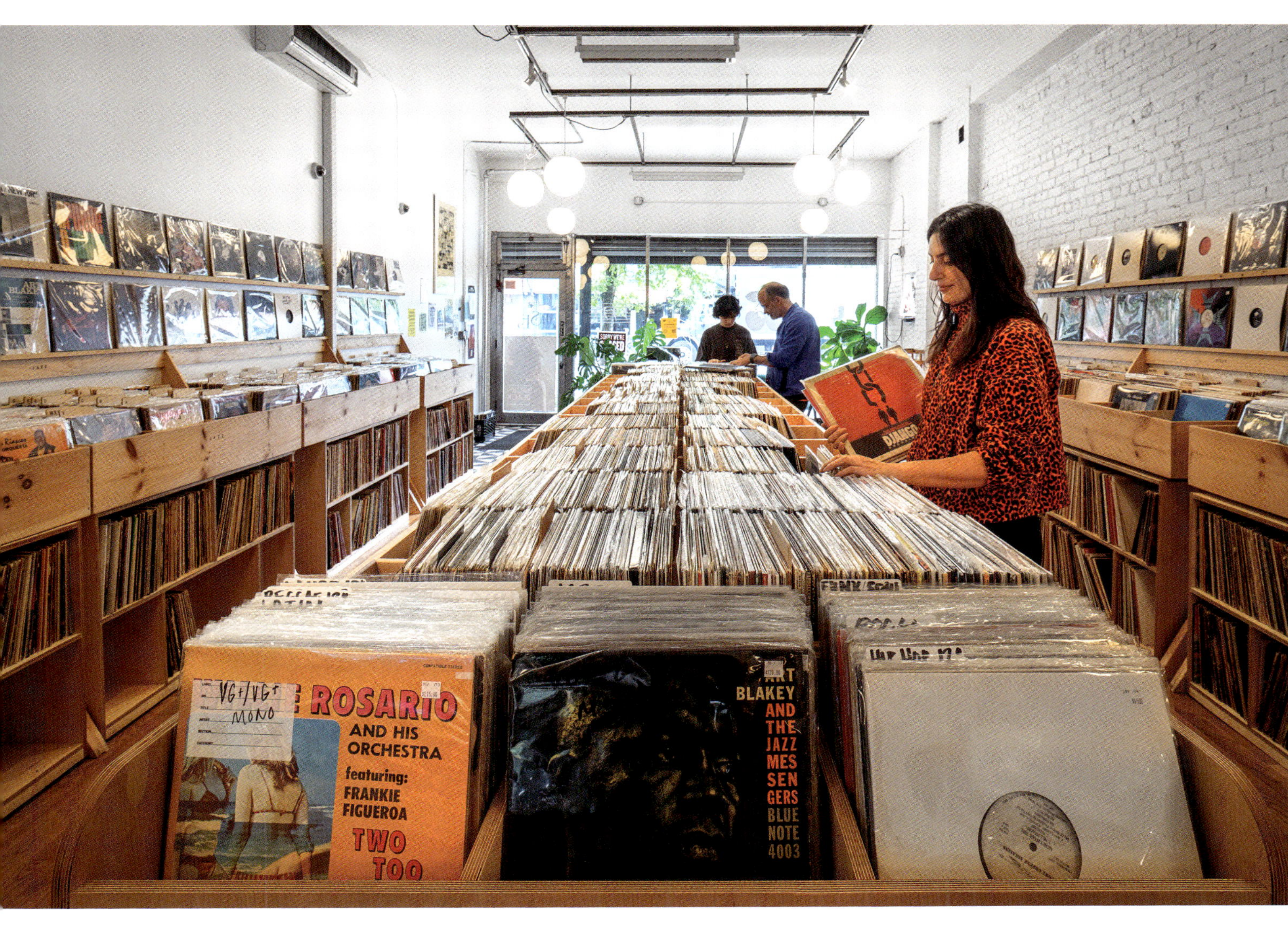

VG+/VG+
MONO
ROSARIO
AND HIS
ORCHESTRA
featuring:
FRANKIE
FIGUEROA
TWO
TOO
BLAKEY
AND
THE
JAZZ
MES
SEN
GERS
BLUE
NOTE
4003
DJANGO

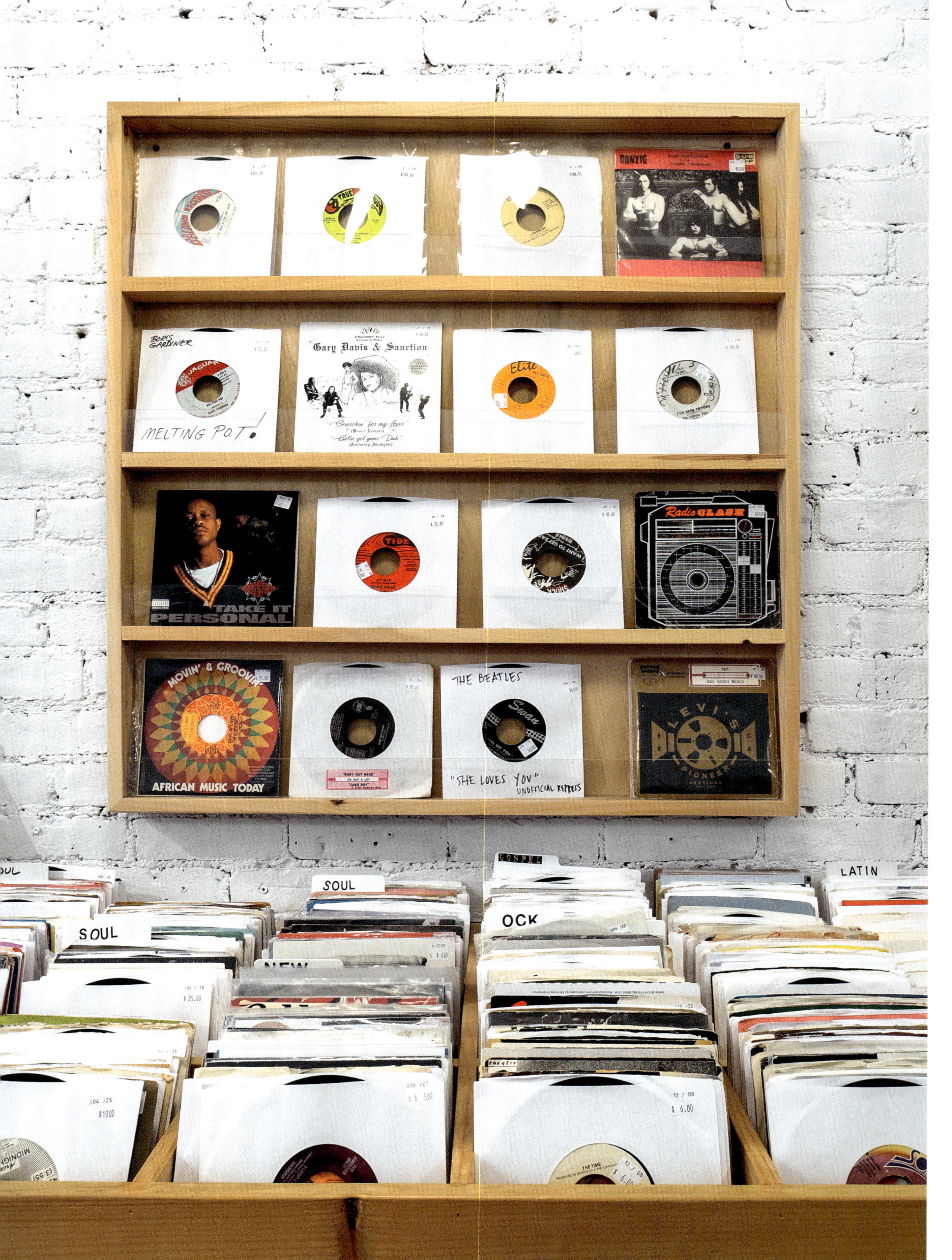

DANZIG
BORIS GARDINER
JAGUAR
MELTING POT!
Gary Davis & Sanction
Elite
TIDE
TAKE IT PERSONAL
Radio CLASH
MOVIN' & GROOVIN'
AFRICAN MUSIC TODAY
THE BEATLES
Swan
"SHE LOVES YOU"
UNOFFICIAL REPRESS
LEVI'S
PIONEER
SOUL
SOUL
GOSPEL
OCK
LATIN

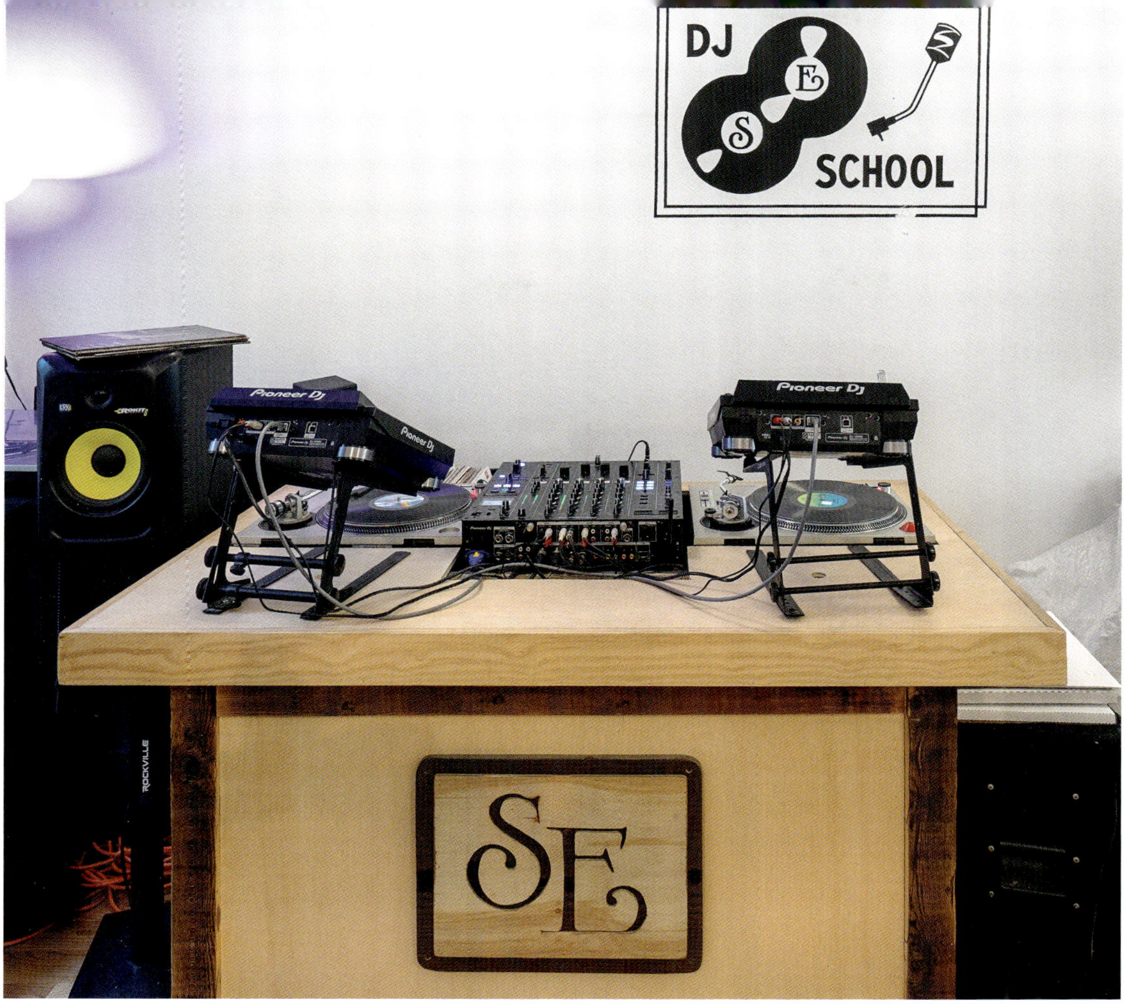

OPPOSITE A corner of the shop is dedicated to an extensive selection of 7-inch vinyl, inc uding a wall of the rarest and highest-value finds.

ABOVE One of Superior Elevation's unique offerings is its DJ school, at which some of the city's top selectors teach students through group and one-on-one private lessons. The shop also often hosts in-house events and sets from local DJs.

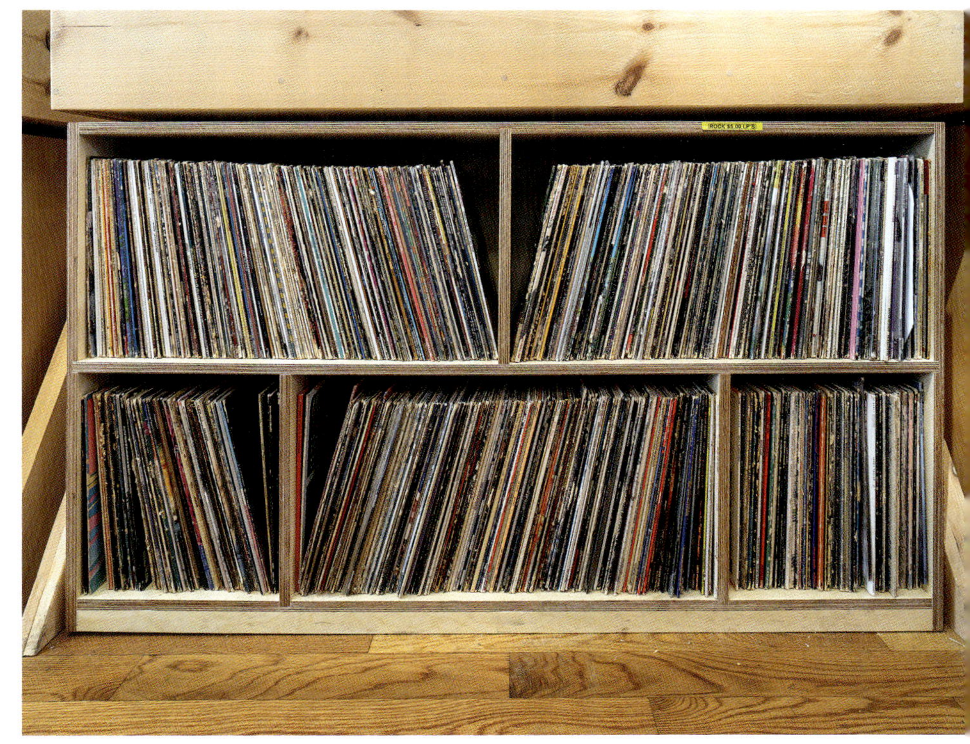

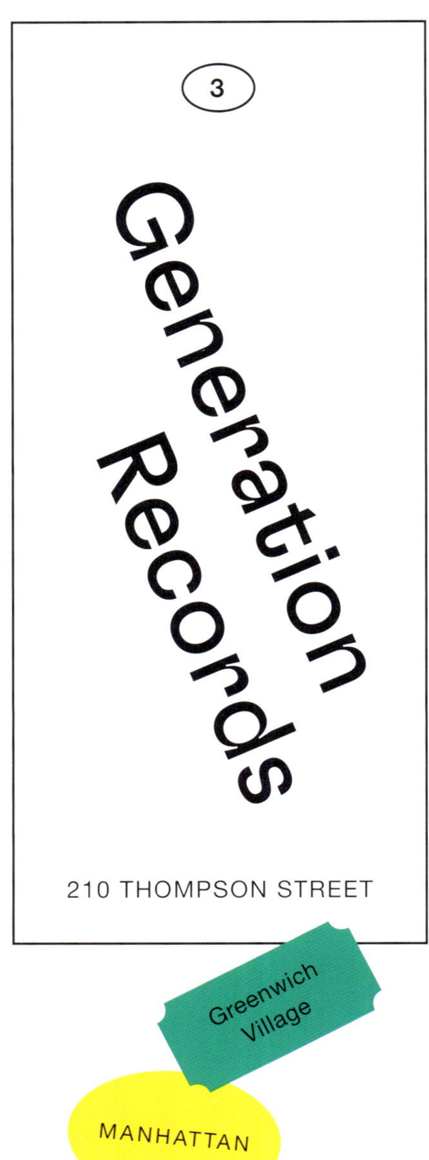

WHEN IT COMES TO THE WEIRD and wonderful world of punk music, Generation Records owner Mark Yoshitomi has two pet peeves. First: hardcore genre nerds who turn their noses up at more popular records; second: anyone who has parachuted into the scene without stopping in a mosh pit first. His Greenwich Village shop stays true to that business, serving as a top-level New York hardcore intro point for local loyalists and traveling tourists alike who won't scoff at a well-kept pressing of Circle Jerks' album *Group Sex*. As for any stolen punk valor? Yoshitomi's past stints on bass with the Casualties and the Krays should cover that, if the Sid Vicious haircut he sported as a preteen and the assortment of iron-on patches he still wears today didn't already.

Although he grew up in Westchester just outside the city, Yoshitomi cut his teeth throughout the '80s coming in from the suburbs to immerse in the roiling punk rock jungle that was downtown Manhattan. His ears perked up to vinyl via a Led Zeppelin collection he inherited when his sister headed off for college, Yoshitomi developed a routine of buying a few records before the Sunday hardcore matinee gigs he frequented, making a circuit of institutions like Bleecker Bob's, Sounds, and FreeBeing. "I almost always had a bag of records with me," he remembers.

Yoshitomi's first job in the field was at the now-defunct Second Coming Records on Sullivan Street, a block away from the storefront on Thompson Street where Generation Records sits today. Generation itself was opened in 1992 by Chris Dunnigan and a team of Second Coming graduates, including Yoshitomi. It proudly specializes in punk, hardcore, metal, and rock, a mirror image of the main team's greatest passion and core commonality. Now a principal partner at Generation, Yoshitomi maintains a few resident twenty-something staffers he can trust to uphold the shop's institutional knowledge of new hip-hop and pop music, but he's not concerned about continuing to draw in a hardcore-focused clientele. From what he can see, as long as there is rock music, the kids will come hunting for it.

Still decorated with original signage from a since-closed sister shop on Bleecker Street, Generation's first floor features new, used, and reissued vinyl by the thousand, as well as a full shelf of memoirs, biographies, and historical novels from every era of punk rock. Follow the Black Flag and Bon Jovi posters down to the basement, and a deluge of discount VHS tapes, 45s, vintage T-shirts, action figures, enamel pins, and more appear, revealing the staff's omnivorous interests. But it all lines up with the ethos of Generation's in-house label, which focuses on key hardcore reissues—like its re-pressing of Agnostic Front's 1983 EP *United in Blood*—and which Yoshitomi proudly considers an acquired taste. As he admitted to the hardcore blog *No Echo* in 2021, "I can't imagine someone liking all the bands."

But at Generation, what customers like is far less important than what they can't live without. The way Yoshitomi sees it, someone with a real love for the game will take the good, bad, freaky, and ugly punk has to offer as one beautiful menagerie. "This stuff is like forty to fifty years old now," Yoshitomi says of some of his favorite punk rock rarities. "And there's still teenage kids looking for it. It's just crazy."

A lifelong distaste for authority doesn't mesh with many careers. But take it from Yoshitomi: If you love vinyl, youthful rebellion and obsession can translate into a dream day job. He's proud to don the old-head badge, but day-to-day life at Generation might just be keeping him young. "I can't even imagine doing anything else," he confirms. "I think the curiosity that people who collect things in general have...that doesn't go away."

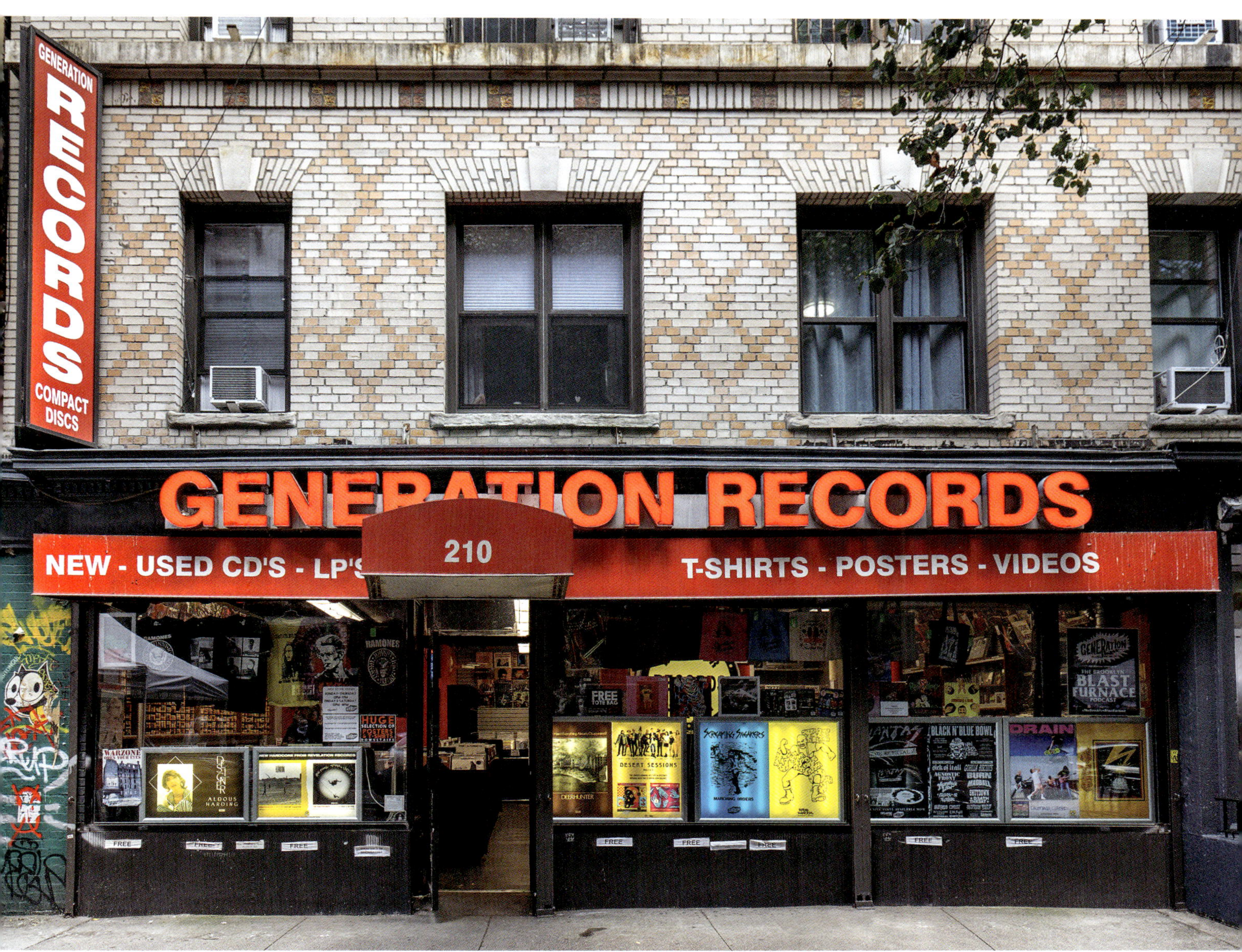

ABOVE Generation Records was founded in 1992 by Chris Dunnigan. It's well-known for its selection of punk, hardcore, and heavy metal, but also carries a variety of genres over its two floors. It's the only shop in New York City that stocks thousands of new vinyl records, reissues, and used vinyl, and also offers CDs, cassettes, and a wide variety of music merchandise.

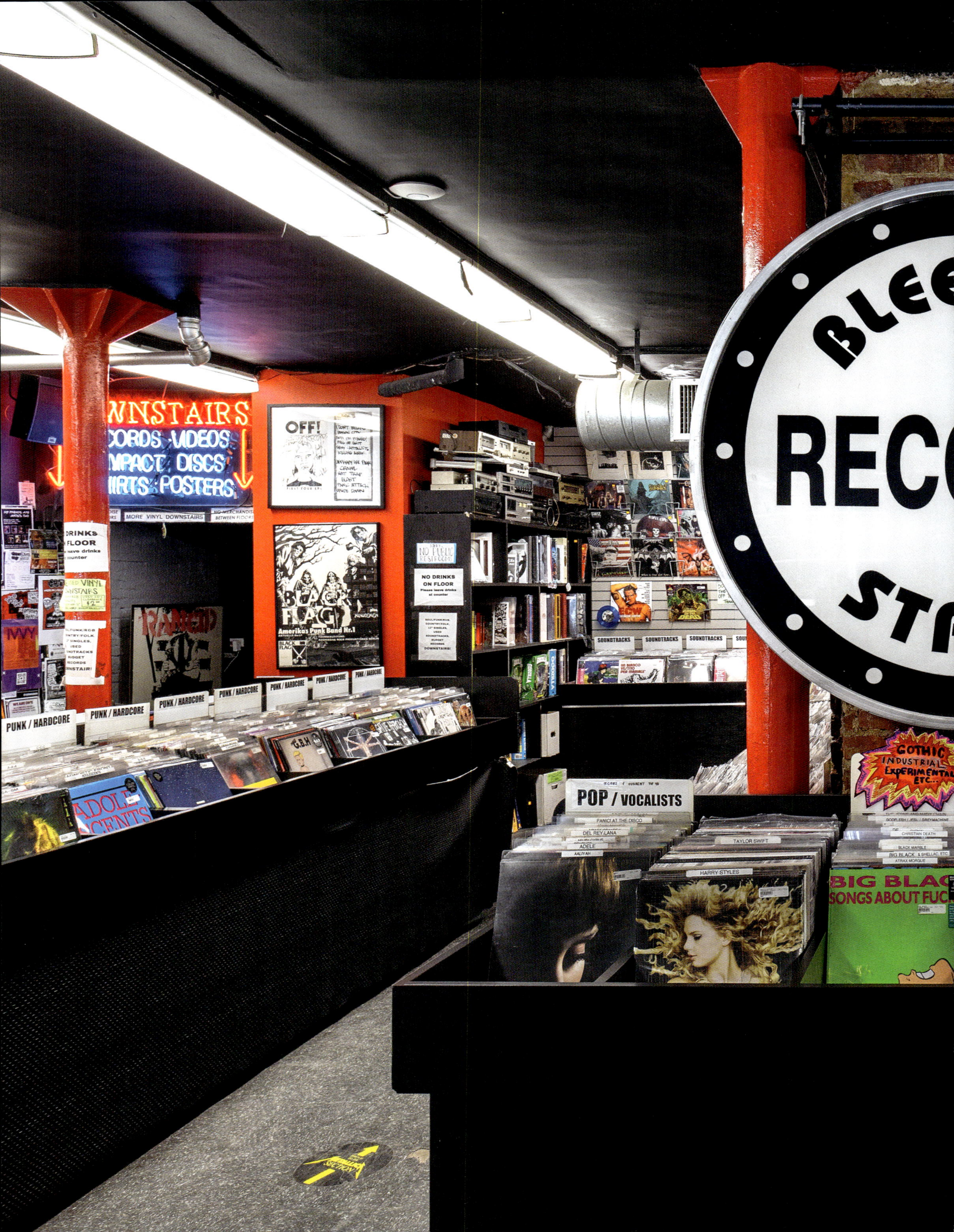

WNSTAIRS
CORDS VIDEOS
MPACT DISCS
IRTS POSTERS
MORE VINYL DOWNSTAIRS
OFF!
BLACK FLAG
Amerikas Punk Band Nr.1
RANCID
NO DRINKS ON FLOOR
Please leave drinks at counter
PUNK / HARDCORE
SOUNDTRACKS
POP / VOCALISTS
PANIC! AT THE DISCO
DEL REY, LANA
ADELE
AALIYAH
TAYLOR SWIFT
HARRY STYLES
GOTHIC
INDUSTRIAL
EXPERIMENTAL
ETC...
CHRISTIAN DEATH
BLACK MARBLE
ATRAX MORGUE
BIG BLAC
SONGS ABOUT FUC
RECO

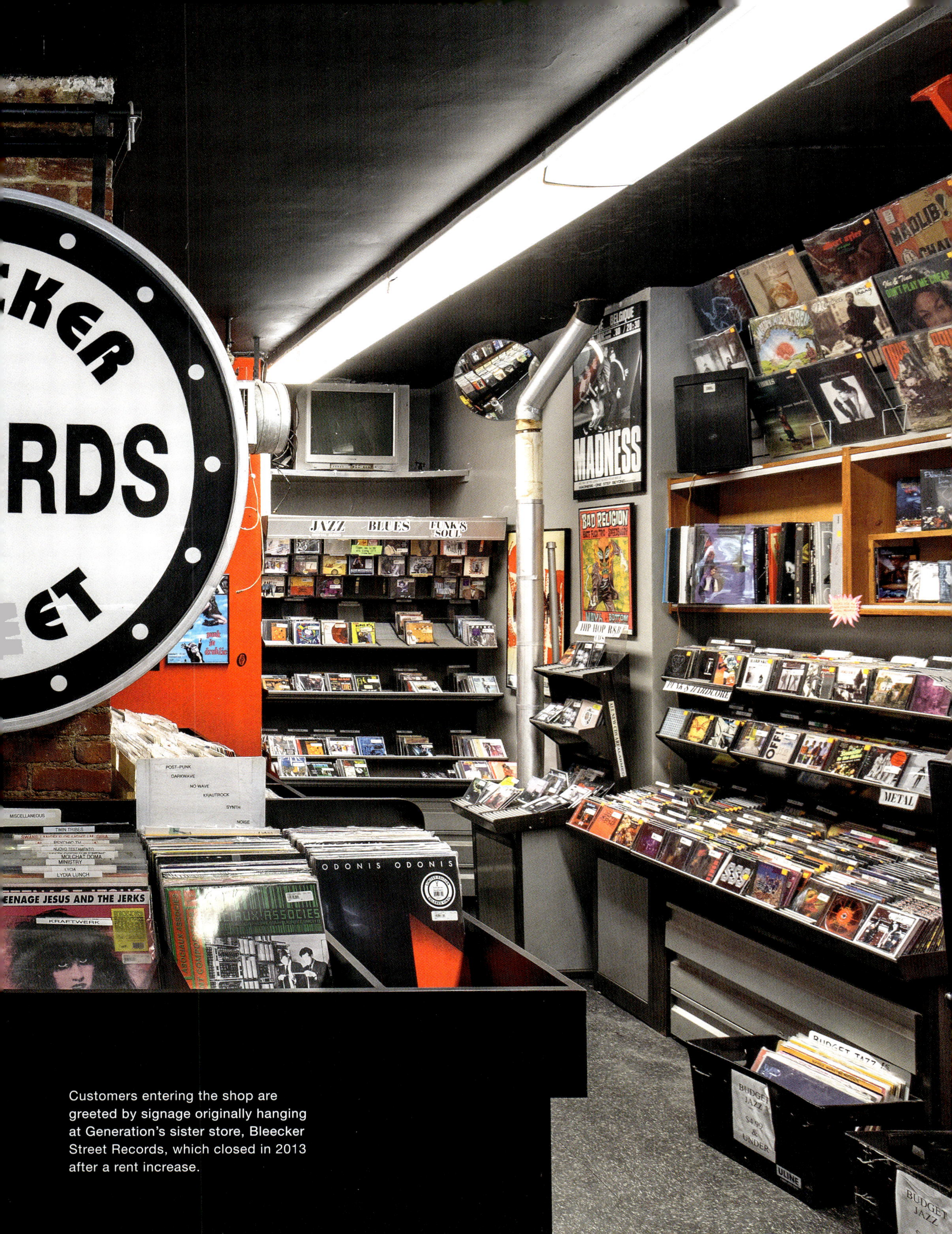

Customers entering the shop are greeted by signage originally hanging at Generation's sister store, Bleecker Street Records, which closed in 2013 after a rent increase.

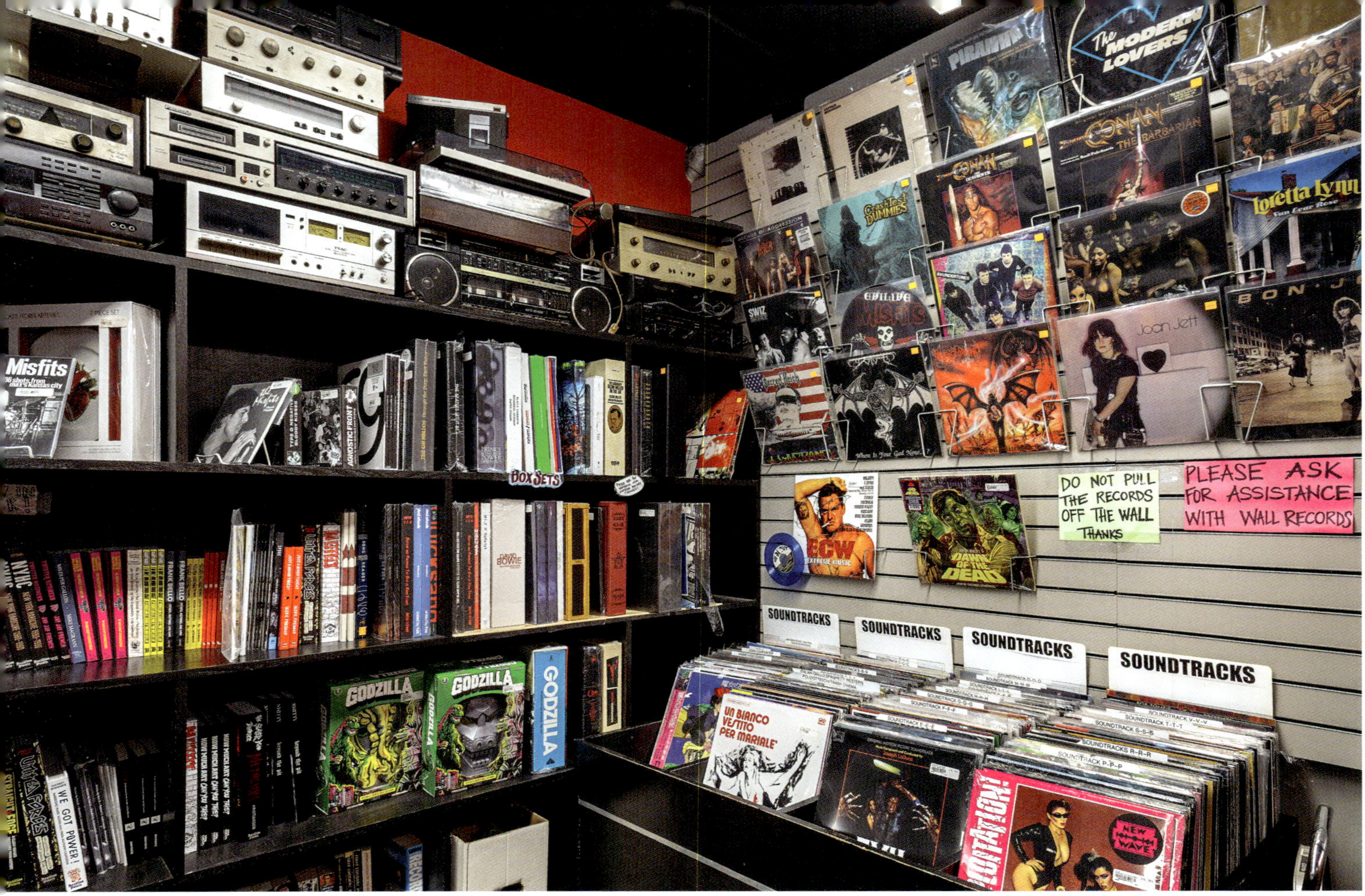

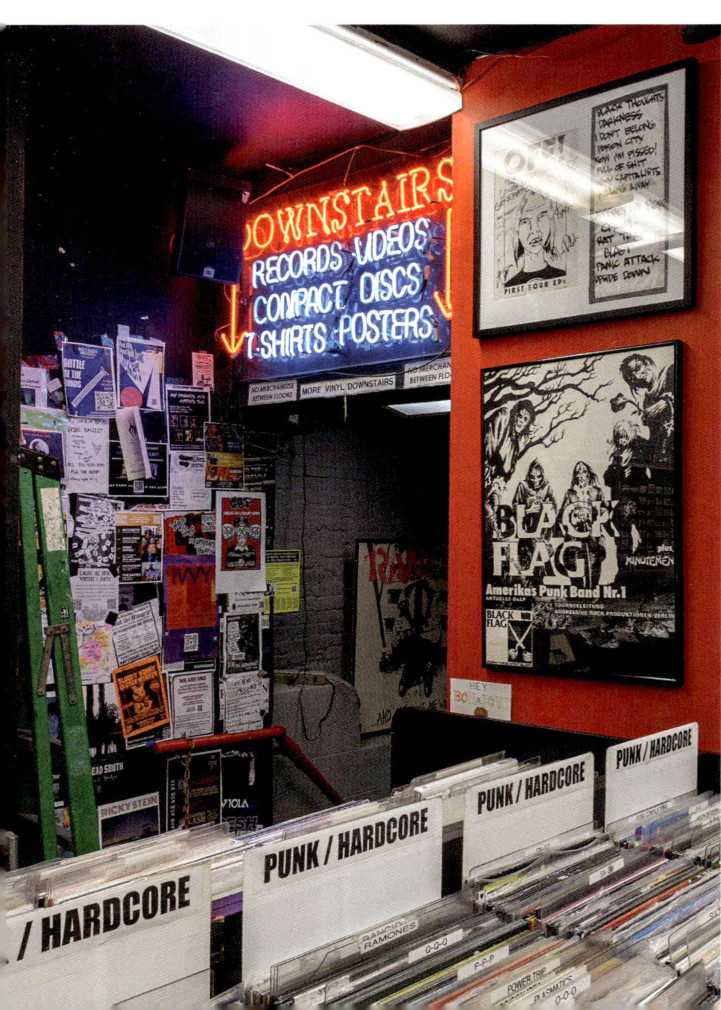
DOWNSTAIRS
RECORDS VIDEOS
COMPACT DISCS
T-SHIRTS POSTERS
BLACK FLAG
Amerikas Punk Band Nr.1
MINUTEMEN
PUNK / HARDCORE
PUNK / HARDCORE
PUNK / HARDCORE
PUNK / HARDCORE
/ HARDCORE

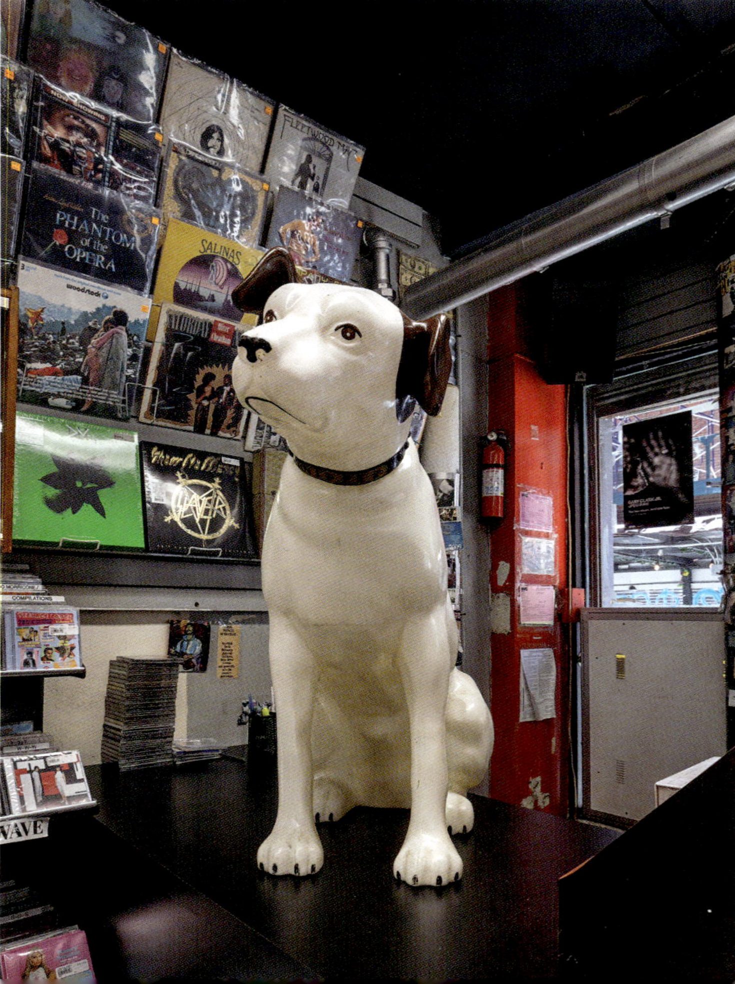
The PHANTOM of the OPERA
SALINAS

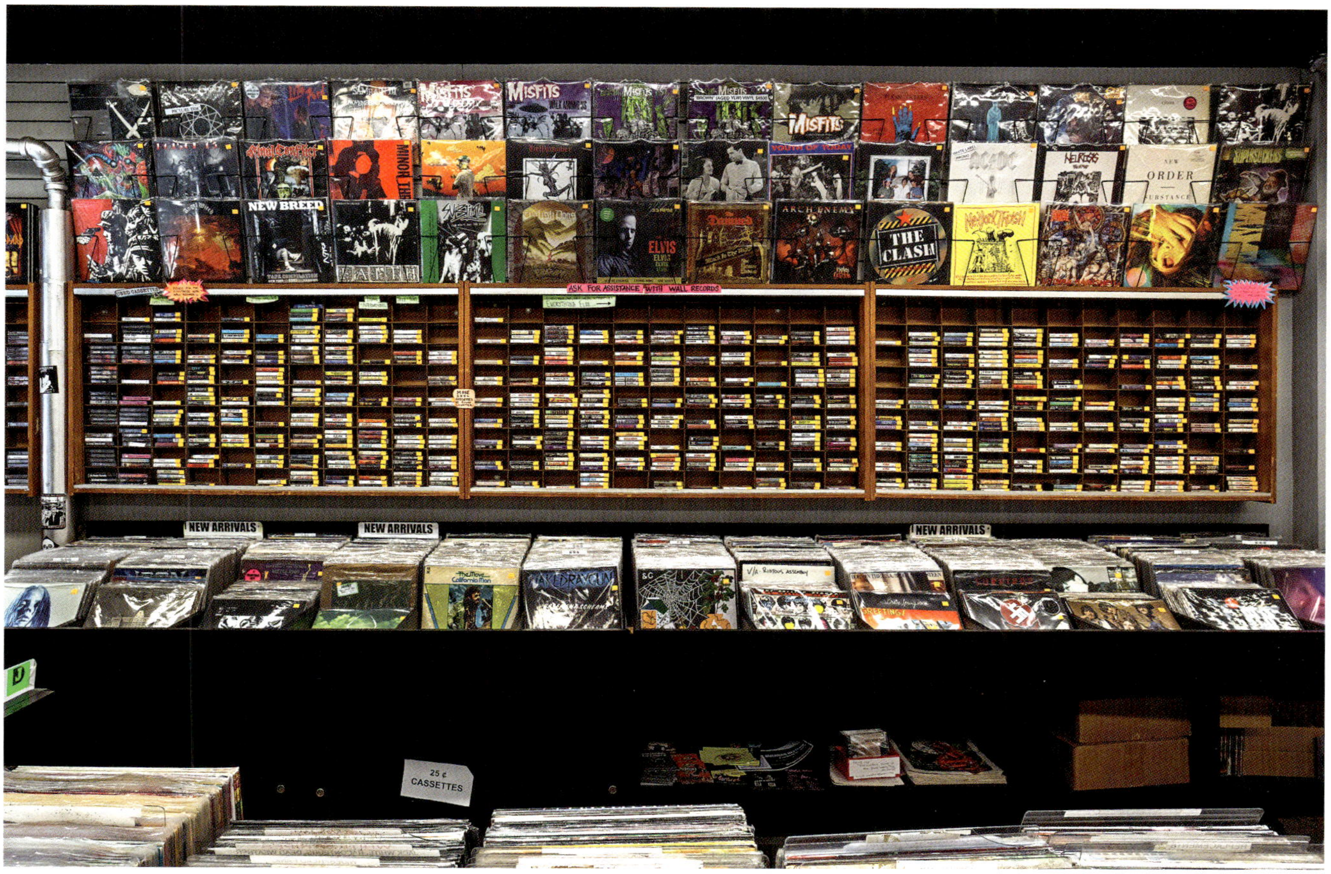

ABOVE A large collection of secondhand cassettes, some being sold for as little as $0.25, can be found on the shop's main floor.

RIGHT Many rare punk, hardcore, and metal titles can be found lining the walls, including a yellow vinyl copy of the second studio album by the Misfits selling for $4,500.

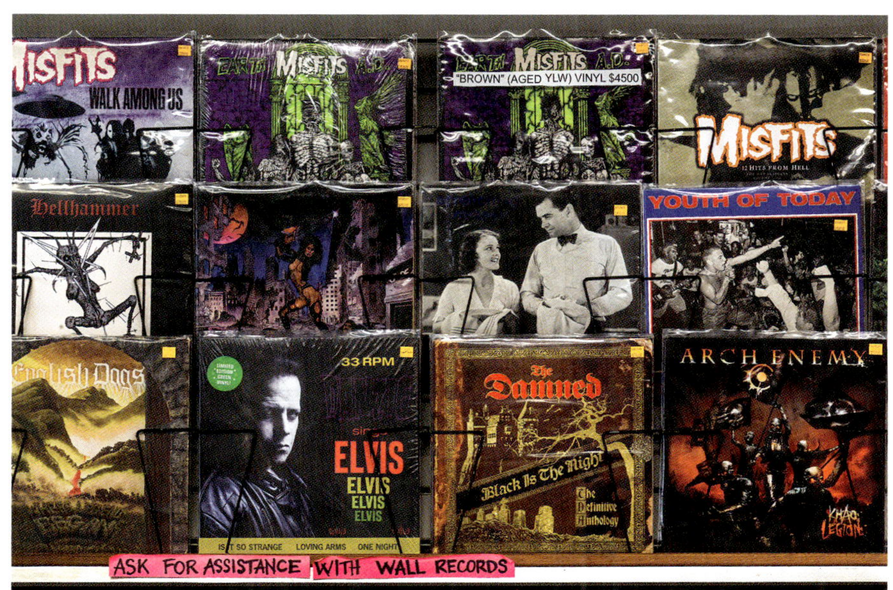

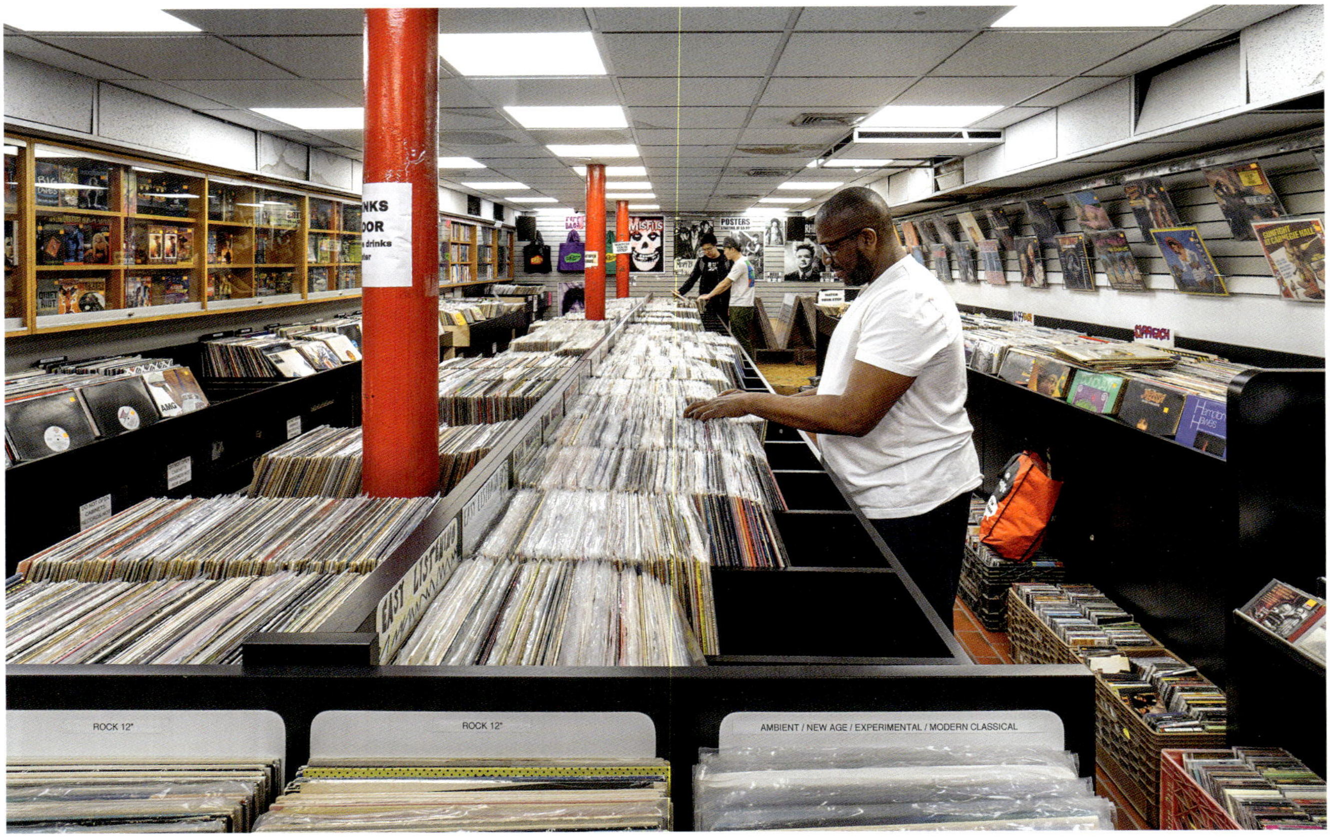

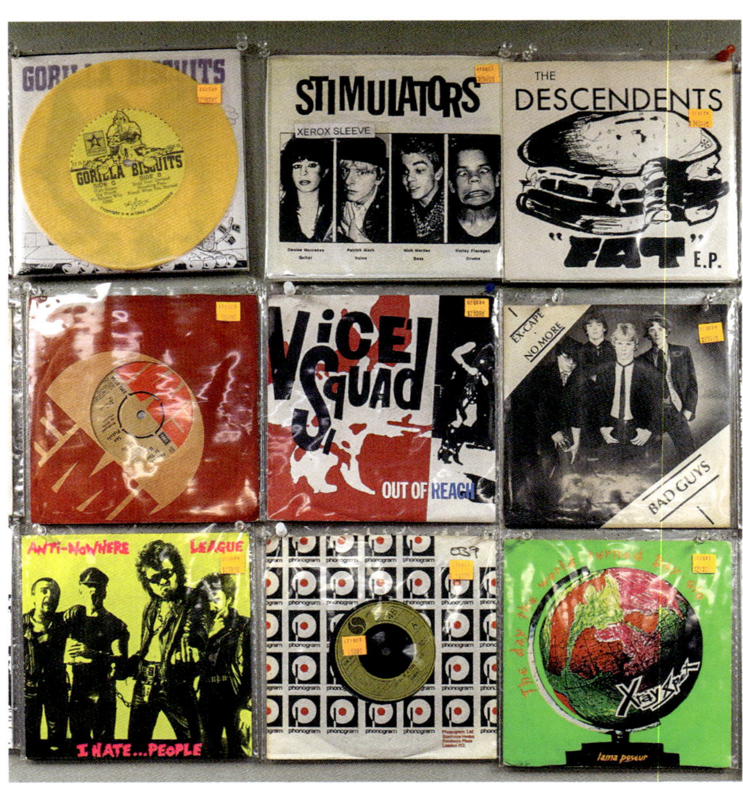
STIMULATORS
XEROX SLEEVE
THE DESCENDENTS
"FAT" E.P.
VICE SQUAD
OUT OF REACH
EX-CAPE
NO MORE
BAD GUYS
ANTI-NOWHERE LEAGUE
I HATE...PEOPLE

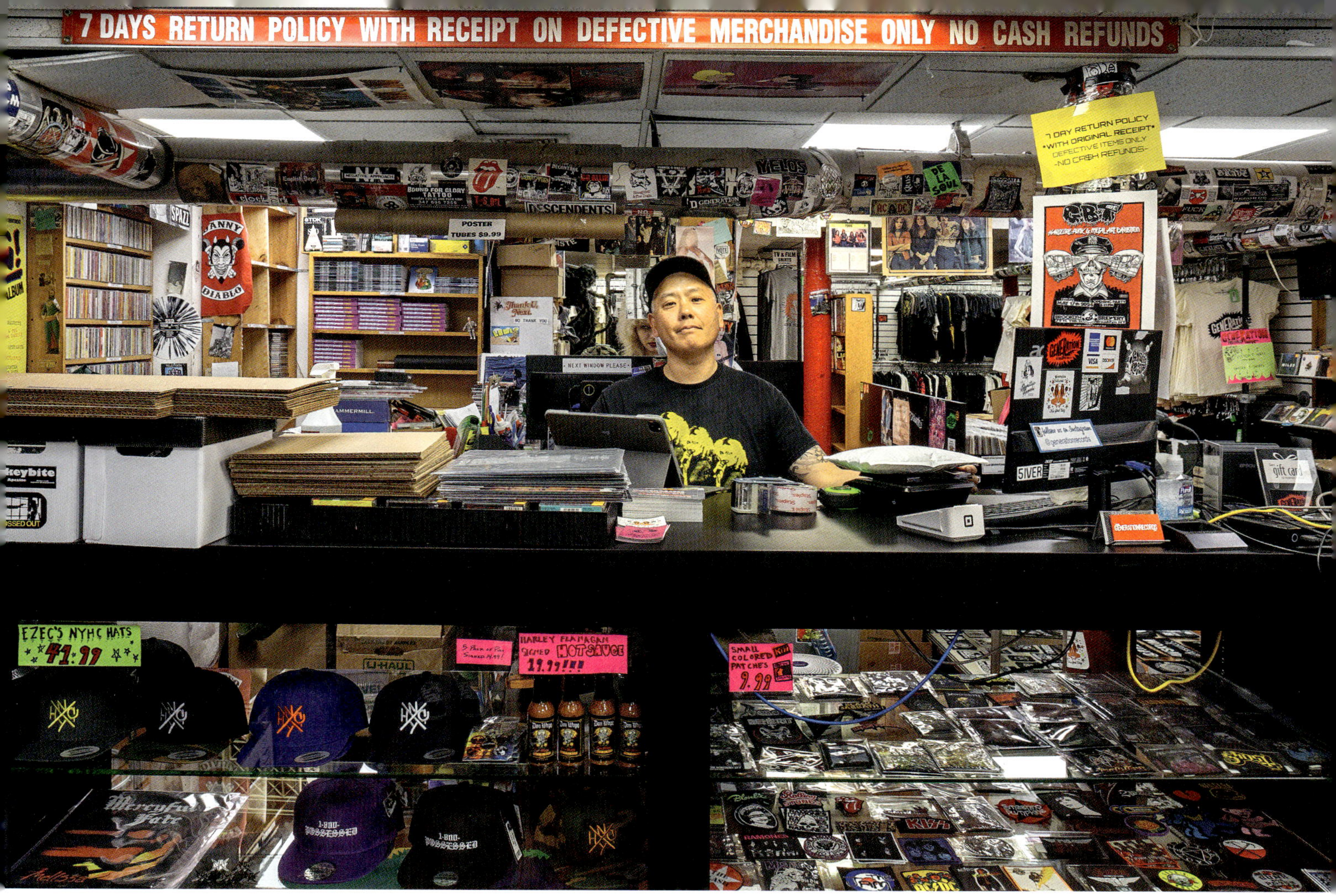

OPPOSITE BOTTOM A dedicated selection of rare punk and hardcore 45s can be found downstairs, including a copy of the *Fat EP* by the Descendents selling for $349.99.

ABOVE Generation Records' principal partner Mark Yoshitomi can be found at the shop most days. He's an avid vinyl collector, a passion that began in his punk rock days as the former bassist of the Casualties.

RIGHT Mark specifically chooses young people to work alongside him "who are passionate about the music of today," and super informed about what the shop carries.

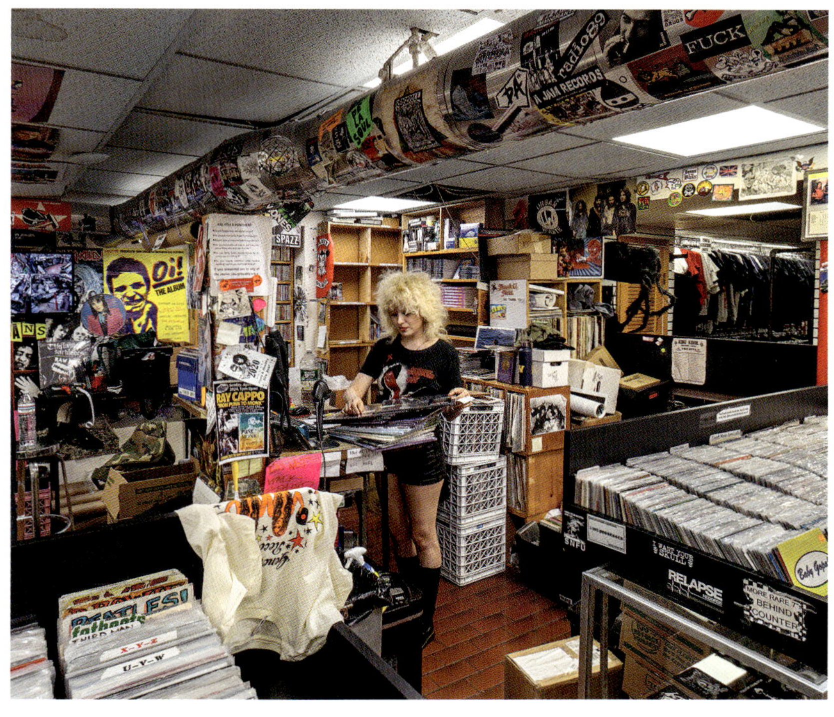

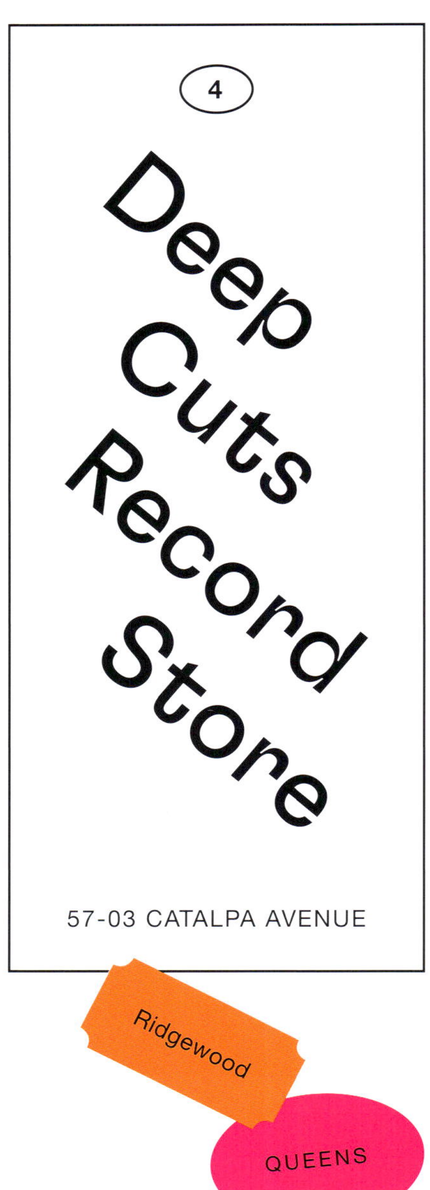

TURNING A PASSION INTO A PROFESSION is no easy feat, but Brandon Perry and John Allen see their decade-plus time spent running the record shop Deep Cuts as a privilege. "I've had a lot of shitty jobs in my life, digging ditches and doing construction," Perry recalls. "Sitting around listening to records all day beats, you know, laying sod down and then doing landscape work."

When he began DJing in high school in Los Angeles, the Colombian American Perry found himself smack at the intersection of flourishing underground hip-hop and punk rock scenes. After trading coasts for New York in 2007, he started spinning regular sets on WFMU, all of which are still compiled meticulously (down to the tracklists) on the independent radio station's website under episode titles like "Totally Bananas." Perry's hour ran just ahead of Allen's. It wasn't long until going on air back-to-back brought them face-to-face, the first steps toward a fast friendship; they quickly began filling in on each other's shows.

The duo opened Deep Cuts in Ridgewood, Queens, in 2012, with the same vim and vigor it takes to rifle through a dollar box at a new haunt or bury yourself in the online music database Discogs' ouroboros of hyperlinks. "I either needed to start putting stuff in storage or open a store," Perry recalls. "Now, I have two storage units and a store."

Inside, the vast assortment of stock runs the gamut from pop to funk, jazz, rock, and more. If any genre specialty rears its head, it's Deep Cuts' Latin rock spread, maintained with just as much care as the shop's altar to the late Tejano icon Selena. A section labeled "Kanye/Clapton/Pantera" borders a series of X-rated '70s and '80s audio erotica. Other highlighted sections include "Neil Fucking Diamond," "Jazz Sax," and "New Zealand." Every category is as wide-ranging as it sounds.

Perry says he prefers LPs to any other format, but Deep Cuts' robust 7-inch singles collection and wall of tapes still show his love for diverse mediums. The shop floor usually consists of one part new releases to two parts used vinyl. Up front near the door, rare performances from rock history captured on VHS are up for sale alongside a few choice Jet Li films. Save for a blown-up vinyl of Bruce Springsteen's *Born to Run*, no wall hangings loom larger than the posters of RuPaul and Dolly Parton smiling down on the store's pristinely preserved offerings.

Deep Cuts also sells local and touring artists' tapes on consignment, keeping only $1 of the profit per sale and sending the rest back to the source on PayPal or Venmo. If the music has been pressed onto some sort of tape or disc, Perry and Allen can find a place for it here.

With its artist-first sales strategy leading the way, Deep Cuts walks the walk when it comes to keeping independent music alive for the next generation. Just ask Perry and Allen's youngest customers. "I have regulars that have been shopping since back when we were in the back of a garage, in the back of the sign-up barn at the music venue," Perry muses. "And now they've grown up, and their kids are shopping with us." (Just not, of course, in the "Adults Only XXX" section).

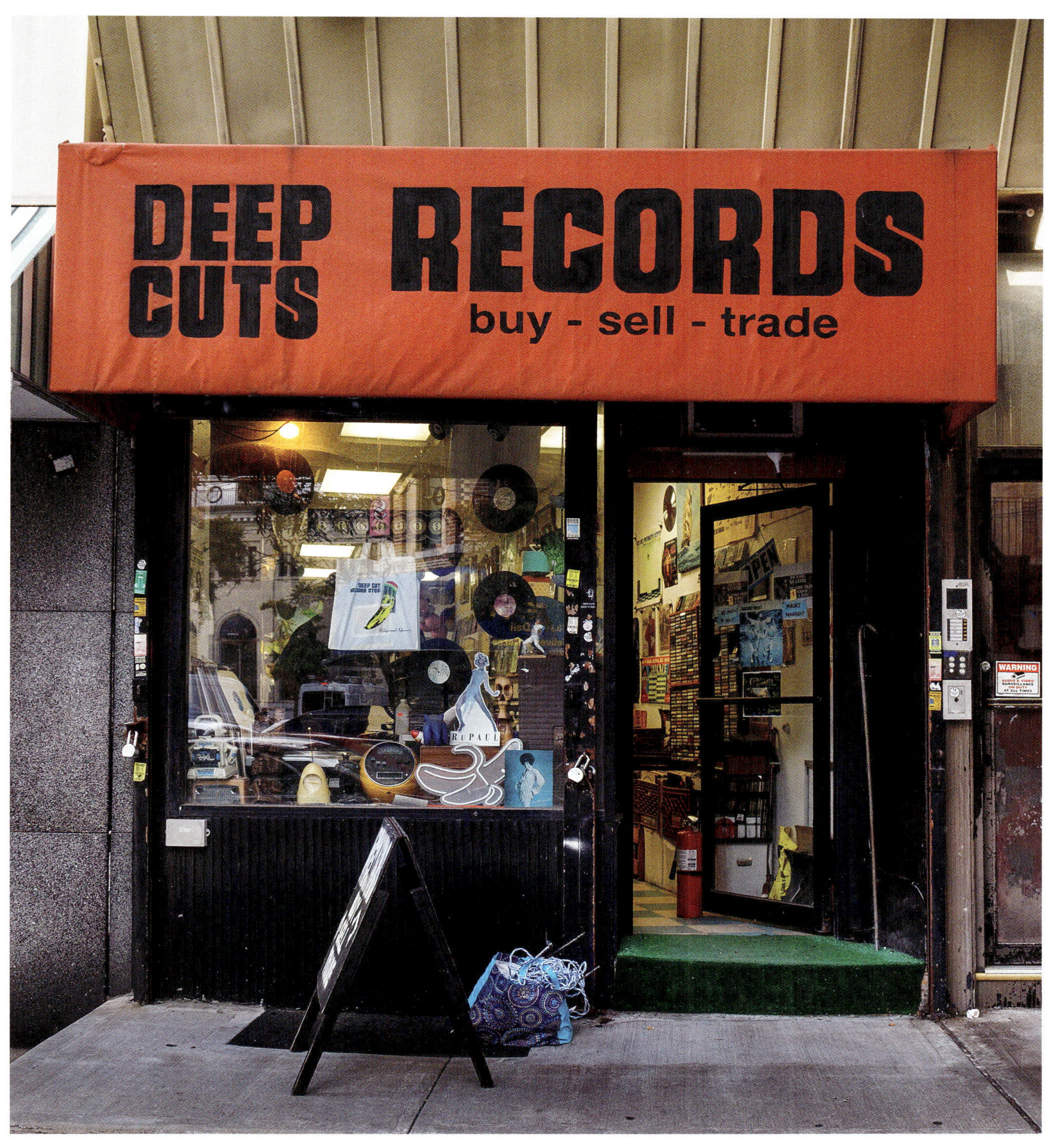

ABOVE Founded in 2012, Deep Cuts is known for its self-described "Warhol Rasta banana" logo. Although the shop, located on a quiet side street, is small in size, it carries an eclectic and wide mix of used vinyl, along with select new vinyl releases, reissues, and an array of used cassettes.

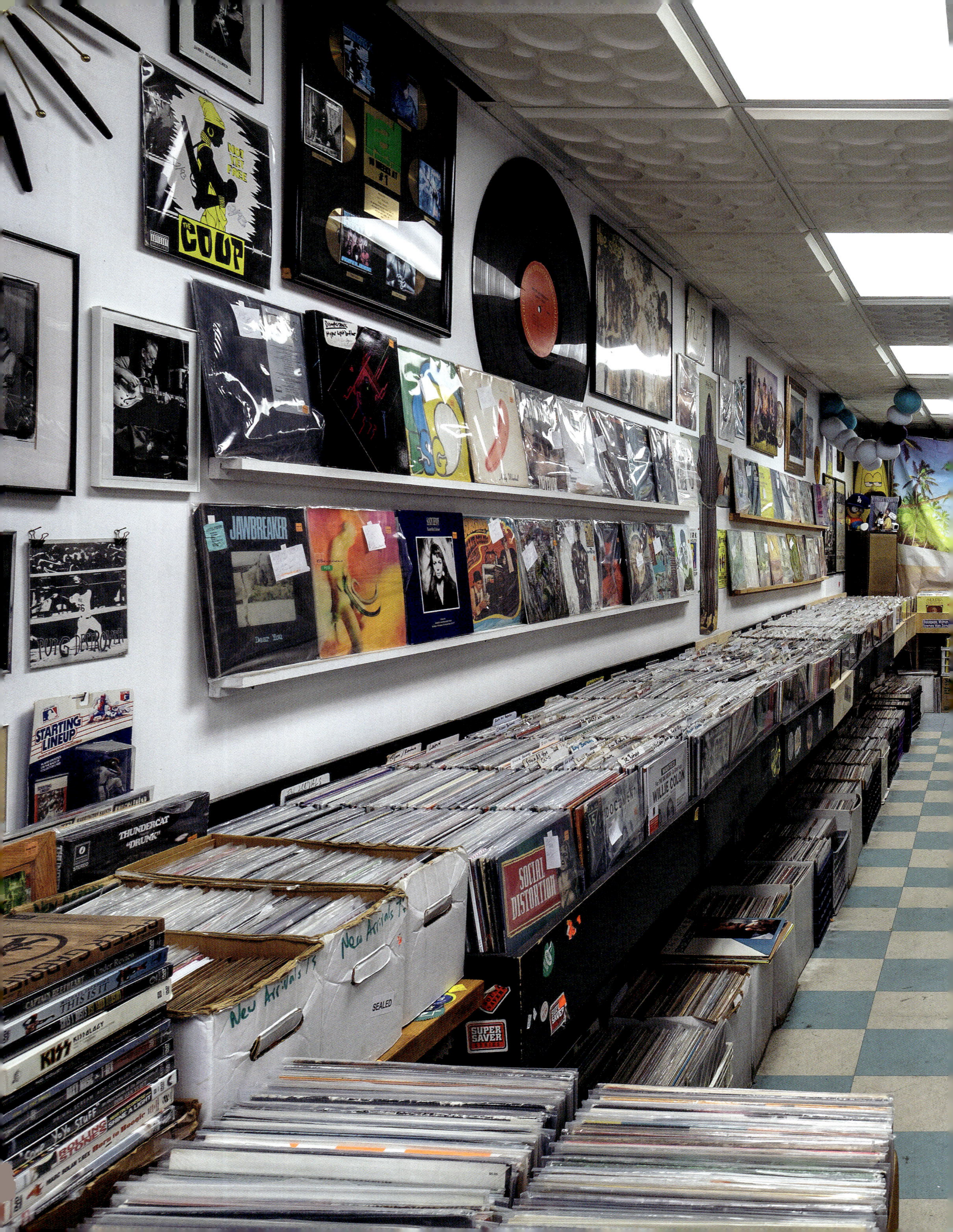

THE COUP
JAWBREAKER
Dear You
STARTING LINEUP
THUNDERCAT
"DRUNK"
SOCIAL DISTORTION
WILLIE COLON
New Arrivals
SEALED
SUPER SAVER
KISS

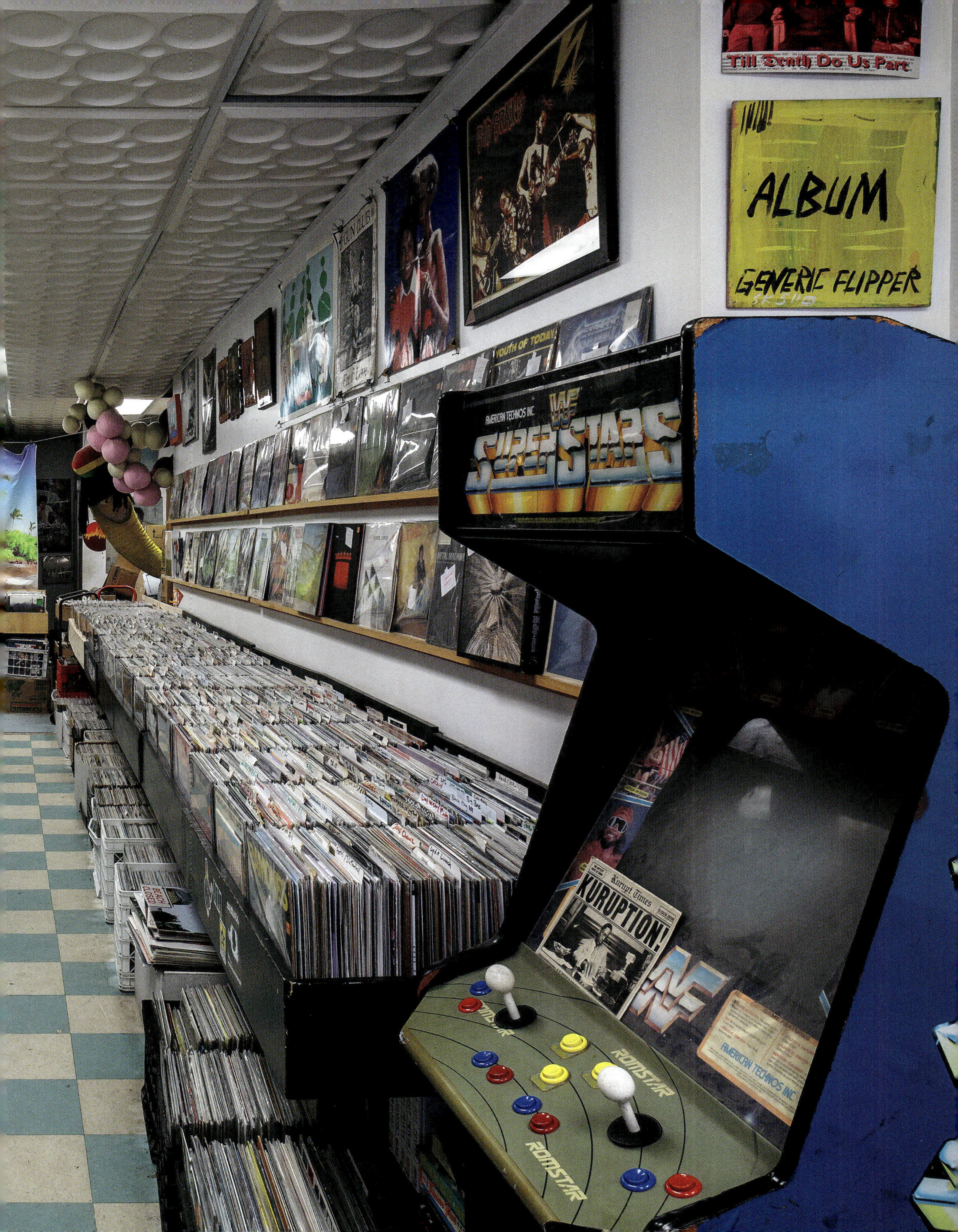

Till Death Do Us Part
ALBUM
GENERIC FLIPPER
YOUTH OF TODAY
AMERICAN TECHNOS INC.
SUPERSTARS
KURUPTION!
ROMSTAR
ROMSTAR
ROMSTAR
AMERICAN TECHNOS INC

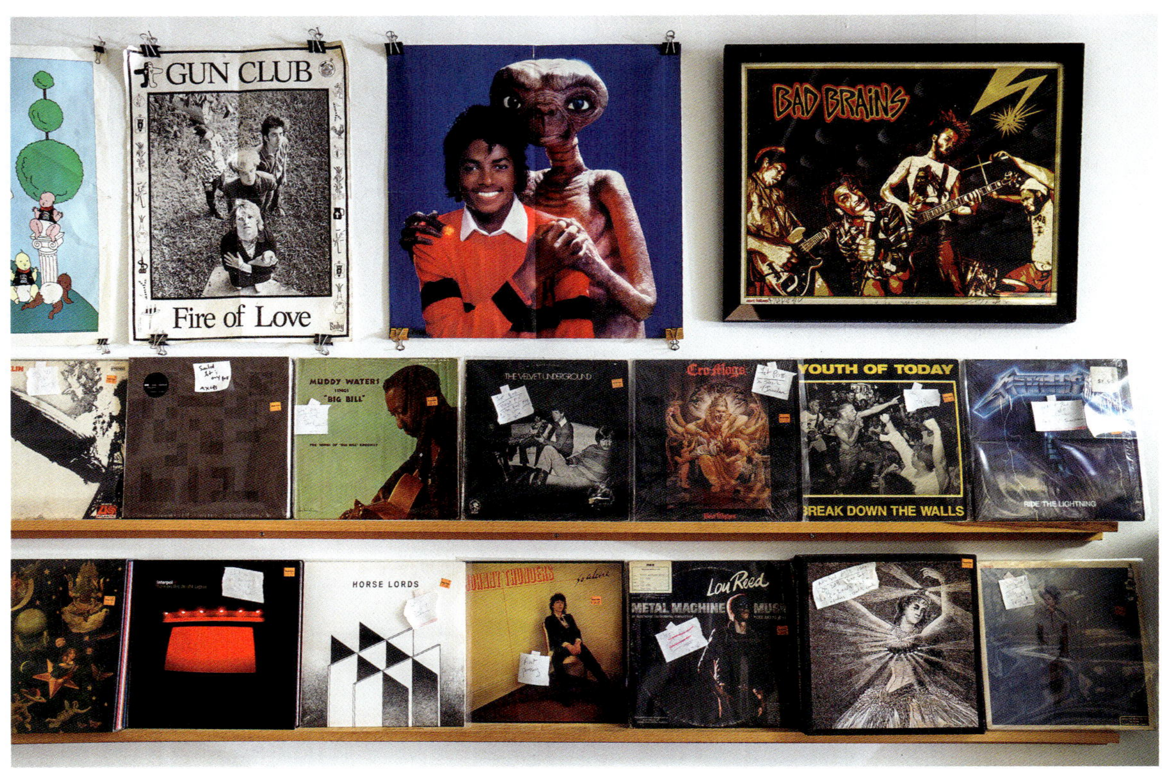
GUN CLUB
Fire of Love
BAD BRAINS
MUDDY WATERS
"BIG BILL"
THE VELVET UNDERGROUND
Cro-Mags
YOUTH OF TODAY
REAK DOWN THE WALLS
RIDE THE LIGHTNING
HORSE LORDS
Lou Reed
METAL MACHINE

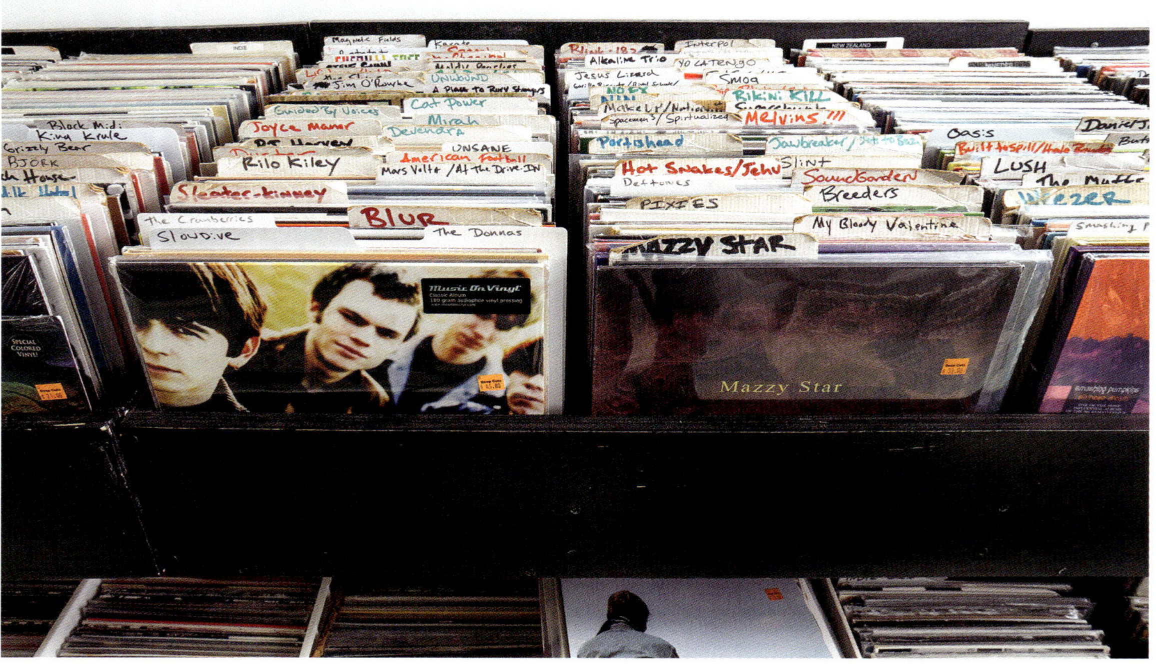
Magnetic Fields
Jim O'Rourke
Unwound
Cat Power
Guided By Voices
Mirah
Joyce Manor
Devendra
PJ Harvey
Unsane
American Football
Rilo Kiley
Mars Volta / At the Drive-In
Sleater-kinney
Blur
The Cranberries
Slowdive
The Donnas
Black Midi
King Krule
Grizzly Bear
Bjork
Alkaline Trio
Interpol
Yo La Tengo
Jesus Lizard
Smog
Bikini Kill
Melvins
Portishead
Jawbreaker
Slint
Hot Snakes/Jehu
Deftones
Soundgarden
Breeders
Pixies
My Bloody Valentine
Mazzy Star
Oasis
Lush
Weezer
Music On Vinyl
Mazzy Star

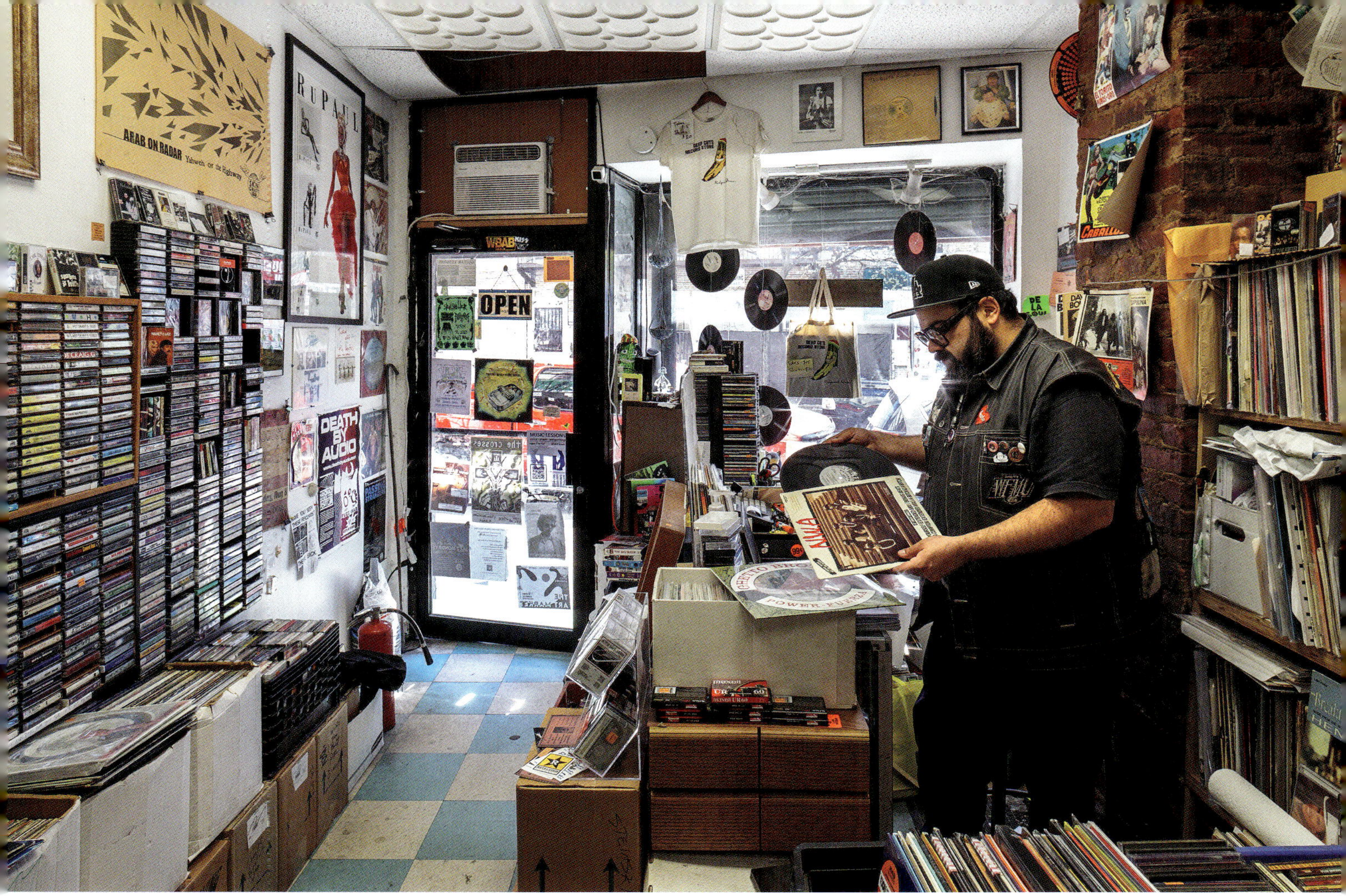

OPPOSITE BOTTOM Handwritten dividers, some with cleverly named categories (like "Bird Talk," "Weird Fuckin' Shit," "Occult/Psychics," and "Dat Gangsta Shit"), help organize the wide variety of music on offer, including salsa, classic rock, reggaeton, Latin, and pop.

ABOVE Co-owner Brandon Perry adds new and used fresh arrivals to the store daily. He also helps support local and touring artists by selling their albums on consignment and giving them almost all of the proceeds.

RIGHT An altar dedicated to Selena, the "Queen of Tejano Music," can be found over the register, along with unique ephemera.

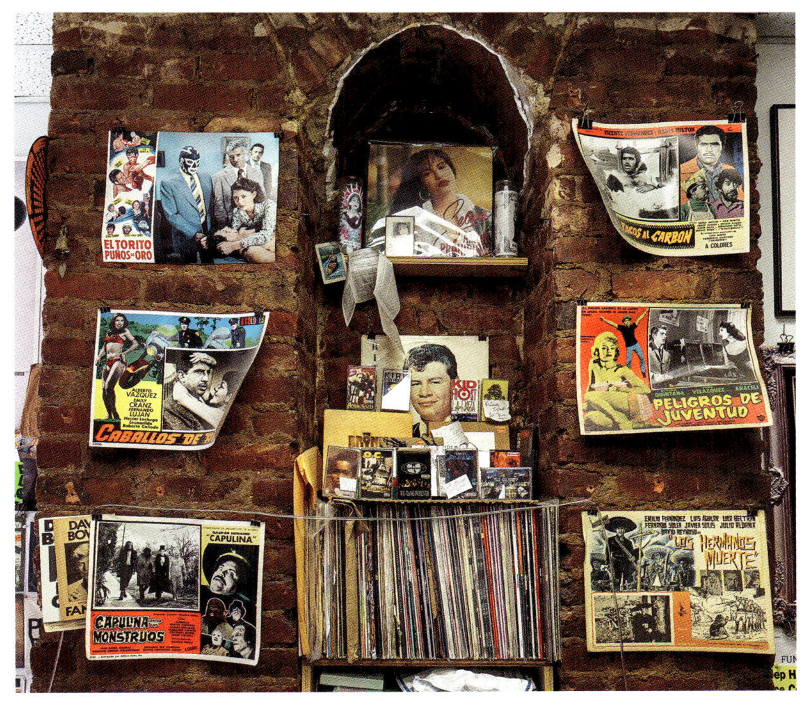

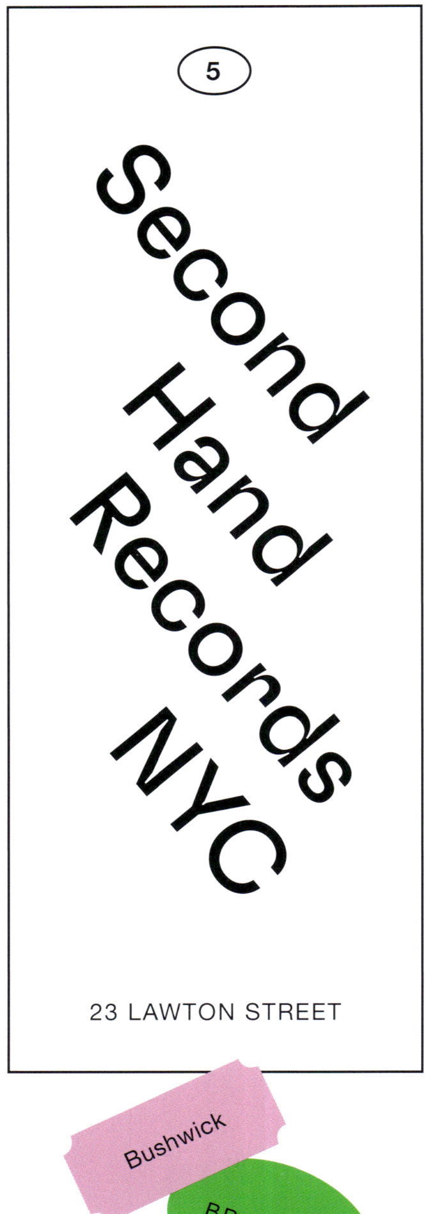

PEOPLE DON'T OFTEN STUMBLE UPON the Bushwick-based Second Hand Records NYC—but Federico "Fatik" Rojas-Lavado, who founded the neighborhood shop in 2016, prefers it that way. Second Hand's first home, on the corner of Myrtle Avenue and Broadway, welcomed plenty of weary travelers from the nearby subway station. Yet Rojas-Lavado finds a certain solace in knowing his newer, off-the-beaten-path location close by, at 23 Lawton Street, invites a certain level of intention. "Being here has recentered the destination aspect of it," he explains. "People come here; they know what they're coming for."

Born in Venezuela, Rojas-Lavado spent his earliest years in Jackson Heights, Queens, before his family settled in Brooklyn. Both his parents studied at Pratt Institute, and he took art and design classes through the prestigious Cooper Union as a high school student. School didn't always fit in with his teenage rhythm, but his older brother's immersion in the mid-'90s New York hip-hop scene did. Via an impromptu education of smuggled tapes and schoolyard listening sessions, Rojas-Lavado encountered a new creative outlet to invest in. Eventually, he decided to do it for a living.

Now, the touring producer and DJ has turned vinyl into a lifestyle. Behind a set of square windows at Second Hand that capture sunlight like a greenhouse, plants, kente cloths, and masks adorn walls of white brick, while Matryoshka dolls, action figures, and mallard duck statuettes find a common habitat atop the Klipsch speakers stationed around the space. Amid the shop's floor stock, which Rojas-Lavado estimates is in the three- to four-thousand record range, old-school hip-hop by artists hailing from up and down the East Coast mingles with an expansive lineage of influences: soul, disco, funk, and jazz. Even without a warehouse's worth of choices, Rojas-Lavado still manages to source an encyclopedic collection, putting his past life as a record distributor to work by personally appraising and pricing every item for sale. He says he tries to be conscious of "rewarding curiosity," and a quick flip through the "Staff Recommended" bin does the trick. (How could any dance music connoisseur resist bringing home a 45 RPM disco extended cut described thusly via a Sharpie note on a white sticker: "Tough, dark and funky Paradise Garage killer"?). Second Hand also operates its own independent record label, selectively pressing EPs available both in person and through its website.

The business may have found a comfortable niche just outside of Broadway's foot traffic, but in 2020, Rojas-Lavado hatched a plan to publicize Second Hand as not just a destination but a meeting place. He began hosting small events for collectors and DJs alike: open decks, after-hours browsing, and an opportunity for regular customers to put personalities to the faces of shoppers featured on the business's photobooth-style Instagram account. Now, a few years in, Rojas-Lavado says the community's response has been rewarding and that not trying to be everything to everyone has served him well. "It's not for everybody, and it's totally fine," he explains. "But for the ones that are comfortable here? It's kind of everything."

Rojas-Lavado recognizes that every customer ends up spending *something* with him, be it money, time, or energy. With that in mind, he's established a shop where fair prices and the finer things comfortably co-exist. "This is a luxury thing. People can listen to music and don't need records for it, which is great," he explains about vinyl. "But this adds texture to it. Polyester's cool, but [there's something] nice about something handwoven."

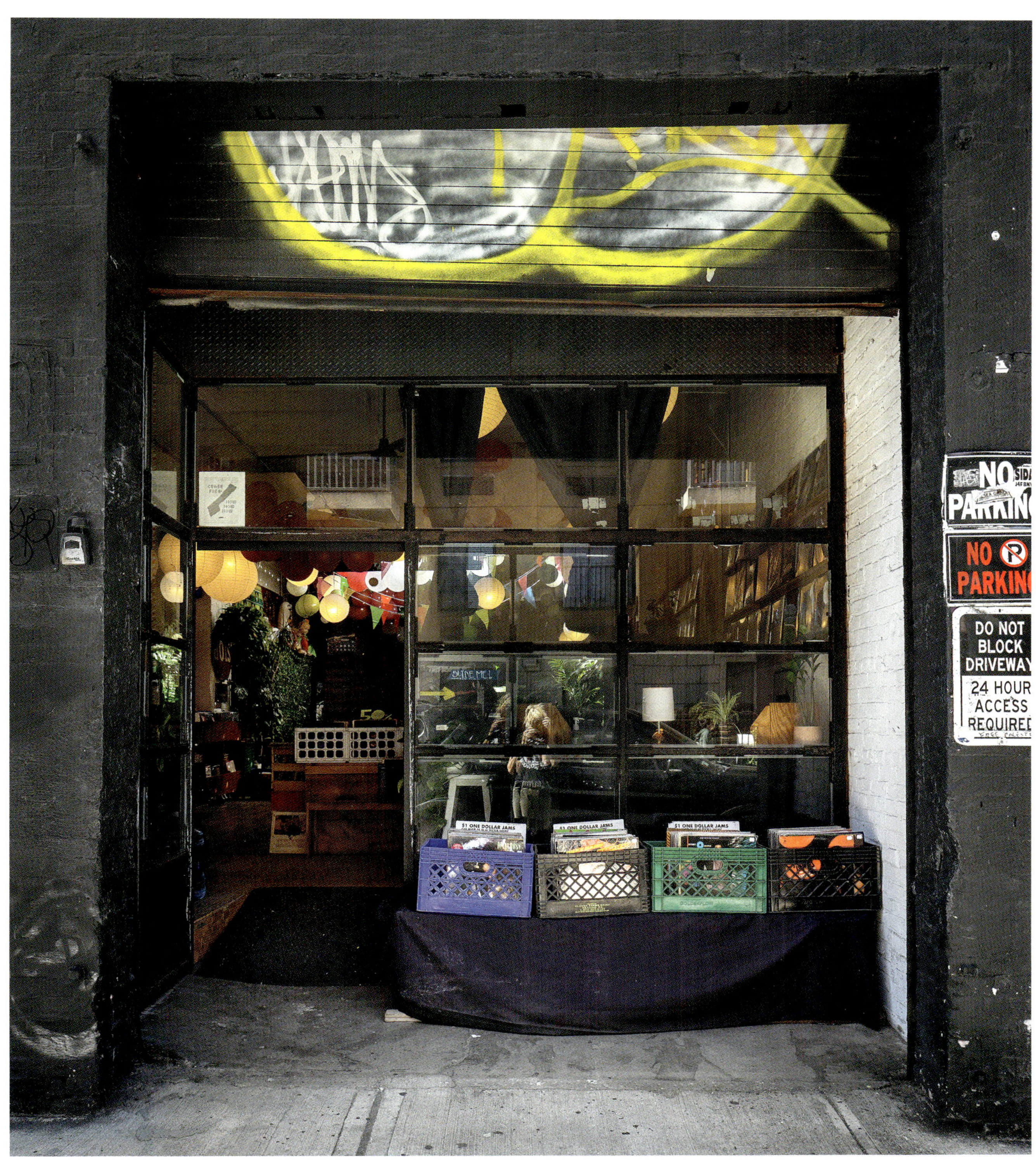

ABOVE Located on a side street in Bushwick off Broadway, Second Hand Records NYC is just a short walk away from the J subway line. It carries a wide variety of used and new vinyl in genres including funk, soul, disco, Latin, rock, house, hip-hop, jazz, and techno.

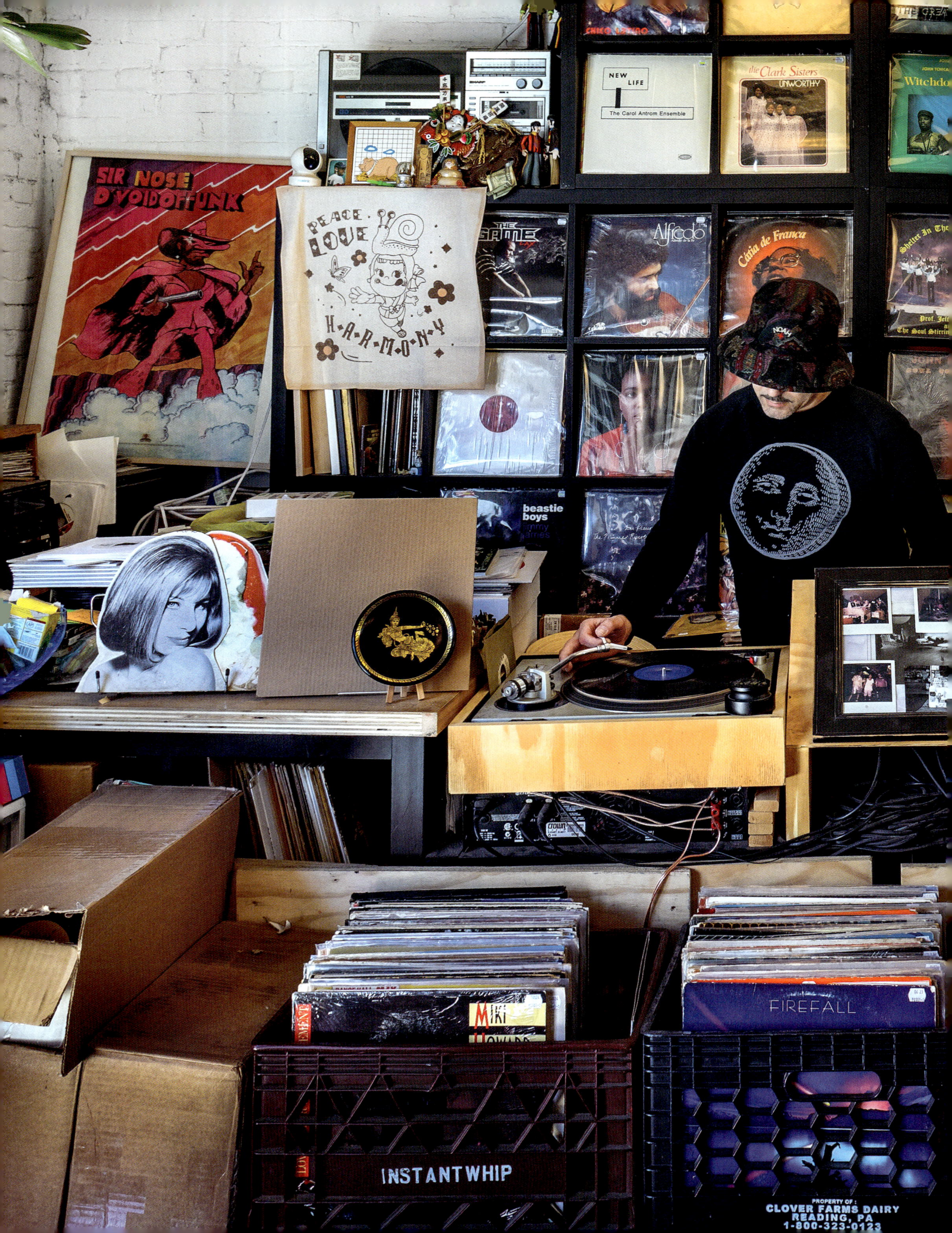

SIR NOSE D'VOIDOFFUNK
PEACE LOVE H-A-R-M-O-N-Y
NEW LIFE
The Carol Antrom Ensemble
the Clark Sisters
UNWORTHY
THE GAME
Alfredo
Cátia de França
NOAH
beastie boys
FIREFALL
INSTANTWHIP
PROPERTY OF:
CLOVER FARMS DAIRY
READING, PA
1-800-323-0123

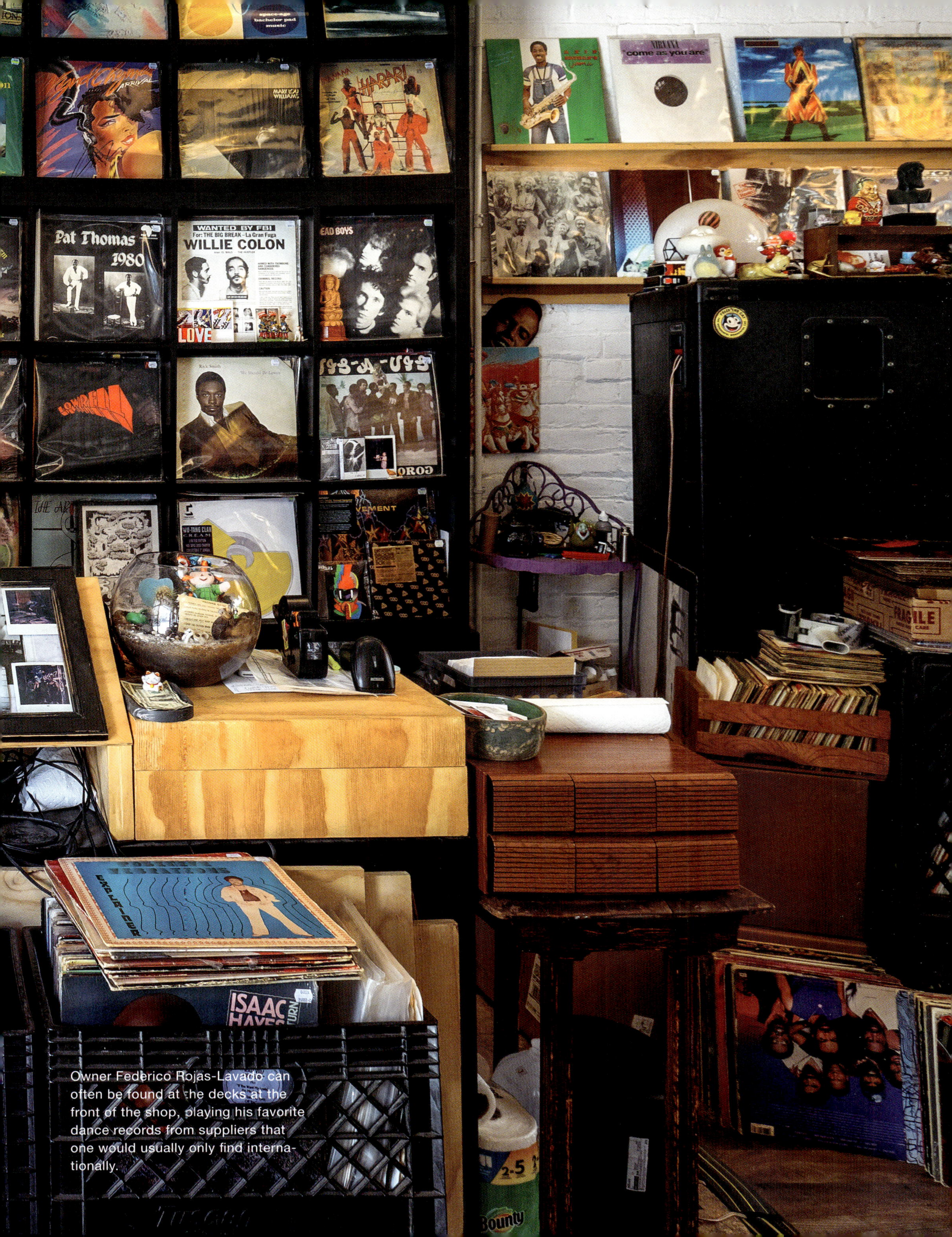

Owner Federico Rojas-Lavado can often be found at the decks at the front of the shop, playing his favorite dance records from suppliers that one would usually only find internationally.

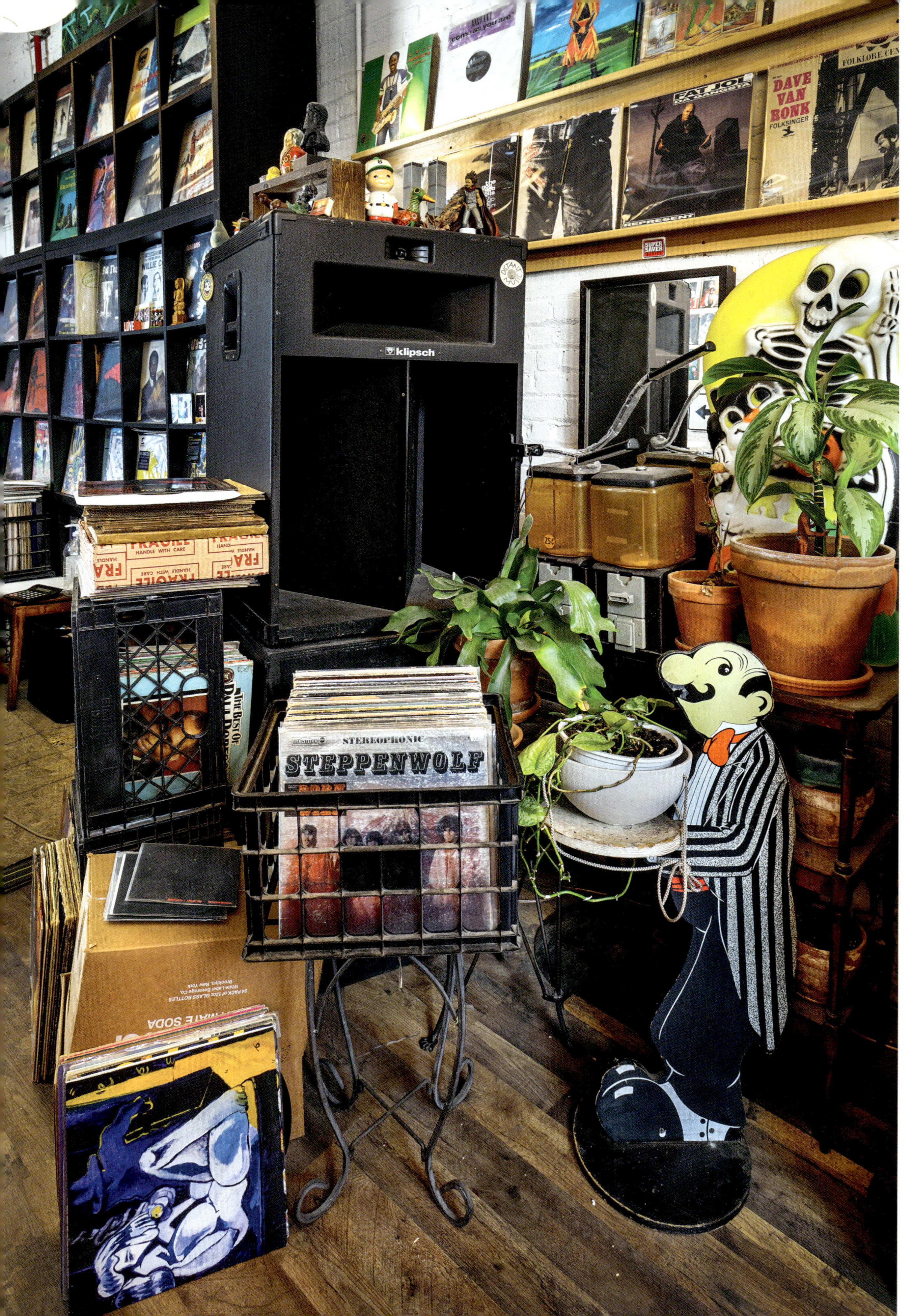

DAVE
VAN
RONK
FOLKSINGER
FAT JOE
klipsch
FRAGILE
HANDLE WITH CARE
STEREOPHONIC
STEPPENWOLF

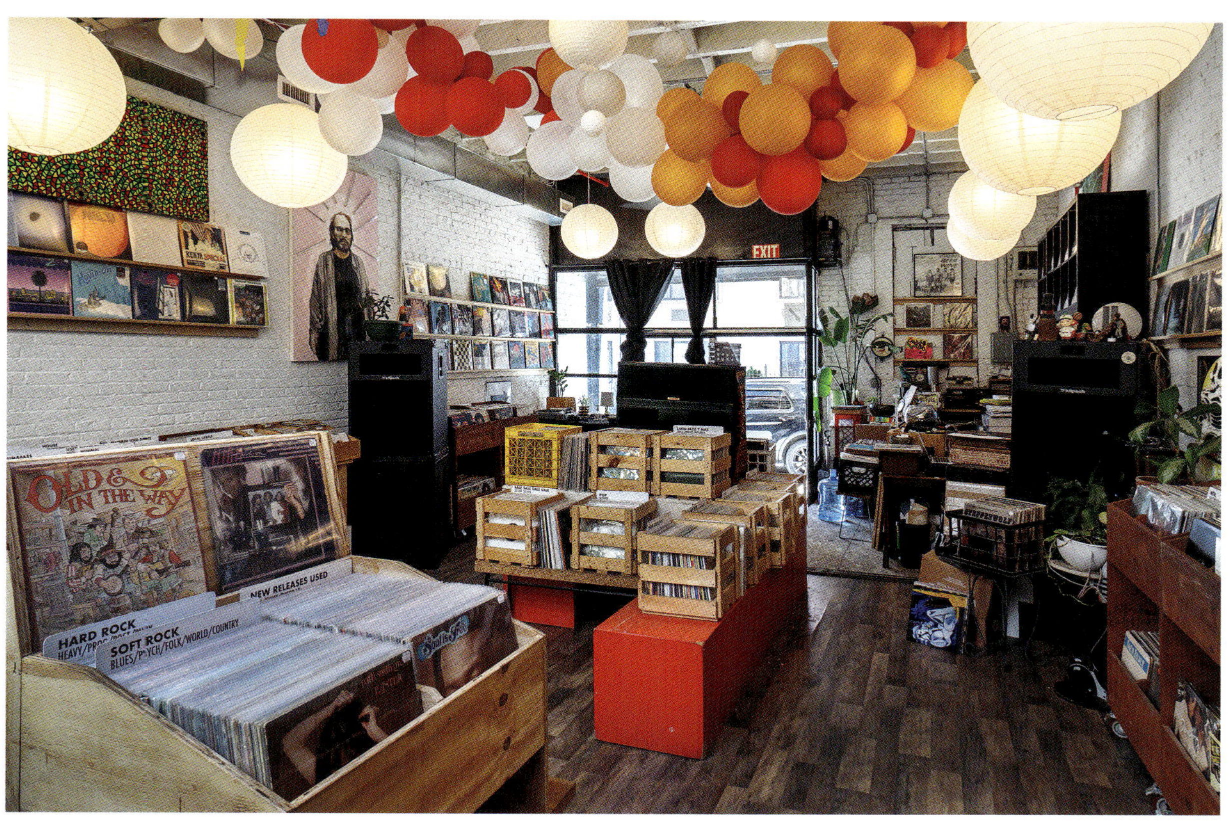
OLD & IN THE WAY
NEW RELEASES USED
HARD ROCK
SOFT ROCK
EXIT

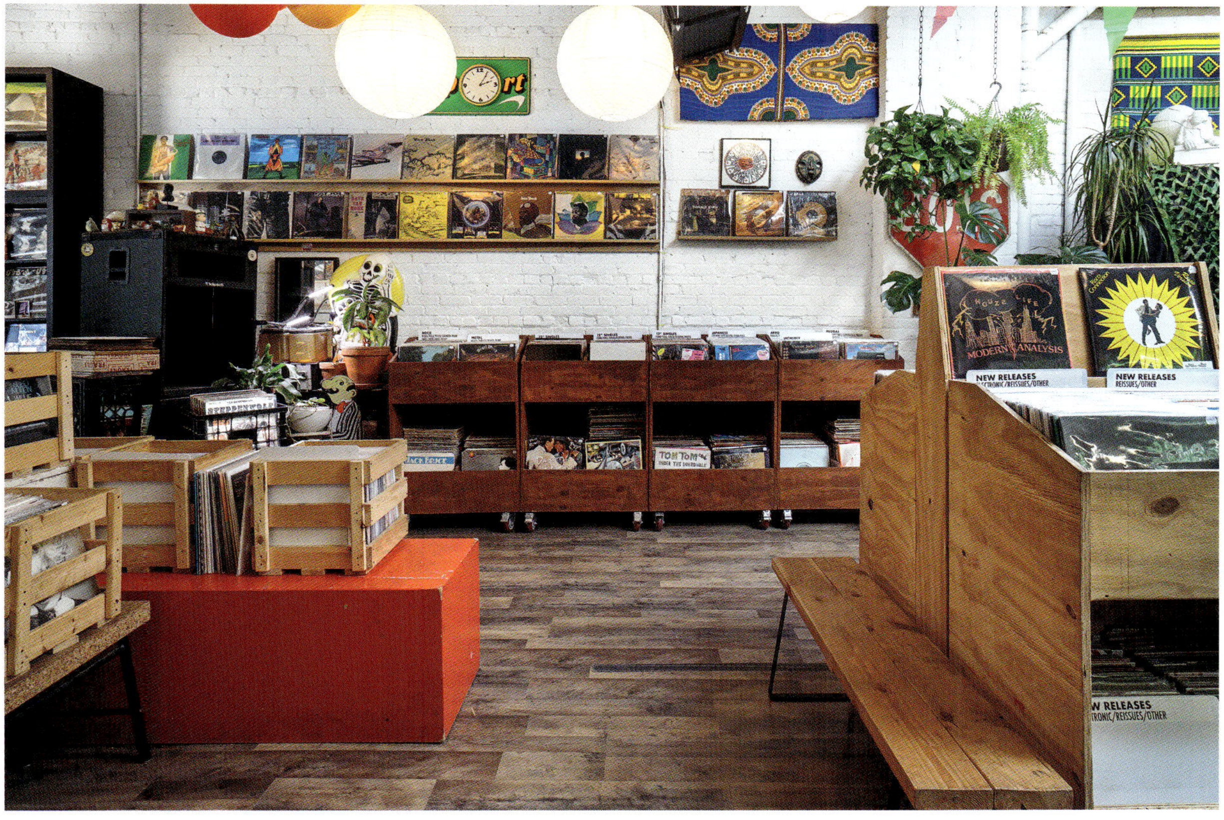
MODERN ANALYSIS
NEW RELEASES
NEW RELEASES

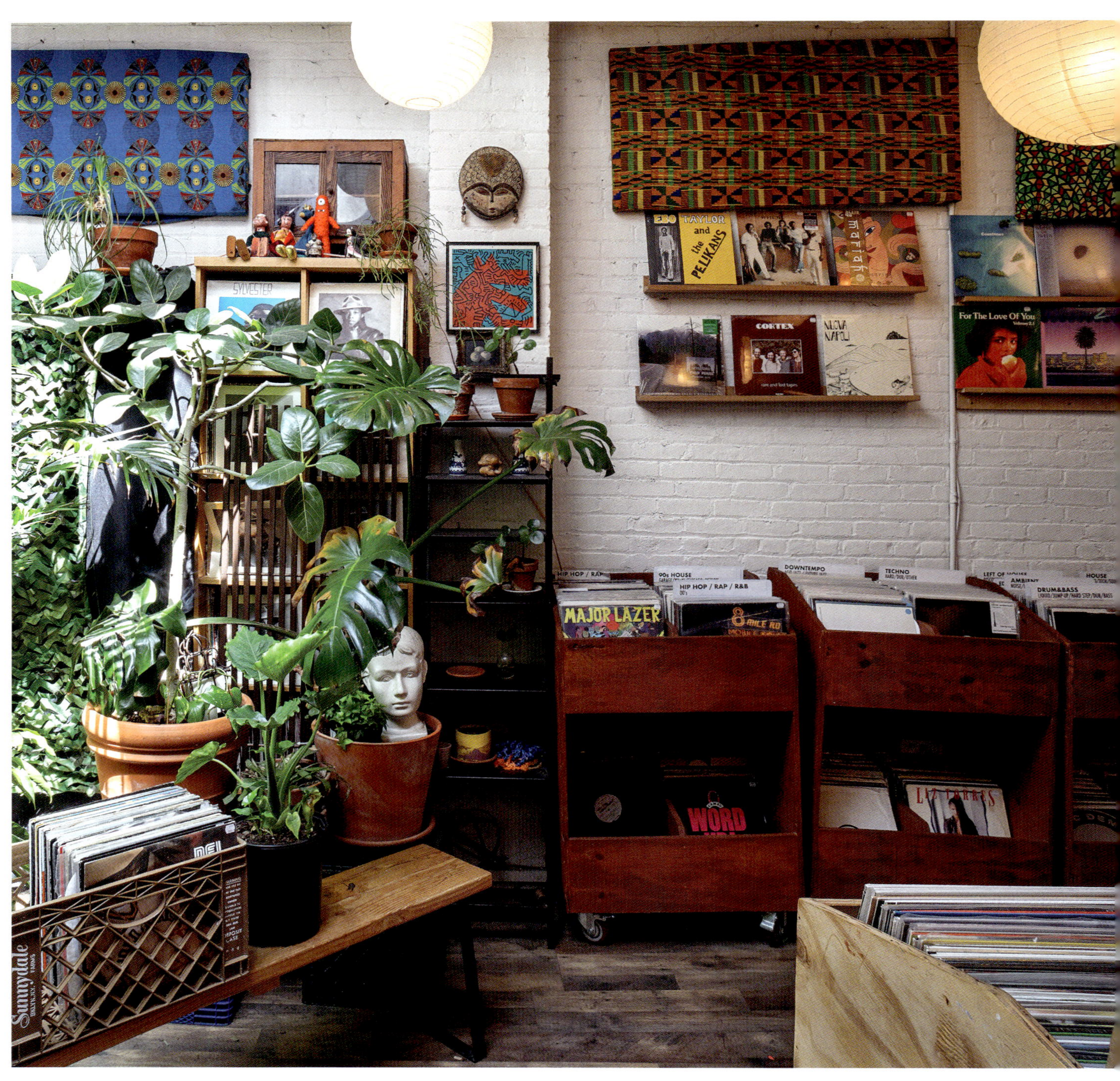
SYLVESTER
EBO TAYLOR and the PELIKANS
CORTEX
NUOVA NAPOLI
For The Love Of You
HIP HOP / RAP / R&B
90s HOUSE
DOWNTEMPO
TECHNO
AMBIENT
DRUM&BASS
HOUSE
MAJOR LAZER
8 MILE RD
WORD
LIZ TORRES
Sunnydale

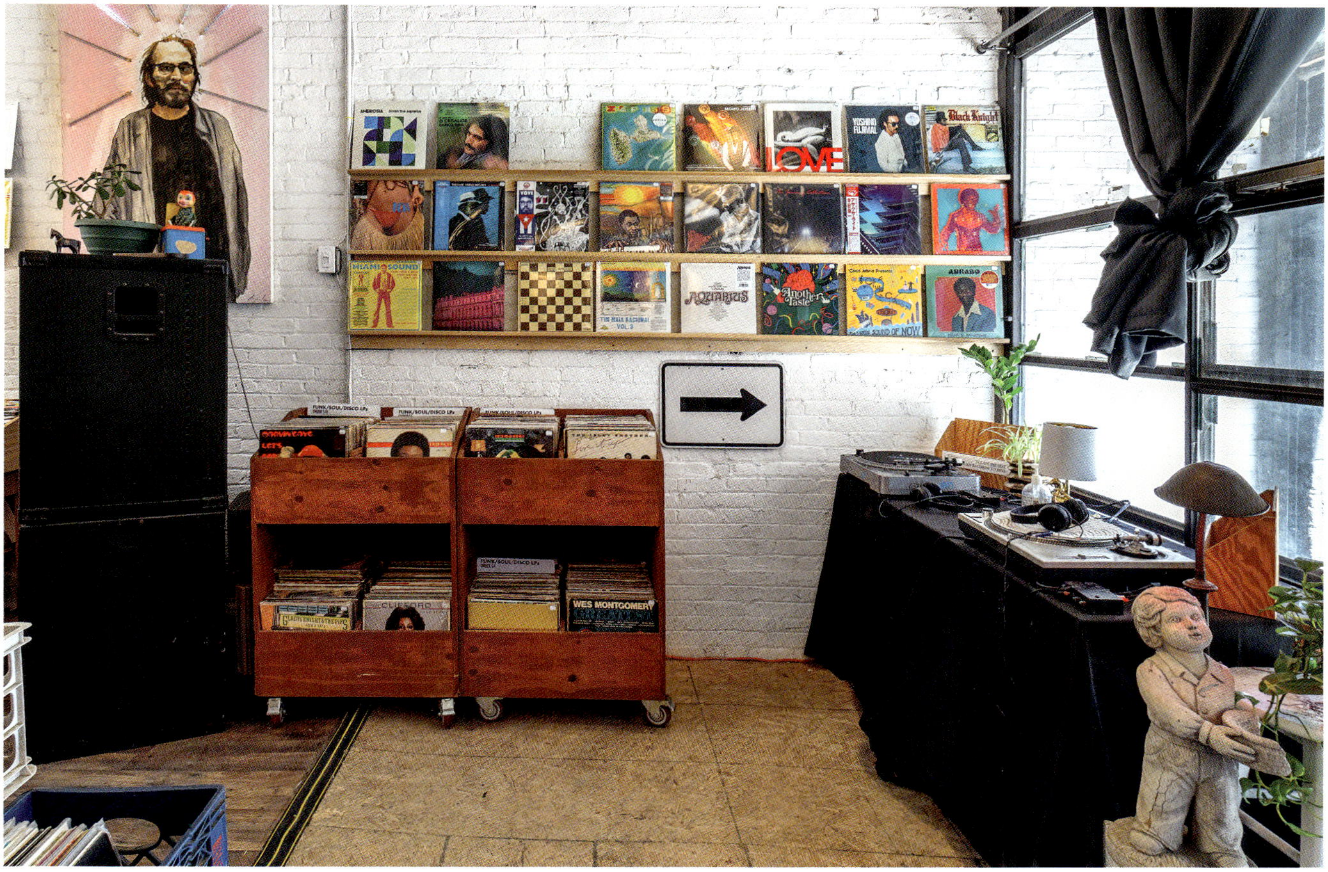

OPPOSITE The large and cheery light-filled space, complete with a jungle of plants, artwork, and balloons, has movable record bins to create even more space for in-store events.

RIGHT Second Hand has its own self-titled label. Uniquely, it also offers pressing and distribution services for local artists and labels, fostering an environment where new and undiscovered music can meet.

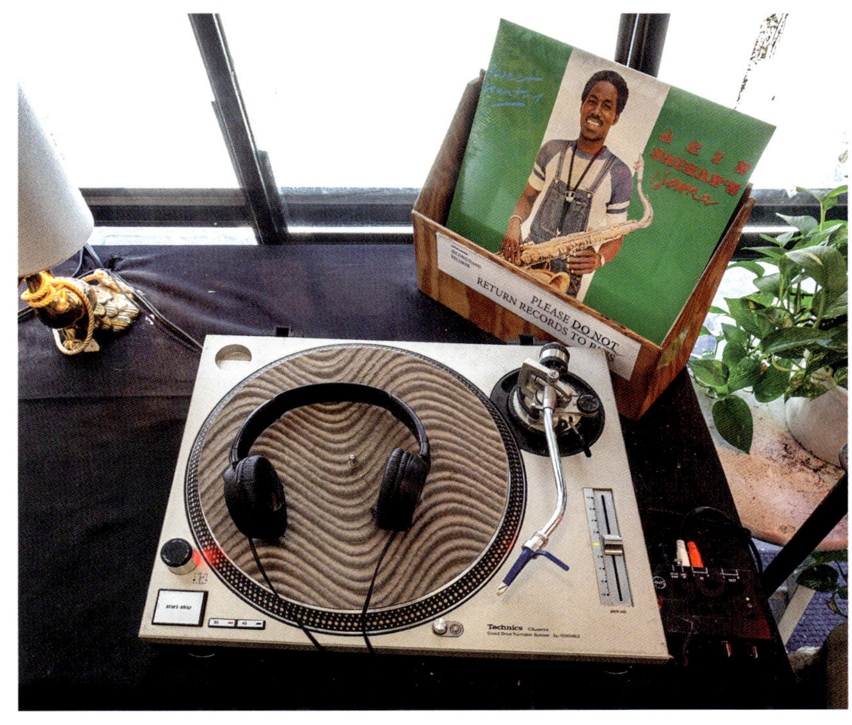

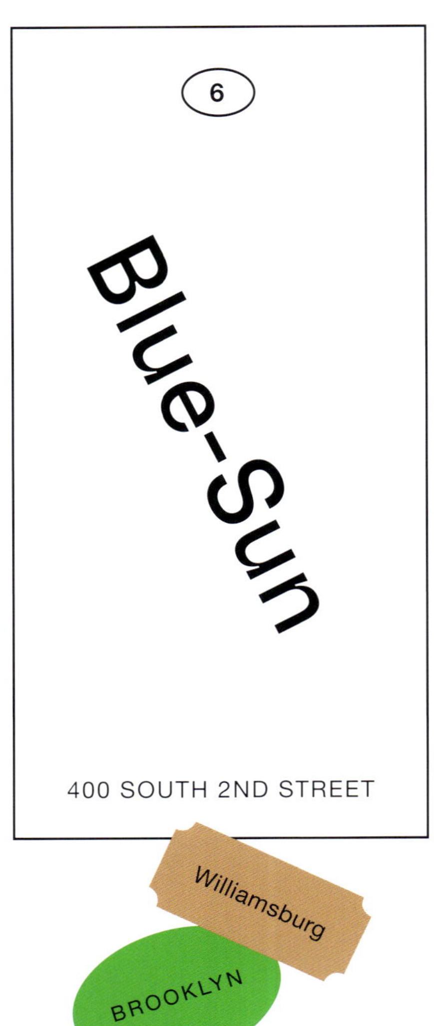

STYLE AND SUBSTANCE DON'T ALWAYS strike a perfect balance—but when they do, the result looks a lot like Williamsburg's Blue-Sun. Established in 2017 by esteemed local selector Billy Teichen, the streamlined collection at Blue-Sun may initially seem spare compared to the controlled chaos of comparable shops. But even though Teichen doesn't trade in anything and everything under the sun, his curation shines plenty of natural light on high-quality vinyl.

With a special eye for jazz, funk, dance music, and disco, the Chicago native has managed to turn Blue-Sun into a Swiss Army knife of genres, with fresh material coming through the doors each day. Wide, open-plan space, combined with ample natural lighting, gives the store a cathedral-like feel. Plenty of customers' prayers are answered thanks to Teichen, who's always happy to provide a recommendation or pearl of wisdom. "My favorite part of my work is the eternal discovery," he says. "That's one of the main reasons I opened the shop. I wanted to explore music as much as possible. I don't make or play music, so listening and collecting was my way to connect and learn."

Nearly equal parts events space and vendor space, any open slot on the store's docket is quickly filled with a wide selection of community activities, ranging from sidewalk garment sales to album release parties, record fairs, custom earplug fittings, ambient sets, and more—so be prepared to leave with more than just records under your arm. "We really welcome every type of person into the shop, not just the record fiends," Teichen says. "We tried to make a space that you want to hang out in and enjoy music."

Blue-Sun is also the only United States stockist currently licensed to sell the high-end Japanese incense brand Kuumba International. Scents like Love Supreme, Clean Air, and Dr Pepper are for sale in sample packs, alongside ashtrays, incense holders, and other ephemera. As part of a clothing line release in 2023, Kuumba and Blue-Sun even collaborated on a bespoke scent named after the store.

A childhood taste for skate videos may have inspired Teichen's move to New York, but it's the community that's kept him there. During his tenure at Blue-Sun's first location on Havemeyer Street (just a few blocks west of where it now sits), Teichen spearheaded plenty of supporting programming, from art and record fairs to online radio sets and socially distanced incense pickups. But since moving to the loftier, high-ceilinged space at 400 South 2nd Street in 2022, he's been able to facilitate bucket-list events, like a live jazz performance from Mitchell Cheng and Everton Isidoro.

These types of endeavors are key to Blue-Sun's strong reputation among veteran musicians and sample-sourcers. Production legends from Large Professor (see p. 215) to BreakBeat Lou to Frankie Bones have all stopped by, and none left empty-handed. In 2024 the rapper Navy Blue even entrusted the shop with limited-edition exclusive versions of his albums *Song of Sage: Post Panic!* and *Navy's Reprise*. And Virgil Abloh, the producer, designer, and visionary behind Off-White, showed his support for years (until his death in 2021) as the proud owner of a red Blue-Sun logo hoodie.

One thing Teichen never promises potential customers? A hold. As he likes to share in regular social media updates highlighting the week's just-ins, "Hesitation will lead to sadness and regret." Plenty of his top-tier titles—lost J Dilla remixes, original Miles Davis pressings, and rare Frank Zappa box sets—head off to new homes before he has the chance to bid them a proper goodbye. But that's part of the beauty of vinyl: there's always the off chance it might walk back through the door.

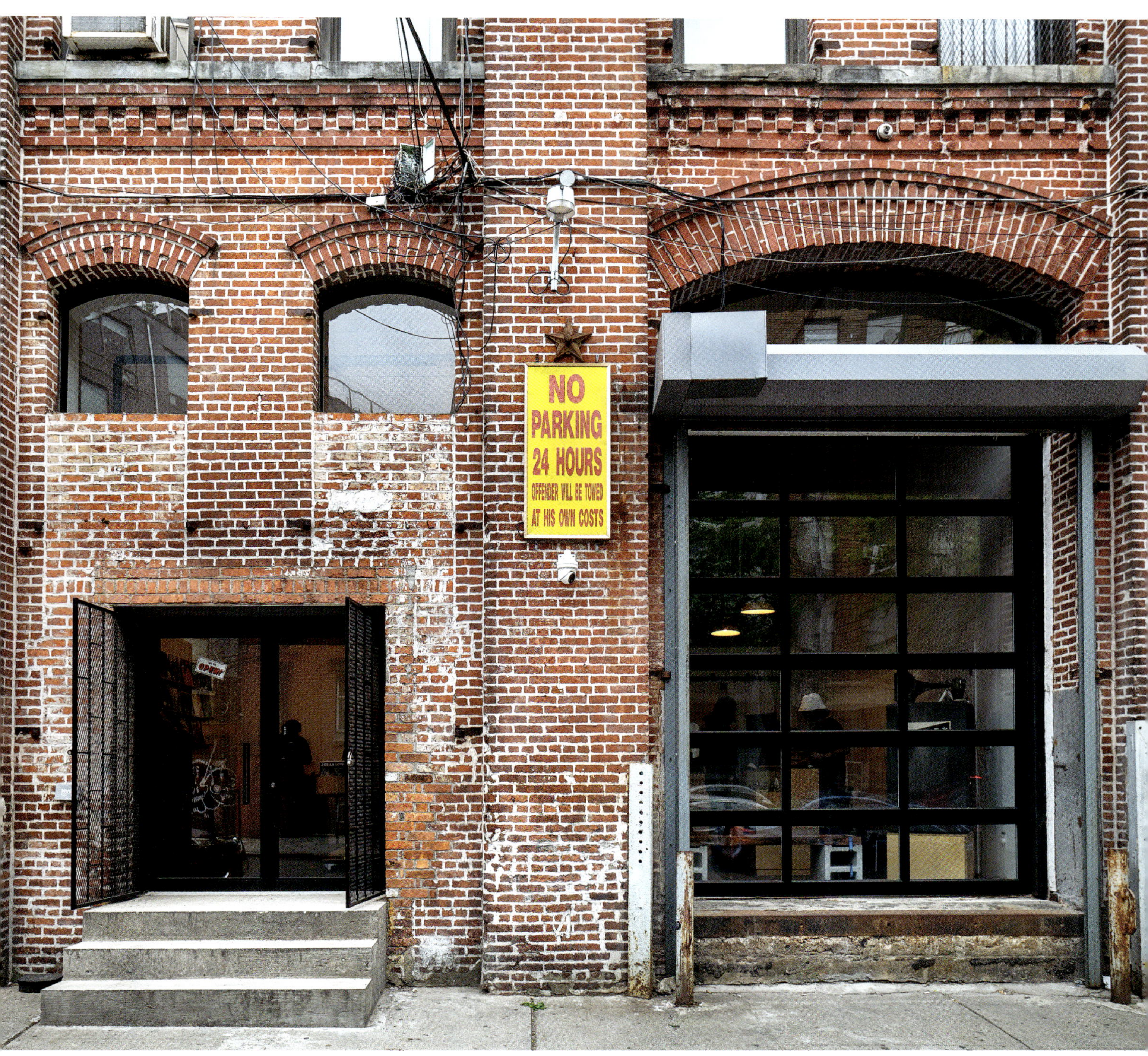

ABOVE Blue-Sun, which was founded in 2017, relocated to a larger, window-filled minimalist space on a residential side street in Williamsburg in 2022.

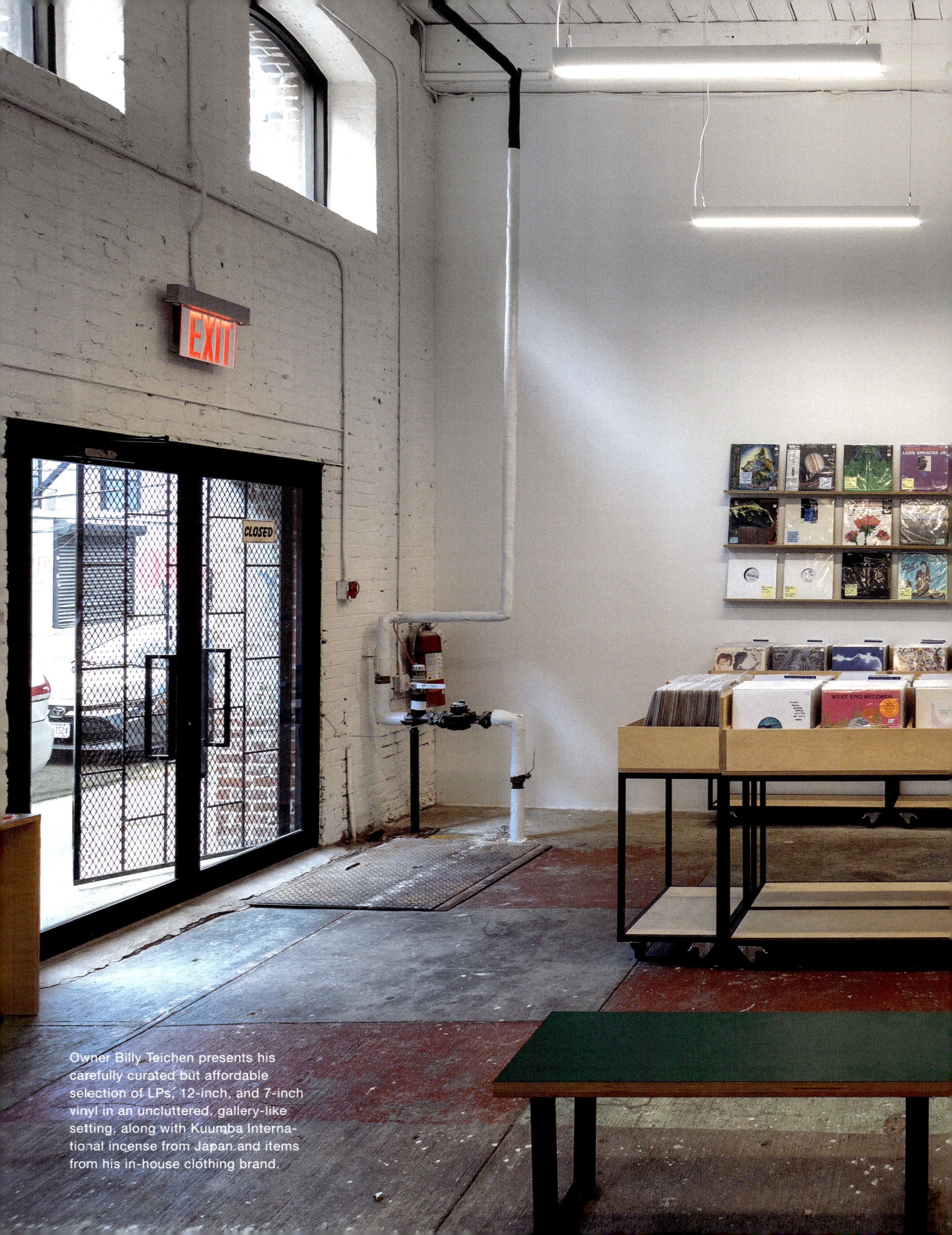

Owner Billy Teichen presents his carefully curated but affordable selection of LPs, 12-inch, and 7-inch vinyl in an uncluttered, gallery-like setting, along with Kuumba International incense from Japan and items from his in-house clothing brand.

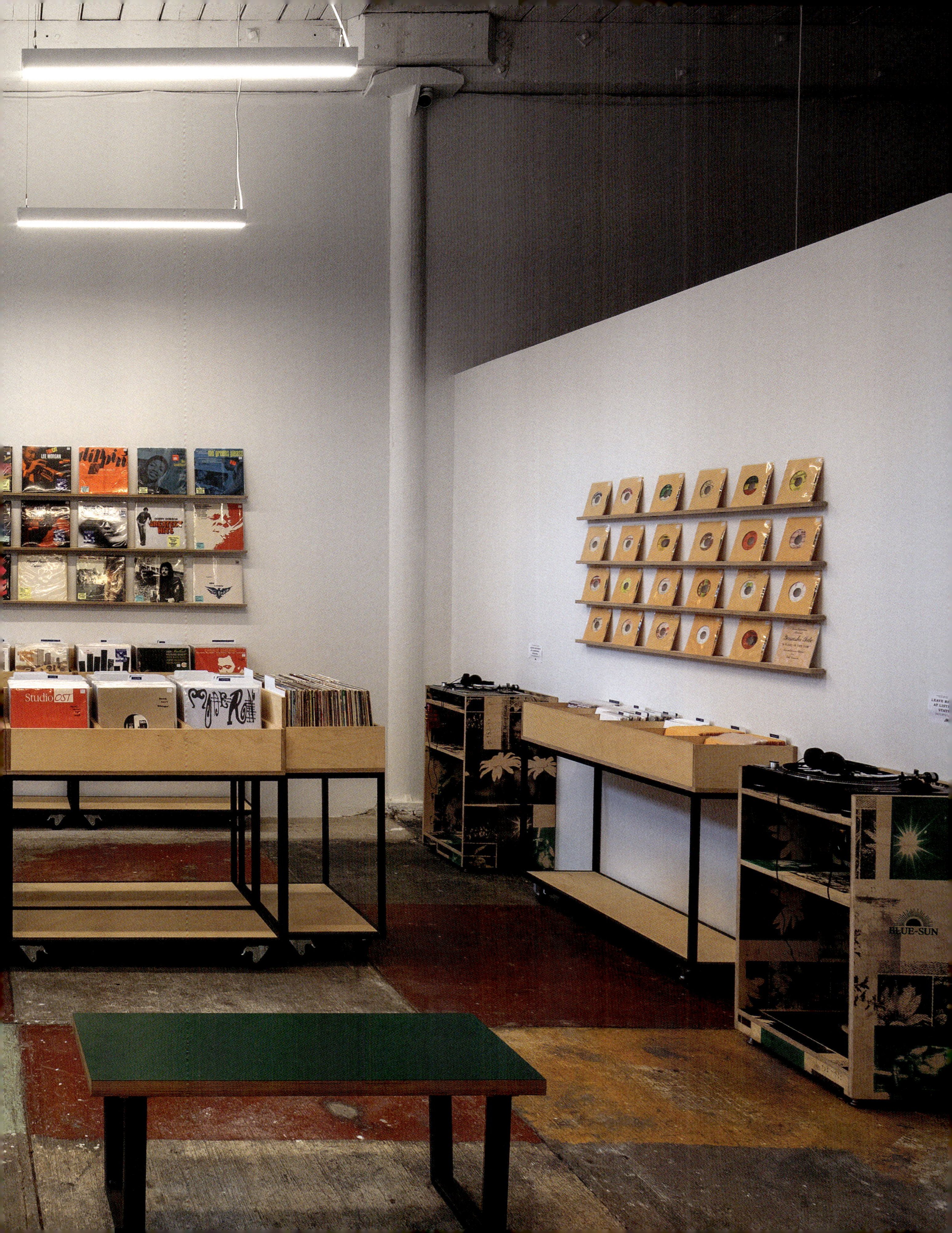
Studio
BLUE-SUN

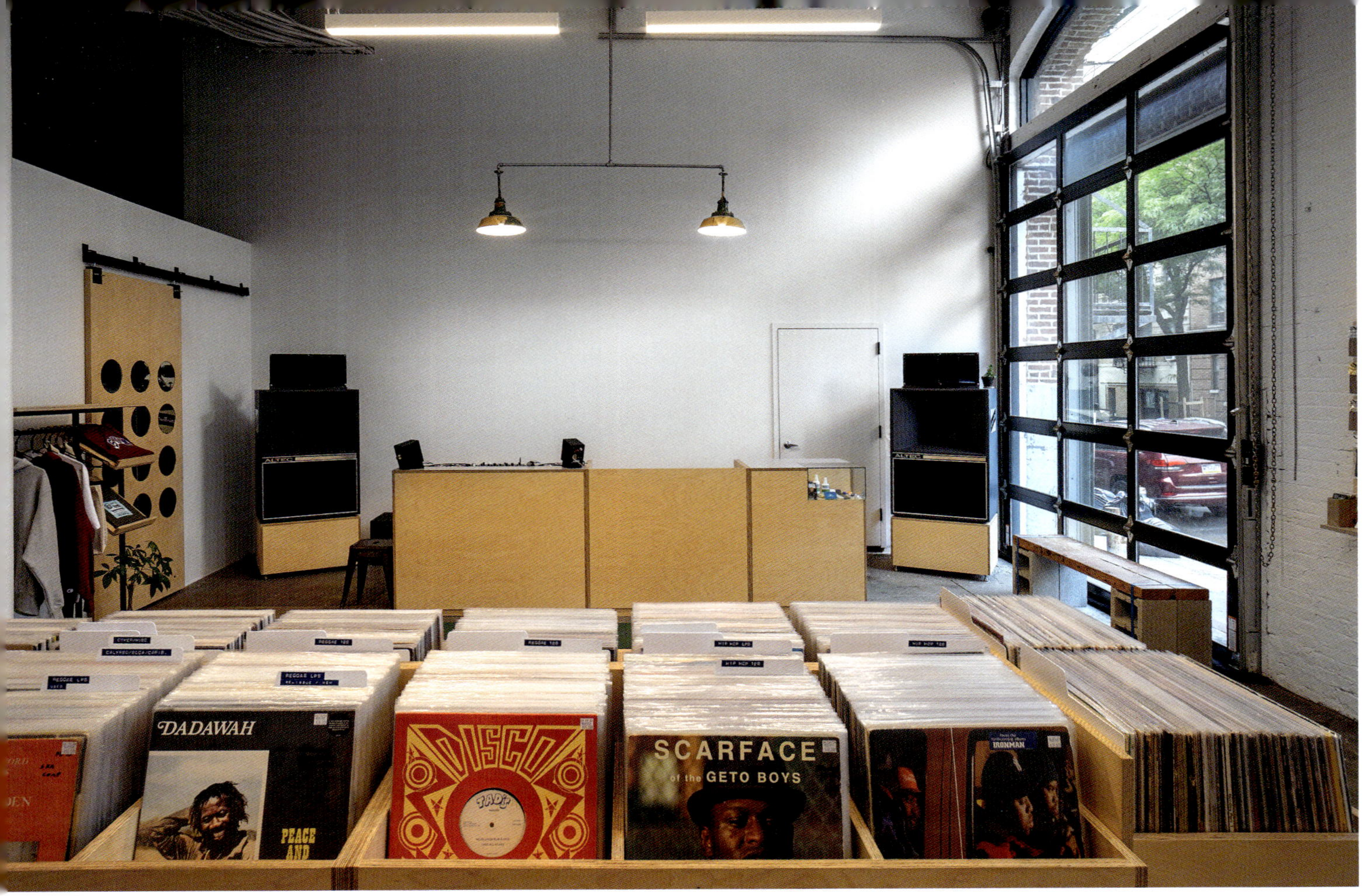

DADAWAH
PEACE AND
DISCO
SCARFACE
of the GETO BOYS
IRONMAN
TOPS 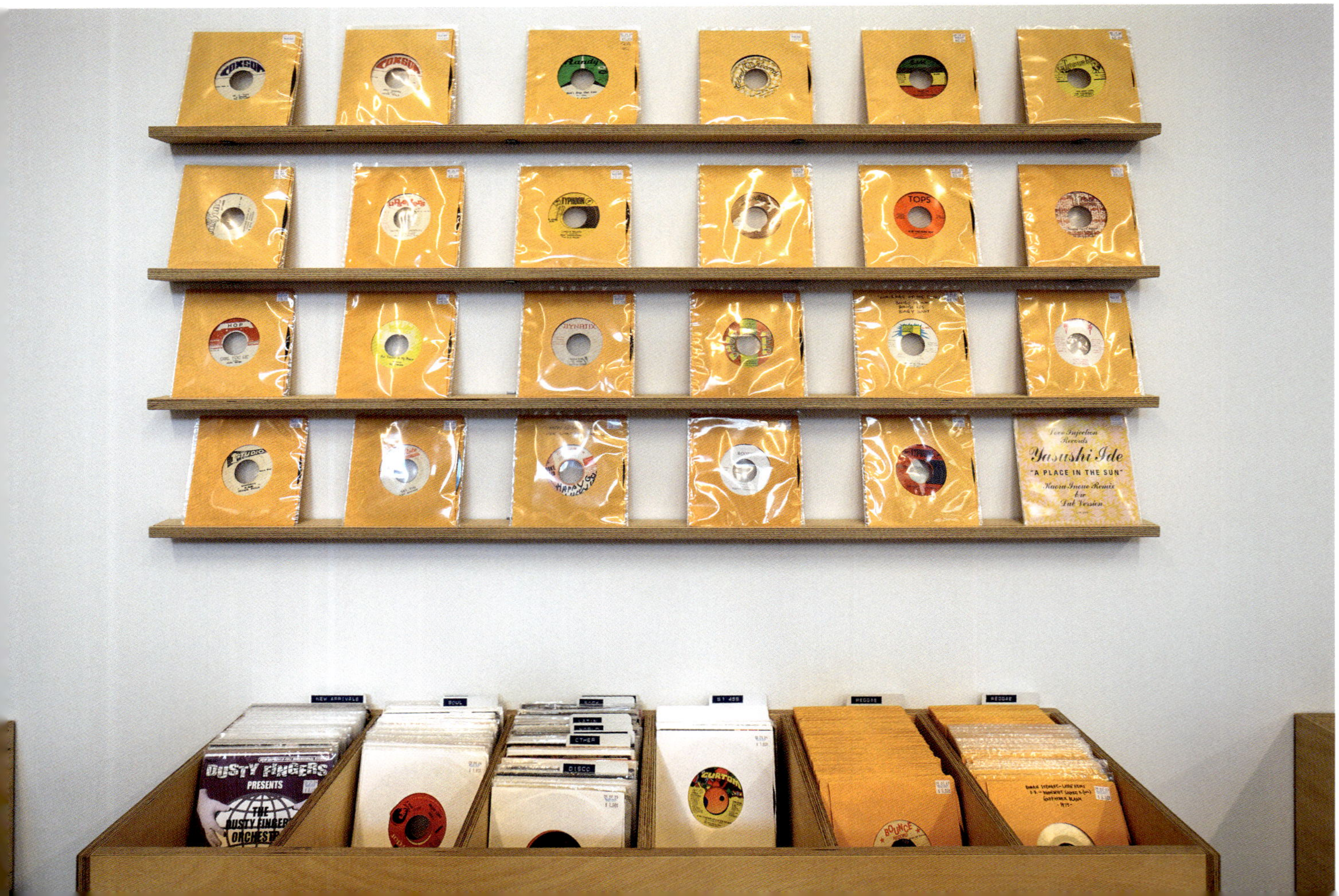
Yasushi Ide
"A PLACE IN THE SUN"
DUSTY FINGERS
PRESENTS
THE DUSTY FINGERS ORCHESTRA
BOUNCE

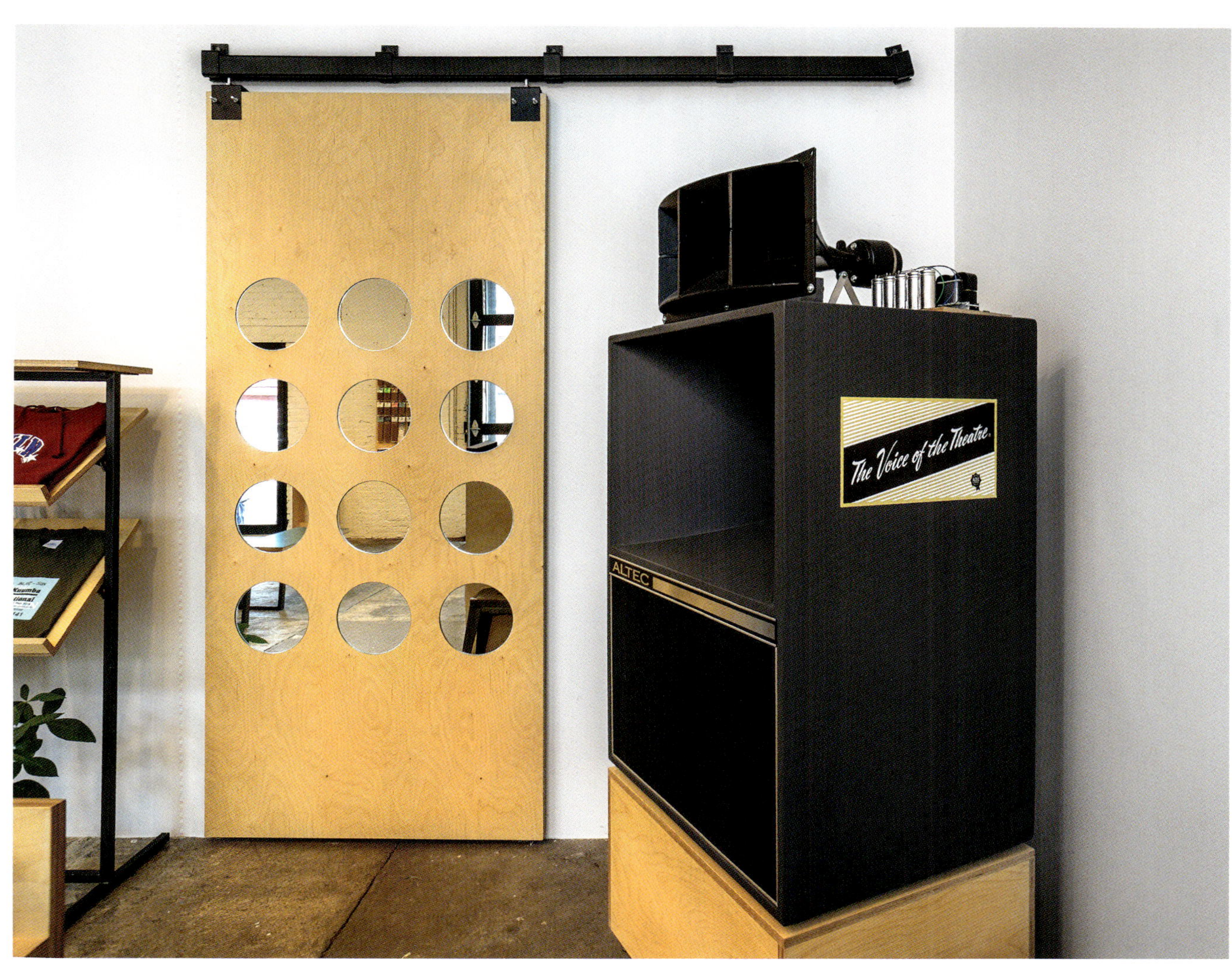

OPPOSITE BOTTOM A large selection of 45s can be found at the shop with a starting price of only $1.

ABOVE A pair of massive Altec Lansing "The Voice of the Theatre" speakers flank the front counter.

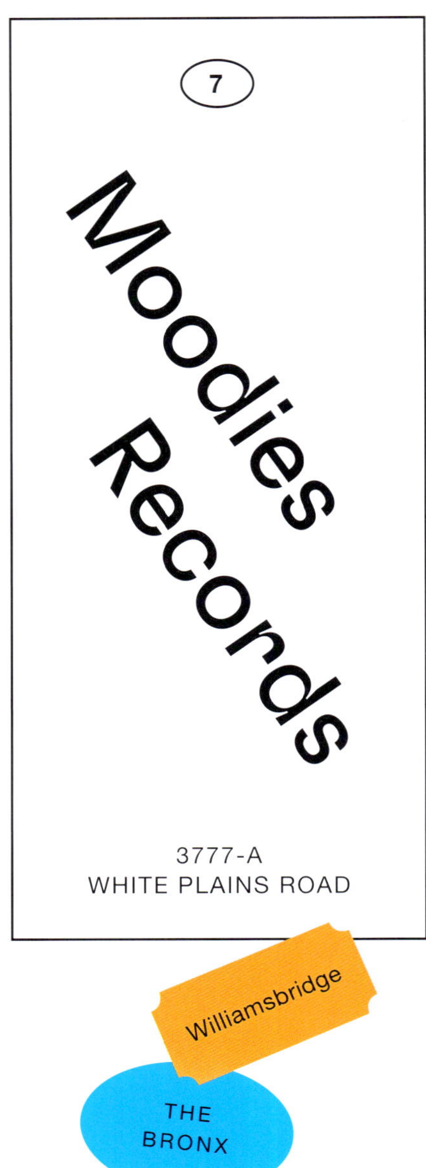

AT MOODIES RECORDS, A KEY LODESTONE in New York reggae history, vinyl isn't a day job but a way to be in the world. A family business that started with a Kingston, Jamaica, kid with a keen ear for music, the store has opened up generations of visitors to a singular collection of diverse Caribbean records curated with a deeply personal touch—and after over five decades, it still has plenty more to teach.

Founded in 1981 by Earl Moodie, the store quickly became a cultural center for a flourishing population of Caribbean immigrants, alongside shops like VP Records (see p. 108). Between 1980 and 1988, over eight hundred thousand Jamaicans emigrated to New York, with the majority placing roots across Brooklyn, the Bronx, and Queens. Moodies grew alongside its changing neighborhood, finding its footing as a business in step with the city's new inhabitants. Counting primarily soundmen and selectors among its early customers, the shop nurtured the very community it belonged to, becoming a landmark reflection of reggae's influence on New York music, not to mention a hub for Caribbean culture, politics, and aesthetics.

Growing up in Jamaica, Moodie loved to tune in to the FM radio stations he could access from the coast: bossa nova from Latin America, jazz and blues from New Orleans, even classical from the BBC in England. After moving to New York in 1969, he began a career in reggae as the lead singer of the Stepping Stones, making the rounds on the club circuits in Brooklyn and the Bronx. His time as a musician inspired a lifelong commitment to empowering local Caribbean artists: listening to their demos; stocking their vinyl; amplifying their shows. The practice has paid off in the form of one of the most comprehensive Jamaican music collections in the world and a staff boasting decades of experience. Longtime manager Peter Gayle has worked at Moodies since he was seventeen years old and will move with the business to its first new location in over fifty years in 2025.

Countless artists have placed their trust in Moodies' curation and heritage. Kool Herc, the Jamaican American DJ who effectively invented hip-hop at a party in the Bronx a few years before Moodies opened, has been a regular for decades. Beenie Man, Bunny Wailer, and Luciano have also paid visits to the store. In 2014 Herc even introduced the late food and culture critic Anthony Bourdain to Moodies as a critical stitch in the Bronx's fabric. "I was so honored he came here," Pierre Barclay, Moodie's nephew, said in an interview with video series *Beyond Obscurity* in 2021. "It was history."

Although Earl Moodie died in 2021, rare records from his personal collection, like a first-edition pressing of Bob Marley's *The Complete Wailers: 1967–1972 Part 1* still animate the store's floor-to-ceiling stock. Moodies has remained in uniquely capable hands with Gayle, Barclay, and Moodie's son, Earl Moodie, Jr., who told interview series Gibbo Presents in 2013 that he joined the store primarily to spend time with his dad. As he put it, "It wasn't about music, and it wasn't about the store—I wanted to get to know my father better." Now, under the care of its second generation of leadership, Moodies shows no signs of straying from the motto its founder held most dear: "Music Is Life."

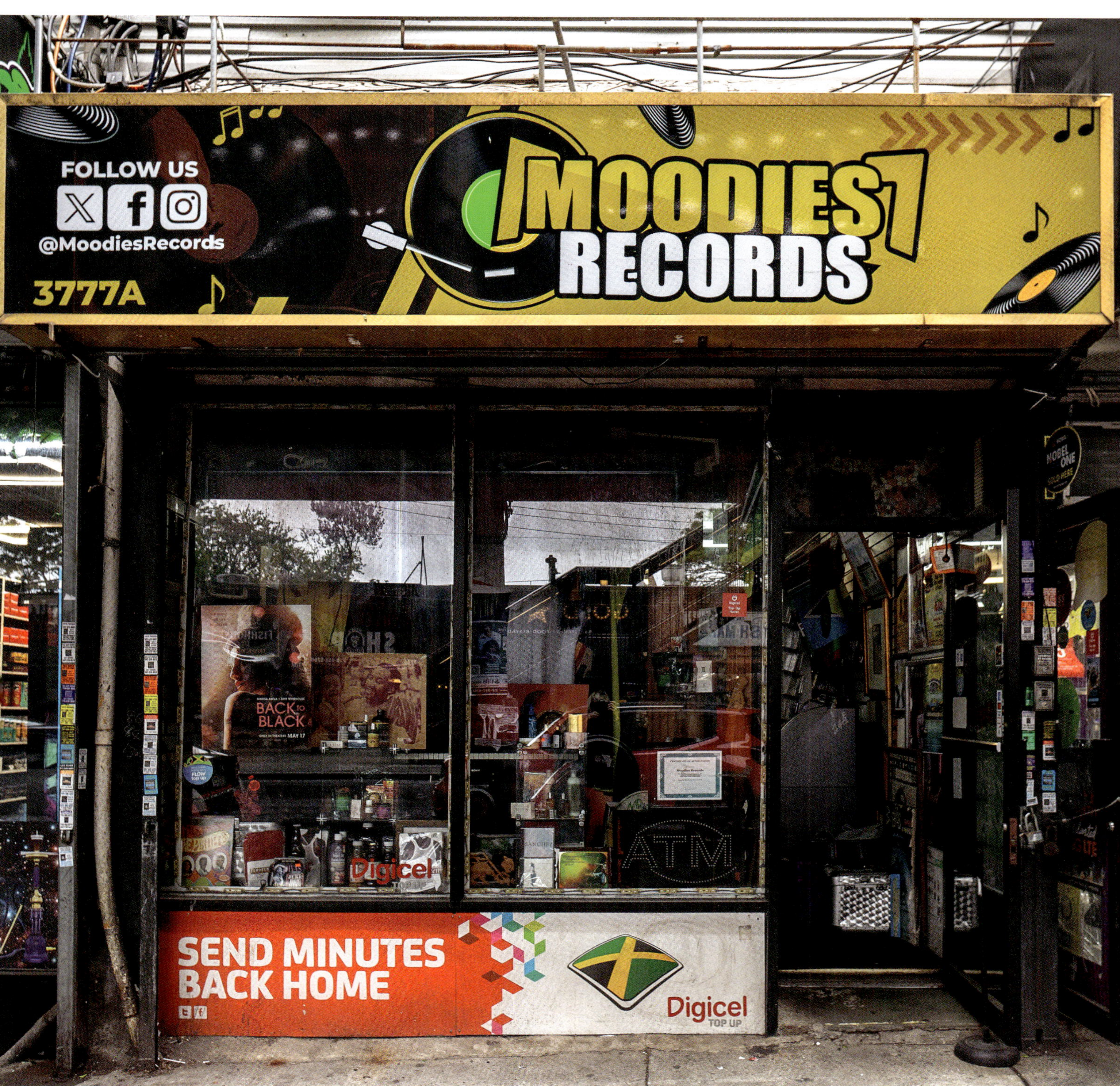

ABOVE Moodies Records was founded by Earl Moodie in the Williamsbridge neighborhood of the Bronx in 1981. Despite its small size, it's become known for its sense of community, as well as its hard-to-find and out-of-print selection of reggae, dancehall, rocksteady, hip-hop, jazz, R&B, and soul music.

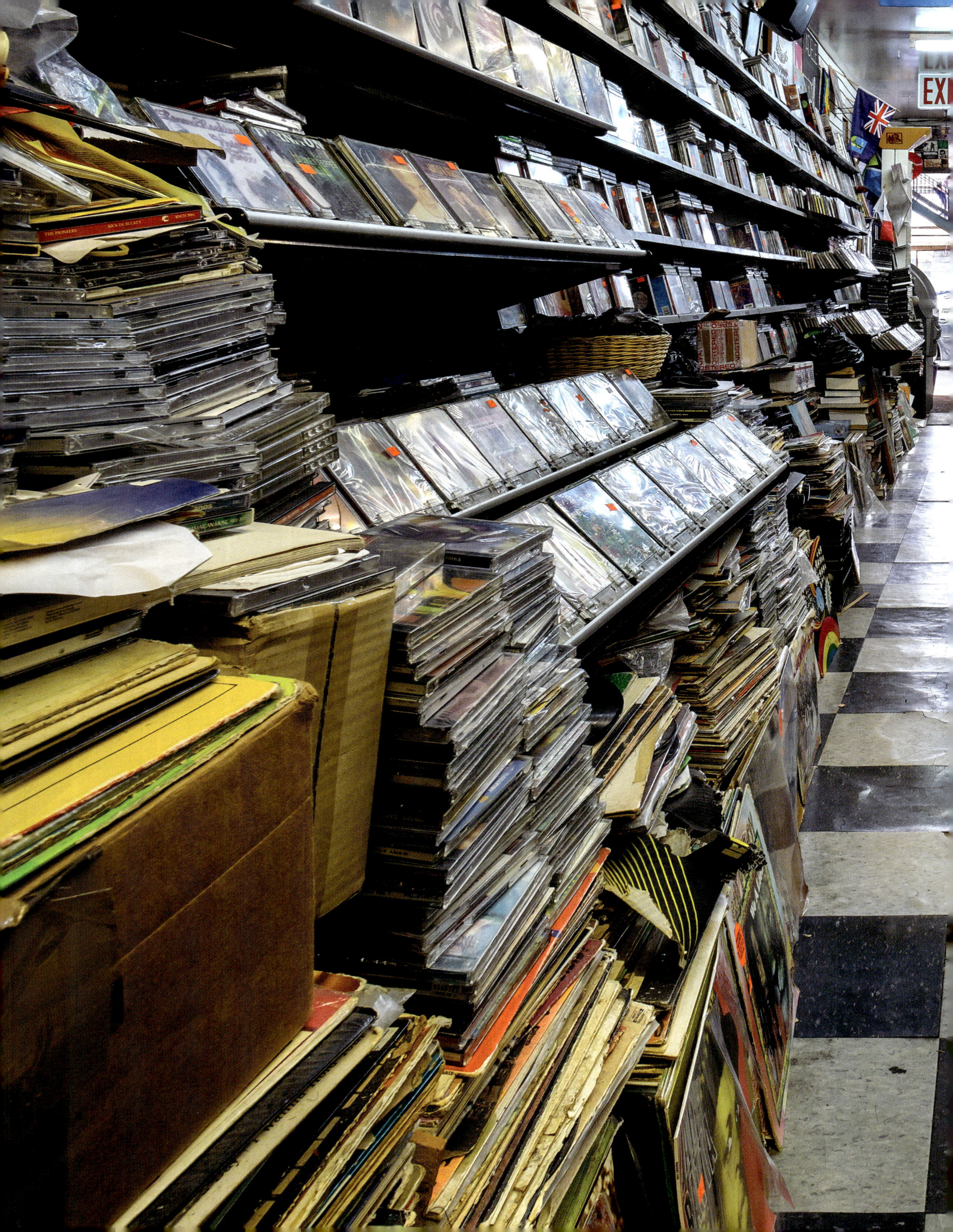

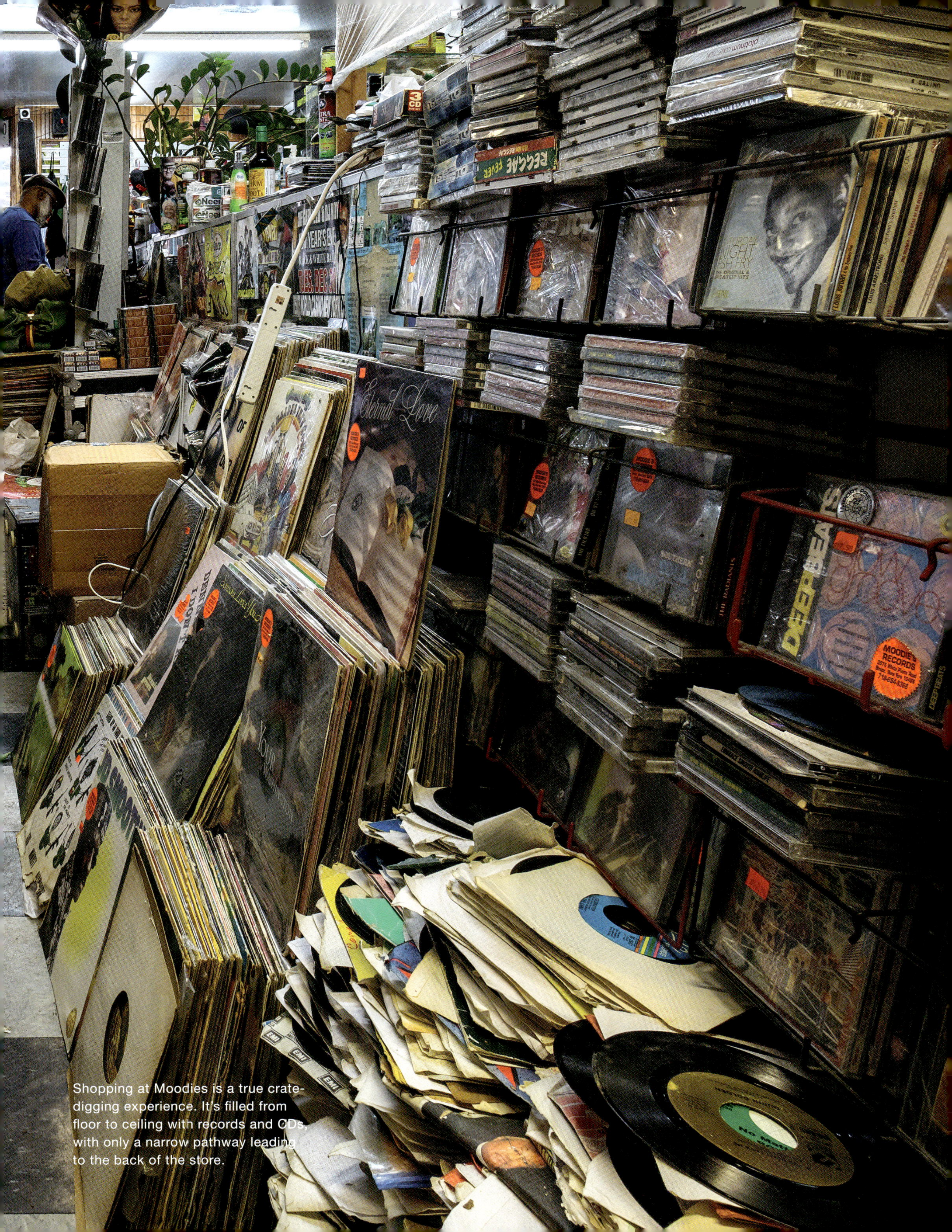

Shopping at Moodies is a true crate-digging experience. It's filled from floor to ceiling with records and CDs, with only a narrow pathway leading to the back of the store.

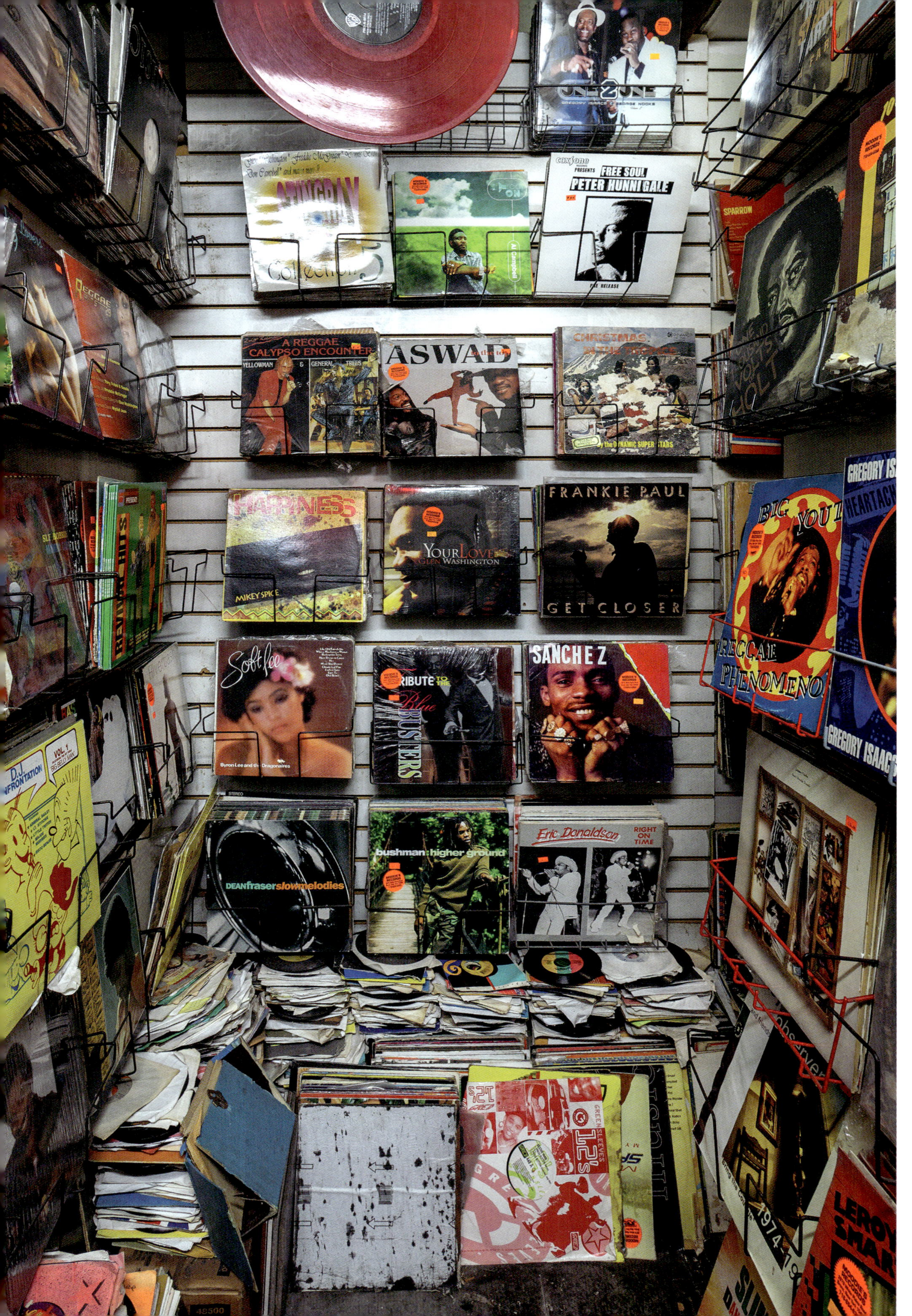

GREGORY ISAACS
PRESENTS FREE SOUL
PETER HUNNIGALE
A REGGAE CALYPSO ENCOUNTER
YELLOWMAN
ASWAD
FRANKIE PAUL
GET CLOSER
HAPPINESS
MIKEY SPICE
YOUR LOVE
GLEN WASHINGTON
SANCHEZ
Byron Lee and the Dragonaires
Eric Donaldson
RIGHT ON TIME
bushman: higher ground
DEANfraserslowmelodies
SPARROW
by the DYNAMIC SUPER STARS

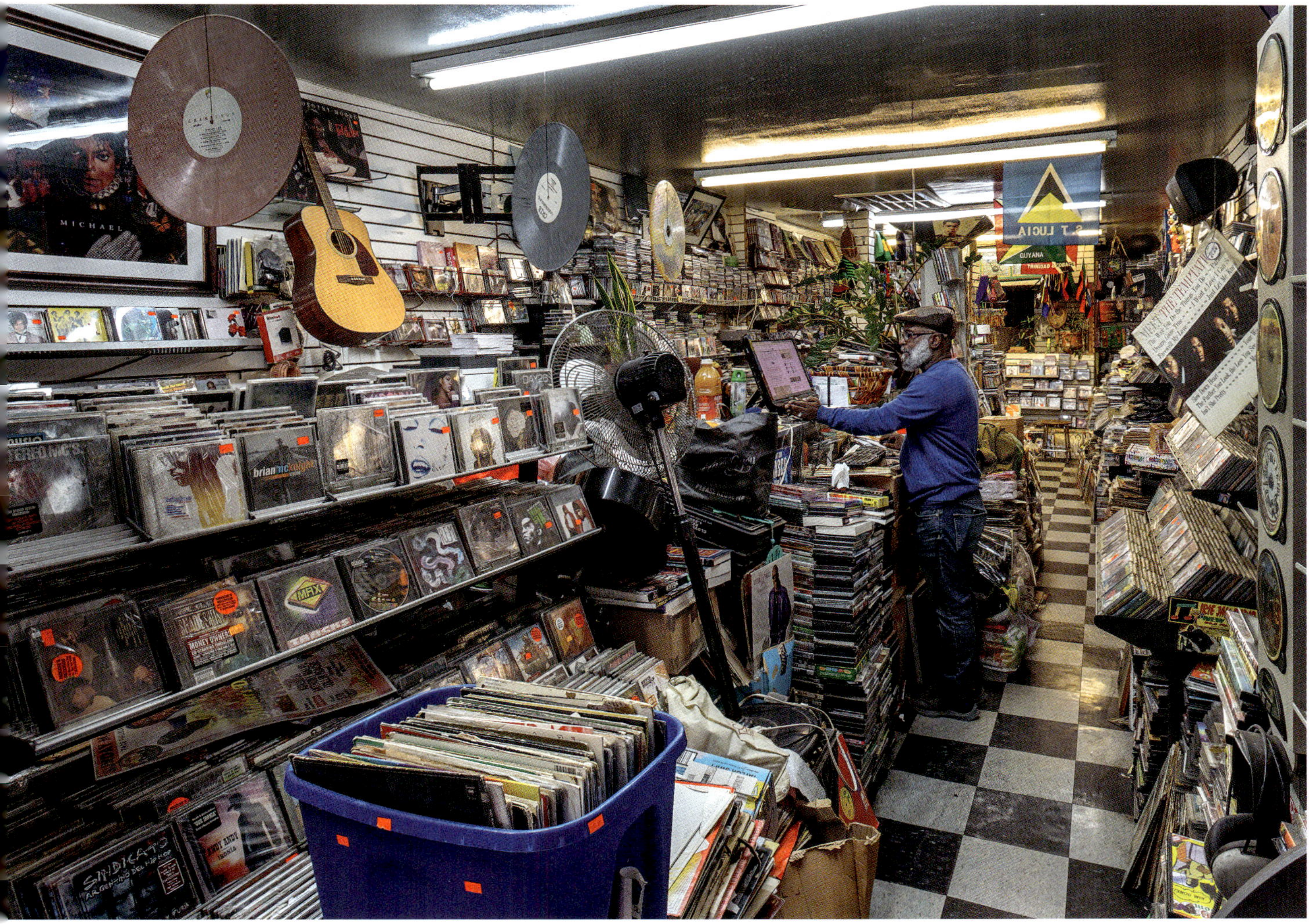

ABOVE Longtime manager Peter Gayle, who has worked at Moodies on and off since he was seventeen years old, promised Moodie before he passed away in 2021 that he would look after the store and keep its motto, "Music Is Life," alive.

RIGHT Rare vinyl from Moodie's personal collection at the shop includes a first pressing of Bob Marley's *The Complete Wailers: 1967–1972 Part 1*, *Catch a Fire* by the Wailers (with its original 1973 Zippo lighter–style hinged album sleeve), and a rare pressing of *Grounation* by the Mystic Revelation of Rastafari.

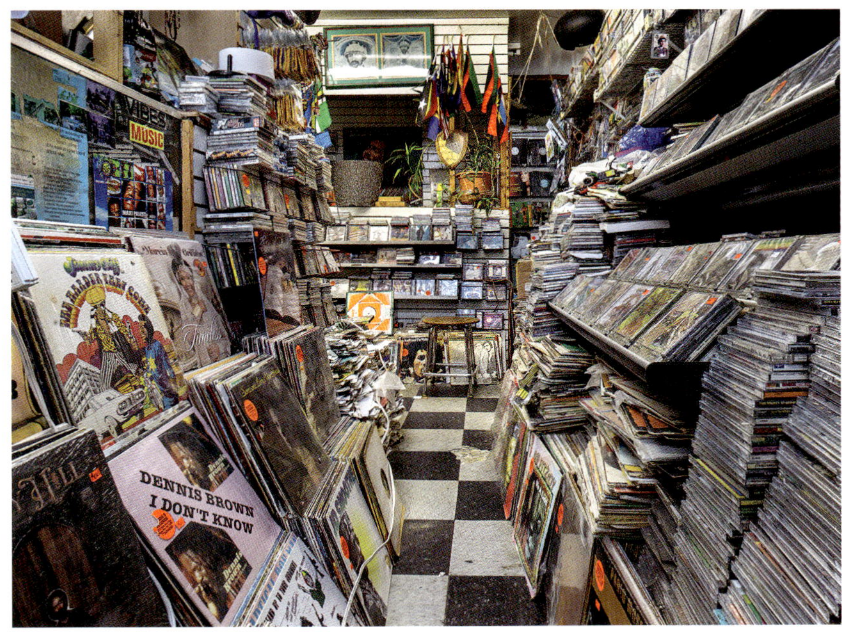

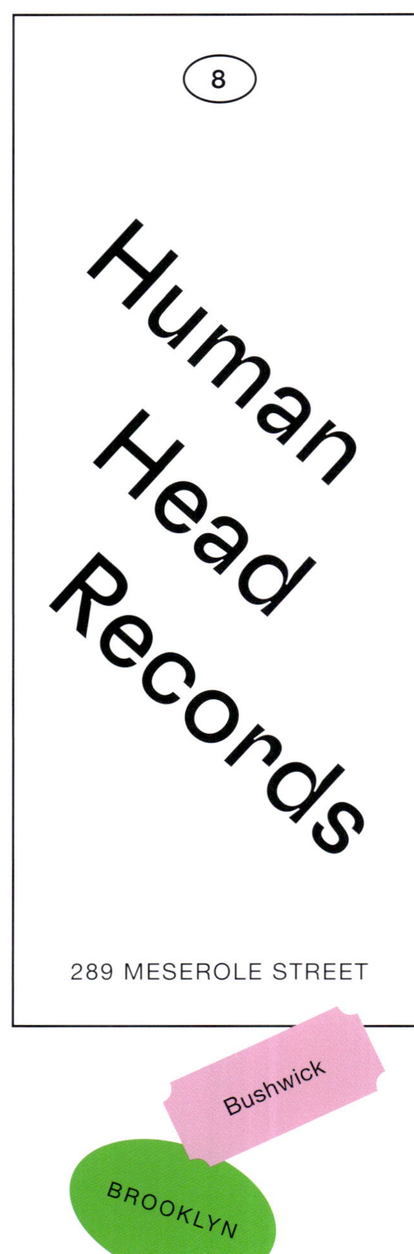

"[IT] STILL FEELS LIKE YEAR ONE in many ways," owner Travis Klein says of Human Head, the Bushwick record shop he co-founded in 2013. As it turns out, maintaining a small business for over a decade evokes many of the same principles as collecting used vinyl: making the old feel new and being as ready to learn from a customer as teach them. But few New York record sellers feel as eternally fresh as Human Head, whose sprawling five-thousand-plus collection forgoes one lane in favor of an entire musical highway.

Initially a hobbyist collector, Klein and his business partner, Steve Smith, turned Human Head from idea to reality in the wake of Hurricane Sandy, when Smith lost a Seaport-area restaurant to flooding. Klein's earliest listening tastes leaned toward Midwest indie and classic rock; Smith hailed from Austin's DIY punk scene. But the generations-deep, melting-pot vinyl community blossoming out of New York forced an open mind. "We learned along the way," Klein recalls.

Following a 2020 expansion, Human Head now sits nestled between a block of warehouses, nightclubs, and studio spaces on Meserole Street. Flinging open the proverbial gates for non–New Yorkers, its expansive collection is also fully available online, where its Discogs page boasts well over sixty thousand satisfied reviews. (This might explain why their unmistakable head-in-a-jar logo, illustrated by White Stripes collaborator Rob Jones and ideated by Smith, allegedly carries some fashion cachet in Japan.) Even the younger, post-internet heads are represented, and can safely rely on the odd rare Travis Scott LP among the rich collections of soul, funk, and disco.

Step inside Human Head's glass-front physical location, and an understated entryway gives way to a crate-digger's cornucopia, catering to the most discerning vinyl devotees and easygoing bargain-bin browsers alike. Eclectic, hard-to-find snags, spanning '70s soul to Nigerian boogie to rare UK monos and West Indian cuts, populate the four-shelf displays manning every wall. The highest-value, and often rarest, LPs hold rotating court across the top rows. But despite the bounty an upward glance reveals, it's difficult to pull your attention away from the waist-level $2 and $5 bins, stocked with rare disco edits the extra-curious listener can test drive on one of the turntables stationed throughout the shelves of plenty.

There's a certain college radio charm to Human Head's warmly lit space, perhaps induced by the thoughtfully hung "Animal House" sign marking where it becomes a vinyl sorting laboratory. In the back, cardboard UHaul box after cardboard UHaul box of records, mostly used, take on a curated shape, a charmingly in-flux layout that adds depth to the store's motto: "Records Before Rent." The shop regularly purchases from walk-in sellers, but also has established international connections with other stores and labels, keeping their rushing stream of inventory at the global forefront without sacrificing the specialist's eye for detail. "We try to identify not only unique, cool sounds," Klein explains, "but also find somebody who offers them."

If any house style does emerge, it's loyal to—and tapped into serious arteries of—the richest Brazilian music of the past fifty years. Klein's wife, who is from the country, spearheaded countless trips that have left Human Head deeply mindful of the region's myriad distinct sounds. The few new releases the shop does carry tend toward reissues, can't-skip Latin, and whatever Berlin-based label Habibi Funk has on the docket.

Like many analog media lovers, Klein is intrigued by the countless diamonds our modern consumerist drive has left in rubbish bins, sharing: "[Americans] have access to this quantity of things that other communities don't have." Fittingly, Human Head consistently sells out and replenishes its inventory—tens of thousands of individual records deep—within six months. It's safe to say this grassroots shop has influenced more than a few tastemakers to try something brand new.

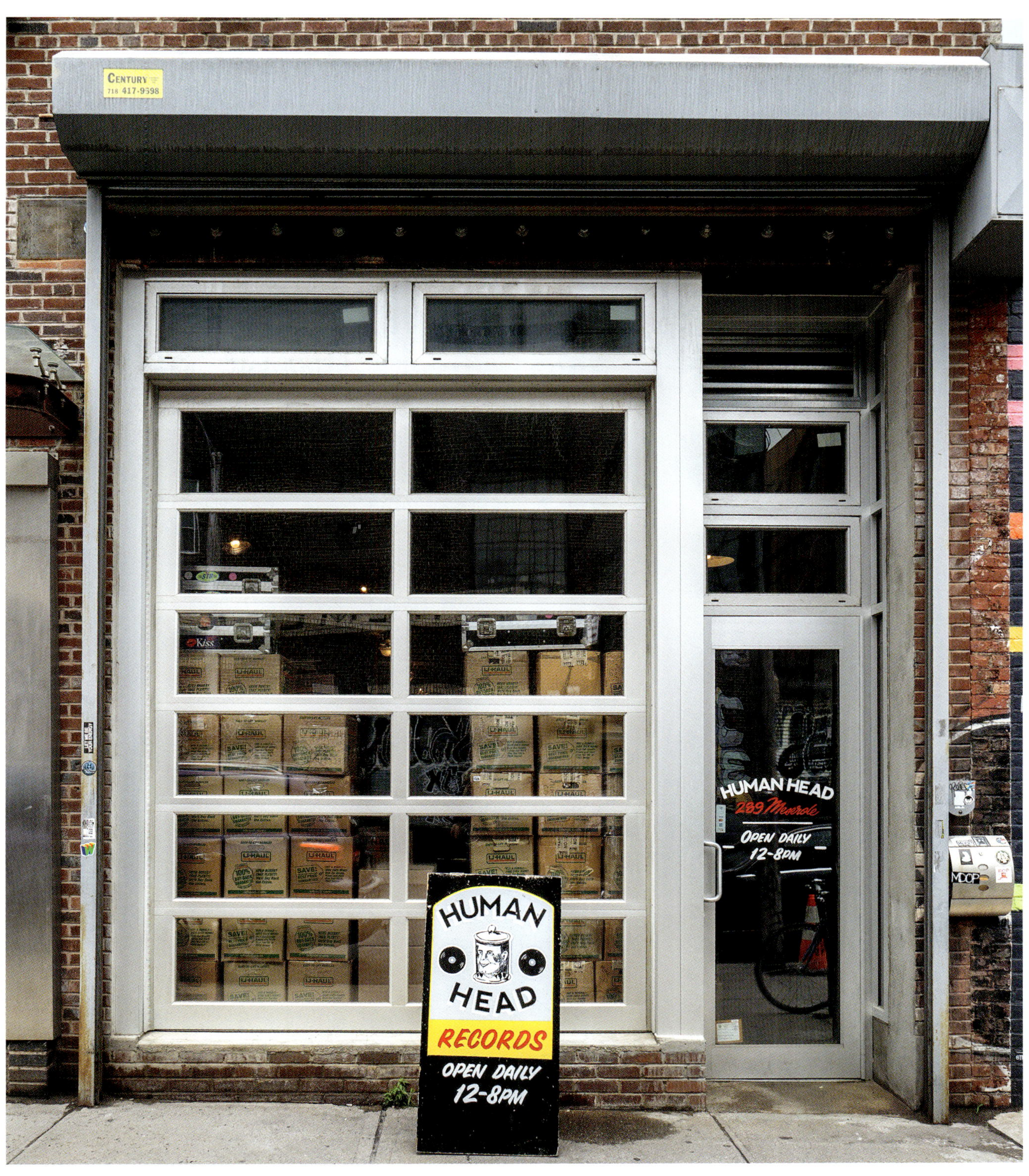

ABOVE Tens of thousands of affordable used vinyl records can be found at Human Head, including obscure and hard-to-find titles across genres like soul, funk, disco, reggae, dub, jazz, Latin, hip-hop, dance, house, and techno.

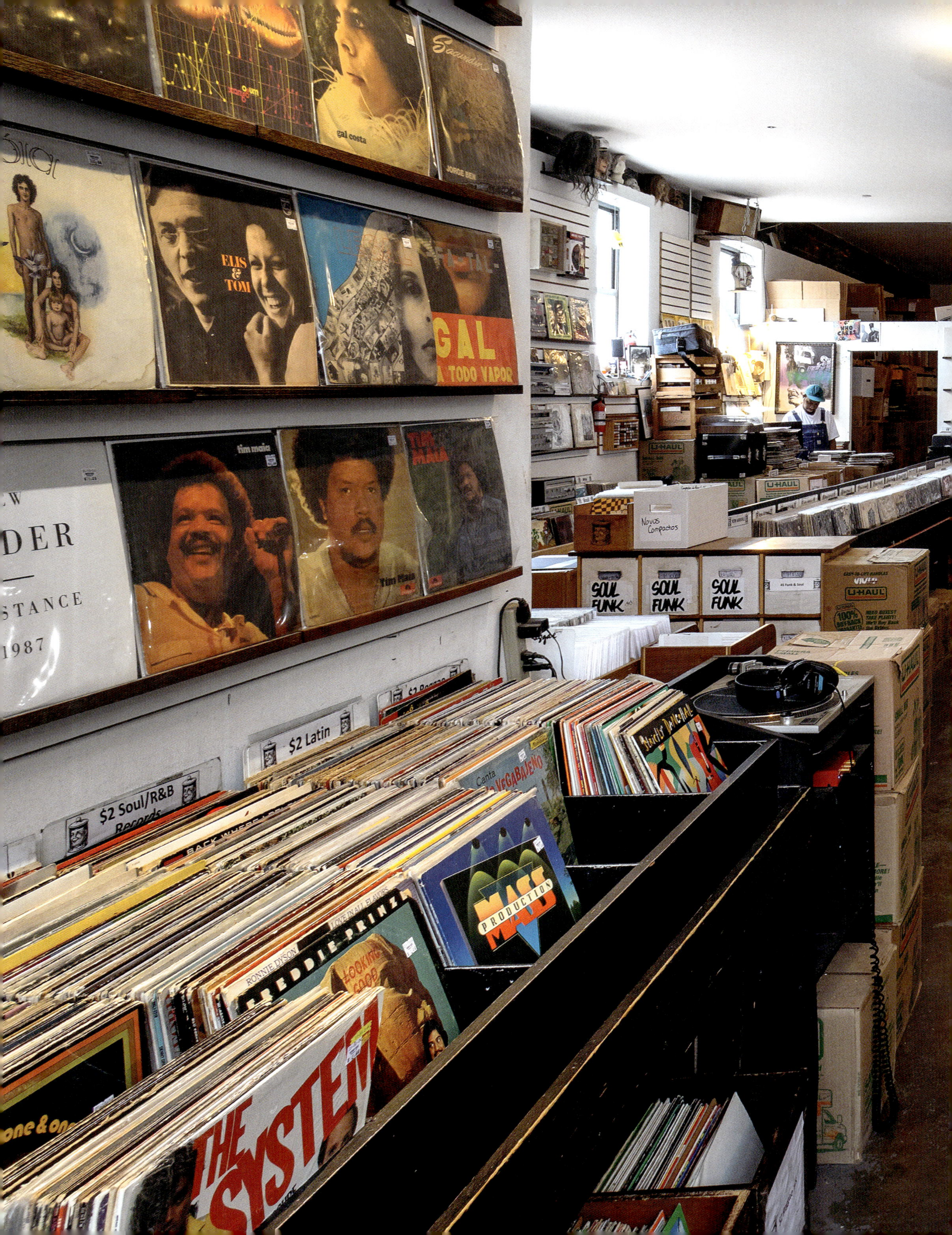
$2 Latin
$2 Soul/R&B Records
SOUL FUNK
SOUL FUNK
SOUL FUNK
Novos Compactos
ELIS & TOM
GAL A TODO VAPOR
tim maia
MASS PRODUCTION
THE SYSTEM
FREDDIE PRINZ
U-HAUL

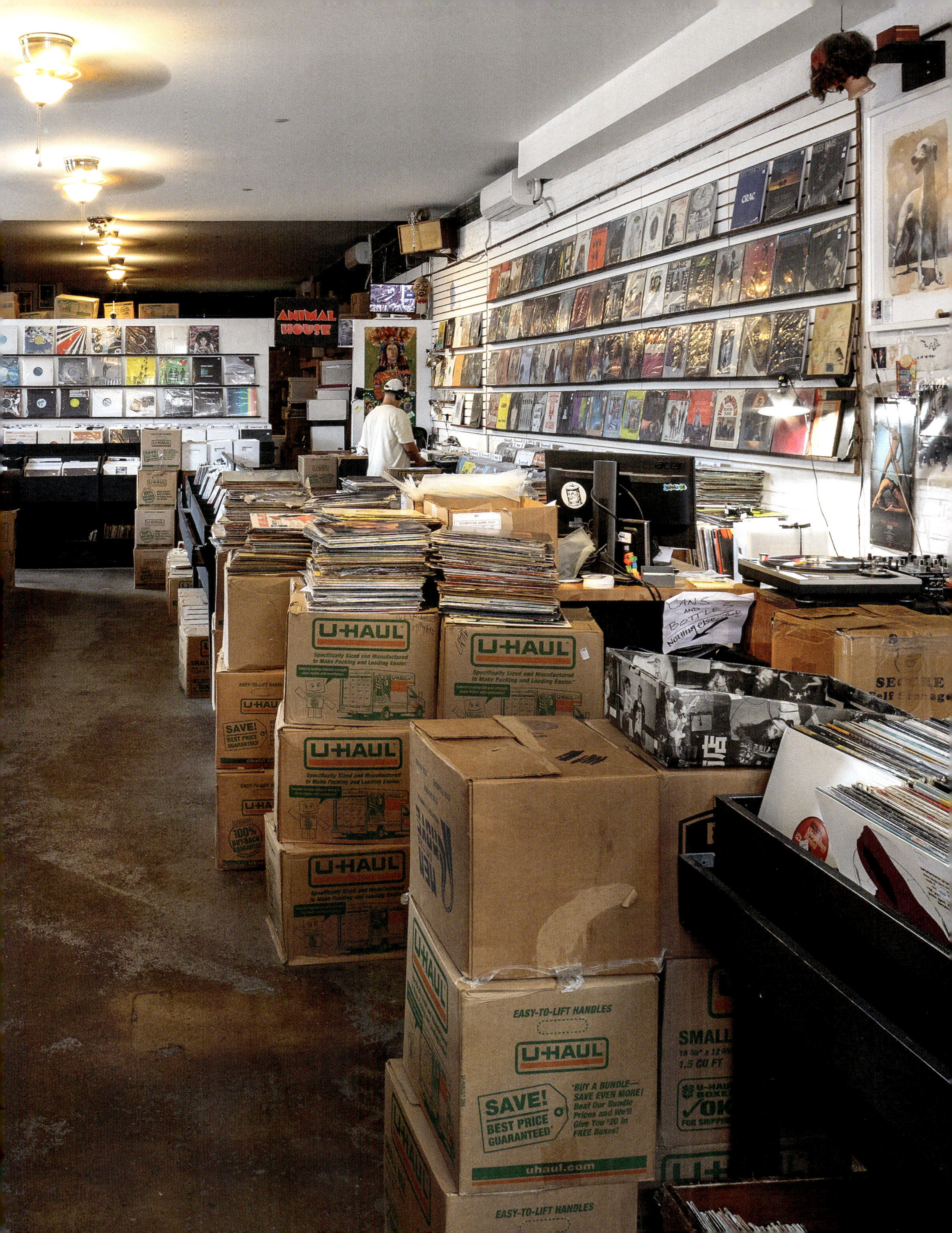

ANIMAL HOUSE
U-HAUL
Specifically Sized and Manufactured to Make Packing and Loading Easier.
EASY-TO-LIFT HANDLES
SAVE! BEST PRICE GUARANTEED
"BUY A BUNDLE— SAVE EVEN MORE! Beat Our Bundle Prices and We'll Give You $20 in FREE Boxes!
uhaul.com
SMALL
1.5 CU FT
SECURE
Self Storage

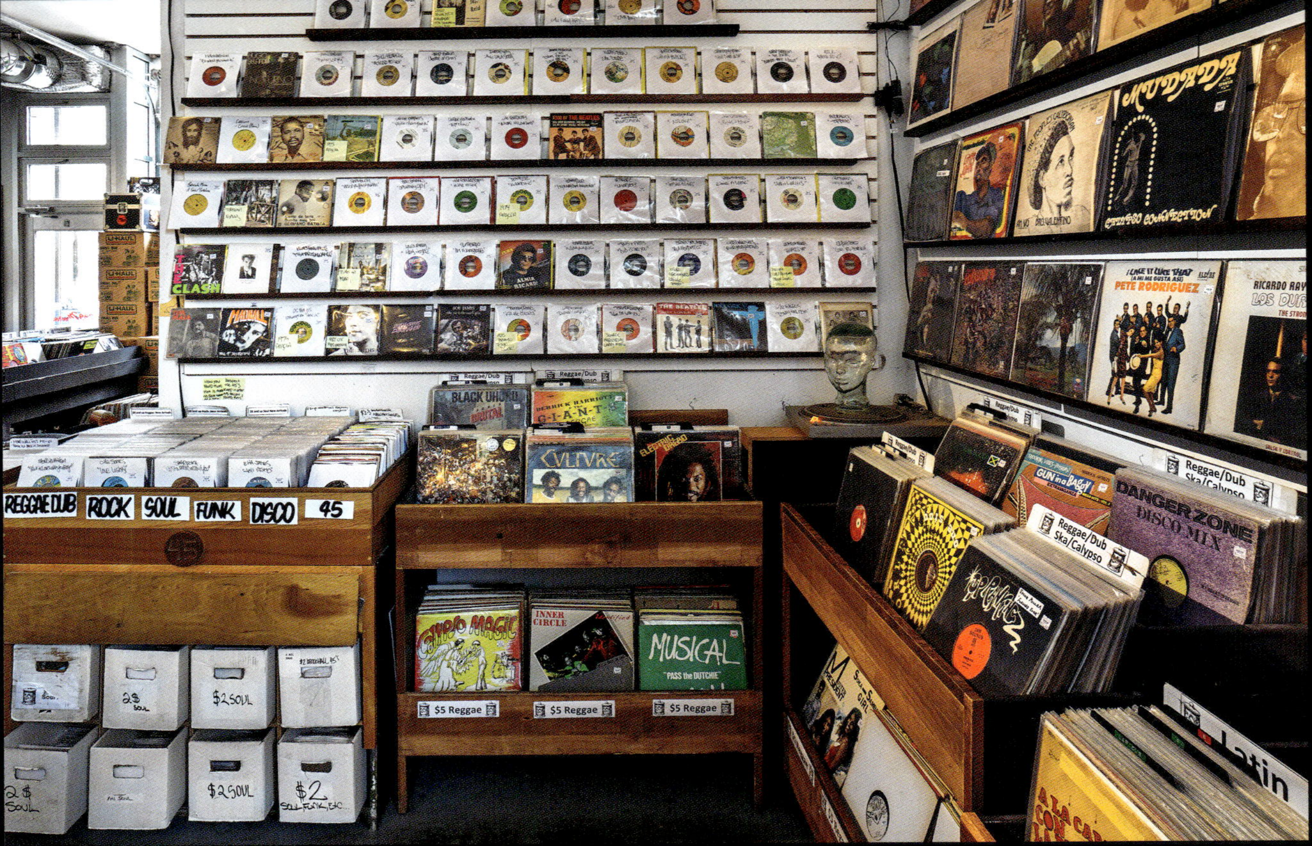

"New York is so special because of the lineage, the history that's here—to this day, there's so many places you can fall into, so many communities you can explore."

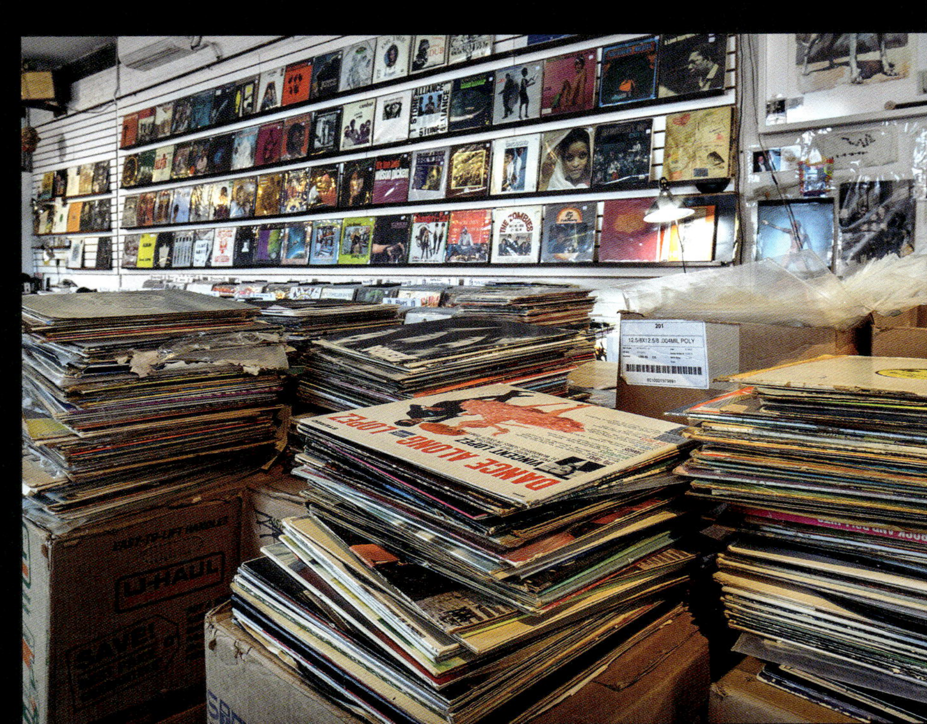

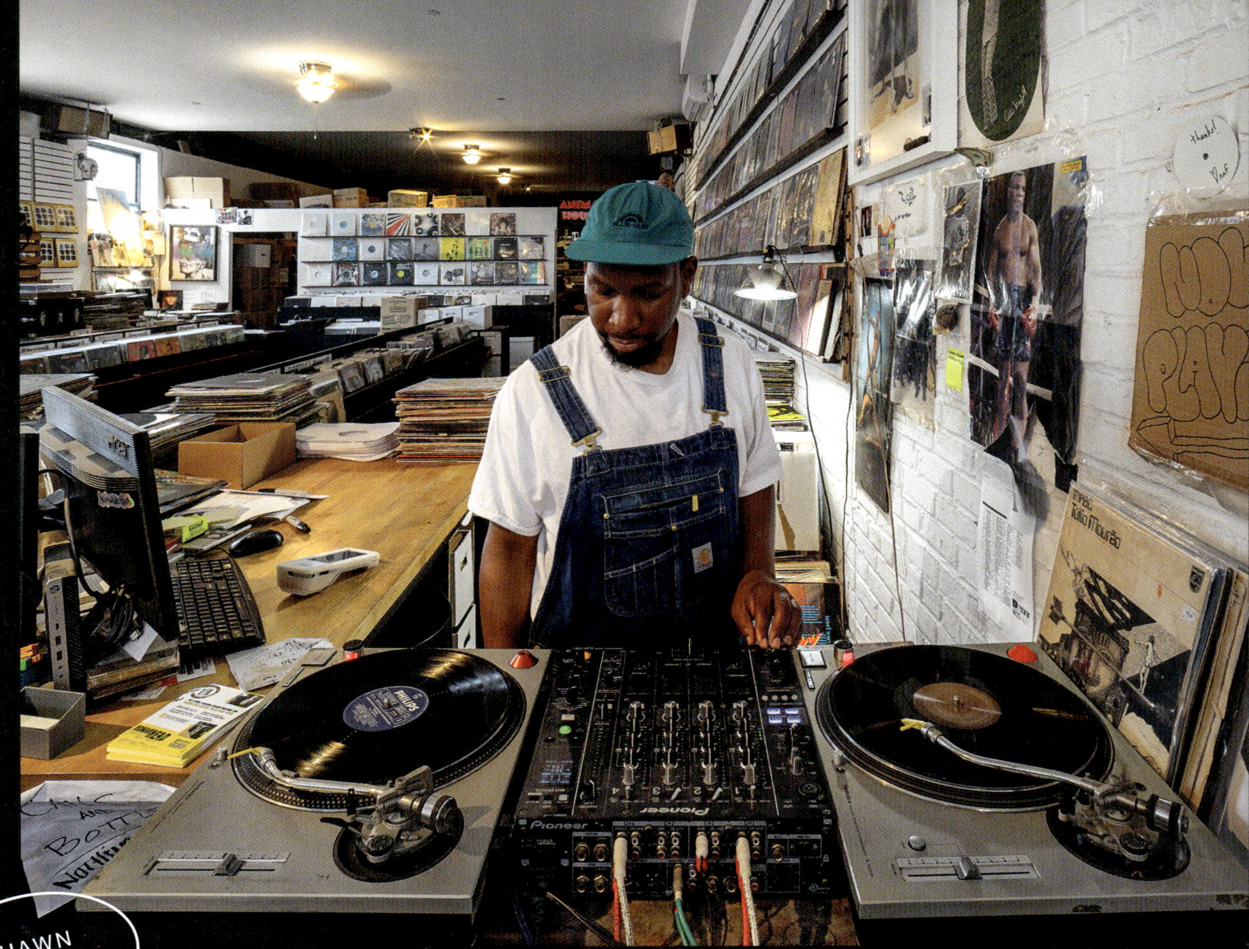

SHAWN DUB

HUMAN HEAD TEAM MEMBER AND RESIDENT DJ AT PUBLIC RECORDS AND THE LOT RADIO

Shawn Wilson's interest in vinyl began as a creative survival skill. As a struggling producer finding his footing in New York, toting around a stack of $1 singles seemed a lot more viable than splurging on Serato DJ Pro software. Known for deep crates and even deeper West Coast roots, Wilson—who's been DJing as Shawn Dub since the early 2000s—began his collection off donations from his mom and grandmother. He moved east to Brooklyn in May 2011, where he's become a sought-after booking in part through the I Love Vinyl crew, a collective he credits with influencing not only his opportunities in New York, but the character of his collection.

From Bay Area hip-hop to Detroit techno, Wilson's mixes show off a sky-is-the-limit approach to discovery. (He thinks his fresh perspective could've been what clinched his first gigs, sharing: "The biggest asset I had was that I had no experience.") It's an itch he scratches as a "lifer" at Human Head Records, where he's been an essential member of the team since 2014. Over the years, he's helped mold the shop's 12-inch selection with his own hands, not to mention pushed its inventory limits across every sliver of dance music. These days, when not at the shop, he's often holed up in the recording trailer at Greenpoint's The Lot Radio, packing smooth-blended classics into his show *Records Before Rent*, or playing tunes as part of his residency at the Gowanus nightclub Public Records.

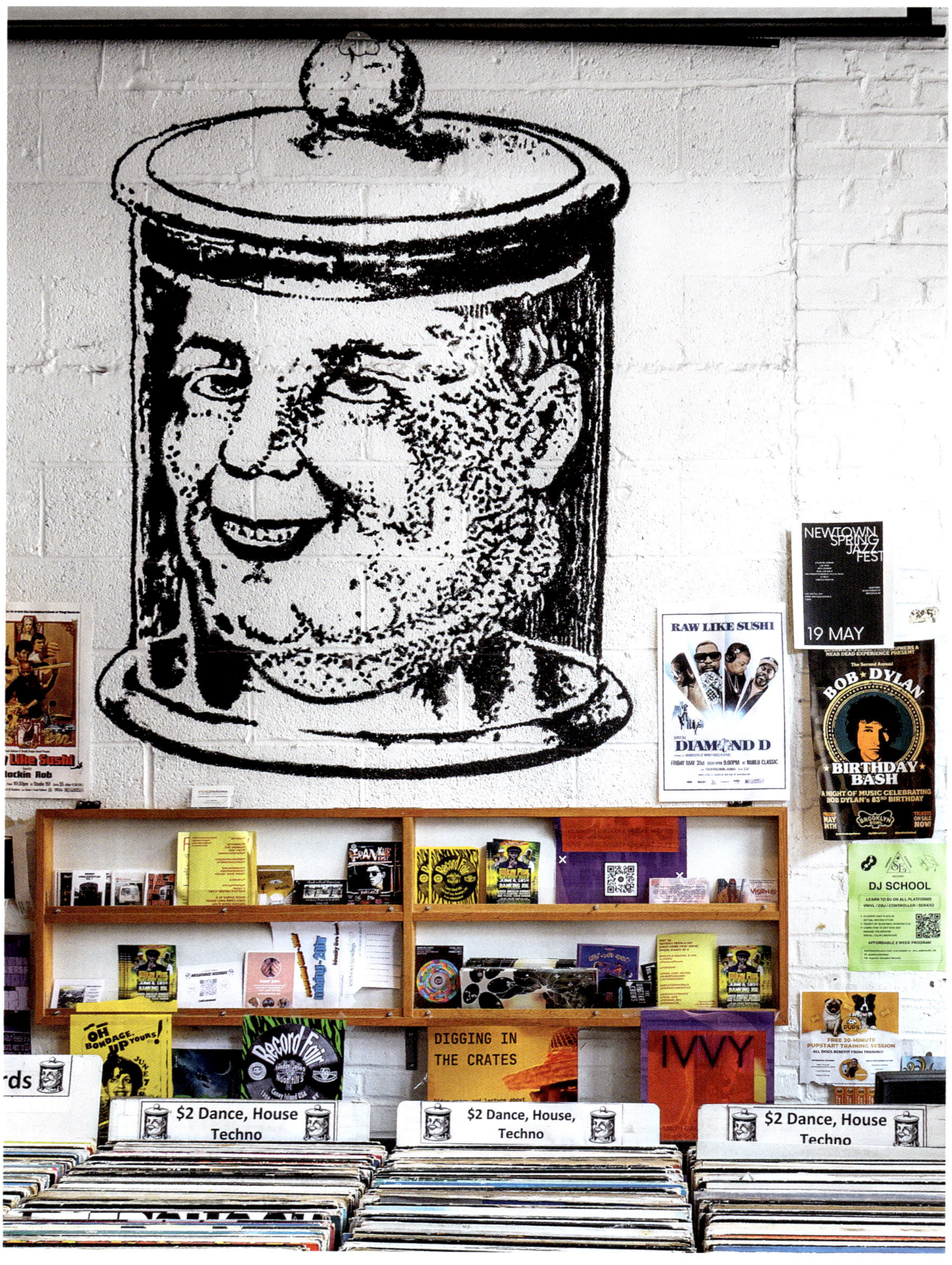

ABOVE Painted on the wall near the entrance is a large head in a jar, which serves as the store's logo.

OPPOSITE BOTTOM A row of new-arrival bins sits in the center of the shop. They are organized by the date each title physically arrives there.

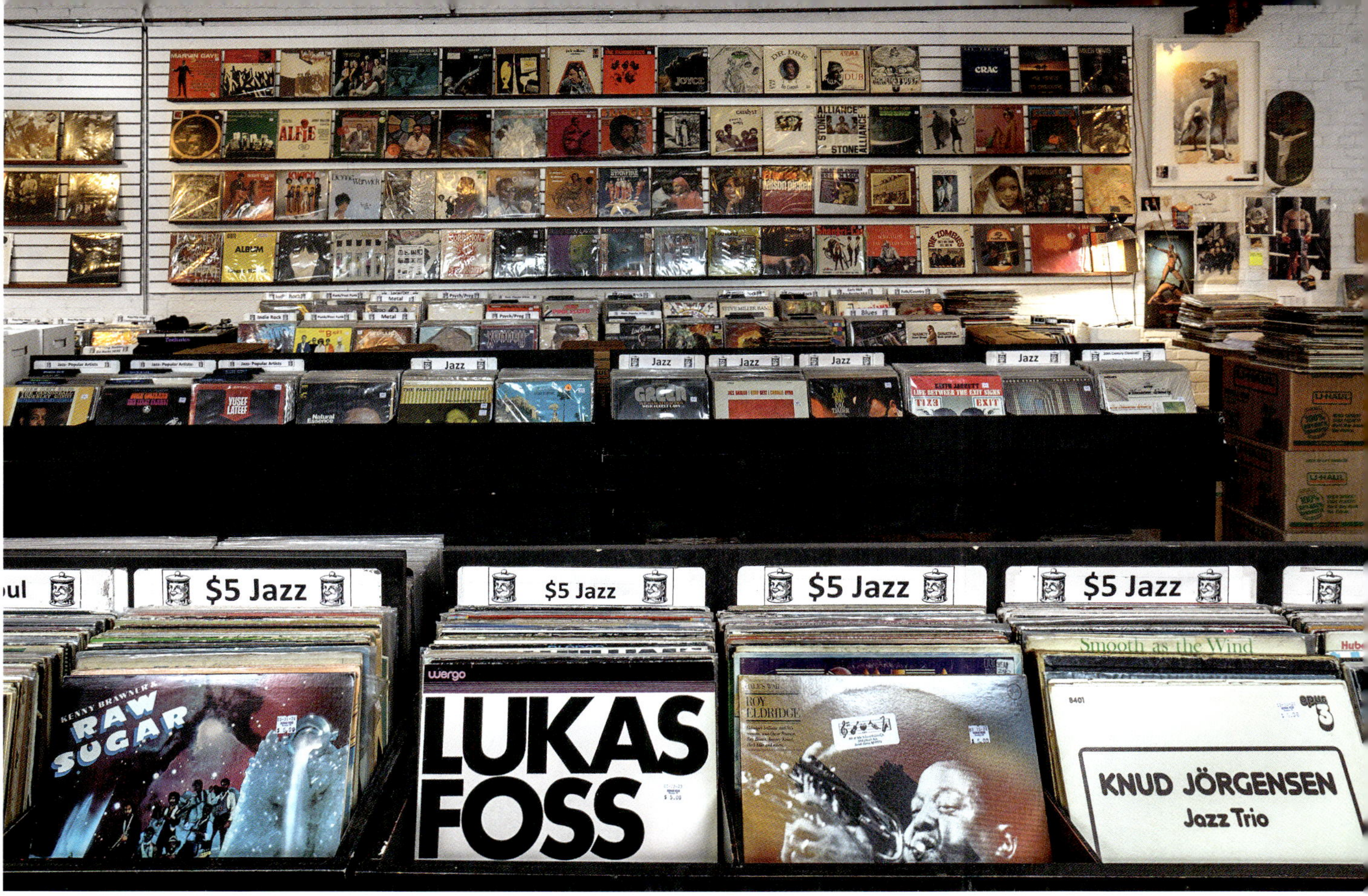

$5 Jazz
$5 Jazz
$5 Jazz
$5 Jazz
Jazz
RAW SUGAR
wergo
LUKAS FOSS
ROY ELDRIDGE
KNUD JÖRGENSEN
Jazz Trio 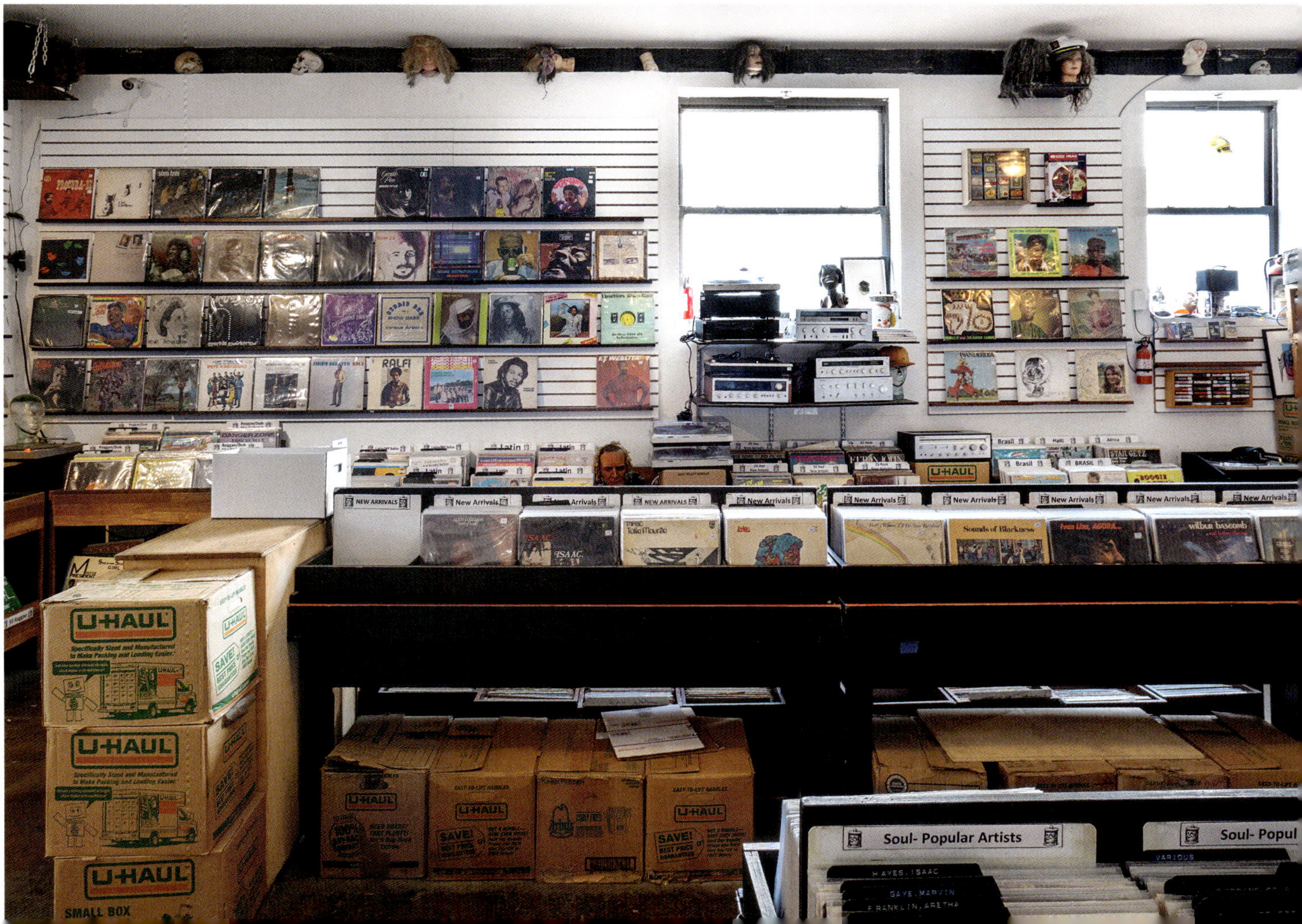
Smooth as the Wind
New Arrivals
U-HAUL
SMALL BOX
Soul- Popular Artists
Soul- Popul

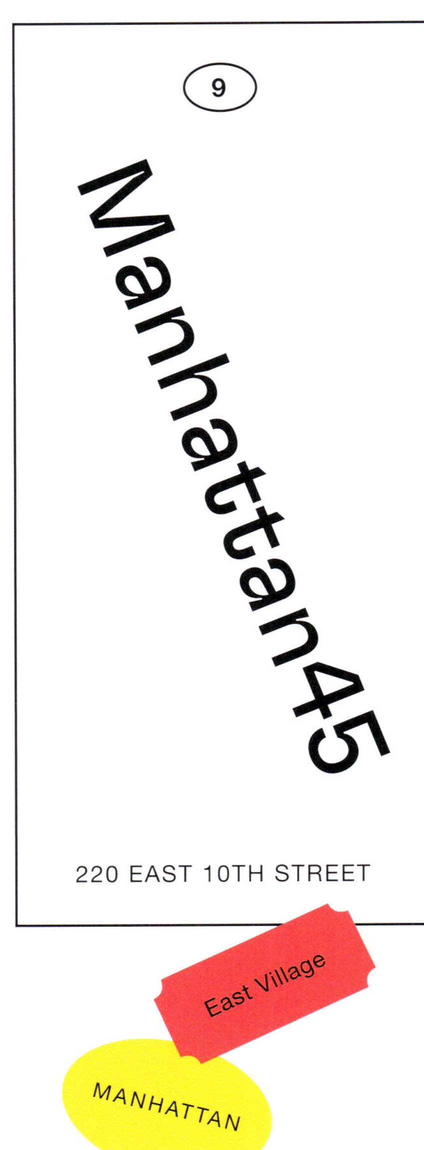

ON AN ISLAND WELL KNOWN for its packed rooms and sleepless nightlife, there's one club music haven in Manhattan without a cover charge or card minimum. Manhattan45 may not have a literal dance floor between its matte black walls, but the set of decks visible from outside the nubby brick storefront betray this electronic music lover's East Village oasis.

Founded in 2020 by Richard Guadagno, Manhattan45 sells only new electronic records, homing in on four main categories: disco, house, techno, and electro. He estimates he listens to thirty to forty titles a day to determine whether each of his shelves is up to snuff. Most of the shop's stock is shipped from Europe, with somewhere between twenty and forty records coming through its clay-red doorway every week or two.

Guadagno says the moments he cherishes most at Manhattan45 are when a customer "who...does not know too much about this music likes what they hear being played in the shop, trusts their ears, and buys it." Decades later, he can still recall being fourteen years old and selecting his first piece of vinyl at Record World, an all-too-apt choice for a Long Island boy who would become a lifelong collector: Billy Joel's *The Stranger*. From there, newfound passions for post-punk and new wave brought him to storied New York shops like 99 Records, J&R Music World, and Bondy's, wallet in hand, eyes and ears open.

Despite its genre focus, expect a substantial appetite for curiosity at Manhattan45, which Guadagno explains he opened to "contribute something positive to the city I love." In addition to pirate-radio-era UK drum and bass, it shelves folktronica, Afrobeats, and lightly abridged discographies highlighting extolled imprints like Toy Tonics, Razor-N-Tape, and Tropical Disco. A set of Pioneer DJ decks complete the record-shop-as-selector's-haven feel: These are not exactly the necessary conditions for more casual crate-browsers.

Guadagno appreciates the multistep process it takes to put a piece of vinyl into someone's hands—mixing, mastering, cutting and lacquering, shipping and distributing, stocking, and eventually, traveling home to a person's collection. Even once a record has found an owner, the format's not one that can be autoplayed or shuffled. "Vinyl makes people slow down and consume music more consciously," he shares.

At Manhattan45, Guadagno explains that "[in] general, the records are 'club focused,' meaning [it's] the kind of music you would hear in a proper club: more visceral than intellectual, music to get you moving." It's a fitting tactic for a business physically located at a nexus of college nightlife, underground music, and cabaret venues. Still, sharing a neighborhood with veteran record shops like A-1 (see p. 8) today, Manhattan45 has roots in a vinyl tradition that goes beyond electronic music.

Although he doesn't discourage a techno-thirsty clientele from being picky, Guadagno's arms stay open to DJs, club regulars, and first-time enjoyers alike. What really motivates him after over three decades of living in New York is getting local customers to catch a rhythm and pick up their feet—and, in the process, remember where they're standing. "Our job is to make New York what it is: about shops that can only exist here," he says of himself and his fellow record store operators. "To give people something energizing...to make them feel, 'Yes, *this* is New York!'"

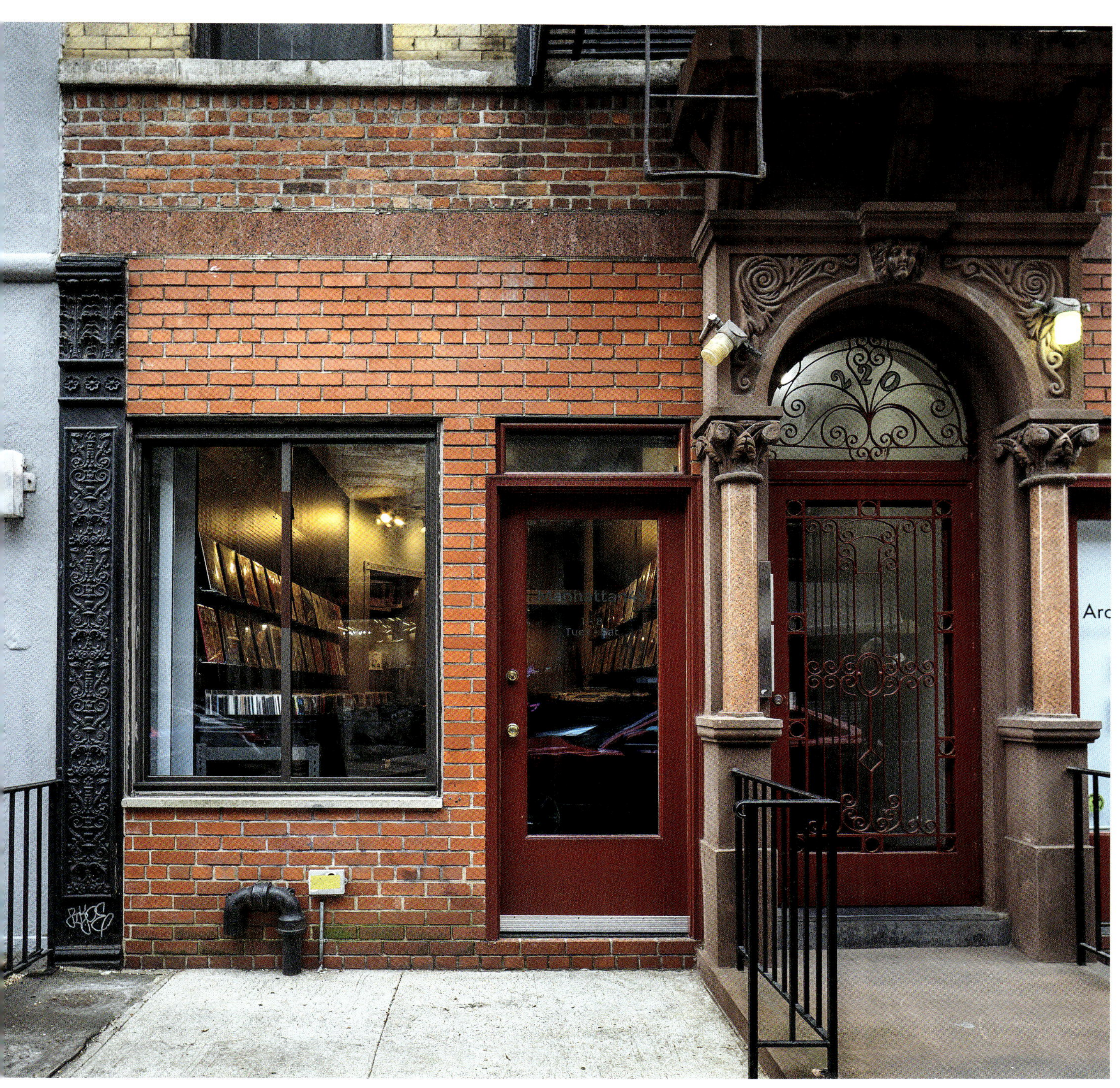

ABOVE Manhattan45 was founded by Richard Guadagno in 2020. It's the only shop in New York City selling solely new—not used—vinyl records, with a focus on electronic dance music, including disco, house, techno, and electro.

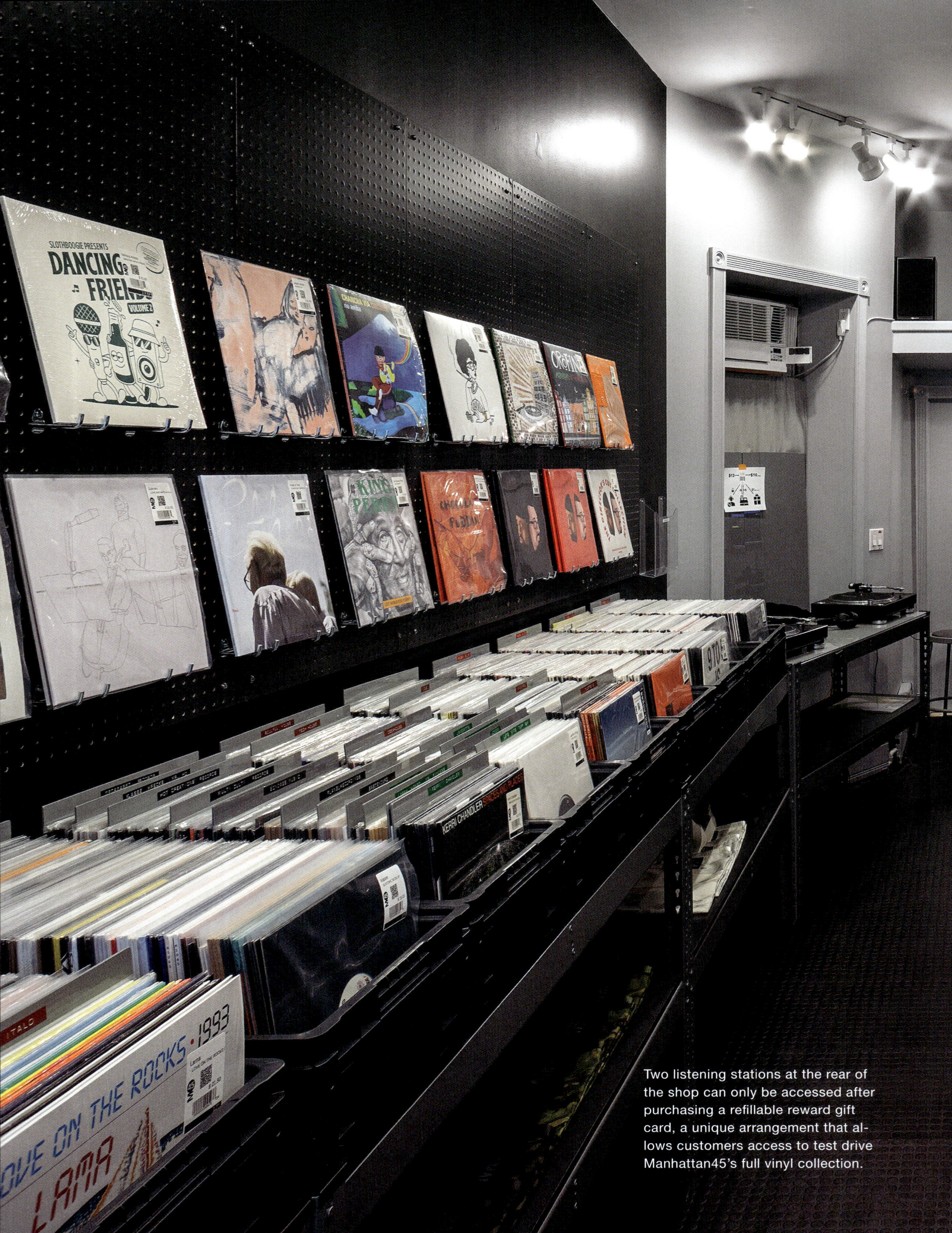

Two listening stations at the rear of the shop can only be accessed after purchasing a refillable reward gift card, a unique arrangement that allows customers access to test drive Manhattan45's full vinyl collection.

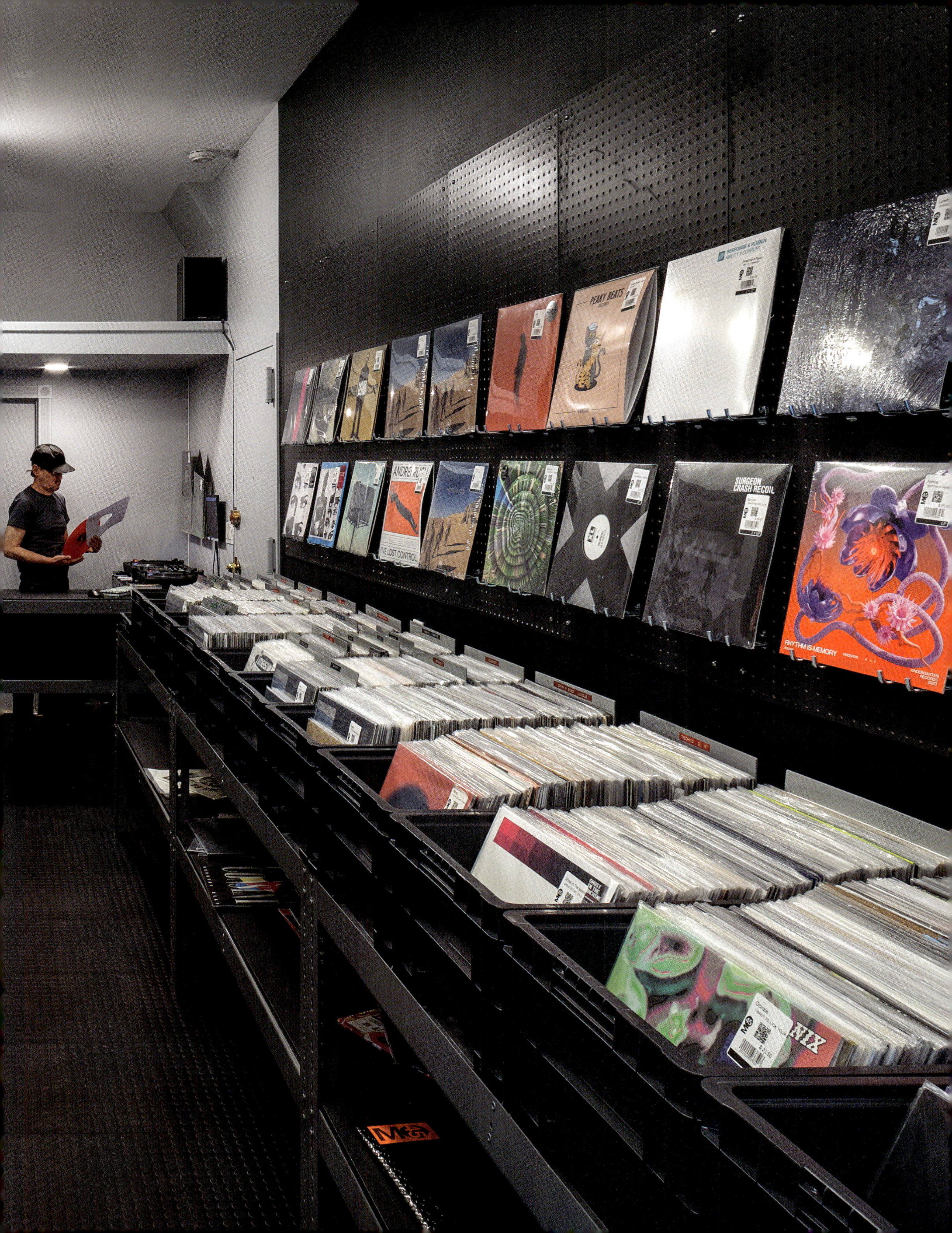
PEAKY BEATS
SURGEON
CRASH RECOIL
RHYTHM IS MEMORY
I'VE LOST CONTROL

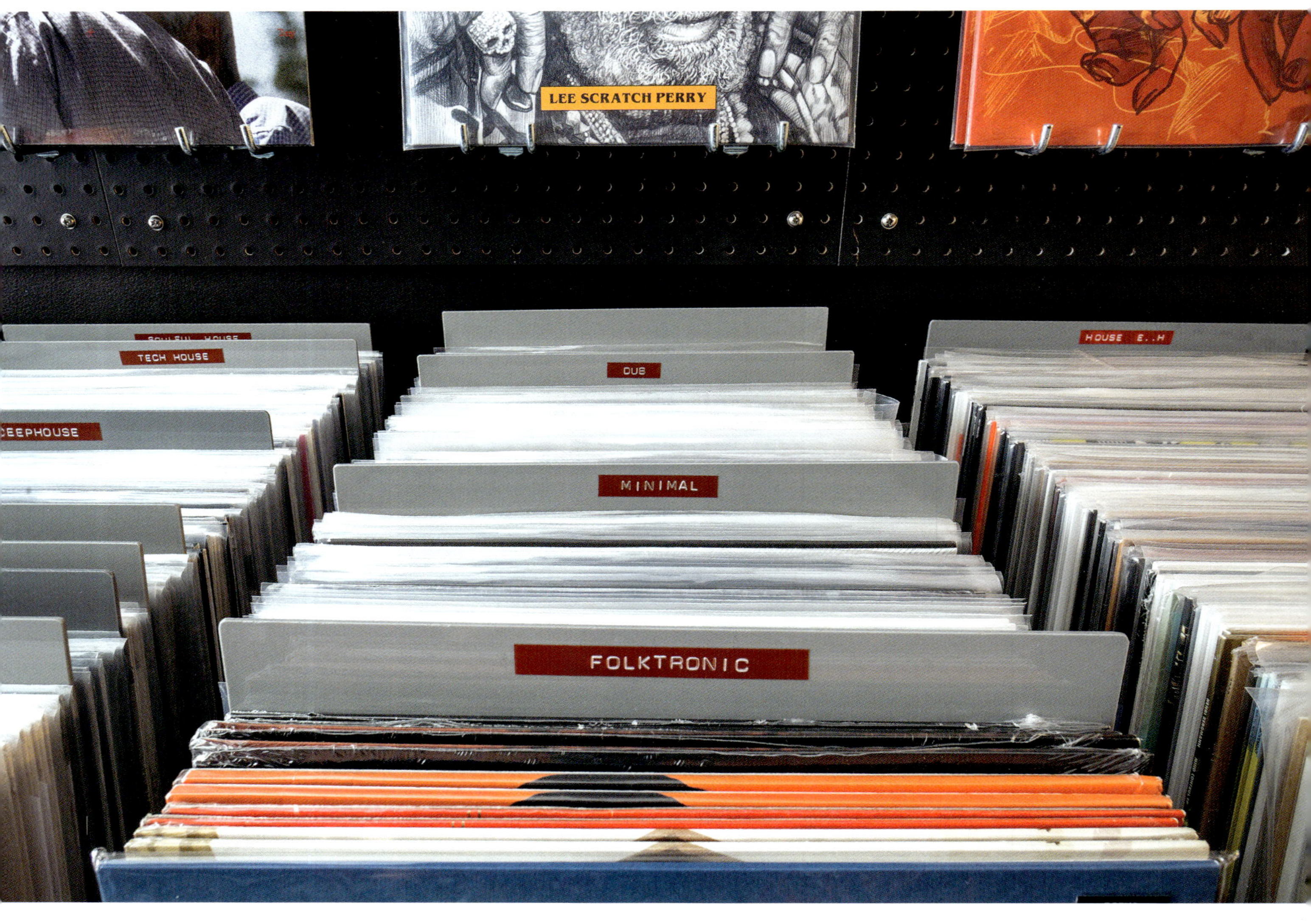

ABOVE The highly curated selection of vinyl is divided into meticulously labeled sections using a vintage Dymo label maker.

OPPOSITE BOTTOM Dance music, including new arrivals, is always playing from the decks at the register so that customers can discover new titles.

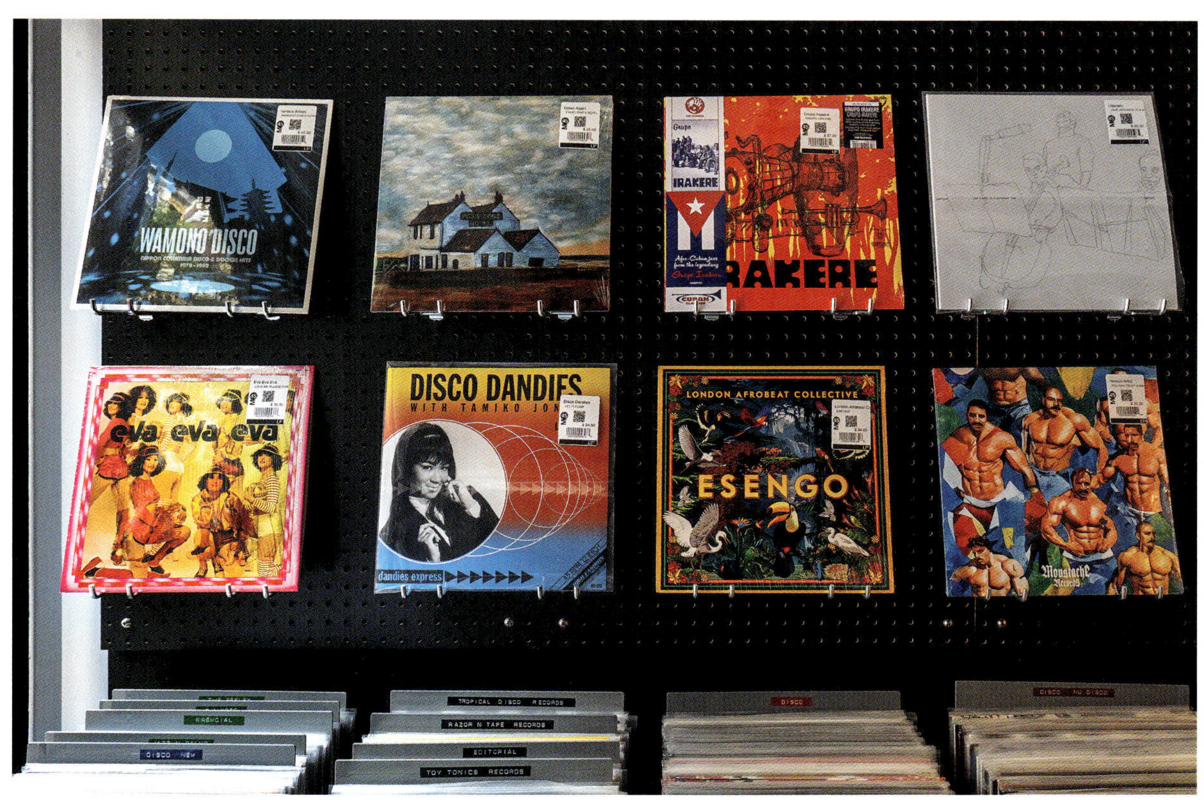
WAMONO DISCO
IRAKERE
DISCO DANDIES
WITH TAMIKO JO
dandies express
eva eva eva
LONDON AFROBEAT COLLECTIVE
ESENGO
TROPICAL DISCO RECORDS
RAZOR N TAPE RECORDS
EDITORIAL
TOY TONICS RECORDS
DISCO NEW
DISCO

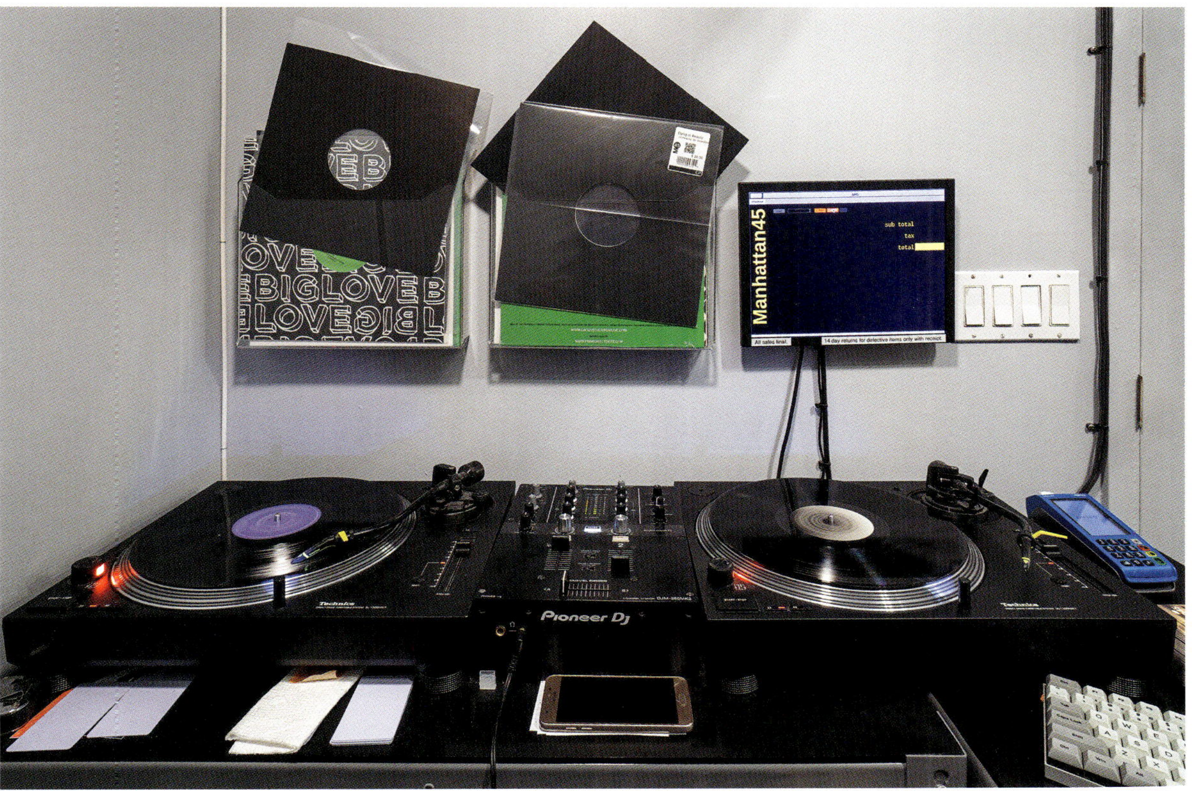
BIGLOVE
Manhattan45
sub total
tax
total
Pioneer DJ

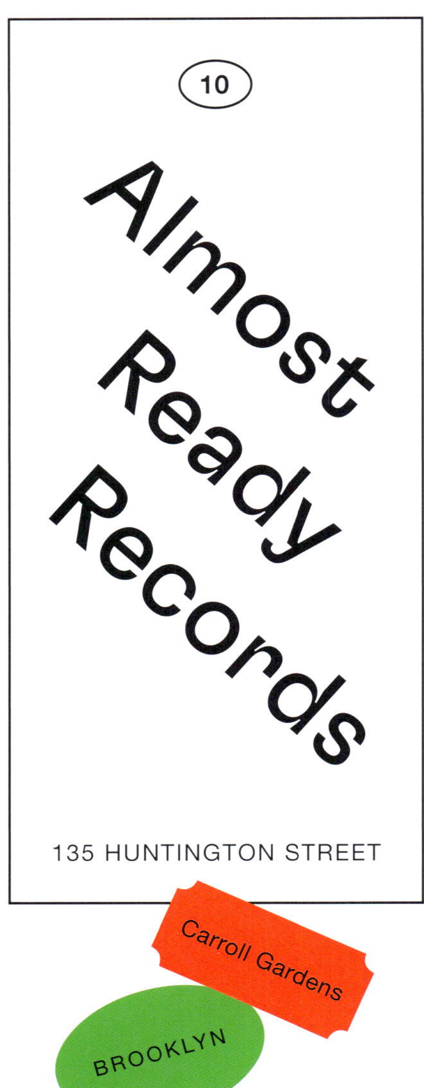

ALMOST READY RECORDS' LOGO, emblazoned on the Technics SL-1200 turntable set up as a listening station at the Carroll Gardens shop, is a pair of claw-like hands clasping at the edge of a storm drain labeled "Brooklyn, New York." It makes a pretty apt metaphor for the uphill battle presented when opening a small business in the city: constant risk for a grimy reward. But at the punk lover's paradise on Huntington Street, disillusionment and creative inspiration go hand in hand. The shop's tagline: "Where the world's lousy with ideas."

Harry Howes and Katherine Ohlweiler co-founded Almost Ready in 2017, an extension of the punk and garage rock label Howes had established in 2007. Like Captured (see p. 114), plenty of Almost Ready's floor stock stems from the eponymous label, whose all-time roster includes acts like Sneaky Pinks, the Normals, Liquor Store, and the Zeros. Yet, despite the punk preference, no genre is fully off the table throughout the five-thousand-plus collection spanning psych rock, funk, hip-hop, soul, jazz, and more (except for, of course, the rare LPs lining all four walls).

Howes's curation strategy at the shop stems from a history of seismic shifts in personal taste. "I've been into music since I was five years old," he told *Montclair Local* in 2023. His first record purchase was a Mötley Crüe album, which made for a strong gateway to Ozzy Osbourne, followed by a stint in high school spent cycling through punk rock bands. But it was boredom with the punk scene that inspired him to found Almost Ready in Hilo, Hawaii, intending to chase the joy of a hobby by making compilation mixtapes for his friends. Figuring it'd be easier to convince an artist to record him a single than a full LP, he got to work. Almost Ready's inaugural 7-inch, featuring tracks from Home Blitz, Boys Club, and Nothing People, arrived in 2007. Today, Howes also leads two other labels, both reissue imprints—Last Laugh Records for American punk, and Mighty Mouth Music for glam, funk, rockabilly, and more.

A regular Record Store Day participant, Almost Ready is one of the few vinyl businesses in New York that experienced a boom during the pandemic, when many quarantined collectors found more time than ever at home with their analog music. In the wake of the Carroll Gardens shop's success, Howes even opened a second Almost Ready branch in Montclair, New Jersey—established in late 2022 with presciently *Brat*-green walls and located in a former women's gym.

These days, Howes is stationed in New Jersey, commuting between his flagship Brooklyn location and Montclair with the support of his trusty hairless pup and Almost Ready's unofficial mascot, Tico. Heading up operations at three different labels makes juggling two different storefronts no easy task either. But Howes knows that, at a record shop, the only real estate that truly matters is the shelf space on the sales floor. "People who want good records don't care where [a store] is," he told the *Park Slope Courier* in 2017, shortly ahead of the Brooklyn location's opening party. "They'll find a way there."

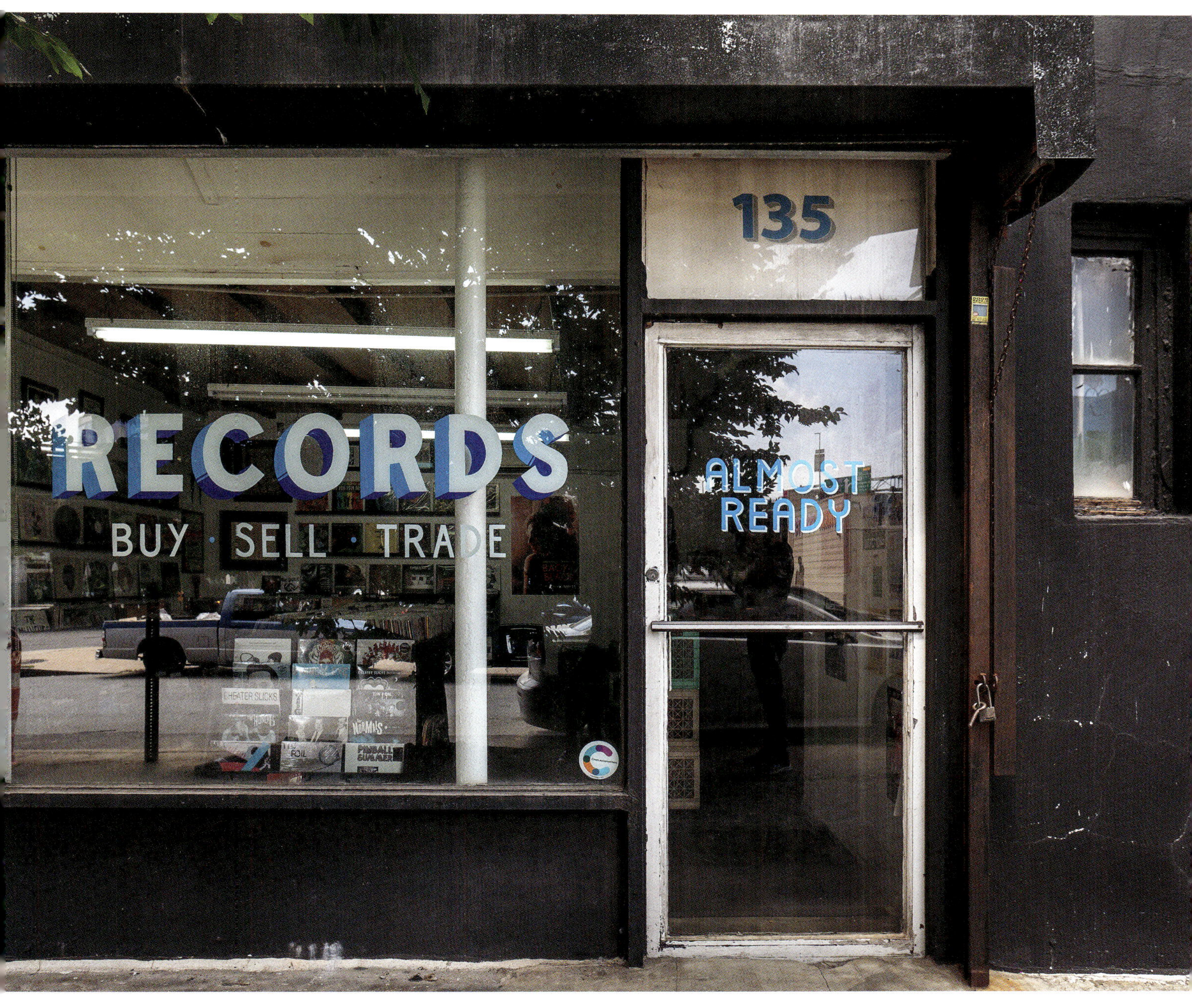

ABOVE Almost Ready Records is an off-the-radar destination for both new and used vinyl, which has been located on a residential side street in Carroll Gardens, Brooklyn, since 2017. Despite its small size, the shop carries many new vinyl releases, including ones from its own in-house record labels, which specialize in garage rock, punk, indie, glam, psych, and reissues.

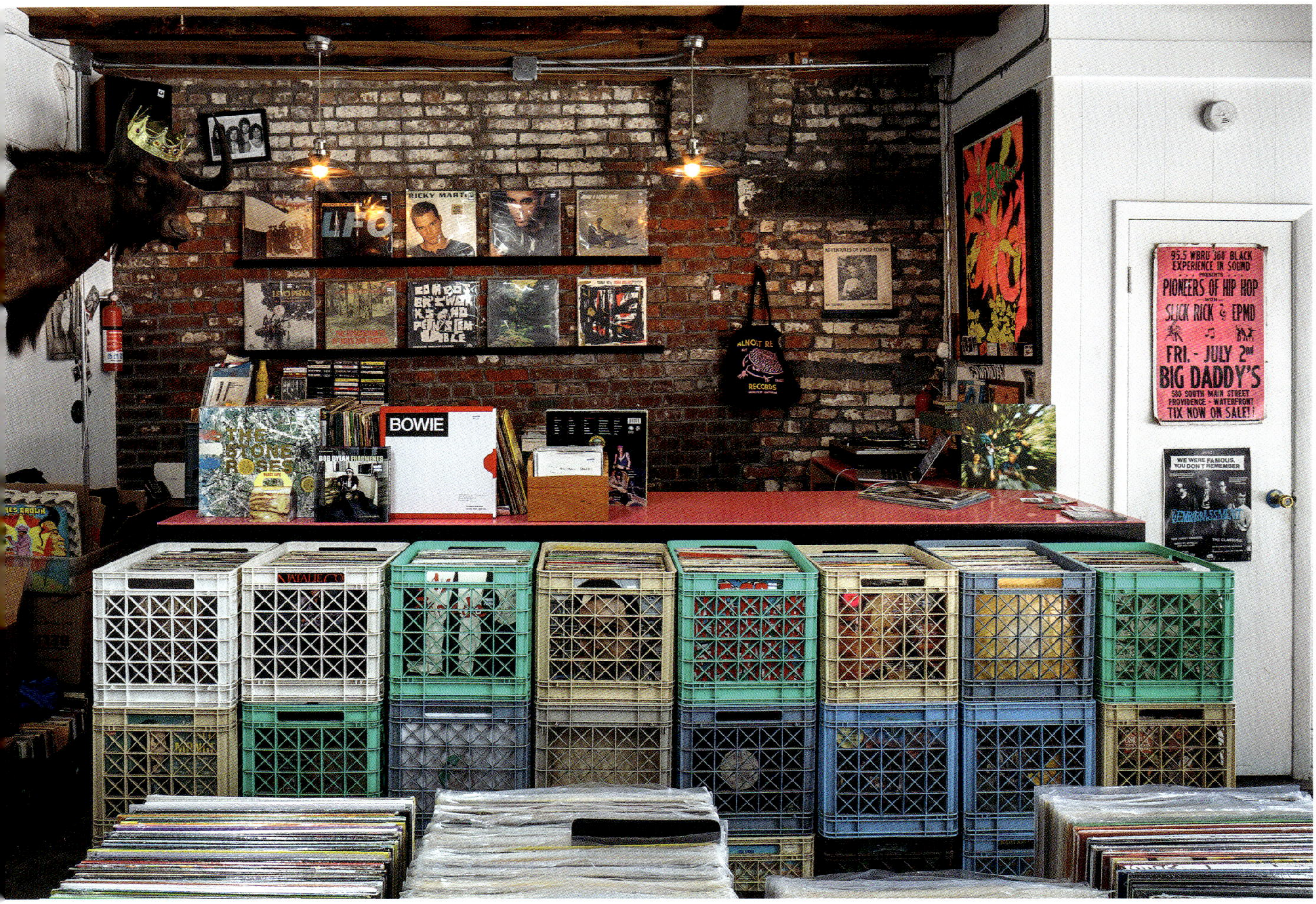

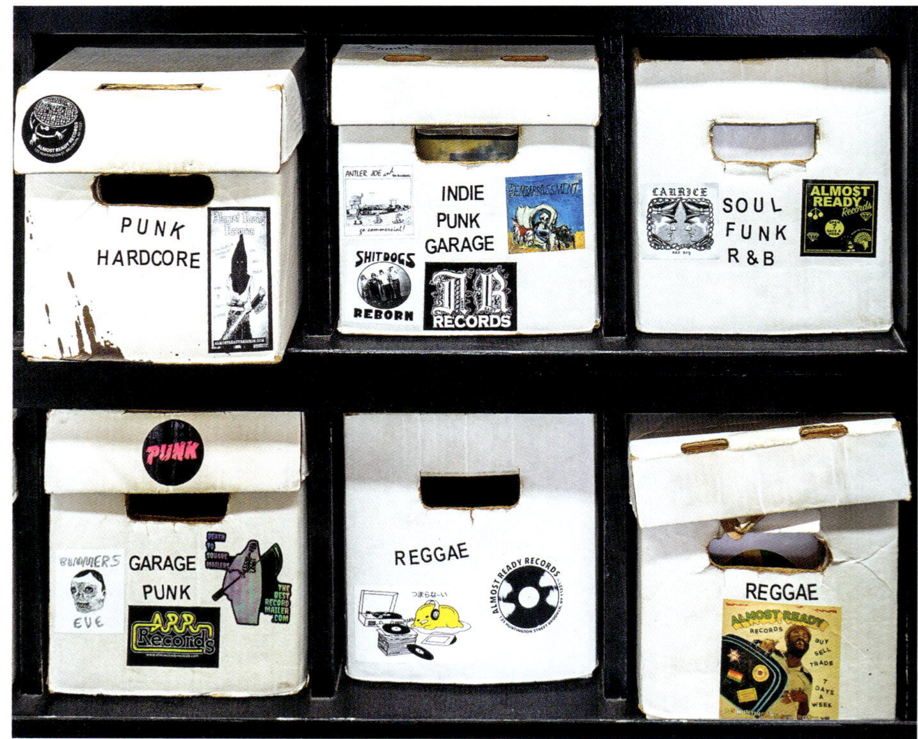
PUNK
HARDCORE
INDIE
PUNK
GARAGE
SHITDOGS
REBORN
RECORDS
SOUL
FUNK
R&B
ALMOST READY
Records
PUNK
GARAGE
PUNK
REGGAE
ALMOST READY RECORDS
REGGAE
ALMOST READY
RECORDS
BUY
SELL
TRADE

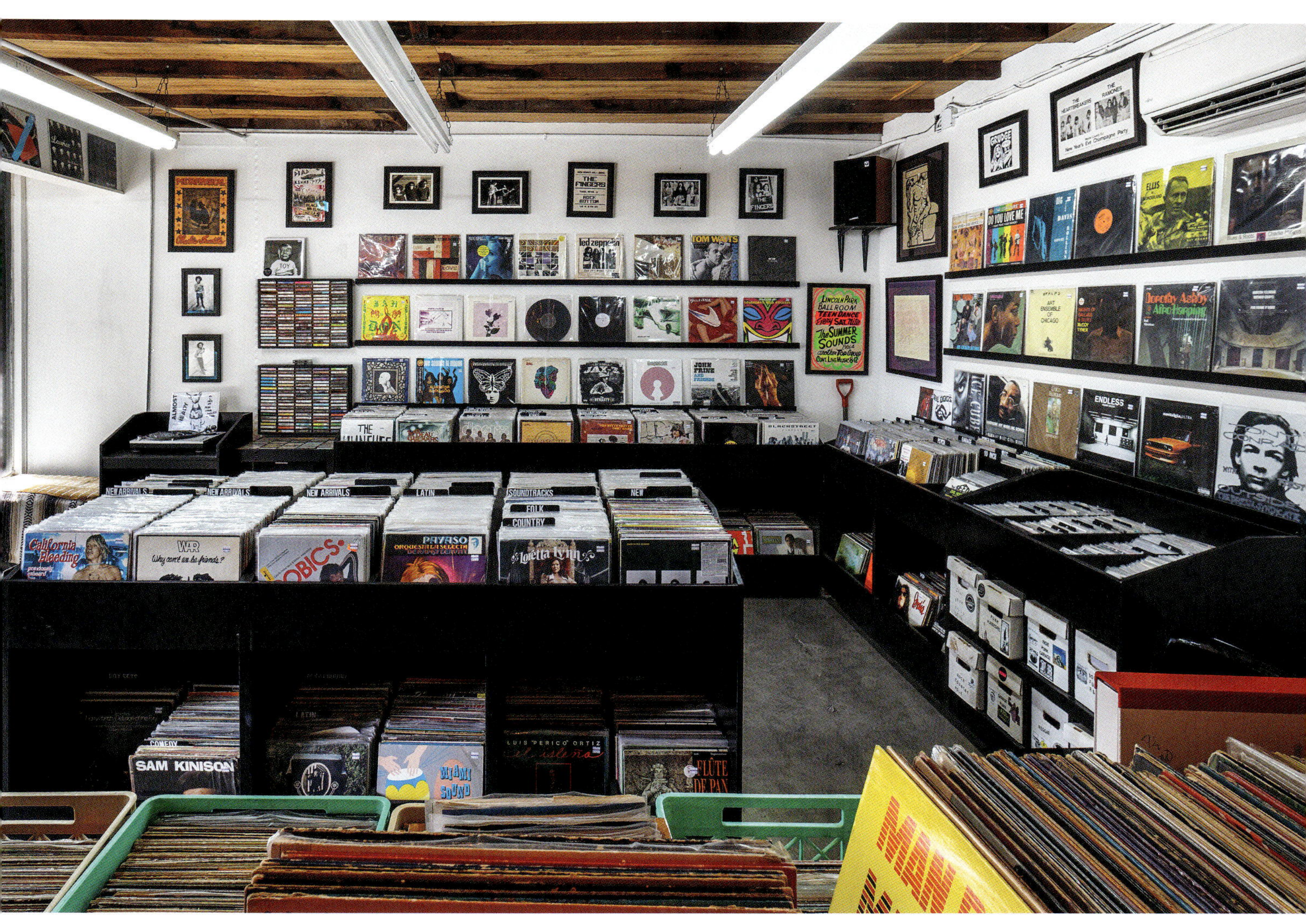

OPPOSITE TOP Almost Ready's walls are lined with collectible new and used vinyl. The shop is a great destination for crate-diggers, with a large selection of affordably priced secondhand vinyl placed in dozens of milk crates by the register, under the watchful eyes of a taxidermied moose head.

ABOVE There are dedicated sections for both 7-inch and 10-inch vinyl, which are organized alphabetically by artist and also divided by genre in marked cardboard boxes.

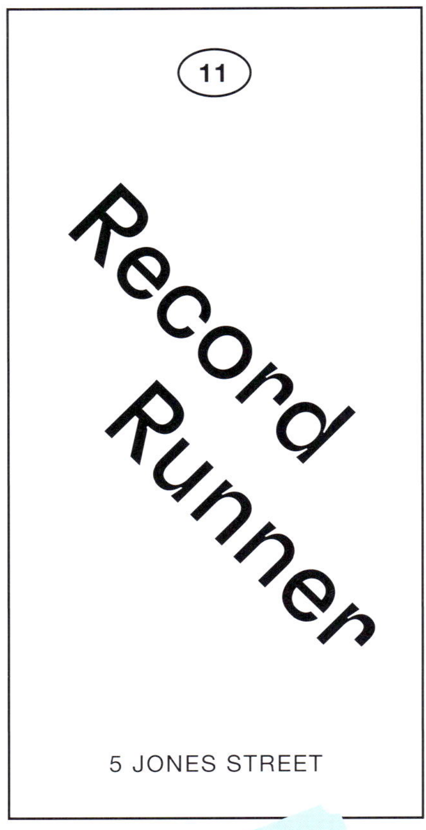

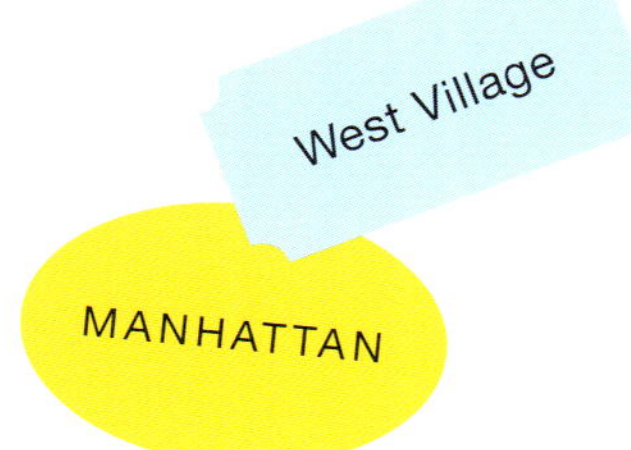

PERHAPS THE MOST FAMOUS PHOTO ever taken of Bob Dylan was shot on Jones Street in lower Manhattan. Eyes slightly downcast, he walks arm in arm with his then-girlfriend Suze Rotolo in the cover image of his classic 1963 record *The Freewheelin' Bob Dylan*. The spot where Columbia Records photographer Don Hunstein captured the shot has become a popular pilgrimage destination for music lovers looking to connect with Dylan's legend. What they might not expect is the record store sitting just steps away at 5 Jones, a piece of history in and of itself.

Established by Greenwich Village native John Pita in 1979, Record Runner wears its decades in the neighborhood like patches sewn on a high-quality vintage jacket. Posters, decals, and portraits line every surface but the floor, with Björk and Janet Jackson watching over shoppers from posters on the ceiling. Pop has always been at the core of the business, with a special eye for '80s cuts from around the world—Pita specifically highlights the shop's Madonna and Mariah Carey selections.

However, the five-thousand-record-strong floor stock may be best known for its devotion to Duran Duran. In 1981 one of Pita's contacts at Capitol Records dropped in with the early-career English group during a press tour; to Pita's surprise, they left a wave of young female customers in their wake. Other, stodgier store owners might have bristled at the unexpected shift in clientele, but Pita got to work getting his hands on every bit of Duran Duran music and memorabilia he could find. To this day, Record Runner saves a significant slice of space for artists like Joy Division and the Cure too. "We became that store where you could comfortably ask for all those kinds of artists, and we created a lot of fans," Pita told the *Village View* in 2024.

His own penchant for music started with his sister's Beatlemania—and just a little bit of mischief. As a teenager, Pita and a friend liked to hop the basketball court fence at St. Luke's School on Hudson Street, shooting hoops until a scolding from the school's gym teacher sent them scampering away. After enough repeat offenses, the teacher invited the duo to help coach basketball. This same teacher encouraged Pita to take up his first part-time job in vinyl, an after-school shift at a small brick-and-mortar on 10th Street.

That gig didn't last, but the store Pita founded on Cornelia Street with a friend in 1979 using his own record collection did. First established as a second location in 1984, Record Runner now exclusively operates from the 5 Jones Street address. In its early days, Pita carved out time to manage the not-so-profitable store while working two other jobs, perplexing his parents, but putting in the hours to pursue his passion. Over four decades later, he has yet to stop.

From under the blue triangular awning shading Record Runner's front window, Pita has watched plenty change in the vinyl business. Once-dominant suppliers like Virgin Megastore and HMV closed down throughout the early 2000s as CD sales skyrocketed, spelling danger for smaller stores. But as Record Store Day, first held in 2008, introduced a calendar of special editions and promotions to a network of independent shops, Pita noticed Record Runner gaining traction among a younger set: college students as keen on new, mainstream releases as signed secondhand gems. Just as he did when Dylan's album cover continued to draw in unassuming folk fans, and just as he did when a flock of Duran Duran disciples came to roost, Pita treated the customer evolution as an opportunity knocking.

The approach hasn't failed him yet. He still remembers the day in 1985 when he struck up a lively conversation about Bruce Springsteen and Japanese vinyl with a new face in the shop. Courting optimism, Pita hoped he'd met a new professional contact, or at least a Record Runner regular. They're still married to this day.

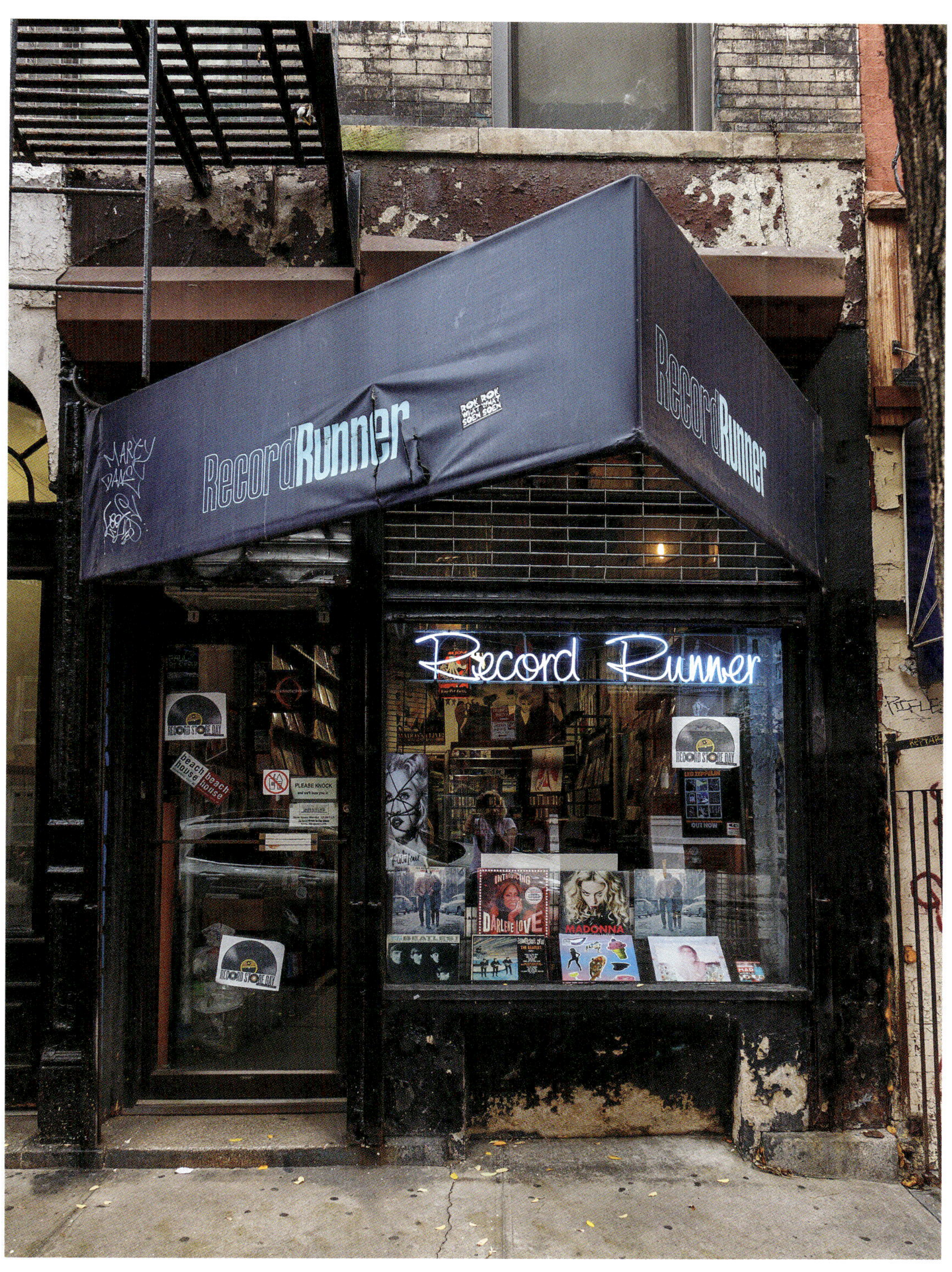

ABOVE Many people first discover Record Runner because they are Bob Dylan fans and want to see the location of the cover photo for *The Freewheelin' Bob Dylan*, which features Bob and his girlfriend at the time, Suze Rotolo, walking down Jones Street. The album is prominently displayed in the front window.

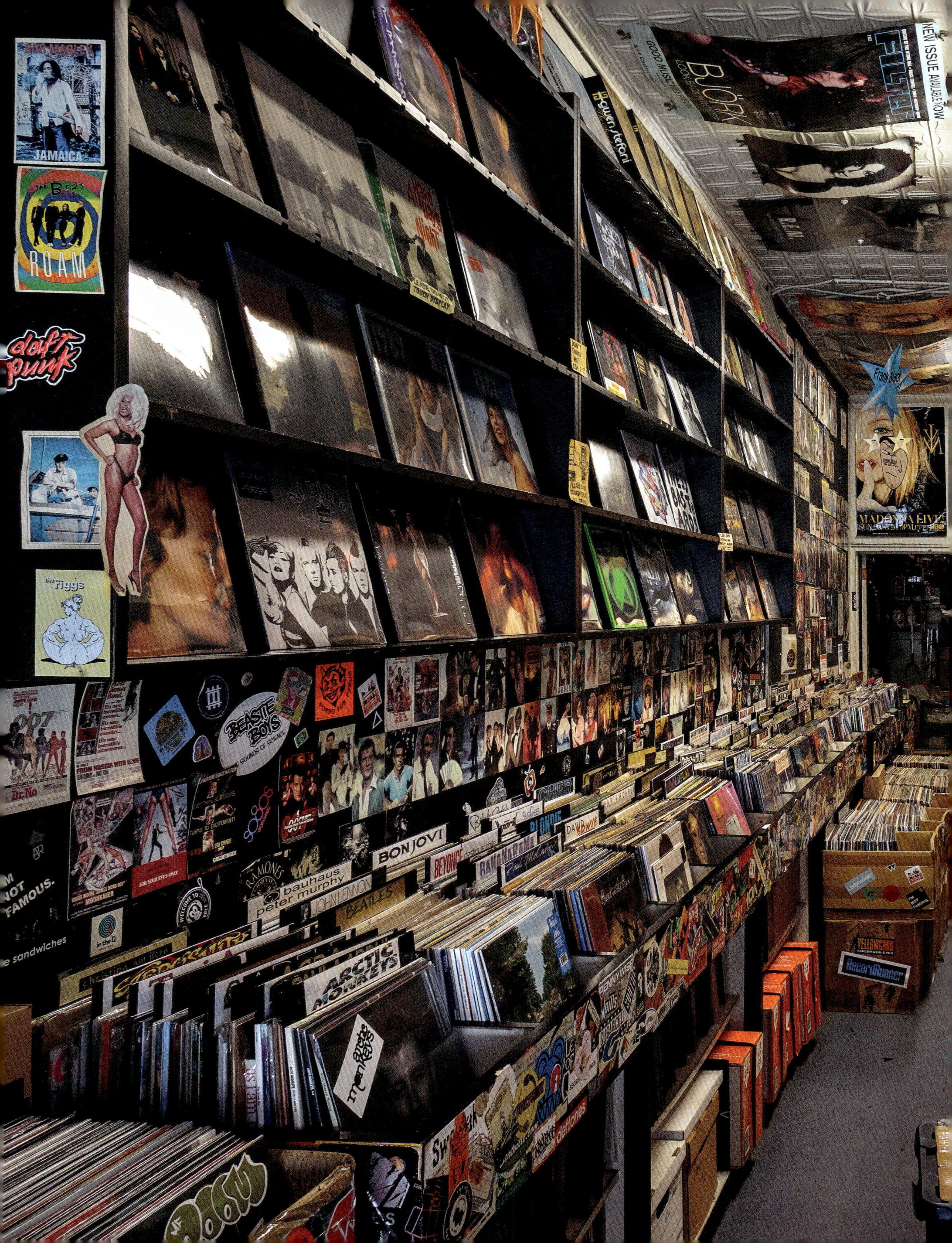
NEW ISSUE AVAILABLE NOW
FILTER
BJÖRK
GOOD MUSIC
gwen stefani
JAMAICA
THE B-52'S
ROAM
daft punk
the riggs
MADONNA LIVE!
007
Dr. No
FROM RUSSIA WITH LOVE
BEASTIE BOYS
SOUNDS OF SCIENCE
FOR YOUR EYES ONLY
NOT
FAMOUS.
sandwiches
RAMONES
bauhaus
peter murphy
JOHN LENNON
BEATLES
BON JOVI
BEYONCÉ
BANANARAMA
BLONDIE
DAVID BOWIE
CHER
ARCTIC MONKEYS
monkees
YELLOWCARD
RecordRunner
deftones

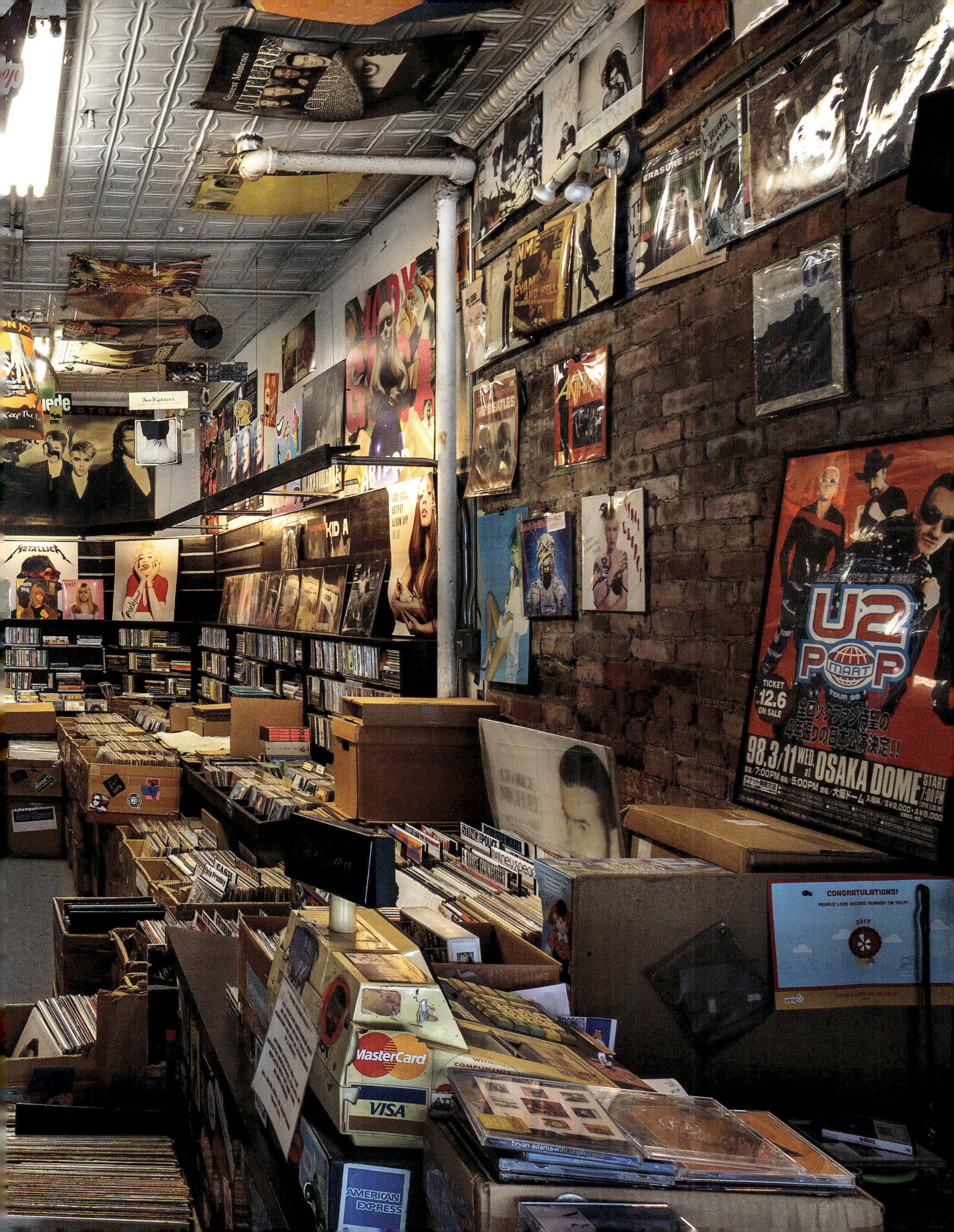

METALLICA
KID A
THE BEATLES
ERASURE
U2
U2 POP MART
TICKET 12.6 ON SALE
98.3/11 WED at OSAKA DOME
CONGRATULATIONS!
PEOPLE LOVE RECORD RUNNER ON YELP!
MasterCard
VISA
AMERICAN EXPRESS

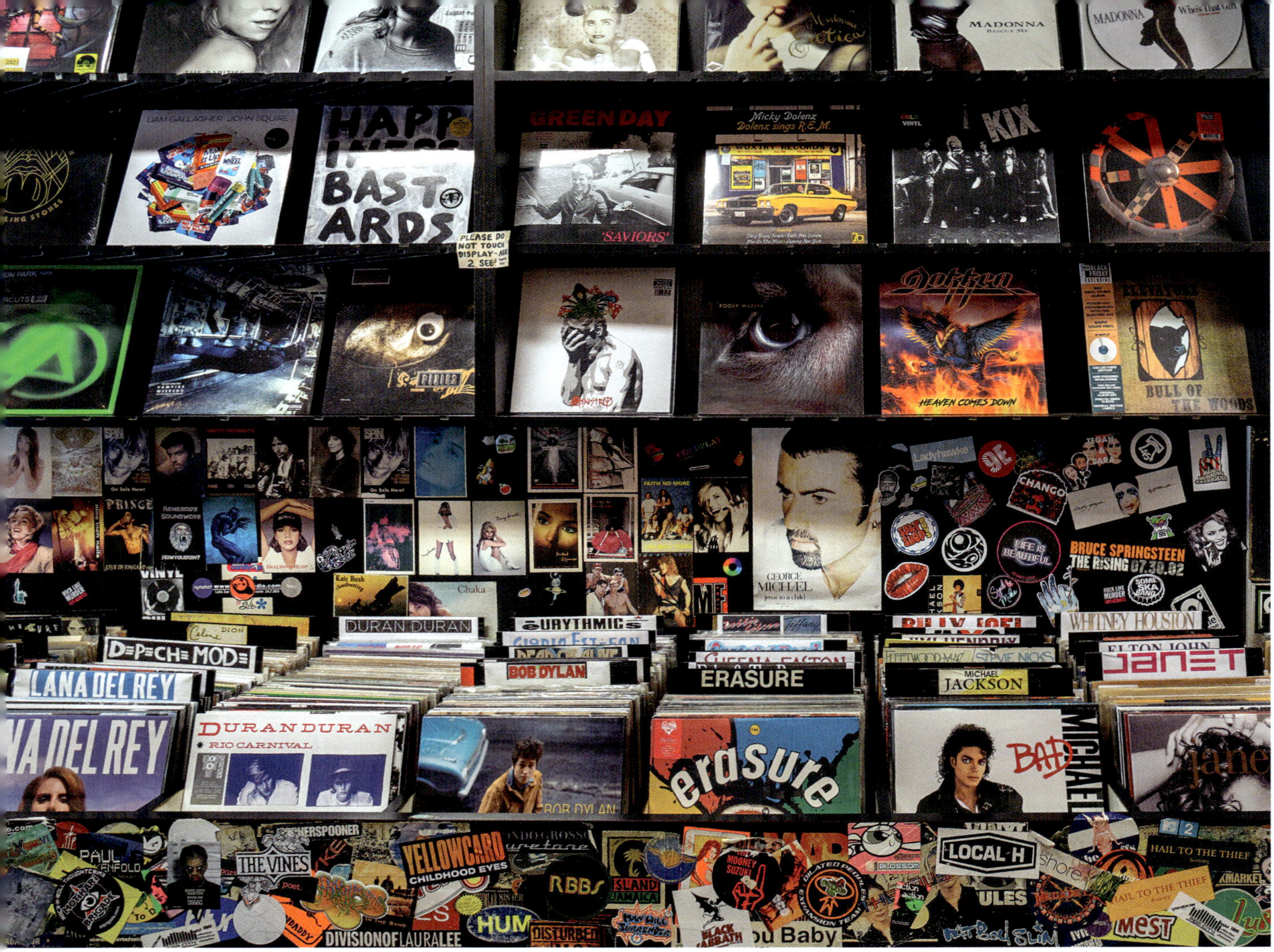

ABOVE Record Runner is one of the first shops in New York City to prominently feature UK imports from pop and rock bands, including Duran Duran, the Cure, Erasure, and the Smiths. To this day, the shop is known for its extensive vinyl selection of '80s and '90s pop artists and has one of the largest collections of rare used vinyl, reissues, and music memorabilia.

RIGHT To attract new young customers, the store also carries many exclusive Record Store Day releases, including albums from Taylor Swift.

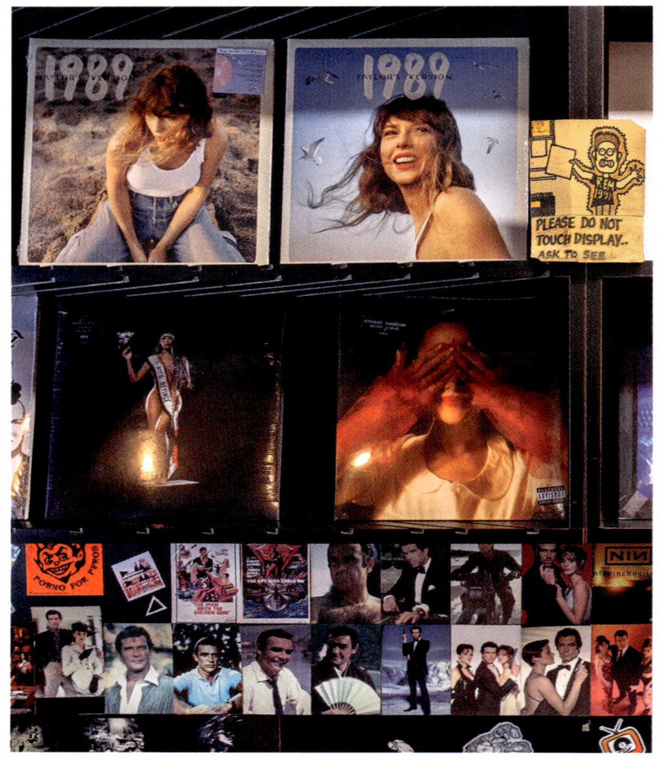

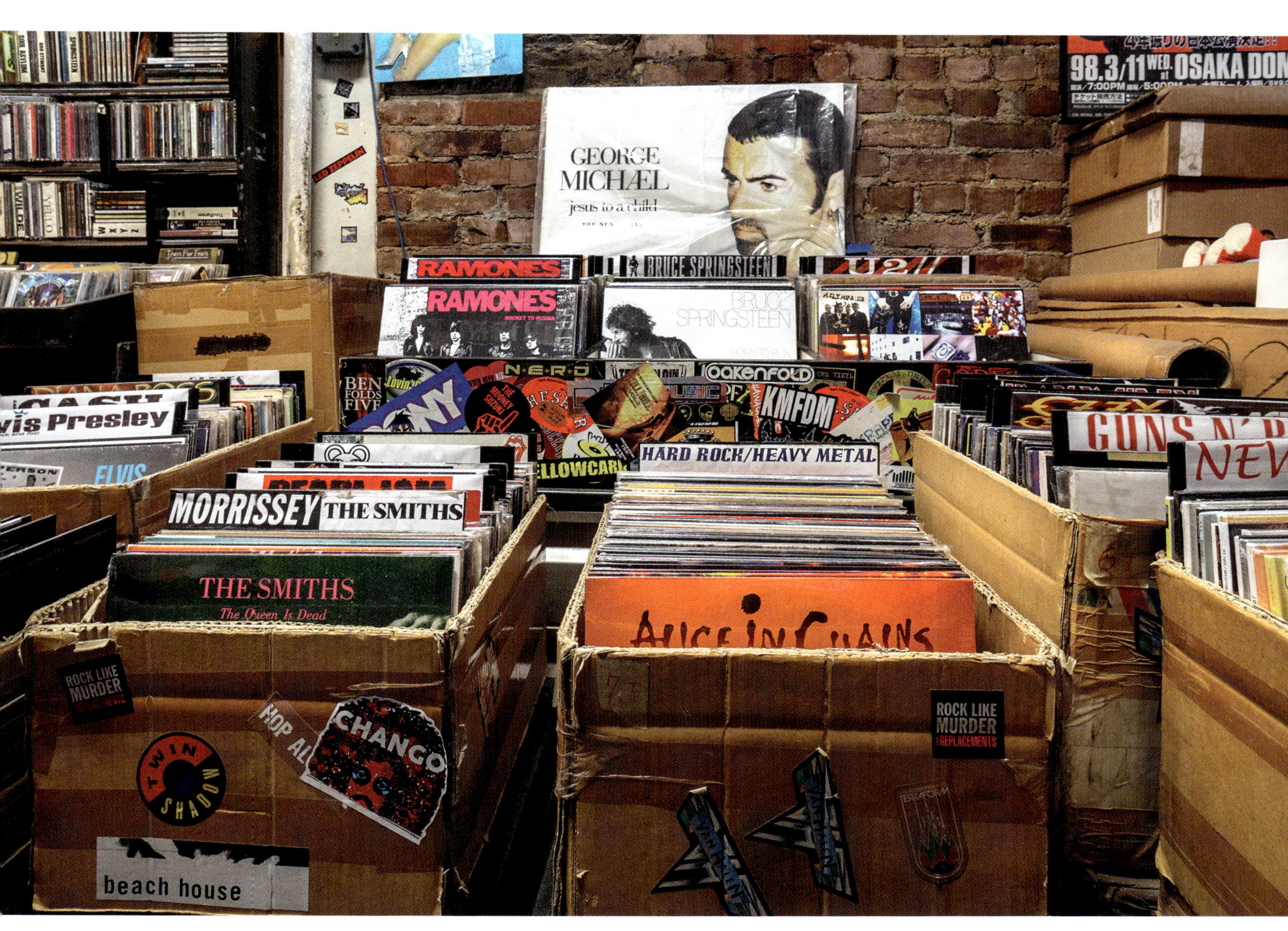
98.3/11 WED. at OSAKA DOM
GEORGE
MICHÆL
jesus to a child
RAMONES
BRUCE SPRINGSTEEN
U2
RAMONES
ROCKET TO RUSSIA
BRUCE SPRINGSTEEN
BEN FOLDS FIVE
N·E·R·D
oakenfold
KMFDM
vis Presley
HARD ROCK/HEAVY METAL
MORRISSEY
THE SMITHS
THE SMITHS
The Queen Is Dead
ALICE IN CHAINS
GUNS N' R
NEW
ROCK LIKE MURDER
ROCK LIKE MURDER
THE REPLACEMENTS
TWIN SHADOW
CHANGO
beach house

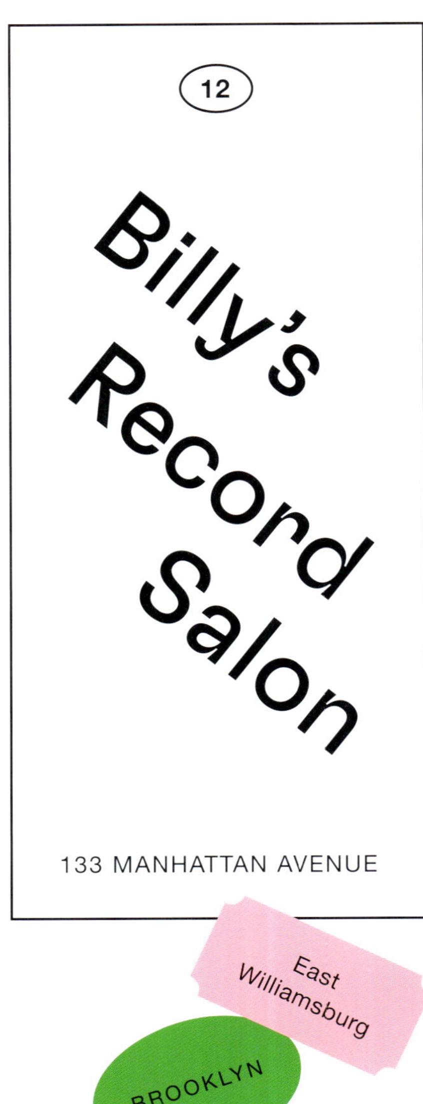

"EASY, LISTENING IS EASY," reads the black typography on a white two-tier stand at Billy's Record Salon in East Williamsburg. "Just listen." This is no empty promise at the light-refracting nook, a jazz oasis marked by a chess set and test turntables located comfortably between "starter pack" crates and idiosyncratic selections hand-picked by Billy Jones (yes, that Billy) himself.

Like the Manhattan Avenue space Billy's has called home since 2023—a former salon that still boasts a painted advertisement for permanent hair relaxer where an awning might be—Jones has lived a few different lives in New York. He moved to Williamsburg in 2002, a time he told the online magazine *Byline* in 2023 that he thinks of as the "calm before the storm." He watched bloghouse and electroclash surge through downtown culture before founding venues Elvis Guesthouse, the Dance, and Baby's All Right (the latter of which is still in operation. Since its five-thousand-square-foot space opened in 2013, Baby's has pulled off standing-room-only gigs from the likes of SZA, Charli xcx, David Byrne, Billie Eilish, and more.)

Ultimately, Jones's passion for jazz outlasted his taste for the indie rock that still enlivens Williamsburg's hipster set. "It's not something I have nostalgia issues with," he told *Byline*. "I can't listen to Radiohead's *Kid A* like I used to...but I can listen to Miles Davis's *Kind of Blue*, and it feels like the first time." There's plenty more than jazz tucked between the sleeves at Billy's, though. On any given day, mint-condition LPs from Charles Mingus, Ornette Coleman, and Alice Clark might intermingle with deeper cuts from Black Sabbath, folk singer-songwriter Fred Neil, and Japanese psychedelic pop auteur Harumi.

Jones's twenty-plus years on the neighborhood's ever-evolving nightlife circuit have honed his preferences toward quality over quantity, and the selection at his clean but cozy shop doesn't suffer for space in the slightest. Walnut-colored Altec Lansing speakers, styled to resemble the '70s and '80s radio sets a listener a generation ago might've used, ring with the day's selected jazz classics. If the intimate living room feel wasn't already potent enough, there's a full-back wicker rocking chair at the window, ready for any weary travelers. The times may change, but good taste and an open mind have an endless shelf life.

Since it opened its doors, Billy's has welcomed zine launches, single releases, DJ sets, and more, cultivating a creative community as keen on experimentation as jazz, the genre at its heart. Outside the shop's eggshell-colored walls, Jones hosts a monthly show on The Lot Radio called *Long Haired Jazz*. On the airwaves, he delivers inventive blends that can often stretch toward two hours long and stay available on YouTube and SoundCloud for playback.

Jones is intimately familiar with how popularity crests and falls in the city, leaving some subcultures and scenes to crash on the pavement. But Billy's Record Salon stands in stark contrast to trend chasing, or even trend forecasting. Despite the thoughtfully selected "Jazz Starter Pack" crates located conveniently close to the test turntables, the store doesn't position itself as an essential guide to jazz or any one kind of music. Instead, it's a completely personalized window into the mind of one of New York's most vaunted curators, the kind of viewpoint not so easily replicated from decade to decade.

Although the fading, hand-painted hair relaxer sign outside plays into Billy's Record Salon's old-is-new charm, the space is best advertised by an unassuming plaque in the bottom corner of its right window, just below its lush 4-for-$10 bins. As suited to the stylish New York shop as a sentimental elder's mantle, it reads "These Are A Few Of My Favorite Things."

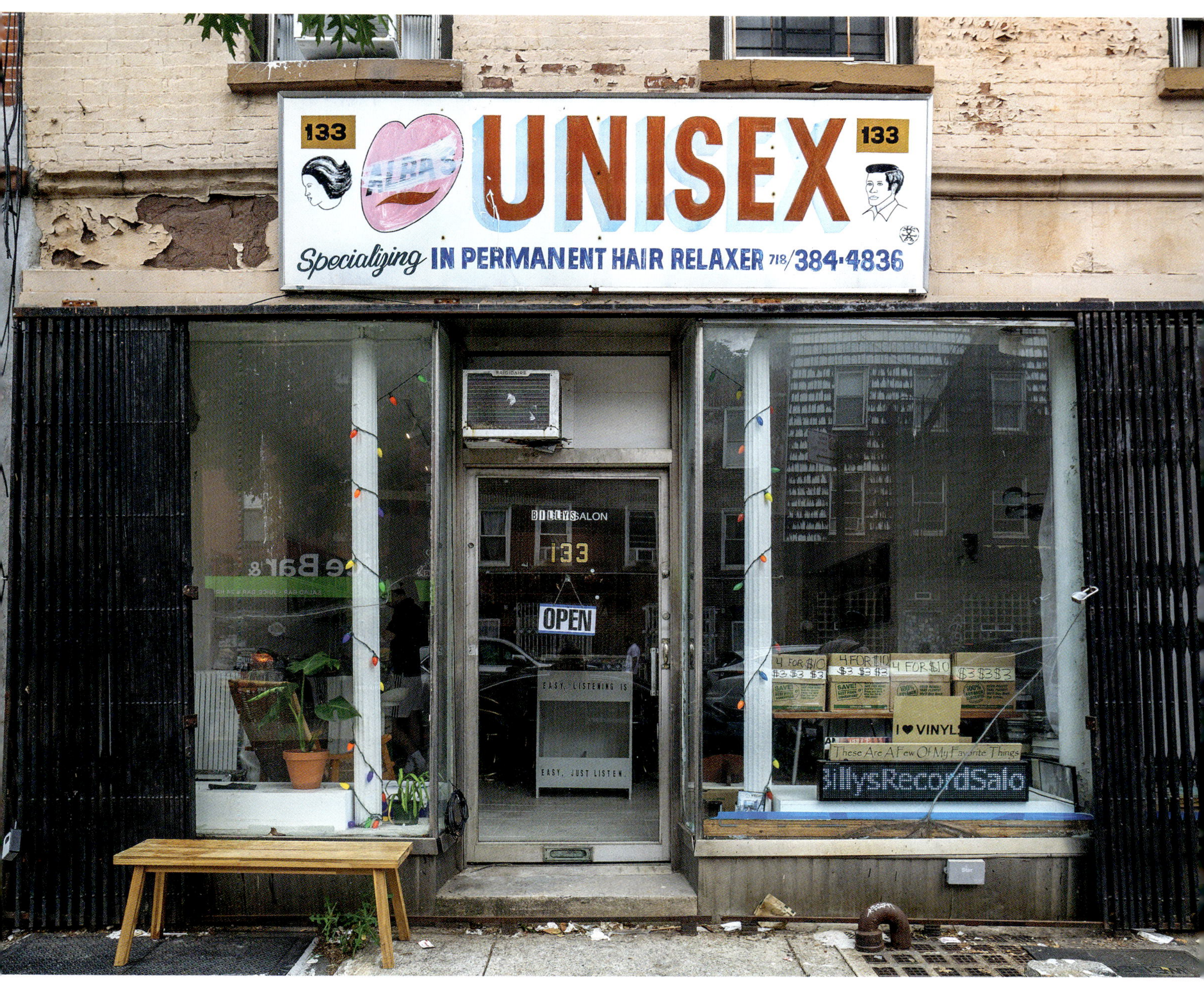

ABOVE Billy's Record Salon was founded by Billy Jones in 2023. He personally curates the store's collection of pre-loved jazz, funk, soul, and reggae. The exterior features a vintage sign for the hair salon that previously occupied the space, and a plaque at the bottom right corner of the window states, "These Are A Few Of My Favorite Things."

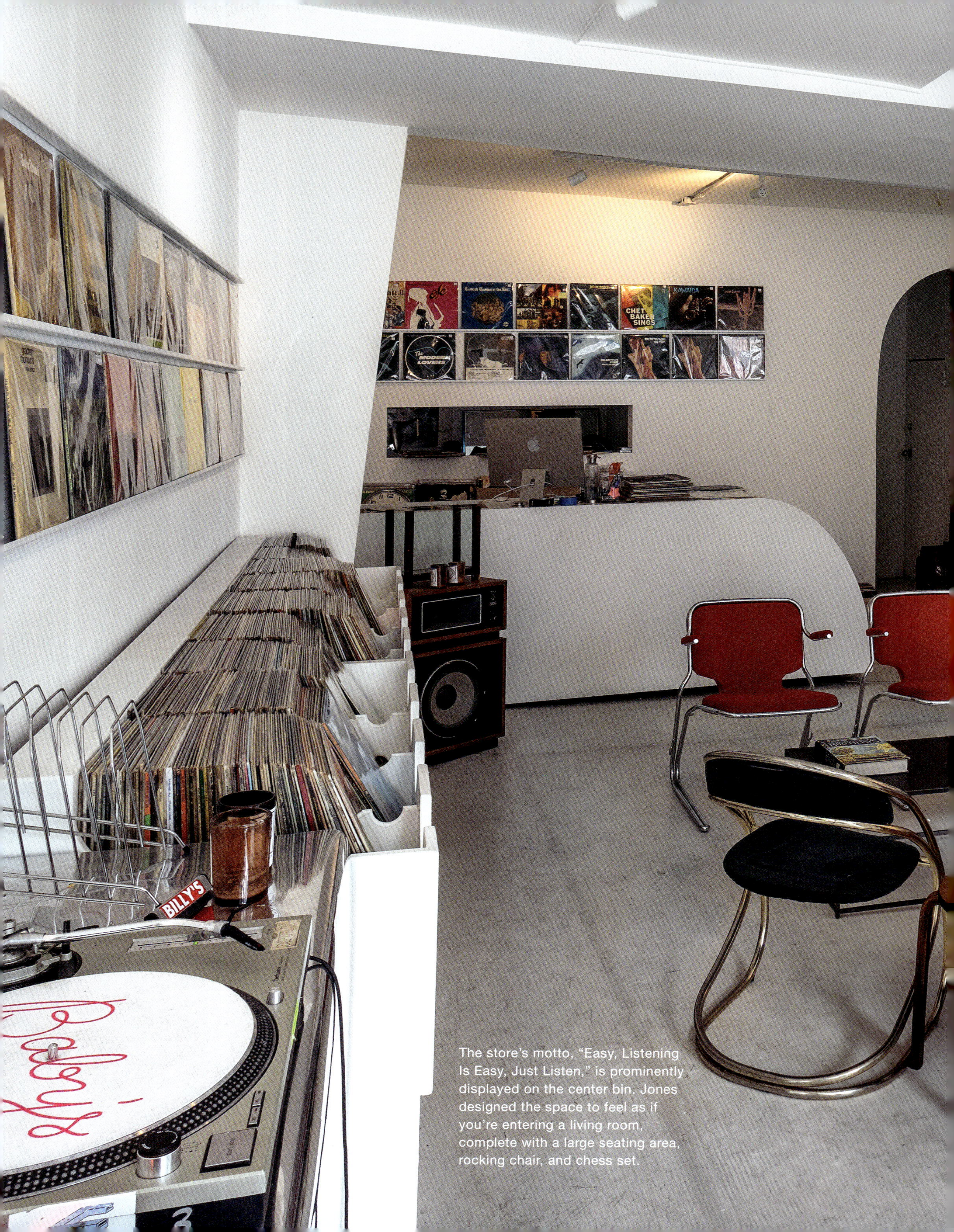

The store's motto, "Easy, Listening Is Easy, Just Listen," is prominently displayed on the center bin. Jones designed the space to feel as if you're entering a living room, complete with a large seating area, rocking chair, and chess set.

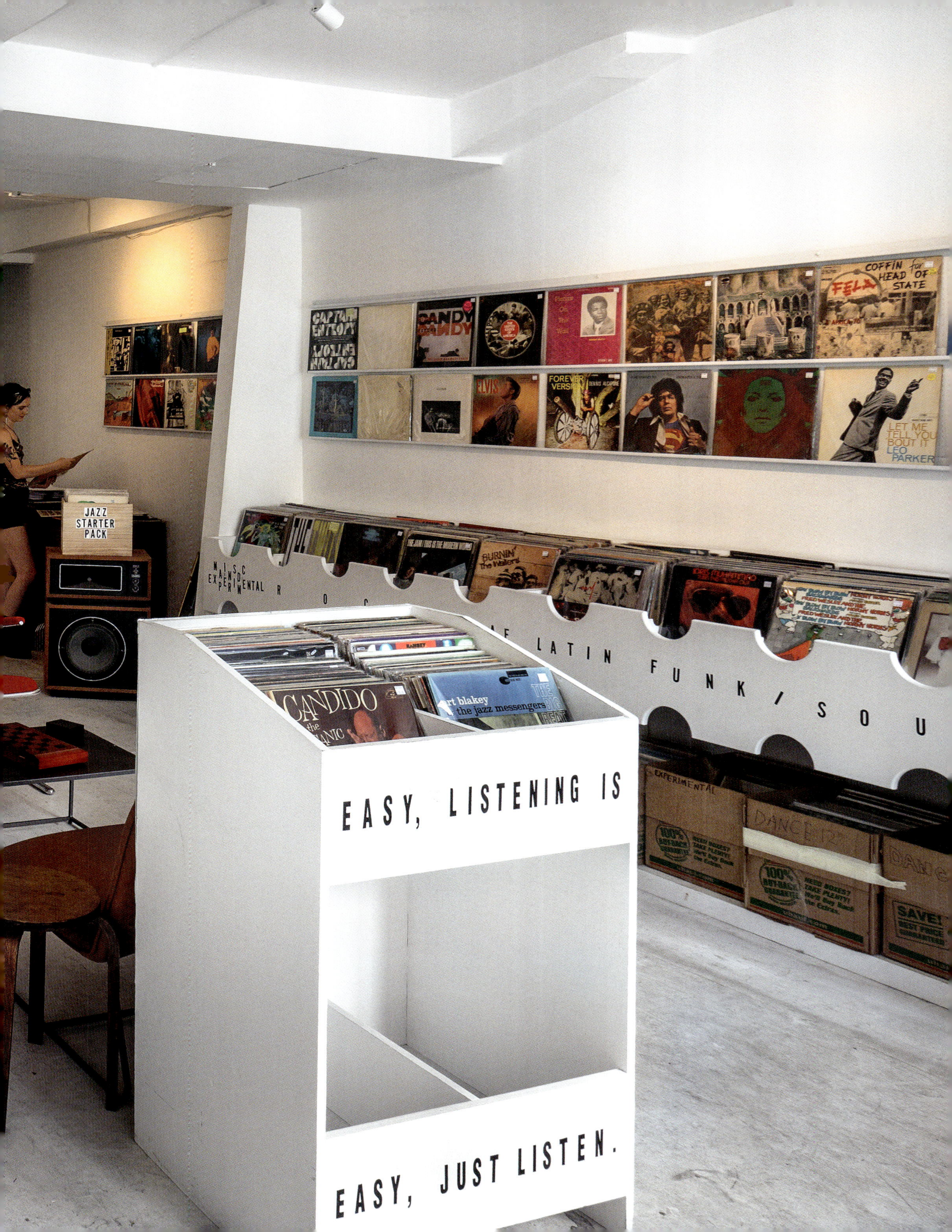

JAZZ STARTER PACK
LATIN FUNK /
EASY, LISTENING IS
EASY, JUST LISTEN.

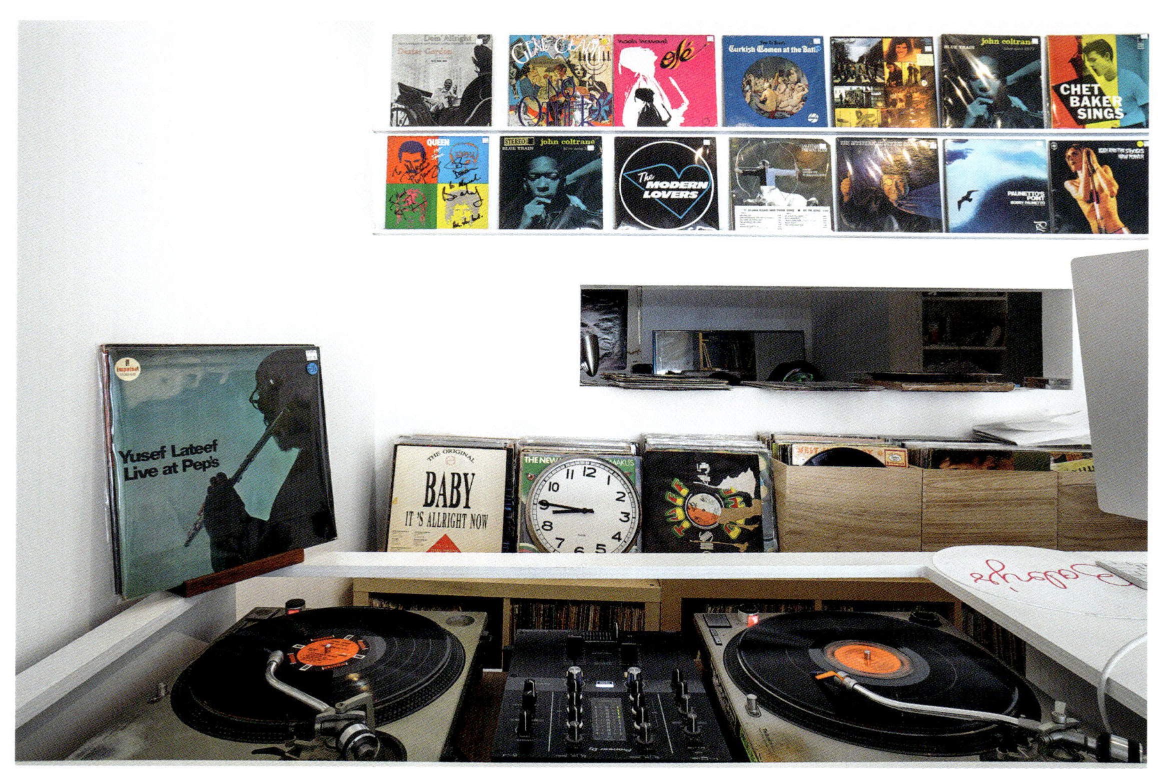
CHET BAKER SINGS
john coltrane
The MODERN LOVERS
Yusef Lateef
Live at Pep's
BABY
IT'S ALLRIGHT NOW

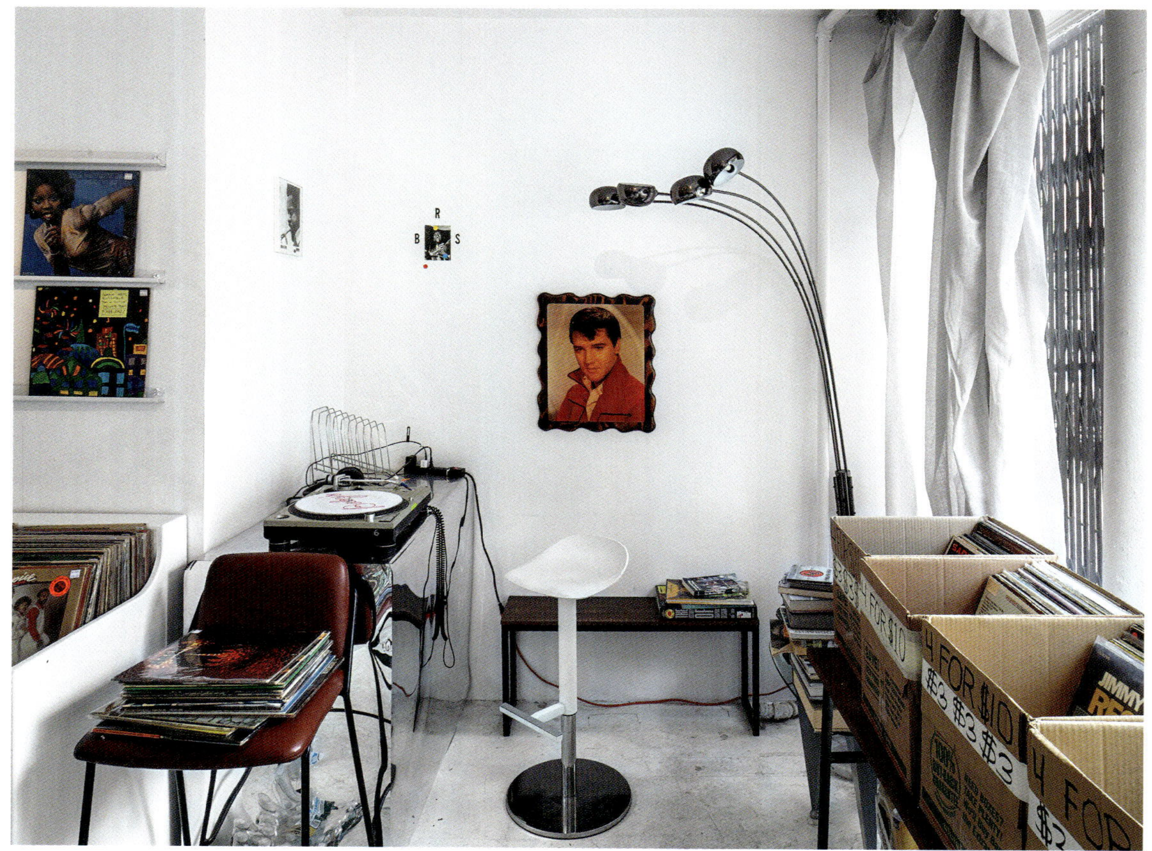
4 FOR $10
$3 $3 $3

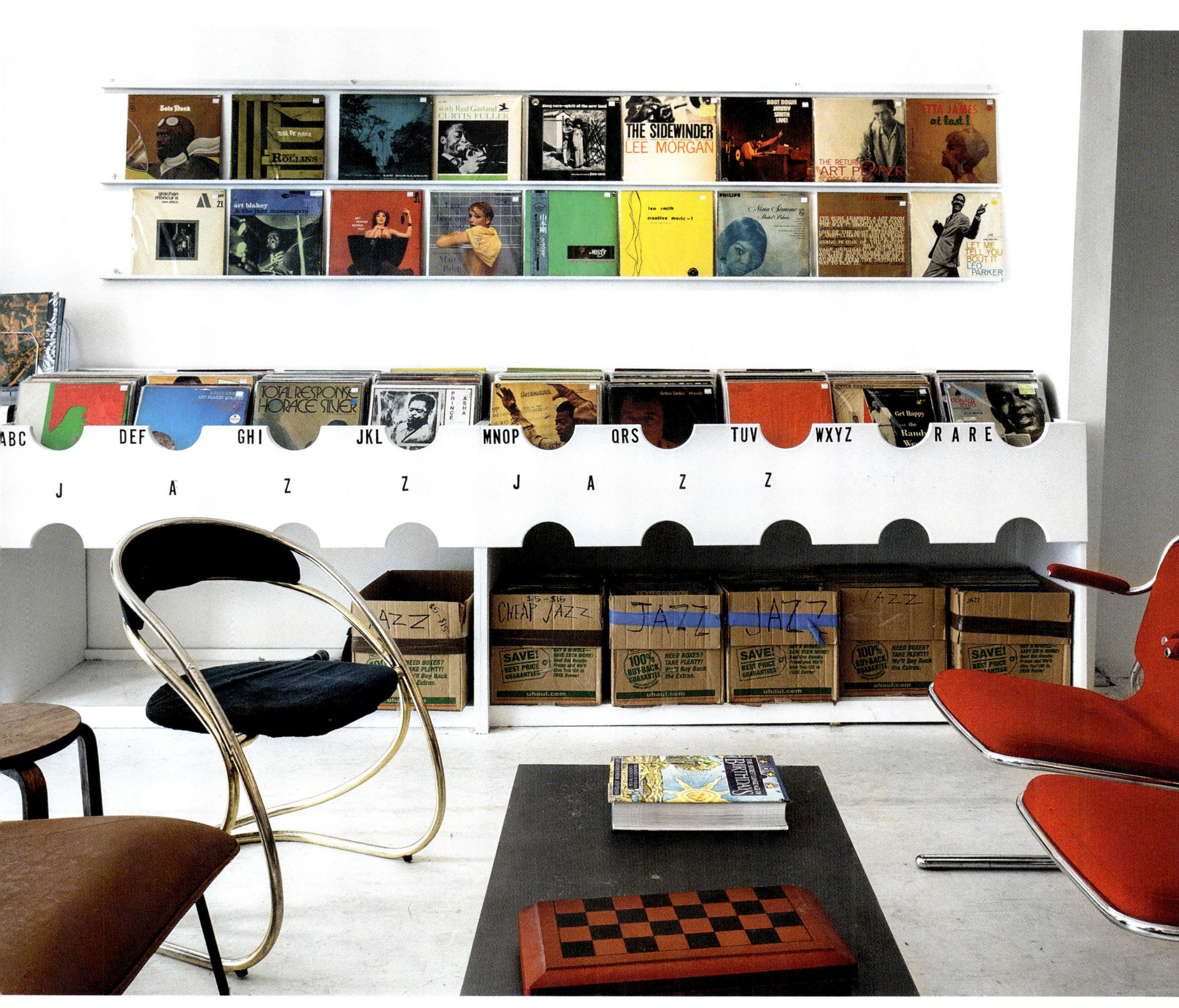

ABOVE The custom-made white wood bins and wall racks keep all the vinyl perfectly organized, including the shop's vast selection of rare jazz.

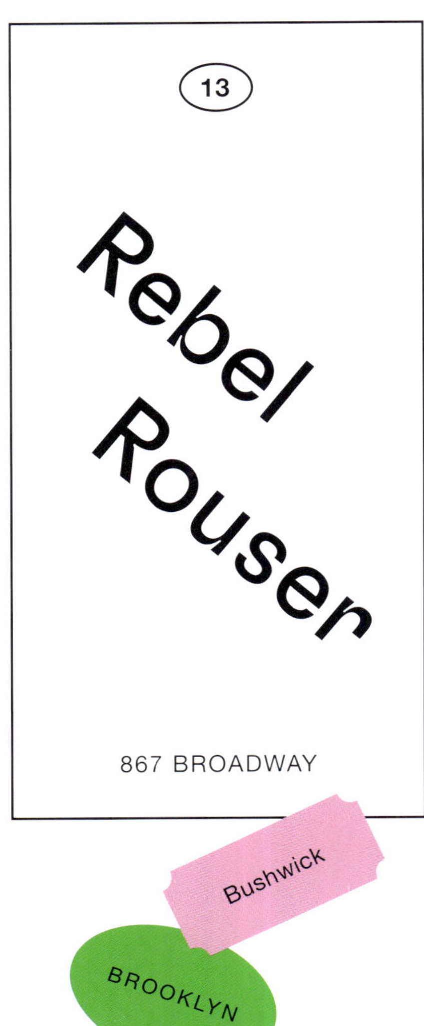

ROCK 'N' ROLL IS THE BE-ALL and end-all at Rebel Rouser, a Bushwick-based shop that shares its name with the twangy 1958 Duane Eddy single. Co-founded by artist Avi Spivak, drummer Josh Styles, and William Martin in 2014, the store specializes in just about anything with a great guitar riff. An assortment of fairly priced LPs spanning punk to power pop line its bright blue walls, overseeing stocked shelves of '60s beat, surf rock, glam, doo-wop, and more. Near the cash register, two well-hatted mannequin heads stand guard on one side of a Stanton turntable for customer listening; a knee-high Dracula statue arranged under a Violent Femmes gig flyer keeps watch on the other side.

Spivak grew up a train ride away from the city in Peekskill, easing the ennui of teenage suburban life with a passion for cartoons, comic books, and punk rock. The first two informed his career as a visual artist (he's become known for his high-contrast, linoleum block print–style drawings); the latter, the store he'd eventually design his own logo for. He discovered the space that would become Rebel Rouser after wandering into a warehouse party on a tucked-away side street fondly referred to as "Punk Alley." Returning mentally over and over again to the unfussy location, lined with stores operating out of repurposed shipping containers, Spivak saw the possibility for a no-bullshit rock 'n' roll hub that Manhattan's rising prices and creeping gentrification had made difficult to imagine. After bringing Styles around to check it out, Spivak put down the first month's rent immediately.

Beyond music, Rebel Rouser also trades in an assortment of rare horror zines, comic books, and vintage fan club flyers—they've sold everything from Black Flag ticket stubs to back issues of the hardcore mag *Outcry*. Plenty of the shop's decor offers a glimpse into Spivak's other life as an artist and cartoonist, collaborating with local establishments like Variety Coffee Roasters, the venue TV Eye, and the independent radio station WFMU. He's also published plenty of print work, from illustrations for periodicals like *Impose* to limited-release zines, like the Norton Records visual history he penned alongside Billy Miller, *Kicksville Confidential*.

Like the limited-release zines he contributes to, Spivak sees Rebel Rouser as a secret treasure that will reward a good eye. As he told online zine *Maximum Rocknroll* in 2015, "It's a little hidden jewel and something you really have to see to believe." Approaching the shop as an artist more than a businessman, Spivak knows well the hard, often thankless work required to make a living off selling art. However, he can't help but trust that the real lovers of rock ephemera, big and small, will come to shop owners who wait. "I've always felt that if you just keep plugging away and working hard and doing interesting work, then the right people will find you," he told the digital magazine *Ponyboy* in 2018.

For over a decade, it's been working—and on an average weekend afternoon, Punk Alley is flocked with shoppers looking for new old memorabilia. Among his well-known fans, Spivak now counts the idiosyncratic, encyclopedic journalist Nardwuar. And in 2020, Miami power pop legend Steve Katz stopped by to deliver a special message signed in black Sharpie on one of his old records: "To Rebel Rouser—Keep Vinyl Alive!"

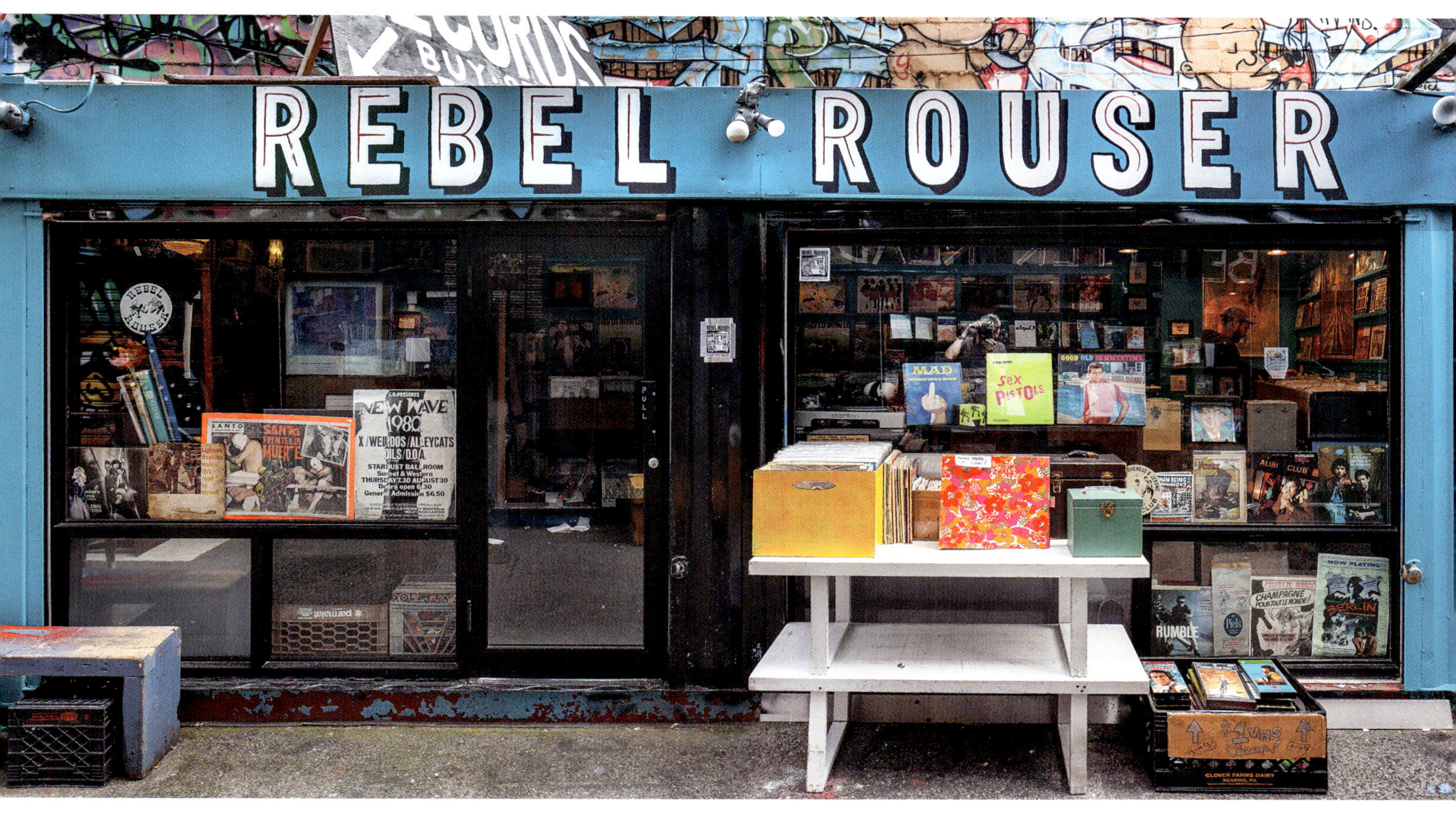

ABOVE Rebel Rouser is one of Brooklyn's most unique record stores, located inside a repurposed shipping container in an alleyway flea market known as Punk Alley. It specializes in records from the 1950s to the 1980s, including a large selection of rare 45s and classic, glam, rock, punk, power pop, psych, funk, and soul LPs. It also sells cassettes, 8-tracks, VHS tapes, pins, T-shirts, and music memorabilia.

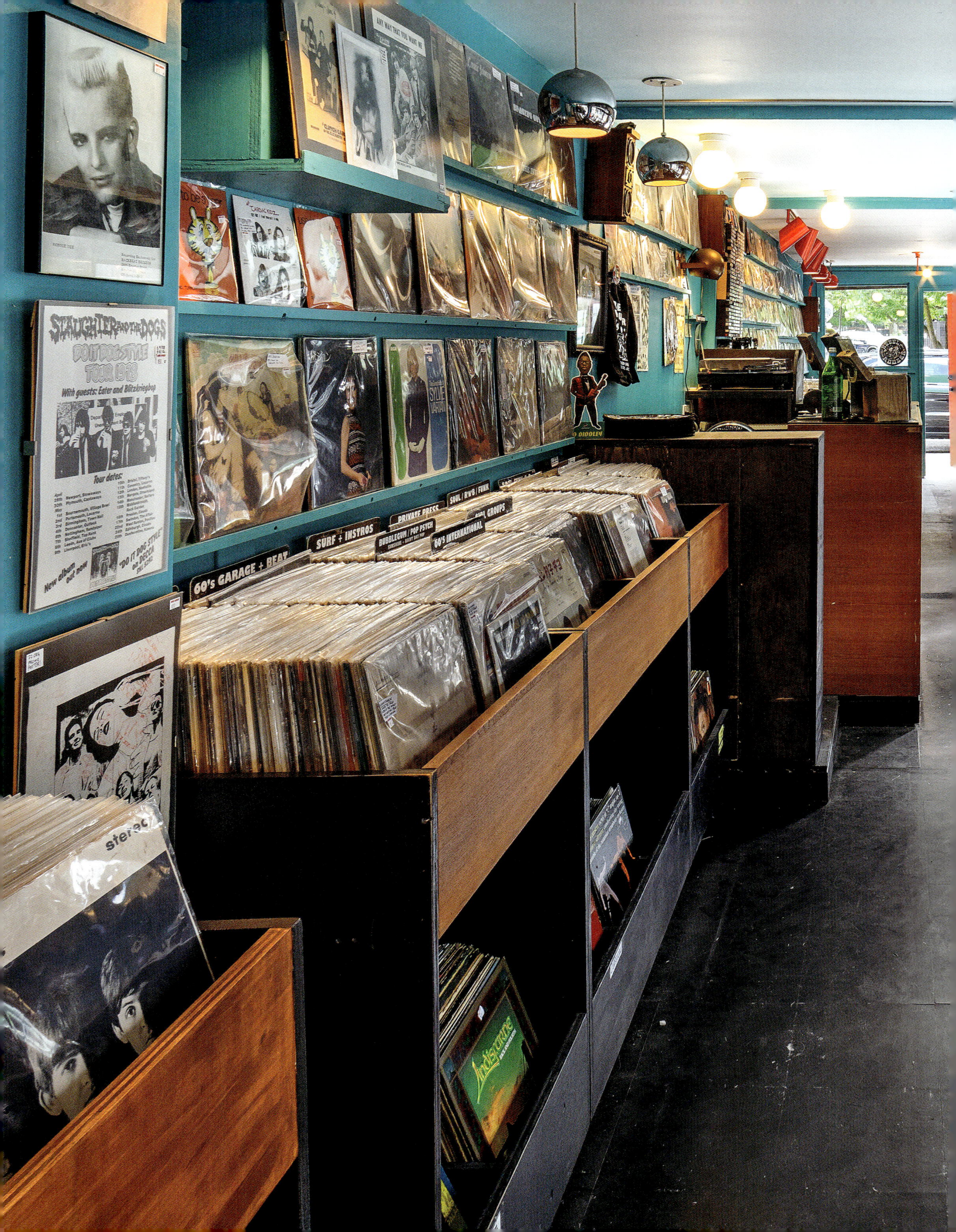

SLAUGHTER AND THE DOGS
With guests: Eater and Blitzkrieg Bop
Tour dates:
New album out now
60's GARAGE + BEAT
SURF + INSTROS
PRIVATE PRESS
BUBBLEGUM / POP PSYCH
60's INTERNATIONAL
GIRL GROUPS
stereo

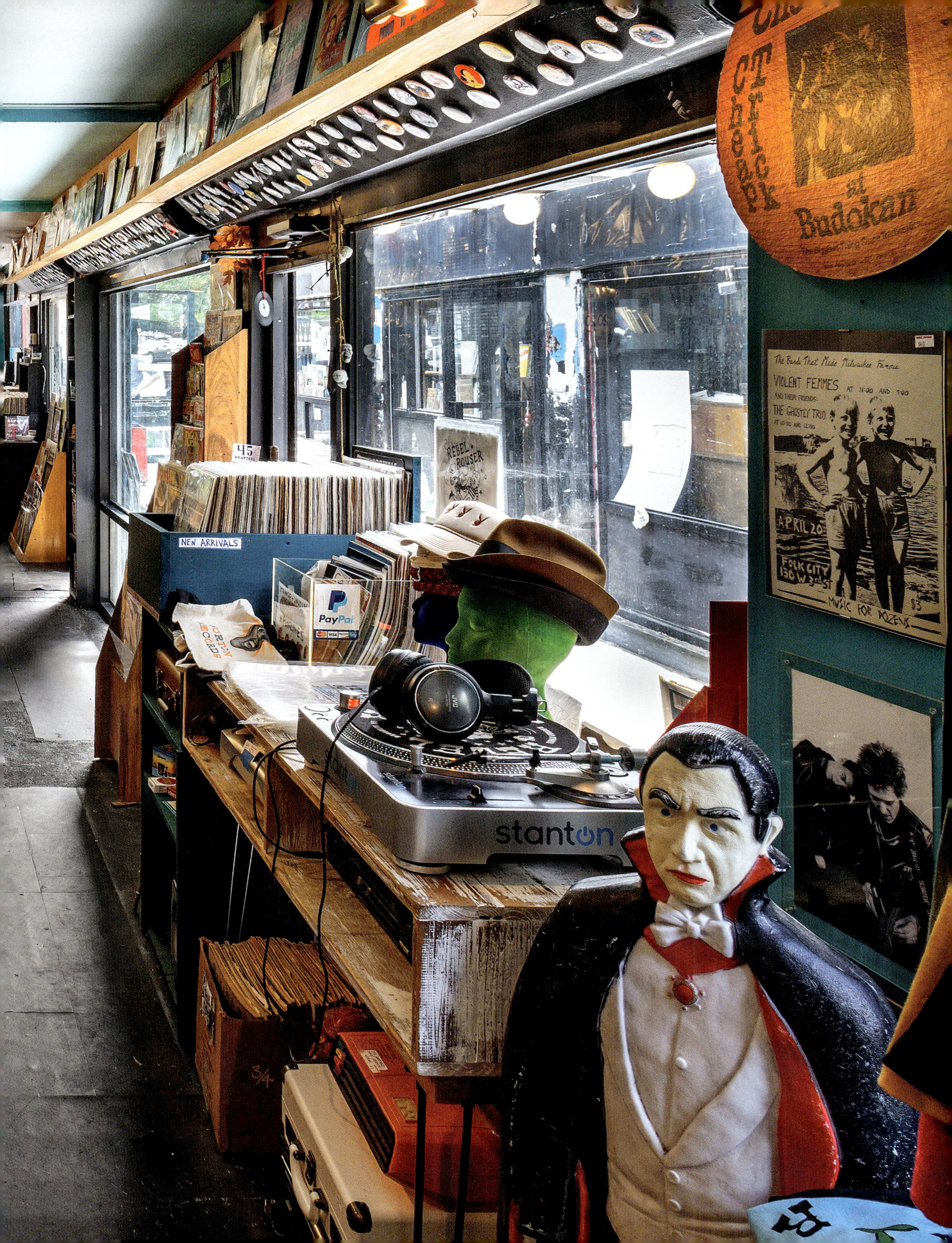
Cheap Trick
at
Budokan
The Bands That Made Milwaukee Famous
VIOLENT FEMMES AT 11:00 AND 1:00
AND THEIR FRIENDS:
THE GHOSTLY TRIO
AT 10:00 AND 12:00
APRIL 20
FOLK CITY
130 W 3rd ST
MUSIC FOR DOZENS
$3
45
REBEL ROUSER
NEW ARRIVALS
PayPal
stanton

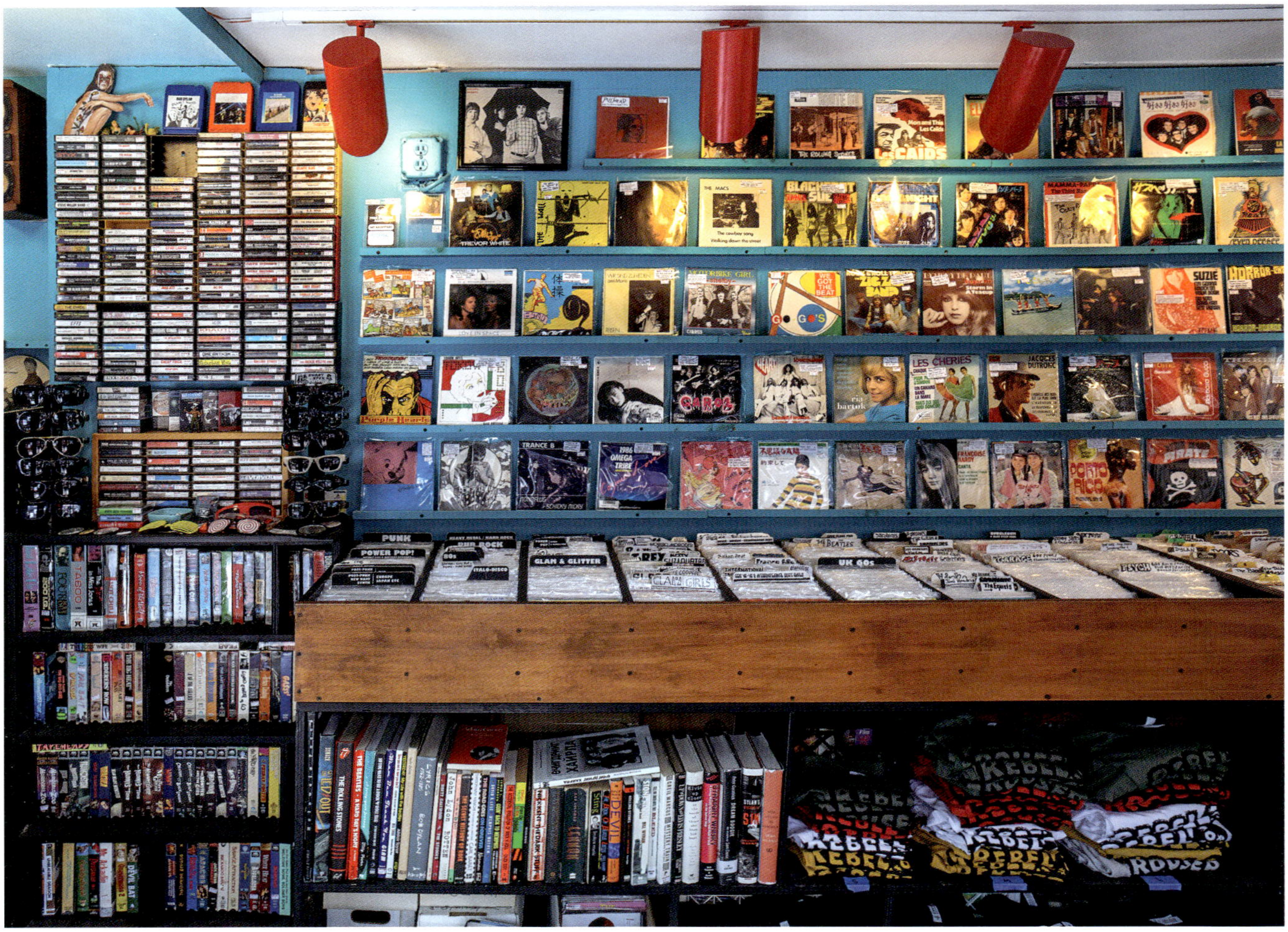

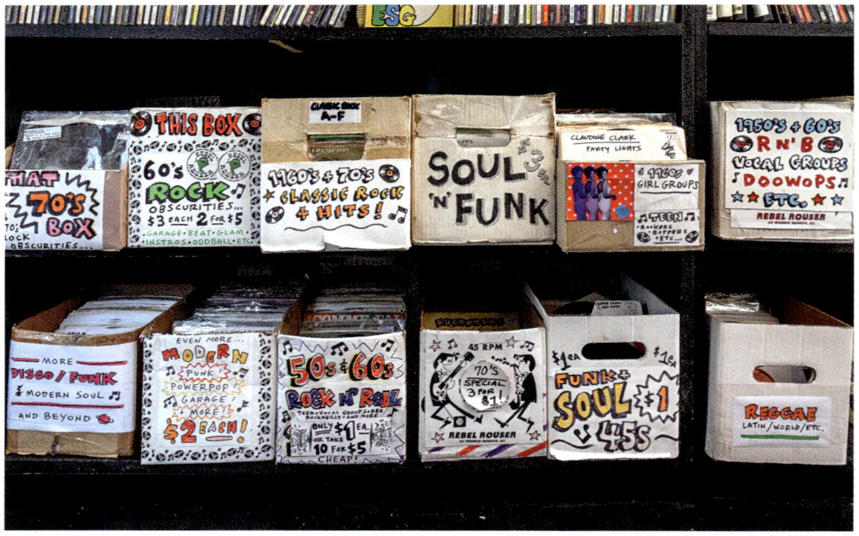

ABOVE Many handwritten dividers help organize the large collection of 45s, including sections for "Power Pop / Denim & Rhinestone," "Glam & Glitter," and "Garage '60s Punk / Janglers / Frat Etc."

OPPOSITE BOTTOM The shop's inventory is all reasonably priced, including rare titles. There are also helpful handwritten stickers placed on the records' outer sleeves indicating genre, condition, and pressing information.

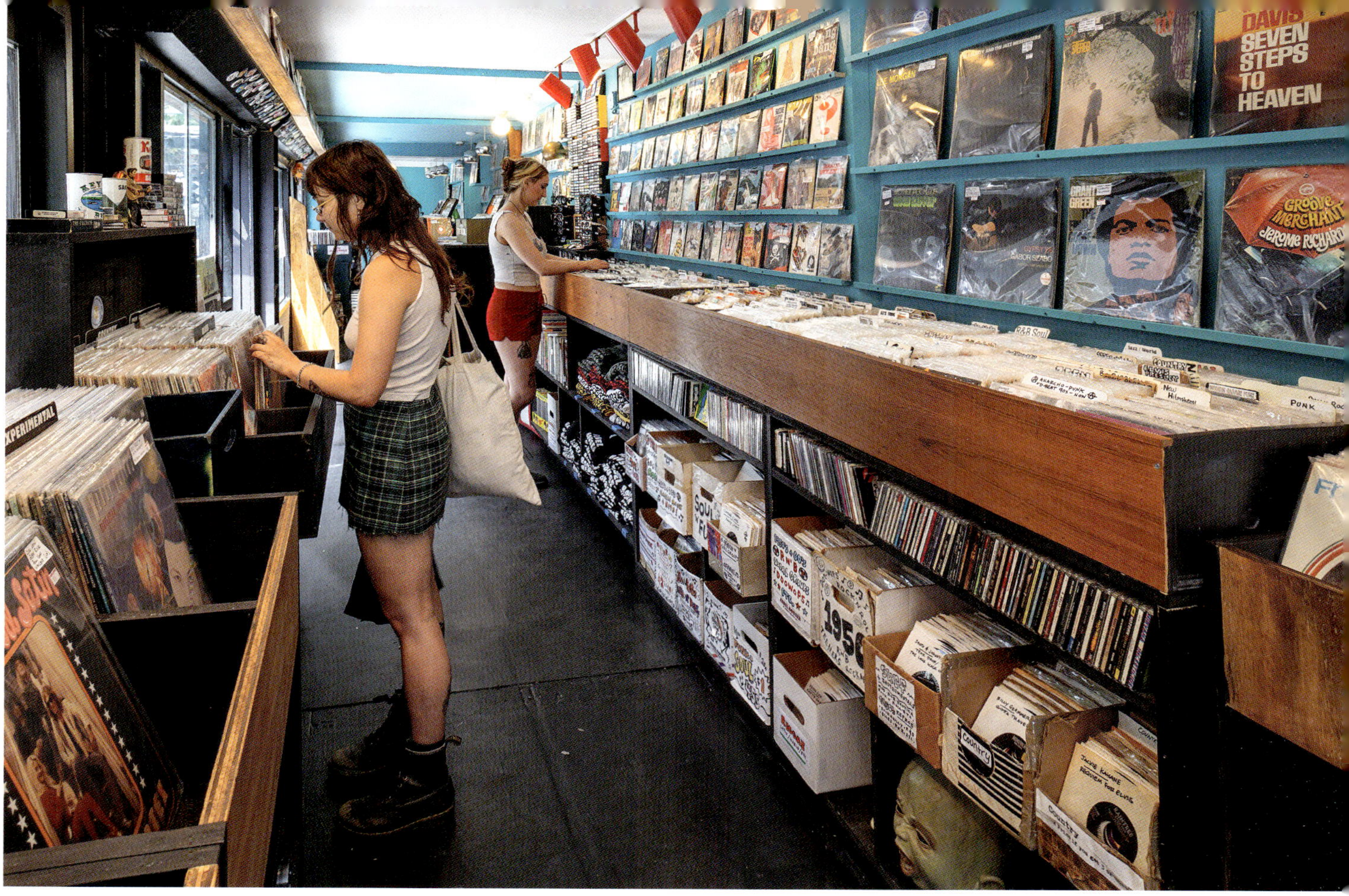

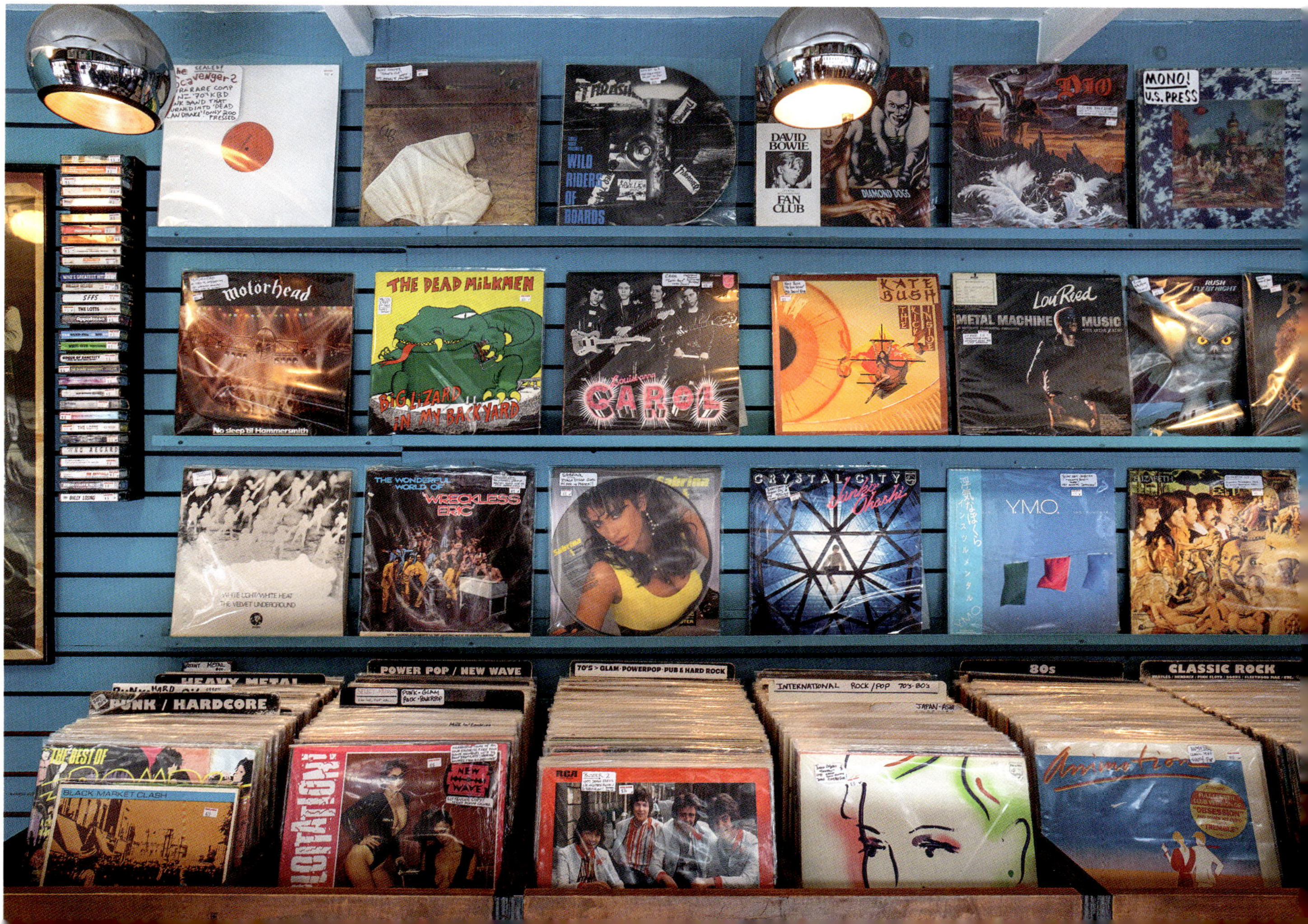

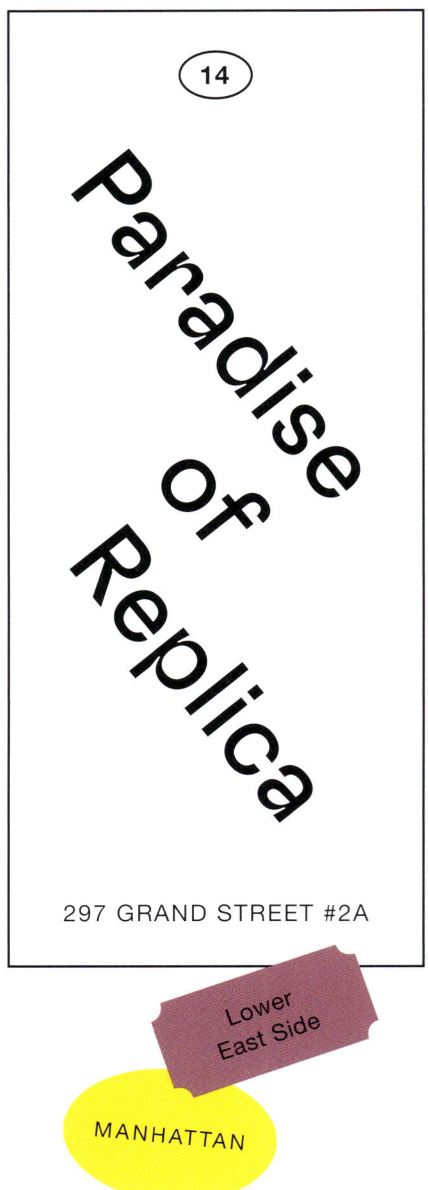

MANY VINYL LOVERS END UP opening record stores as a means to house the unruly fruits of their lifelong digging labors, once they've outgrown a bedroom closet or basement corner. But for DJ, filmmaker, and Paradise of Replica founder Kyle Molzan, a taste for vinyl came later, after online music exploration led him to places even his USB couldn't go.

Molzan's shop is named after a 1989 record by the Japanese avant-pop group After Dinner (whose band name also inspired a left-of-center radio program Molzan hosted with friends after graduating from Pratt Institute). Born in Fort Myers, Florida, he originally came up the coast for film school, where he crucially discovered composer and film scorer Ryuichi Sakamoto's Yellow Magic Orchestra, a common gateway to Japan's robust musical history. Eager to level up his local sets with vinyl-only gems, he found himself rabbit-holing into minimal dub, techno, and ambient—anything with a synth, really.

Venture up the flight of stairs that leads to door 2A, and you'll find that Paradise of Replica's robin's-egg blue walls conjure the effect of stepping into a soft-lit spa. But there's nothing laid back about the lean, mean assortment of options here, carefully curated enough to court the odd bedraggled tourist, but eccentric enough to please the most esoteric—and highest-stamina—of hobbyists.

Although the onset of Covid-19 forced many physical media retailers to close, Paradise of Replica came to fruition amid the emptiness of lockdown solitude. In 2020, when Molzan's DJ gigs and film projects dried up, he just wanted something to work at. While waiting for the world to reopen, he amassed thousands of records. With the idea for a shop buzzing at the back of his mind, he got his collection up to twelve thousand pressings strong; half of that personal cache became Paradise of Replica's original stock. The store opened to customers in November 2021.

Its second-floor space does limit walk-in customers, but Molzan erases any potential purchasing deficit with the internationally imported collections that make up his stock. However, he views these sorts of buys less as blind bets than mystery bag opportunities. Past-life jobs at NYC's physical media churches, including the independent movie theater Film Forum and the now-defunct rental shop Kim's Video, trained Molzan's eye toward not just the rare but the unfamiliar. After all, what's the fun in running a shop if you're not expanding your own horizons? "Half of it is just for me to know," he shares of his bulk buys. "Just to hear what the hell it sounds like."

Take stock of Molzan's inspired spread, and you'll want to hear what the hell it sounds like too. From Donna Summer bootlegs to rare Japanese ambient and city pop, all the twists and turns his methods of discovery have taken throughout the years are on full display in the shop's offerings. However, his devotion to deep cuts never morphed into a gatekeeper complex. "When I started the store, my sister was like, 'You should probably go into selling records, because you like telling people more about records than you do keeping them,'" he explains. The sharing was the best part.

Since Molzan first took his sister's advice, he's acquired a few different collections, expanding the store's reach into the curatorial realm. A substantial stack of punk and hardcore came from artist Richard Kern, whose 1995 photobook *New York Girls* cemented the provocateur as a Manhattan legend. Molzan also purchased a boatload of pre-'60s folk and jazz from the late painter and collagist Duncan Hannah, a pillar of the '70s art scene who Molzan got to know just prior to Hannah's death in 2022.

Whether meeting new customers or maintaining bonds with weekly shoppers, Molzan has managed to re-create the same creative camaraderie he found missing post- (and even pre-) lockdown. "I didn't meet that many people that I could talk about film and music with," he recalls of his life before Paradise of Replica. "I was just like an isolated guy in a basement." Now, he's made his way into a community—and all it took was settling in on the second floor.

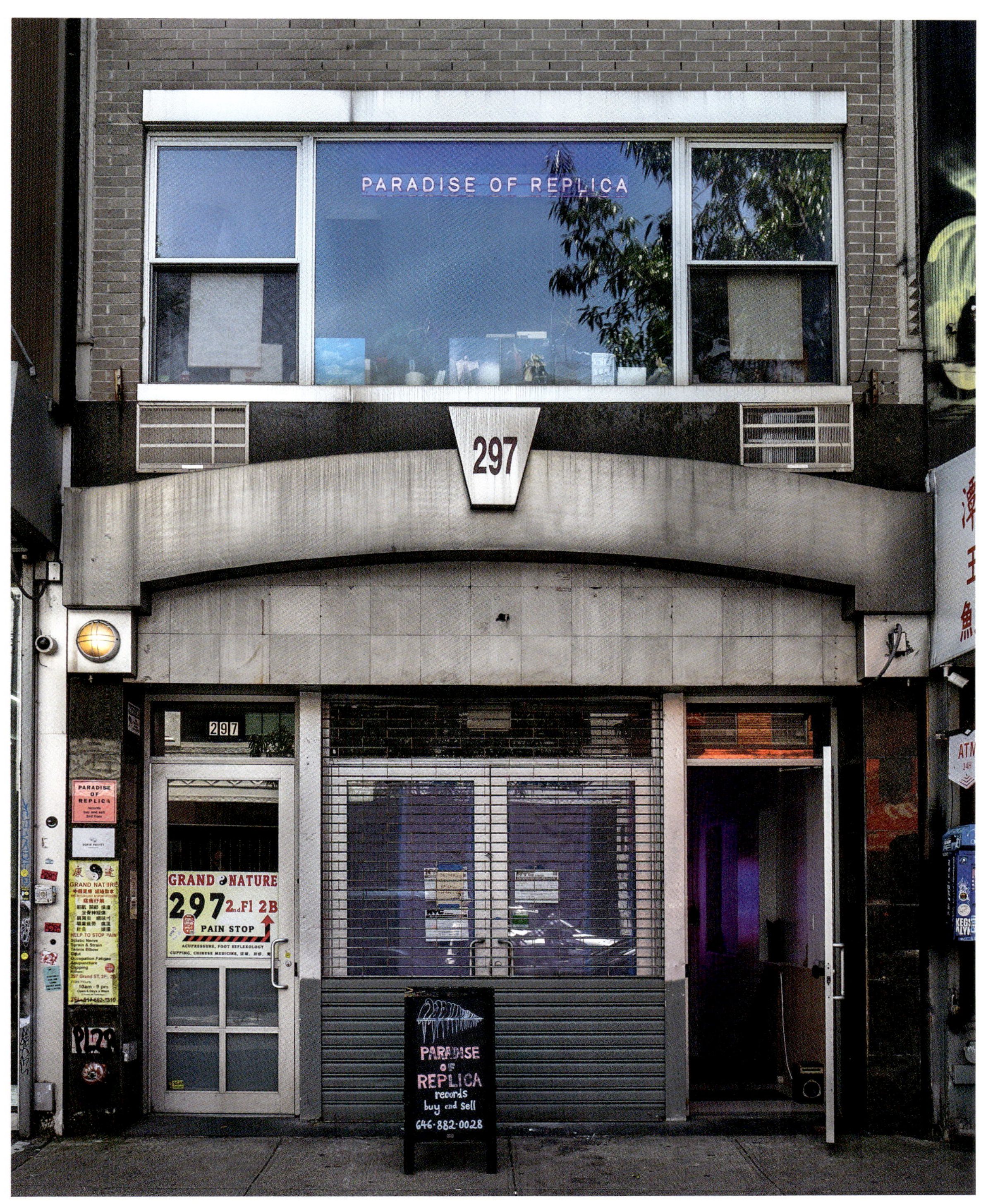

ABOVE Locatec on the second floor of a bustling Chinatown street, Paradise of Replica was founded by Kyle Molzan, who personally curates the shop's living room–like setting. Musically, he focuses on the 1980s, with lots of synth pop, ambient, and experimental-leaning jazz, mixed with Japanese technopop rarities.

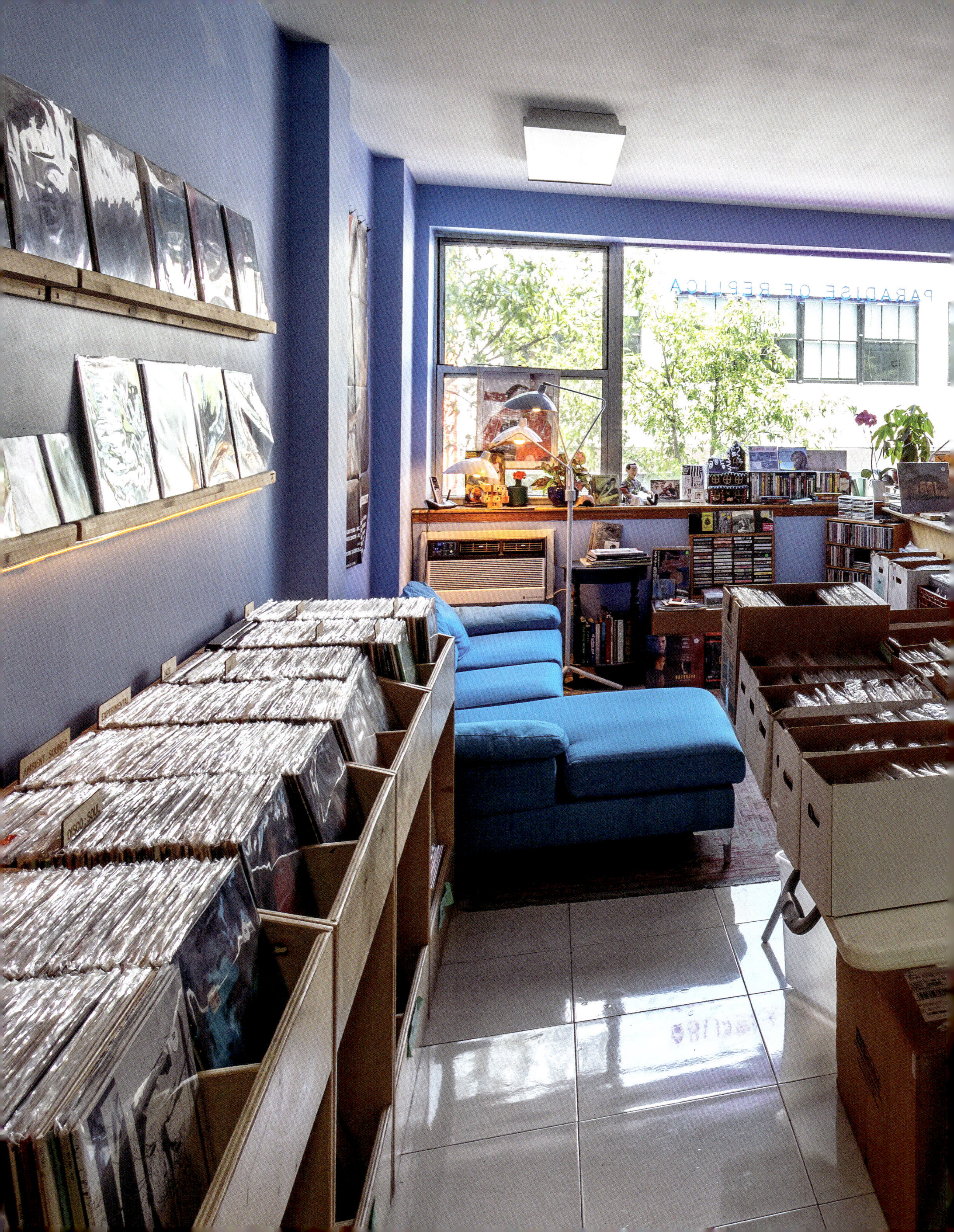
PARADISE OF REPLICA
JAZZ
EXPERIMENTAL
AMBIENT : SOUNDS
DISCO : SOUL

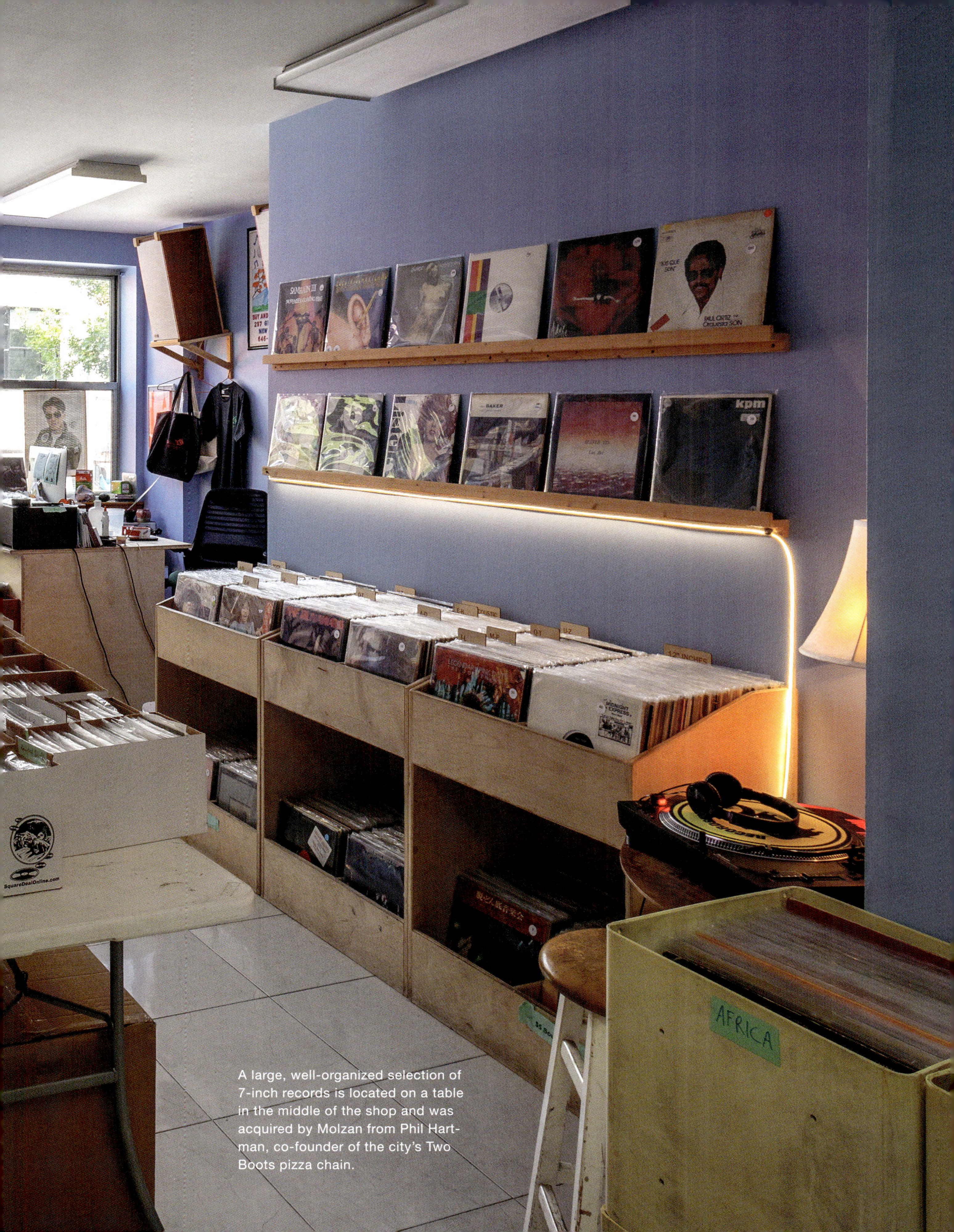

A large, well-organized selection of 7-inch records is located on a table in the middle of the shop and was acquired by Molzan from Phil Hartman, co-founder of the city's Two Boots pizza chain.

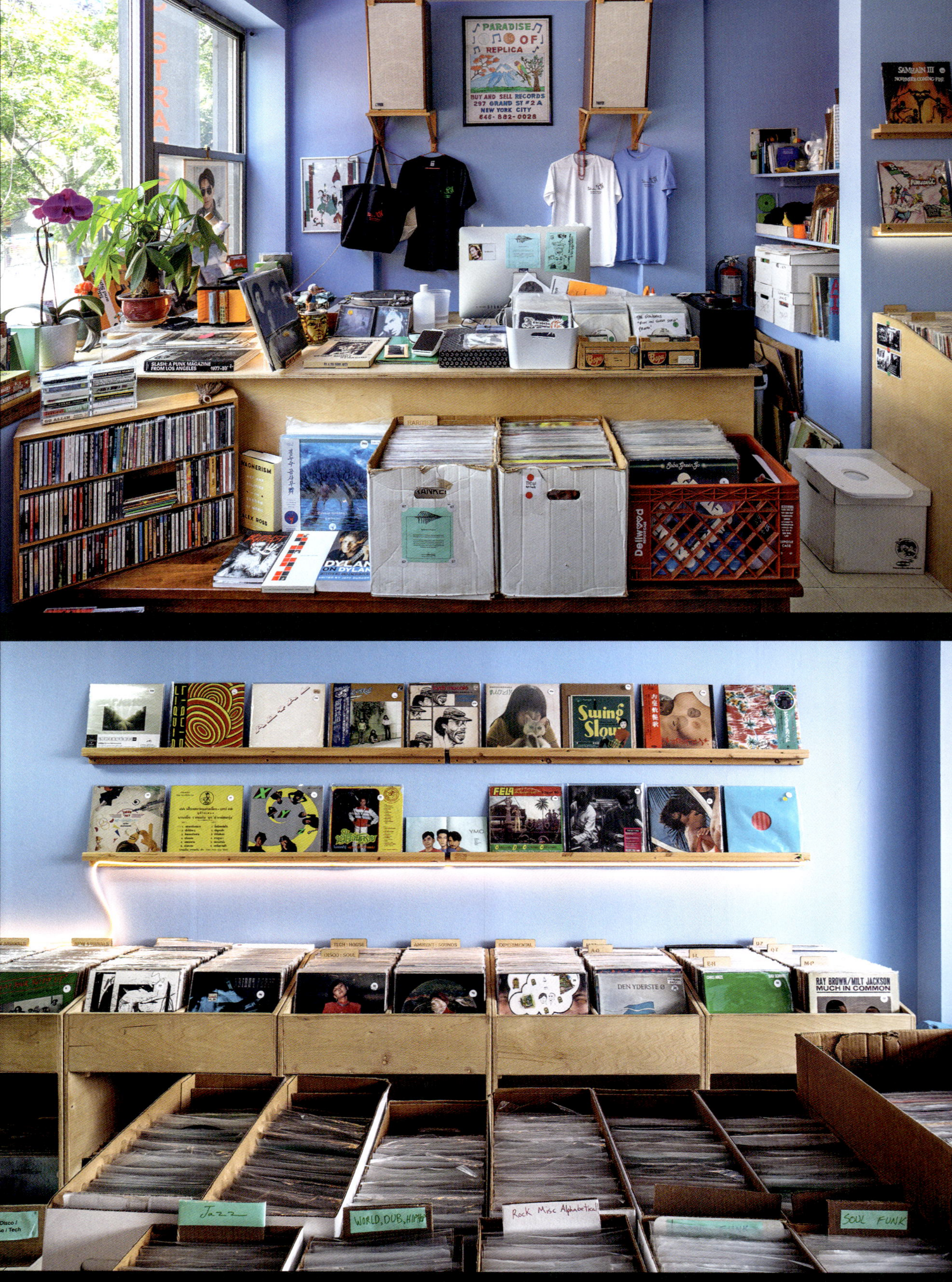
PARADISE OF REPLICA
BUY AND SELL RECORDS
297 GRAND ST #2A
NEW YORK CITY
646-882-0028
Jazz
Rock Misc Alphabetical
SOUL FUNK

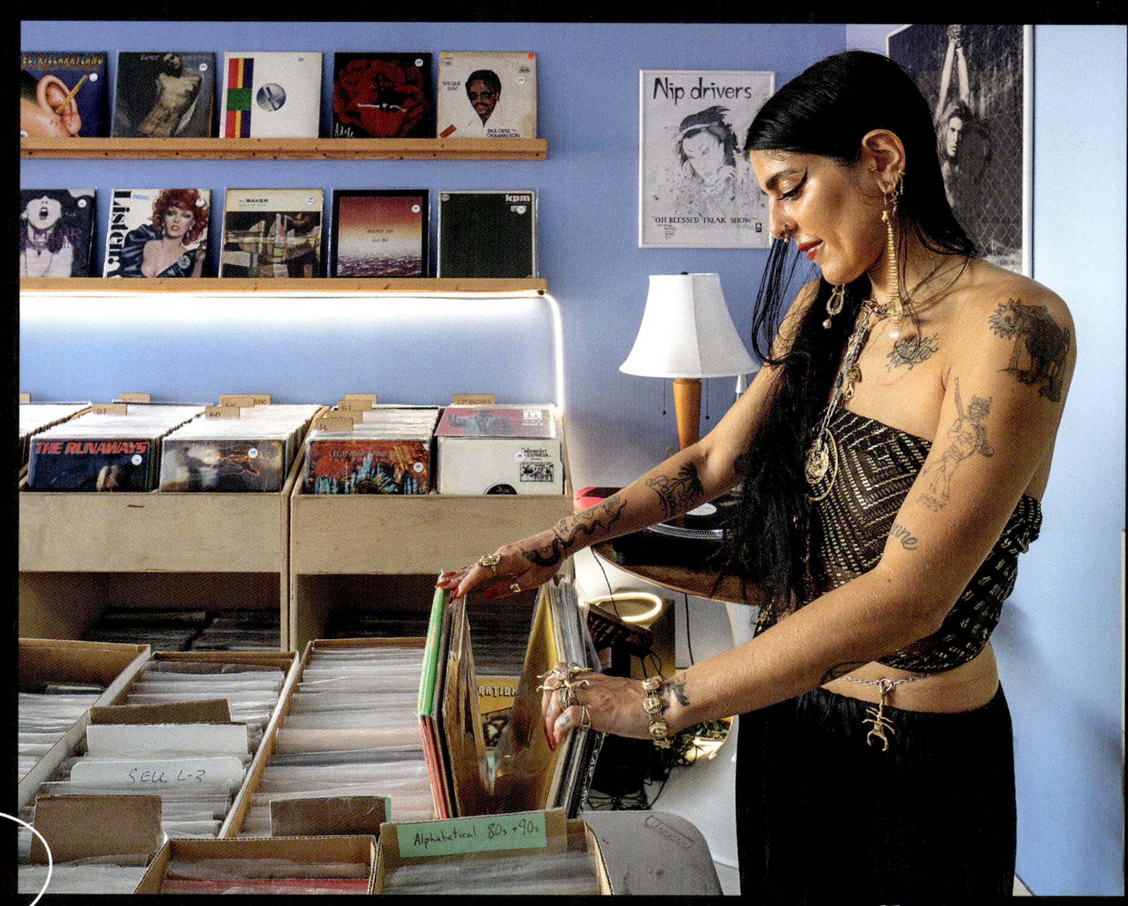

KRISTINE BARILLI

"I will forever advocate for the dig, but it's nice when your local record dealer hands you some gems."

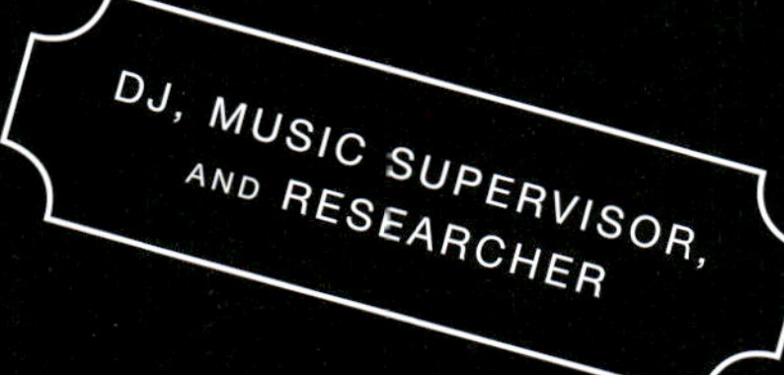

Kristine Barilli fondly recalls the routine that defined her first New York apartment: rave until morning, then wander in a daze to dig for vinyl at Chelsea Flea Market. A music supervisor, researcher, and resident DJ at Greenpoint landmark The Lot Radio, her hunt for hidden heat has taken her across the Middle East, Europe, Tokyo, and Bangkok—and that doesn't even include a yearly pilgrimage to Utrecht's famed record fair. Although she big-ups A-1 Record Shop (see p. 8) for their "wonky 12-inch" selection and Superior Elevation (see p. 18) for their donation-based DJ school, her favorite spot to dive deep in the city is Paradise of Replica, where owner Kyle Molzan serves as "the master sorcerer of all things off-kilter and special," she explains. Barilli, who focuses on snagging private-press and oddball one-offs to enliven her mixes, trusts a tangible selection like Molzan's even more these days, as a growing crop of producers forgo DJing on wax entirely. He's not just a taste ally in a cold world of mainstream mid—Molzan reminds Barilli that the rare-record business, from Thailand to Texas, has a lot left to give. "There will always be people who devote their lives to preserving this tradition," she shares.

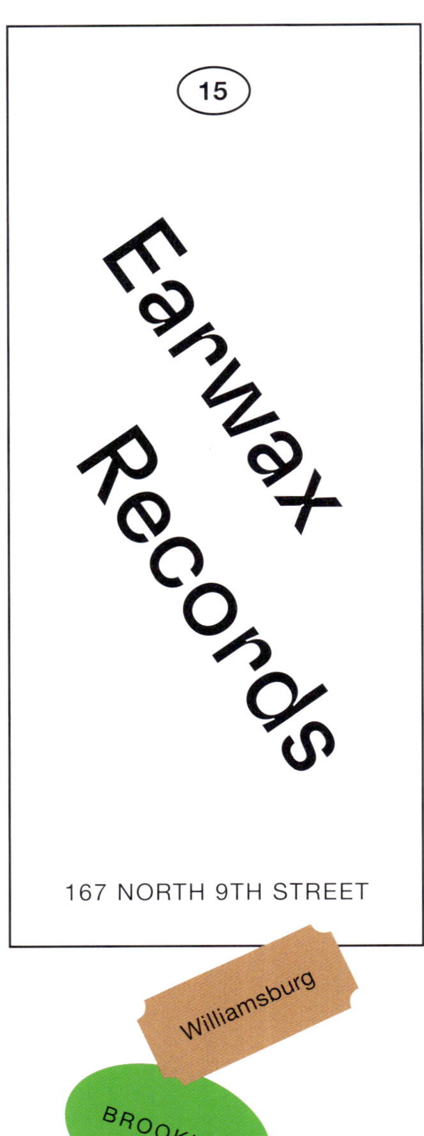

"I'M A BIT OLDER THAN MOST of the record shops," says Fabio Roberti, who runs the longest-standing one in Williamsburg. Earwax has outlived plenty of Brooklyn record stores and influenced plenty more—but half a lifetime into business ownership, Roberti hasn't lost sight of what shoppers are searching for.

Founded by Tom Schmitz in 1990, Earwax still mainly qualified as a hobby when the Argentina-born Roberti joined his friend in 1996 and became a partner in 2000 (Roberti has been its sole owner and proprietor since 2007.) Originally a filmmaker and photographer, Roberti brought a technical expert's eye for equipment to the space. For any listener whose collection may have outpaced their tools, Earwax offers a selection of turntables, integrated amplifiers, receivers, and speakers.

When the store first came to Williamsburg, the neighborhood wasn't the same mini-metropolis Roberti finds himself navigating today. Its main drag, Bedford Avenue, was still "sleepy working class," as he remembers it, dotted with a few bakeries and dive bars. As apartments thinned out into warehouses near the East River, few businesses maintained storefronts, and even fewer Brooklynites had extra income to spend. But when Earwax expressed interest in a space with a new landlord on a waterfront strip, the shop initiated a chain reaction of local commerce. "It was like a magnet for other businesses, because we were already on the strip," Roberti recalls.

A 2013 move ultimately brought the store to its current location on North 9th Street. Recognizable for its ooze-green, red, and white neon sign and orange mid-century modern chair positioned up front, Earwax is a true generalist's heaven. However, there's also plenty of room for more collector-forward items, such as back issues of music magazines in print like *The Wire*. Between the cabinets and plastic crates insulating the space, expect an encyclopedic selection of new releases spanning rock, electronic, jazz, funk, soul, pop, punk, reggae, and even country and musical scores. This is the rare store where the soundtrack for the movie *Wicked* and the latest Tinashe album rub elbows with vintage hi-fi speakers and turntables.

Roberti personally owns thousands of records, and he keeps an eye on how his customers and sellers alike treat the media they bring into their possession. That being said, he laments the gallerist's approach that some of his clientele have to album collecting—Earwax's wares are meant to be heard, not just displayed.

Over the years, Roberti has watched CDs, cassettes, and MP3s fall in and out of fashion, and stocked his store in accordance—but wax remains the backbone of the business. Even when he first began dealing in used vinyl given up by collectors chasing the CD boom, he was always able to gather quality goods in pristine shape for their age. He's begun restocking cassettes again after noticing a surge in interest among his younger market. And, at a time when he thought Covid-19 might spell the end of vinyl's decades-long run as a staple of Williamsburg's original hipster cool, its popularity came back in full force. "By the late summer [of 2020], people were coming in buying records like I hadn't seen in over fifteen years," he recalled.

Like many people who hang around Brooklyn long enough, Roberti is a DJ, and after years spent sourcing listener requests, the wants and whims of the public have become second nature. He may have a few years on some of the other shops in town, yet, as he points out, "I have records that are seventy-five years old, and they still play perfectly well."

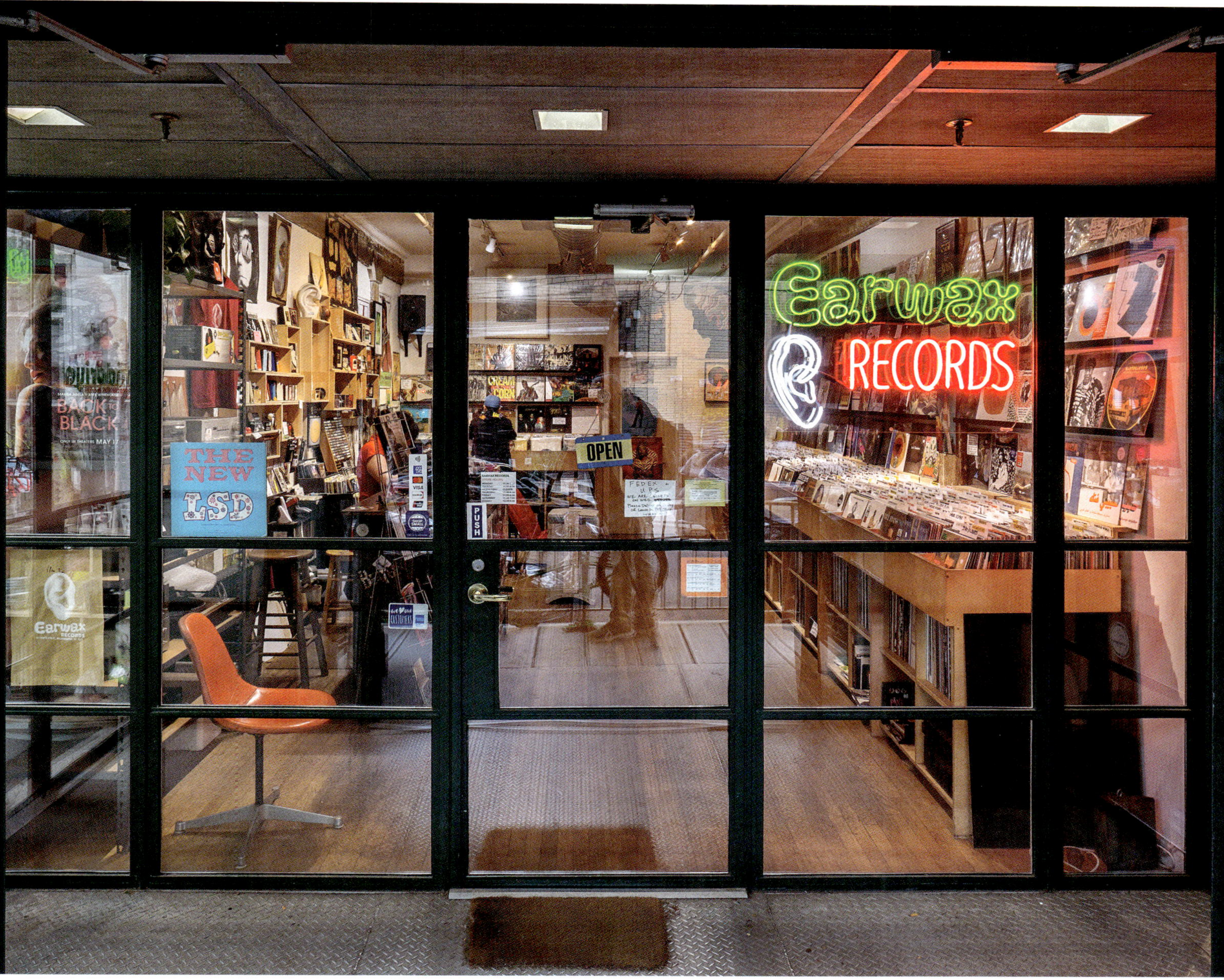

ABOVE Founded in 1990 and located in a recessed storefront up a staircase in Williamsburg, Earwax is one of the oldest record stores in Brooklyn. As a testament to its longevity, its main focus is on new releases, including new pressings of popular music, classic rock, punk, soul, funk, and jazz, as well as some experimental and avant-garde.

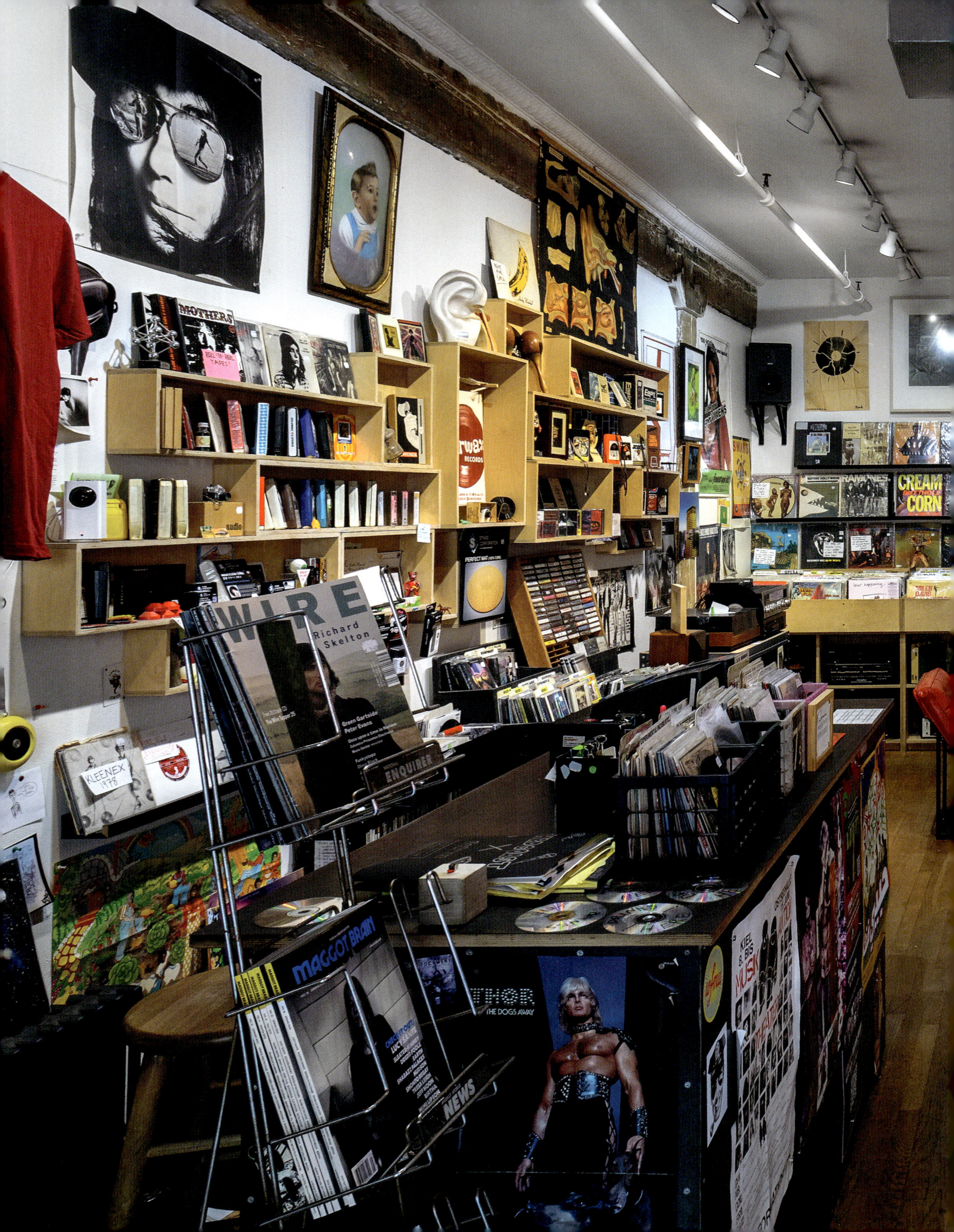
MOTHERS
REEL-TO-REEL TAPES!
KLEENEX 1978
WIRE
Richard Skelton
Green Gartside
Peter Evans
ENQUIRER
MAGGOT BRAIN
NEWS
THOR
THE DOGS AWAY
PERFECT MAT
RAMONES
CREAM CORN
audio

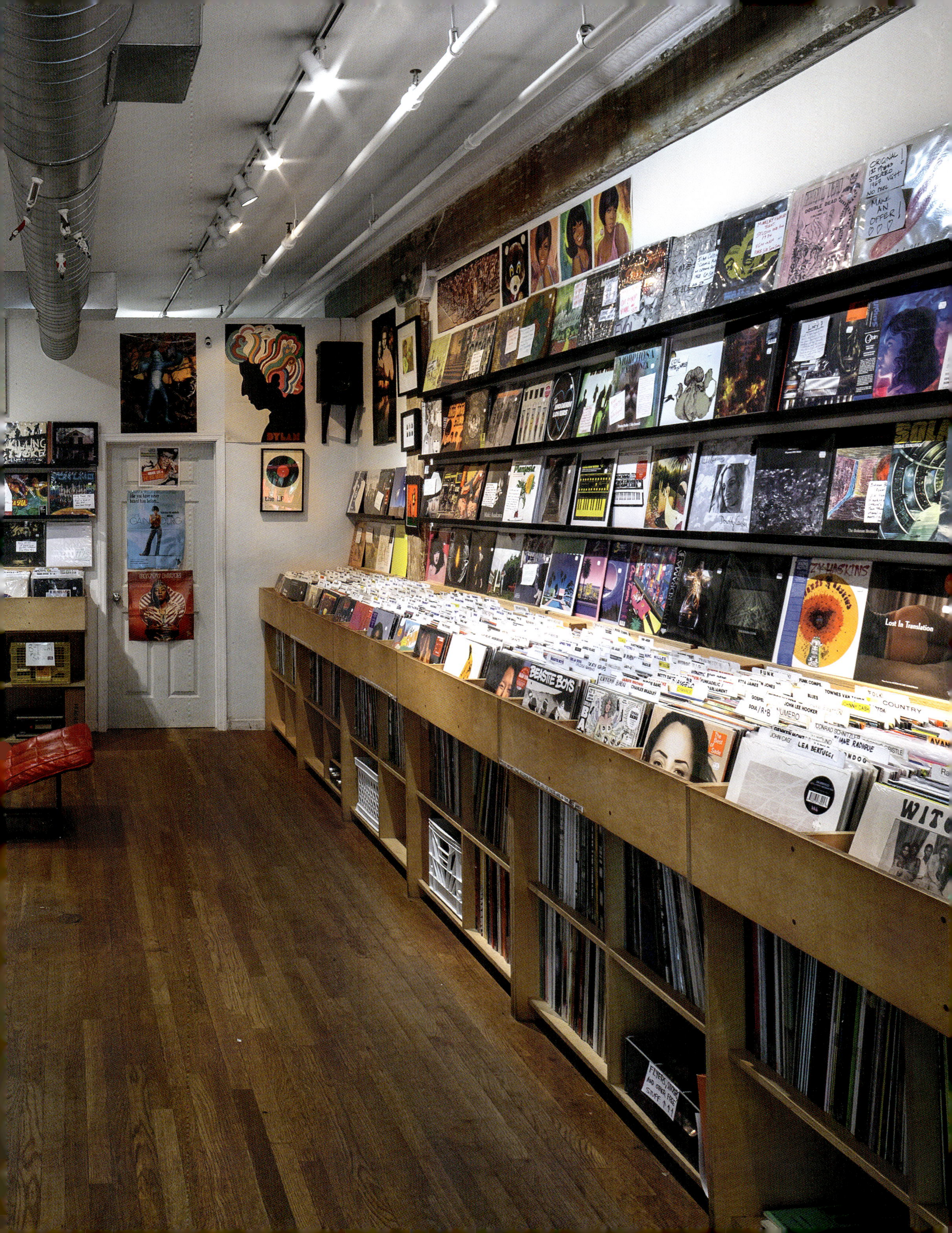
DYLAN
BEASTIE BOYS
Lost In Translation
FUNK
FUNK COMPS
GOSPEL
BLUES
COUNTRY
SOUL/R+B
JOHN LEE HOOKER
LEA BERTUCCI
JOHN CAGE
NUMERO
MAKE AN OFFER!

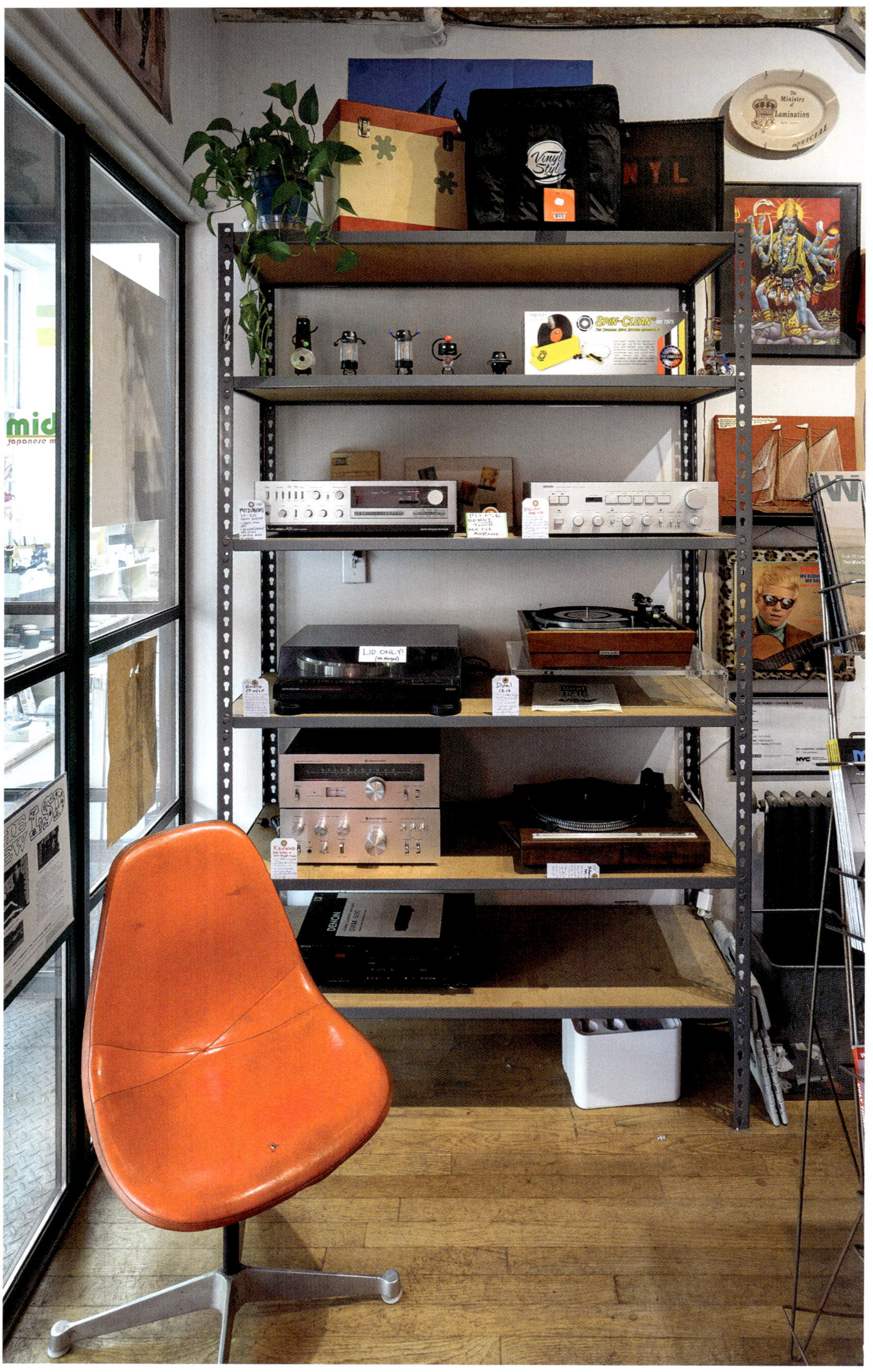
SPIN-CLEAN
LID ONLY!

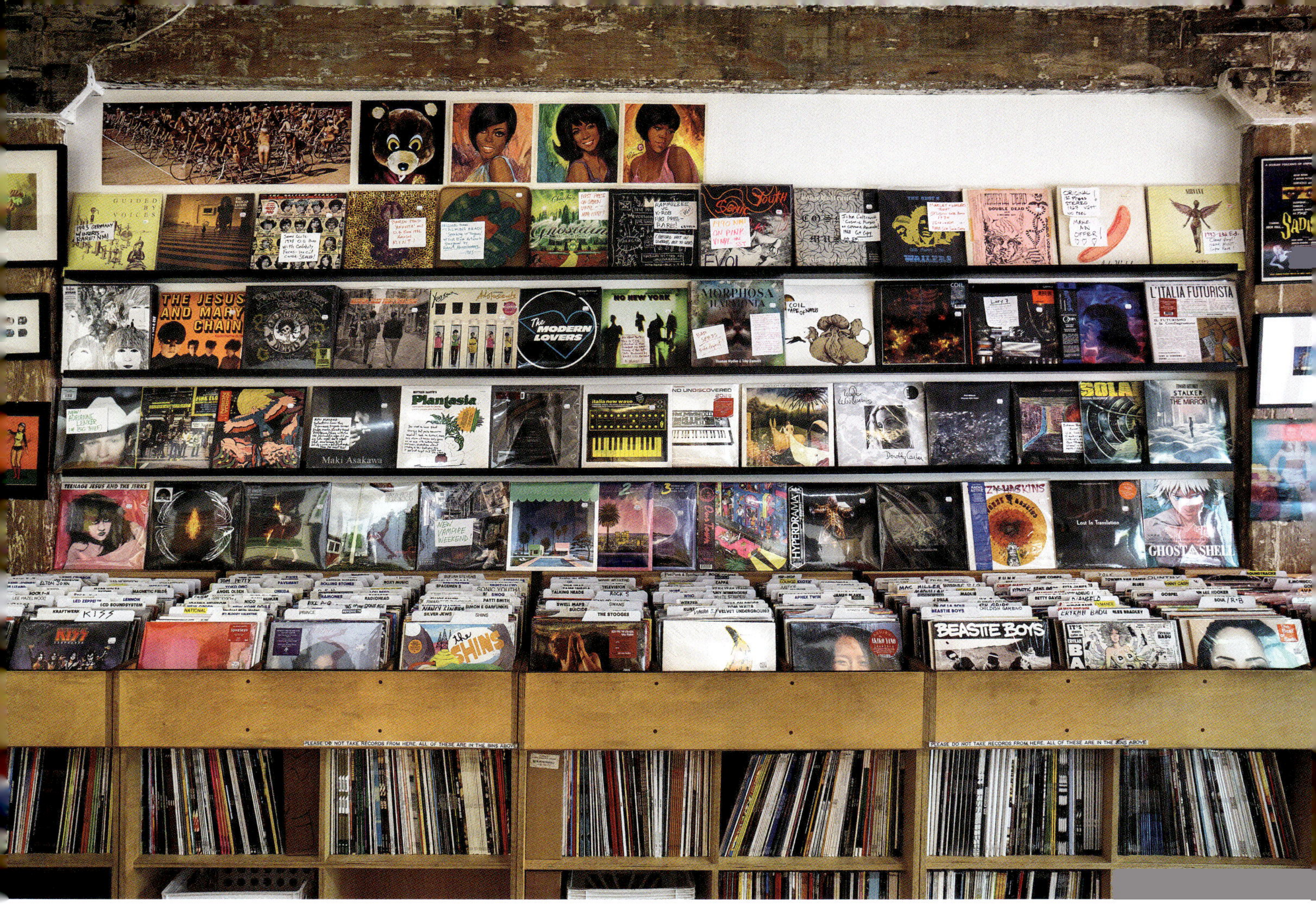

OPPOSITE Earwax also sells a selection of vintage stereo equipment including turntables, receivers, cassette players, and amps.

ABOVE Handwritten sticky notes placed on the records' outer sleeves help those unfamiliar understand the genre and pricing of the titles. For example, there's a rare first press of *Rammelzee vs. K-Rob* with a VG+ (Very Good +) rating selling for $3,999.99, and a reissue of *No New York* on which a note states, "This is *the* collection of the greatest No Wave bands of the late '70s. Produced by ENO Ltd. reissue. A MUST!"

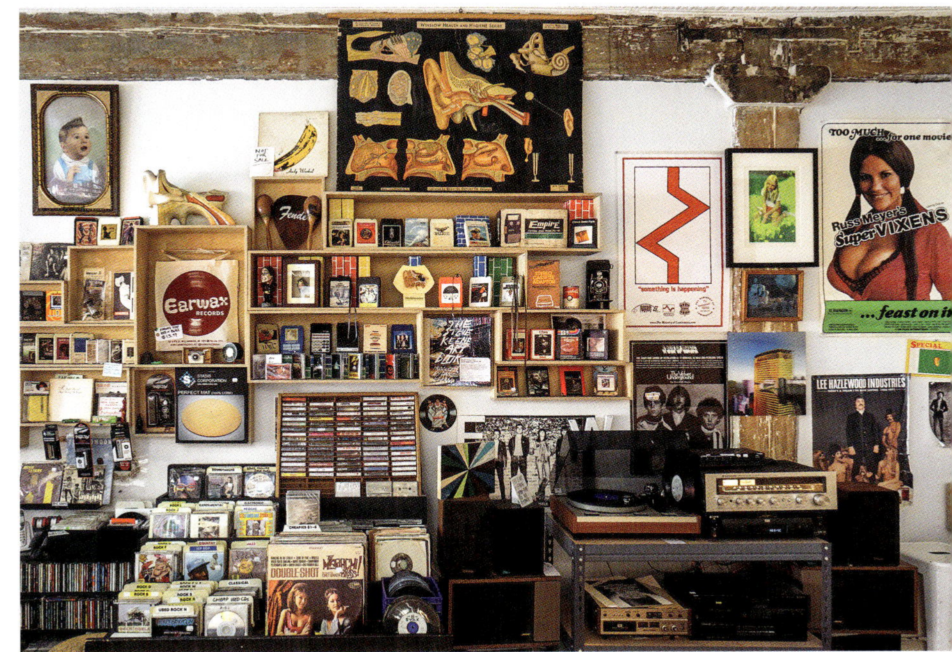

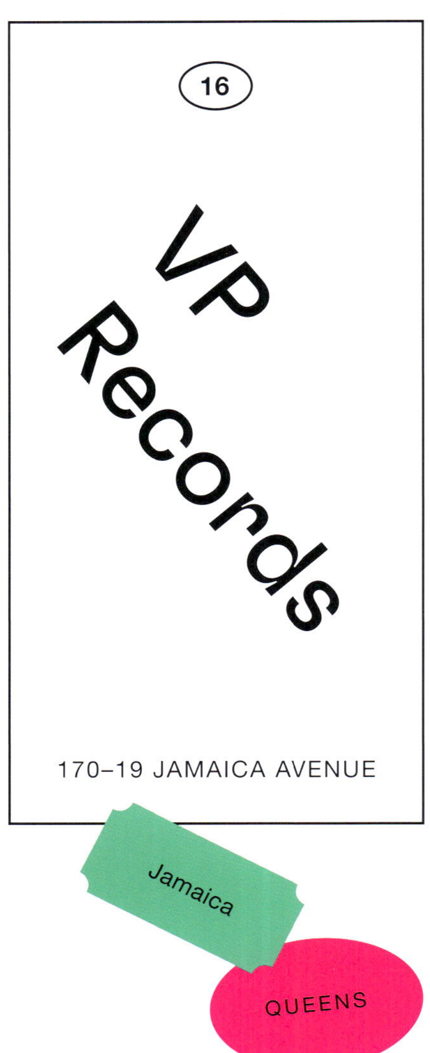

VP RECORDS' ORIGIN STORY ISN'T just pivotal to the history of New York's Jamaican diaspora, but to the evolution of Jamaican music itself. The local institution, which opened in Queens in the late '70s, might not have been the first space in the city to play the Caribbean country's riddims, yet the visibility it has provided Jamaican music across the past half-century is hard to overstate.

After all, VP Records co-founder Pat Chin, a.k.a. Miss Pat, didn't earn her title as the "godmother of New York reggae" just anywhere. Born in Jamaica in 1937, she met her future husband Vincent "Randy" Chin in Kingston, where the couple opened their first brick-and-mortar resale shop, Randy's Record Mart, in 1958. There, they sold used records Randy obtained at his job restocking jukeboxes. An early example of a one-stop-shop model, Randy's not only hawked hard-to-come-by records at a fair price but also sold merch, equipment, and other retail items. But perhaps its most enduring innovation came when Randy established a recording studio on the shop's second floor in the '60s. Sometimes called "the Jamaican Motown," Randy's studio saw icons like the Heptones, Bob Marley and the Wailers, and countless others come through its doors.

As their transatlantic client base strengthened and the Chins' eyes turned toward the growing Jamaican community in New York, the couple began migrating their developing family north. By 1979 Randy, Pat, and their four kids—Clive, Christopher, Randy Jr., and Angela—had settled in the city. That same year, VP (Vincent and Pat) Records opened its doors as close to home as they could find an ocean away: on Jamaica Avenue in Jamaica, Queens.

The label born out of the modest storefront, also called VP Records, is the largest independent reggae imprint in the world today and was crucial in introducing the style to a global audience. To build it, the Chins tapped into Queens's long history as a hub of international distribution, the result of an airport-adjacent location and historically cheap rent. Transforming their Kingston business model into an international endeavor, the family has pressed contemporary Jamaican music releases, from rocksteady to ska, for nearly half a century.

Today, VP's flagship shop also serves as a cultural center, offering a hub for intimate performances and educational events. The Chins' daughter Angela oversees a sister shop in Florida, while their sons Christopher and Randy Jr. run the VP label from offices in Miami, Kingston, London, and right at home in Queens. Over its decades in operation, VP Records has shepherded then-ascendant stars like Lee "Scratch" Perry, Yellowman, Sean Paul, Gyptian, and even Estelle to major crossover careers that have seen dutty riddims win American Grammys. But VP's many branches haven't outgrown its roots.

When Randy Sr. died in February 2003 after a lifetime in the family business, Miss Pat wanted to honor her partner the right way. She chose to start a foundation that supports music and arts education for underprivileged youth, an endeavor that emphasizes their shared commitment to fledgling artists at the start of their careers.

As long as Miss Pat is stocking shelves with VP compilations and re-presses from the archival reggae imprint Greensleeves, she'll also be outstretching a hand to any aspiring reggae musician who dreams of honing their craft and upping their taste level. "I'm still doing the same things that I started doing [in the late '70s]: develop the young artists, and give back," she shares. "I continue doing it because I saw the need, and the opportunities; that if you help a person to develop a talent, they will be ever grateful to you. That was really ingrained in my parents and my grandparents. Always give back."

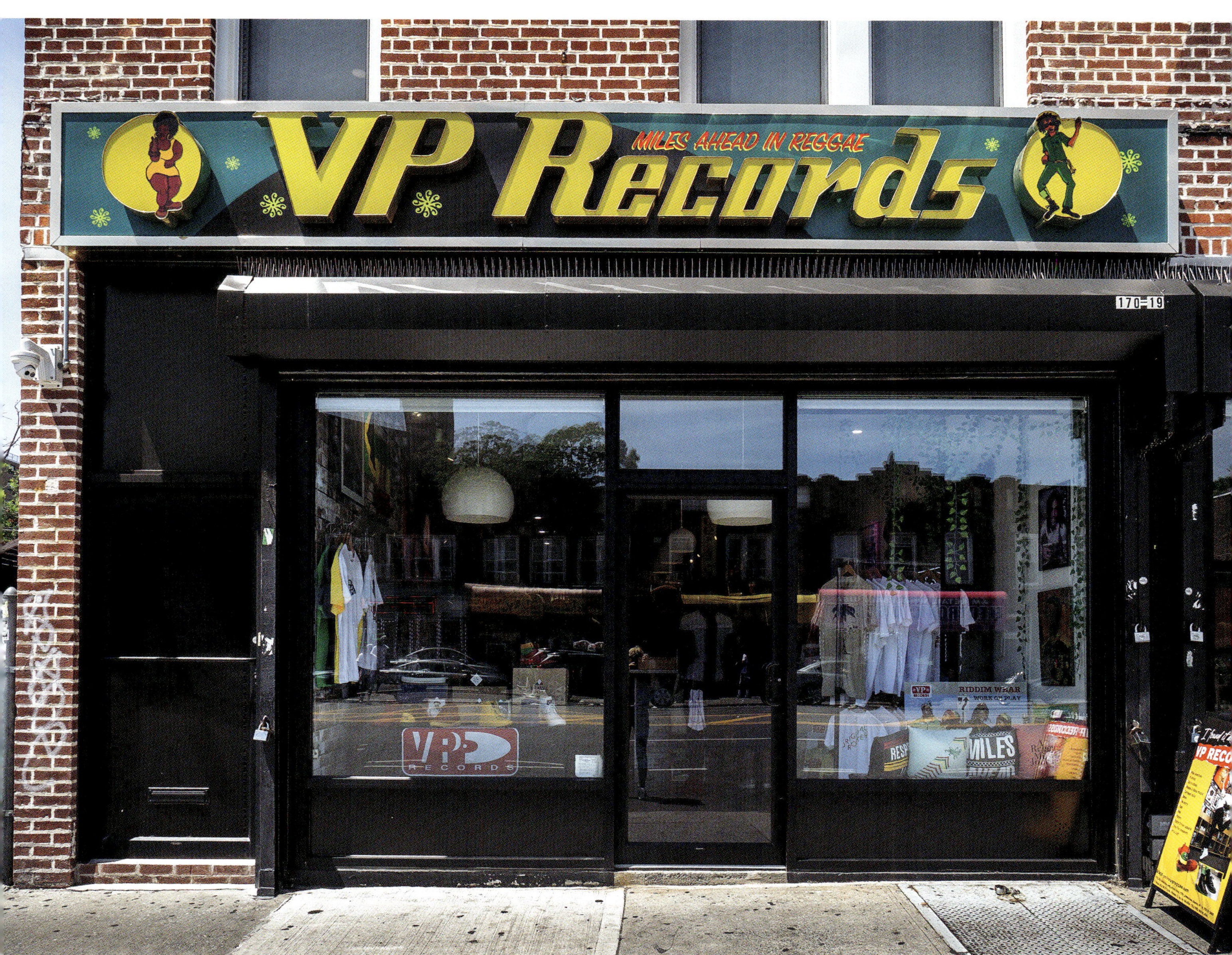

ABOVE Named after its founders Vincent and Patricia (a.k.a. Miss Pat) Chin, VP Records first opened in Jamaica, Queens, in 1979. It's the largest independent distributor of reggae, dancehall, and soca music in the world. The shop not only carries both new and used vinyl, CDs, and cassettes, but is also a lifestyle store, selling Caribbean clothing, books, poster prints, and other music-related merchandise.

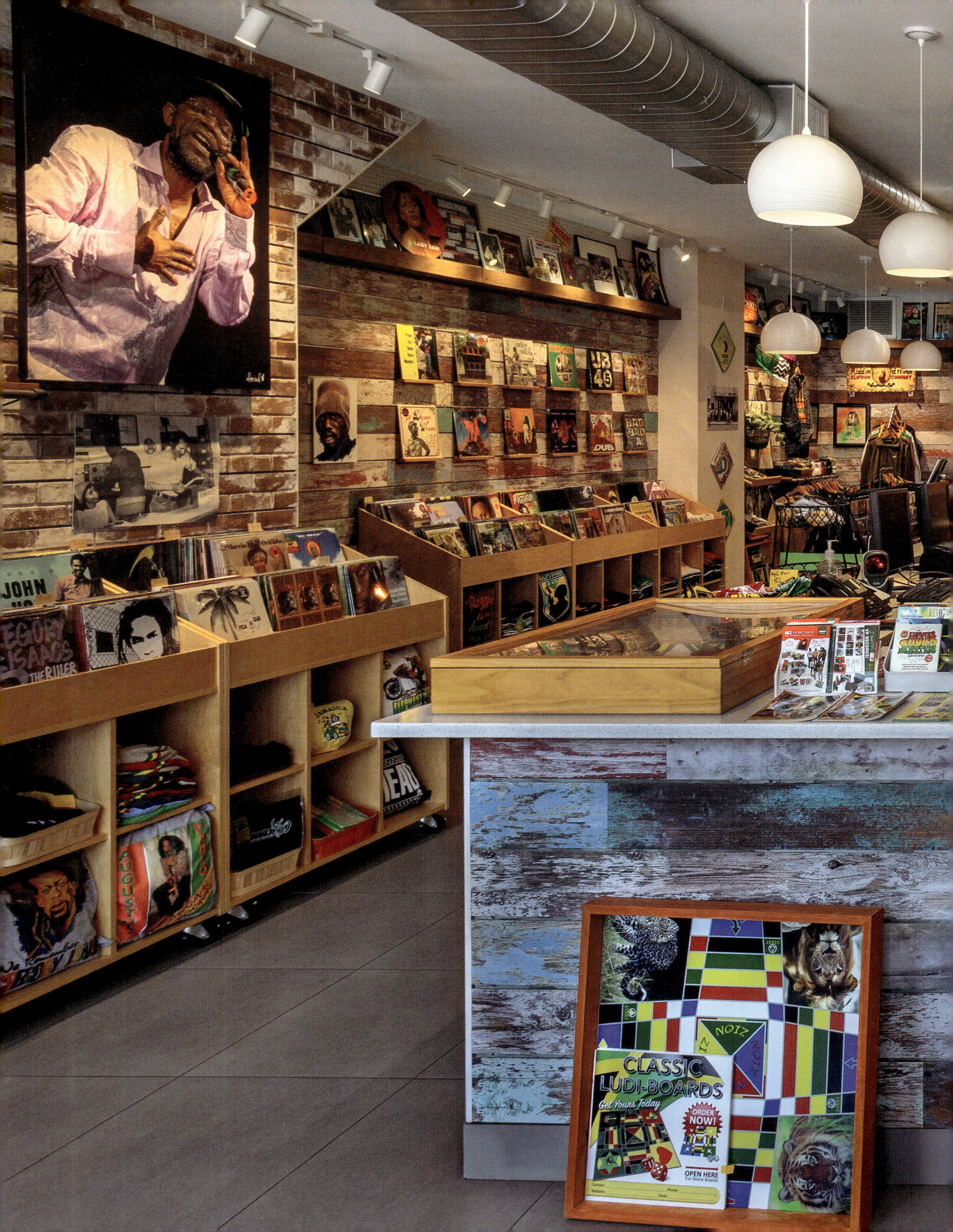
CLASSIC
LUDI-BOARDS
Get Yours Today
ORDER NOW!
OPEN HERE
For More Boards
NOIZ
JOHN
EGORY ISAACS
THE RULER
UB 45
DUB

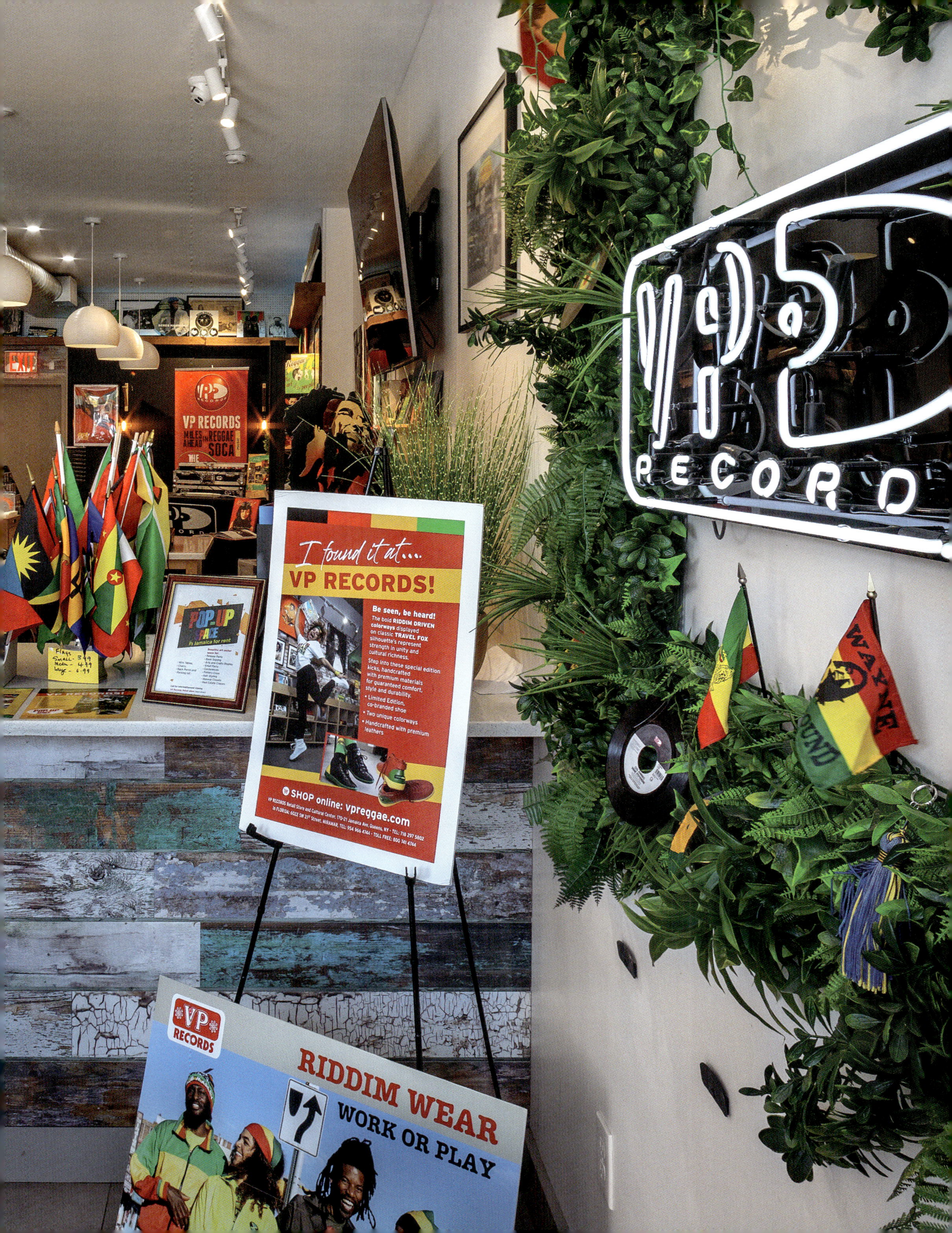
EXIT
VP RECORDS
MILES AHEAD IN REGGAE SOCA
POP-UP SPACE
I found it at....
VP RECORDS!
Be seen, be heard!
SHOP online: vpreggae.com
RECORD
VP RECORDS
RIDDIM WEAR
WORK OR PLAY

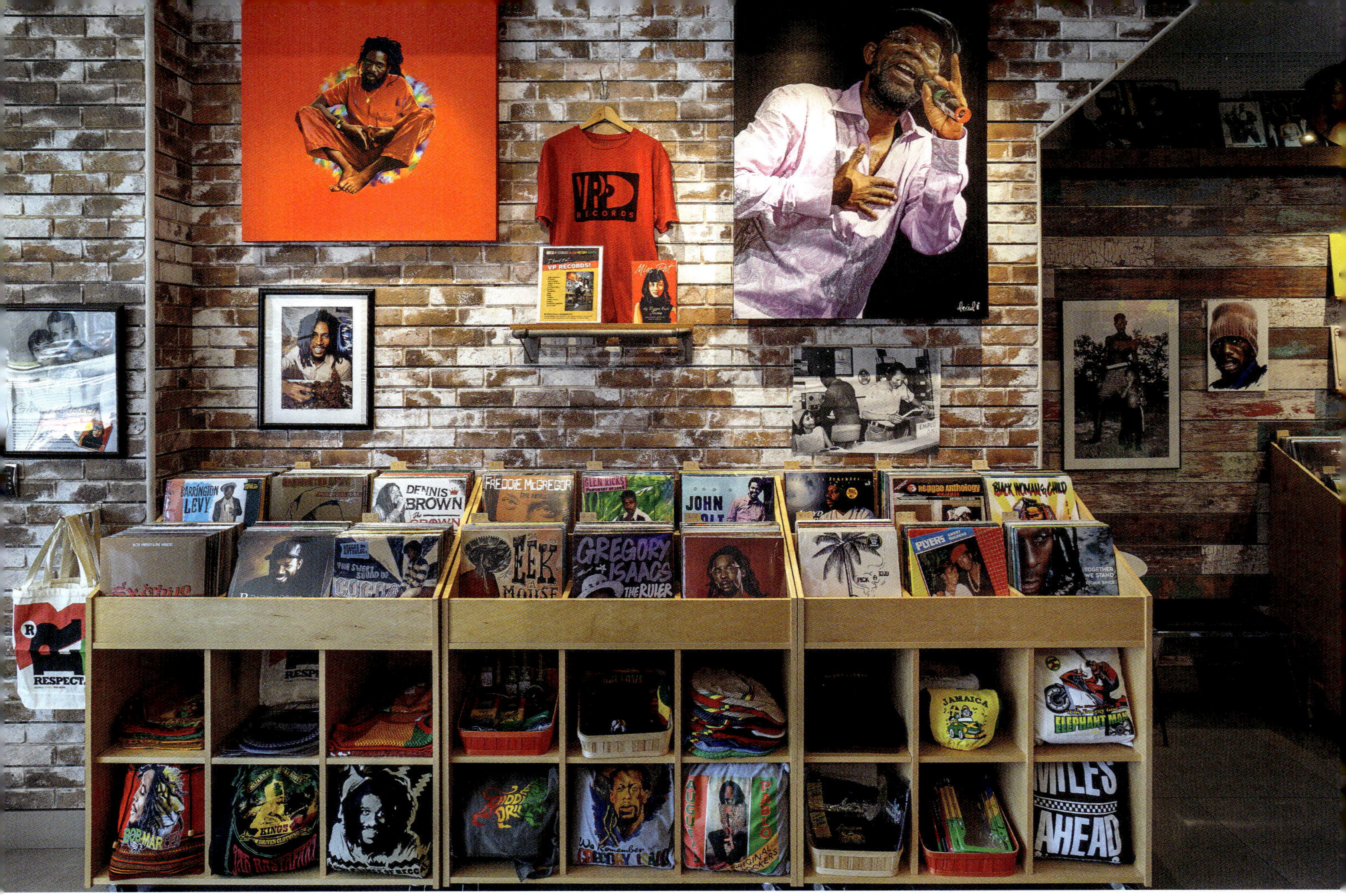

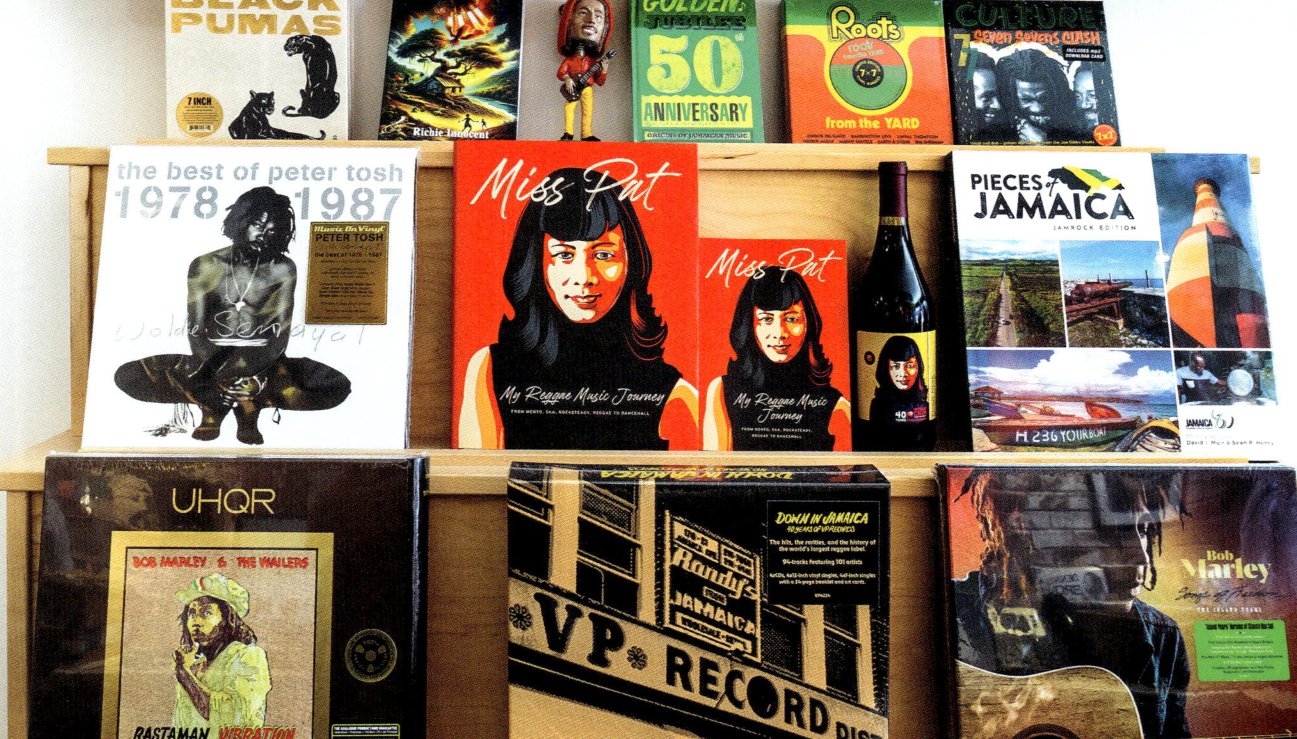
BLACK PUMAS
PERSEVERANCE
GOLDEN
JUBILEE
50
ANNIVERSARY
Roots
from the YARD
the best of peter tosh
1978 1987
Miss Pat
My Reggae Music Journey
Miss Pat
PIECES of JAMAICA
UHQR
BOB MARLEY & THE WAILERS
RASTAMAN VIBRATION
DOWN IN JAMAICA
VP RECORD DIST.
Bob Marley

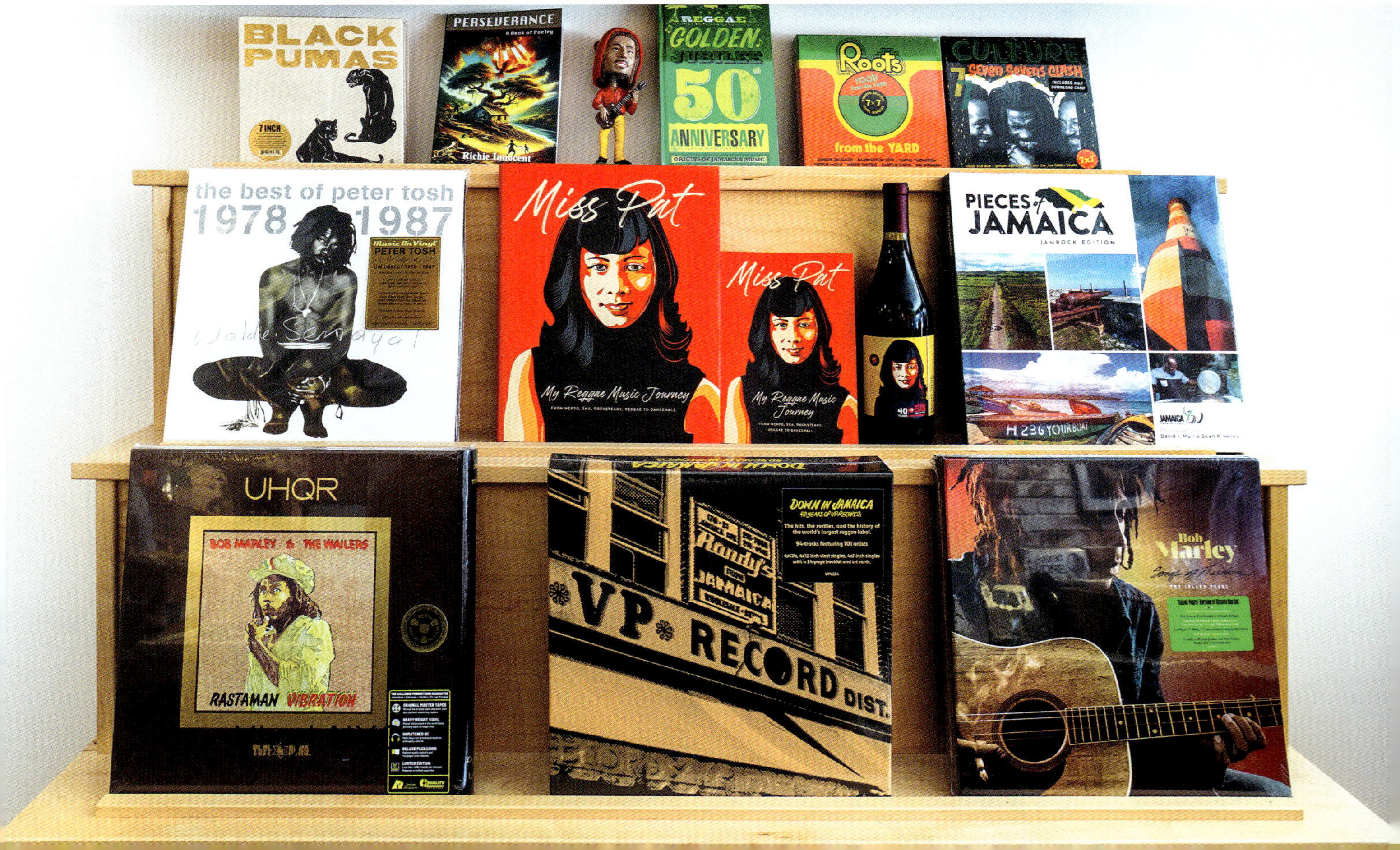

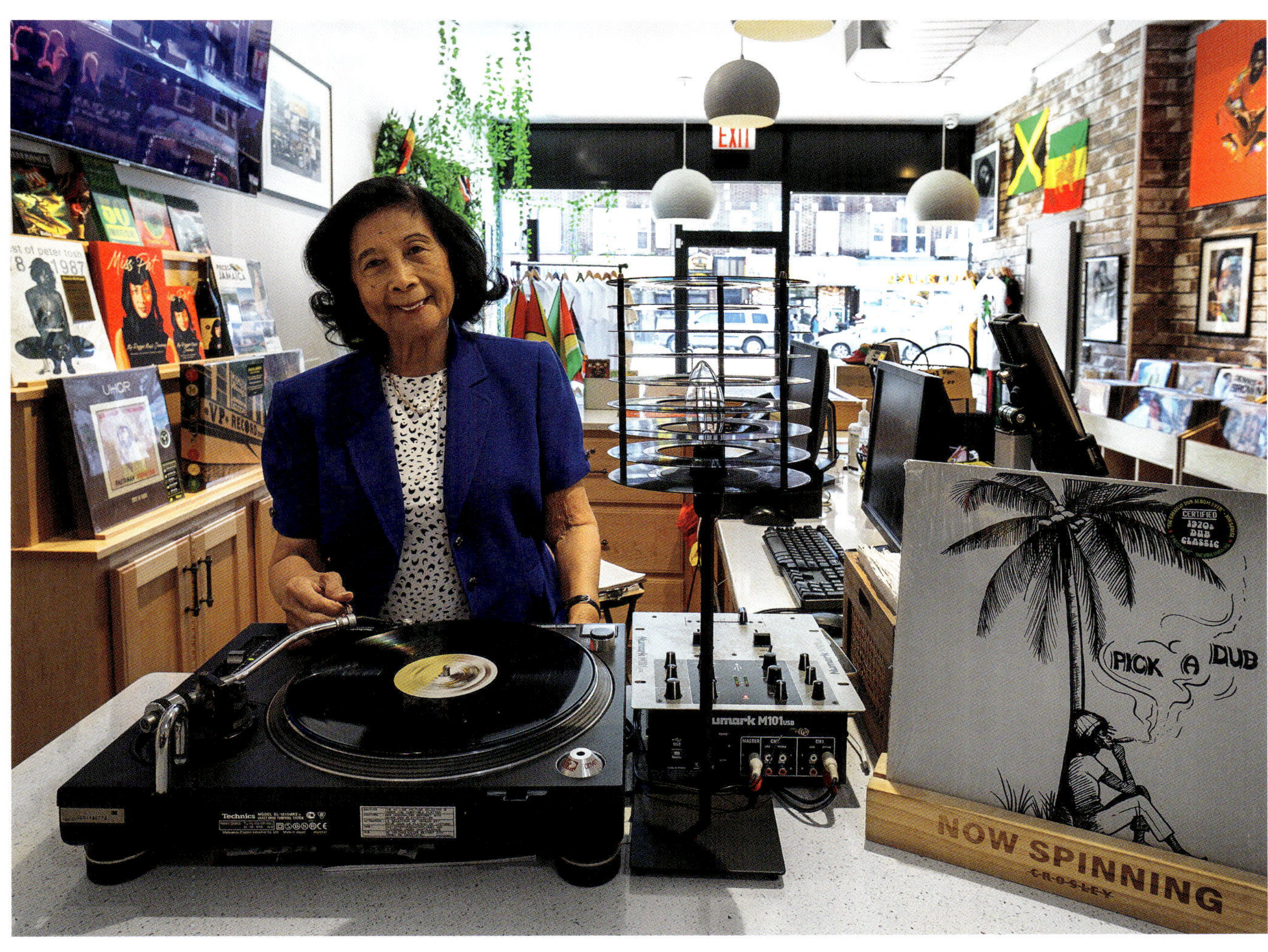

OPPOSITE BOTTOM One of the box sets available at the shop is *Down in Jamaica: 40 Years of VP Records*, which features 101 different artists, including Sean Paul, Beenie Man, Lady Saw, and Shaggy. Its ninety-four tracks pay chronological homage to the shop's history as the world's largest reggae label.

ABOVE Miss Pat is not only the face of VP Records but takes the time to give back to the community, hosting Record Store Day events, artist meet-and-greets, and book signings.

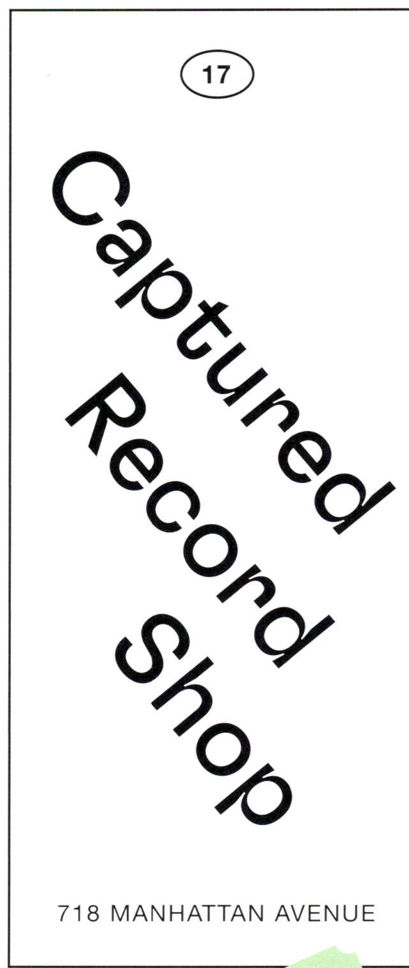

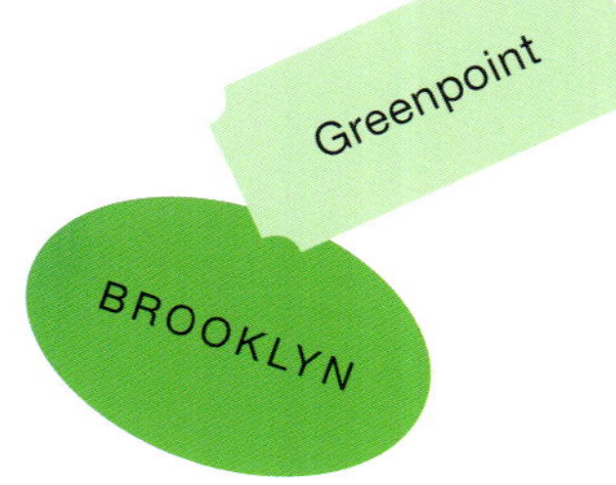

AFTER CAPTURED RECORD SHOP'S FOUNDER Mike Sniper finishes up a DJ set at one of his regular haunts around the city, he's been known to tip his favorite bartenders with a 12-inch record. At his Greenpoint store, which originated as a basement offshoot of his famed indie label of the same name, the humble 45 has uniquely high status—rows of new and notable green-sleeved EPs at the shop's center promise: "All Genres, Additions Daily."

While in art school, Sniper's regular lunch breaks spent browsing at the now-closed Midnight Records in Chelsea ended up getting him a job offer at the shop's in-house label. "That's when I realized most successful record labels are run by people like me," he told *Merry-Go-Round Magazine* in 2018. "They all come from record store backgrounds, not necessarily from studying the music industry directly." He started the Captured Tracks label in 2008, funding its first releases off the sales of a rare collection of power pop reissues amassed via both his first imprint, Radio Heartbeat, and a side job at Academy Records (see p. 208). In some ways the Academy basement served as the first real Captured Tracks office.

Captured Tracks would go on to break millennial stars like Beach Fossils and Wild Nothing, placing early bets on 7- and 12-inch releases and earning some serious scenester cred along the way. But as far as Sniper is concerned, collectors' bragging rights couldn't have less to do with his record shop. "Going someplace, talking to someone about music, getting a recommendation, listening to it at a shop, and then buying it," he told *SLUG Magazine* in 2015, "is more what [vinyl is] about than having that object."

The camaraderie of working in music has called to Sniper ever since he started his first punk band in high school. "It was another reason to hang out with friends who like the same stuff," he told the website 12 Songs Project in 2024. He ended up playing professionally with a few post-punk outfits, like the DC Snipers and Blank Dogs, but never quite got in the hustling rhythm of tours and rehearsals.

Once tucked away on a quiet, residential corner of Calyer and Leonard Streets, Captured Record Shop has maintained a laid-back vibe even after a move to bustling Manhattan Avenue. A front-of-store lounge area is dotted with wooden crates containing back issues of niche and sometimes-discontinued music publications like *Creem* and *Sounds*. Rows of 45s and LPs are organized under umbrellas like "Sophistopop" or "Exotica," and a lane of new arrivals front and center has the label "Stop Here First!"

For many vinyl collectors, new releases simply lack the time-flecked personality of vintage pressings. But the Captured Tracks label's focus on amplifying its small but mighty roster gives the shop's new and notable bins some refreshing character. Sniper and his team dedicate substantial floor space to sections of sealed DIIV, Perfect Pussy, and Mac DeMarco cuts. (A cassette wall that may encompass another store's entire tape collection barely fits its DeMarco offerings alone.)

Over its years in operation, Captured Tracks has expanded into a full-on label group, Omnian Music. But no matter how big the business gets, the ethos behind it—and in turn, some of the most influential indie acts of the 2010s—comes right from the record store playbook Sniper picked up in college, one he hasn't yet put down. As he explained to *Merry-Go-Round*, "It's mostly about an ear when you're working with independent music. You have to be willing to take chances. You have to be a little crazy."

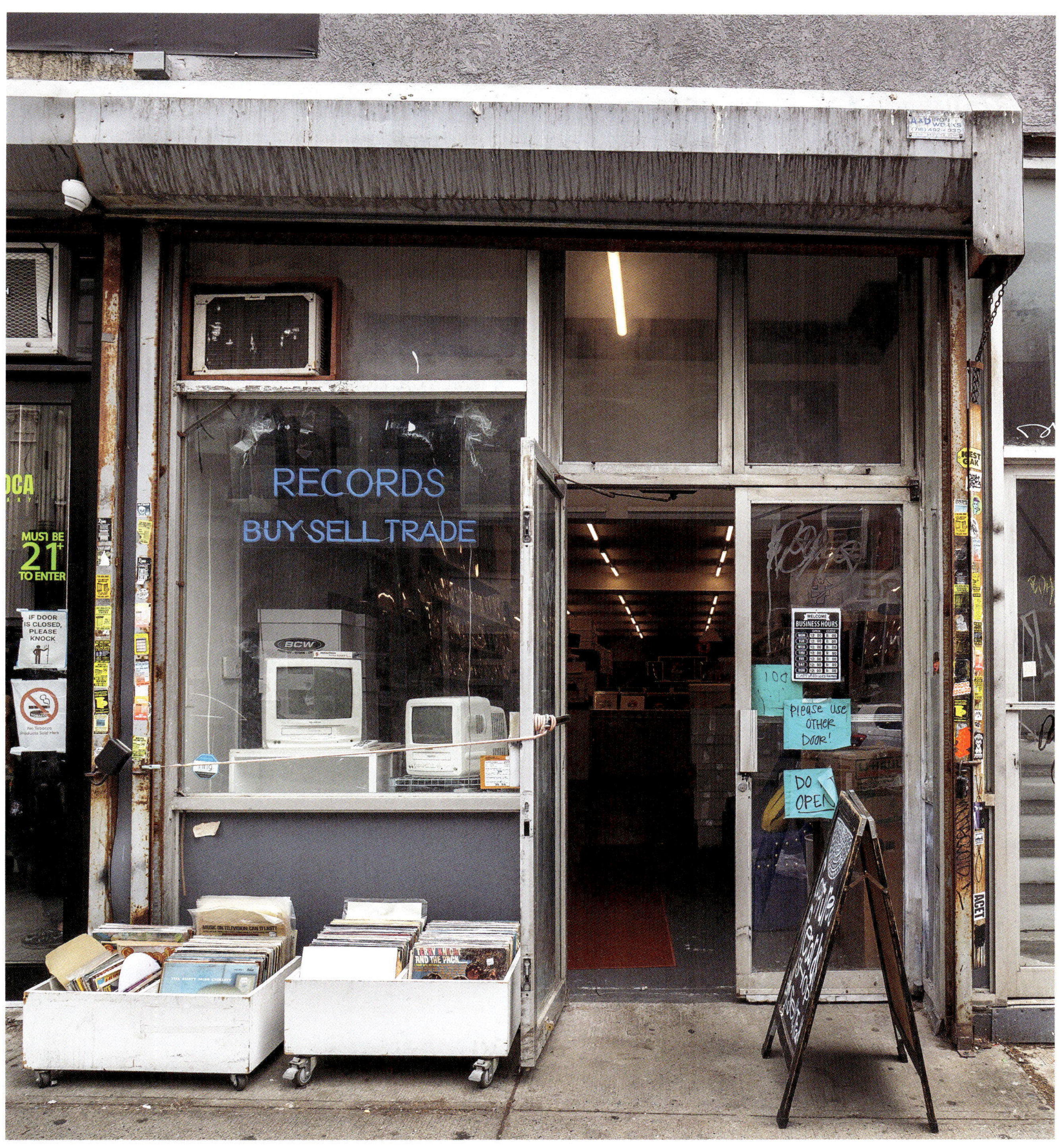

OPPOSITE Founded by Mike Sniper, Captured Record Shop is the flagship store of the indie rock record label Captured Tracks (responsible for releases by artists including Mac DeMarco, DIIV, the Lemon Twigs, and Juan Wauters). The shop stocks both new and used vinyl of all genres, with a large focus on hip-hop, soul, electronic, and a massive collection of singles and 45s.

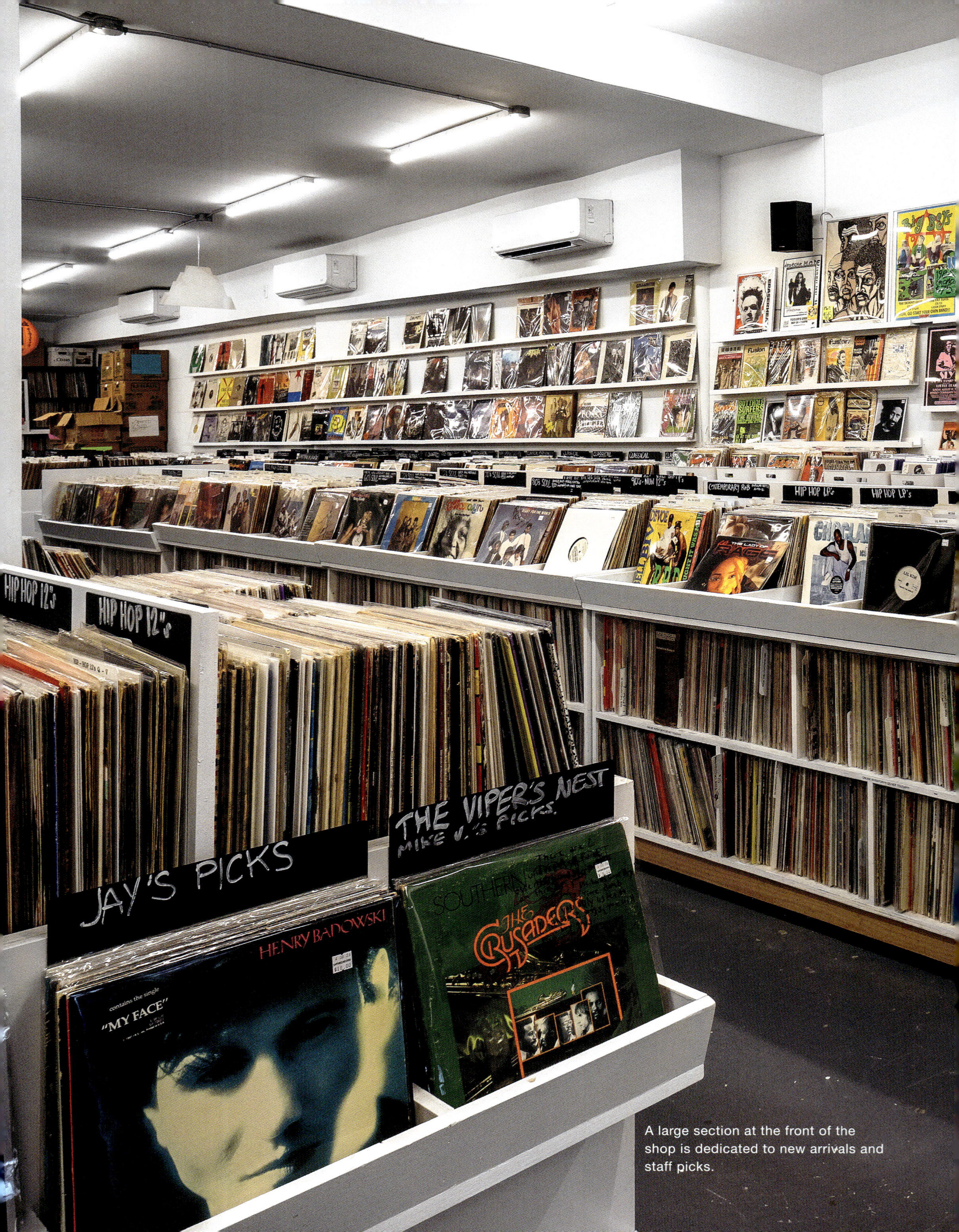

A large section at the front of the shop is dedicated to new arrivals and staff picks.

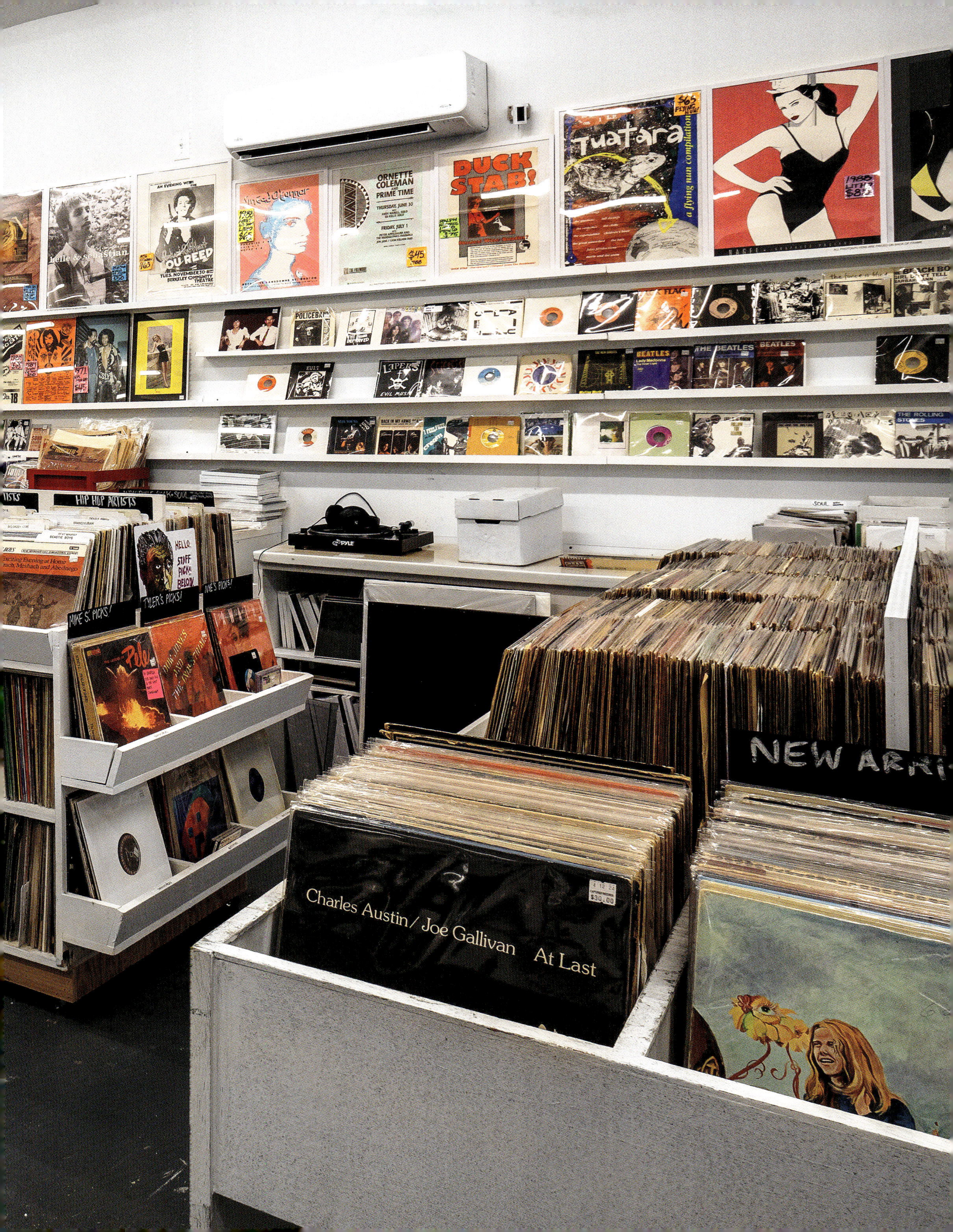
Tuatara
a flying nun compilation
DUCK STAB!
ORNETTE COLEMAN
PRIME TIME
belle & sebastian
LOU REED
HIP HOP ARTISTS
MIKE S. PICKS!
TYLER'S PICKS!
HELLO. STAFF PICKS BELOW
BEATLES
THE ROLLING STONES
PYLE
Charles Austin / Joe Gallivan At Last
$30.00

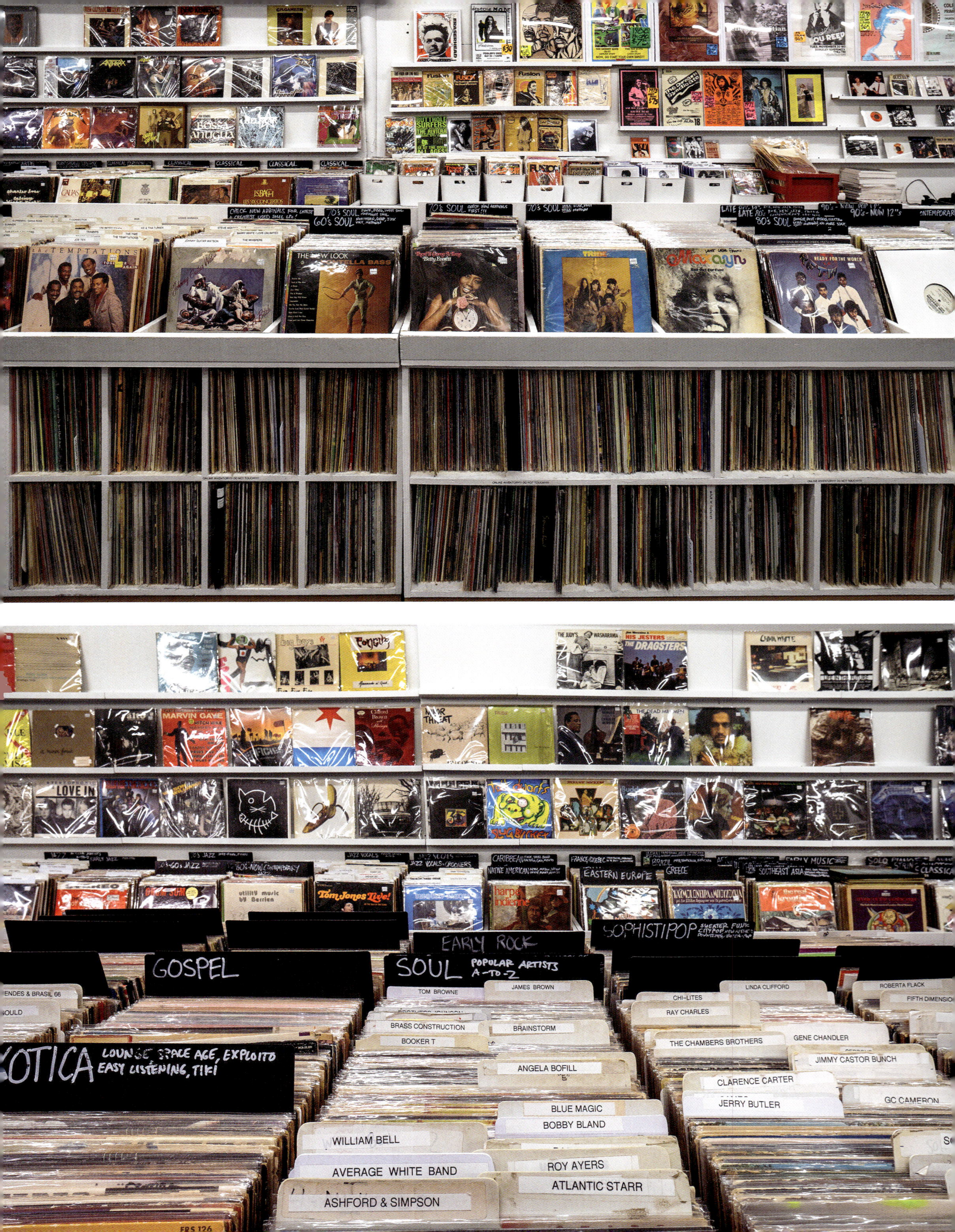

CHECK NEW ARRIVALS FOR LATEST GREATEST USED SOUL LP'S!
60'S SOUL
70'S SOUL
80'S SOUL
90'S - NOW 12"S
EARLY ROCK
SOPHISTIPOP
EASTERN EUROPE
GREECE
SOUTHEAST ASIA
GOSPEL
SOUL POPULAR ARTISTS A-TO-Z
OTICA LOUNGE SPACE AGE, EXPLOITO EASY LISTENING, TIKI
TOM BROWNE
JAMES BROWN
BRASS CONSTRUCTION
BRAINSTORM
BOOKER T
ANGELA BOFILL
BLUE MAGIC
BOBBY BLAND
WILLIAM BELL
AVERAGE WHITE BAND
ROY AYERS
ATLANTIC STARR
ASHFORD & SIMPSON
CHI-LITES
RAY CHARLES
LINDA CLIFFORD
ROBERTA FLACK
FIFTH DIMENSION
THE CHAMBERS BROTHERS
GENE CHANDLER
JIMMY CASTOR BUNCH
CLARENCE CARTER
JERRY BUTLER
GC CAMERON
MARVIN GAYE
THE DRAGSTERS
Tom Jones Live!

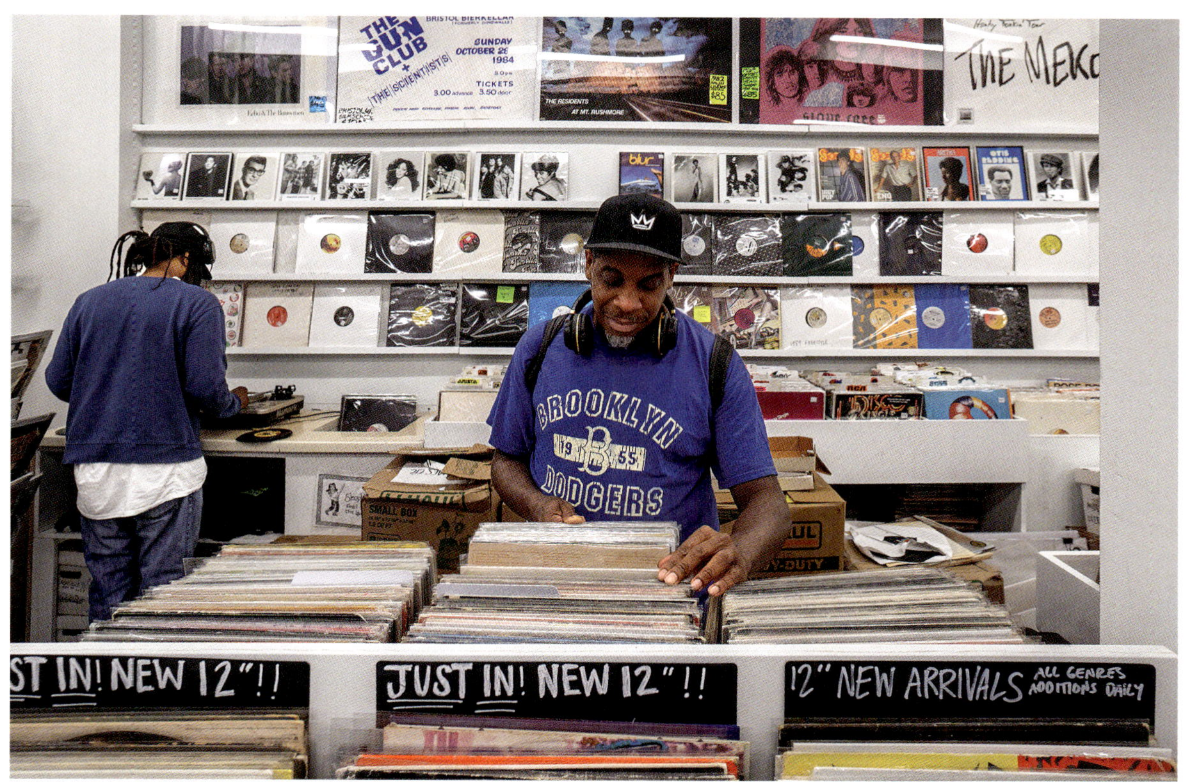
THE GUN CLUB
+
THE SCIENTISTS
SUNDAY
OCTOBER 28
1984
TICKETS
THE RESIDENTS
AT MT. RUSHMORE
blur
OTIS REDDING
BROOKLYN
19 55
DODGERS
SMALL BOX
ST IN! NEW 12"!!
JUST IN! NEW 12"!!
12" NEW ARRIVALS
ALL GENRES
ADDITIONS DAILY

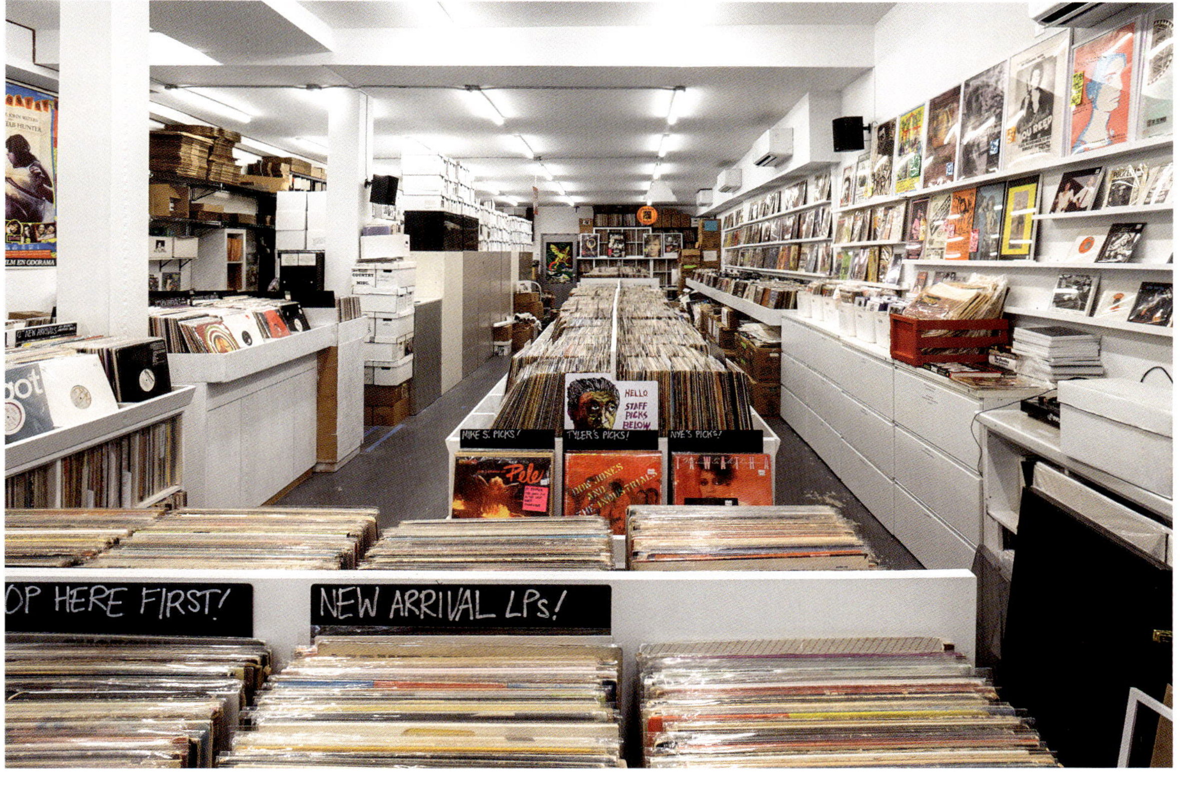
MIKE S. PICKS!
TYLER'S PICKS!
HELLO
STAFF
PICKS
BELOW
OP HERE FIRST!
NEW ARRIVAL LPs!

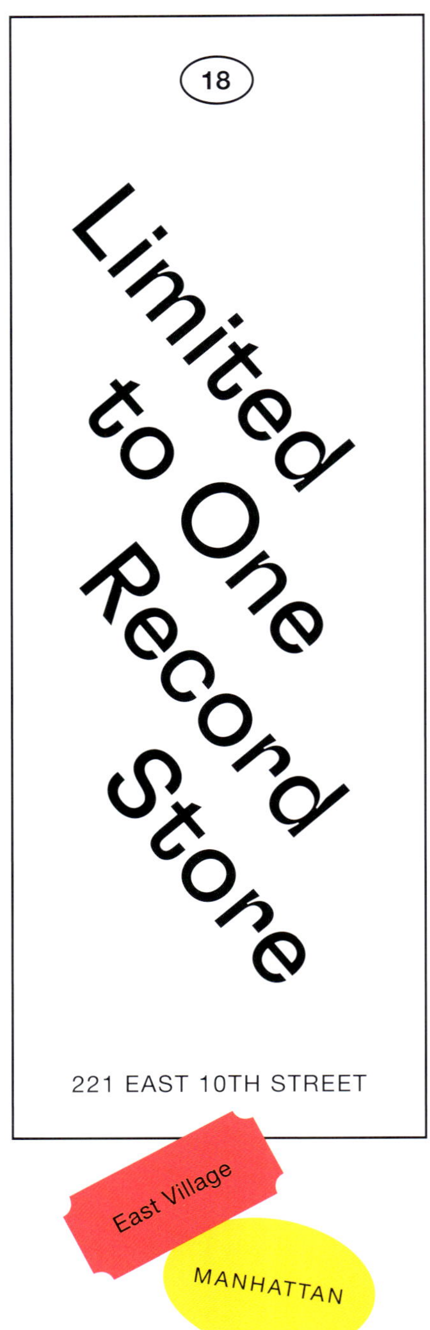

QUALITY, NOT QUANTITY, IS THE MISSION at Limited to One, yet another gem in the East Village's well-documented crown of record stores. Even though the streamlined, minimalist shop specializes in rare and uber-niche records, founders and co-owners Kristian Sorge and Nichole Porges aren't the types to greet you with an upturned nose or a list of backhanded recommendations. "I never understood that 'my taste is better than yours' record worker," Sorge shares. "I want people to come here and feel welcomed. I don't think there's such a thing as guilty pleasures." Indeed, guilt doesn't loom large whatsoever over Limited to One's vibrant, community-oriented, below-ground-level universe.

When Sorge and Porges opened the store in 2017, they weren't concerned about competition in an area buzzing with record shops. In fact, the group of collectors and wholesale buyers interacting across a few-block radius made them extra eager to establish a haven for the most discerning—and sometimes, newest—of vinyl lovers. Track IDs aren't hard to find here: A turntable by the glass storefront plays the sounds of the day, displayed for purchase on a notch marked "Now Spinning."

Born in New Jersey, Sorge boasted a serious penchant for CD and record collecting from the time he could walk. "I was pretty obsessive about the music I liked," he recalls of his childhood. It was in the mid-2000s that he revisited his youthful pastime with a fully developed palate and recognized a drought in the market when it came to the newer, post-'80s music he'd grown up with on MTV. Where were the strange and abrasive '90s hardcore records, the small-imprint demo cassettes, and the individuals who made up the demand for it?

Looking around, he knew what he wanted Limited to One to be: "a shop that focused on mostly limited and hard-to-find records." He isn't just interested in high-value reissues or special-edition pressings, but also the music paraphernalia other stores might not be willing to pick up. A row of demo tapes and cassettes from Limited to One-affiliated labels receives prime real estate next to the cash register, while across the slim aisle sits a bin of free zines, flyers, and papers—a little library of materials gathered from their countless deals with area indie labels.

Covid-19 presented Limited to One with the same challenges and changes that thousands of small businesses remember all too well. Yet there was also opportunity. Before the pandemic lockdown, Limited to One never experimented with mail-order services. Today, the shop operates a Patreon program where online subscribers can pay for a monthly record box curated by Sorge and Porges themselves and tailored to personal tastes and preferences.

If there's one thing Limited to One's stock prioritizes today, it's indie labels of all kinds: rock, hip-hop, electronic, metal, and more. A special affinity for offbeat and rare emo, hardcore, and punk records becomes clear as you sift through the slick array of music on offer. Even though the shop opens its arms to customers disillusioned by the vinyl industry's increasing prioritization of new-release LPs, it's still a welcome haven for the most unpretentious shopper to spend a few minutes while on their lunch break. As long as listeners are happy and the lights stay on, Sorge and Porges want anyone and everyone to experience the first-rate community service at a store like theirs—if the prominently positioned doorway sticker reading "All are welcome" didn't tell you that already.

"You get a better experience when the people who love the business are running it," Sorge explains. "It's as simple as that: The mom-and-pop stores look after their people. They're going to help the community, they're going to give back, they care about their neighbors. They care, genuinely."

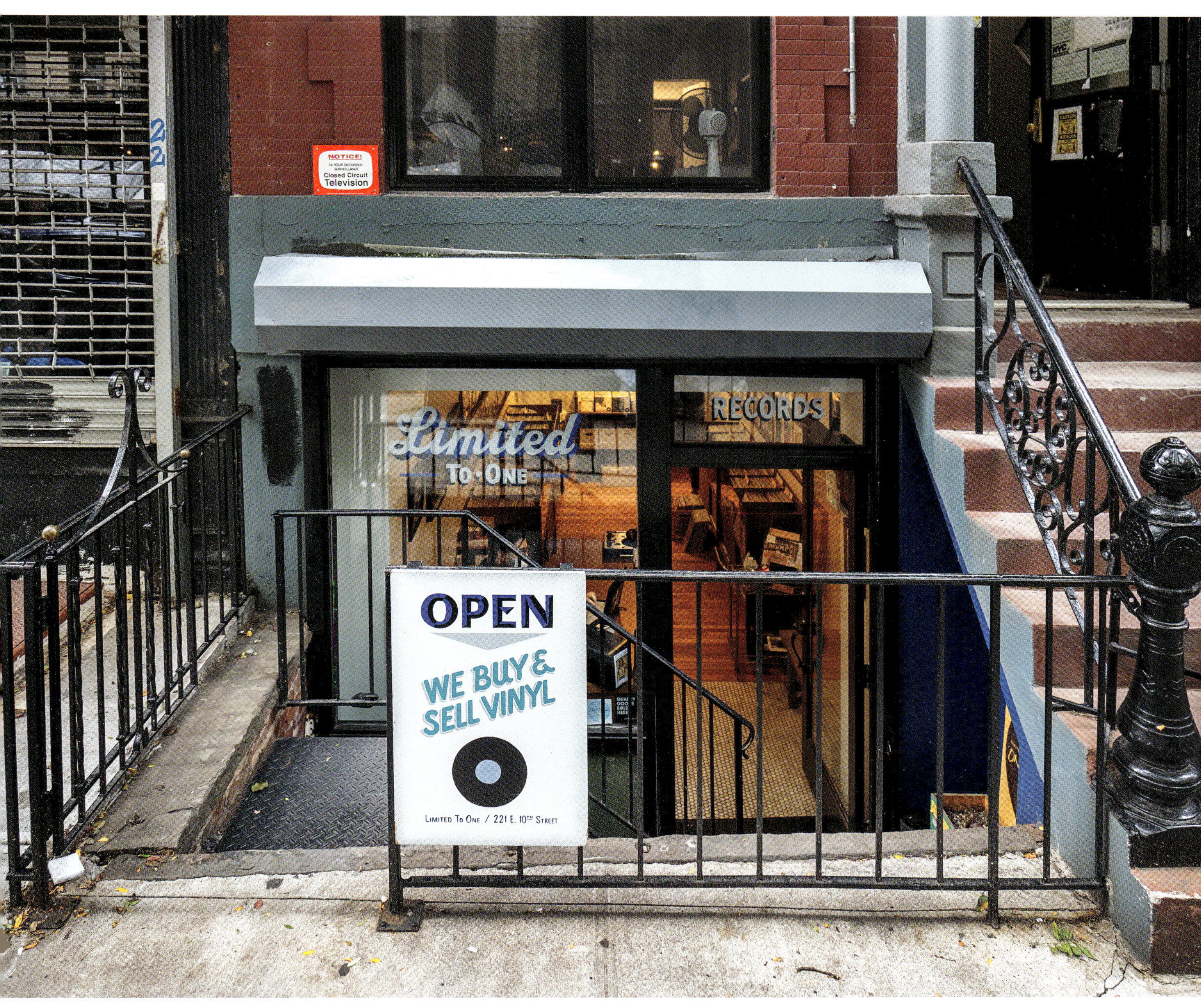

ABOVE Limited to One is a basement-level shop founded by husband-and-wife team Kristian Sorge and Nichole Porges in 2017. Its unique focus is limited and hard-to-find vinyl (hence the name), concentrating on independent music from 1985 to the present, including rock, hip-hop, punk, and hardcore.

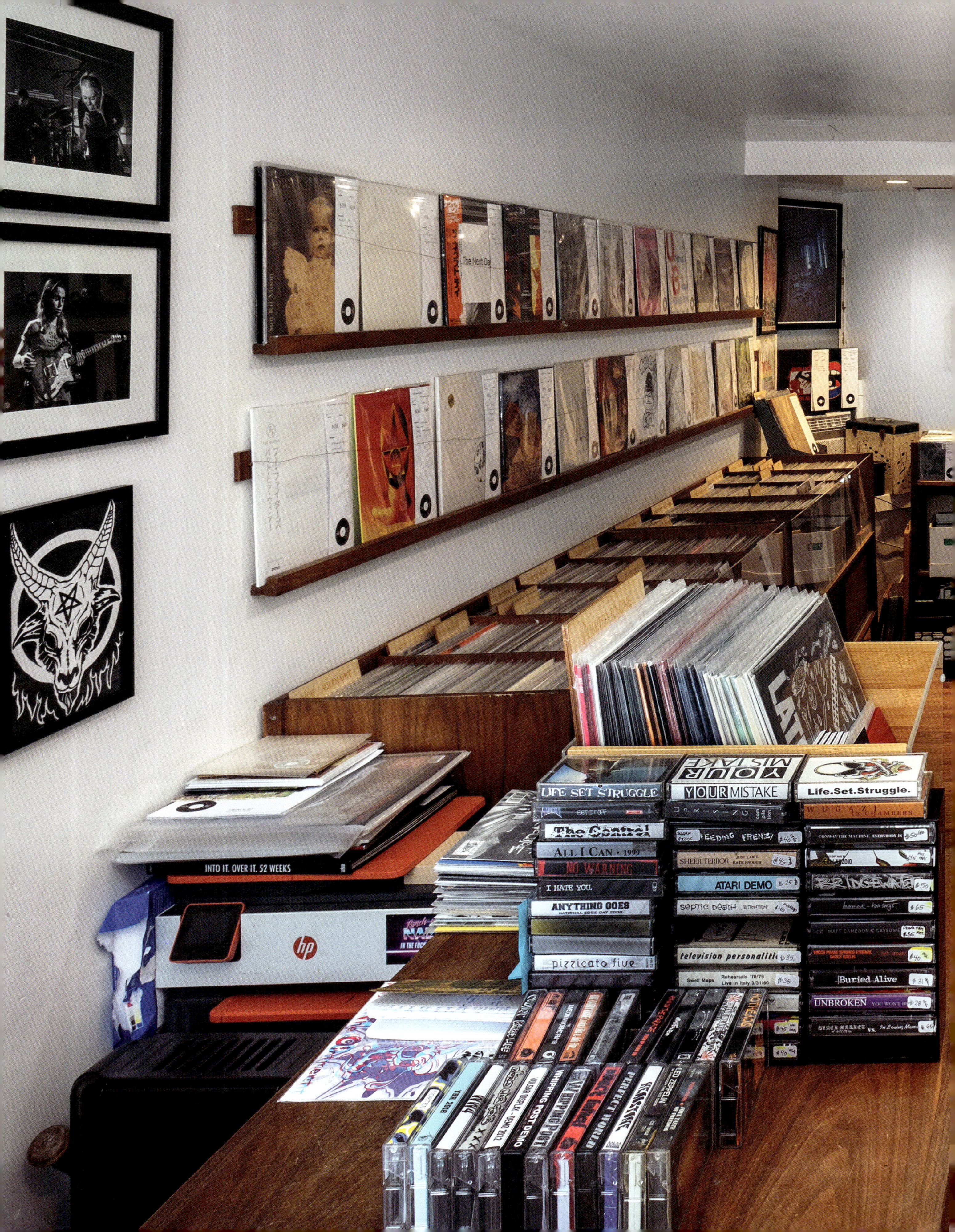
The Next Day
INTO IT. OVER IT. 52 WEEKS
LIFE SET STRUGGLE
YOUR MISTAKE
Life.Set.Struggle.
The Control
ALL I CAN · 1999
NO WARNING
I HATE YOU.
ANYTHING GOES
pizzicato five
FEEDING FRENZY
SHEER TERROR
ATARI DEMO
septic death
television personalities
Buried Alive
UNBROKEN
hp

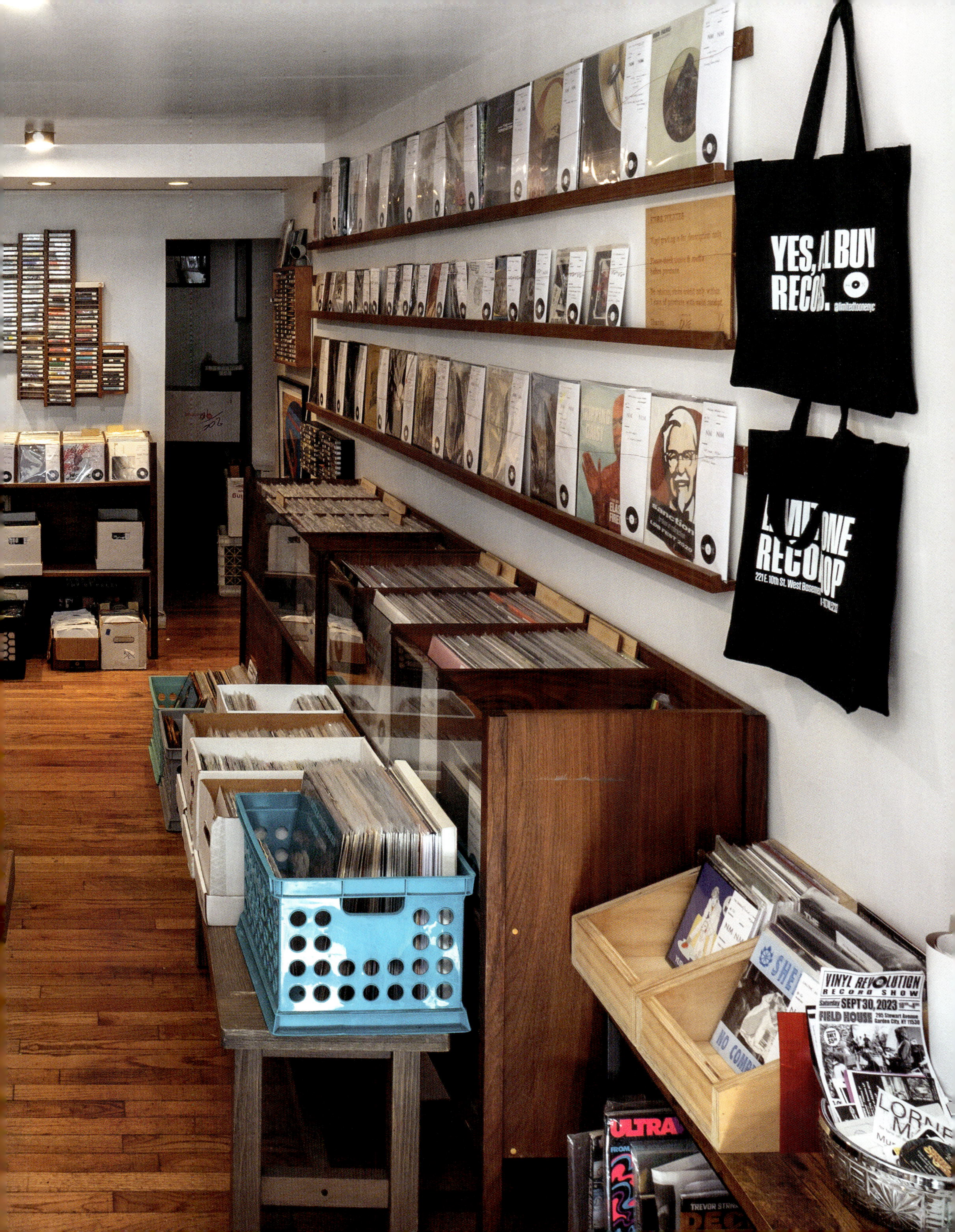

BUY
221 E. 10th St.
VINYL REVOLUTION
RECORD SHOW
Saturday SEPT 30, 2023
FIELD HOUSE
ULTRA

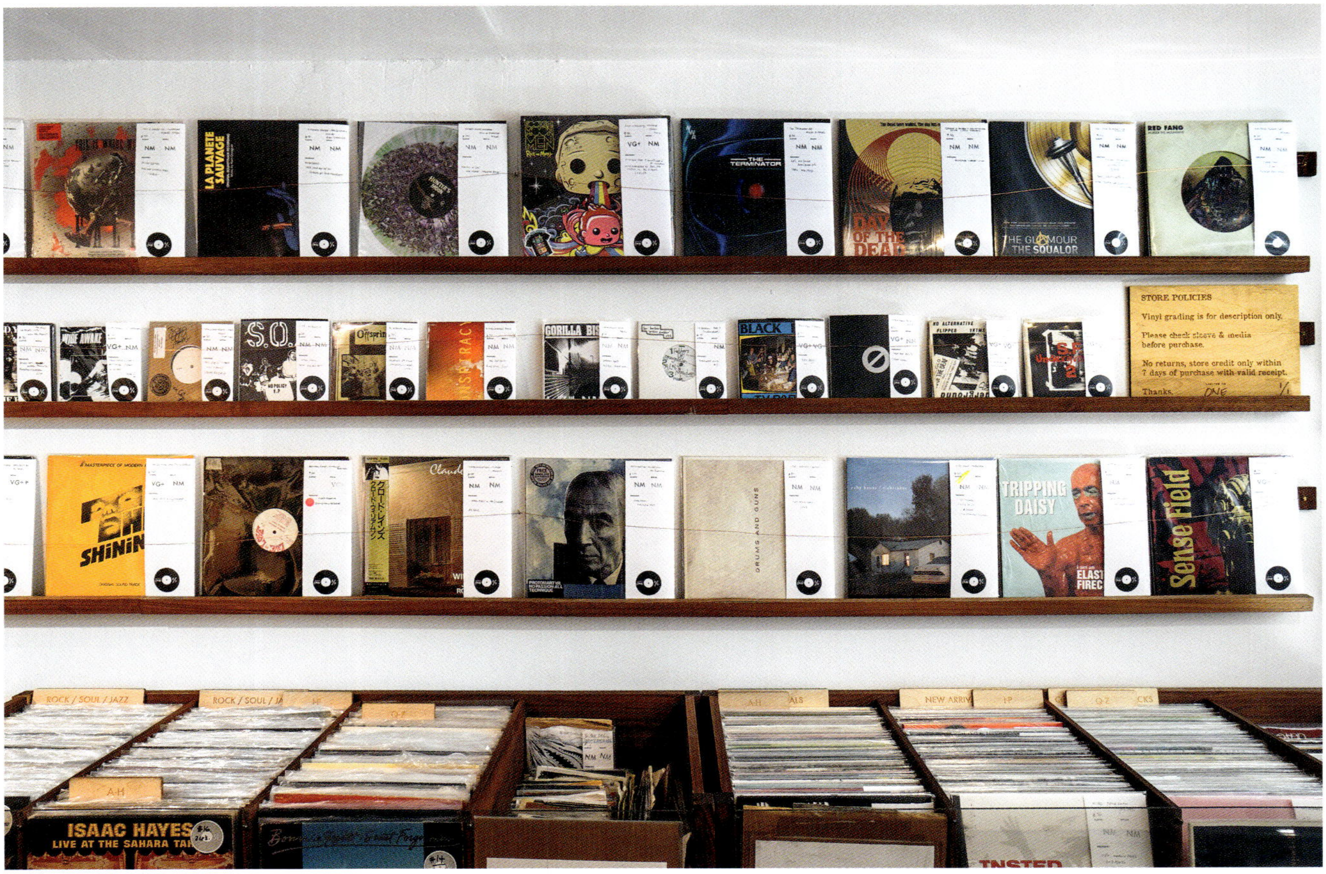

ABOVE The meticulously organized shop places a slip of paper on each record identifying the title, price, sleeve and media condition, and any pressing notes. Limited to One mainly only sells vinyl with a condition of VG+ and above.

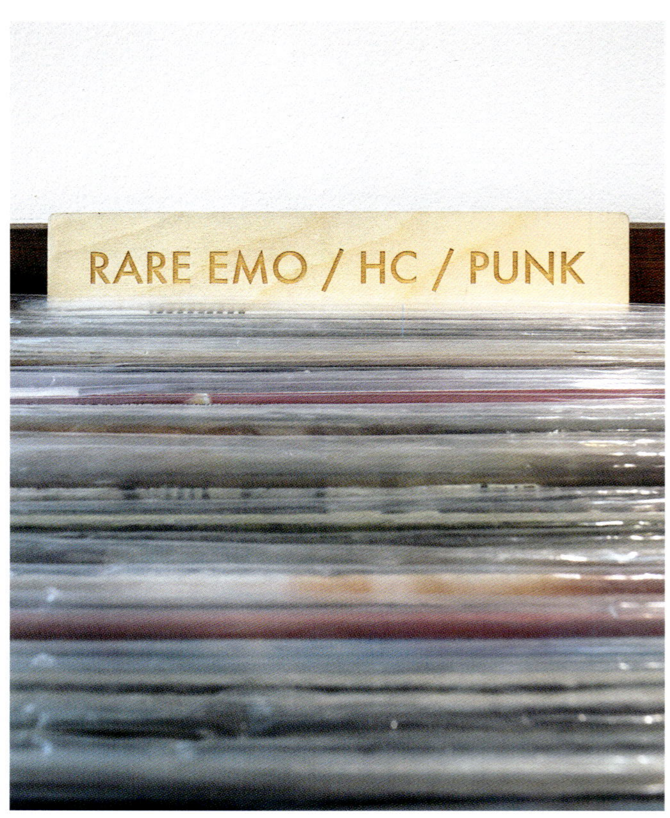

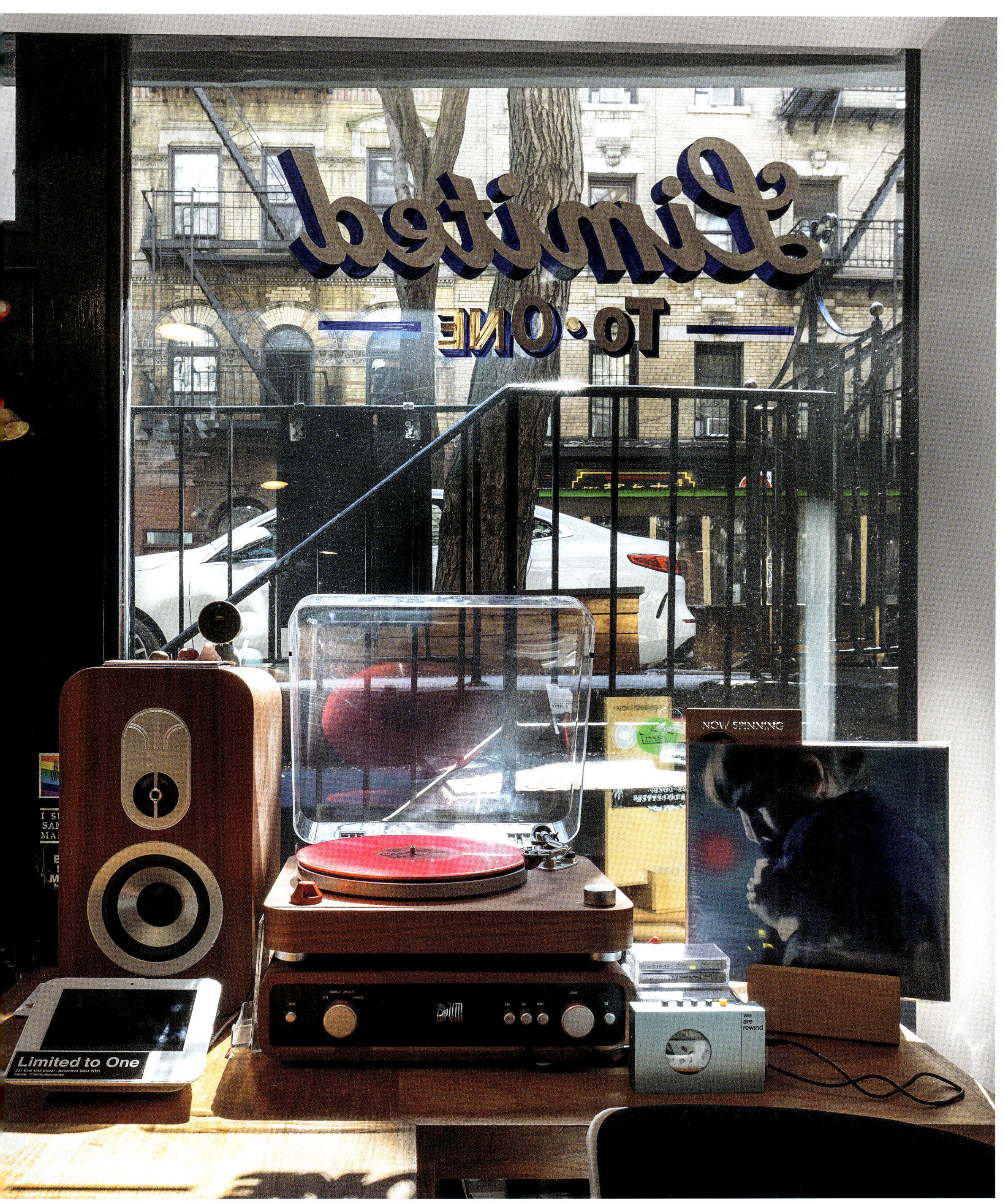
NOW SPINNING
Limited to One
we
are
rewind

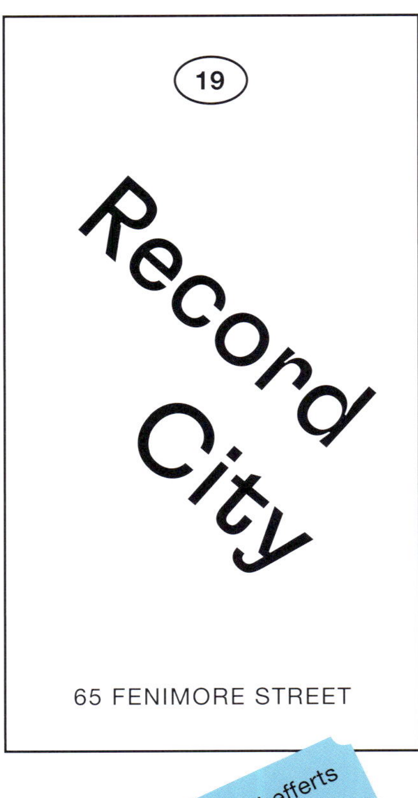

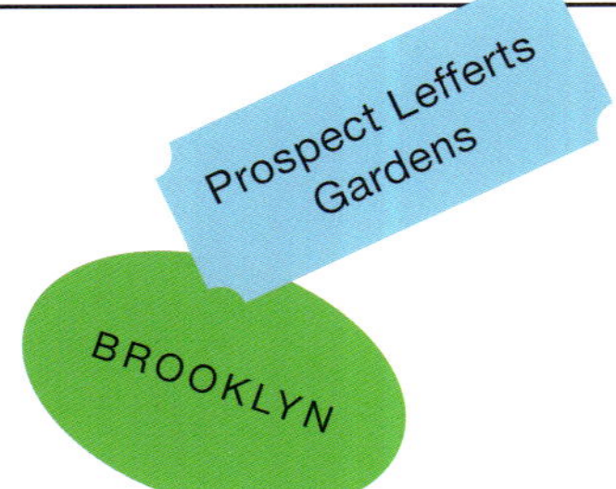

ON THE EDGE OF PROSPECT PARK, only blocks away from Drummer's Grove, the famed area where local musicians improvise together, one record store's reggae roots have grown and spread into branches as leafy and layered as those shading the park's landmark boathouse.

Record City is the brainchild of DJ and one-time label head Ian Clark. As a kid in the late '70s and early '80s, he was glued to the then-brand-new *Yo! MTV Raps* segments on the influential cable channel. A lifelong love affair with hip-hop soon began, and in the same beat, he found himself devoting all his spending money to choice tapes and LPs that targeted his fledgling interests. He traces this passion back to its roots in the jazz, funk, and soul music that his most-revered MCs were mining for samples.

But it was reggae that transformed Clark's hobby into a profession. He helped found the reggae reissue imprint DKR in 2009, but by 2016 turned his focus to expanding an online resale business, Infinite Bass. He opened Record City at 65 Fenimore Street that same year, filling the square interior with a small-batch selection that reaches across eras, genres, and styles. Whether it's underappreciated rocksteady or a $1 folk record, the lithograph of a palm tree perched behind Record City's cash register promises "Vinyl Sounds Better."

Following the "go with what you know" principle, Clark chose to establish Record City in Brooklyn's Little Caribbean area in the hopes of catering to the diasporic communities there, many of whom he could imagine patronizing a shop specializing in the islands' most influential musicians. However, he learned quickly that interest in reggae crops up among customers primed to explore a broad canopy of sounds and textures. Although he doesn't deny Record City's reverence for the genre, he's careful not to box in his store's primary focus. Whether you're a steel drum aficionado or a first-time flyer, it has waters worth wading into—and a new tide of records washes in every Thursday.

"Part of the mission is not just to make people feel welcome, but to have records of all price points, where the dollar bins are actually interesting and good," Clark explains. He's come to learn that snap-profiling a customer isn't likely to determine their taste in LPs. "In my experience, it doesn't matter where you come from, there's always people of different backgrounds in the dollar bins," he says.

One collector he won't soon forget, an older Jamaican man downsizing to move to a nursing home, gave Clark a treasure trove of vintage country western, including over three hundred Merle Haggard pressings. He's made innumerable connections like this over his years of trading, whether they began through a walk-in, a phone call, or sheer coincidence. "I've had some really great friendships form," he muses. No matter the unreliable East Coast weather, for a minted collector looking to up their 12-inch game, it's always blue skies overhead at Record City's parkside chest of curiosities.

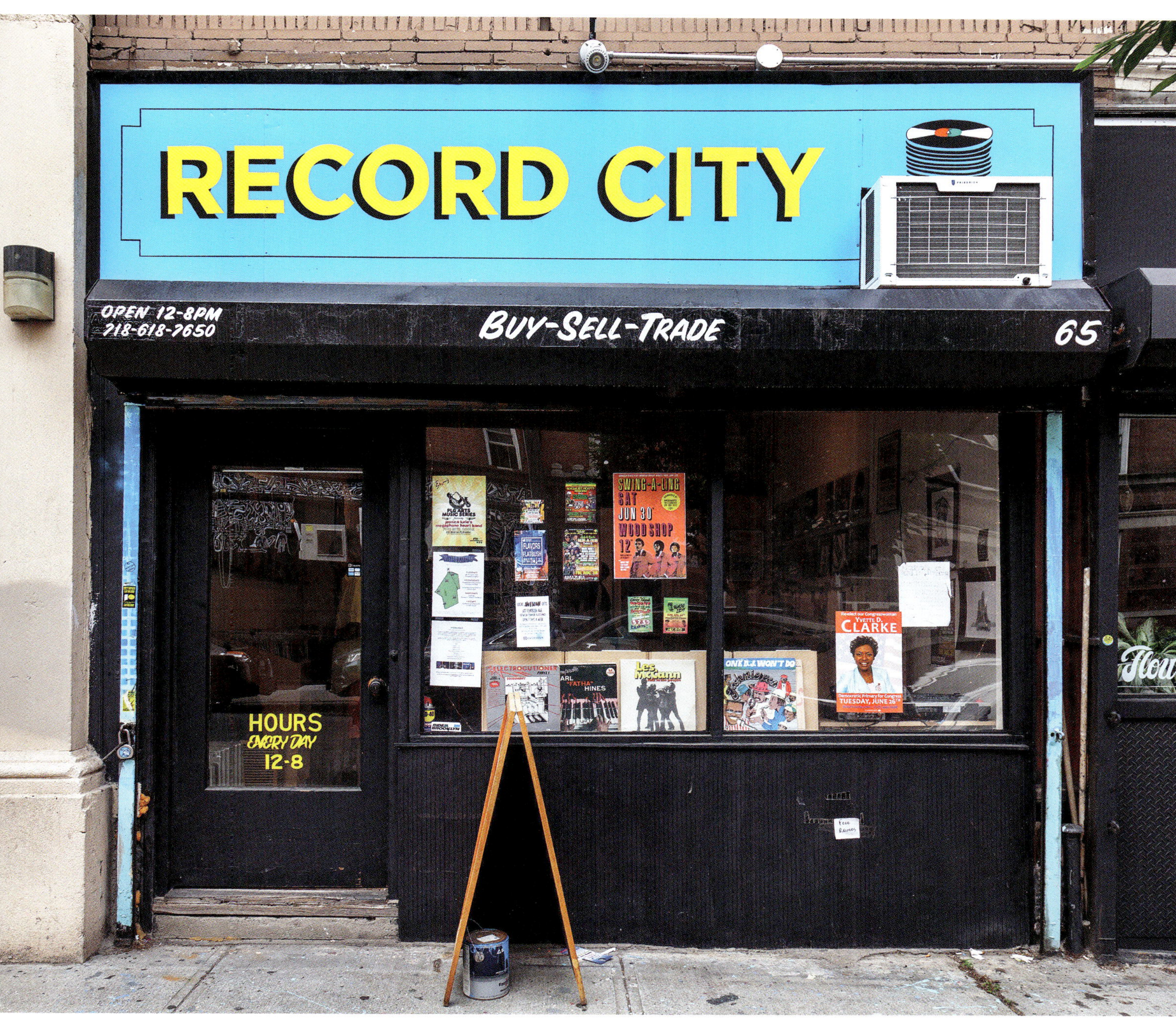

ABOVE Record City, with its brightly colored hand-painted signage, is located on a tree-lined residential street in the historically Caribbean neighborhood of Prospect Lefferts Gardens. Founded by Ian Clark in 2016, the shop has become well-known for its collection of rare reggae and soul LPs and 45s, but it also carries jazz, rock, hip-hop, dance, and records with Caribbean and Calypso flavor.

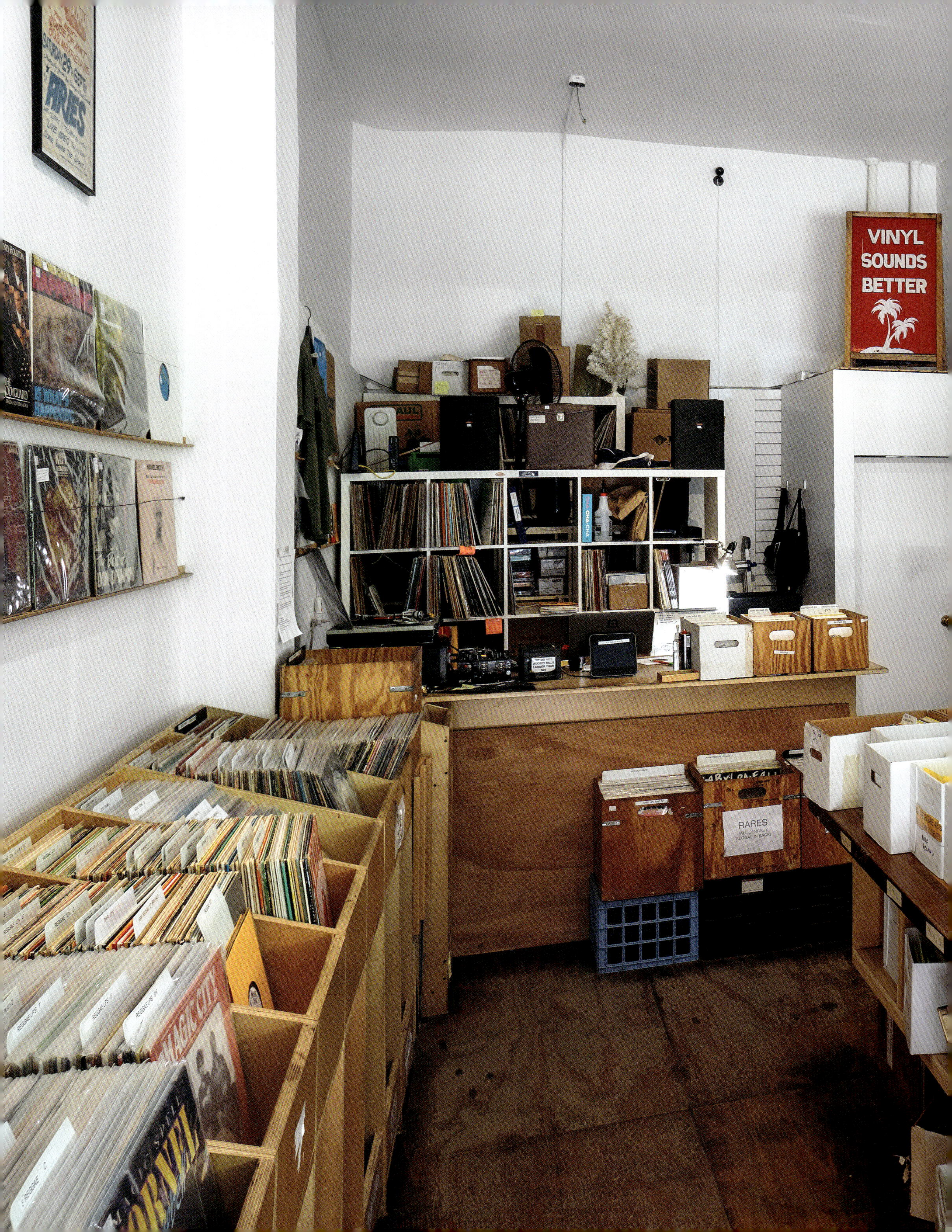
VINYL
SOUNDS
BETTER
RARES

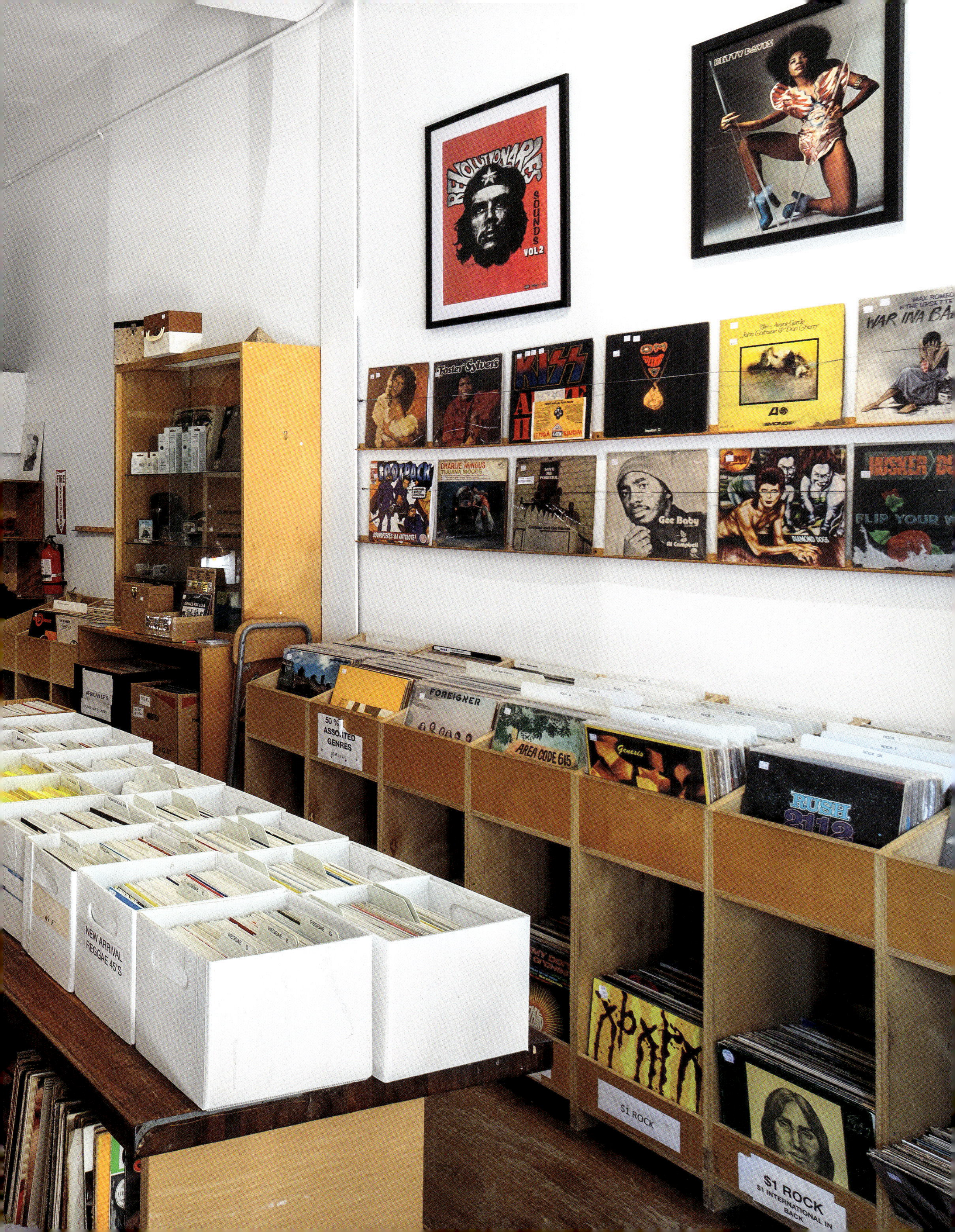

REVOLUTIONARIES
SOUNDS
VOL 2
BETTY DAVIS
Foster Sylvers
KISS
The Avant-Garde
John Coltrane & Don Cherry
CHARLIE MINGUS
TIJUANA MOODS
Gee Baby
Al Campbell
DIAMOND DOGS
FOREIGNER
50 %
ASSORTED
GENRES
AREA CODE 615
Genesis
RUSH
2112
NEW ARRIVAL
REGGAE 45'S
$1 ROCK
$1 ROCK
$1 INTERNATIONAL IN
BACK

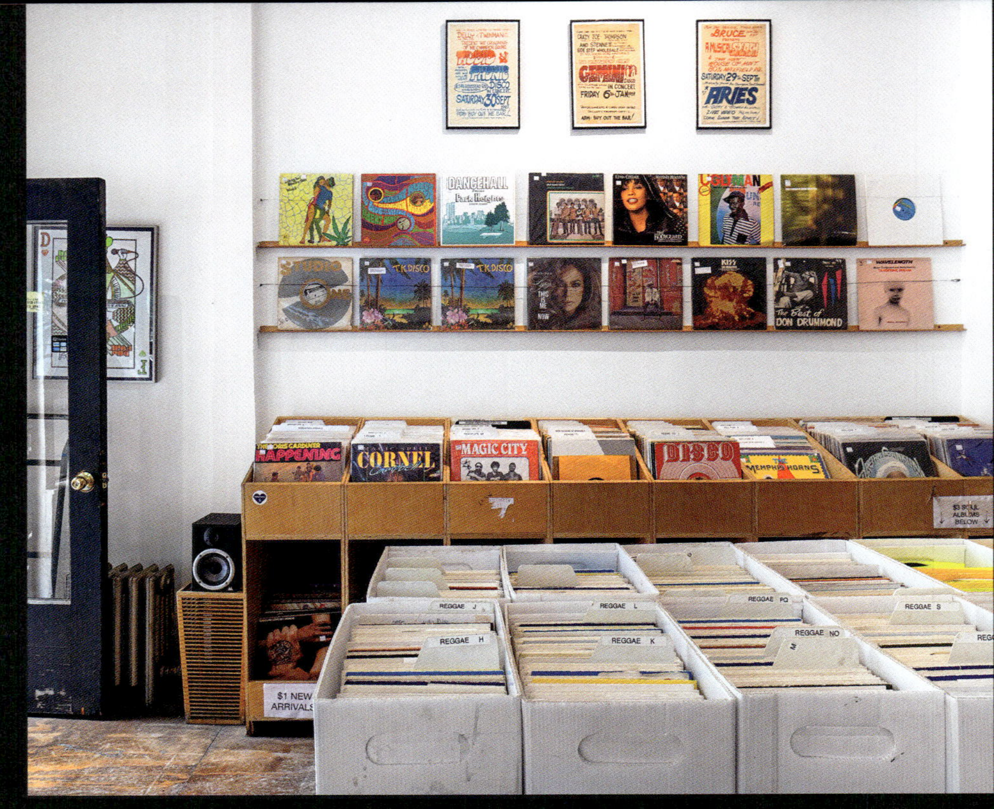
ARIES
DANCEHALL
CORNEL
MAGIC CITY
DISCO
$1 NEW
ARRIVALS
REGGAE H
REGGAE K
REGGAE L

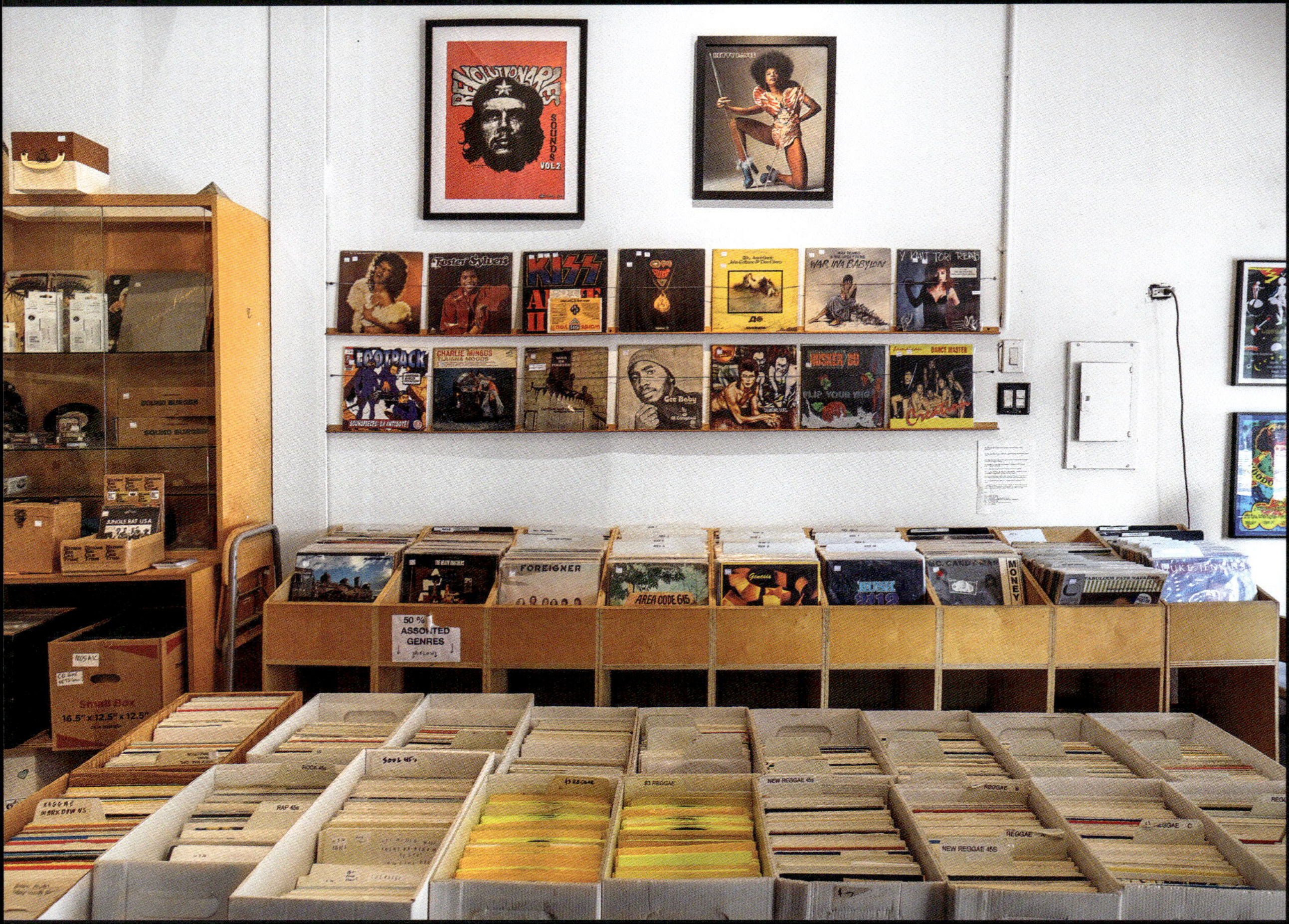

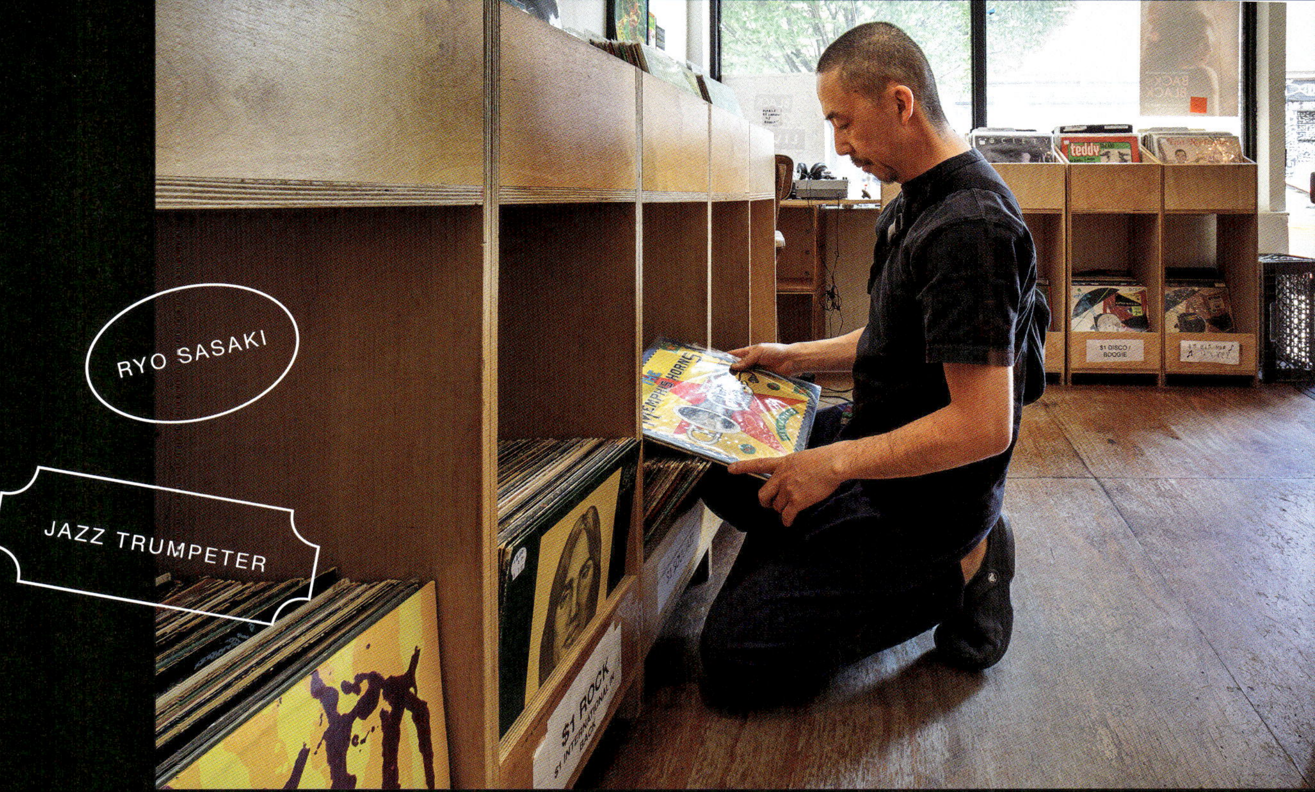

“The point of jazz to me is having a conversation with the people playing with you up there and just putting a message out.”

Trumpeter Ryo Sasaki first began studying his instrument as a teenager in Tokyo, but he fell in love with it against a backdrop of the Manhattan skyline. Watching a TV Christmas special recorded in New York at age fourteen, he can recall looking on, rapt, as Wynton Marsalis performed some of the first jazz music he'd ever heard. Hooked, Sasaki eventually enrolled at Boston's Berklee College of Music to train with jazz luminaries like Darren Barrett, Tiger Okoshi, and Charles Lewis, before making for the city where he'd first seen Marsalis.

Since kicking off his professional career in 2000, Sasaki has brought his talents to local institutions like Blue Note, Minton's Playhouse, Smalls, Saint Peter's Church, and the Carlyle. When he's not traveling between gigs with a trumpet case in hand, Sasaki takes in the season at the Metropolitan Opera, logs miles on one of his annual fall bike trips, and pores over the new arrivals at his well-loved rotation of vinyl shops, among them Prospect Lefferts Gardens' Record City.

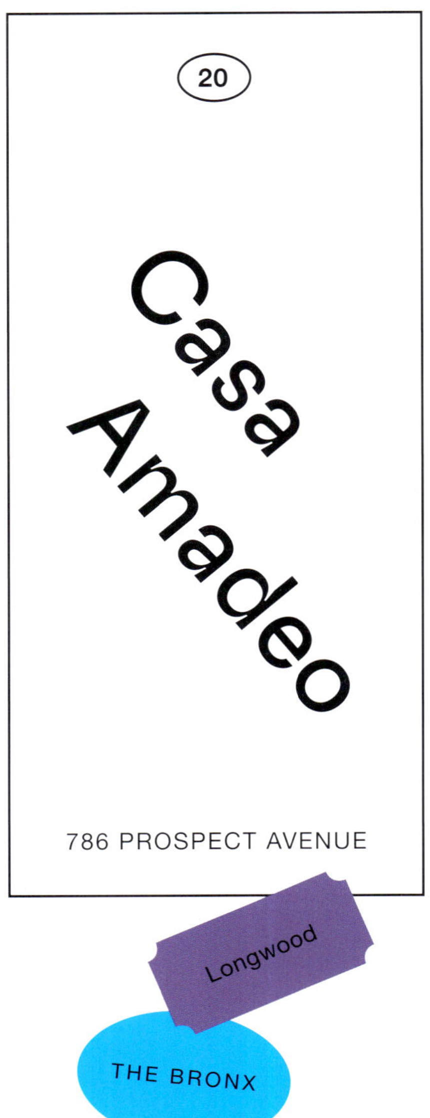

THE LONGEST CONTINUOUSLY RUNNING LATIN music store in the city, Casa Amadeo has been described as a "microcosm of the Puerto Rican experience in New York" by the National Park Service—perhaps best encompassed by the duo of immigrant artists who started it all.

Born in Aguadilla, Puerto Rico, siblings Rafael and Victoria Hernández emigrated to East Harlem in 1919. Already accomplished musicians in their own right, Rafael played with James Reese Europe's 369th Infantry Regiment "Hellfighters," an African American military band credited with introducing jazz to greater Europe. Meanwhile, Victoria opened what may have been the first Puerto Rican–owned music store in all five boroughs, Almacenes Hernández. By the time they sold the business in 1939, Rafael had become one of the highest-profile Latin American composers in the country.

They opened their second shop, Casa Hernández, in the Bronx in 1941. Downstairs, the street-level storefront was stocked with salsa, bachata, and merengue; upstairs in her apartment, Victoria taught piano lessons. In 1969 the Hernández's sold the store to Miguel "Mike" Amadeo, who changed its name and has held the reins there six days a week, twelve hours a day, ever since. The composer, singer, and guitarist, who is now in his nineties, first came to New York from Puerto Rico at thirteen. Since picking up his first guitar at sixteen, he's written over three hundred songs for musical icons from Celia Cruz to Tito Nieves, who also happens to be Amadeo's nephew.

Today, the majority of Casa Amadeo's collection comes directly from Latin artists, not collectors. In turn, Amadeo's sage wisdom draws musicians from around the world to visit, looking for notes on a new demo or intel on a guaracha deep cut. A career like Amadeo's can't easily be summarized, so he often turns to a printed *Daily News* profile of him displayed proudly on the shop's front window, where a pull quote reads prominently: "There is not a single Latino musician who has not received help from him."

Amadeo's formidable tenure and reach means he's witnessed more change in the vinyl economy than any other record store owner in the city. (Before he owned Casa Amadeo, the business was selling records when major labels like Columbia still depended on brick-and-mortar shops to foster audiences and break careers, becoming a pivotal taste-making space during the Bronx's early '50s mambo surge.) When CD sales began to surpass vinyl, Amadeo built up the shop's hundreds-deep collection. And in 2020, when a three-month closure and dwindling weekly profits threatened business as he knew it, an unexpected spike in acoustic guitar sales righted the ship. (The majority of buyers, Amadeo notes, were pandemic-weary parents hoping to cheer up their cooped-up kids.)

For all that's changed, some things have stayed the same. Casa Amadeo has retained its original Neo-Renaissance architecture, the array of painted wooden maracas on display at the counter, and its defiant absence of an online store that encourages music lovers to visit in person. Amadeo, after all, plans to be there—with almost six decades logged behind the cash-only counter, he doesn't intend to leave the shop for anywhere but the grave. "I'm facing life here until God decides," he told *New York* magazine in 2020.

Amadeo may not be waiting behind the door to greet his customers forever—but, due to a change in the Bronx's very geography, he'll always be there to guide them. In 2014, over seventy years after Casa Amadeo first opened on Prospect and Longwood Avenues, New York's City Council voted to rechristen the corner Miguel Ángel (Mike) Amadeo Way.

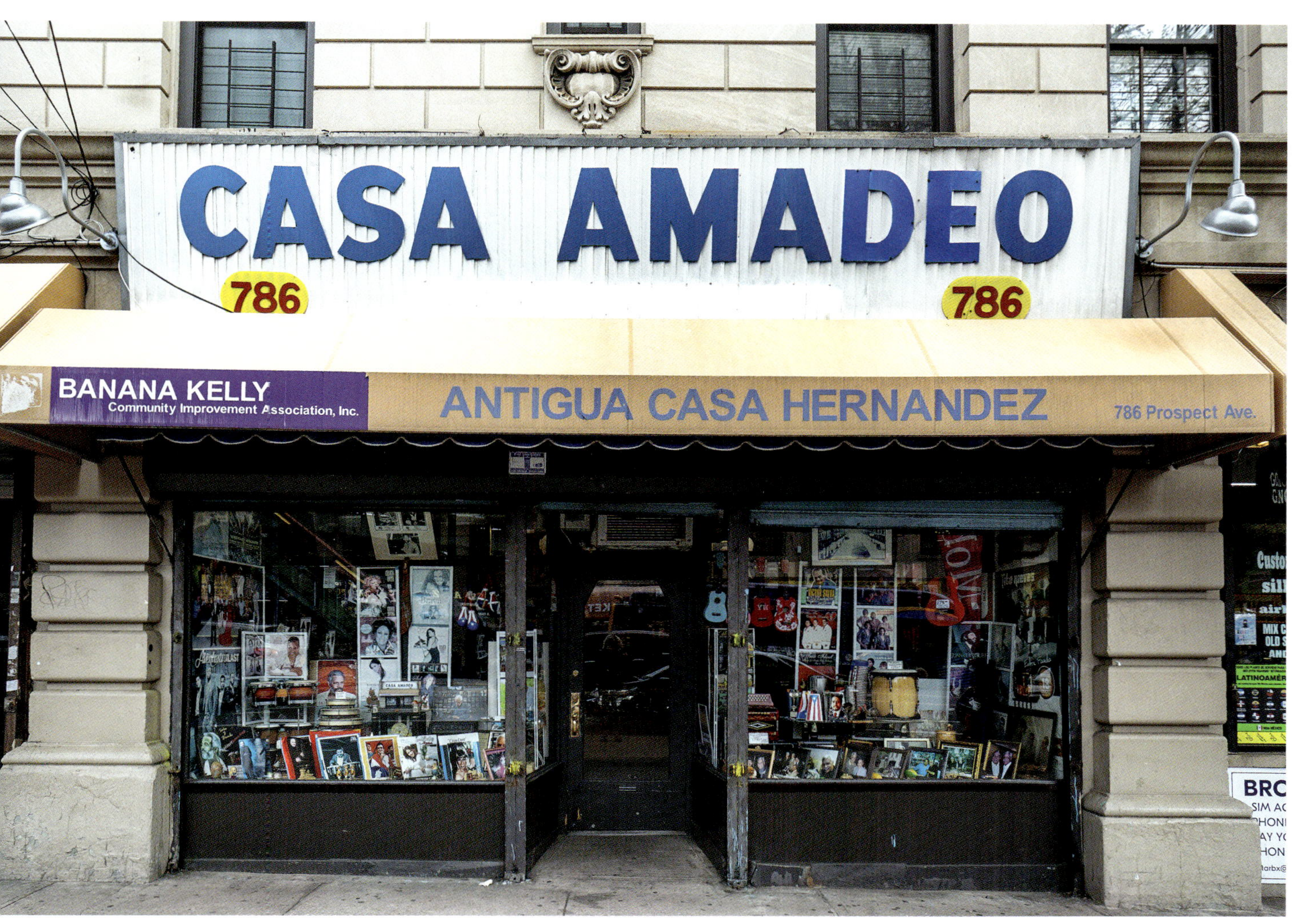

ABOVE Casa Amadeo was founded (under the name Casa Hernández) in 1941 and is the first Puerto Rican music shop, and the longest-running Latin music store in New York City. It carries a wide selection of vinyl and CDs, as well as Latin and Caribbean musical instruments.

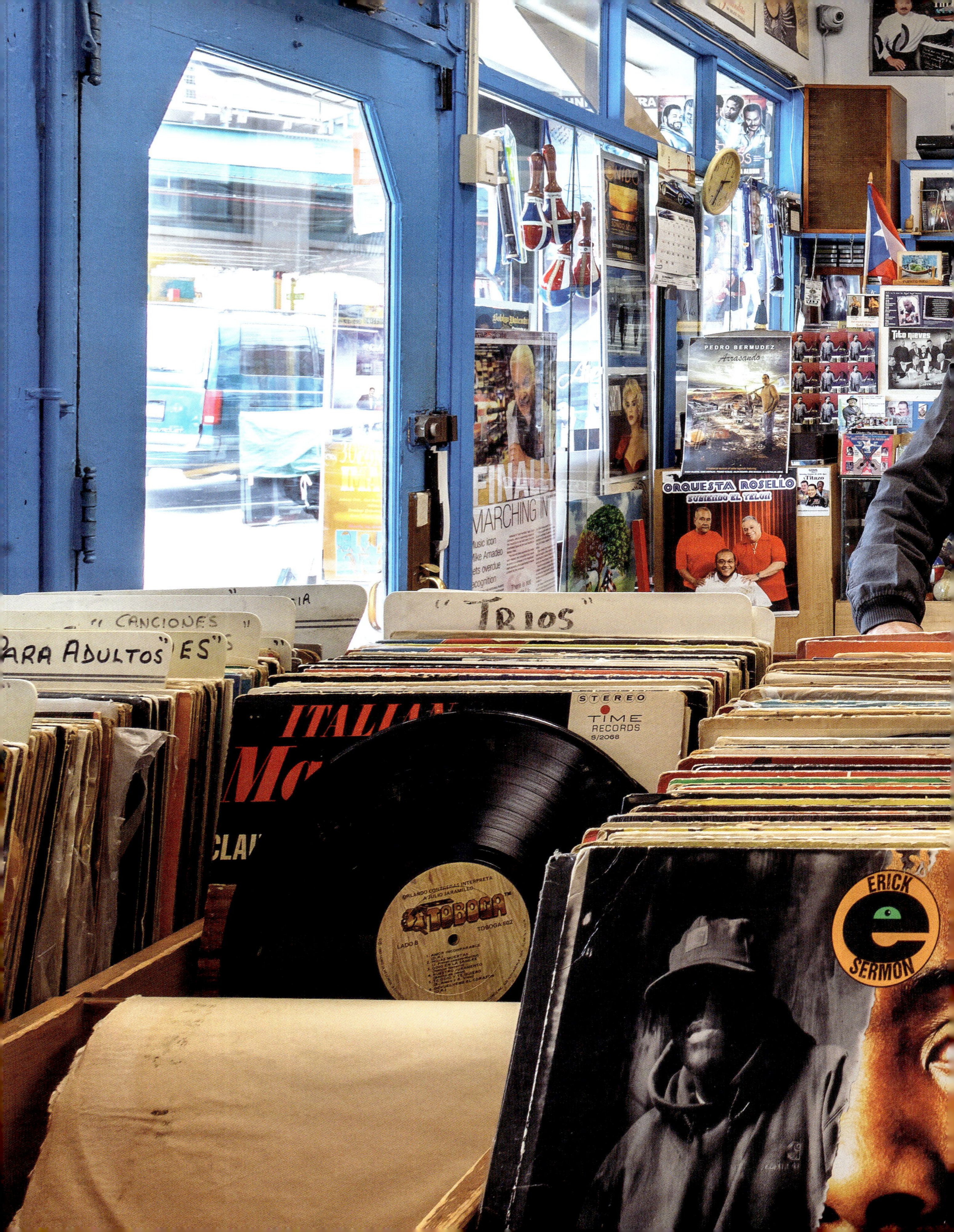
" CANCIONES
ARA ADULTOS"
" TRIOS "
STEREO
TIME
RECORDS
S/2068
ITALIAN
ERICK
SERMON
TOBOGA
PEDRO BERMUDEZ
Arrasando
ORQUESTA ROSELLO
SUBIENDO EL TELON
Tito nieves
MARCHING IN

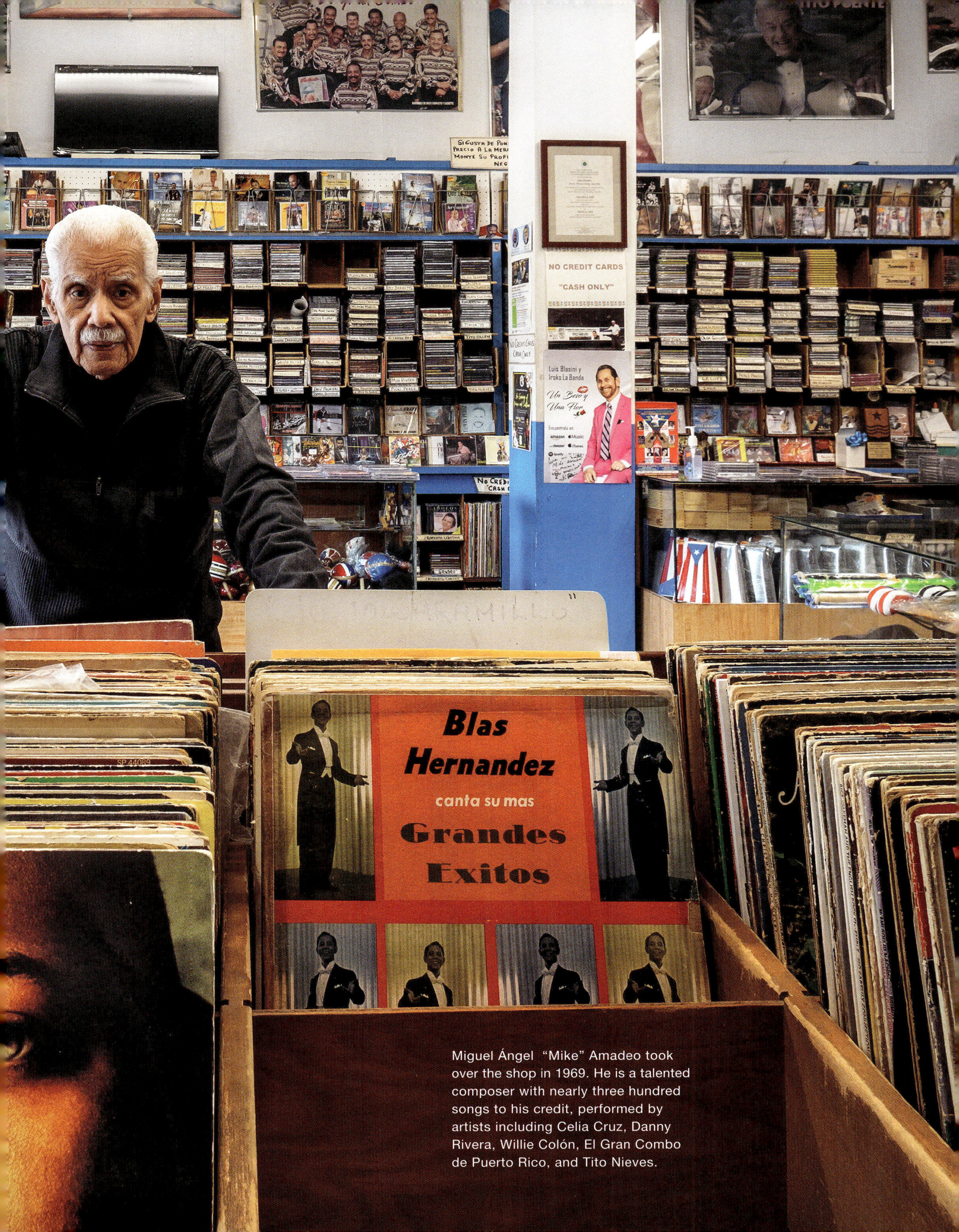

Miguel Ángel "Mike" Amadeo took over the shop in 1969. He is a talented composer with nearly three hundred songs to his credit, performed by artists including Celia Cruz, Danny Rivera, Willie Colón, El Gran Combo de Puerto Rico, and Tito Nieves.

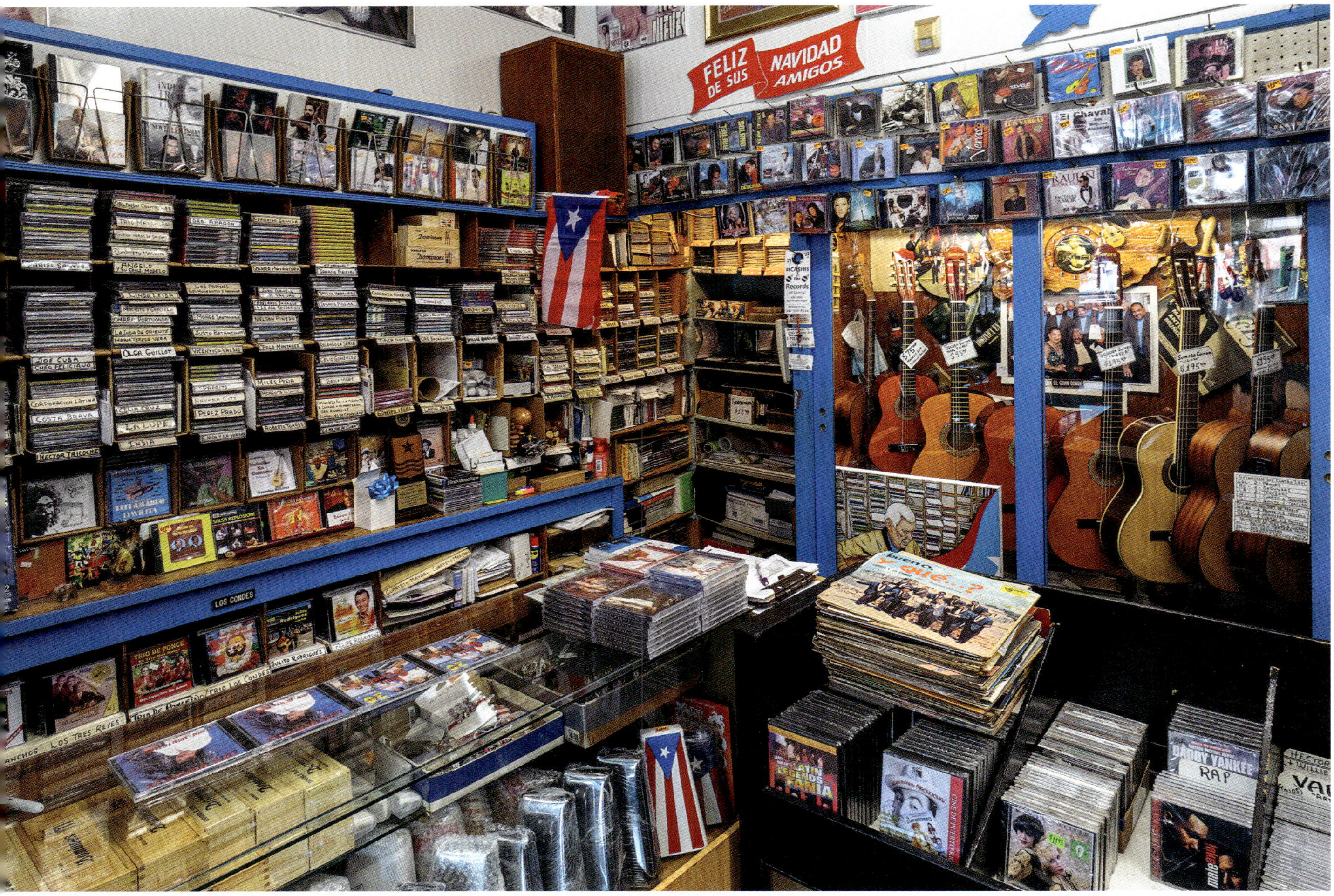

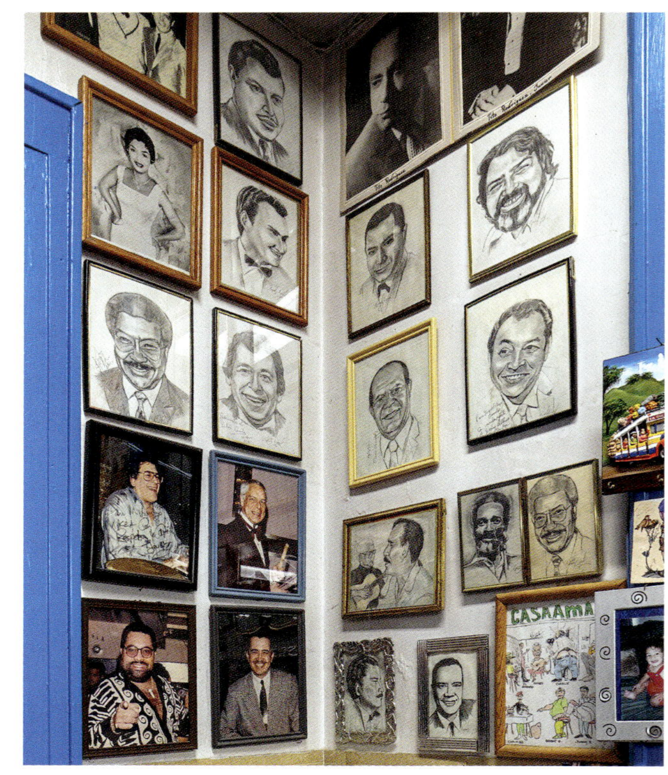

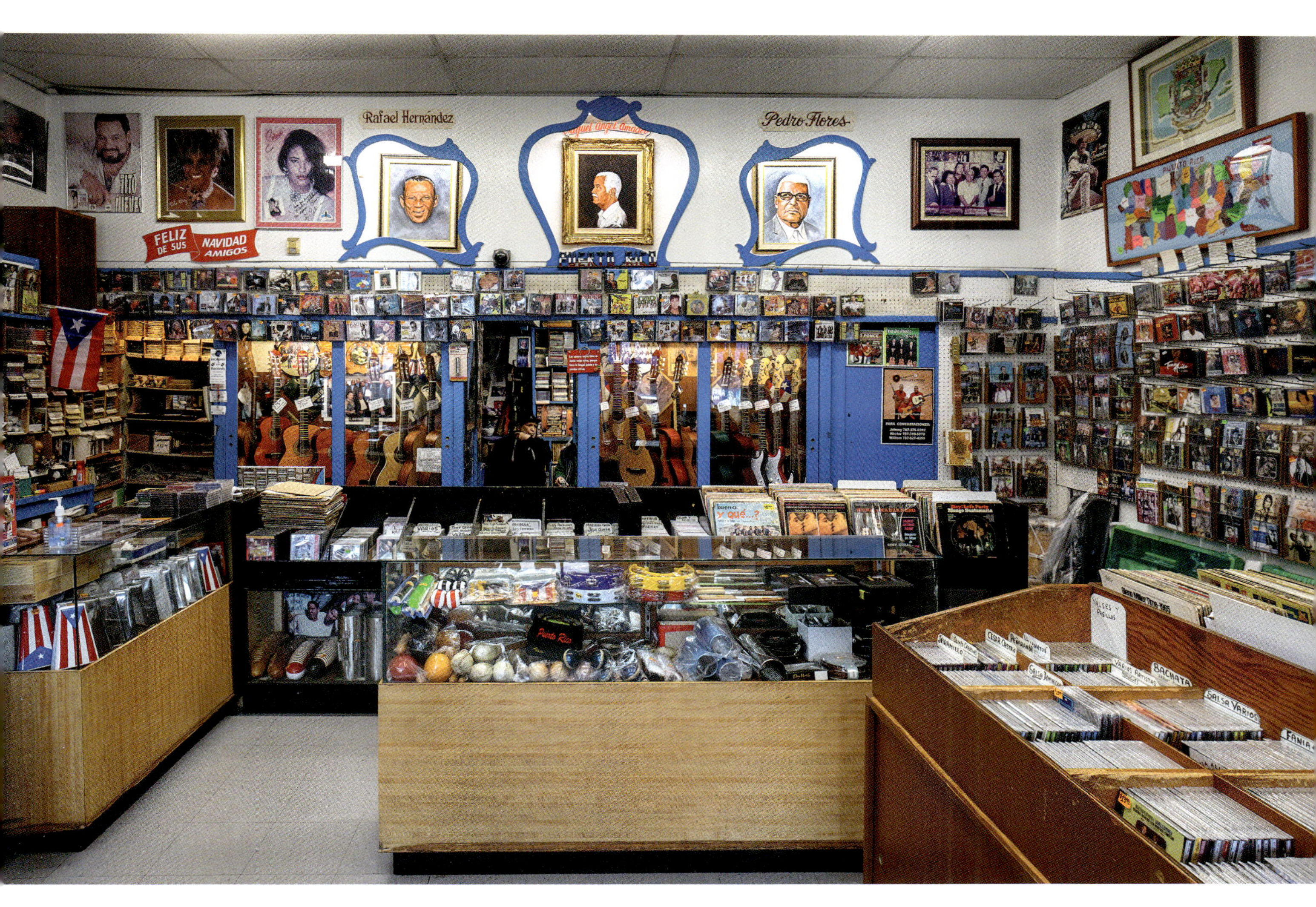

OPPOSITE BOTTOM Portraits of many of the artists Mike Amadeo has worked with line the walls of the shop, including Virginia López, who recorded his composition "Tu Promesa de Amor."

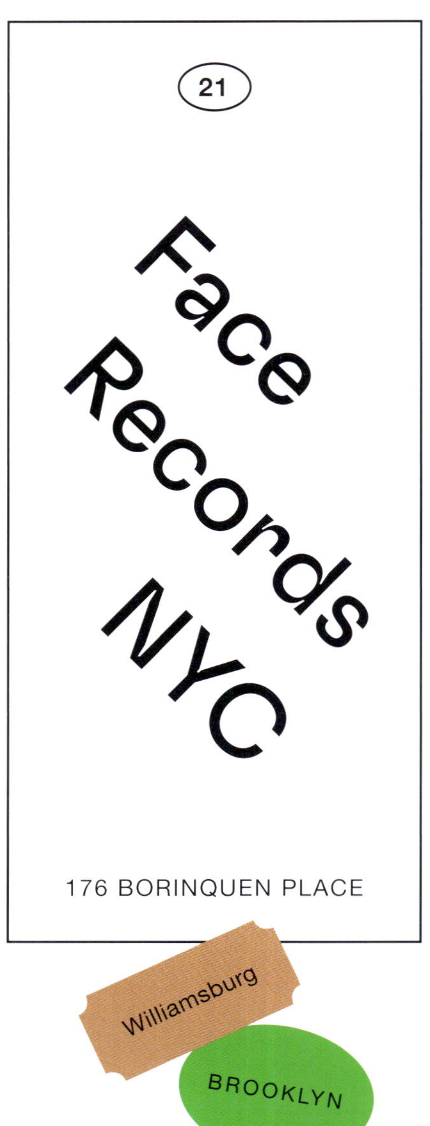

"I'M LOOKING FOR A PARTICULAR EP that was released like ten years ago," a Reddit post titled "Seeking Rare Japanese Titles in the US—Any Good Stores I Should Consider?" reads. "Are there any good stores in the US, particularly on the East Coast, that specialize in Japanese releases? Don't even know if that's a thing." Responses seem to confirm the original poster's doubt, laying out alternate strategies like eBay or a direct shipment from the country. But the highest-voted answer is also the surest: "Check with Face Records in NYC."

When Face opened its Brooklyn storefront in 2018, it was the only all-Japanese, all-vintage vinyl shop in the United States. But its roots trace back to Kanagawa, Japan, where it was founded in 1994 by Shinichi Takei. Originally a mail-order business focused on secondhand resale, Face opened its first brick-and-mortar location in Tokyo in 1996, and has since expanded into a premiere destination for Japanese city pop, rock, and more. The store even boasts an extensive selection of anime soundtracks and American vinyl pressed in Japan, oft-understocked genres that many rare collectors hold as personal holy grails.

Producer and collector Yu Mamiya oversees Face's NYC location, where the passion for vinyl he cultivated as a teenager in Tokyo reaches its final form. Although he recalls an early affinity for jazz music, he truly learned how to crate-dig by studying the hip-hop producers he'd often find himself shoulder to shoulder with once he made his way to New York. Over the years, rappers and producers like the Alchemist, Erick the Architect, A$AP Ferg, and the late Ka have all stopped in to peruse Face's wares. Their sharp eyes and stamina impressed Mamiya, inspiring him to dive into production himself. Today, he's released songs with Large Professor (see p. 215), Freddie Gibbs, and more.

Hip-hop artists may have a long-standing home at Face, but the heart and soul of the shop's inventory lies with the hard-to-find, high-quality jazz and city pop it built a reputation on in Kanagawa. (City pop, a warm and optimistic blend of soft rock, disco, and boogie, grew to prevalence in 1980s Japan in response to a booming economy and expansive urban development.)

It may not be Tokyo in the 1980s, but there's still plenty to be excited about at Face's Williamsburg location. A browsing session can be as likely to reveal a signed Japanese pressing of Kendrick Lamar's *DAMN* as city pop legend Miho Fujiwara's *California Crisis*, an anime soundtrack that also serves as a genre pillar. Prices can climb throughout Face's selective stock, especially when their robust selection of original mint-condition vintage pressings comes into play. But the payoff from a visit to 179 Borinquen Place can be unquantifiable. In mid-2024, for example, lucky shoppers had the chance to meet Fujiwara herself on a rare trip to New York; she was signing records any moment she wasn't busy browsing for new discoveries to deepen her own collection.

Face's inception as a mail-order business has translated seamlessly into its robust Discogs shop, an online union between its US and Japan locations. The service proved essential in 2020 when the store had to close down for four months due to the Covid-19 pandemic. But it also serves as a reminder of how city pop continues to uniquely capture vinyl collectors across the world, becoming a touchstone for younger listeners through reissue campaigns and YouTube compilations. Whether by walk-in or Wikipedia rabbit hole, a new crop of American kids will come upon the classics just as a young Mamiya did in Tokyo. When they do, they'll learn quickly: On the stateside hunt for Japan's very best, there's only one store to check with first.

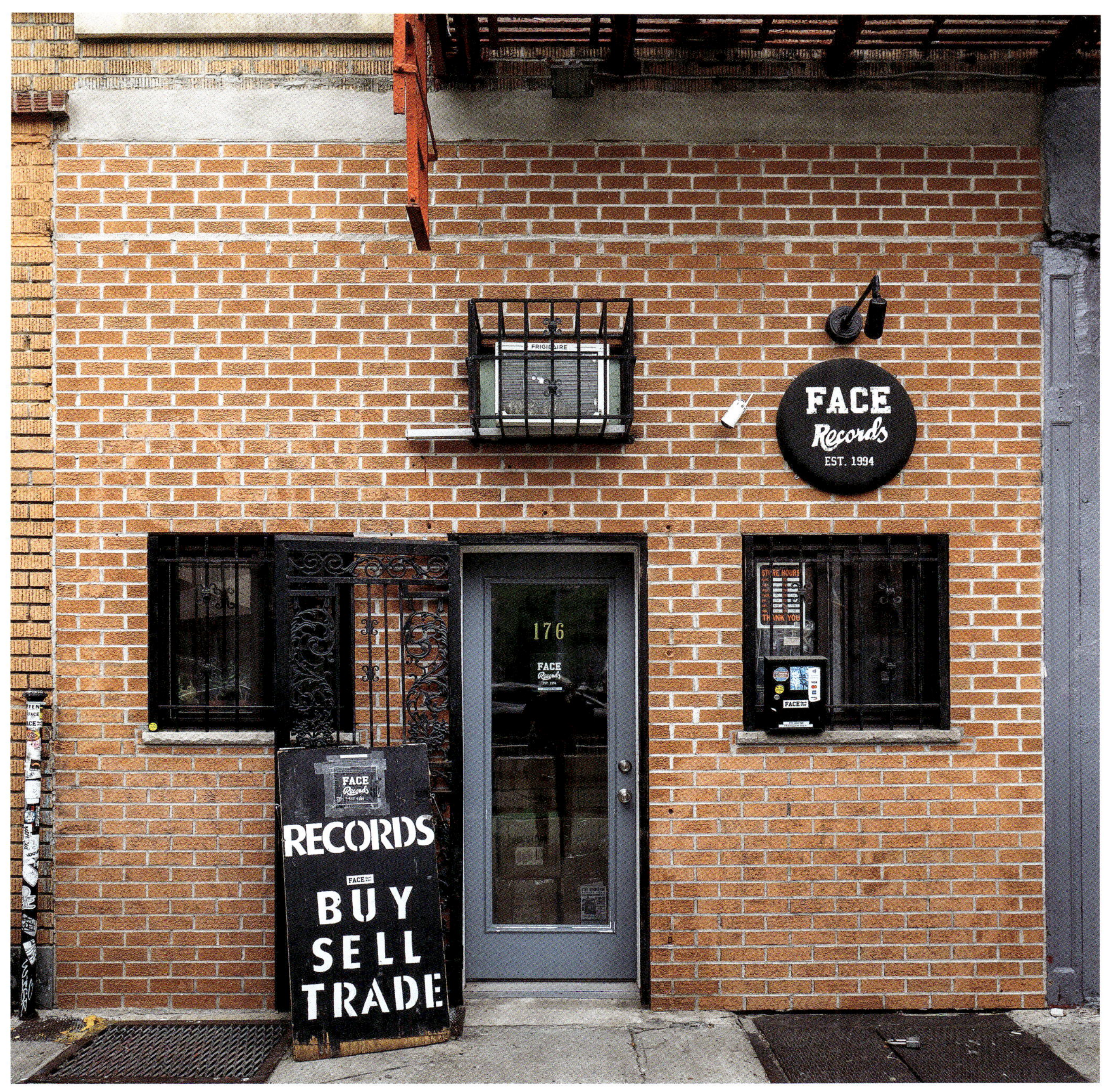

ABOVE Behind this storefront is one of the most hyper-specialized vinyl shops in New York City. Face Records sells a curated selection of rare and sought-after titles by Japanese artists, including Masayoshi Takanaka and Tatsuro Yamashita, as well as Japanese pressings of jazz, rock, city pop, soul, funk, hip-hop, and anime soundtracks, often featuring obi strips (paper bands wrapped around vinyl albums released in Japan).

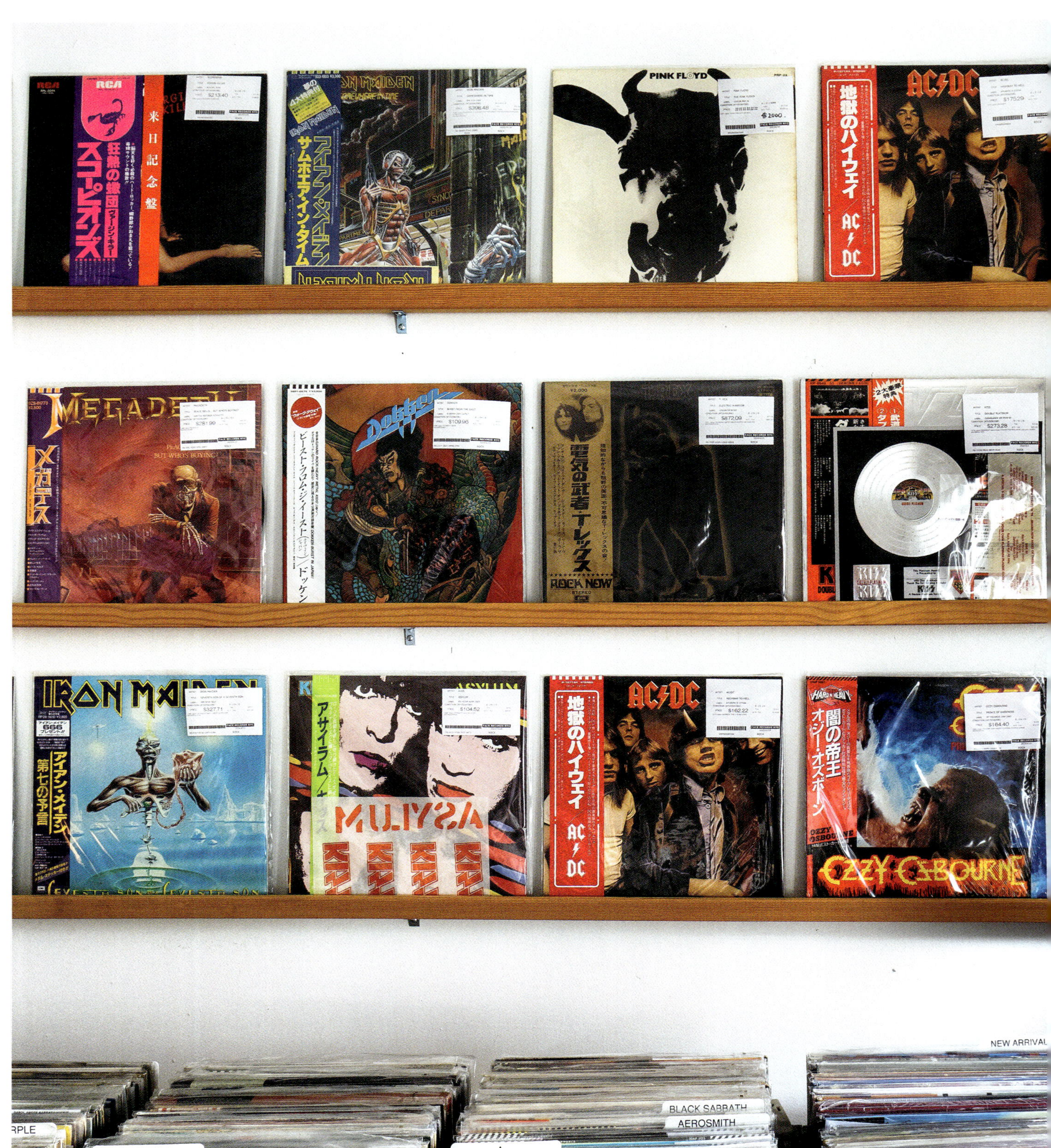
RCA
スコーピオンズ
狂熱の蠍団
PINK FLOYD
AC/DC
地獄のハイウェイ
AC/DC
サムホエア・イン・タイム
アイアン・メイデン
ビースト・フロム・ジ・イースト
ドッケン
電気の武者
T・レックス
ROCK NOW
アイアン・メイデン
第七の予言
アサイラム
AC/DC
地獄のハイウェイ
AC/DC
闇の帝王
オジー・オズボーン
OZZY OSBOURNE
NEW ARRIVAL
BLACK SABBATH
AEROSMITH
A

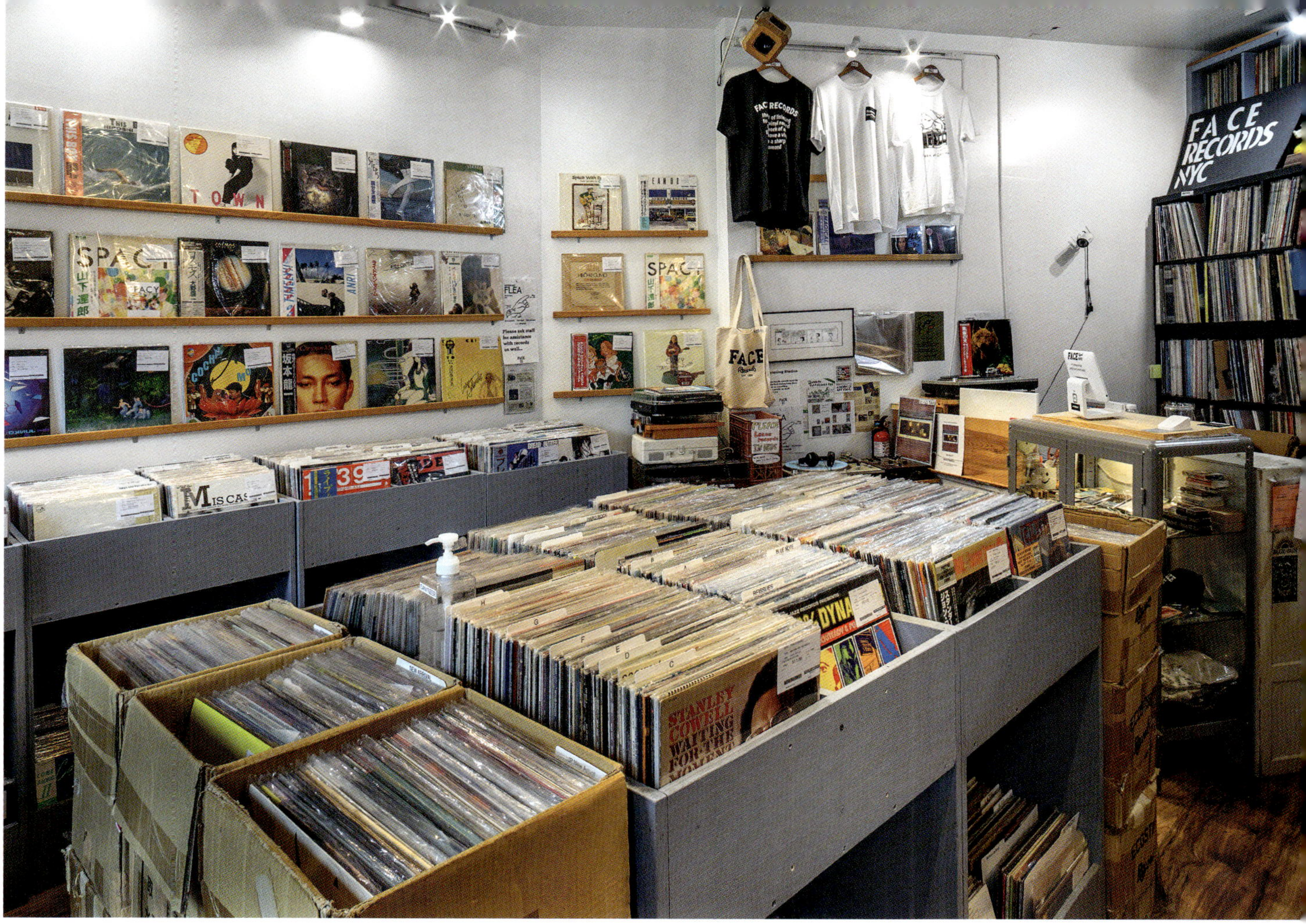

OPPOSITE The most valuable and in-demand records displayed along the wall include a rare pressing of Pink Floyd's 1971 promotional-only sampler EP *The Pink Floyd*, selling for $2,000, and a Japanese pressing of T. Rex's *Electric Warrior* for $872.09, with its original obi strip.

RIGHT Yu Mamiya, a Japanese beatmaker who manages the shop, updates the stock regularly with new arrivals from Japan. He also helps label each title with the artist's name, genre classification, and condition of the jacket, vinyl, and obi strip.

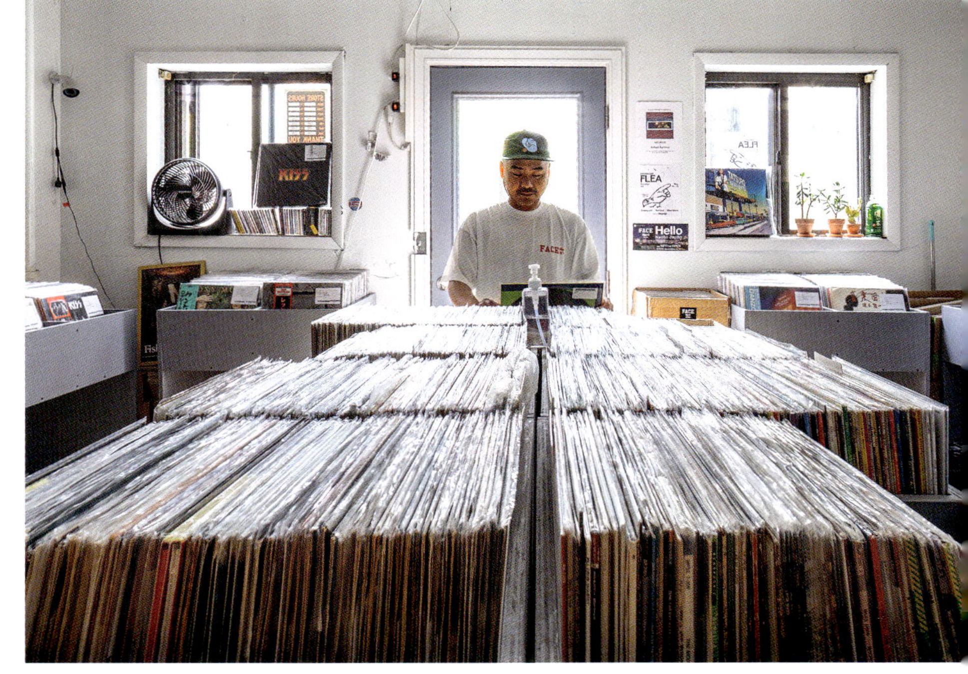

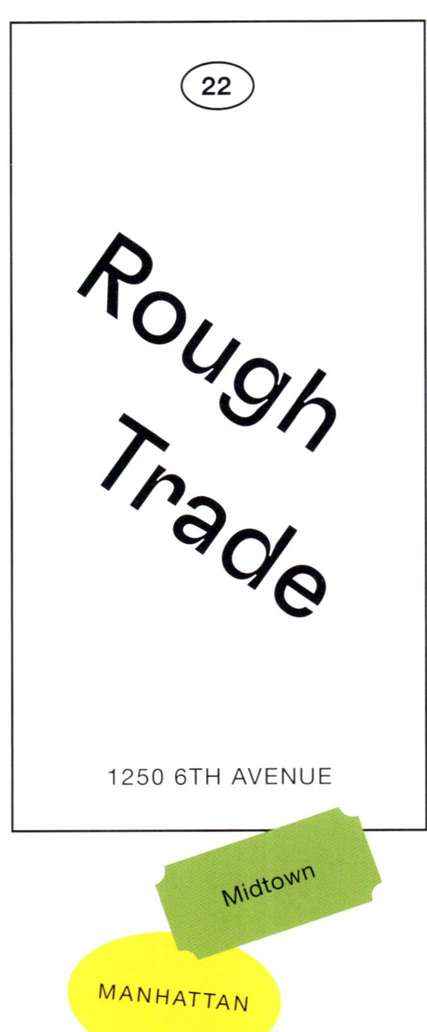

EVEN IF 30 ROCKEFELLER PLAZA'S famous statue of a bronze Atlas shouldering the weight of the world relays independence, its neighboring high rises don't quite scream counterculture. But as Rough Trade co-owner Stephen Godfroy explains, that's exactly what made it a perfect spot to relocate to after leaving a nearly ten-year-old Brooklyn location mid-pandemic.

Before Rough Trade developed into the indie label behind Arcade Fire, the Raincoats, ANOHNI, and more, it was a record store in West London. Founded by Geoff Travis in 1976, the initial location reached great heights on the burly shoulders of the city's burgeoning punk scene. It drew inspiration from San Francisco's City Lights, an independent bookstore, publisher, and nonprofit that treated its operation as a meeting place and marketplace in equal measure. Rough Trade would become, as Godfroy explains, "the epicenter for the DIY music movement" in the British capitol, developing a format that buoyed a leap across the pond in 2013 to Williamsburg. Hurricane Sandy delayed the original opening, but it was a lease agreement change that later confirmed the need for a move to Manhattan. (Rough Trade's West London location still stands today, alongside a flagship East London shop and a central London location, with a used-only shop nearby.)

Opened in June 2021, Rough Trade's current Midtown spot maintains its original gathering-minded intentions, hosting album signings, listening parties, live performances, and more—events that draw crowds as impassioned as the wide-eyed ones that congregate around Broadway stage doors just a few blocks away. "If music is my religion," begins a quote from famed British DJ Don Letts displayed over the shop's gold-rimmed entryway, "then Rough Trade is my church."

Godfroy, too, sees the store as "a place of worship," and treats his work as seriously as any servant of a higher power might. "It's a privilege, a joy, something that never grows old, an evergreen reward that inspires hope and faith in humanity," he says of his role as Rough Trade's head of US business. The hub of the label that launched the Strokes is nothing to joke about in New York, and although Godfroy's first record purchase at nine years old—Survivor's *Eye of the Tiger*—might not have been "indie," he wised up quickly to the label first established during his toddling years. "Prior to [working at] Rough Trade," he shares, "all of my money was spent at Rough Trade."

Hallowed history aside, the aesthetic at the store is less cathedral fresco and more community church bulletin—a pillar at the center of the sales floor encourages, "Got A Band? Leave Your Band Sticker." In addition to a genre-neutral catalog from the label's roster past and present (Rough Trade stocks everything, save straight classical), the shop regularly maintains a selection of around one-thousand used records. A Greenpoint-based fulfillment warehouse helps deliver the roughly forty-five thousand other titles consistently available through its online store and Discogs page.

Rough Trade caters regularly to big-name clients, many of whom receive weekly inventory lists. But discretion and equal treatment have remained at the business's core, no matter how much its profile has grown. The closest it comes to a red carpet is a photobooth, the source of a neighboring wall's neat cluster of black-and-white images depicting the many musicians who've come through the doors, from Helado Negro to Charli xcx.

"A sense of place in time and space is marked by the actual, the physical," Godfroy shares. "A vinyl record is the ultimate music document...one that importantly can be owned, bequeathed, [passed] down from generation to generation." By the looks of the customers lining up around the block for album signings to the overlapping decal stickers touting what might be the next big thing, Rough Trade doesn't need to worry about longevity. Its commitment to generational education and preservation has more than earned it its spot on the ground floor of one of Manhattan's most globally recognizable landmark sites.

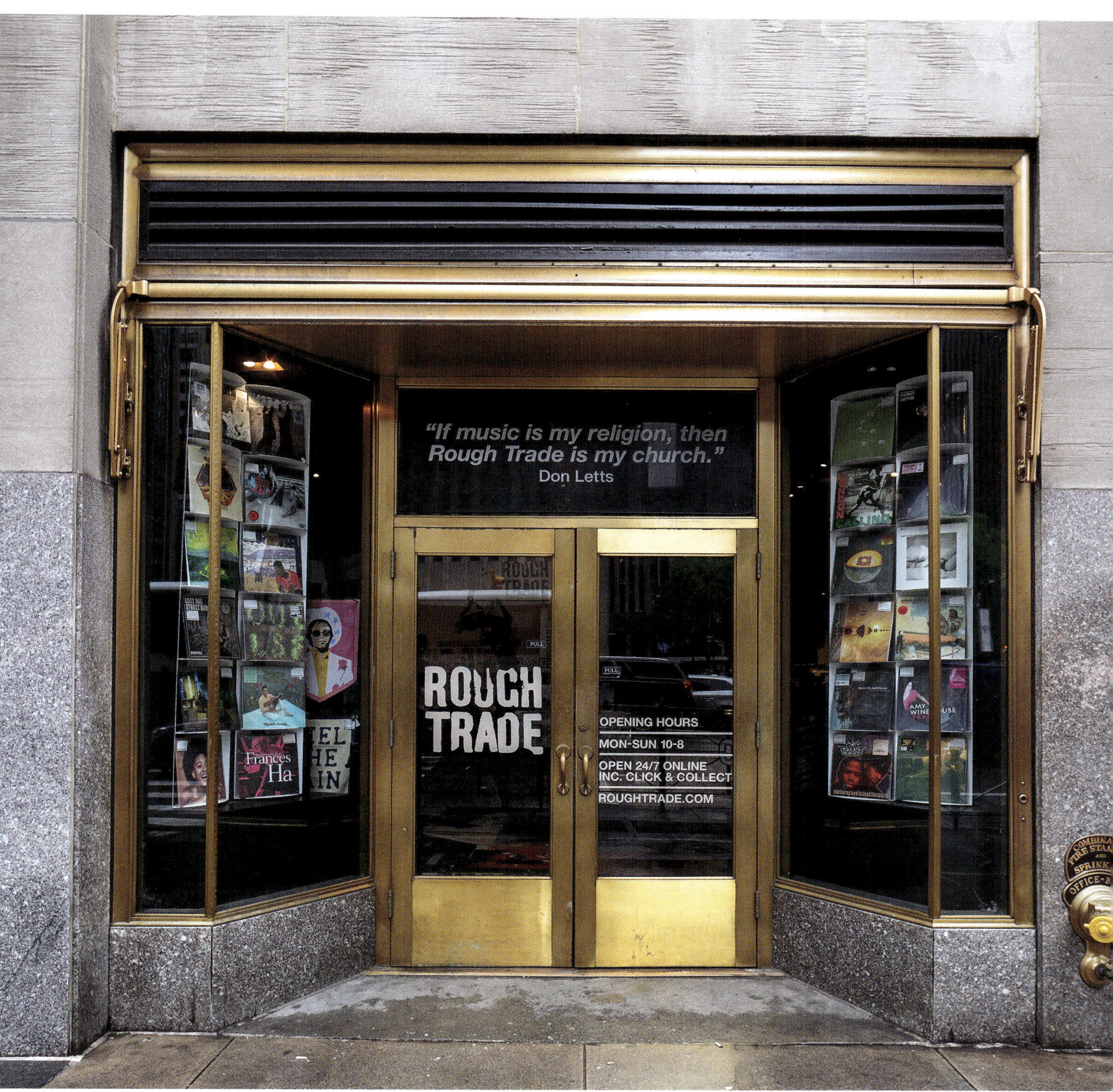

ABOVE Rough Trade opened in 2021 within the Rockefeller Center complex. The shop is large and stocks a vast inventory of both new and used vinyl records, as well as books and music merchandise. Due to its unique location, it often holds concerts on the plaza and even inside the famed Rainbow Room.

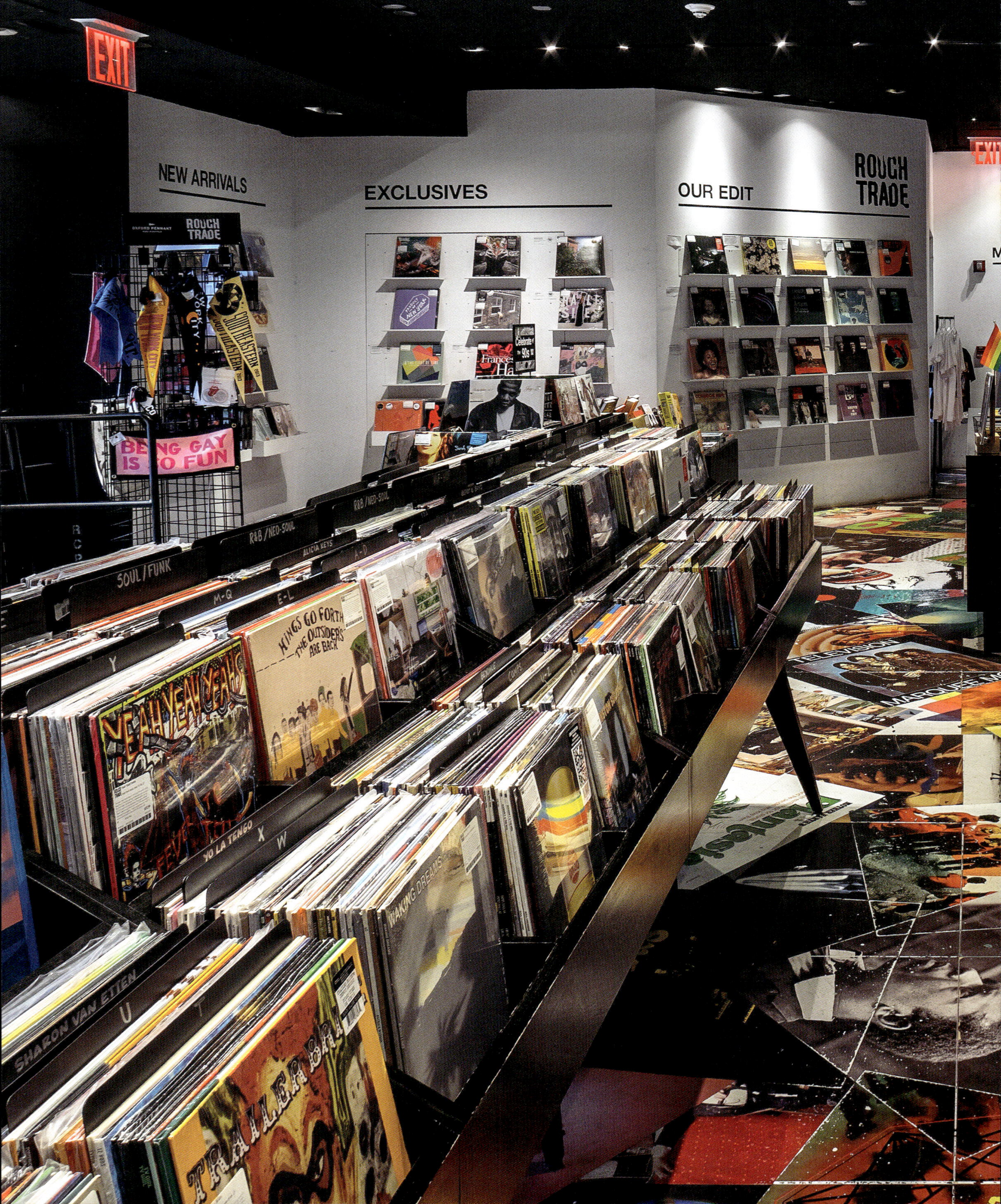
EXIT
NEW ARRIVALS
EXCLUSIVES
OUR EDIT
ROUGH TRADE
BEING GAY IS SO FUN
R&B/NEO-SOUL
SOUL/FUNK
YEAH YEAH YEAHS
KINGS GO FORTH
THE OUTSIDERS ARE BACK
YO LA TENGO
SHARON VAN ETTEN
WAKING DREAMS
TELEVISION
MARQUEE MOON

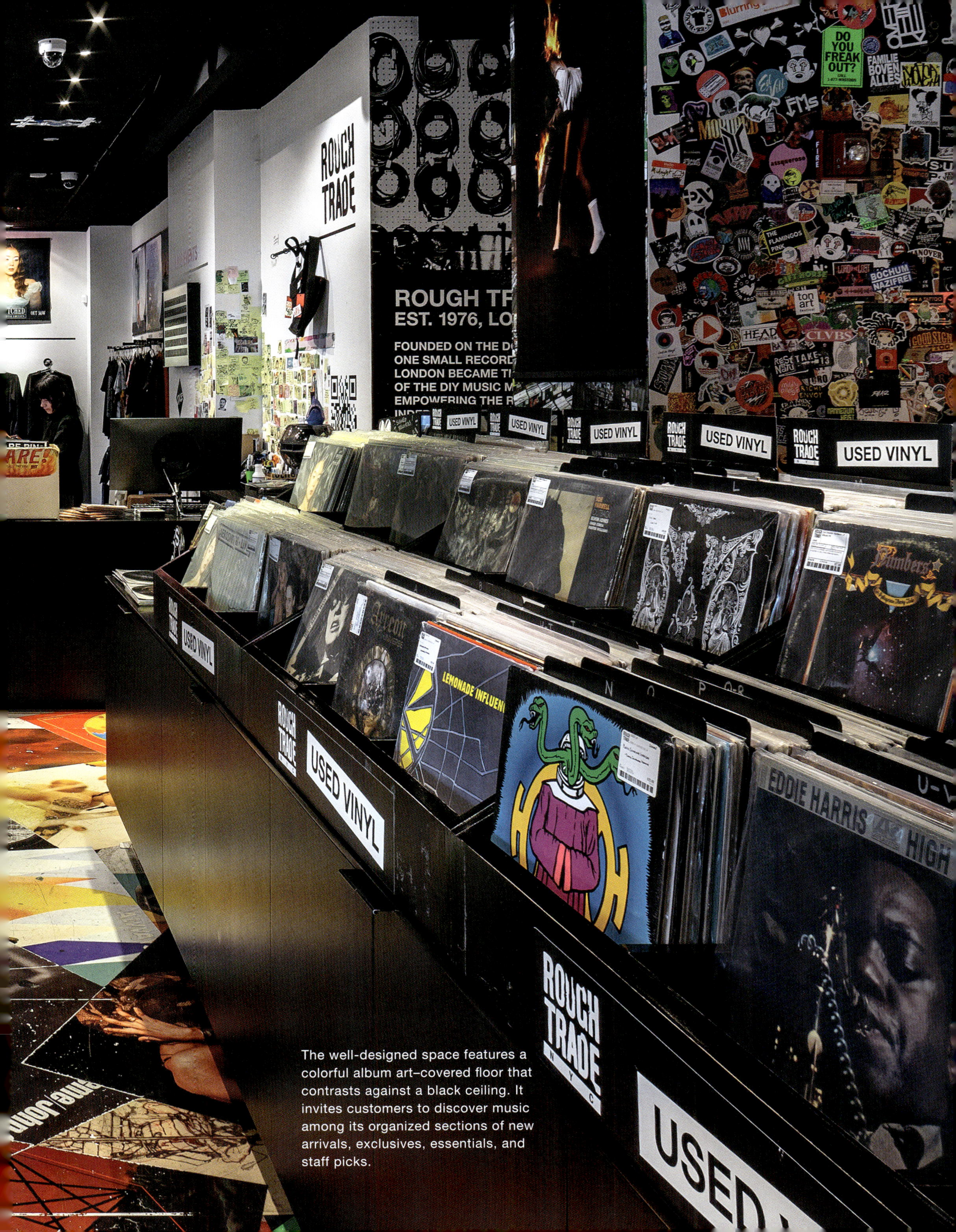

The well-designed space features a colorful album art–covered floor that contrasts against a black ceiling. It invites customers to discover music among its organized sections of new arrivals, exclusives, essentials, and staff picks.

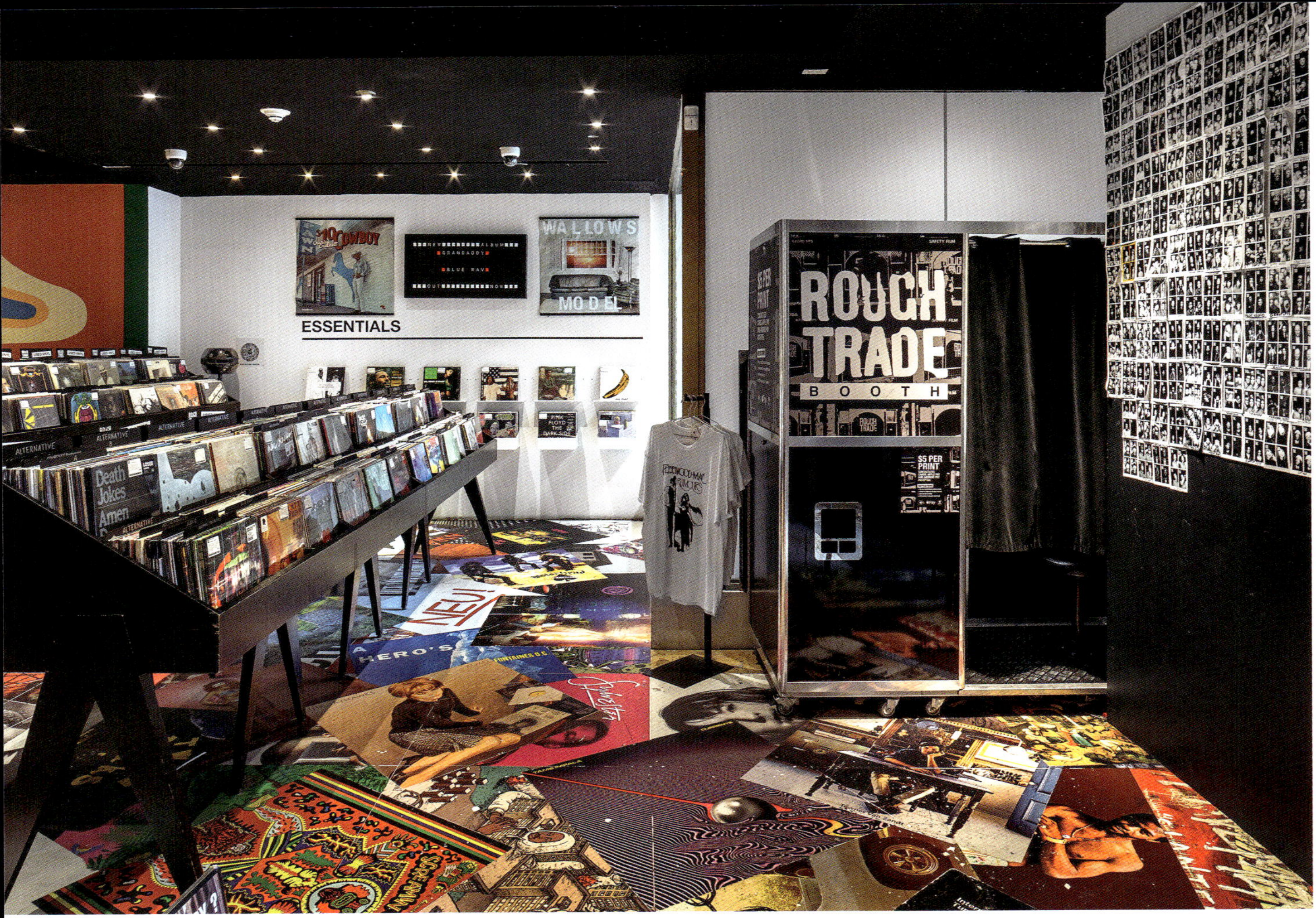

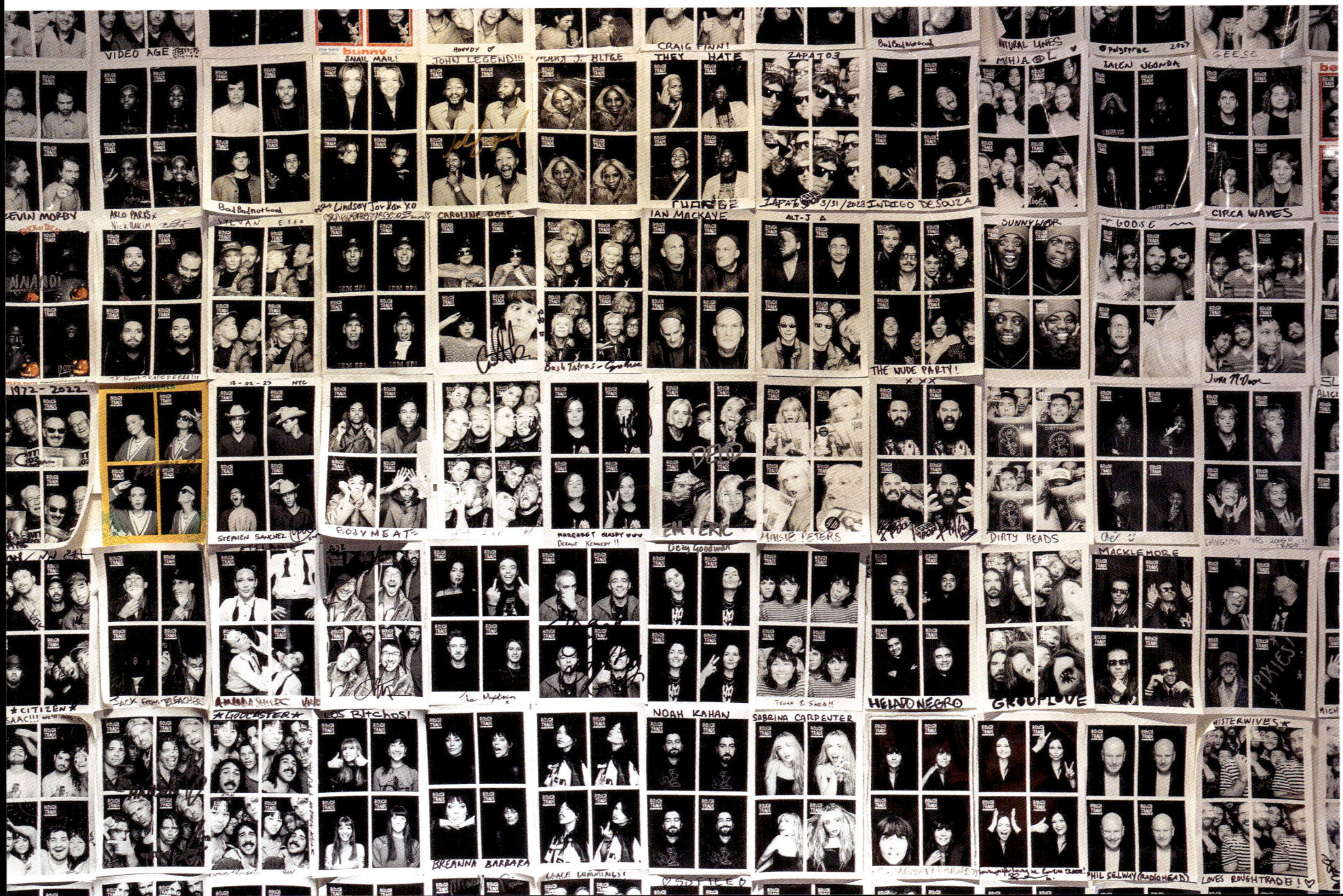

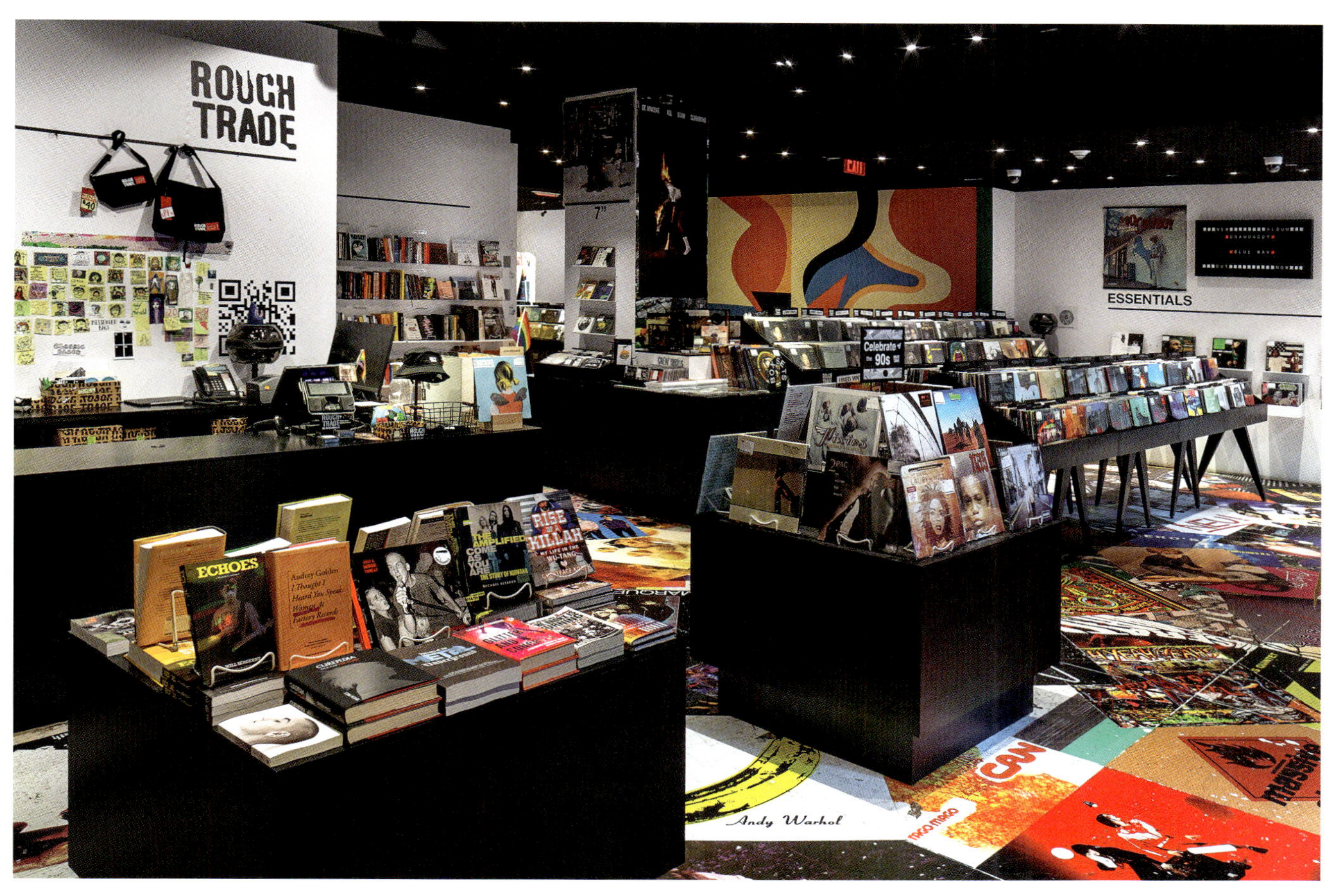

OPPOSITE BOTTOM A black-and-white photo display shows many of the musicians who have done in-store signing events and concerts at Rough Trade, including John Legend, Mary J. Blige, Macklemore, and Sabrina Carpenter.

ABOVE Signage designed to mimic vintage analog train station arrival and departure boards, found throughout the store, alert browsers to new albums. Custom Post-it notes drawn by the staff further help shoppers find new artists and music selections currently playing in-store.

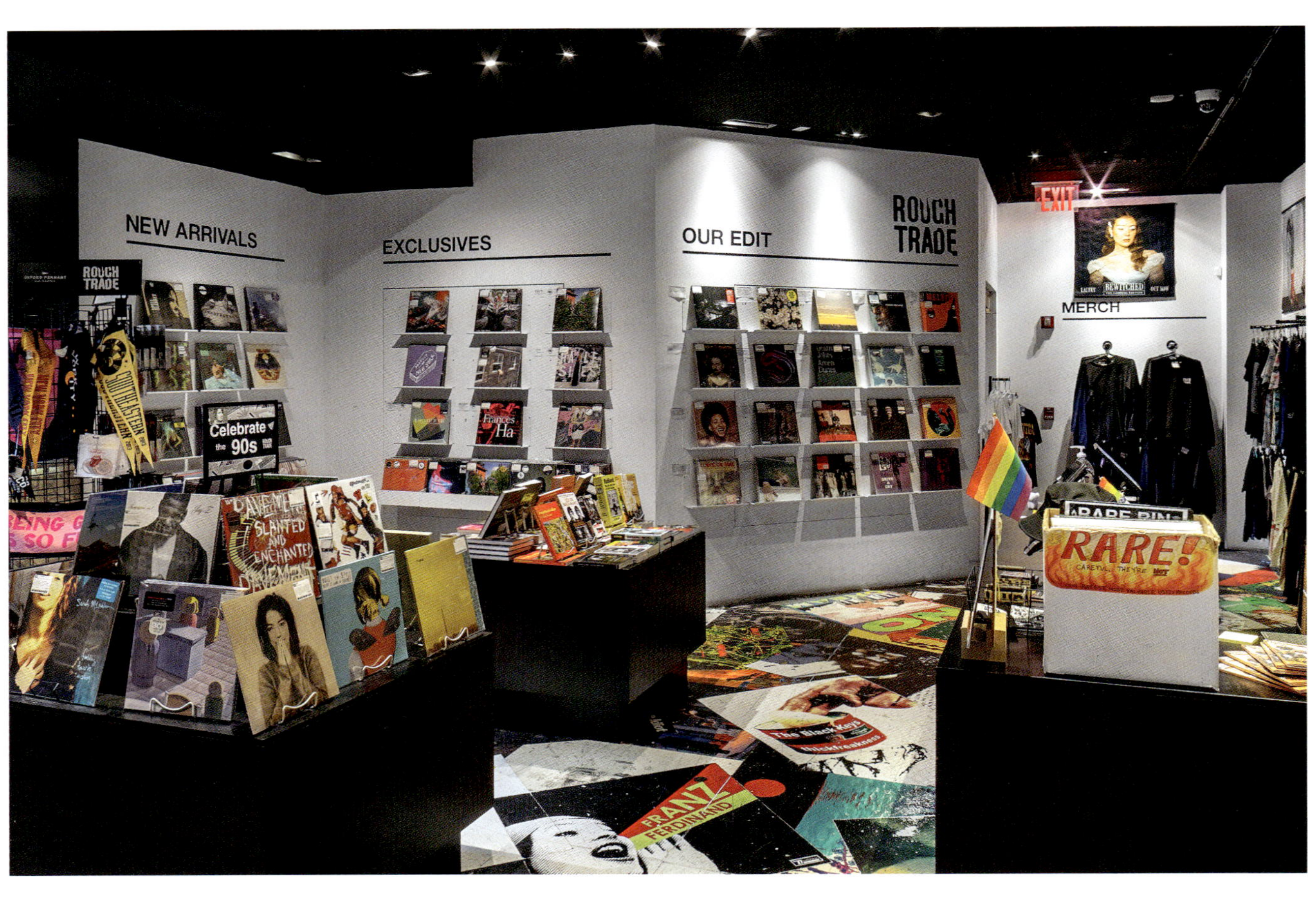

OPPOSITE TOP Rough Trade fosters a sense of community among independent record labels and emerging artists. It even devotes a pillar in the middle of the shop where musicians can "Stick 'Em Up! Got a Band? Leave Your Band Sticker."

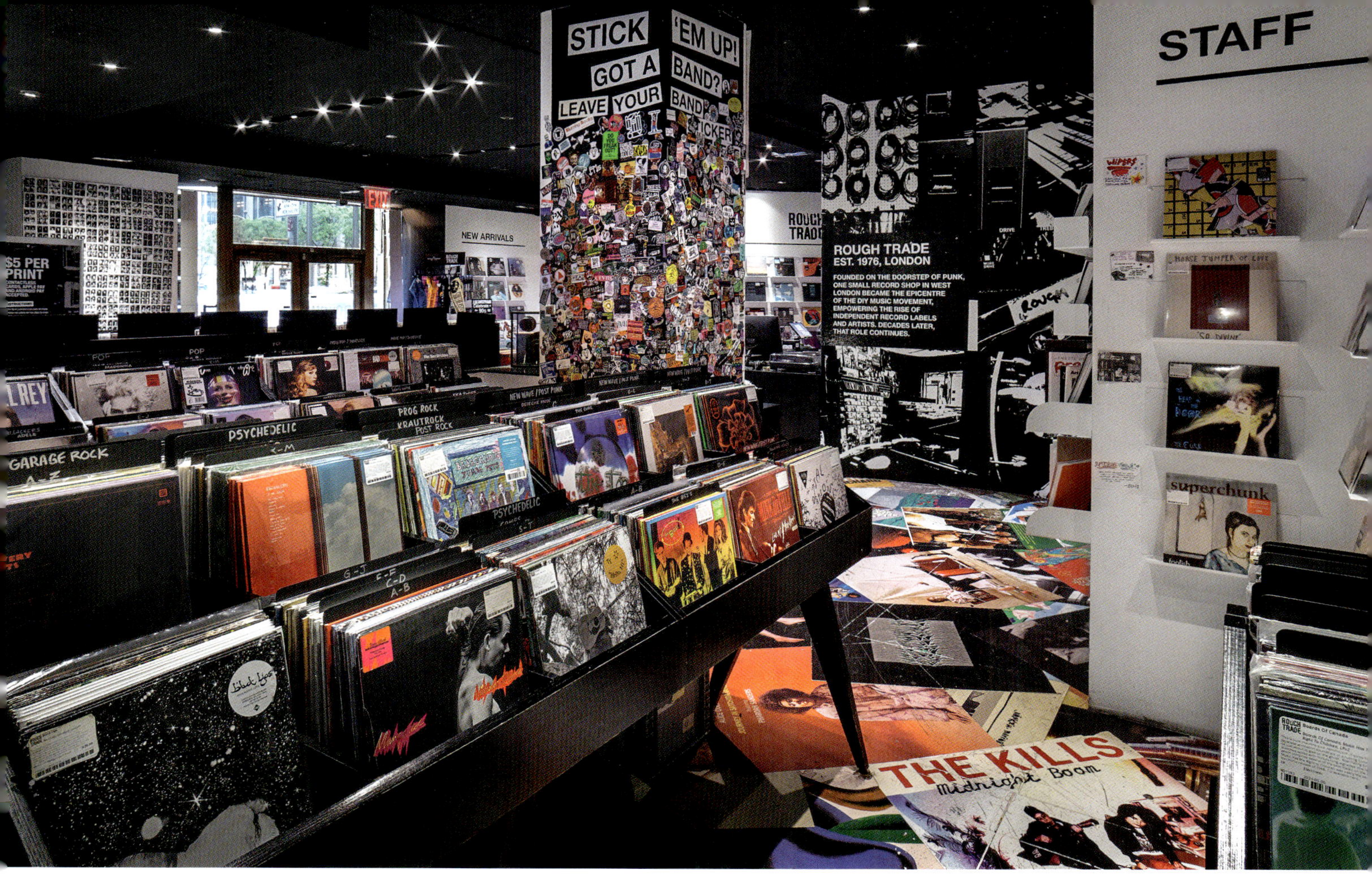

STICK 'EM UP!
GOT A BAND?
LEAVE YOUR BAND STICKER
STAFF
ROUGH TRADE
EST. 1976, LONDON
FOUNDED ON THE DOORSTEP OF PUNK, ONE SMALL RECORD SHOP IN WEST LONDON BECAME THE EPICENTRE OF THE DIY MUSIC MOVEMENT, EMPOWERING THE RISE OF INDEPENDENT RECORD LABELS AND ARTISTS. DECADES LATER, THAT ROLE CONTINUES.
NEW ARRIVALS
PSYCHEDELIC
GARAGE ROCK
PROG ROCK
KRAUTROCK
POST ROCK
THE KILLS
Midnight Boom
superchunk

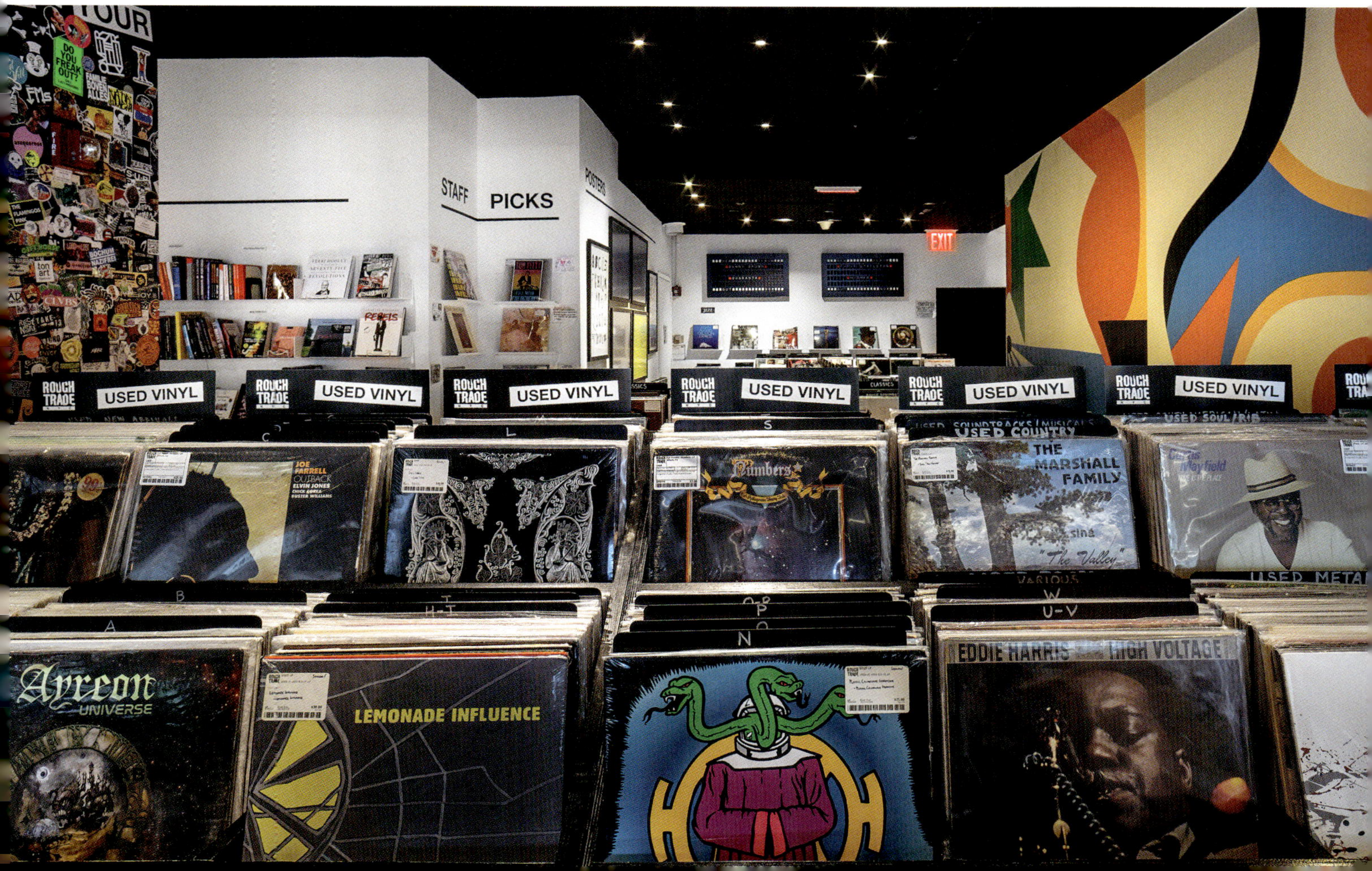

STAFF PICKS
POSTERS
EXIT
ROUGH TRADE
USED VINYL
USED COUNTRY
THE MARSHALL FAMILY
Numbers
Ayreon
UNIVERSE
LEMONADE INFLUENCE
EDDIE HARRIS
HIGH VOLTAGE

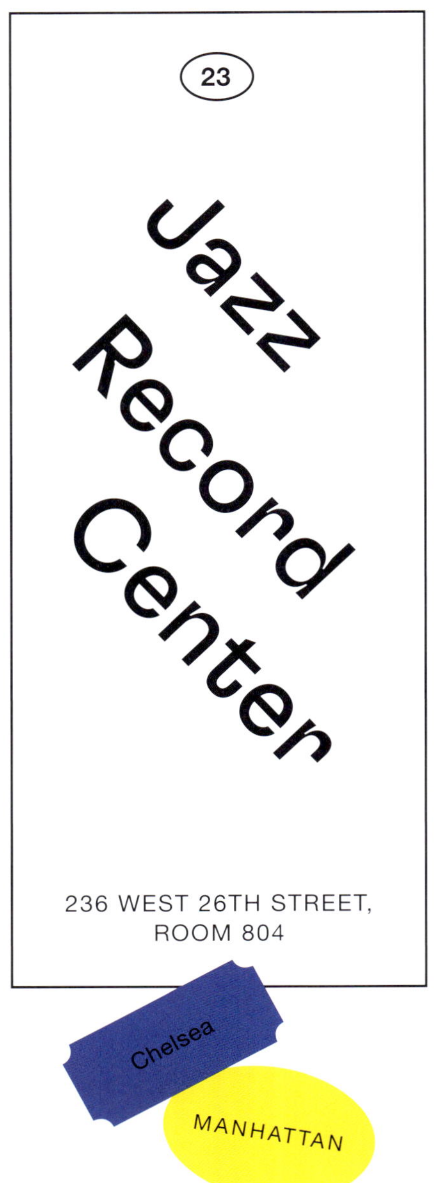

"HOW CAN I MAKE YOUR DAY BETTER?" Fred Cohen says as he answers the desk phone from Manhattan's Jazz Record Center. On the other end of the line, a caller is hoping to pick the veteran store owner's brain on a few archival concerts, inquiring about his personal top ten. Calls like this come often for Cohen after over four decades behind the counter. But few other collectors in the city can provide jazz lovers with the kind of comprehensive crash course and sense of camaraderie as him—as long as they're willing to look eight floors up to find it.

Passion over profit has always been the motto at Jazz Record Center, which Cohen has run since 1983. Tucked away in the unassuming Room 804 of its Chelsea building, the store doesn't cater so much to curious passersby as to students of culture, ready to begin or expand their jazz education in one of the genre's capitals. Early-genre avant-garde works from Baby Dodds and Red Allen have as much of a place on Cohen's shelves as major hits from Duke Ellington and Louis Armstrong, for example. "From day one, my focus was to represent all jazz," he says, "even stuff that doesn't sell." He operates the store single-handedly, save for some weekend help, and looks forward to playfully countering people who stop in with a strict list of essential albums. He urges them instead to look beyond digging creds toward the real beauty of collecting: discovering the music they *actually* like.

Raised by a chorus-member mother alongside a pianist sister in Boston, Cohen wasn't lacking for musicality in the home. But it was at eleven or twelve when he overheard composer Charles Mingus playing from the sitting room at a friend's house that he was hooked. (Despite Jazz Record Center's intentionally wide berth, Cohen's personal collection contains exclusively Mingus's music.) He began his career as a rehab counselor, but after eleven years, burnout set in; he didn't know exactly what came next. Then, the owner of Jolly Roger, a record shop on Columbus Avenue, called with a proposal: she needed a lease takeover. She had mainly traded in classical, which didn't interest Cohen—but his inner child, forever transfixed by the tones of Mingus's stand-up bass, had a lightbulb moment. "Important, well-known experts and writers in jazz that I asked about opening a store at that time—all of them said I was stupid," Cohen recalls. Yet he gave himself a year to get his bearings anyhow, building up a collection of vinyl, CDs, concert films, biographies, and other ephemera.

After originally opening Jazz Record Center in a 12th Street walk-up in 1983, Cohen moved to the mixed-use co-op on West 26th Street (where the business is still located today) in 1992. Some of his most frequent regulars stop in every day. Plenty of the visitors he buzzes up into the space are looking for guidance or recommendations, but he also values the peaceful, private browsing experience his shop can offer. It's part of why he doesn't ever plan to descend to a street-level location.

An authorized Blue Note dealer, Cohen has a unique relationship with the pioneering New York jazz label. He literally wrote the book on buying Blue Note vinyl, a detailed and user-friendly guide to identifying different pressings that he still carries at the store. But many other Jazz Record Center disciples have found their way to Cohen through his long-running vinyl auctions, which regularly draw bids in the thousands of dollars for treasures like rare Hank Mobley and Charlie Parker pressings.

Cohen's collection may hold world renown, but after so many years in business, his favorite moments at Jazz Record Center are still the ones that teach him something new. He remembers fondly the customer who brought in a copy of Duke Ellington's *Masterpieces*, turning Cohen from a skeptic to a believer. He hopes to pass some of that wisdom on to the younger faces he now sees frequenting the shop: that the "good taste" one holds to be self-evident should always be subject to change. "The ones that buy records just to put on the shelf," Cohen explains, "you've got to scratch them a little bit."

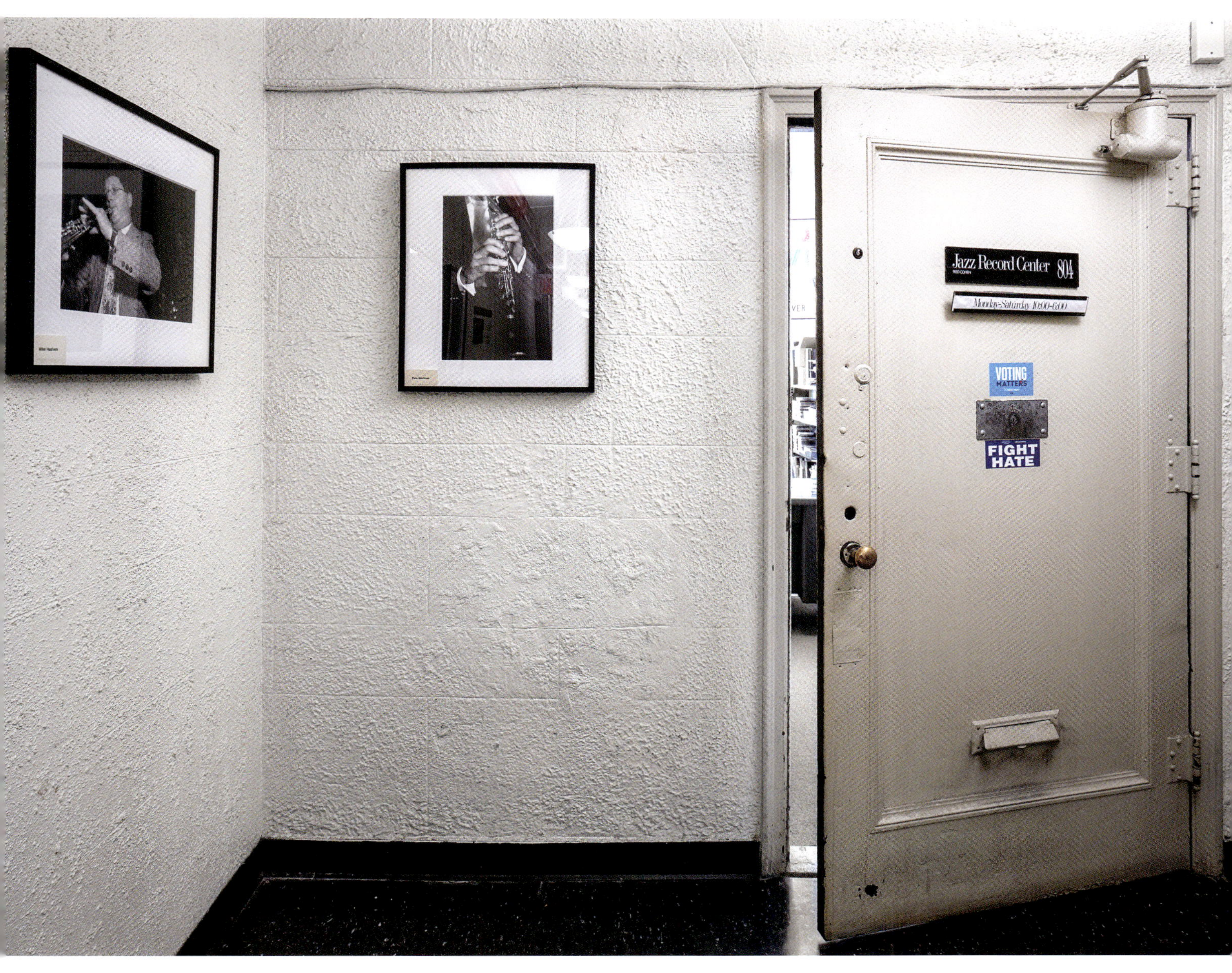

ABOVE Despite its out-of-the-way location on the eighth floor of a commercial building in Chelsea with no exterior signage, Jazz Record Center has attracted devoted fans of the genre since 1983. It carries a wide offering of rare and reissued jazz LPs, including a large selection of Blue Note records as well as CDs, DVDs, books, posters, magazines, and ephemera.

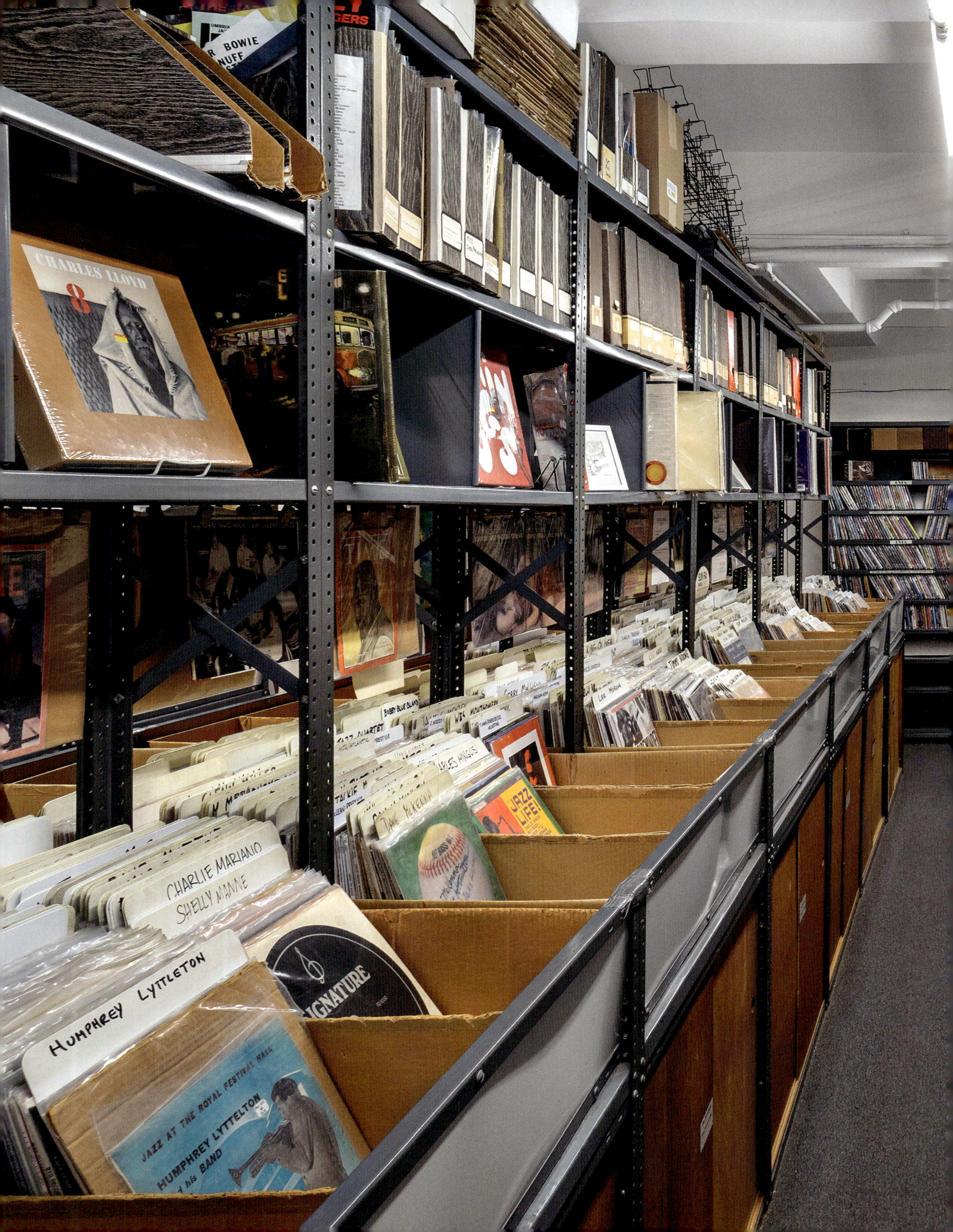
CHARLES LLOYD
8
CHARLES MINGUS
JAZZ LIFE!
CHARLIE MARIANO
SHELLY MANNE
HUMPHREY LYTTLETON
SIGNATURE
JAZZ AT THE ROYAL FESTIVAL HALL
HUMPHREY LYTTELTON
and his BAND

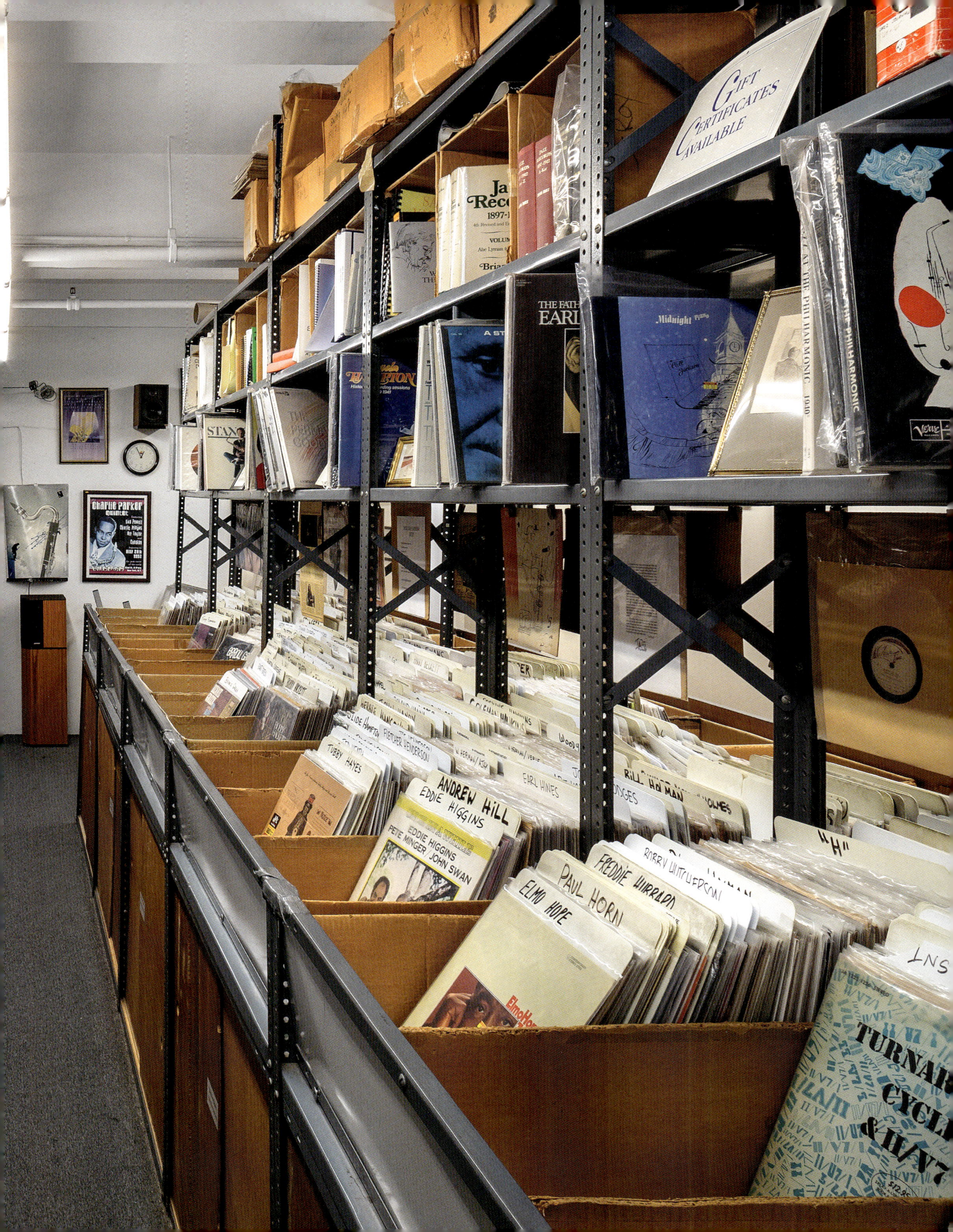
GIFT CERTIFICATES AVAILABLE
Charlie Parker
Midnight
EARL HINES
TUBBY HAYES
FLETCHER HENDERSON
ANDREW HILL
EDDIE HIGGINS
EDDIE HIGGINS
PETE MINGER JOHN SWAN
ELMO HOPE
PAUL HORN
FREDDIE HUBBARD
BOBBY HUTCHERSON
"H"
Verve

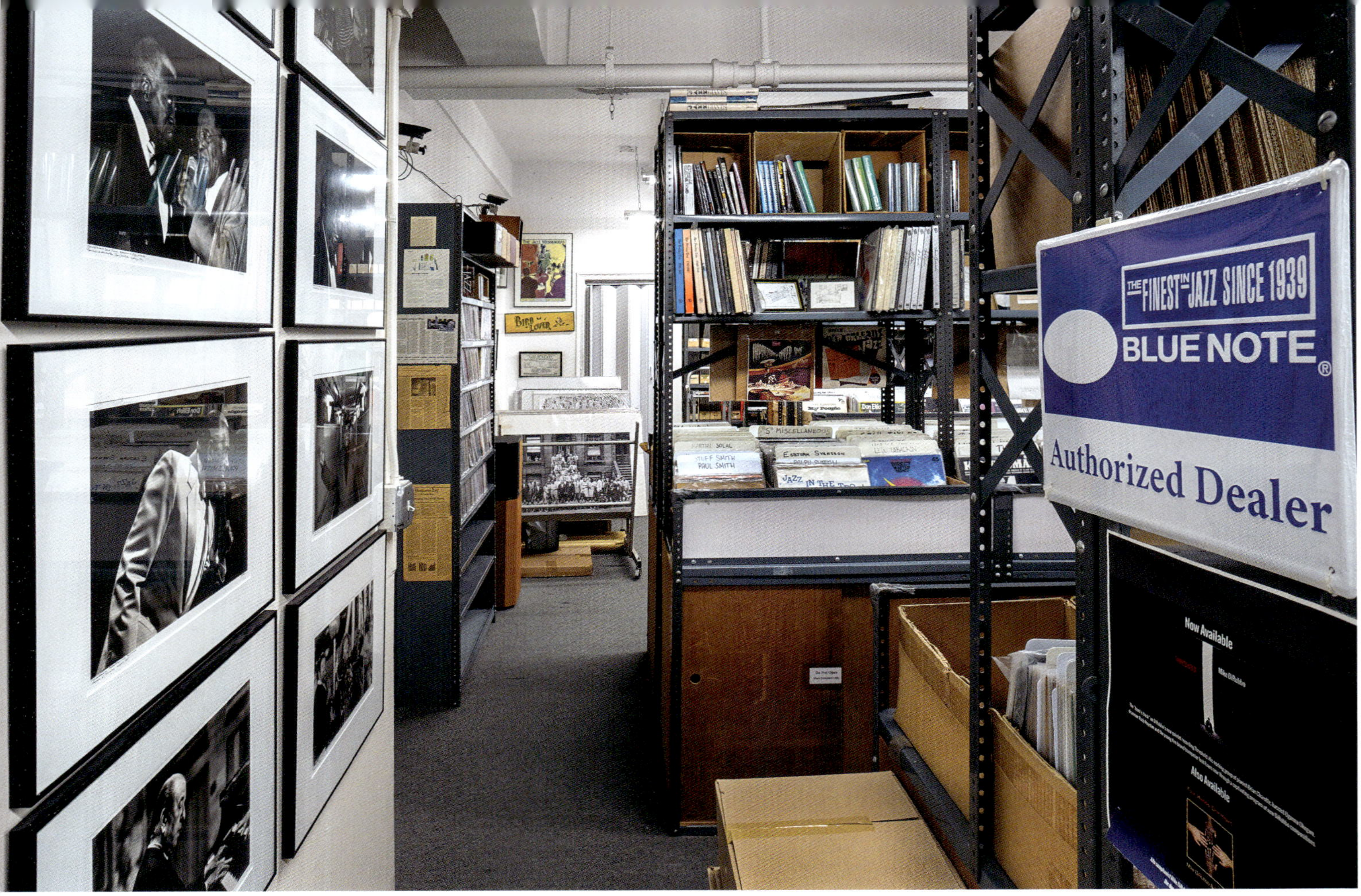

THE FINEST IN JAZZ SINCE 1939
BLUE NOTE
Authorized Dealer
RECORDS

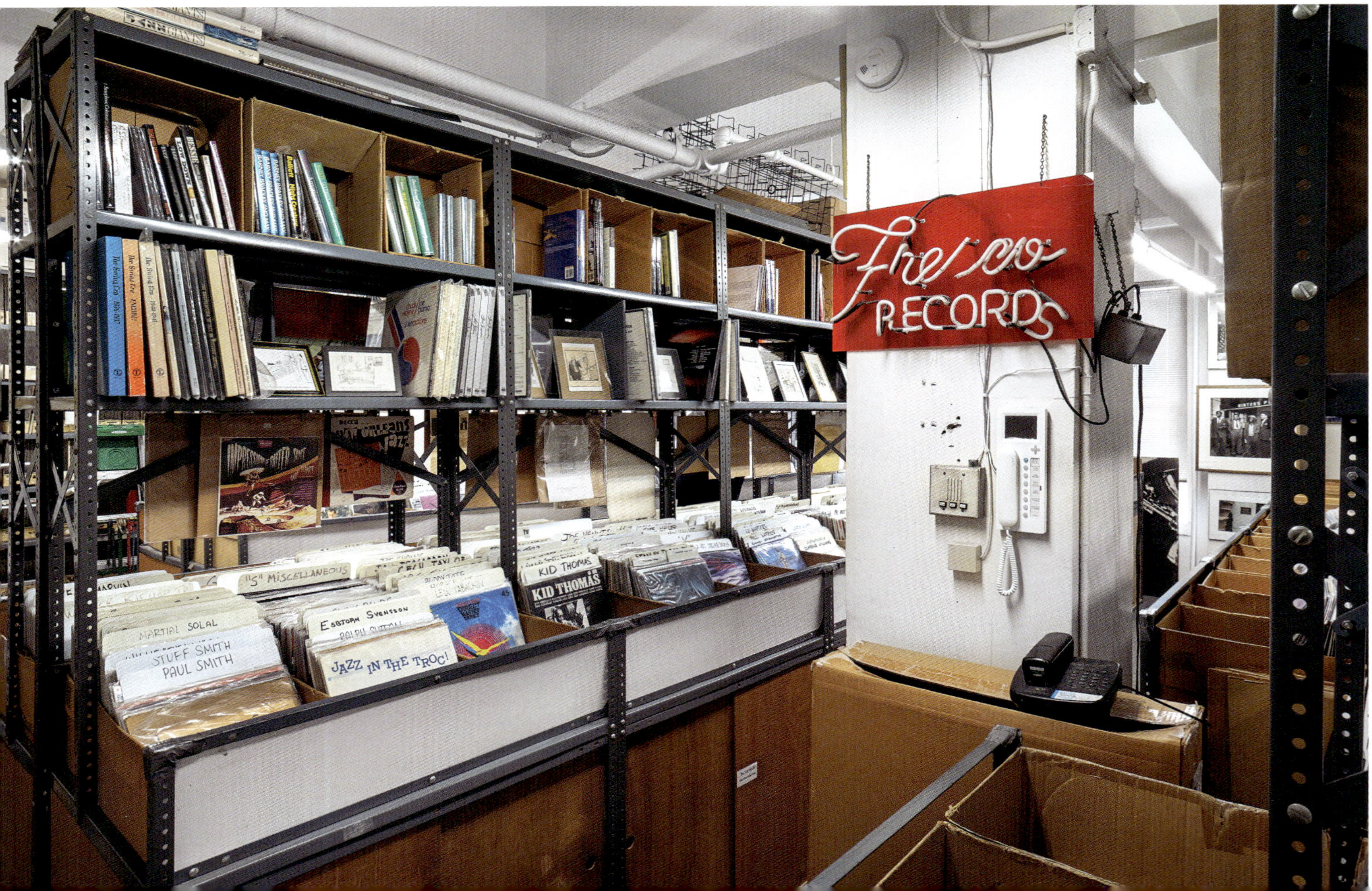

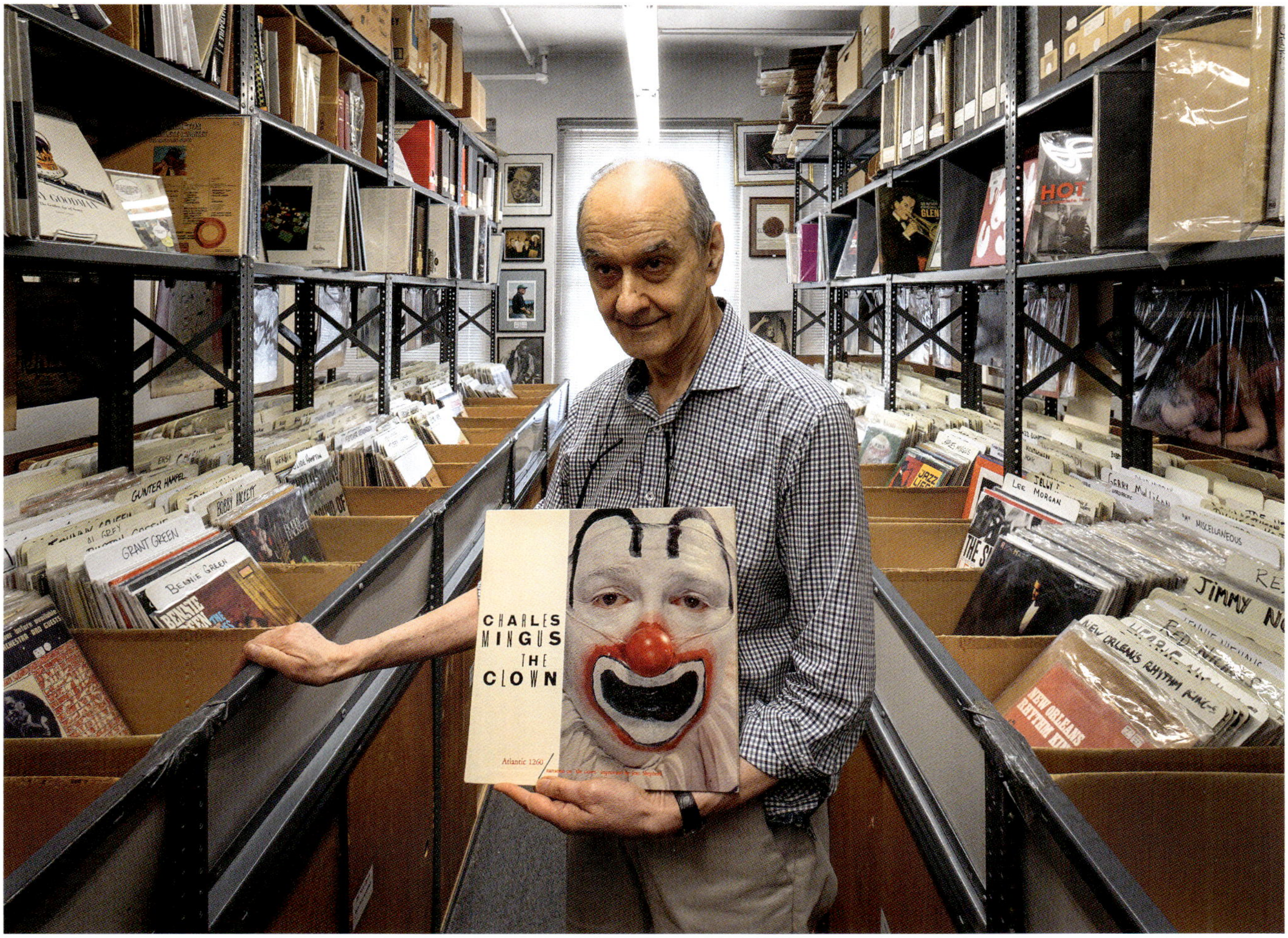

OPPOSITE BOTTOM Thousands of vinyl records are meticulously organized in bins that sit on industrial metal shelving with handwritten dividers listing the artist names.

ABOVE Owner Fred Cohen holds one of his most treasured albums from his personal vault, a rare copy of Charles Mingus's *The Clown.*

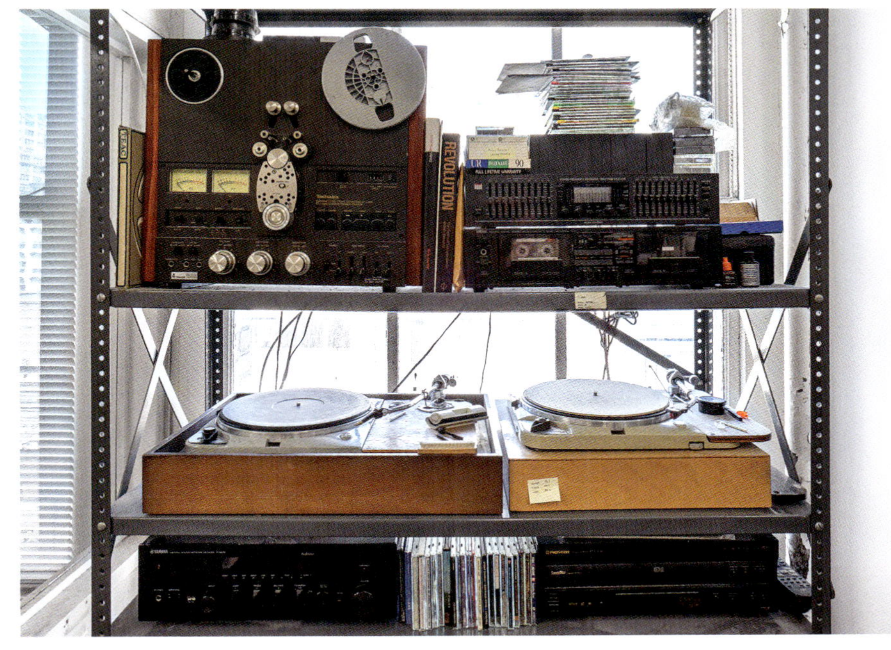

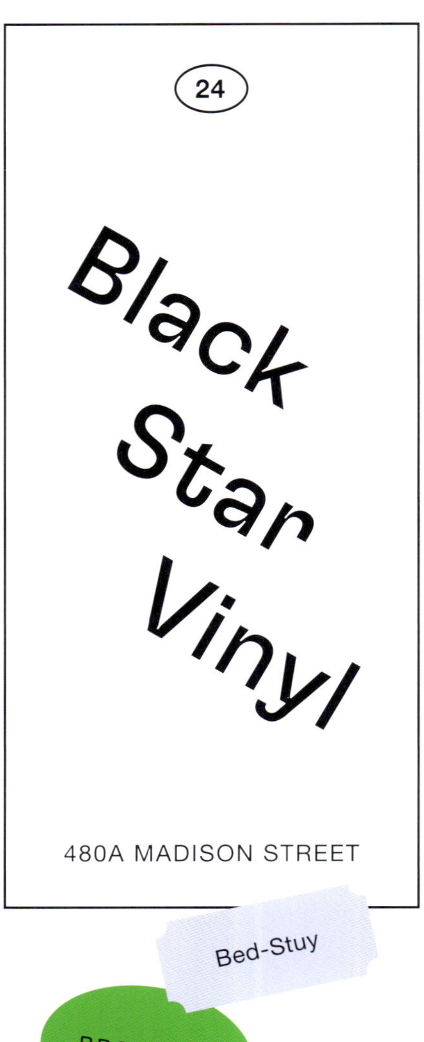

WHEN MARTIN BREWER AND SONYA FARRELL founded the record and antique shop Halsey & Lewis in 2017, they made sure it was easy to spot by putting a signature sunshine-colored bench out front. For five years, the yellow beacon marked a well-loved meeting place in Bed-Stuy—but when they learned their landlord had other plans for the building in 2021, they had less than a week to leave it behind. Brooklyn's ongoing gentrification had finally caught up to the small, Black-owned business—but a fundraiser spearheaded by progressive city councilman Chi Ossé, social media personality New York Nico, and countless area donors provided an escape route.

Raising $35,000 in just a few days, Brewer and Farrell's community rallied to fund their relocation to 480A Madison Street, just off Marcus Garvey Boulevard. To celebrate a new era next to the pioneering Jamaican activist's eponymous roadway, Halsey & Lewis became Black Star Vinyl—a tribute to Garvey's Prohibition-era shipping company, Black Star Line. But Black Star had already been well on its way to honoring Garvey's legacy, by organizing the shop around the principles of mutual aid. "I think everybody adds to it," Brewer told CBS in 2022. "If you need something, I can help you...and vice versa."

In turn, Black Star is just one arm of Brewer and Farrell's work promoting health, happiness, and connection in Brooklyn's Black community. At the height of the Covid-19 pandemic (when they were still operating as Halsey & Lewis), the pair introduced a #ShareTheHealth campaign, organizing friends and store regulars to donate masks, sanitary items, and other basic resources to local homeless shelters. Together, they also run the nonprofit Let's Get on the Bus, which sponsors and organizes free trips for school-age children to the National Museum of African American History and Culture in Washington, DC.

When choosing Black Star's new location in 2022, Brewer paid special attention to the neighboring Raymond Bush Playground and Herbert Von King Park, two popular outdoor gathering spaces he hoped would help his shop thrive. Born in Philadelphia in the 1970s, Brewer grew up listening to the local radio station WDAS Philadelphia, of which civil rights leader Andrew Young once said, "[N]o station in America...worked harder, longer, and with more dedication for Black people." "They promoted community and activism," Brewer told the retailer West Elm's culture blog in 2022, "and what they did then is what I want to do now."

Like a tapestry of Brewer's East Coast childhood, Black Star's music collection spans jazz, soul, funk, rock, and hip-hop, with especially comprehensive offerings from the '70s and '80s—and a clear affinity for Nina Simone. But the self-described "sundries" store is also stocked with candles, crystals, plants, lamps, and La Colombe coffee. One white wall, lined with shelves of palo santo and sage, disappears behind a patchwork of Polaroids featuring Black Star customers smiling brightly, LPs or lattes in hand.

With every new Polaroid added to the wall, Black Star continues to build an environment as warm and inviting as that original yellow bench. It's no surprise, then, that an homage to its first location has a prominent place behind the shop's doors. Hanging on a wall flanked by Prince and J Dilla box sets, the original Halsey & Lewis sign watches over the sales floor, a reminder of the Bed-Stuy corner where it all began.

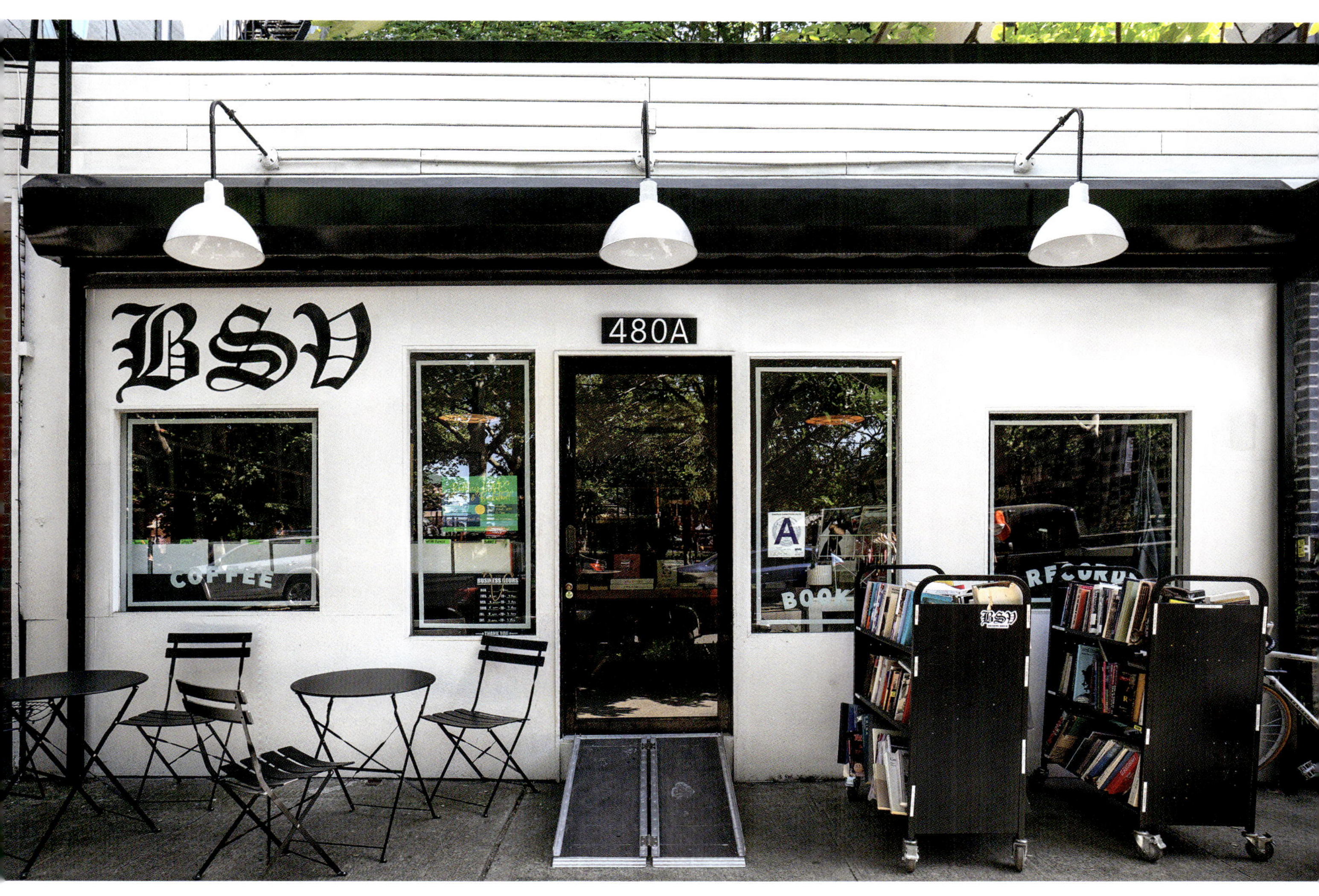

ABOVE Black Star Vinyl is located on a tree-lined street in Bed-Stuy, directly across from a busy playground with basketball and handball courts. It not only carries a curated selection of new and affordable used vinyl records, it also sells books, candles, incense, and vintage clothing, along with freshly brewed coffee and pastries.

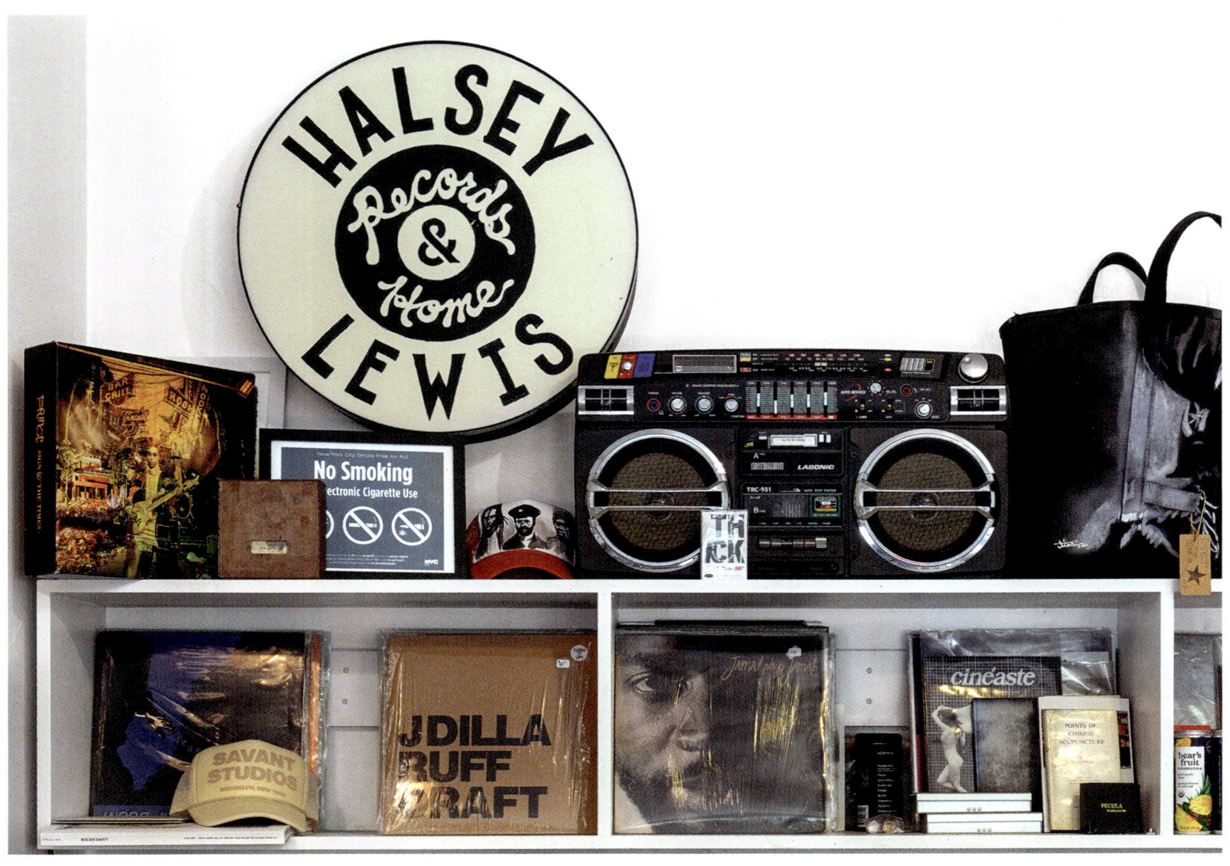
HALSEY
Records
&
Home
LEWIS
No Smoking
J DILLA
RUFF
SAVANT
STUDIOS
cinéaste

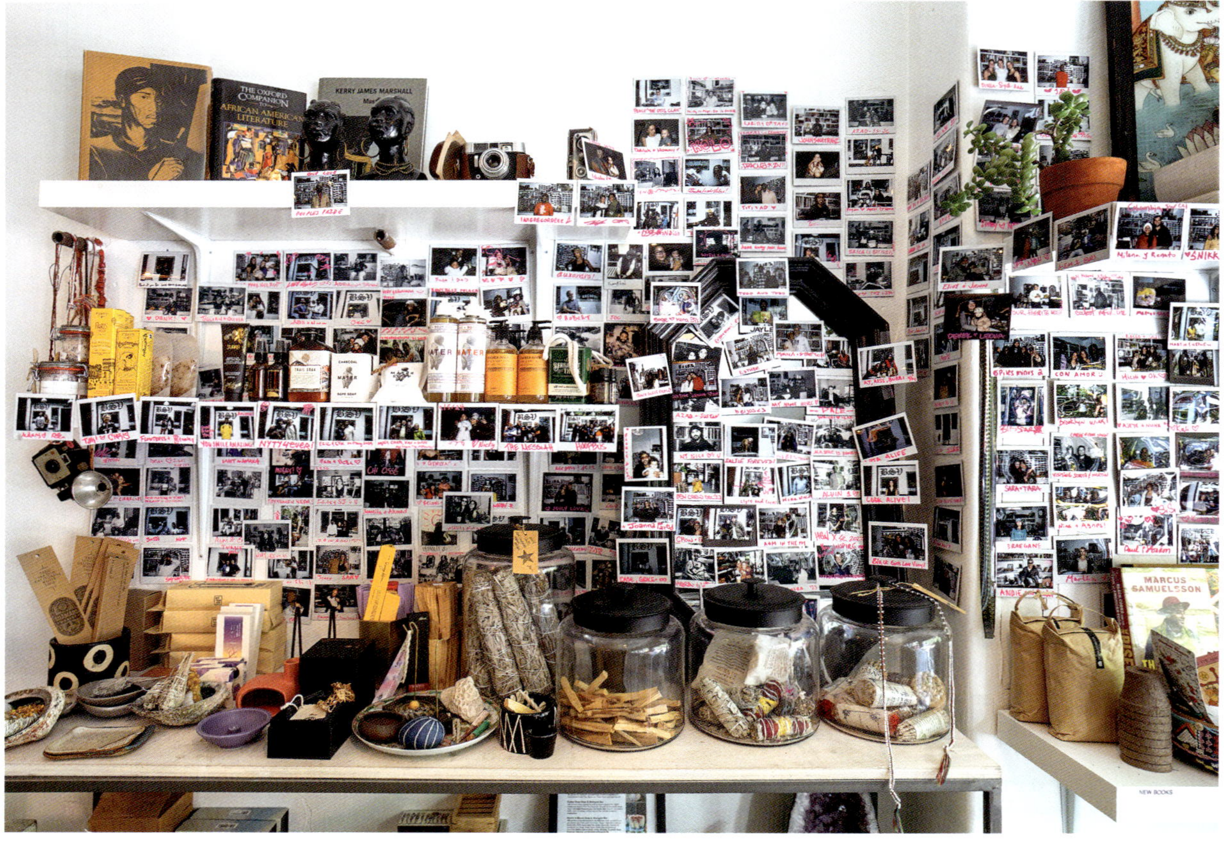
THE OXFORD COMPANION
AFRICAN AMERICAN LITERATURE
KERRY JAMES MARSHALL
MARCUS
SAMUELSSON

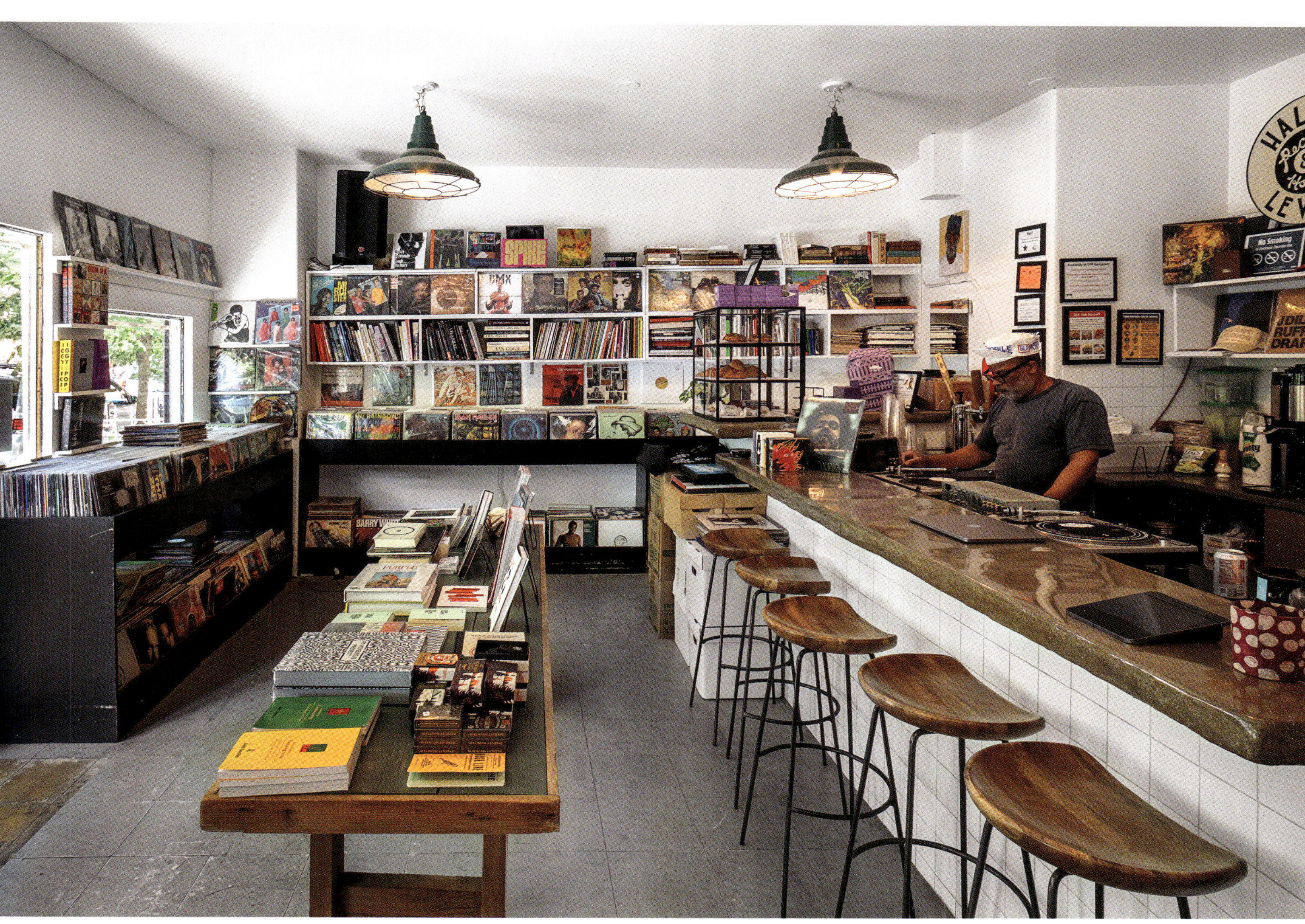

OPPOSITE TOP Displayed on a shelf behind turntables is the shop's original signage from when it was called Halsey & Lewis (due to its former location on Halsey and Lewis Streets).

ABOVE Co-owner Martin Brewer not only personally selects the shop's eclectic vinyl LPs and 45s, he welcomes customers to sit, listen, and talk about music over a cup of coffee.

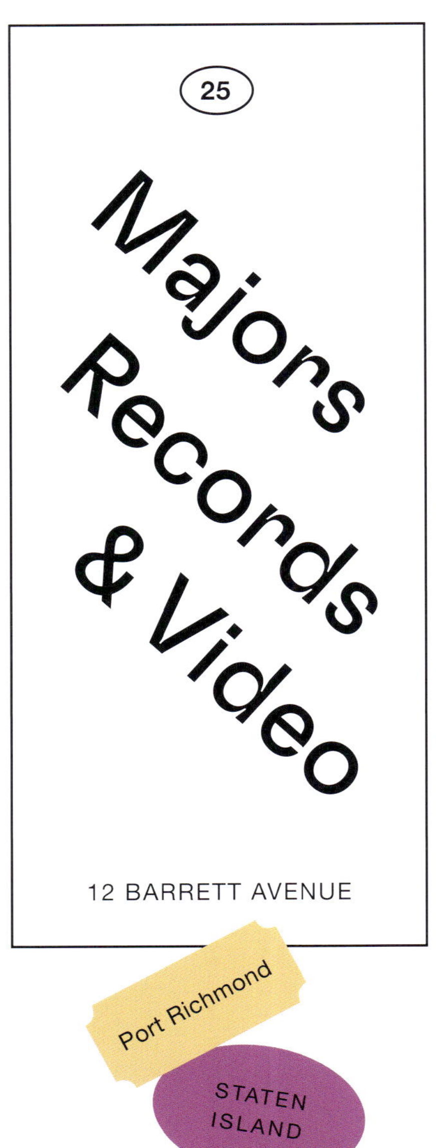

AT THE LAST RECORD STORE ON Staten Island, 99-cent DVDs and Casio boomboxes share the shelves with a generalist's treasure trove of new and used vinyl LPs, 45s, and more. A sandwich board stationed outside the swinging double doors asserts "If You Want It…WE GOT IT! And If You Don't…WE'LL GET IT!" That's no empty promise—fresh records have been coming through the entrance of Majors Records & Video nearly every morning for over five decades.

Located in Port Richmond, Majors isn't just the only remaining vinyl store in the borough—it's also one of the oldest in all of New York City. Co-founder Ed Pavia had initially opened up his first shop in Brooklyn in 1961 before moving to the North Shore, where he got a front row seat to a generation's worth of changes in the physical media market. In 1982 Majors became the first retailer on Staten Island to stock CDs, and in 2008, it participated in the inaugural Record Store Day, an annual drive partially responsible for turning a younger set of music lovers back toward vinyl. (An older generation need not fear, though—Majors still offers a 10 percent veterans' discount.)

It took forty-plus years for New York's creeping rents to pull Pavia away from Majors' original location. In 2014 he reluctantly decided to close the store, lamenting to the *Staten Island Advance* at the time: "Suddenly what was such a vibrant business became a thing of the past, a dying breed." But the interview itself ushered in a realignment of the stars—within days after the story ran, Pavia had a number of viable offers on the table. Majors reopened for good a few months later just half a block away, at 12 Barrett Avenue, with Pavia paying roughly half his previous rent for an even bigger space. Clearly, even the area's landlords understood something Pavia knew well to be true of Majors: "We have a long list of people who want to know where we are going to," he told the *Advance*.

Today, Majors has served over three hundred thousand customers and counting. Among them is one of Staten Island's greatest exports: Wu-Tang Clan, which formed in the early '90s out of a Warren Street apartment just twenty minutes away from the store. Founding producer RZA allegedly grew up shopping at Pavia's emporium—and in 2019, scenes for *An American Saga*, a Hulu series about Wu-Tang's birth, were filmed inside Majors.

The shop's reverence for physical media goes hand in hand with its brick-and-mortar mentality—don't expect this selection to be available online. After all, where else could one find a thousands-strong collection of resurfaced vintage DVDs? Majors even offers repair services, urging customers not to throw away the scratched vinyl, CDs, or DVDs they already own before entrusting it to the store's staff, including current manager (and music producer) Steve Hubbs. The preservation of both Majors' business and the model it relies upon remains the store's biggest motivation for opening every day at 9 a.m. (except Sunday): the conviction that vinyl just has something special to offer. "Independent record stores like Majors are like a casino," a statement on its website reads, "where you put down your money and you always win." In kind, blue bunting hanging at the back of the store spells out "S-H-O-P S-M-A-L-L."

Big-box competitors like Best Buy, Blockbuster, and even Barnes & Noble have come and gone since Majors first opened up, but the Staten Island staple isn't showing any signs of slowing. With over half a century in the business down, the store has eyes and ears trained on the future, inviting customers on its website to "come join us for the next 40 years."

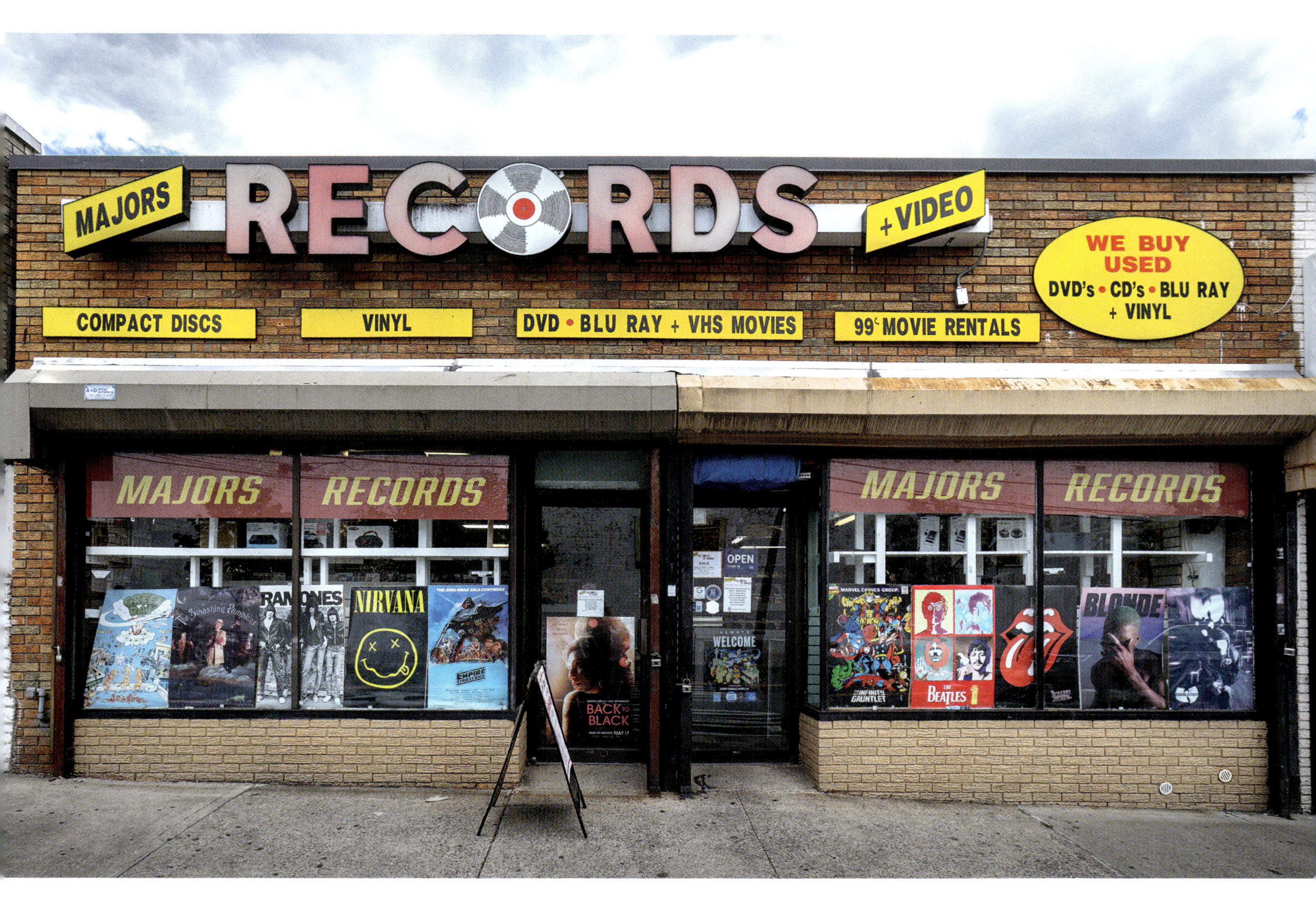

ABOVE Located on a side street off busy Forest Avenue is Staten Island's oldest family-owned record store, Majors Records & Video.

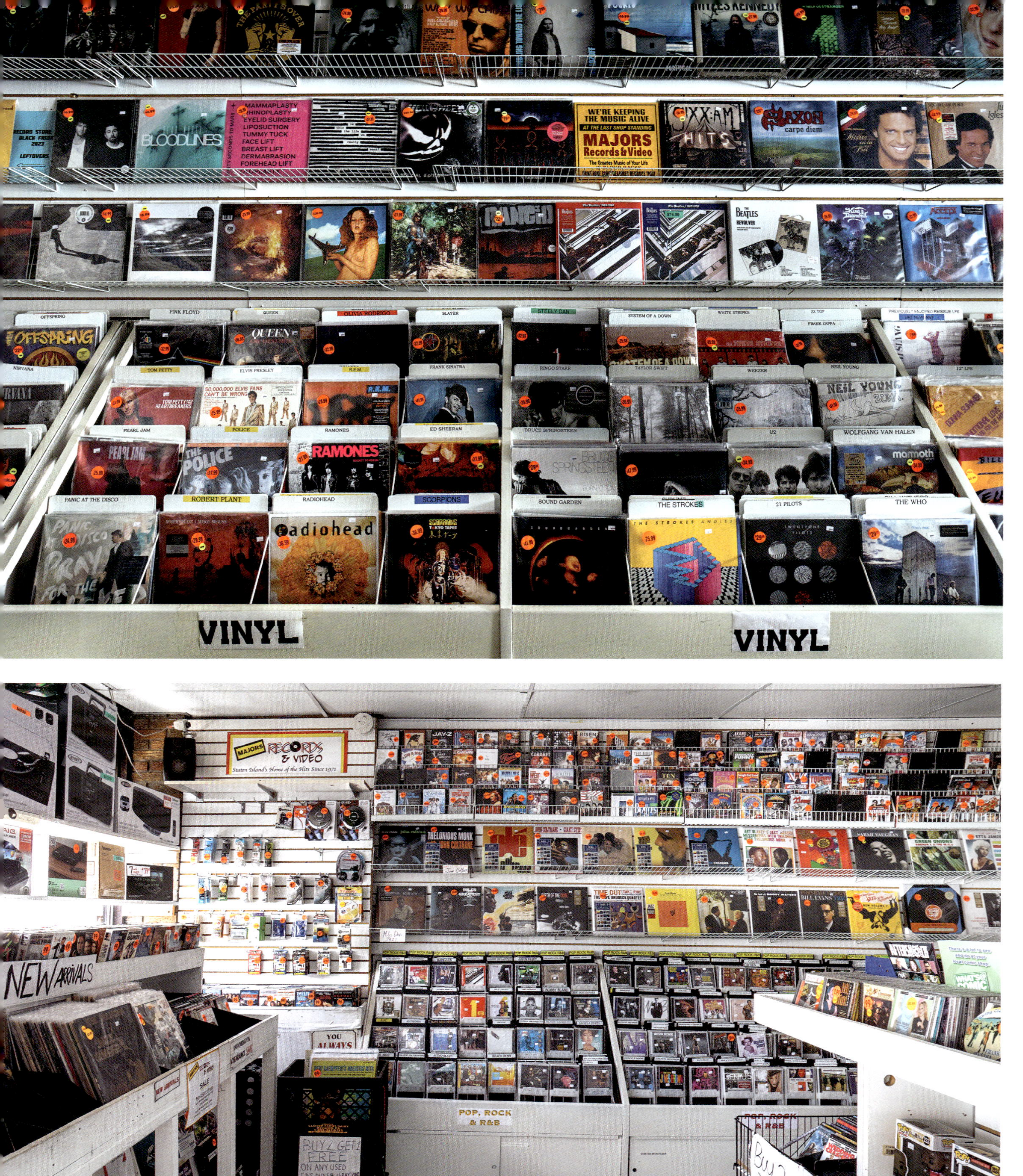
VINYL
VINYL
MAJORS RECORDS & VIDEO
Staten Island's Home of the Hits Since 1971
NEW ARRIVALS
POP, ROCK & R&B
Buy 2 Get 1 FREE

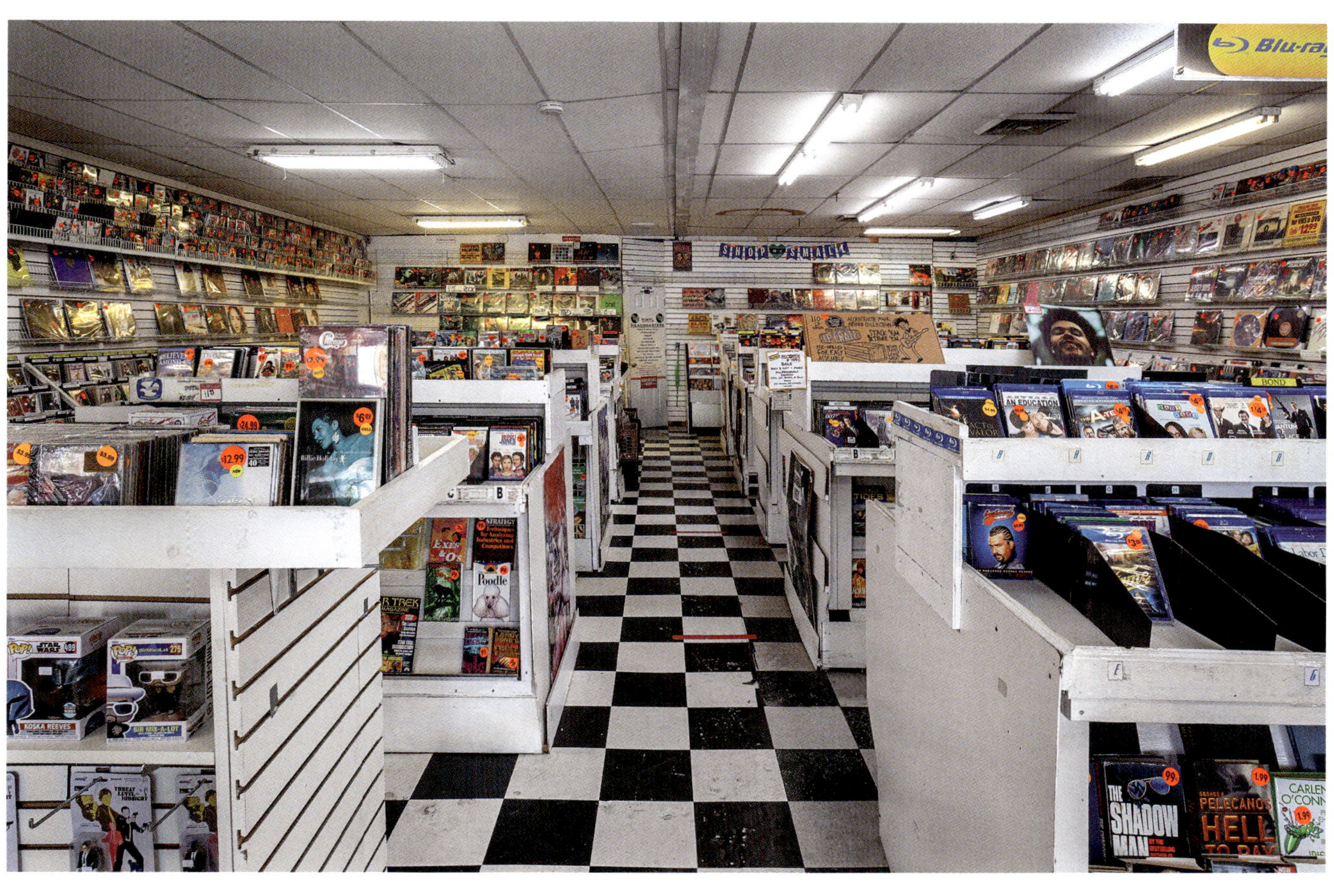

OPPOSITE TOP As a testament to the shop's longevity, new and used collectible vinyl spanning every genre can be found lining its walls and bins, alongside many exclusive Record Store Day releases.

OPPOSITE BOTTOM Majors has a wall of vinyl devoted to jazz, blues, country, and oldies, plus a large inventory of both new and used CDs and DVDs, as well as turntables, needles, and stereo equipment.

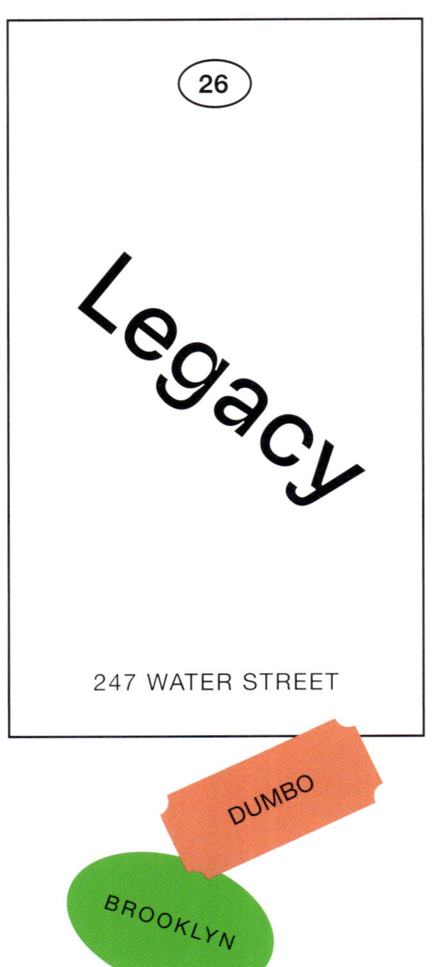

LEGACY MAY NOT BE THE OLDEST record shop in Brooklyn, but few endeavors embody such dedication to the long game and the lasting cultural imprint the most beloved small businesses leave. A store, event space, and community center, when the DUMBO retailer opened in 2021 it was one of only a few Black-led record shops in Brooklyn. "We have things that are devalued in other places that are cherished in our community," co-founder Victorious De Costa told *CBS News* in regard to the store's stock in 2023.

All three of the business's founders—De Costa, Haile Ali, and Barkim Salgado—trace their roots back to the Caribbean. This intrinsic connection inspires Legacy's offerings, a purchasable paean to Black music past and present. Reggae and soca are especially plentiful across the three-level wooden cabinets on display at the store, but out in the world, Ali—now Legacy's sole owner and operator—hears their R&B section lauded most.

Ali grew up in Brooklyn's Crown Heights neighborhood—like so many new-generation record shop operators, he got interested in vinyl as a burgeoning hip-hop producer digging for samples to sustain his beat-making. "That's how I fell in love with the mood that vinyl created, the patience," he recalls. "Before I even decided to chop up any records, I listened to a whole collection that I was gifted." A lion's share of that collection became part of Legacy's first-ever sales floor stock. Today, the airy space on average contains around 1,600 items at a time. "What we love to say at Legacy is 'You may not always get what you're looking for, but you'll always leave with something you love,'" Ali explains.

The DUMBO location was De Costa's idea. Although the rent wasn't cheap and brick-and-mortar music businesses weren't numerous there, Ali felt it was important to set up a stronghold somewhere Black communities had historically been excluded from. "Who we are, as a people—we also need to have stores on the Fifth Avenues of the world. We have to occupy spaces where money is being spent," he asserts.

Legacy's long-overdue hub for Afro-Caribbean sounds in DUMBO has earned it its flowers from far beyond the borough's reggae community. Musicians like Rae Sremmurd, Mahalia, Metro Boomin, Burna Boy, Yo Gotti, and GloRilla have all held meet-and-greets at the 247 Water Street location. Yet whether or not it catches media attention, Legacy dresses to impress every visitor, from those leaving with an armful of purchases to those passing time on the orange leather couch by the window. The shop has hosted all sorts of events, from candle-making classes and first dates to the flourishing vinyl club Liner Notes. Its employees have cleared the floor for wedding engagements and receptions too.

Ali is thrilled to see his initial vision grow from preserving history to making it—but he never wanted to limit Legacy to silent, solo shopping. The store's collector meet-ups, multidisciplinary workshops, and entry-point dense section of modern hip-hop and R&B reflects a core value he still works from today: Every curatorial choice has a staff of real human beings behind it. "We thrive off of our authenticity," he explains. "We thrive off of people coming in and seeing how human we are."

Leaving a lasting positive imprint is not just Legacy's namesake but its mission. After all, Ali points out, that's what the best records do. "Music itself, whether it's liked or not liked, it's always a reflection of the time," he says. "No matter the genre, if it was pressed on vinyl, it's gonna last." He sees a long tenure of coaxing customers beneath the Brooklyn Bridge in the store's future. But for now, he is content: He's quite familiar with the prosperity a little patience can bring.

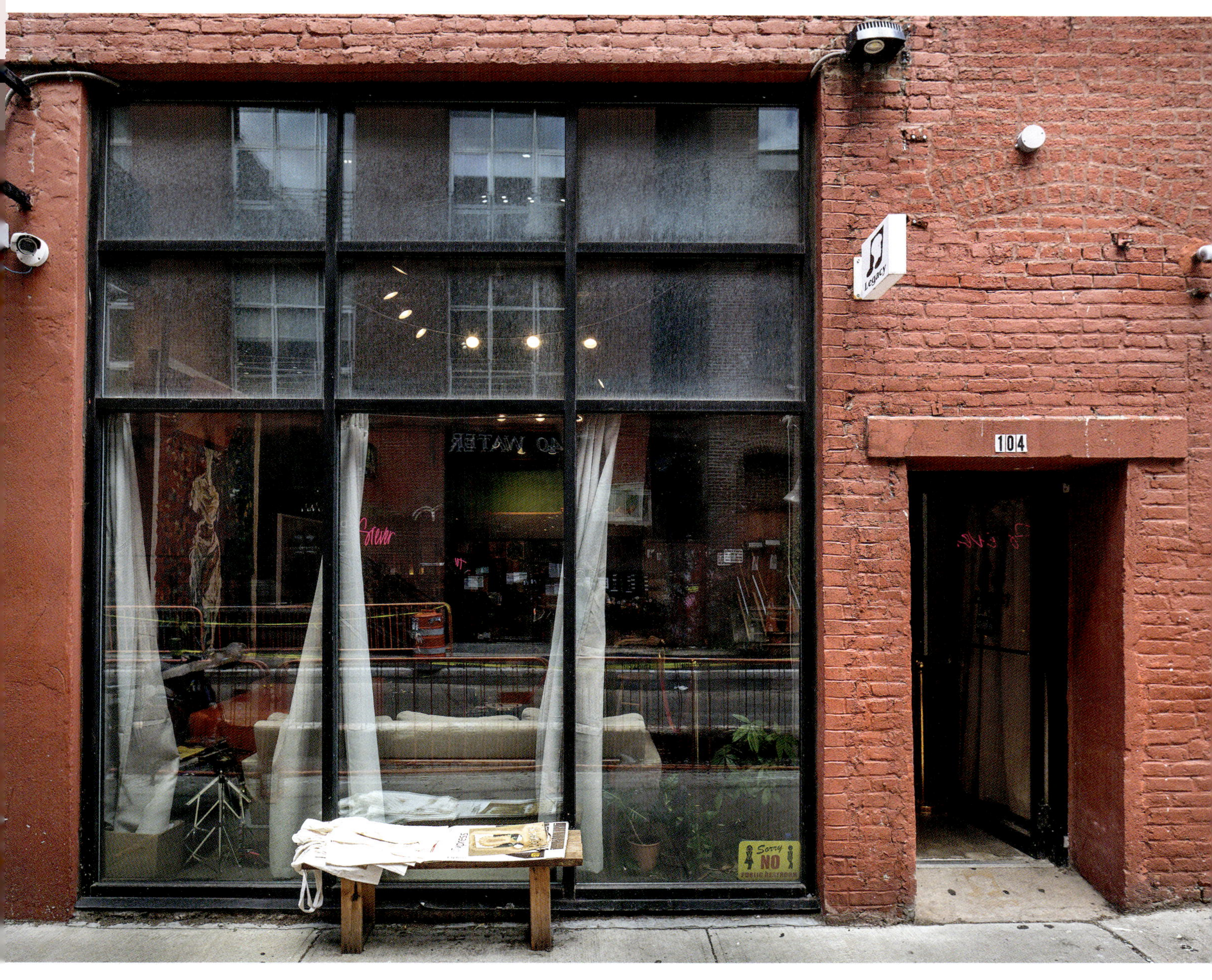

ABOVE Legacy was founded in 2021 in Brooklyn's DUMBO water-front neighborhood. Its glass facade and understated signage provide few clues to the treasures inside, including a large collection of R&B, soul, funk, hip-hop, and jazz records.

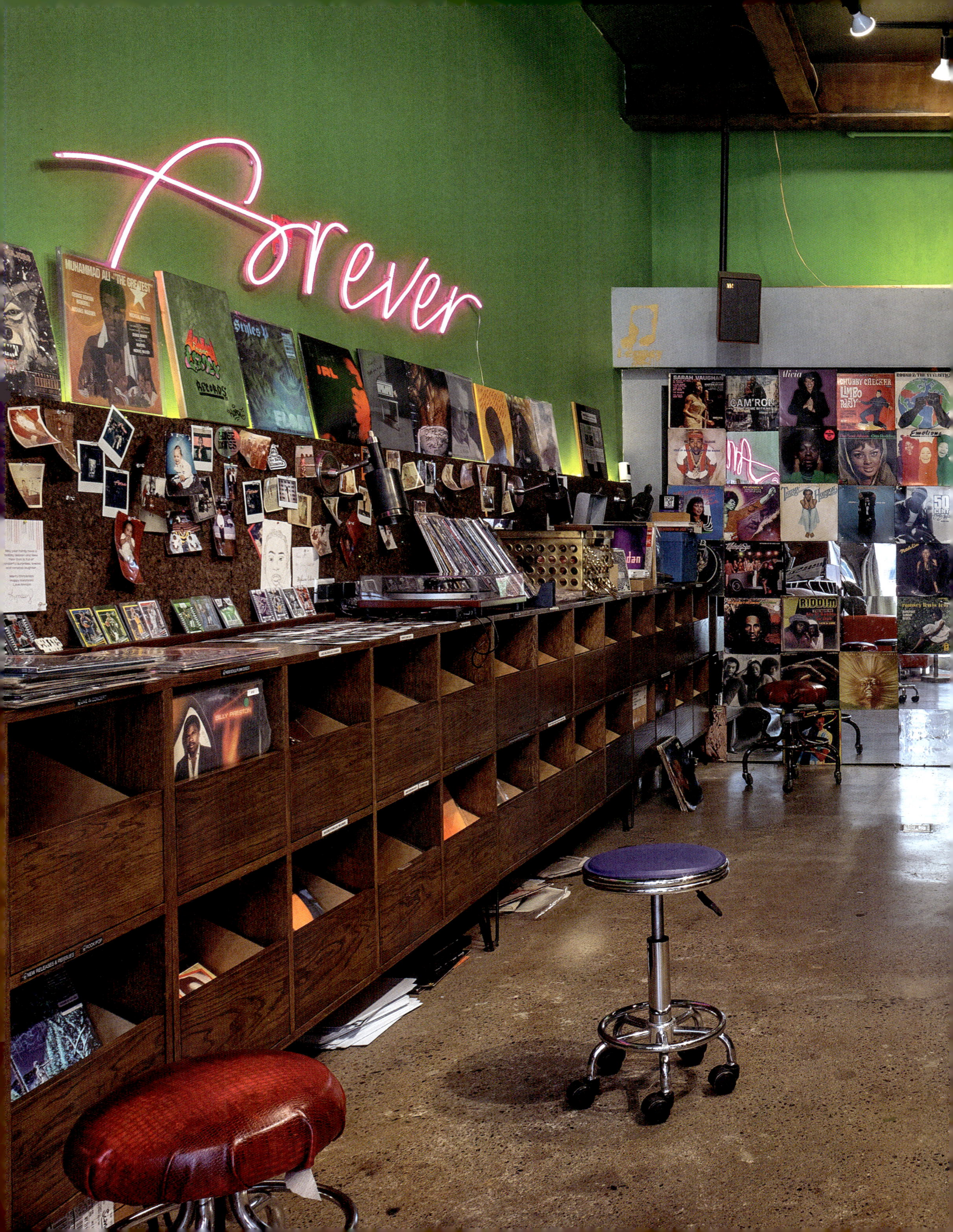
Forever
MUHAMMAD ALI "THE GREATEST"
SARAH VAUGHAN
CAM'RON
Alicia
CHUBBY CHECKER
LIMBO PARTY

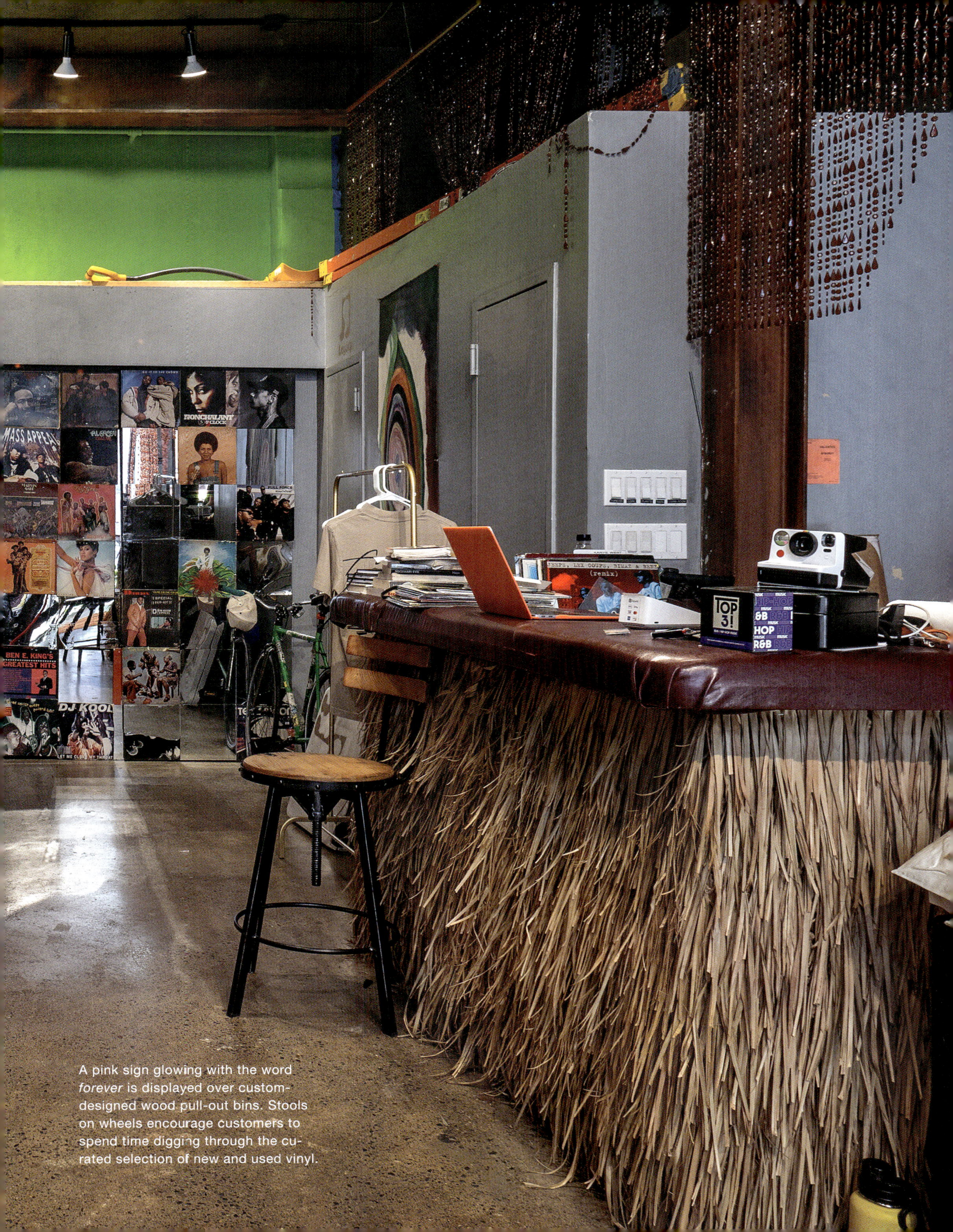

A pink sign glowing with the word *forever* is displayed over custom-designed wood pull-out bins. Stools on wheels encourage customers to spend time digging through the curated selection of new and used vinyl.

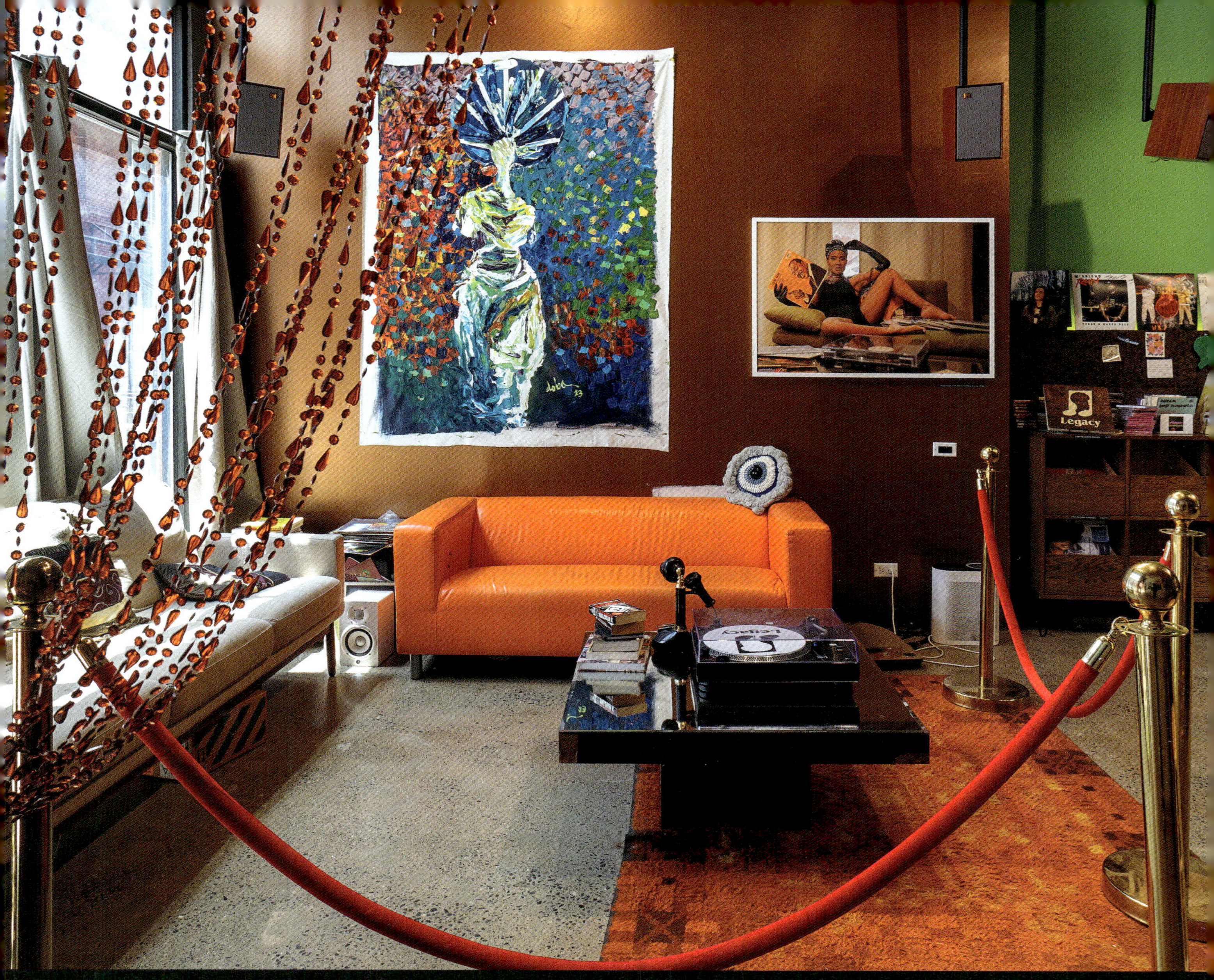

"People like to talk about music, but sometimes they don't have the space to nerd out. There's something rudimentary, more real, about a record that helps someone connect with something larger. Just put the needle down."

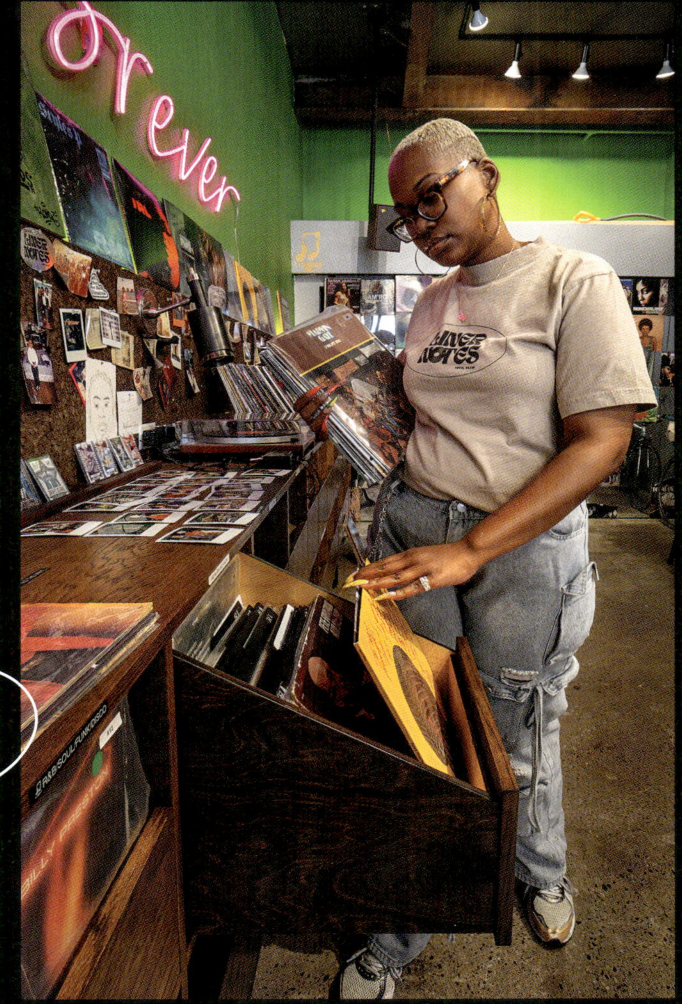

ZOË WIGGINS

CULTURAL CONSERVATOR, ARCHIVIST, AND DJ

Zoë Wiggins is a lifelong record collector and veteran Legacy volunteer—it's where she celebrated her first Record Store Day. Brought up in Jamaica, Queens, among a family of musicians, she fondly recalls her grandfather Johnny Robinson, a '70s soul crooner, regularly mailing her his demos throughout her childhood. She discovered vinyl as a teenage A Tribe Called Quest fan, dipping into the jazz, soul, and funk LPs behind her favorite sample loops. This inspired her to grow up into an adroit curator and DJ, not to mention the leader of a monthly vinyl collector's club born out of Legacy, Liner Notes. Emboldened by the store's ambitious programming, she founded the club in 2023, hoping to reach DUMBO's diverse community with a group, as her Instagram page (@linernotesvinylclub) explains, "where music lovers and connoisseurs share passion, stories within the community, and celebrate the music and history of Black artists."

The club's inaugural meetup was an in-store record show-and-tell. Since then, it has hosted game nights, live shows, selecting workshops, and magazine launches. In just a few years of operation, attendance has already quadrupled. For Wiggins, that means an even greater chance to distribute essential wisdom to the next generation. "I see vinyl as a cultural conservatory for Black artists," she told the pop-culture-focused *Ralph Magazine* in 2023.

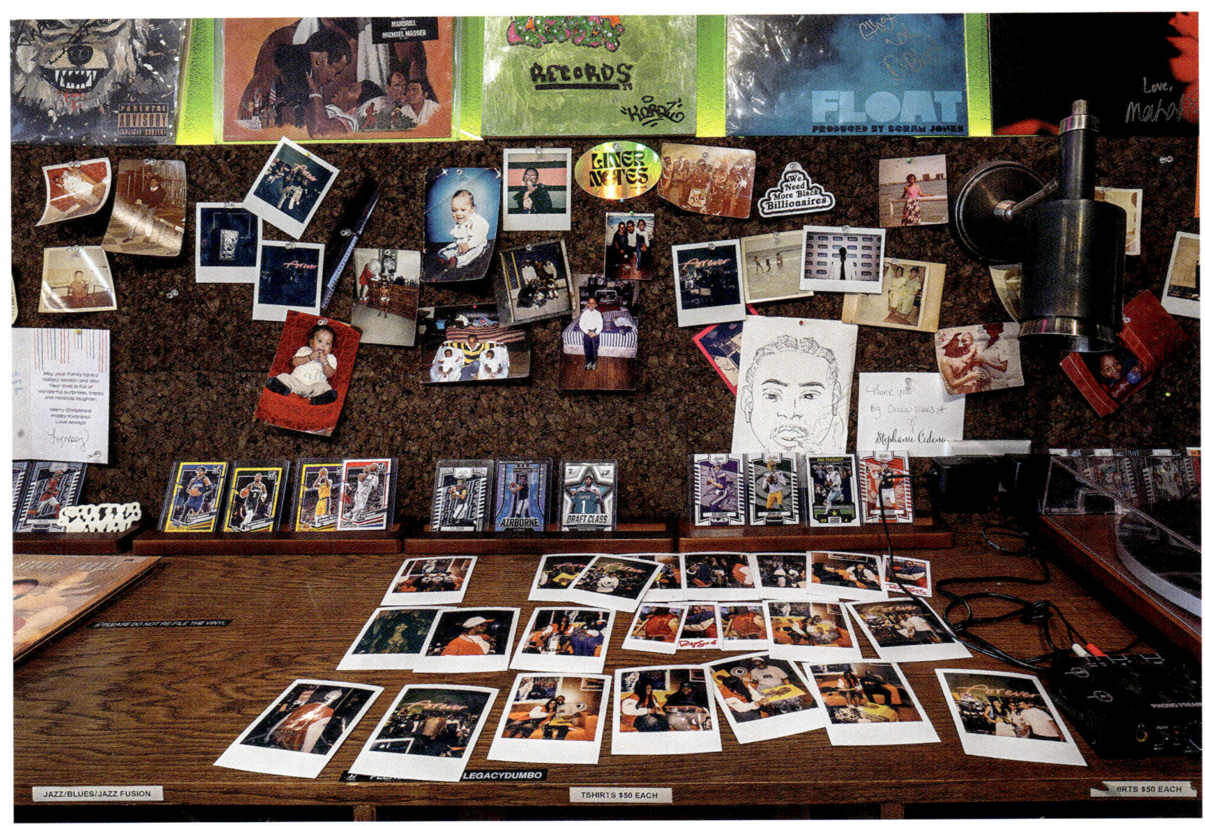
RECORDS
FLOAT
LINER NOTES
We Need More Black Billionaires
AIRBORNE
DRAFT CLASS
JAZZ/BLUES/JAZZ FUSION
LEGACYDUMBO
TSHIRTS $50 EACH

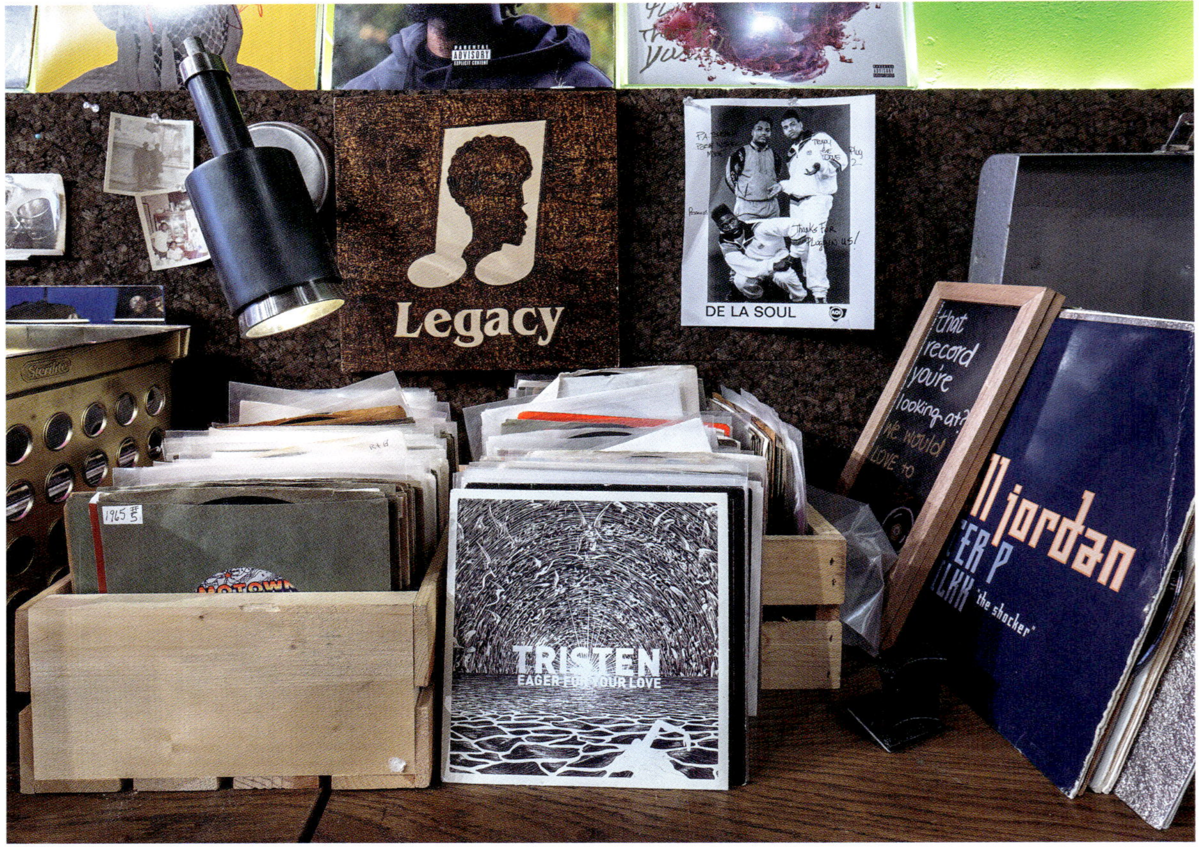
Legacy
DE LA SOUL
TRISTEN
EAGER FOR YOUR LOVE
MOTOWN
"the shocker"

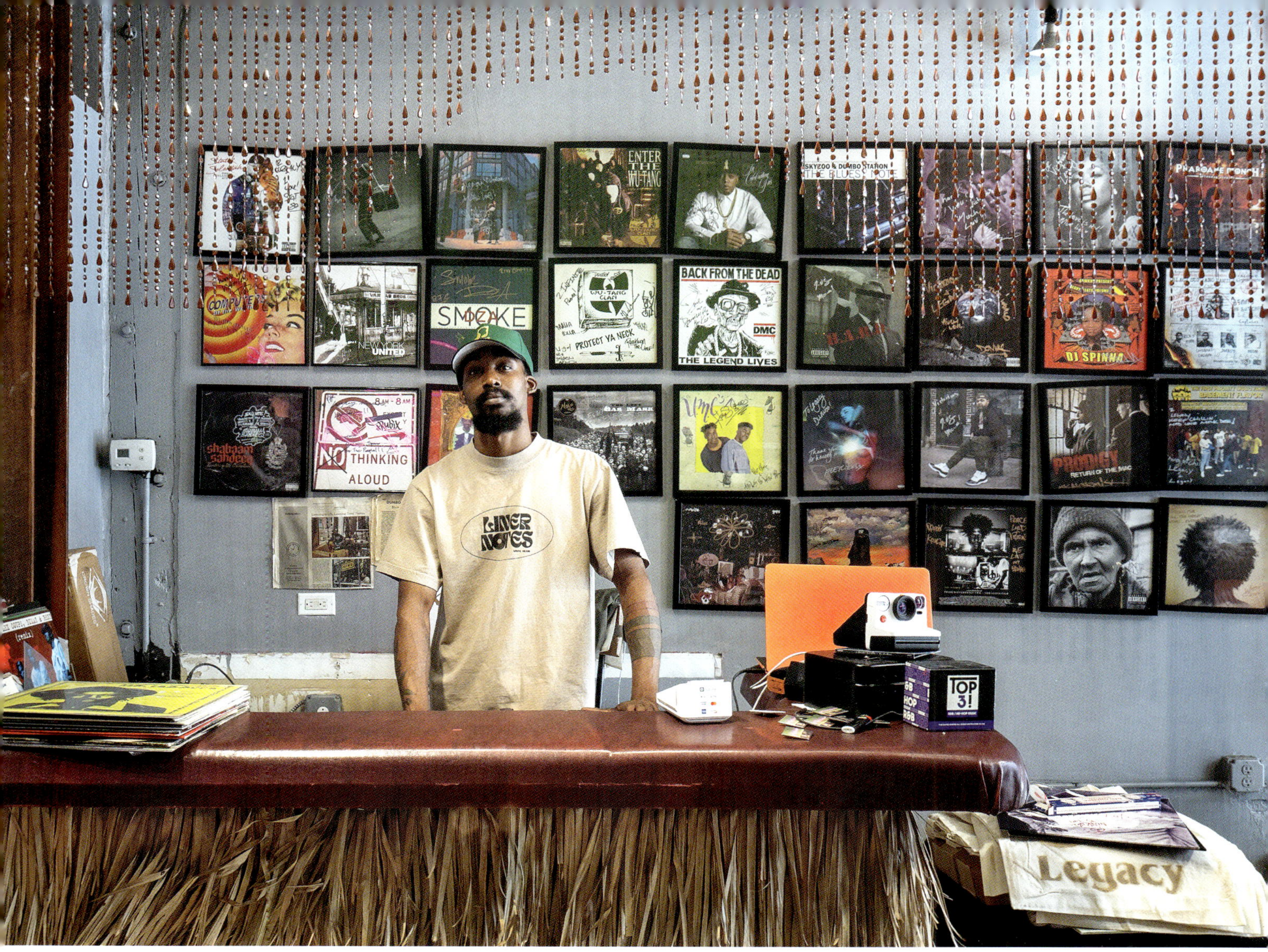

OPPOSITE BOTTOM Small bins of used 45s are displayed alongside the logo for the shop, whose motto honors the "Legacy" of where records come from.

ABOVE Rapper and producer Haile Ali, who co-founded the shop, in front of his personal collection of framed album covers—many signed by hip-hop legends.

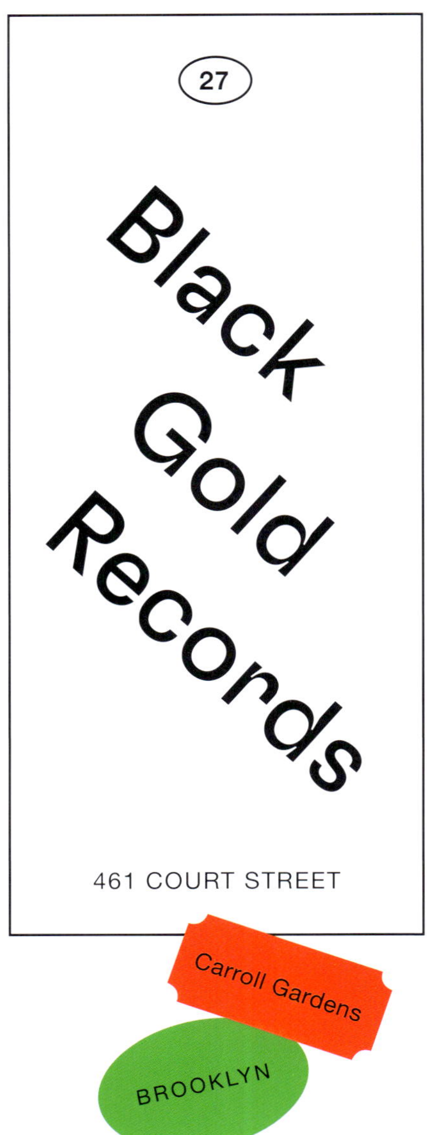

AT THE TURN OF THE TWENTY-FIRST century, fanfare over MP3 files and gateway-to-streaming platforms like Napster had the eyes, ears, and pockets of quite a few entrepreneurial music fans hoping to make a living off what they loved. But childhood friends Jeff Ogiba and Mike Polnasek placed their bets on vinyl records, the final form of a joint passion for collecting nearly as long-standing as their friendship. As Ogiba puts it, "We figured out that it was the [format] that made sense to us."

Business partners since 1995, Ogiba and Polnasek parted ways for a few years before coming back to each other, with fresh perspectives and new wax treasures unearthed from attics, basements, and dollar bins. It was time for another shot, and the duo opened Black Gold Records at its current Carroll Gardens location in 2010 (what's that song about making new friends but keeping the old?).

The "mystery of discovery," as they explain, has fueled Ogiba and Polnasek throughout their careers, and a desire to pass along their experience stands out in Black Gold's curation. Well-aware of the stereotypical two-pronged entryway to record selling that dictates record lovers either get their start in punk rock or hip-hop, the pair are no more willing to stick to one lane than they are to stock one subgenre.

If the two bunting flags caressing Black Gold's hand-painted (and aptly colored) gold leaf window lettering didn't exude enough old-school weathered decorum, the taxidermied buck's head overseeing the coffee and pastry counter should do the trick. But the faded glory the shop conjures isn't washed up or washed out, just well-worn: it's that sensation of stepping back in time and realizing the past is very much still alive. Expect a healthy selection in the store's wooden bins, where prices are fair and turnover is quick. ("We've been into music for so long," Polnasek says, "that it just turns into good and bad music—you stop judging it by genre.") Gathered together in a glass case, paper-sheathed 45s rub elbows across from the month's choice of stereo cassette tapes stacked neatly above an LED-lit diorama, empty but for two triceratops figurines facing each other, as if in conversation.

In catering to the whole spectrum of sounds, the shop has drawn in some familiar faces. In 2011 frequent buyer Q-Tip of A Tribe Called Quest fame told *The New York Times* Black Gold was his "favorite record store." Questlove and Large Professor (see p. 215) have also dropped in. But while Ogiba and Polnasek appreciate the accolades, they also emphasize how important bantering with the median customer is to their practice. Don't expect pretentiousness behind the register here. "We like to learn as much from our customers as we talk to them about our own knowledge," Polnasek shares.

Immersing in the neighborhood's tight-knit community of small business owners hasn't hurt either, with Polnasek explaining: "We all support each other and prop each other up." Especially during the hotter months, he notes the way the area unfurls into the sidewalks and streets; he loves that Black Gold's storefront becomes part of an amalgam of curiosity and convivence. But hey, if you're not connecting with the brighter side, there's always the option to leave with one of the shop's trademark crewneck T-shirts, emblazoned with the slogan "Record Collecting Ruined My Life."

Shaking off the dust is a part of any good vinyl collector's project: learning to discover—and more often than not, rediscover—the next tossed-aside classic from "some guy's uncle that made the record in his garage and pressed a hundred copies of it by himself," as Polnasek says. Black Gold proudly offers that service to both toe-dippers brand new to vinyl and bin burrowers with years of experience. But after over a decade of running a business together, what really keeps the door swinging is Ogiba and Polnasek's shared drive to practice their oldest and best-loved hobby. "We both grew up with that work ethic," Polnasek says. "Where it's like, if you are pure, love something, and you're really interested in it, you can do it."

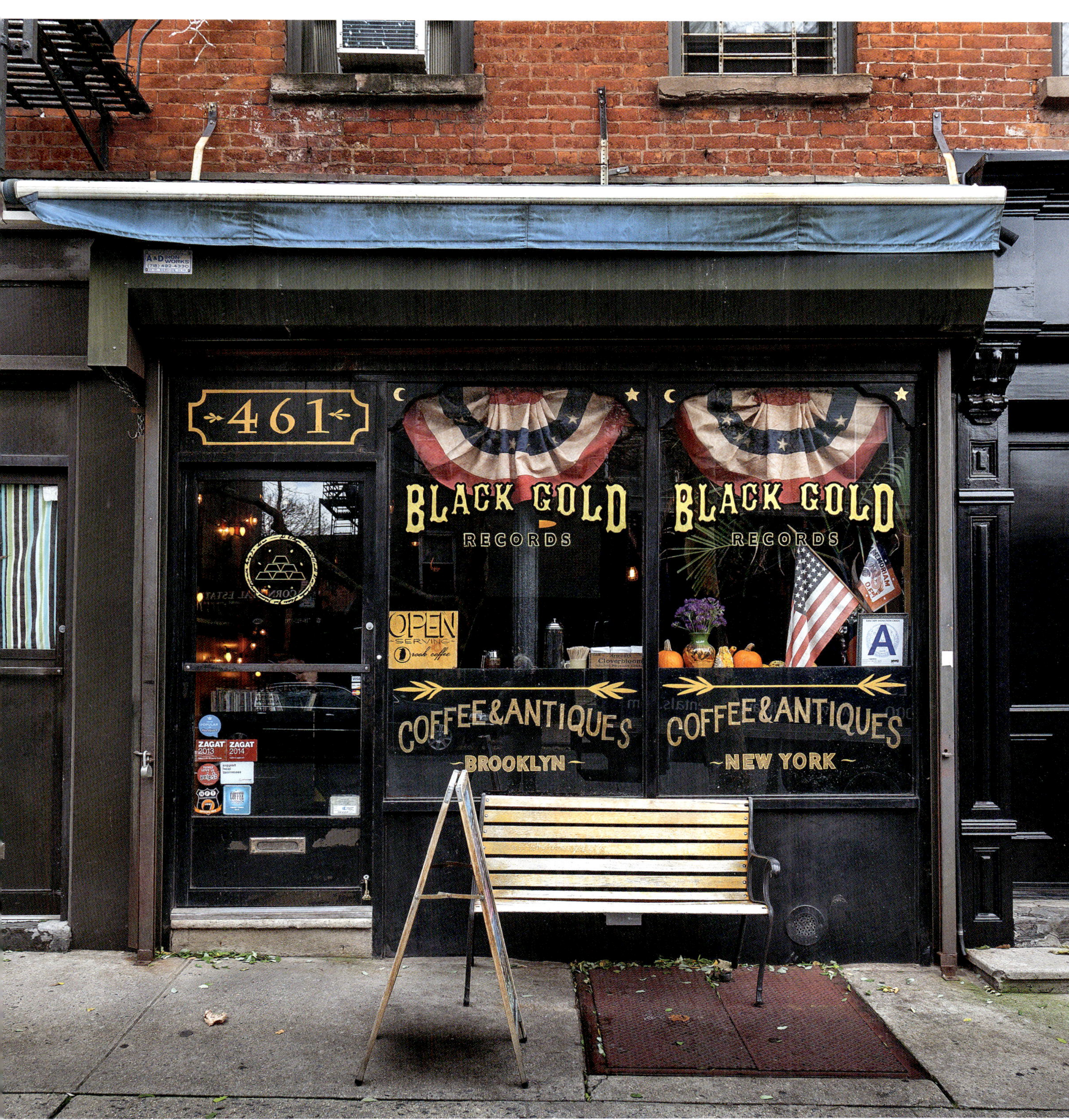

ABOVE With its welcoming hand-painted gold leaf signage, Black Gold Records offers up vinyl, antiques, and coffee, creating a uniquely vintage crate-digging experience.

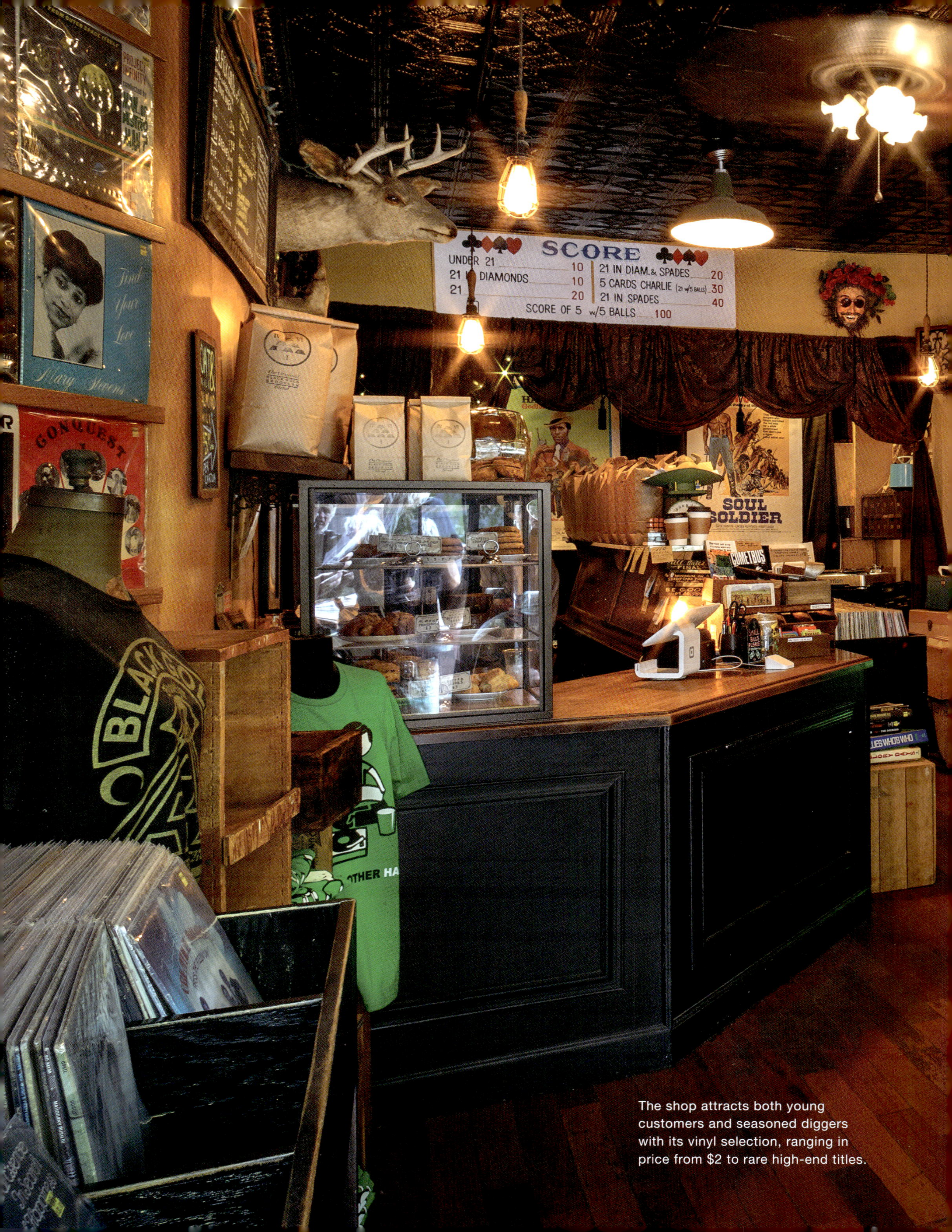

The shop attracts both young customers and seasoned diggers with its vinyl selection, ranging in price from $2 to rare high-end titles.

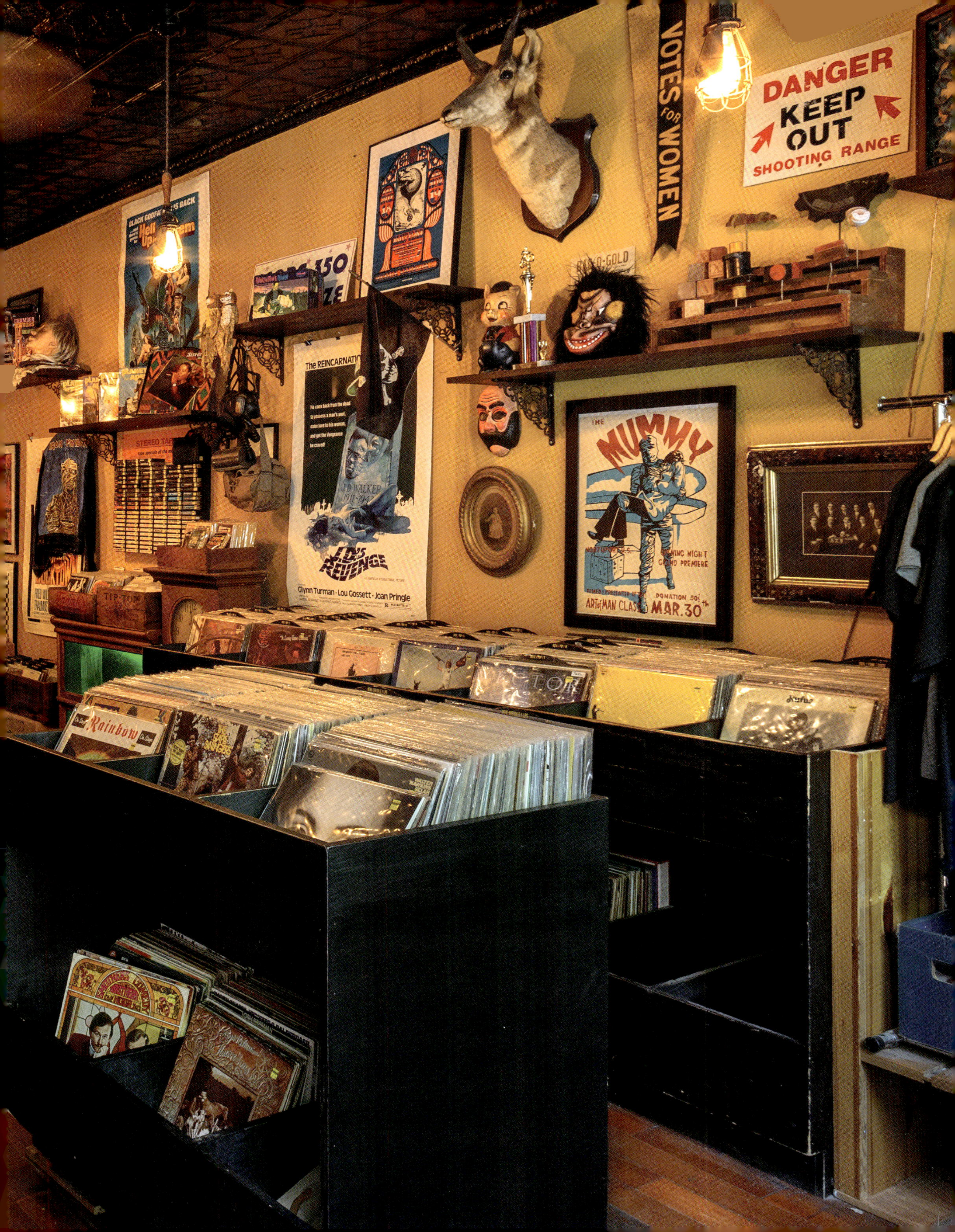

DANGER
KEEP
OUT
SHOOTING RANGE
VOTES FOR WOMEN
THE
MUMMY
Glynn Turman · Lou Gossett · Joan Pringle
Rainbow

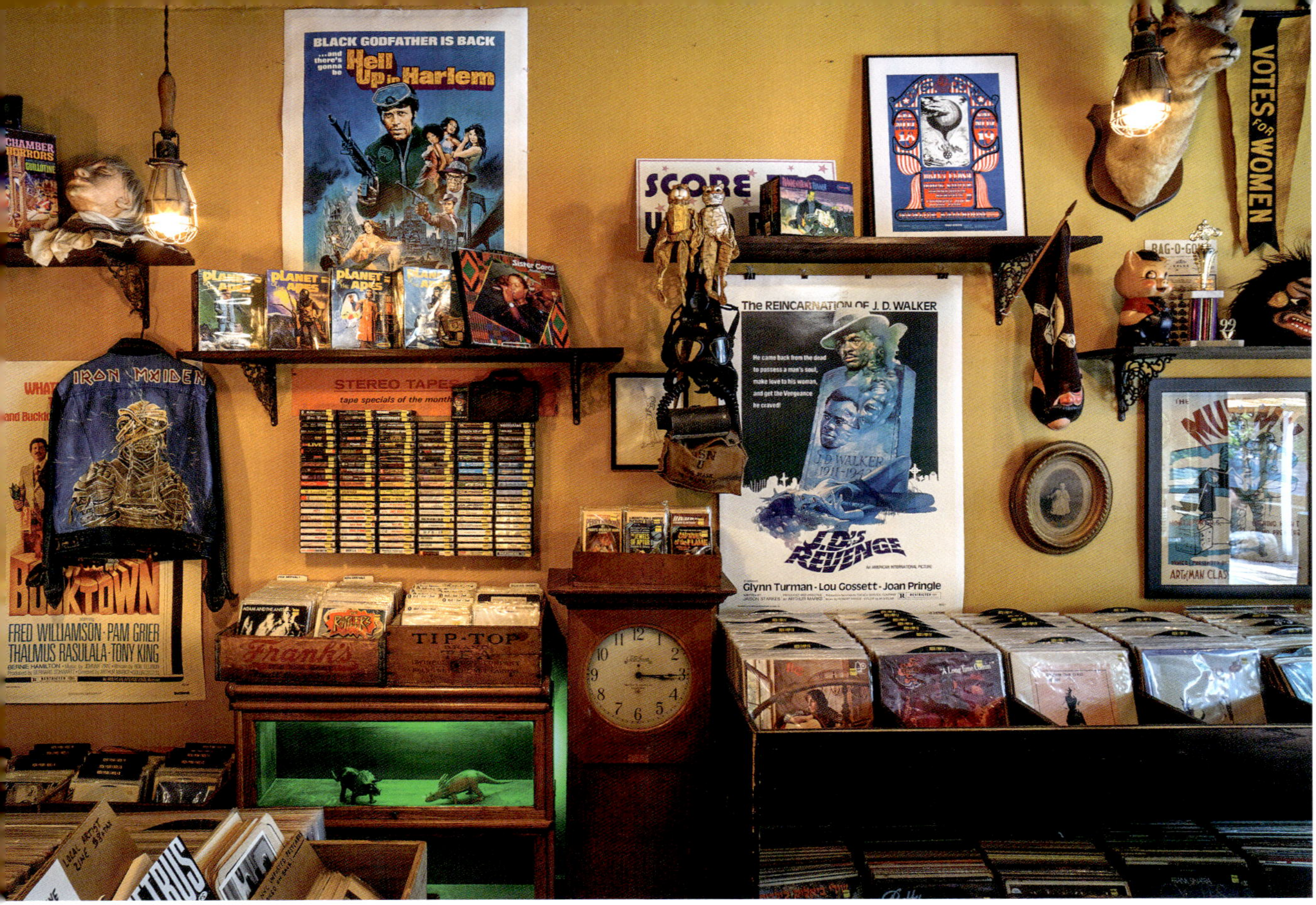

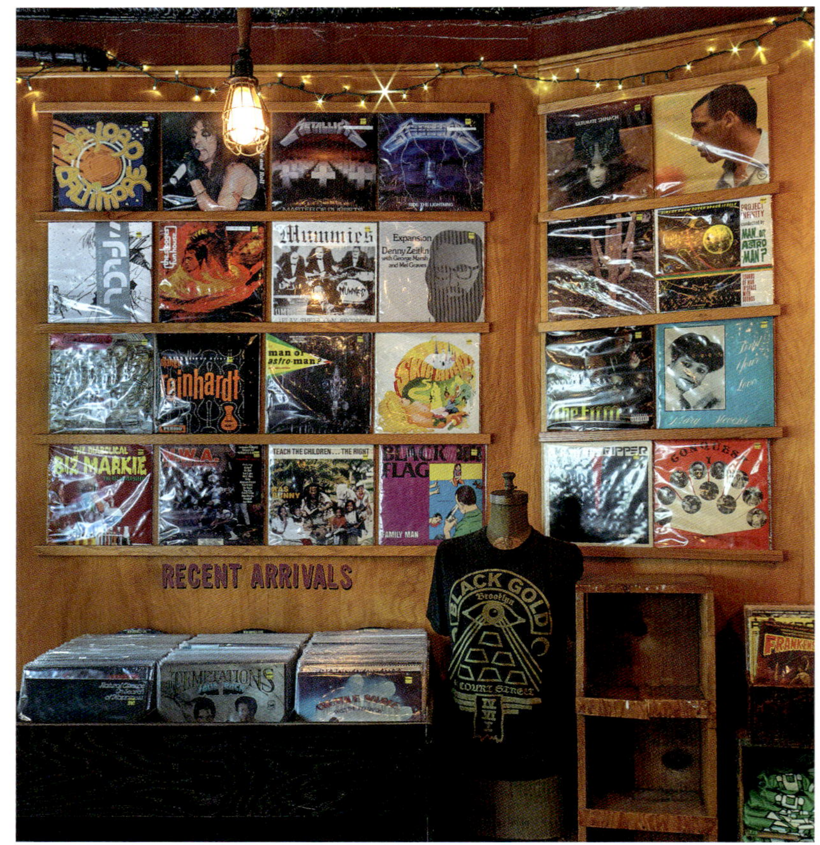
RECENT ARRIVALS

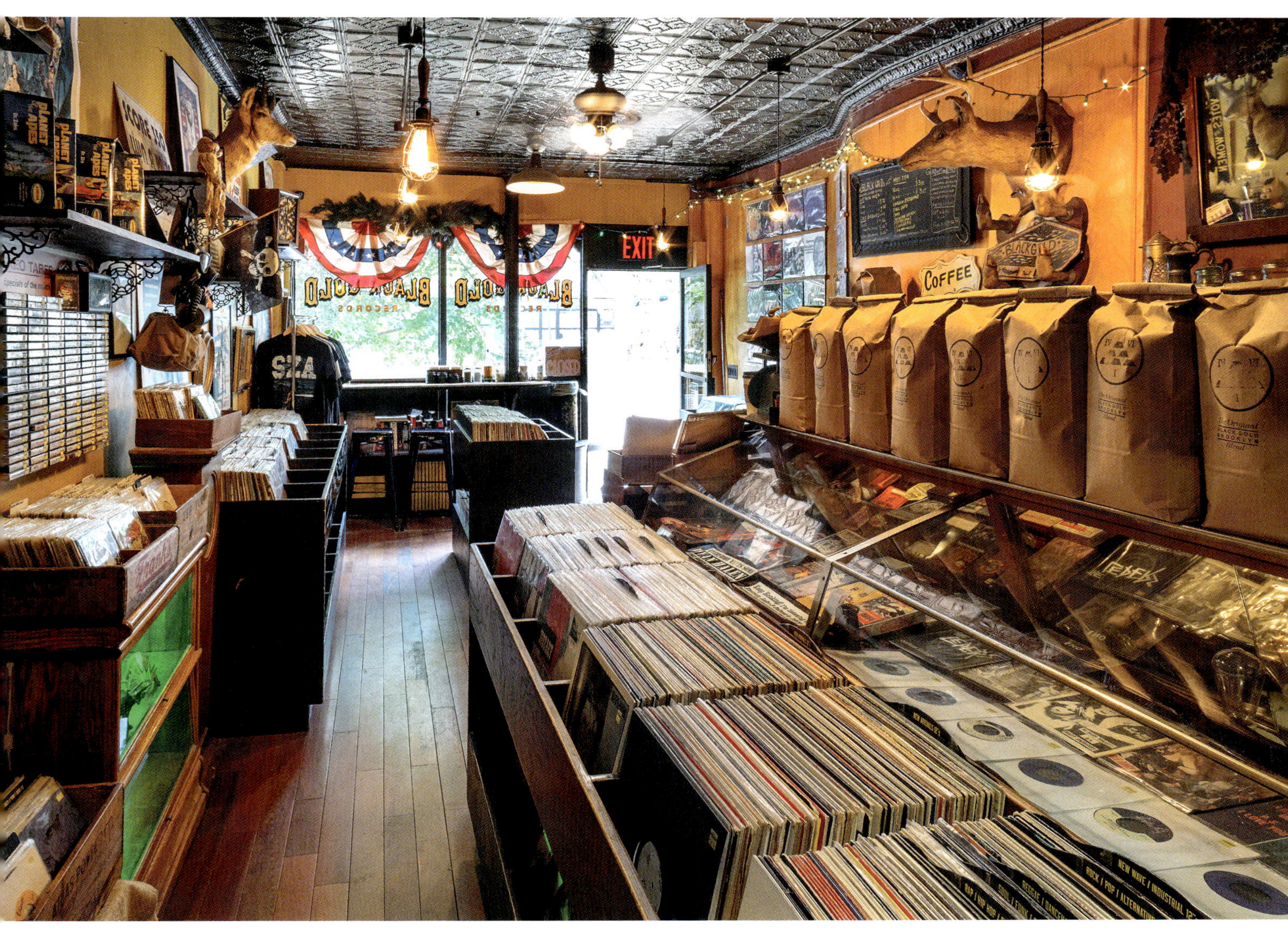

OPPOSITE TOP The interior is lit by vintage work lights and customers are watched over by taxidermied animal heads. Black Gold not only sells vinyl, but it also stocks a small selection of cassettes, as well as vintage T-shirts, jean jackets, and posters.

ABOVE Although the shop is small, it regularly stocks over a thousand 12-inch funk, disco, hip-hop, reggae, dub, and dance records, as well as a diverse selection of 45s, including punk and Motown classics.

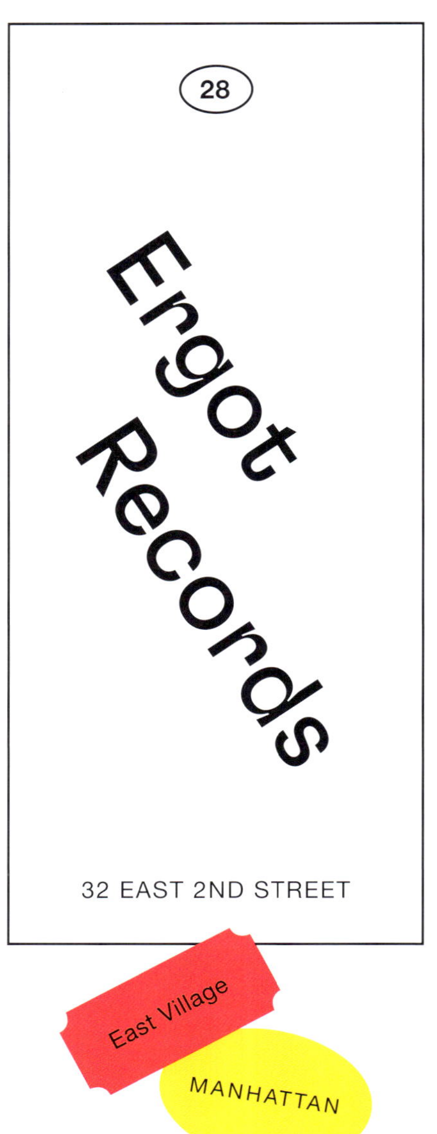

IT ONLY TOOK A FEW YEARS of owning his own record shop for Adrian Rew to be brought to tears. Until he was twelve years old, the Chicago native exclusively listened to the Beatles, with a special preference for "The White Album" and *Magical Mystery Tour*. Eventually, his father decided it was time to introduce him to one Sergeant Pepper, bringing Rew to their local spot Reckless Records for his first-ever CD purchase. Fast forward a couple of decades, and Rew sold a boy and his father the same album from the vinyl selection at the shop he owns and operates in Manhattan, Ergot. "[It] was the kid's first record-buying experience," he remembers. "I cried a little bit."

These types of moments are rare but not unsurprising at Ergot, an East Village nook steeped in the neighborhood's crate-digging tradition and rooted in the love that inspired Rew to pick up his first records. Despite his upbringing as the son of a '90s post-rock musician forging an independent career in the wake of Nirvana, Rew still got his start with the staples. After his Beatles-only era, he eventually gave Led Zeppelin, the Ramones, and Marvin Gaye a try. He had a habit of pocketing the $1.50 his mother allotted for the subway ride to school and biking instead, bringing the change to a local discount record shop for his regular treasure hunt.

Rew still recalls a period before he opened Ergot when, trawling the legendary dollar bins at A-1 Record Shop (see p. 8), an employee noticed his selections captured a blind spot the team needed help with. A-1 offered him a job, which he maintained for a few years before moving to a cherished role at an arts nonprofit. Eventually, the Covid-19 pandemic, in all its chaotic disruption, presented him with the crossroads he needed to pull the trigger on a lease for his own store in 2021. "Turns out I can do a lot of the meaningful work that I did [at the nonprofit] within the context of my store," he says.

Ergot's inventory is 90 percent used, with a focus on New York's circa-1970s avant-garde and post-minimalist traditions—Rew's certain the shop promises one of the best selections from the era in the area. Inside the ground-floor location, framed by two tables lined with free and discount bins positioned like columns, a large poster highlighting French yé-yé icon Catherine Ribeiro stands watch over the expanse of punk, techno, disco, house, soul, noise, and anything and everything else that draws Rew's well-trained eye. Rows and rows of records slot together like pieces in a taste-profile puzzle, dreamily top-lit by soft, unencumbered rows of candle-esque bulbs. To Rew, loving Isaac Hayes and break-y '90s drum and bass go hand in hand. After all, the latter style might not even exist without the volunteer archaeological work of vinyl-only DJs, who were instrumental in discovering the samples and beat loops that would go on to birth entire genres. As Rew puts it, "Nonprofessional archivists are doing this cultural work—discovering music once neglected, music of the past that may hold a key to the future."

In a market as historically competitive as lower Manhattan's, Rew wants to ensure Ergot continues catering to the individuals who can't find their cup of tea anywhere else. "I tell myself [that] for every ten normal functioning people I might alienate, I might save the life of one already-alienated person who needed some weird stuff. I think it's important too, in a neighborhood like the East Village that it's still pretty cool, but has changed a lot," he muses. "It's important for people to walk in the door and hear some freaky shit."

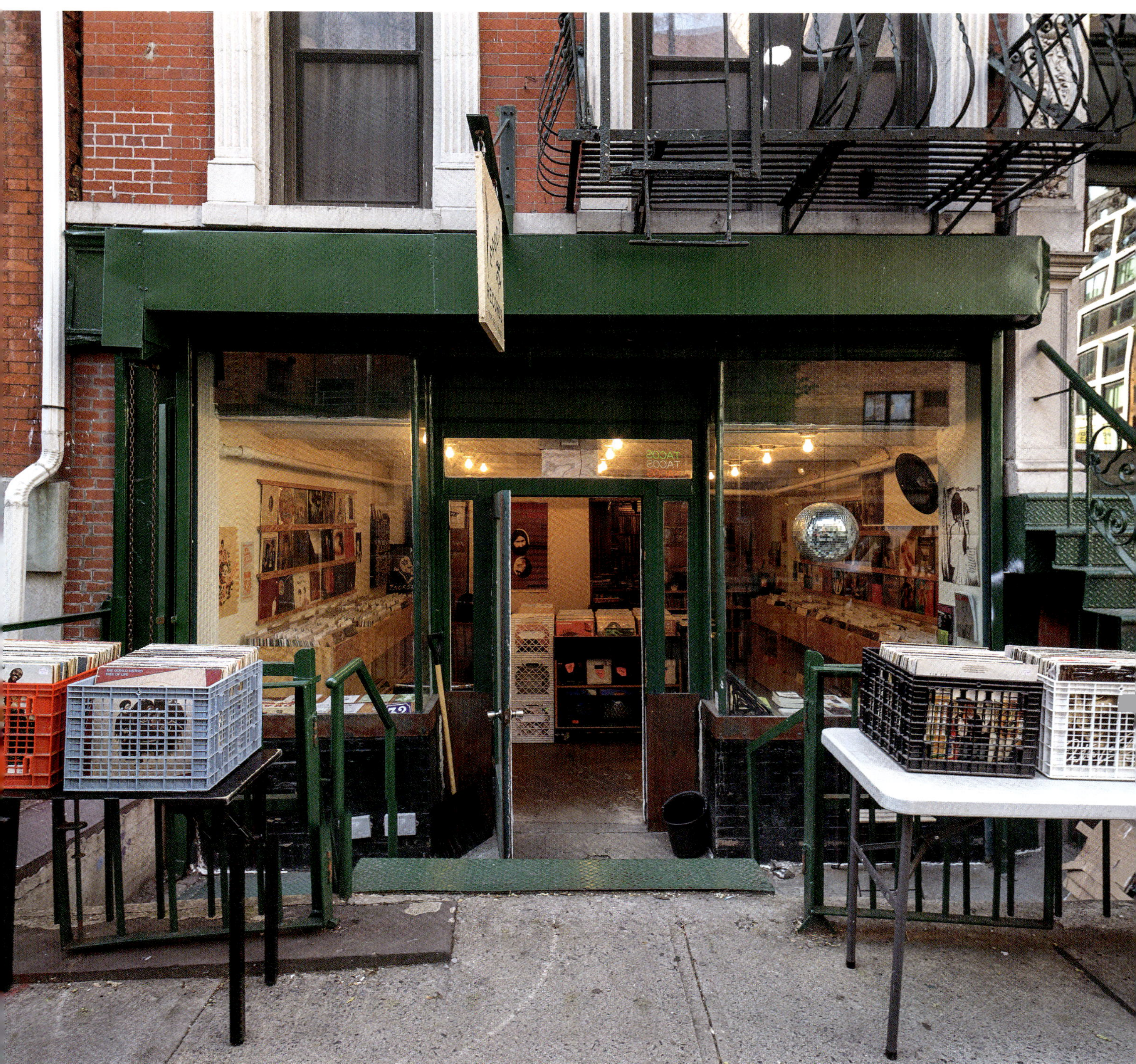

ABOVE Occupying the ground floor of a tenement building, Ergot Records specializes in secondhand vinyl as well as a limited number of new and reissued records, with a concentration on experimental music. The disco ball that hangs in the front right window once belonged to Macaulay Culkin and was purchased at an estate sale. Small tables set up outside the shop daily sell LPs for $1 and up.

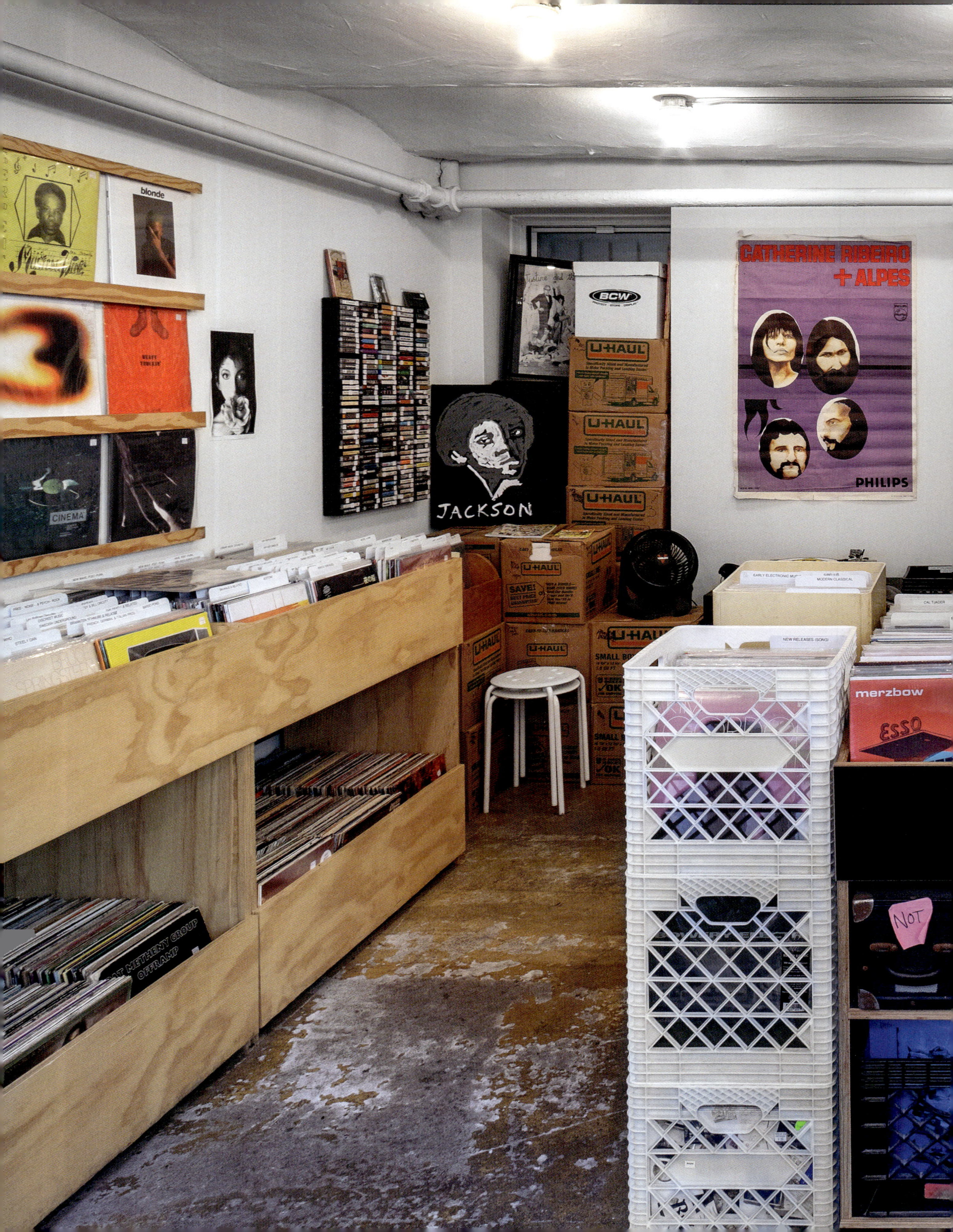

CATHERINE RIBEIRO
+ ALPES
PHILIPS
JACKSON
U-HAUL
BCW
merzbow
ESSO
NOT
blonde
CINEMA

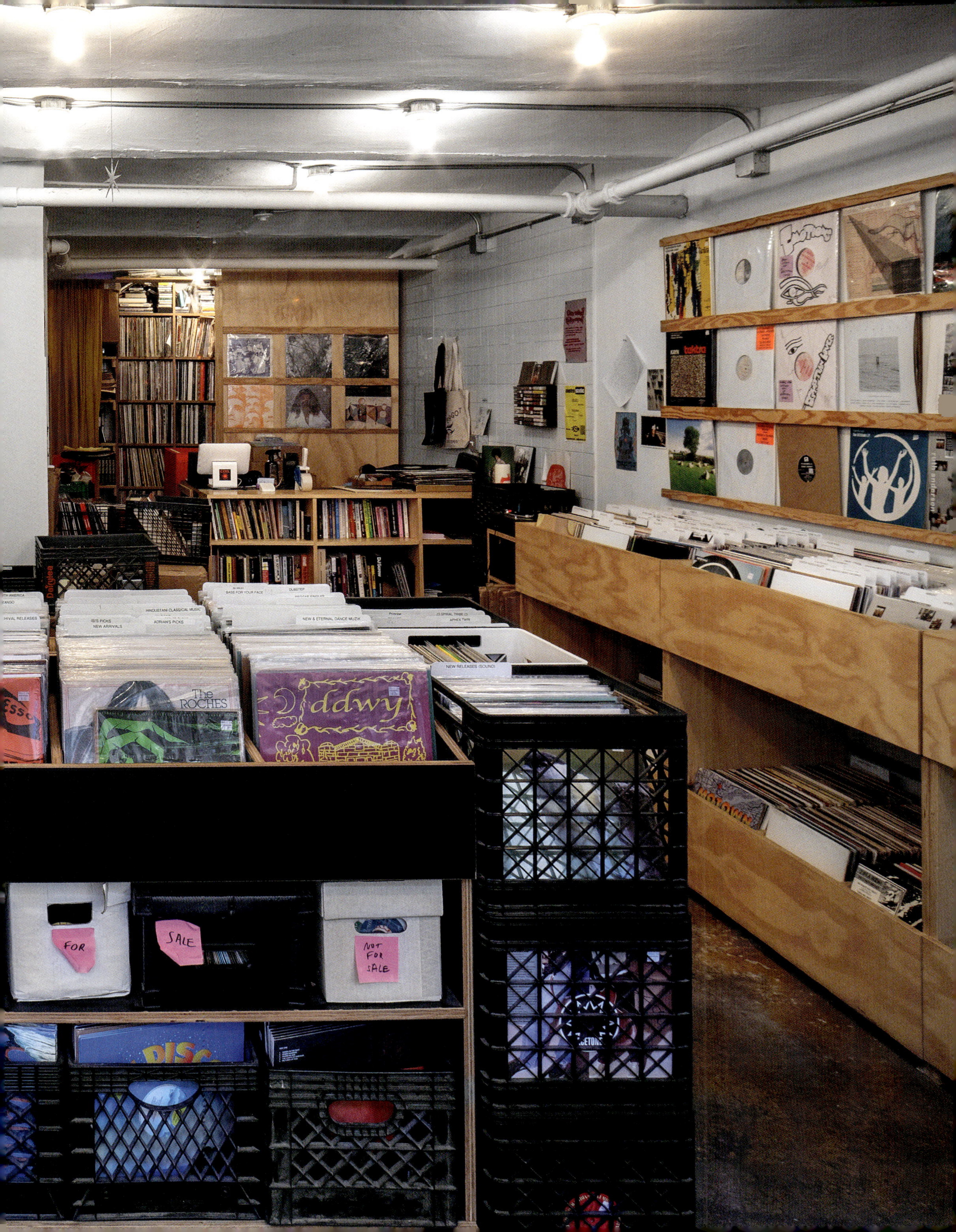
The ROCHES
ddwy
FOR
SALE
NOT FOR SALE

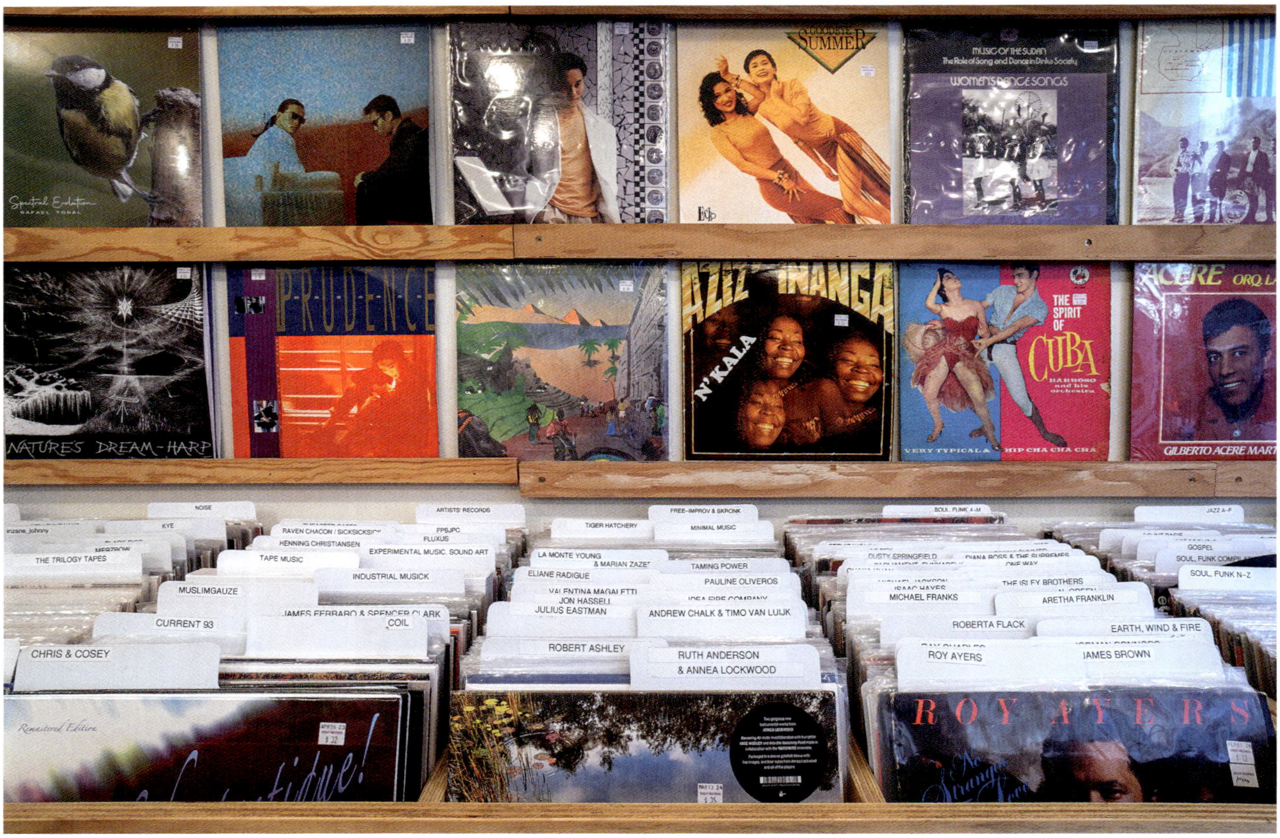

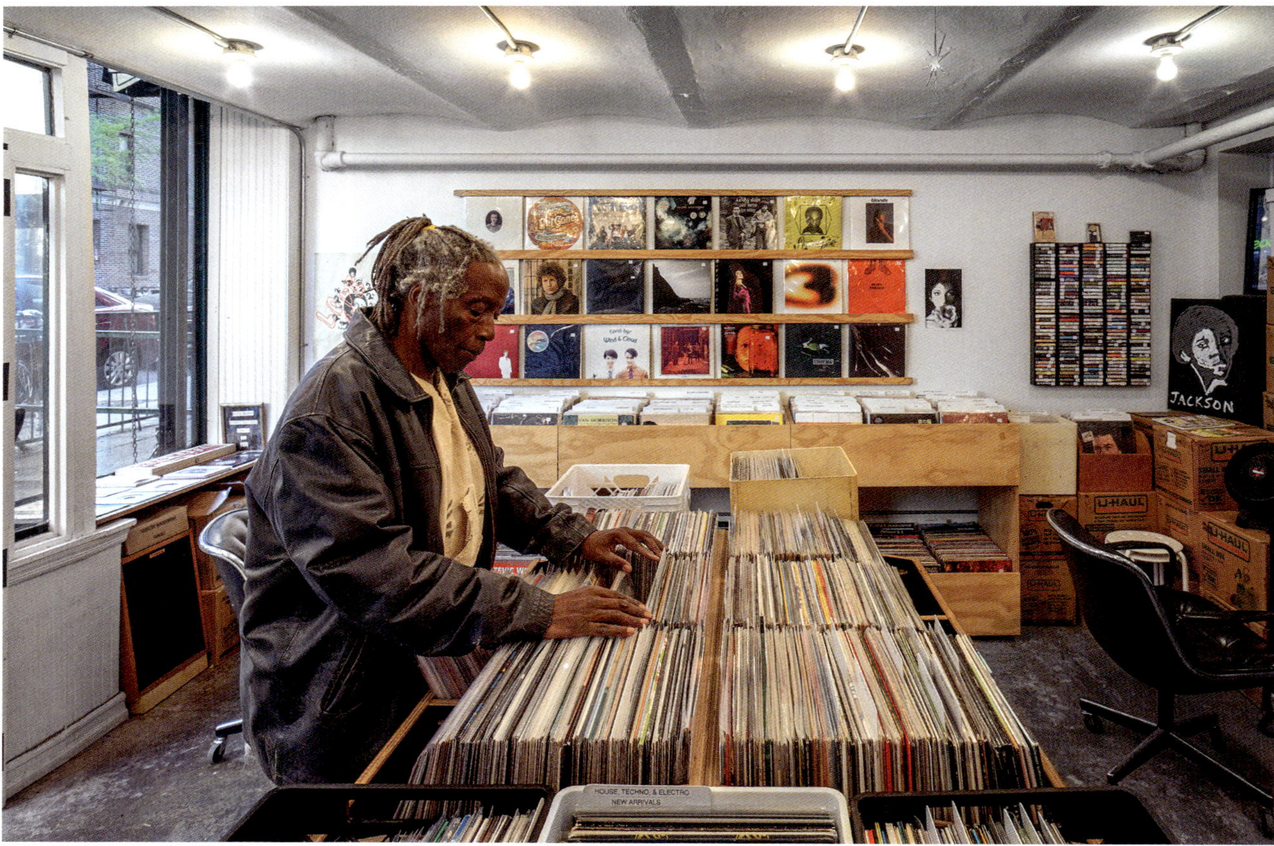
JACKSON
U-HAUL
HOUSE, TECHNO, & ELECTRO
NEW ARRIVALS

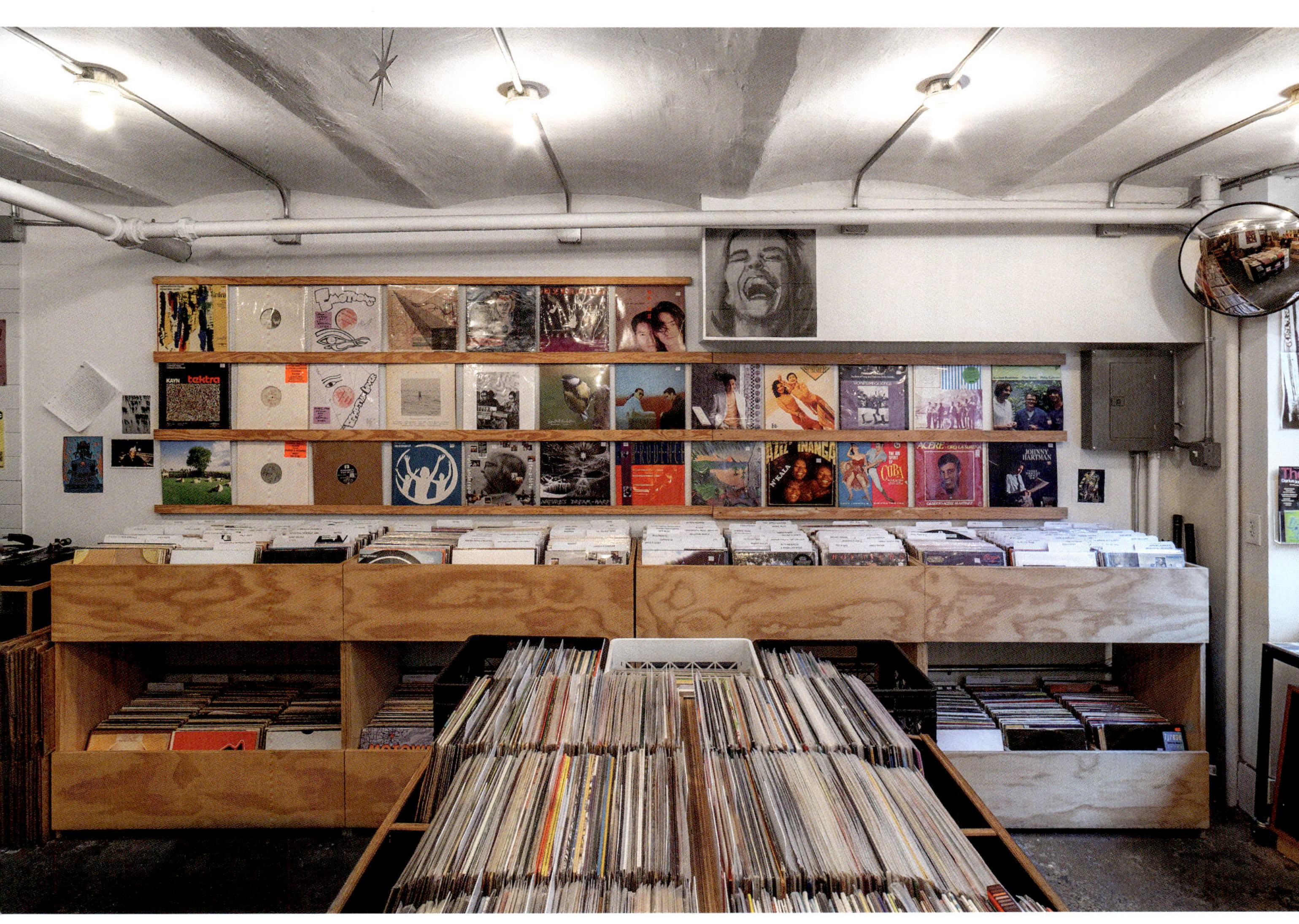

OPPOSITE TOP Walls display the most sought-after and rare titles, including punk, house, rock, disco, and avant-garde, while plywood bins neatly organize LPs and 12-inch vinyl by artist name and genre.

ABOVE Floor-level bins are a true crate-digger's paradise, offering $1 and up "Cheap Electronic, Disco, Reggae and Rock, 12-inch and LPs."

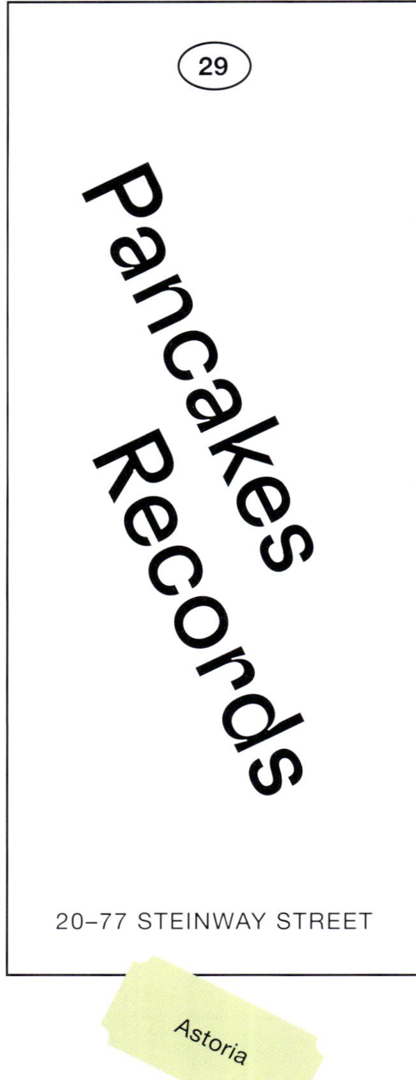

AJ PACHECO WAS JUST A KID when he came up with the phrase that, decades later, he'd emboss across the marigold awning of his own Queens storefront. Over countless afternoons spent poring over vinyl with friends, he developed a shorthand for the act of turning a record from its A- to B-side—not to "flip it," but to "pancake it." This core memory made an apt name for the shop he opened in Astoria in July 2023, which is dedicated to the kinds of replayable masterpieces well worth switching from side to side.

The narrow sanctuary behind Pancakes' double-windowed storefront has plenty of those types of treats on offer. Touting an even mix of new and used vinyl, its collection of Greek music is especially robust, a nod to the large diasporic community that converges off the nearby RFK and Hell Gate Bridges. But like many shop owners, Pacheco and his partner in work and life, Tanya Gorbunova, initially explored the record business as a means to tussle with increasingly wily personal collections, grown substantially during their tenure at Astoria's HiFi Records & Café. From Future to Blondie, Rush to Pharoah Sanders, a generation's worth of new releases and reissues live between these rows of vinyl. "There is not a decade that isn't represented in the store," Pacheco told the *Astoria Post* when Pancakes first opened.

Pancakes' self-designation as a "friendly neighborhood record shop" goes beyond offering a broad selection too. Monthly, they organize a gallery series highlighting local visual artists, plus put on live music events. In their first year of business, Pacheco says they hosted between forty and fifty different performers in their back room space, separated from the main shop by a velvet curtain. They share information about these events with passersby the old-fashioned way: on a regularly updated lunch board, where performance dates are scrawled out in multicolored chalk.

"Part of being a store in a neighborhood is to provide things for the neighborhood," Pacheco told the Instagram account Astoria Storefronts, which highlights local businesses, in 2024. And if Queens faces any overarching deficit these days, it's of accessible third spaces—places people can go that are neither home nor work—many of which have been pushed out or priced up as rents continue to skyrocket. "One of those things [people can experience here] is obviously music," he explains, "but another part of that is a place to hang out."

The wealth of knowledge (and contacts) Pacheco and Gorbunova gained as managers at HiFi Records before its closure made opening Pancakes a logical transition. Motivated to carry on the trade they had learned in an establishment all their own, Pacheco decorated the store top to bottom with toy dinosaurs collected throughout his childhood (one especially girthy brontosaurus perches atop a record listening station between Pancakes' two rooms). San Francisco folk-rock group Osees and their brushstroked artwork are also prominently represented.

An artist in her own right, Pacheco's mother painted the business's ink-black logo: a stack of vinyl-striped hotcakes with a long trail of syrup resembling a tonearm spilling out of it. It's a clever allusion to the other definition Pacheco gives "pancakes" within his and Gorbunova's universe, as noted on their website: "stacks of delicious flat discs for aural consumption."

Even after just a few years in business, plenty of Astoria collectors have already developed a taste for what the duo has to offer. "I feel like we've been around forever because we've had this relationship with our community," Gorbunova told the *Astoria Post*. "A lot of the people that came out on the first day were people that we've known for years that were coming into HiFi—we feel really lucky." Whatever you do, arrive at this sonic buffet extremely hungry.

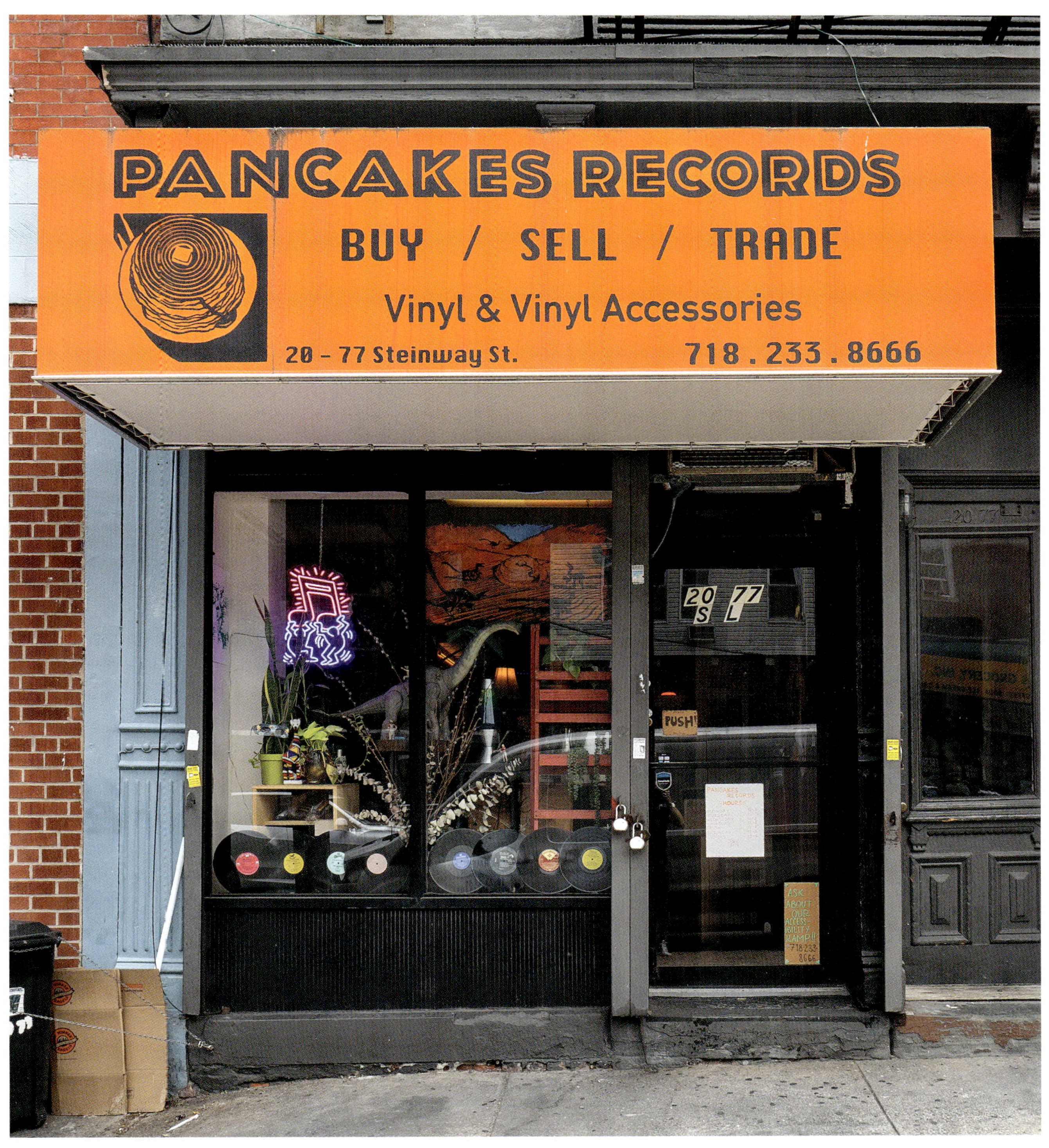

ABOVE Pancakes was co-founded by AJ Pacheco and Tanya Gorbunova. They chose the name because, when their friends get together and listen to records, they say "pancake it" instead of "flip it" when they want to hear the B-side. AJ's mother, an accomplished artist, even designed the pancakes for their logo.

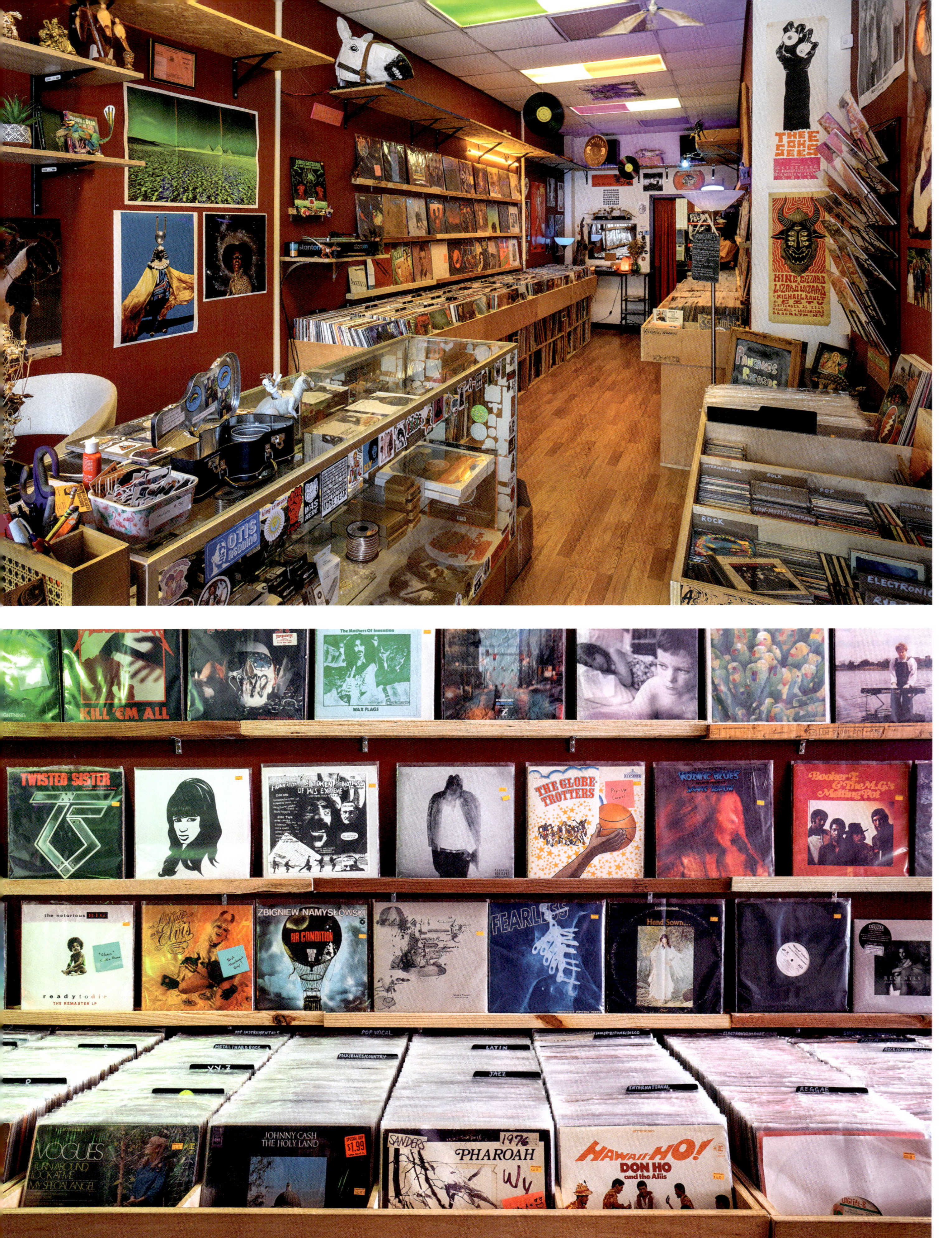

THEE OH SEES
KING GIZZARD & THE LIZARD WIZARD
OTIS REDDING
ROCK
POP
ELECTRONIC
KILL 'EM ALL
The Mothers Of Invention
TWISTED SISTER
THE GLOBE TROTTERS
Booker T. & The M.G.'s Melting Pot
the notorious B.I.G.
ready to die
ZBIGNIEW NAMYSŁOWSKI
AIR CONDITION
METAL/HARD ROCK
LATIN
JAZZ
INTERNATIONAL
REGGAE
VOGUES
TURN AROUND LOOK AT ME MY SPECIAL ANGEL
JOHNNY CASH
THE HOLY LAND
$1.99
SANDERS
1976
PHAROAH
HAWAII HO!
DON HO
and the Aliis

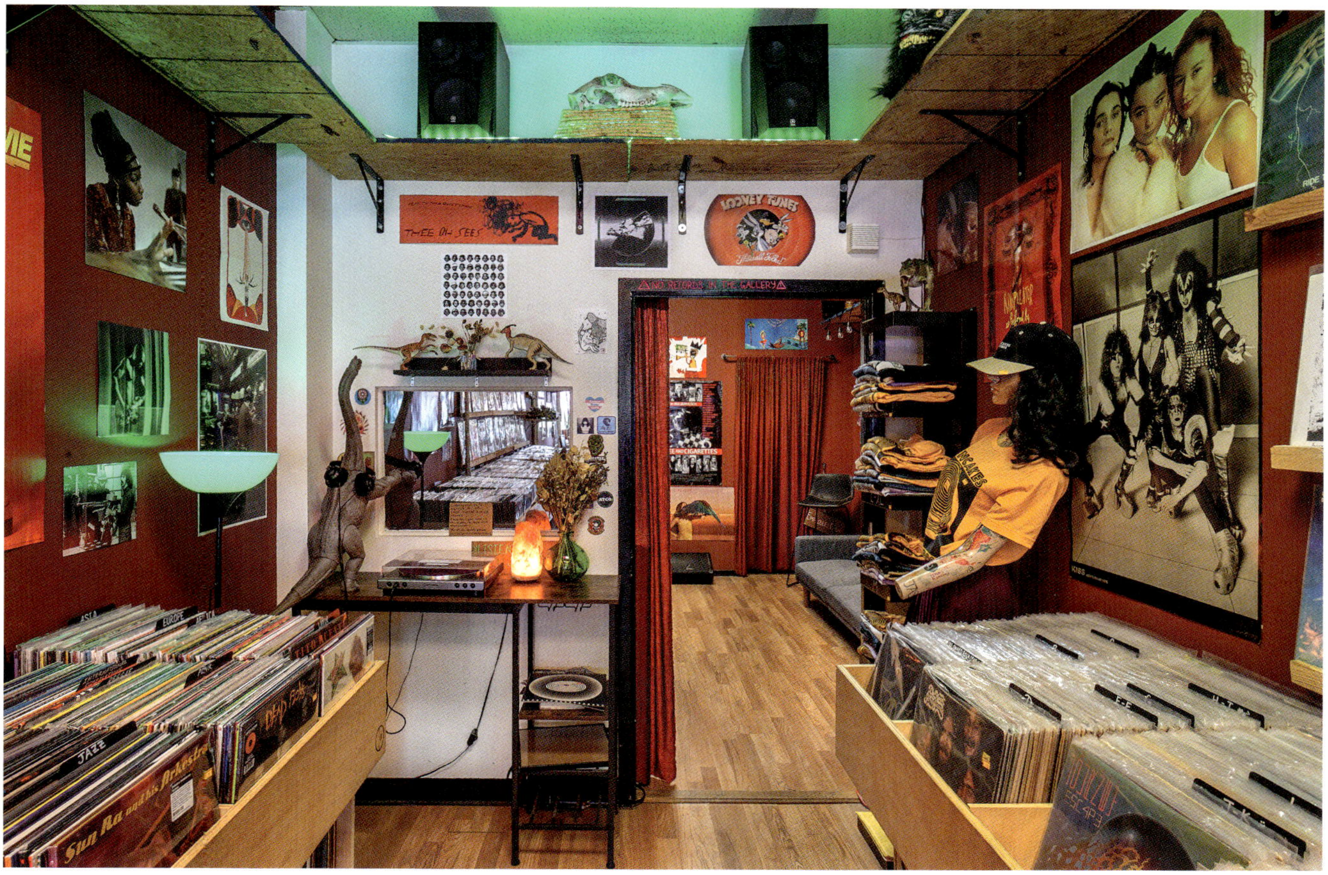

OPPOSITE BOTTOM Pancakes sells both new and used vinyl, with a heavy concentration on new releases. It also offers a wide selection of international music, including a dedicated section for Greece, catering to Astoria's historically large Greek population.

RIGHT The shop is cheerfully decorated with dinosaurs, which were all AJ's childhood toys, including figures from popular movies like *Godzilla* and *Jurassic Park*.

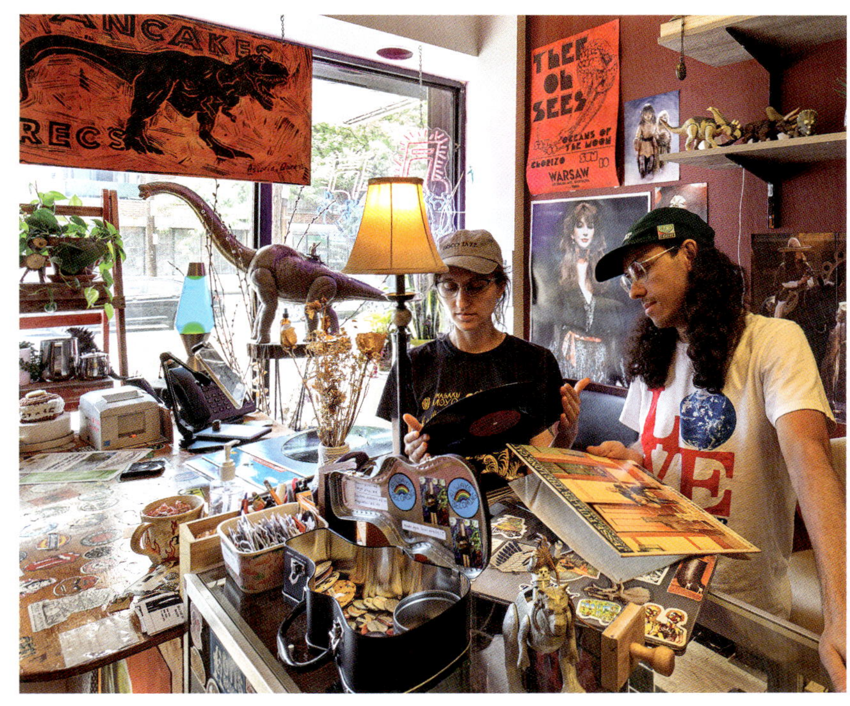

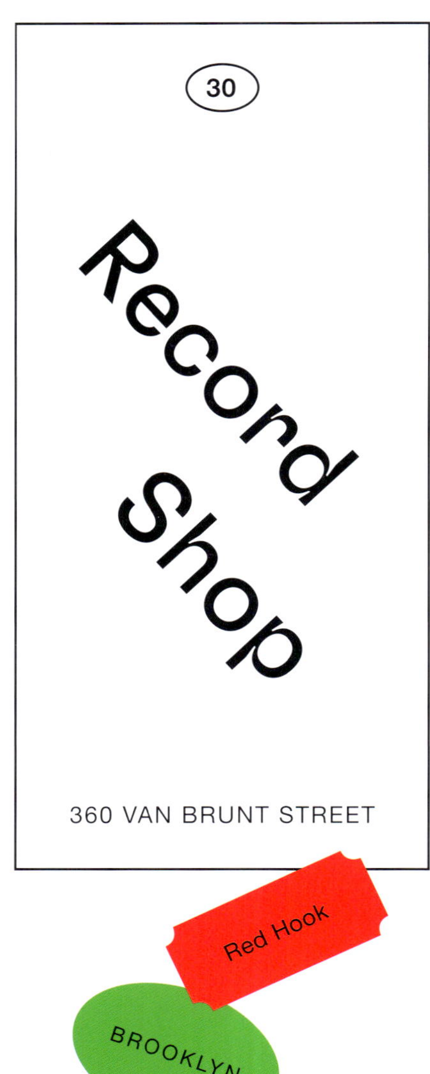

BEFORE BENE COOPERSMITH MOVED INTO 360 Van Brunt Street, it had already been a French restaurant, a spin studio, a volunteer office for Occupy Wall Street, a Spanish library, and a saxophone repair shop. When Coopersmith approached building owner Scott Pfaffman about turning the space into a record store to house his overflowing vinyl collection, Pfaffman had seen half a dozen businesses come and go since the '90s. But Coopersmith, a carpenter, had a confidence in the building that rubbed off. "I don't think this space is cursed," he told the *Red Hook Star-Revue* in 2015, shortly after opening day. "I think I just needed to help make it smile again." At the time, he was still mulling over what to call his new record shop. That was over a decade ago.

Record Shop, Red Hook's only dedicated vinyl store, promises the kind of quintessential Brooklyn experience that can often feel lost to time. Formed from a base of his personal collection, Coopersmith's eclectic offerings feel balanced without major curation. Aretha Franklin classics mingle with $2 '80s workout mixes and rare soul test pressings; a healthy protest music selection co-exists with a bin of "Pop!" collectible bobbleheads; and winding potted plants infuse every hand-labeled row of records with an extra pump of personality. A mobile of a wooden airplane hangs from a quiet corner stocked with an array of books and one black bongo drum.

Raised in Newtown, Connecticut, by a singer-songwriter father, Coopersmith first landed in the city at eighteen. Eventually moving to Verona Street in 2009, he spent his early years in Red Hook frequenting the legendary saloon Sunny's, which has stood in the neighborhood since the 1890s. But his passion for vinyl—and reputation among New York's record collectors—took root during the regular Sunday shifts he worked for years at Park Slope's 5th Avenue Records (which opened in 1972). It was there he began to understand the dig as much more than just a gateway to listening, sharing with the *Star-Revue*, "Sometimes just holding a record and imagining what it contains is even better than listening to it."

If a customer's imagination happens to fail them, however, Coopersmith is happy to step in with a recommendation. He can often be found surveying the shop from out front, turning passersby into buyers with a little kindness and conversation. A listening station set up by the window comes opposite a red vinyl chair, conjuring the feel of a school desk primed for exploration—the within-reach tambourine on the windowsill nearby doesn't exactly scream "Keep to yourself." "Nobody should feel intimidated here," Coopersmith told the *Star-Revue*. "I just want to open up the door and see what kind of conversation happens."

Every record store needs some sort of signature pull to survive an often-unforgiving business: a genre specialty, an events series, or an aesthetic lane. At Record Shop, that signature is Coopersmith. Director Dustin Guy Defa, a former roommate, even based a lead role in his acclaimed 2017 ensemble short film *Person to Person* on the idiosyncratic store owner—and Coopersmith appeared as himself. Set over a single day in New York, the film follows a series of characters as they experience all the mundane and magical experiences the city has to offer. Opposite Michael Cera, Tavi Gevinson, and Abbi Jacobson, Coopersmith plays Benny, a vinyl collector who finds himself on a wild-goose chase around town, searching for a rare new pressing to add to his collection. When creating the role, Defa didn't just choose Coopersmith because he was a friend but because he was a prime example of the unique and passionate business owners across disciplines who work to make the city special. "To me," he told *Vice* in 2015, "Bene is New York."

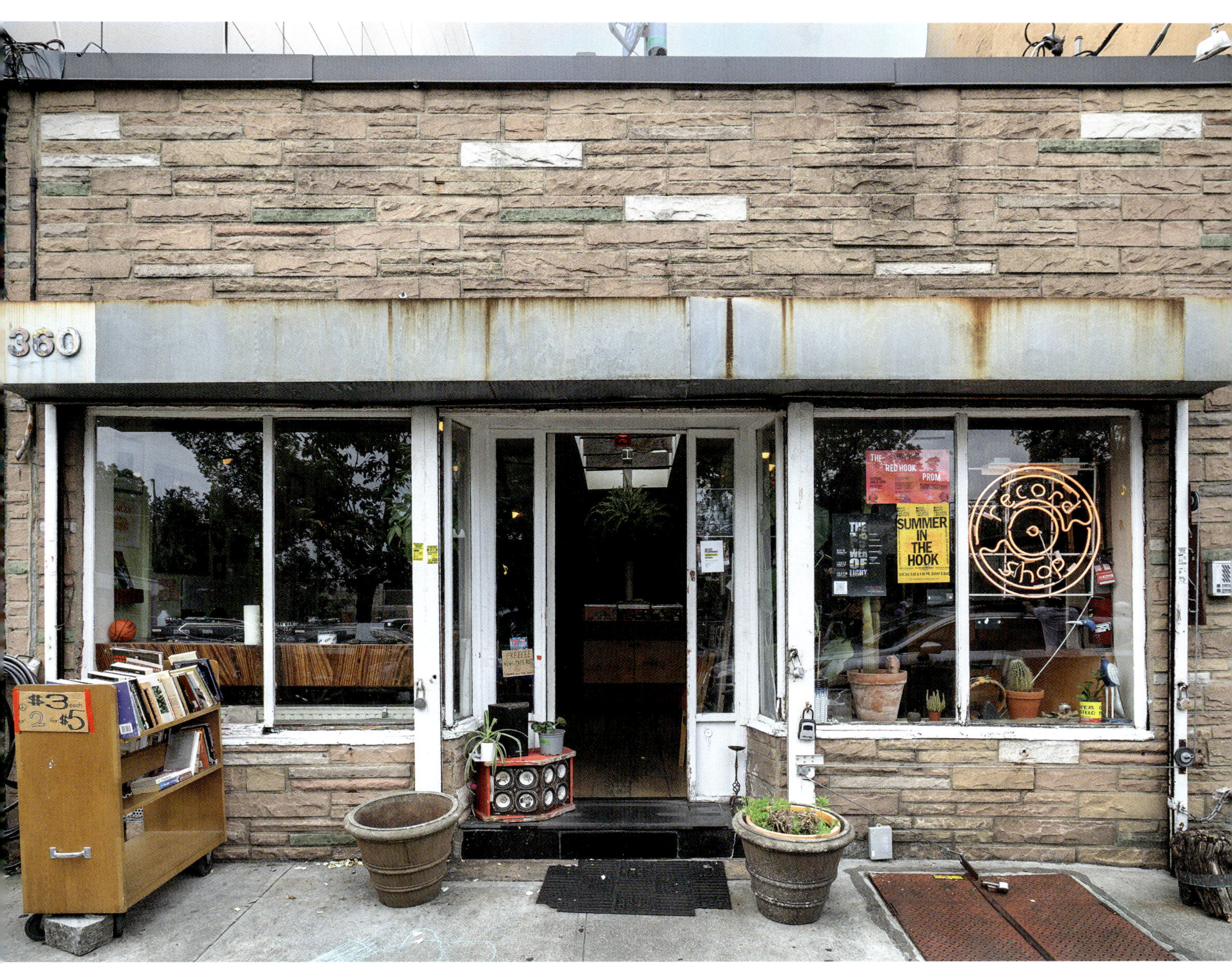

ABOVE Record Shop is Red Hook's only vinyl outlet. It's known by locals as equal parts community space and record store. It has a custom-designed neon sign hanging in the window, which was crafted by Moon Sign, a nearby graphics and neon shop.

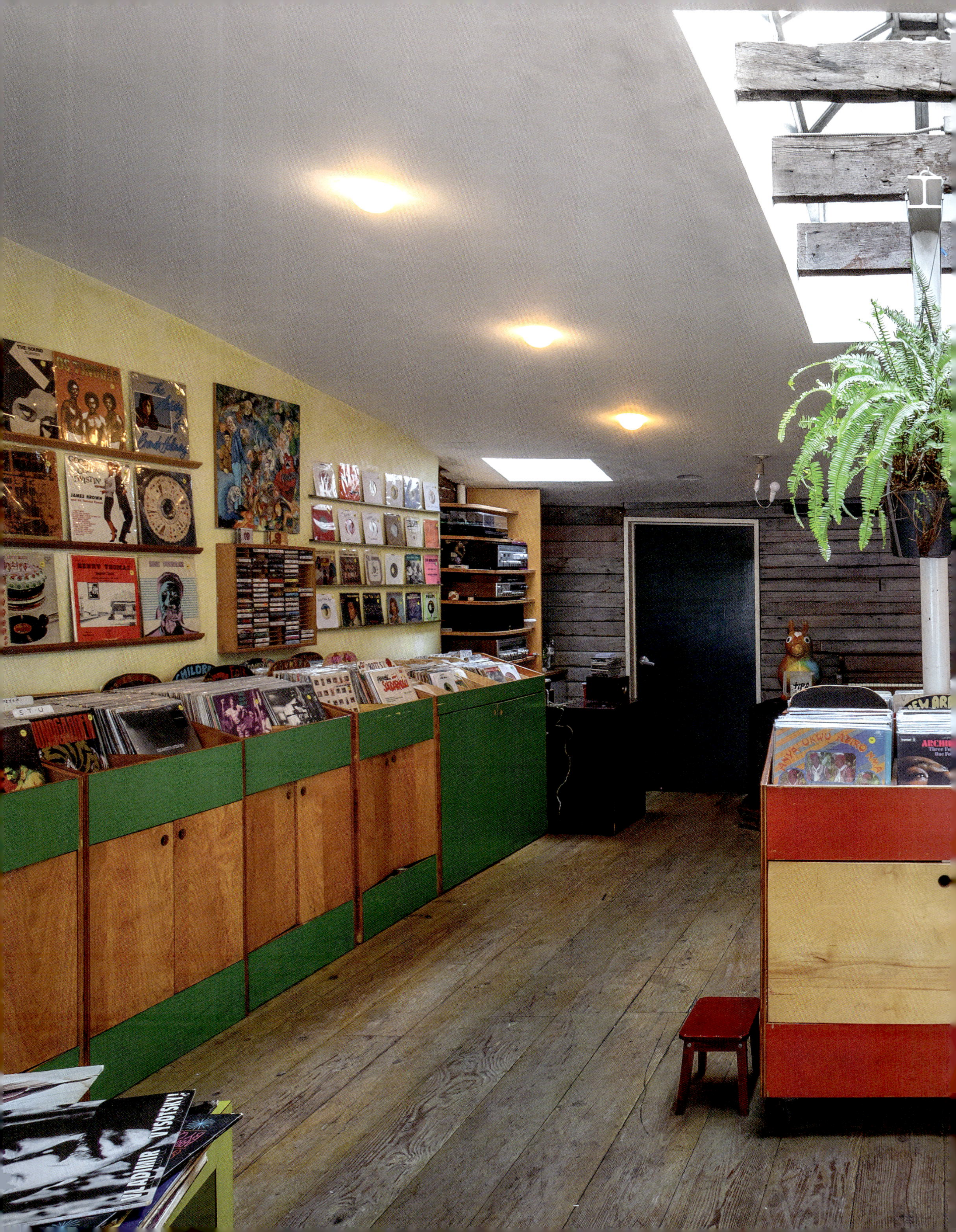

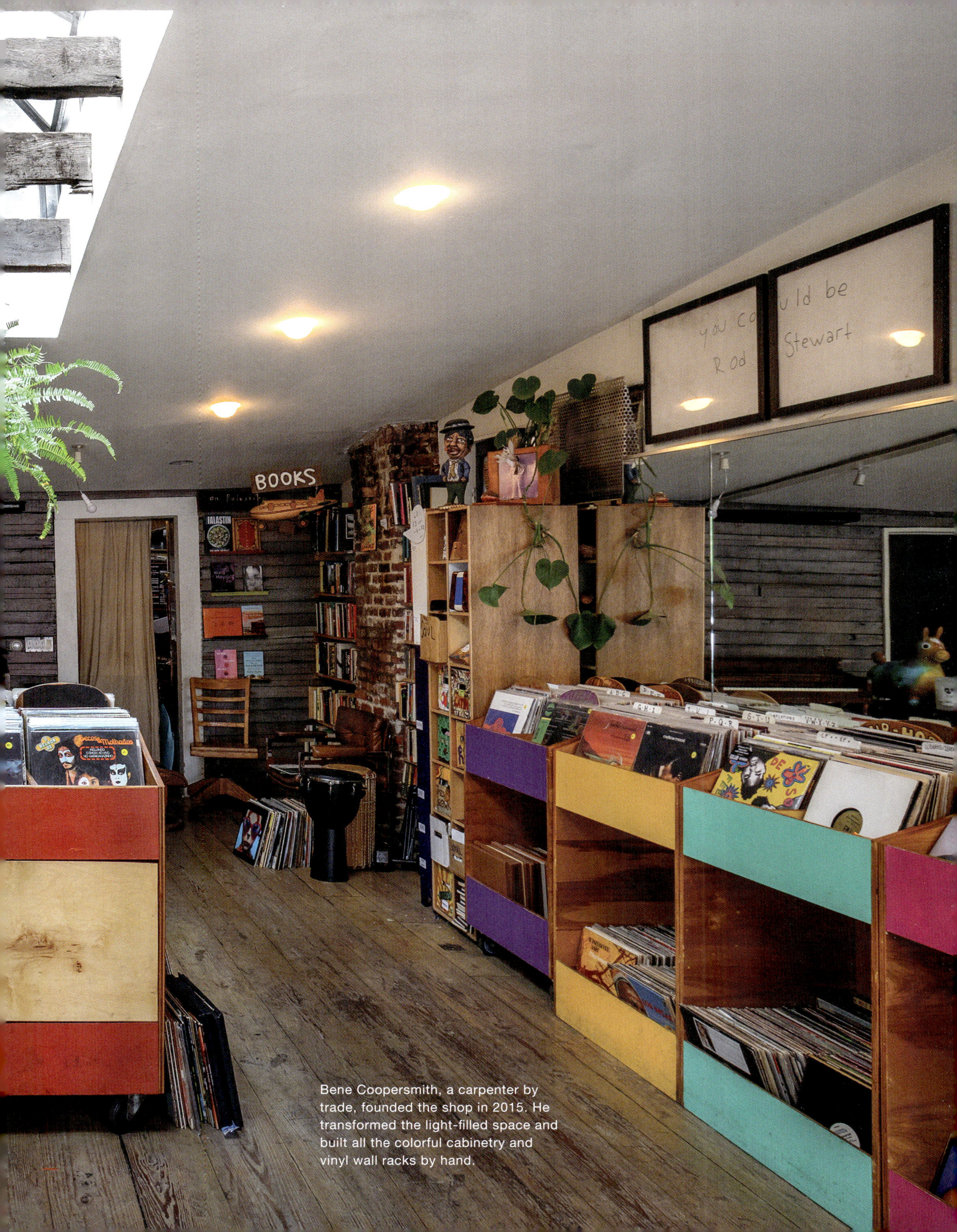

Bene Coopersmith, a carpenter by trade, founded the shop in 2015. He transformed the light-filled space and built all the colorful cabinetry and vinyl wall racks by hand.

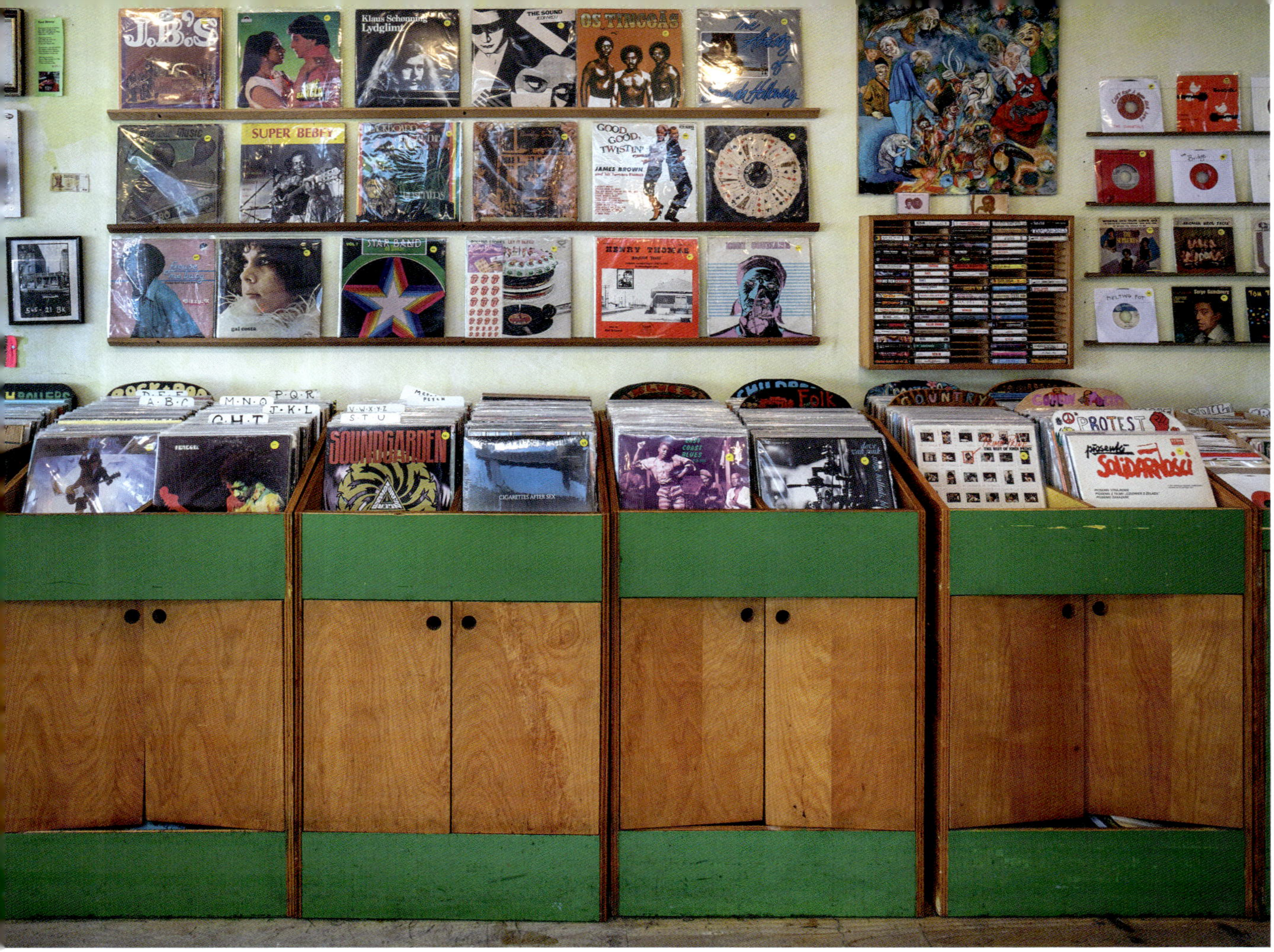

J.B.'S
SUPER BEBEY
SOUNDGARDEN
PROTEST
COUNTRY
Folk
TOTES
$15
HIGH ROLLERS
Hot Tub
record
shop
565-21 BK
Excuse me baby
gal costa
A·B·C
D·E·F
PROPERTY

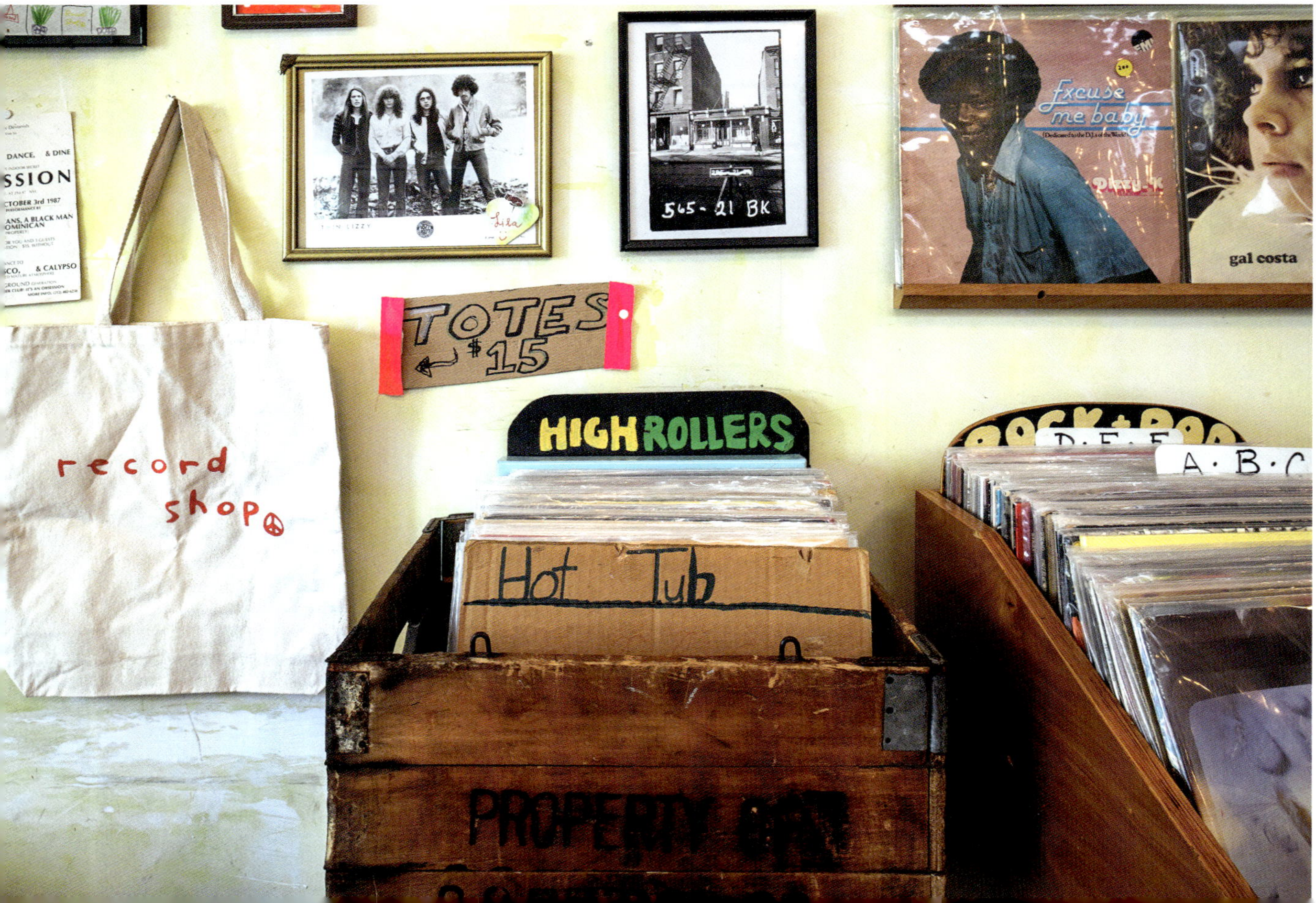

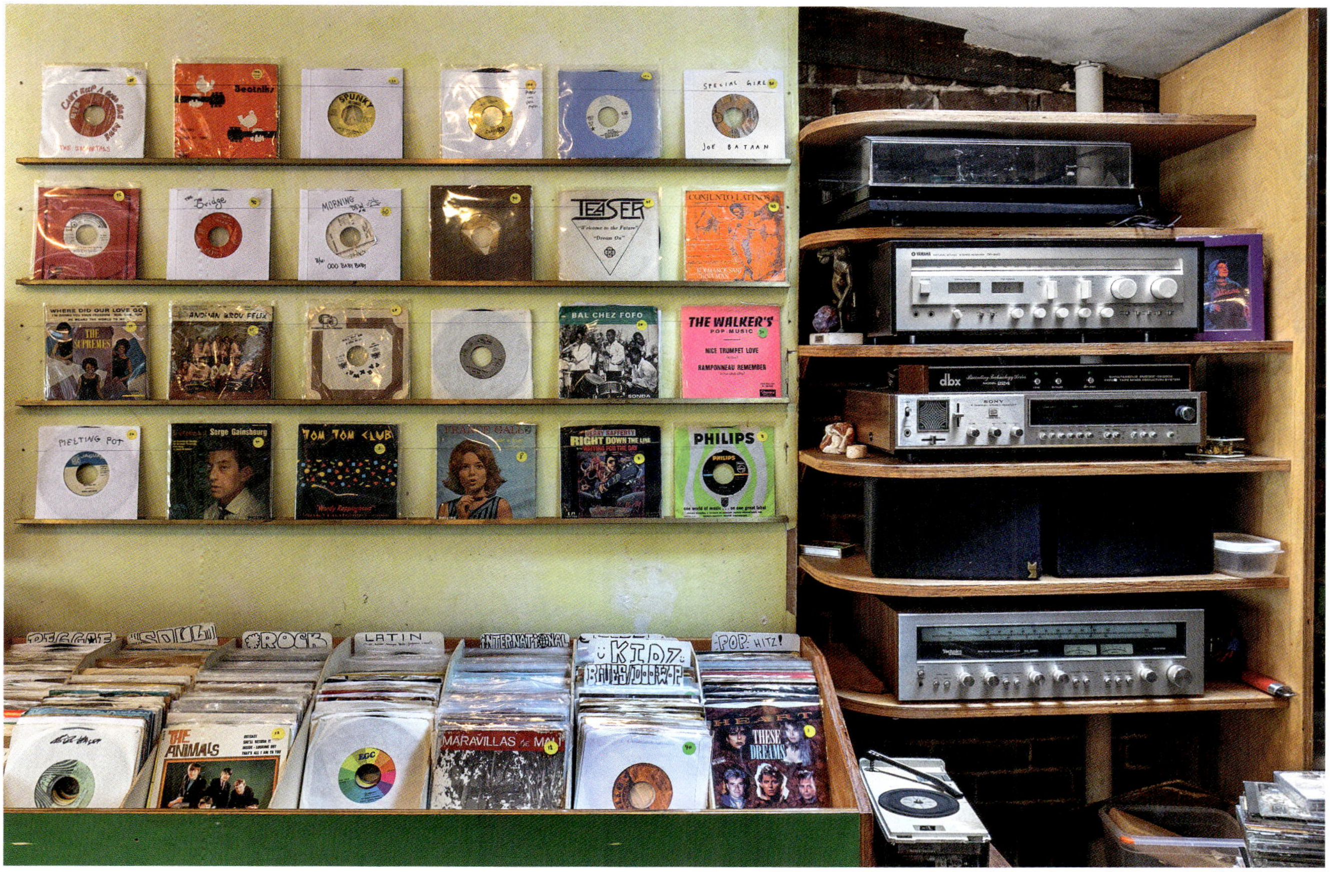

OPPOSITE BOTTOM A vintage wood crate holds the cheekily named "High Rollers / Hot Tub" section for rare valuable vinyl.

ABOVE Handwritten dividers help organize the large selection of 45s, including a special section for "KIDZ."

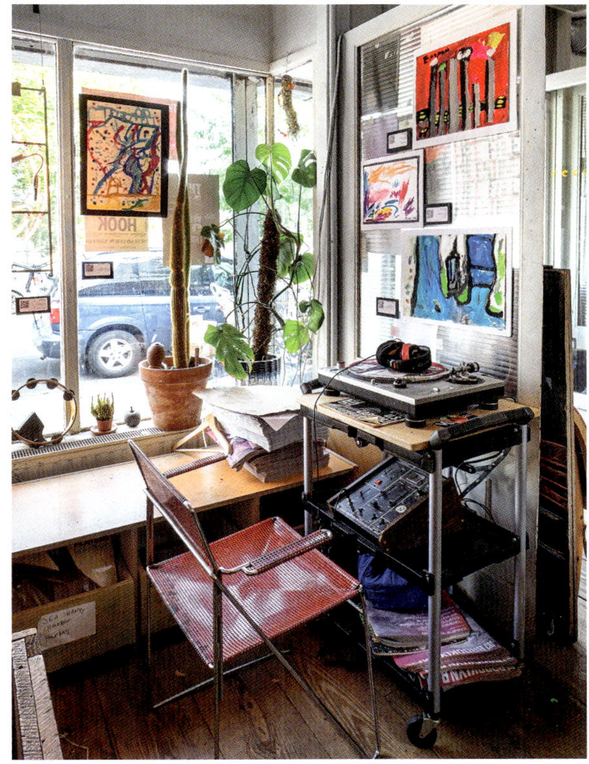

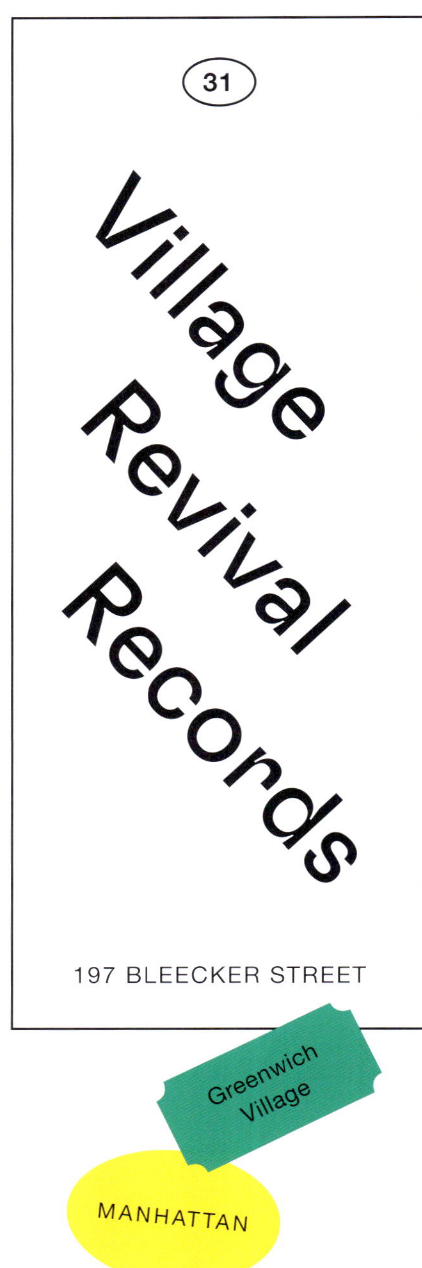

AS A LITTLE BOY GROWING UP in Palestine, Jamal Alnasr and his portable radio were attached at the hip. He could count the number of artists he knew by name on his fingers back then, like Madonna and Boney M. When he settled down in New York (after a few years spent living in Jordan) at seventeen in 1990, he angled for a part-time job at his uncle's record shop on Bleecker Street and quickly realized just how much he didn't know. At first, Alnasr felt out of place when customer queries on Bob Marley, Barbra Streisand, and Louis Armstrong left him stumped—who were these unfamiliar performers that seemed to be a part of every local's vernacular? Then, he felt determined. "I made a promise to myself: I was going to learn all of it," he told the blog *Humans of New York* in 2021.

Step inside Alnasr's downtown shop, Village Revival Records, and it's not so hard to believe he achieved that goal somewhere on the way to the sprawling, genre-indiscriminate collection, which boasts over two hundred thousand records. (Yes, you read that right.) He co-founded his first store, Village Music, with a former business partner in 1994. In paying for a space to lease and cabinets to fill, Alnasr realized he hadn't saved any money for records to sell. So, on opening day, he turned his personal assortment of rare LPs into Village Music's inaugural stock, raking in $5,000 and a surer way forward. After a rent hike in 2017, Alnasr let Village Music go and returned to Palestine, unsure exactly what came next. But after selling some family-owned real estate, he gave his store a second lease on life, and a slightly altered name to match.

Some industry-wise Village Revival regulars have estimated the worth of Alnasr's collection at 197 Bleecker Street to be in the hundreds of thousands of dollars. But the wooden door leading to its basement, when left slightly ajar, reveals a further untold number of items waiting to hit the shop's floor. From Juicy J mixtapes to Eastern European accordion concertos to Sufi whirling music to obsolete 78 RPM records, Alnasr lives up to his self-identification as a "greedy" listener, telling CBS in 2021, "I'd like to have everything around me." In the upper reaches of one Village Revival alcove, reams of sheet music from Bach, Handel, Puccini, and more are stacked to the ceiling.

In 2022 Alnasr sent an unlikely friend home with the compilation *Palestine Lives! Songs from the Struggle of the People of Palestine*: the model Bella Hadid, whose own family fled Palestine as refugees in 1948. Hadid is far from the only high-profile guest he's charmed, though. Alnasr counts Rosalía, André 3000, and countless others among his regular customers. A pre-fame Lana Del Rey even began shopping with him as a college student. (A signed copy of her 2012 debut *Born to Die* at the shop reads: "To Village Music and Jamal, lots of love.")

To maintain his stock, Alnasr watches new releases like a hawk, but also regularly purchases private collections, many of which he doesn't have to dig too hard for. Given the strength of Village Revival's reputation these days, the rare gems tend to walk themselves through the door. "I don't find them," he told *Pitchfork* of his customer base in 2023. "They find me."

Like many neighborhood stores, Alnasr closed for a period during 2020's Covid-19 quarantine; in early 2024 he spent a month without heat, wearing a winter coat behind the counter. He's all too familiar with fighting price gouging, precarious plumbing, and the countless other surprises that come with Manhattan living. But he's never considered closing the curtain on his Greenwich Village community. The main difference between the omnivorous music-loving teenager on the trail of Barbra Streisand and the grown-up guardian of one of Manhattan's most lauded collections are the hundreds of customers Alnasr has converted to friends. "When people come to my store to learn about music, it's like a mirror," he told *Humans of New York*. "I see myself in them. And it's a beautiful connection."

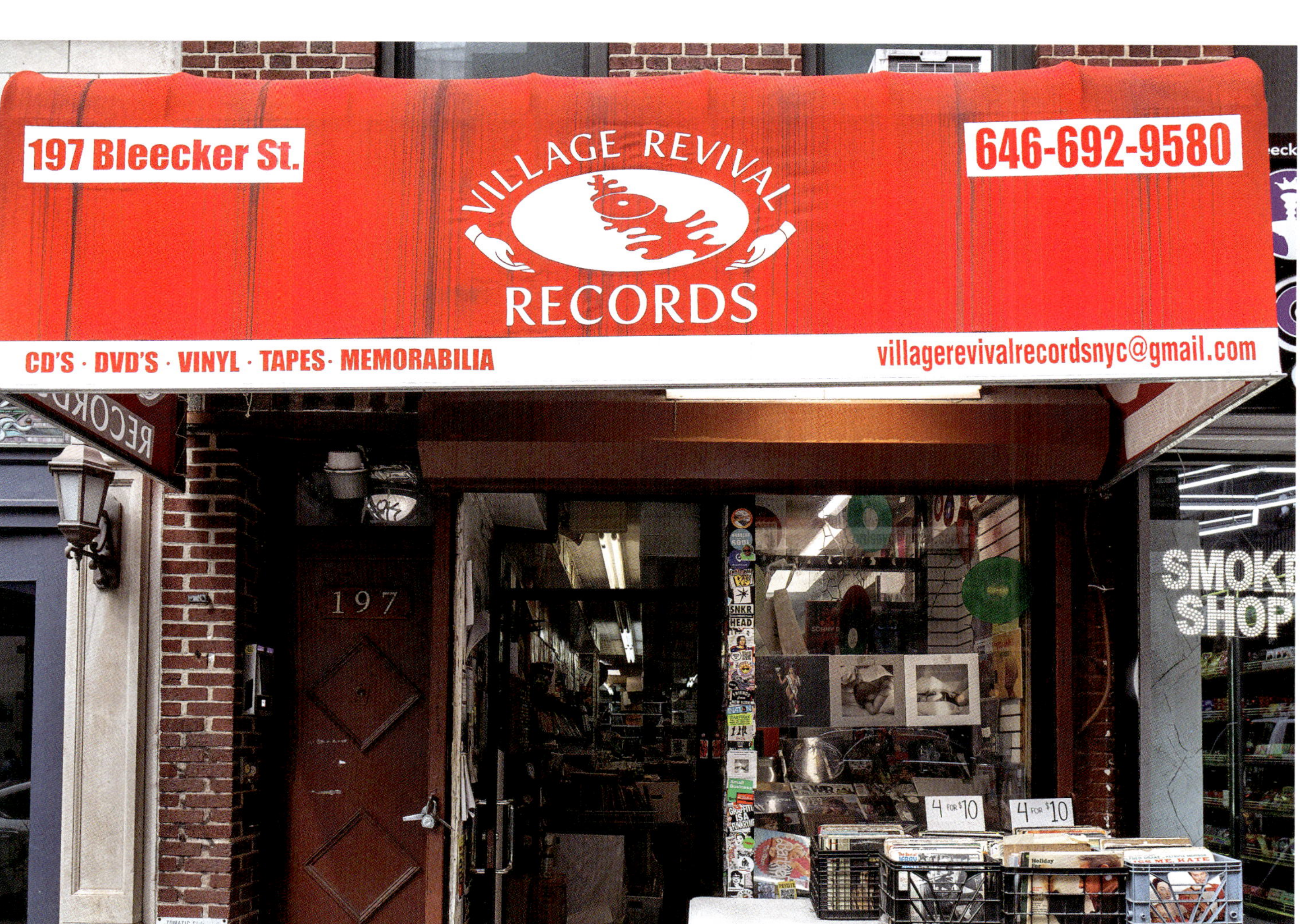

ABOVE Located in the heart of Greenwich Village, Village Revival Records has welcomed customers since its beginning as Village Music in 1994. Its window display showcases the many new vinyl records available inside. The cavernous store is also a destination for crate-diggers, as it stocks a huge selection of used LPs, 45s, and 78s in all genres, including the four-for-$10 bins set up outside.

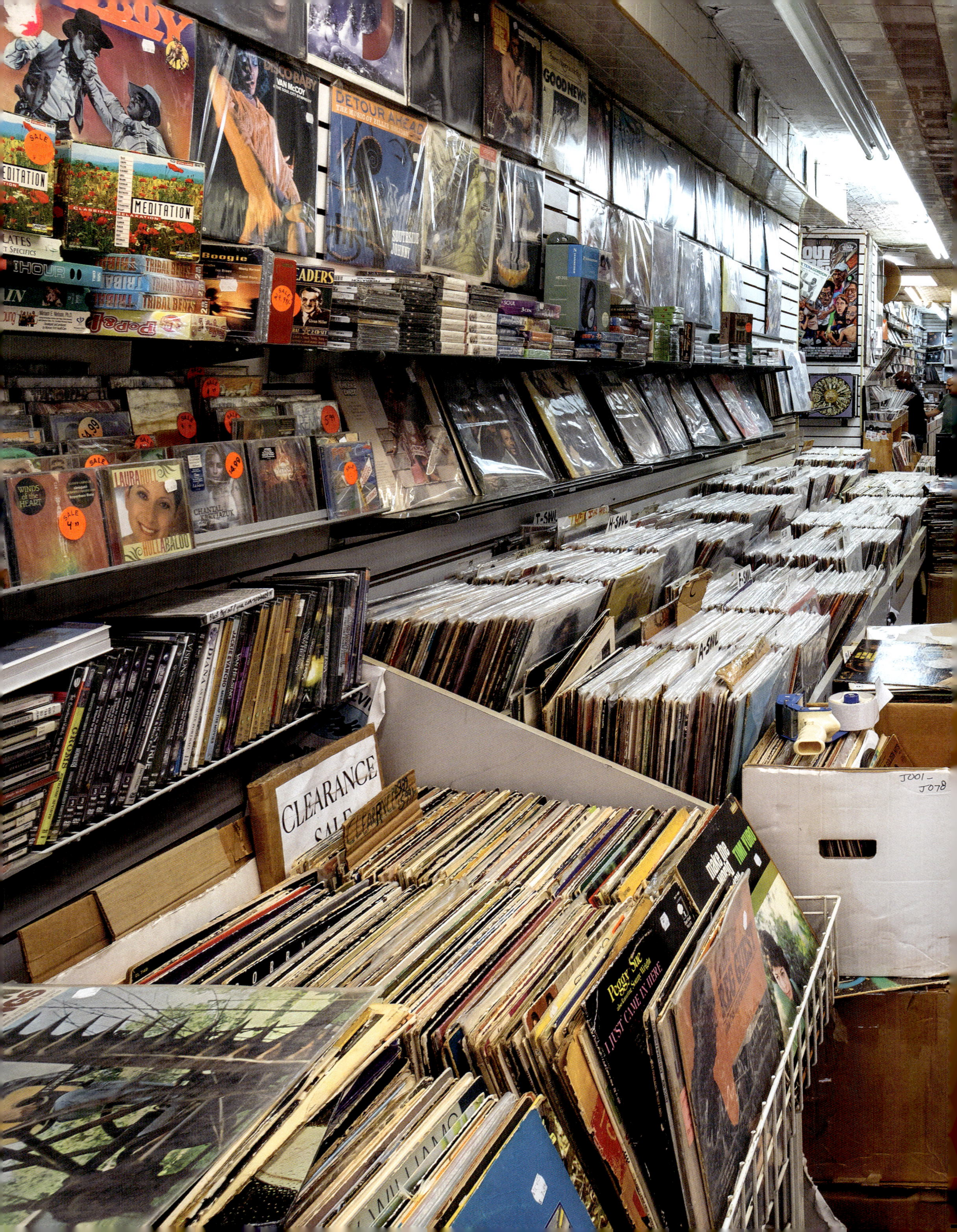
DETOUR AHEAD
GOOD NEWS
MEDITATION
TRIBAL BEATS
LEADERS
LAURA HULL
HULLABALOO
WINDS of the HEART
SALE
4.99
T-SOUL
A-SOUL
CLEARANCE SALE
JOO1-JO78
Peggy Sue
I JUST CAME IN HERE

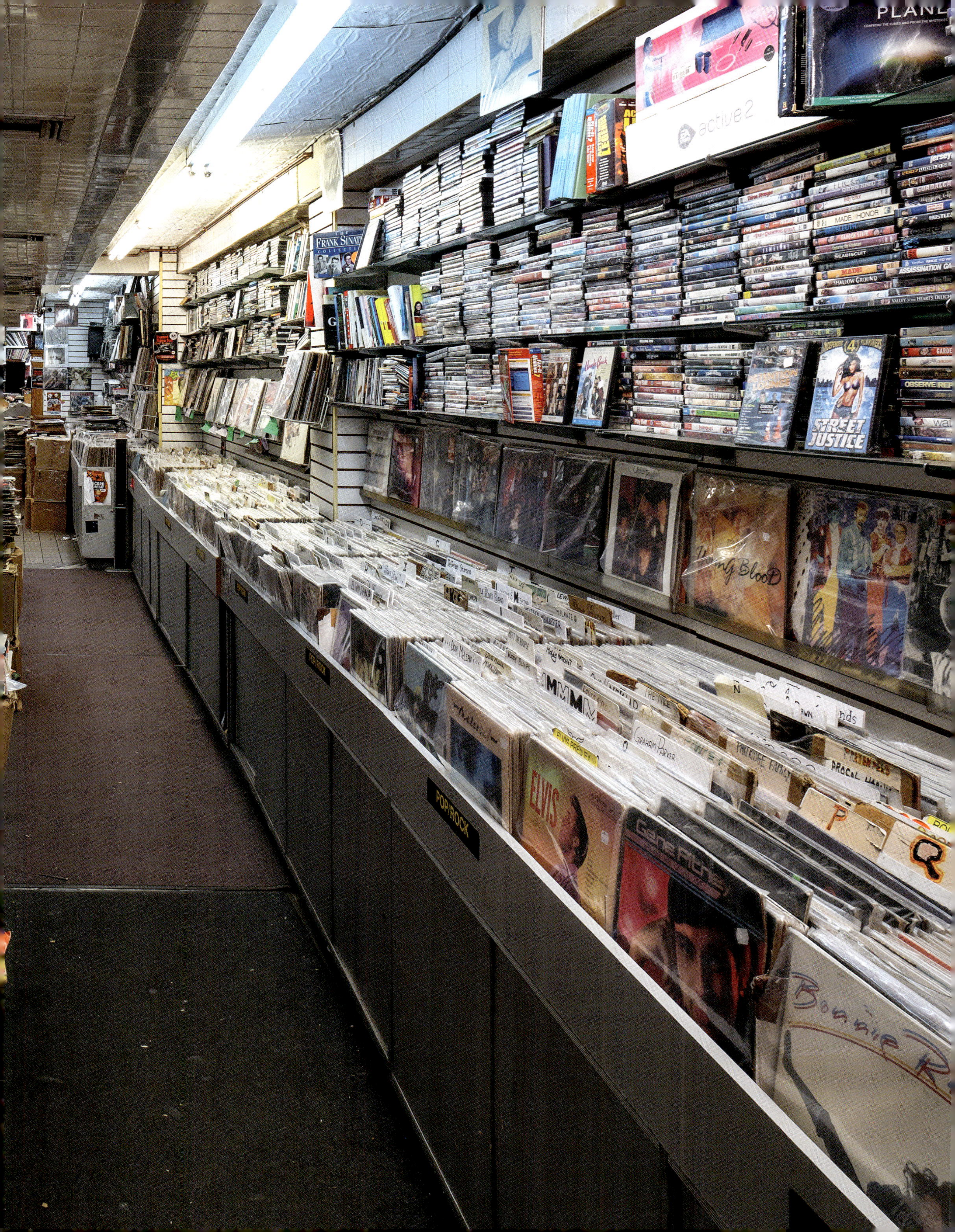

active2
SEABISCUIT
WICKED LAKE
STREET JUSTICE
POP/ROCK
ELVIS

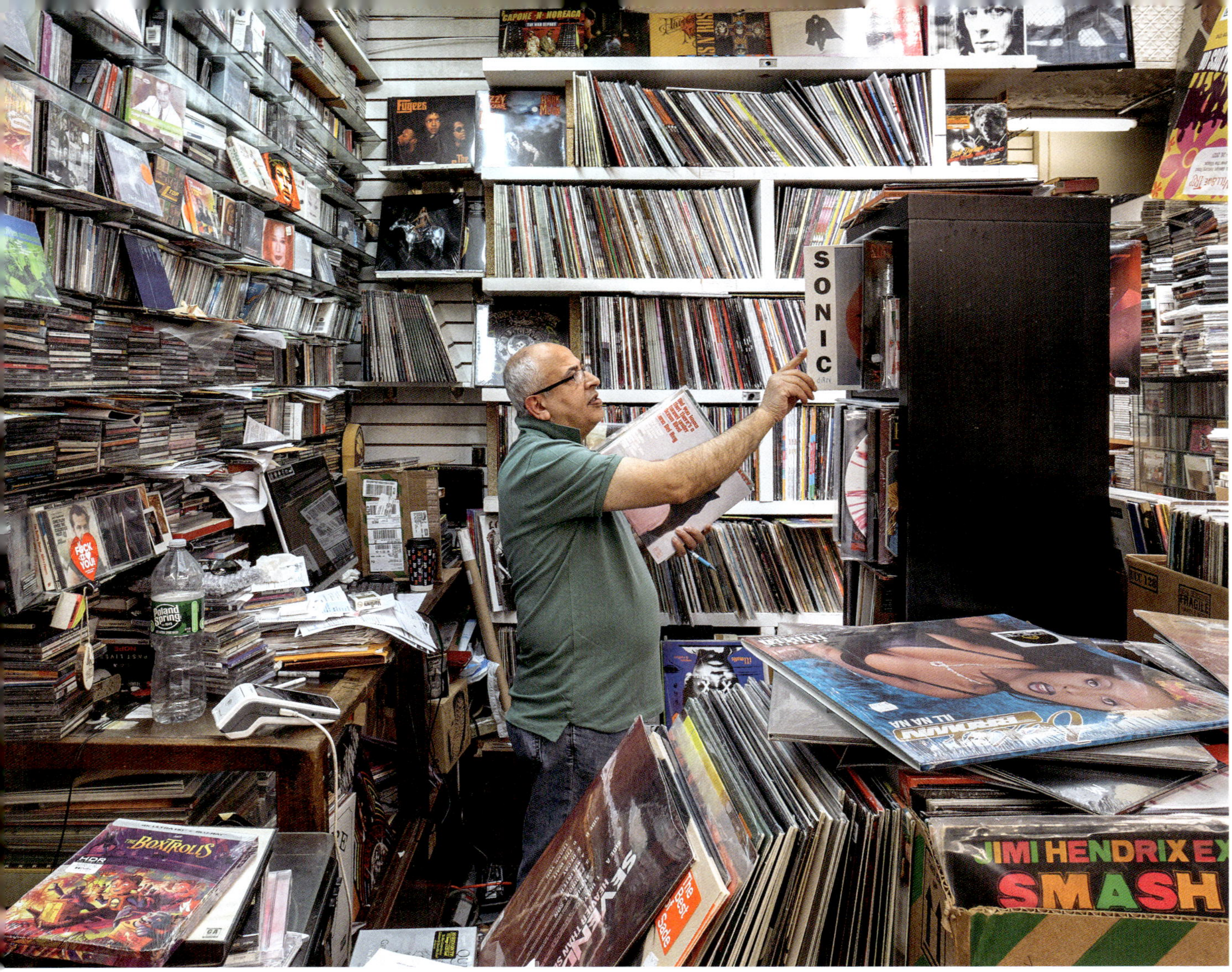

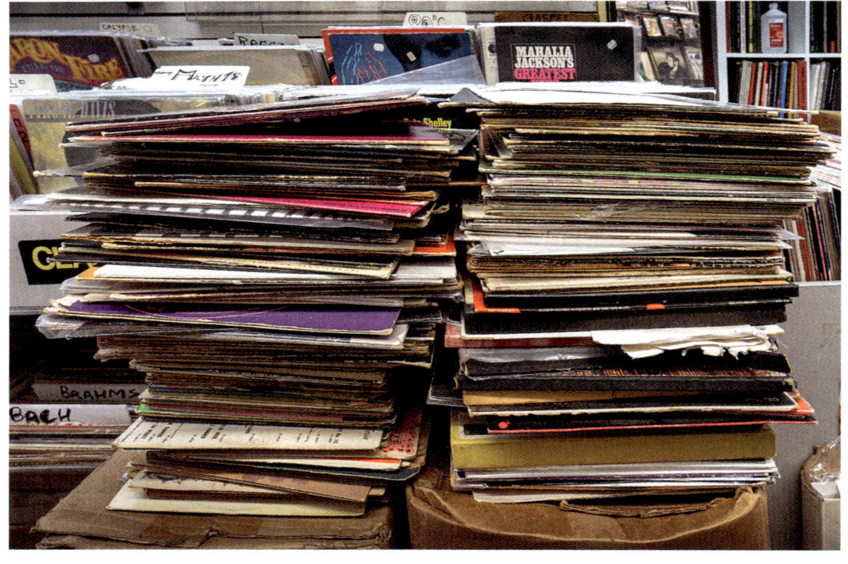

ABOVE Even though the store contains over two hundred thousand records, owner Jamal Alnasr knows exactly where to locate everything. If you don't see what you're looking for, be sure to ask Jamal, as he keeps some of his most prized vinyl stored in the back room behind the register.

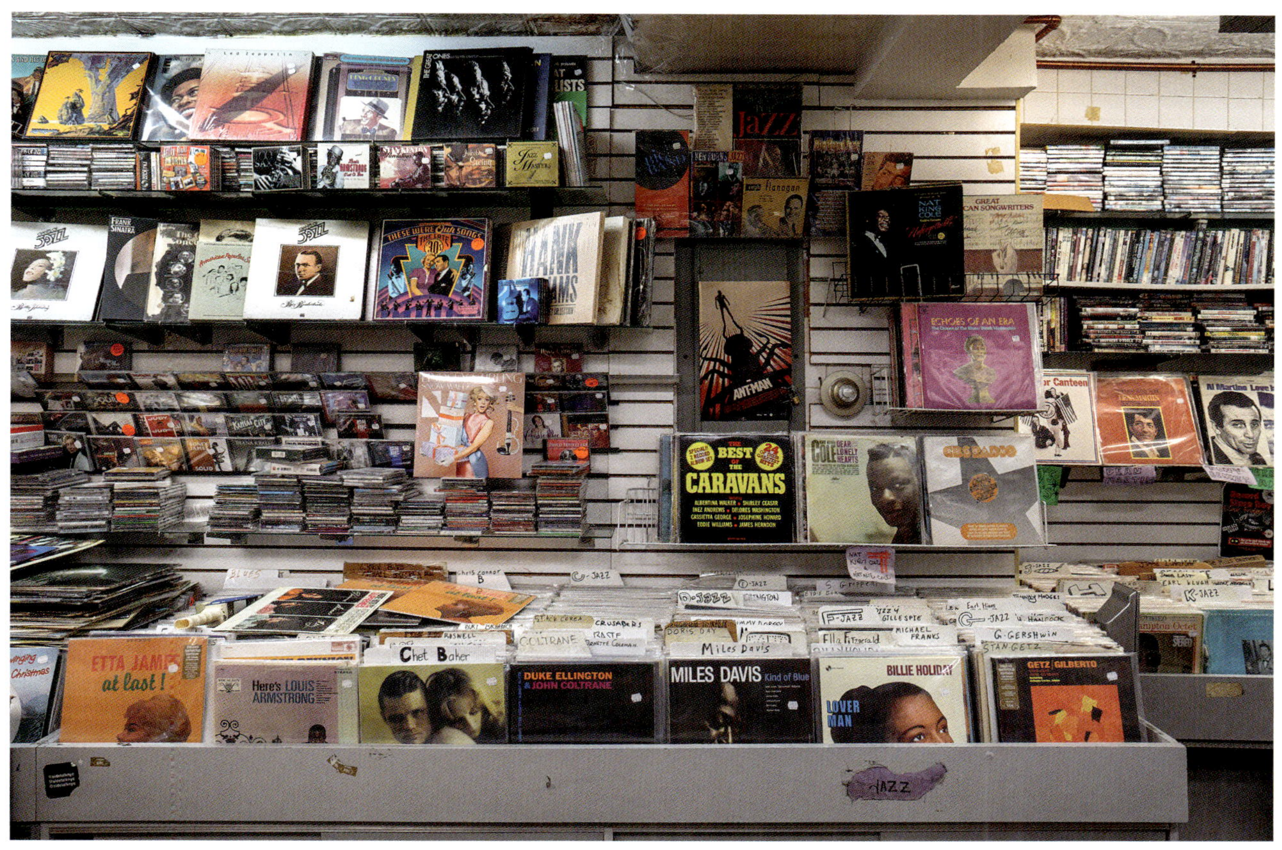
THE BEST OF THE CARAVANS
ECHOES OF AN ERA
ETTA JAMES at last!
Here's LOUIS ARMSTRONG
Chet Baker
DUKE ELLINGTON & JOHN COLTRANE
MILES DAVIS Kind of Blue
BILLIE HOLIDAY
LOVER MAN
GETZ/GILBERTO
JAZZ

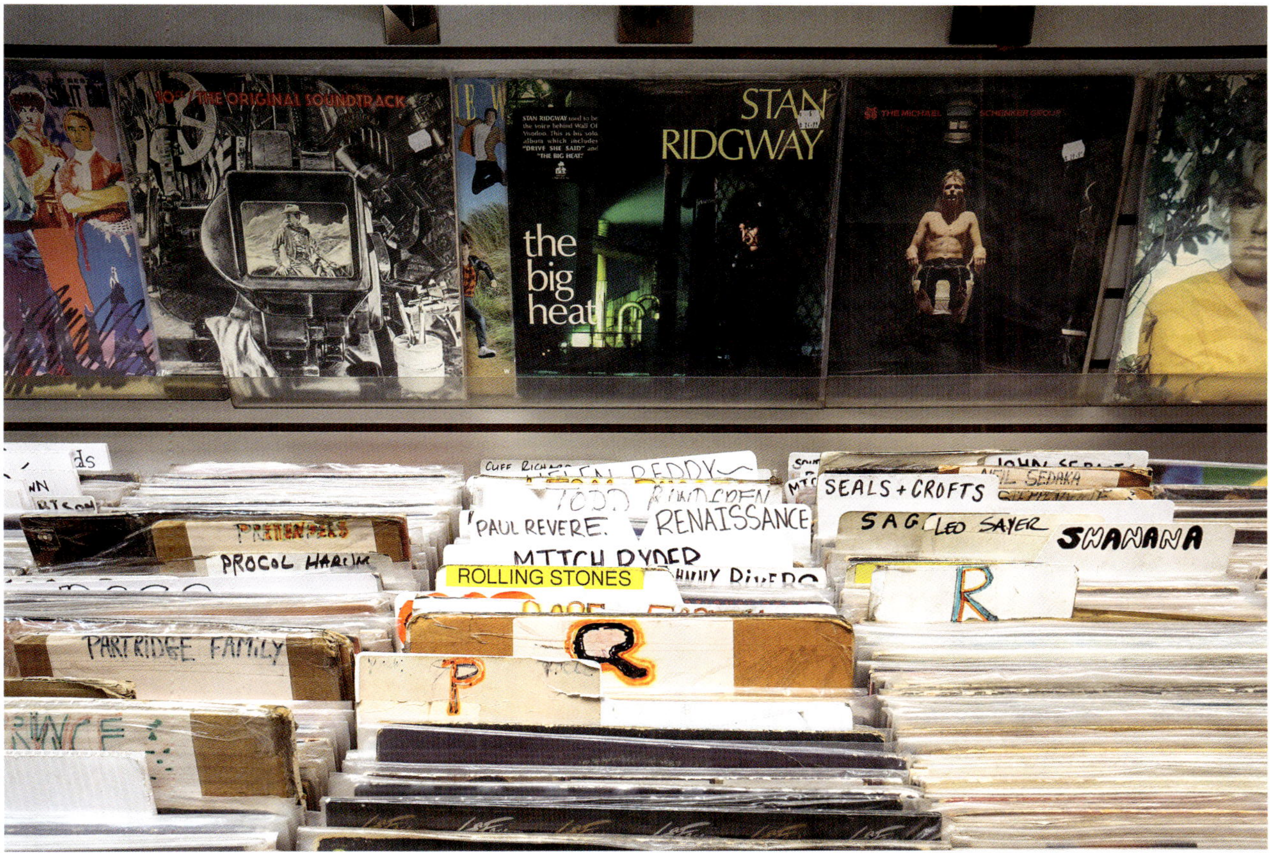

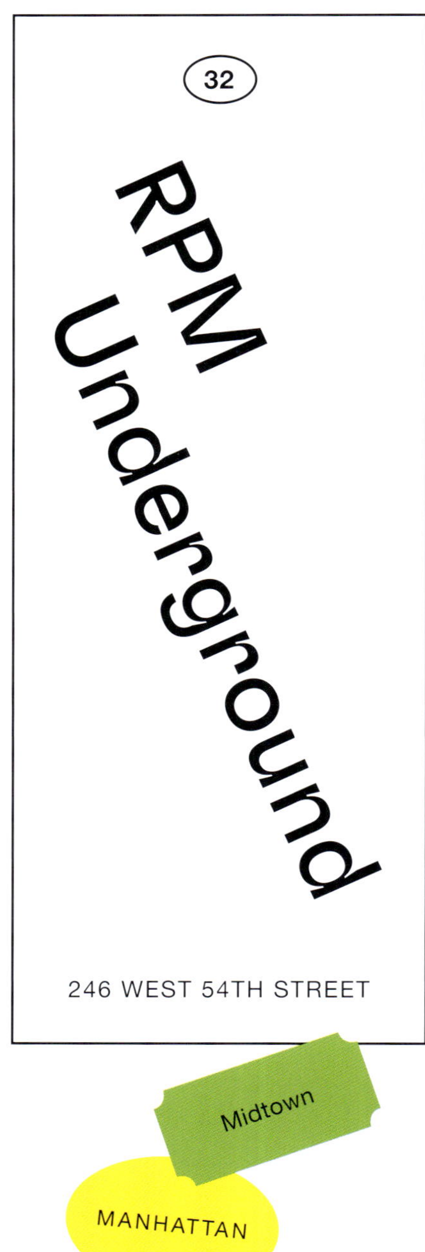

WHEN SAM HUH DESCRIBES THE "mom-and-pop shop" he manages out of a two-floor space on 54th Street, he's not talking about the type of cozy, one-counter corner the moniker immediately conjures. RPM Underground and its internal record store are unique amid their few Midtown-based peers (that is, small, independently run businesses without franchise attachment). And Huh, who opened the store with Raj Banik in 2019, wouldn't have that any other way.

Every piece of decor at RPM Underground has been sourced from Huh's personal collection, compiled across thirty years. "If you ever come to my place," he shares, "you will recognize it from the decorations...I love a lot of energy." That means hand-carved LP holders and vintage audio equipment on display amid rows of pop, rock, funk, opera, musical soundtracks, and more. In one downstairs room, a Cubist Marilyn Monroe sucks in a pouty breath across from a painting of Mount Rushmore. Between two other rooms, a full-size canoe hangs upturned along the ceiling.

RPM Underground specializes in classic Americana from every inch of the continent, and its collection of Brazilian records is also especially vibrant. Across surprisingly cavernous reserves (in Midtown, no less!), Huh estimates the store has twenty-thousand-plus different pieces of wax to its name at any given time, with new sellers bringing through stock every day. The spread at its maze-like location only represents a portion of the total holdings, though—thirty minutes outside the city, a storage warehouse helps Huh replenish his rapidly-circulating collection.

Although the breadth of its repertoire may not immediately meet the eye at street level, don't mistake this space for a hideaway. A stratified wooden box affixed to RPM Underground's front door holding free LPs gets the Broadway treatment here, illuminated beneath the red-and-gold glow of a flashbulb marquee. And for anyone reluctant to go gentle into the night with just a few new samba rock records, Banik heads up a downstairs area equipped with eighteen private karaoke rooms, each themed after a different pillar of pop music history. Priced by the hour and catering to parties as small as four and as large as five hundred, the venue frequently shelters off-duty Broadway stars testing (and resting) their pipes away from the crowd. In 2022 Broadway actor Syndee Winters told *New York* magazine the space was "one giant time capsule of why people love music."

Beyond handling plenty of karaoke nights, RPM Underground regularly transforms its quarters into a venue for comedy shows, political debate viewing parties, and more. Expanding the scope of what sorts of events and communities it caters to doesn't just keep regulars coming back. It guarantees Huh and Banik can build relationships with an increasingly diverse group of sellers and patrons, the ripples that help the business thrive. "There's so much to learn...there's no way you can know everything. So I never get bored," Huh shares. "Every day, every hour, I learn something new."

RPM Underground is for those music lovers who see the intellectual journey on the way to a great purchase as equally valuable to the destination—as well as anyone looking to belt out Cher tunes with 499 of their closest acquaintances behind the doors of a true Manhattan original. Now *that's* showbiz, baby.

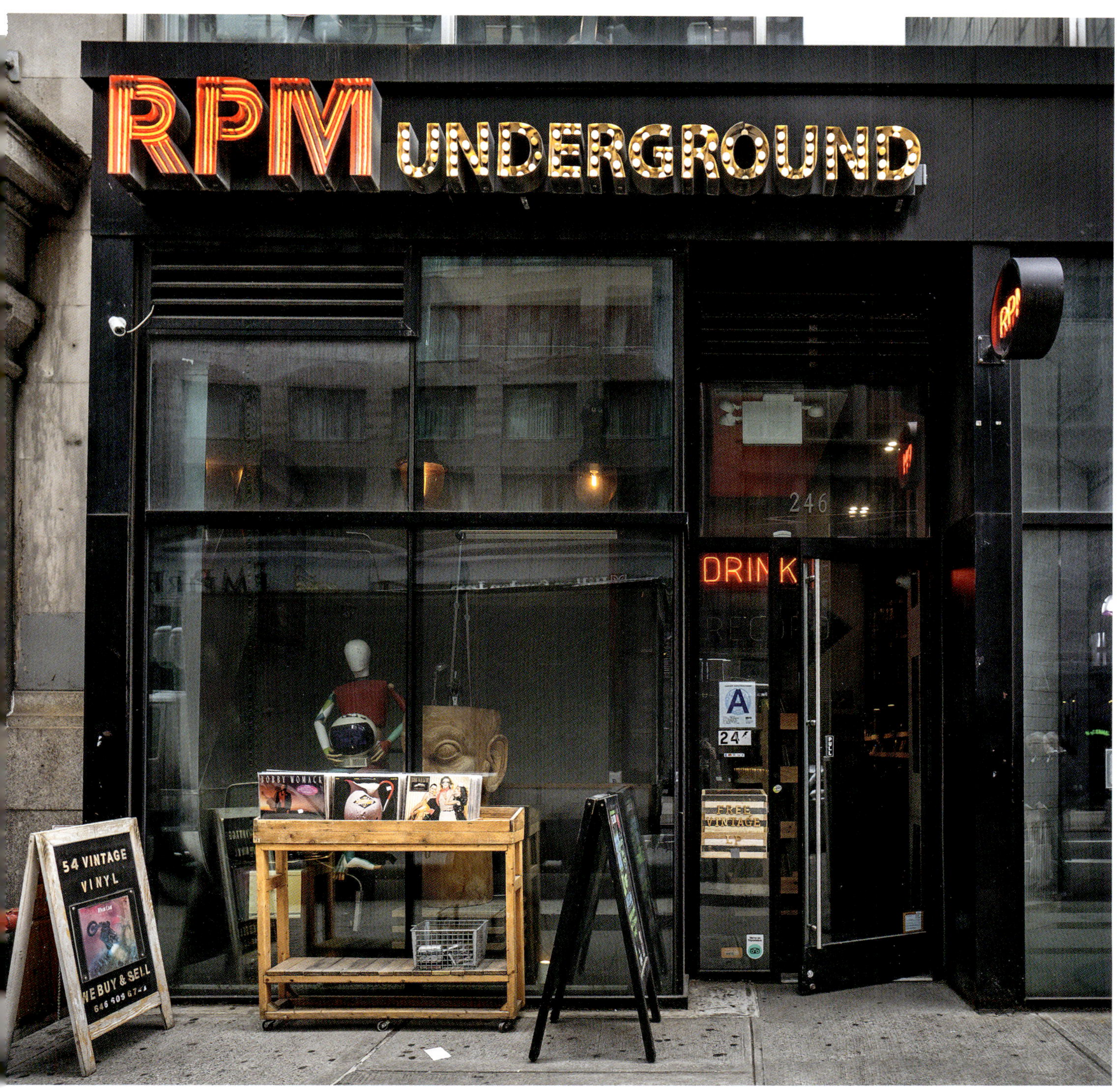

ABOVE Located on a side street in the Theater District, RPM Underground is a unique bi-level space featuring a ground-floor record store and an underground speakeasy with eighteen private pop-themed karaoke rooms. The record shop sells new and used vinyl, concentrating on classic American rock, pop, jazz, blues, and soundtracks.

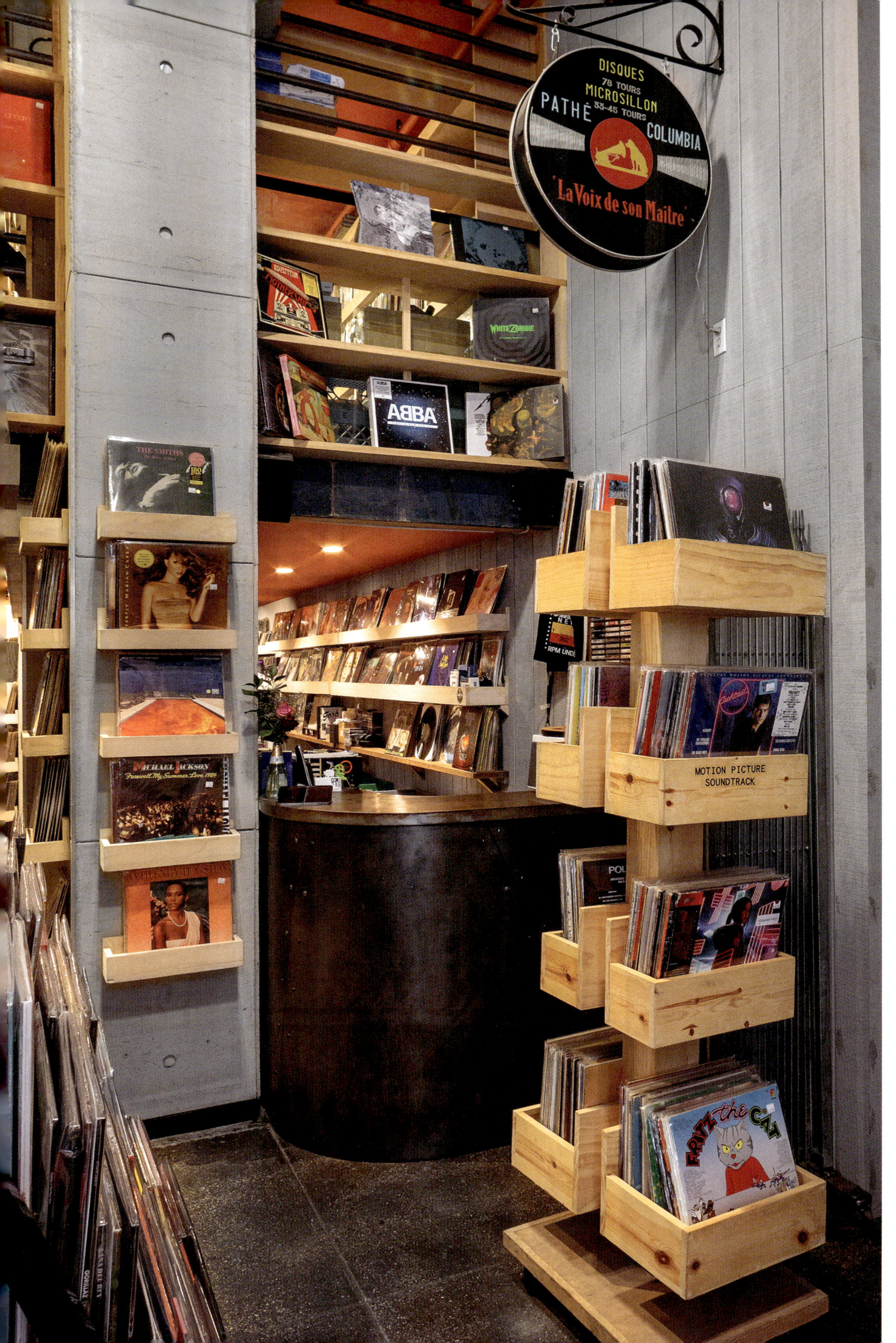
DISQUES
78 TOURS
MICROSILLON
33-45 TOURS
PATHÉ
COLUMBIA
"La Voix de son Maître"
MOTION PICTURE
SOUNDTRACK
ABBA
THE SMITHS
MICHAEL JACKSON
Farewell My Summer Love 1984
FRITZ the CAT

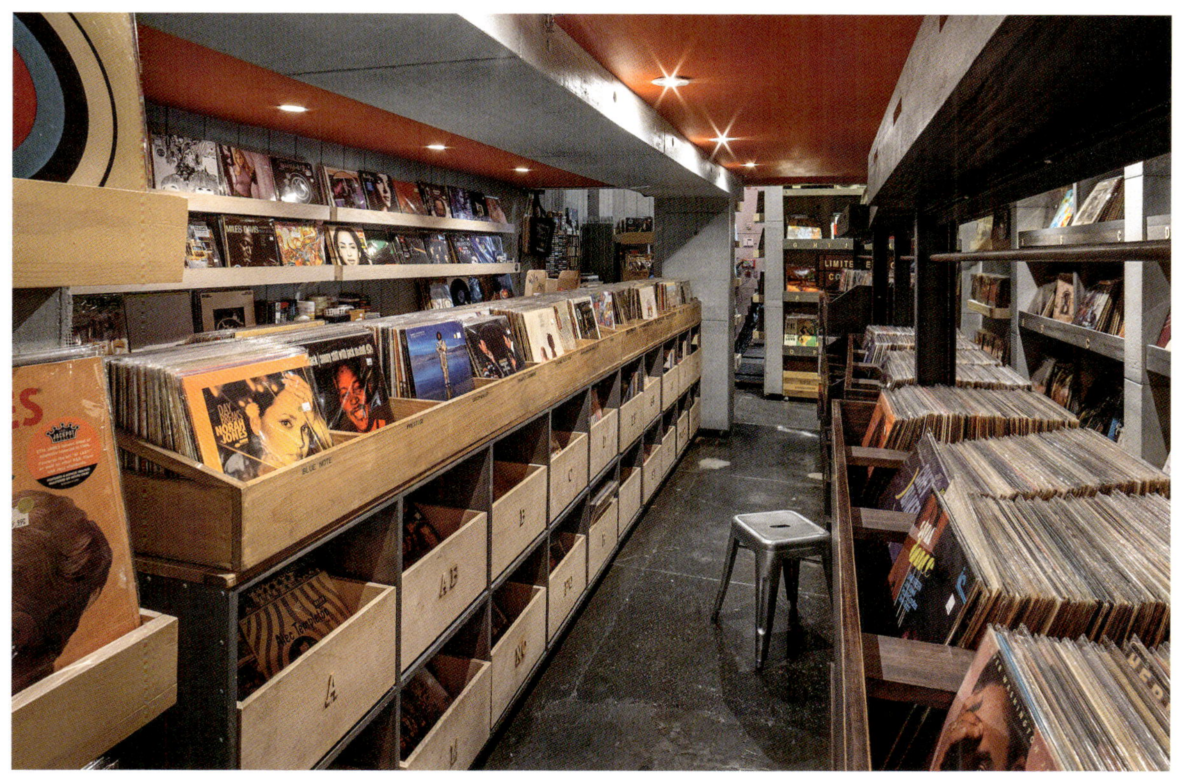

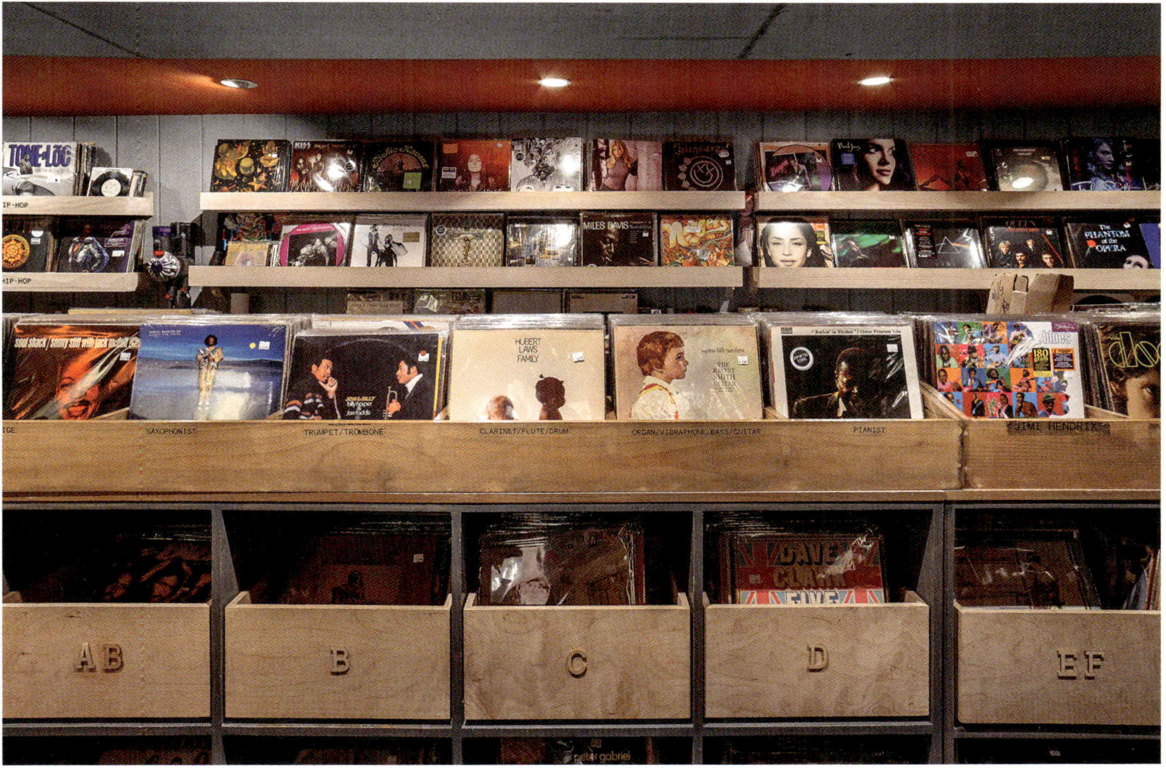

BOTTOM Custom-designed cabinetry, including bins and pull-out drawers all labeled alphabetically and organized by genre, keep the small space easy to navigate.

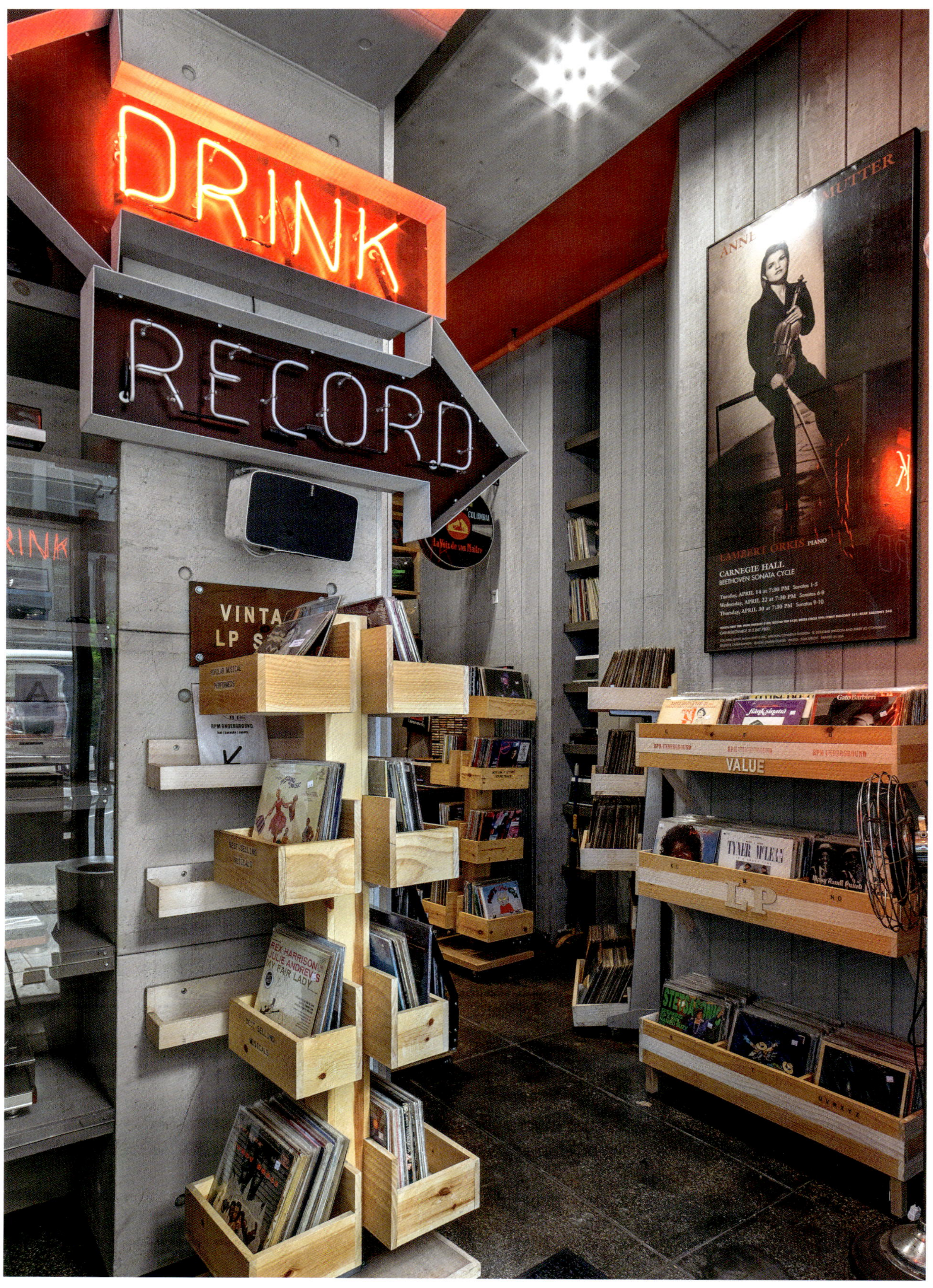
DRINK
RECORD
LAMBERT ORKIS PIANO
CARNEGIE HALL
BEETHOVEN SONATA CYCLE
REX HARRISON
JULIE ANDREWS
MY FAIR LADY
VALUE
LP

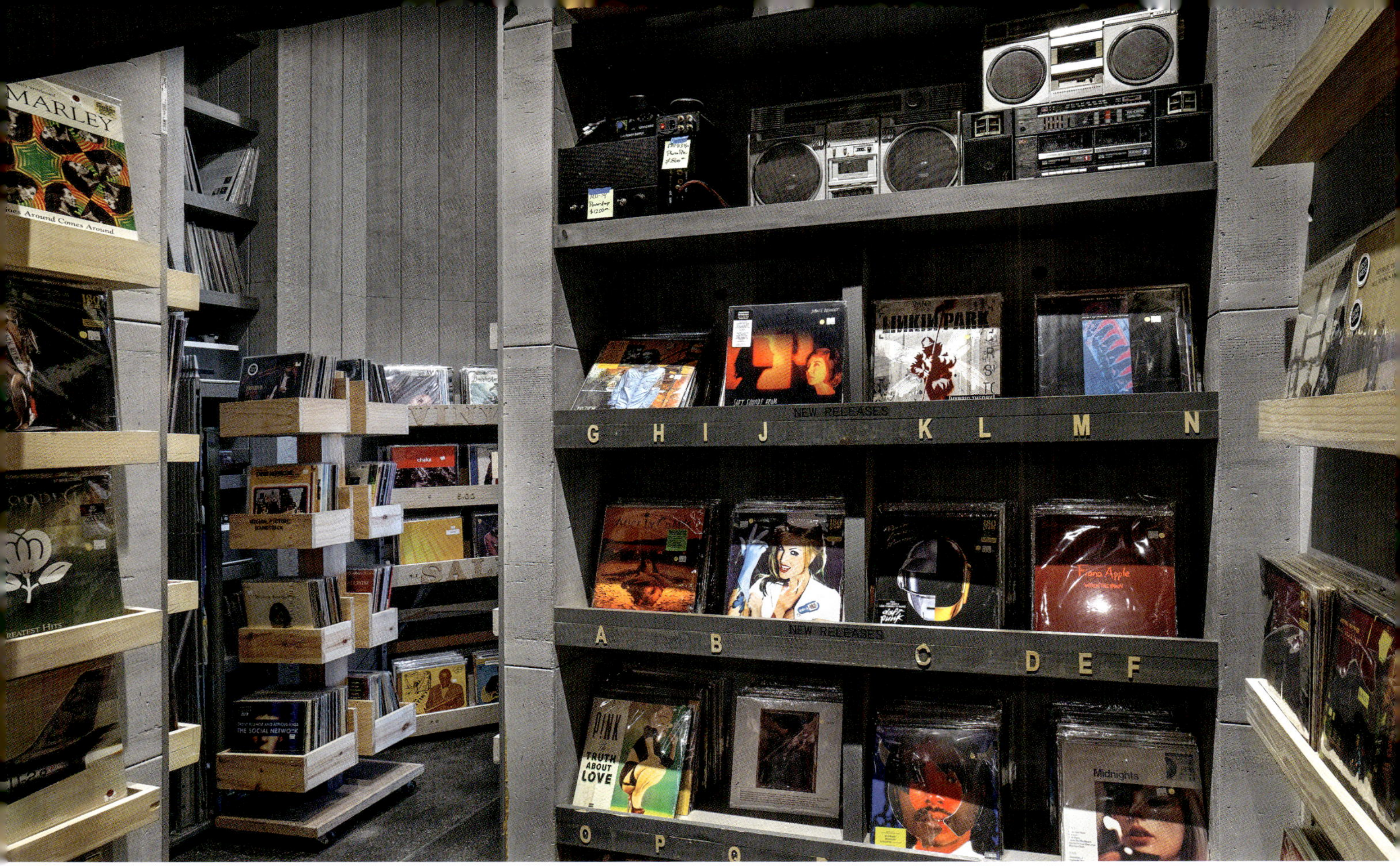

OPPOSITE Neon arrow signage near the entrance directs customers to DRINK downstairs, or shop for a RECORD upstairs.

RIGHT A large selection of Broadway and other musical soundtracks on vinyl can be found downstairs, alongside jazz, blues, soul, and funk CDs.

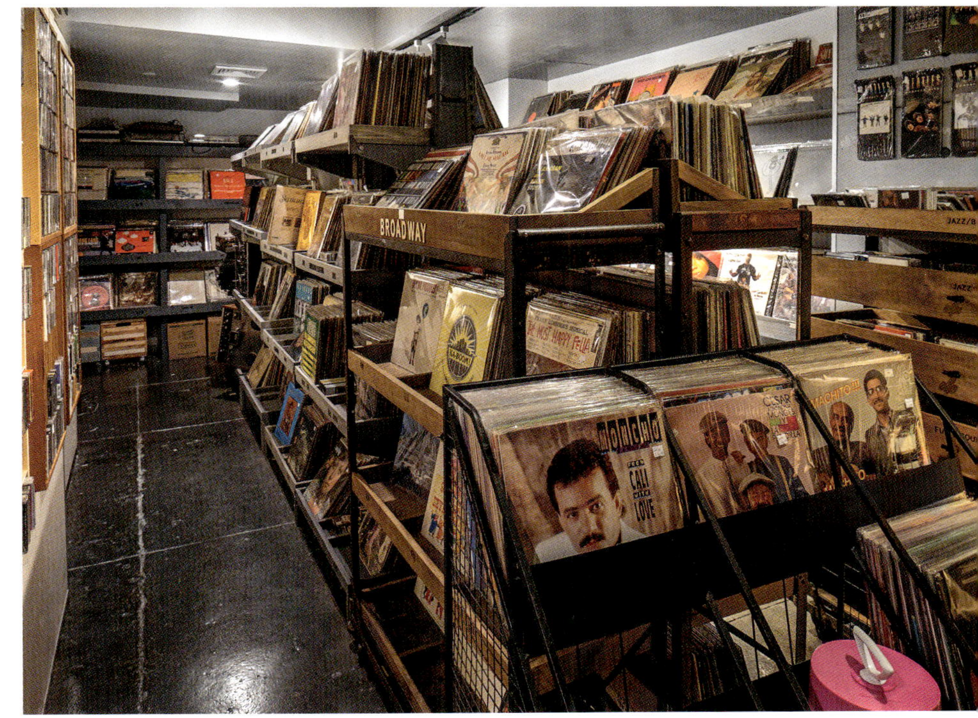

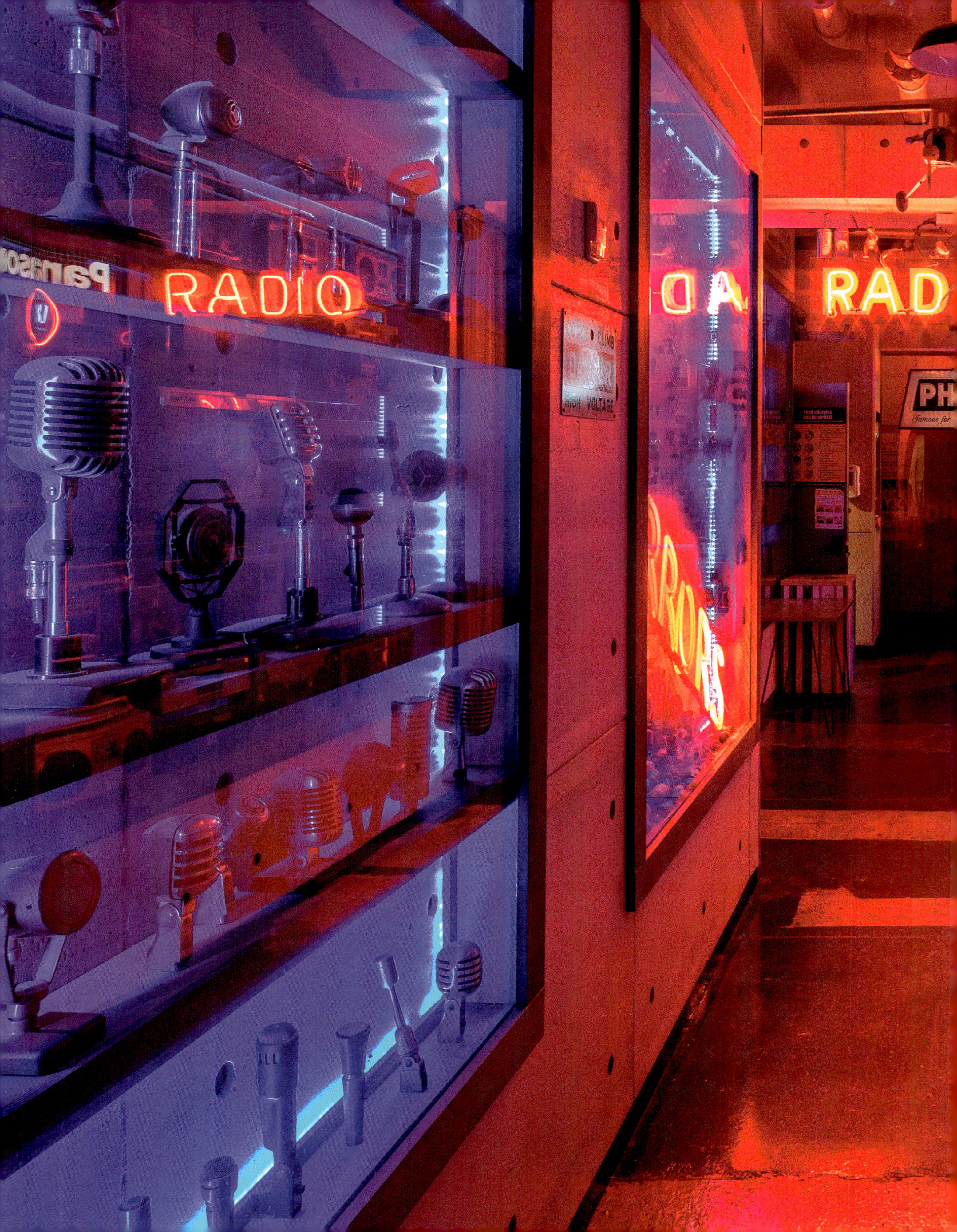
RADIO
HIGH VOLTAGE
RAD
PH

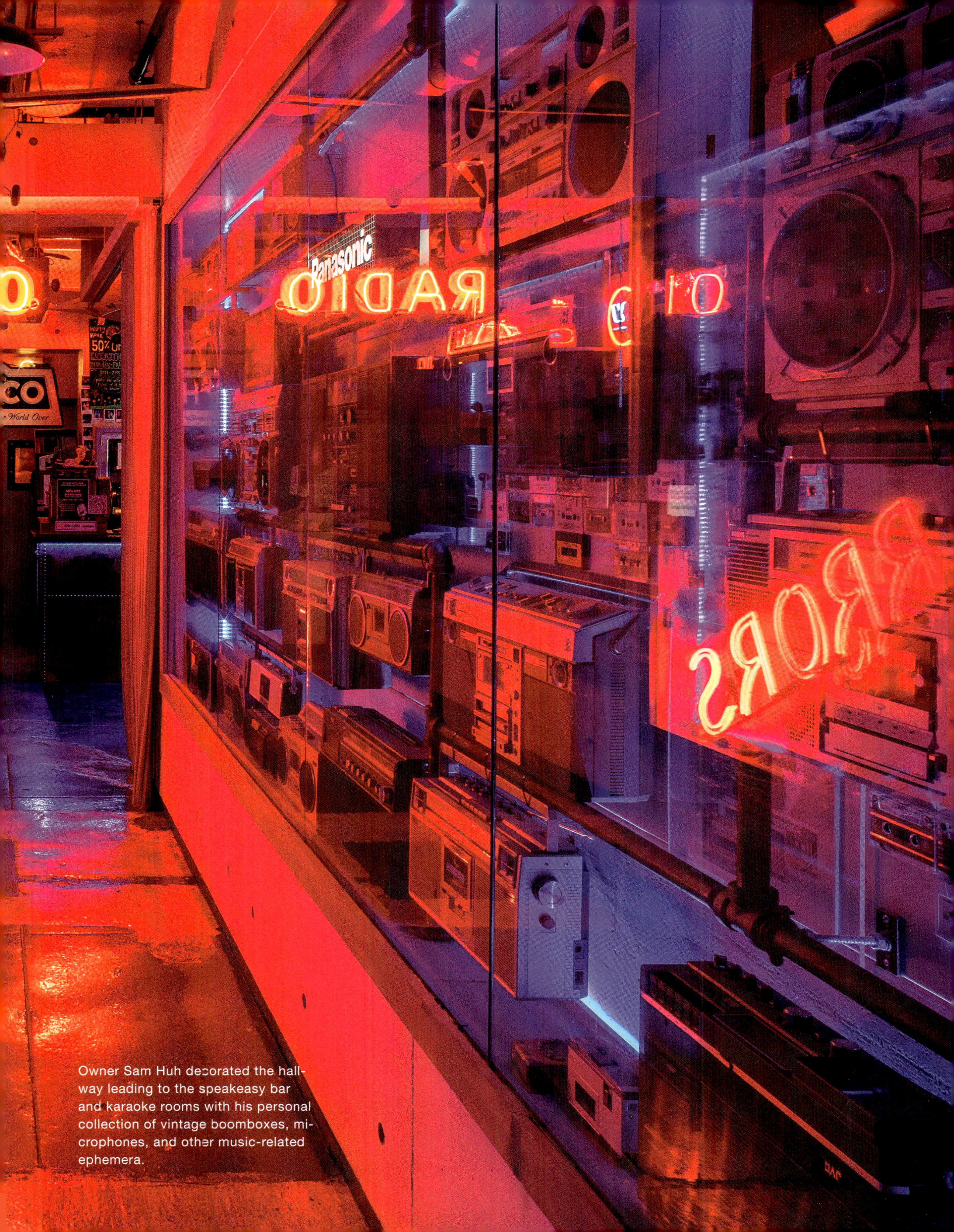

Owner Sam Huh decorated the hallway leading to the speakeasy bar and karaoke rooms with his personal collection of vintage boomboxes, microphones, and other music-related ephemera.

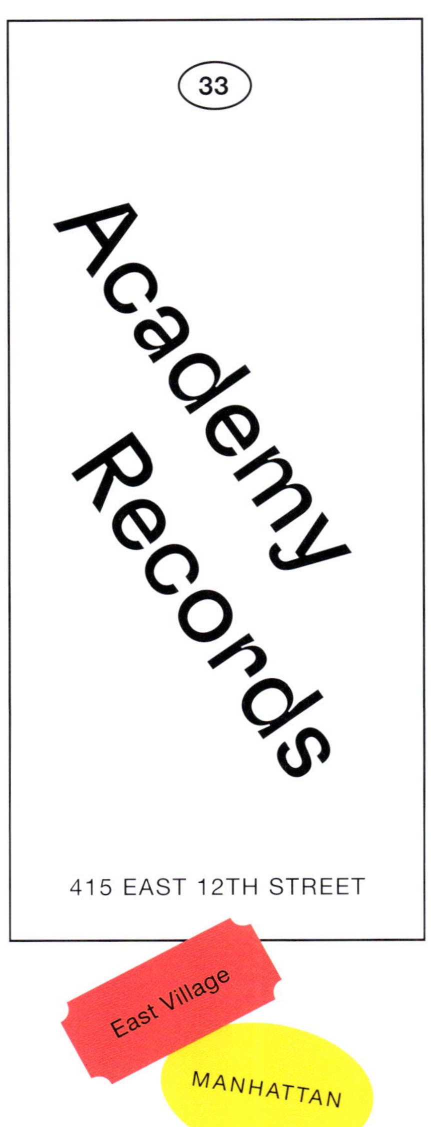

WHEN MIKE DAVIS FIRST OPENED Academy Records in the East Village, he says there "definitely weren't thirty record stores in New York City." But then again, when he first came upon the bookstore that would transform into Academy, it wasn't a record store either. This was the early 1990s, when the original Academy sold only a few cardboard boxes of vinyl. The shop "was buying so many book collections, and records were often just there for the taking," Davis recalls. During this period, the nostalgia market for vinyl hadn't yet reared its head, and even well-respecting collectors were happy to unshoulder the newly christened "dinosaur technology."

After seven or eight years of stopping in on his daily route as a bike messenger, Davis spontaneously inquired one day with an employee: "You guys need help with the records here?" It was pure cosmic timing, as the staff member working on Academy's spare records business had given notice that morning. A good word was put in; Davis got the job. However, he traces Academy's true inception as a record store back to the year 2000, when he—now with a few employee hours under his belt—suggested its vinyl bins graduate to their own space. Then, in 2001, Academy Records proper welcomed customers for the first time. "The opening day was crazy," Davis recalls. "More than half the records in the store sold."

In 2008, after their building faced instability due to planned development, Davis and his team moved to 415 East 12th Street, where Academy lives today. "It's sort of a family. I don't have a landlord looking to maximize profit," Davis shares of the current space, which is in a co-op building. Location stability means everything for a shop like Academy, which predominantly stocks used gems acquired from eager walk-ins. "We have days where it's just four, five, or six hours straight of people waiting to sell records," Davis says.

The first group that dominated Davis's personal record collection as a kid was Parliament Funkadelic. George Clinton's seminal catalog with the group is now paramount amid the East Village shop's offerings, alongside other icons like James Brown and Howling Wolf. But don't be surprised to encounter sealed Master P and Ghostface Killa LPs, or private-press R&B and Peruvian garage 45s amid the Italo disco and Detroit ghettotech.

When Academy first opened, its average collector was on the hunt for samples or breaks to fuel new waves of electronic music and hip-hop. But Davis is accustomed to change. "When I first started in the early 2000s, you couldn't give Led Zeppelin or Fleetwood Mac records away," he recalls. "Now, I wish I could buy a pallet of them." (It's not like Davis himself doesn't wield rock cred, though—as a bassist for the band Angel Rot, he says he "probably played at CBGB like twenty times.")

In the same way he jumped at the chance to give Academy its own stage in 2001, Davis leaped into a deal to start up a sister location, Academy Annex, that opened in Brooklyn in 2003. Initially based in Williamsburg before a move to Greenpoint in 2013, the warehouse-esque space is high-ceilinged and equally highly stocked: to-be-sorted boxes are piled as far as the eye can see. The Annex's formative role in the local indie scene hasn't been limited to counting the city's brightest collectors and selectors among its customers, either. Multiple labels—including independent radio staples like Captured Tracks (see p. 114) and Sacred Bones—have also formed out of conversations that have taken place at the Annex.

Past and present, bookshop or multilocation record store, Davis knows community means everything in his industry. "I've had employees who got married, who started bands together, businesses together," he says, continuing, "[Academy Records] has been a meeting place." It's no surprise, really, when one of the joys of records is touch; the chance to get closer to the artists who created the songs that mean the most to us. "Somebody made something, and then they're presenting it to you," Davis muses. "There is some human interaction, buried deep in there."

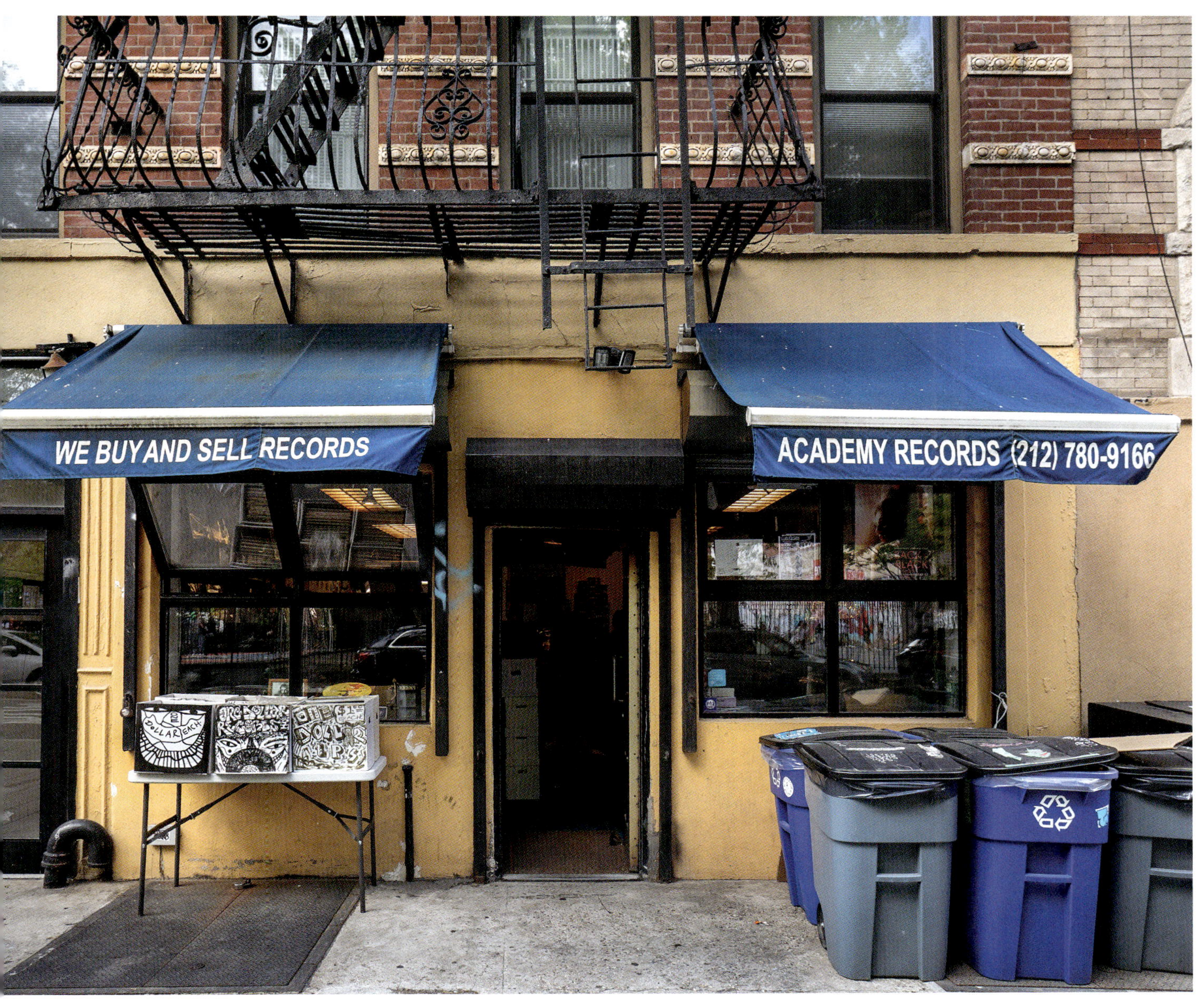

ABOVE Academy Records was founded in 2001 by Mike Davis and moved to its current location on a side street off First Avenue in the East Village in 2008. It sells both new and secondhand vinyl and cassettes in a well-balanced variety of genres including jazz, rock, hip-hop, compilation, and punk.

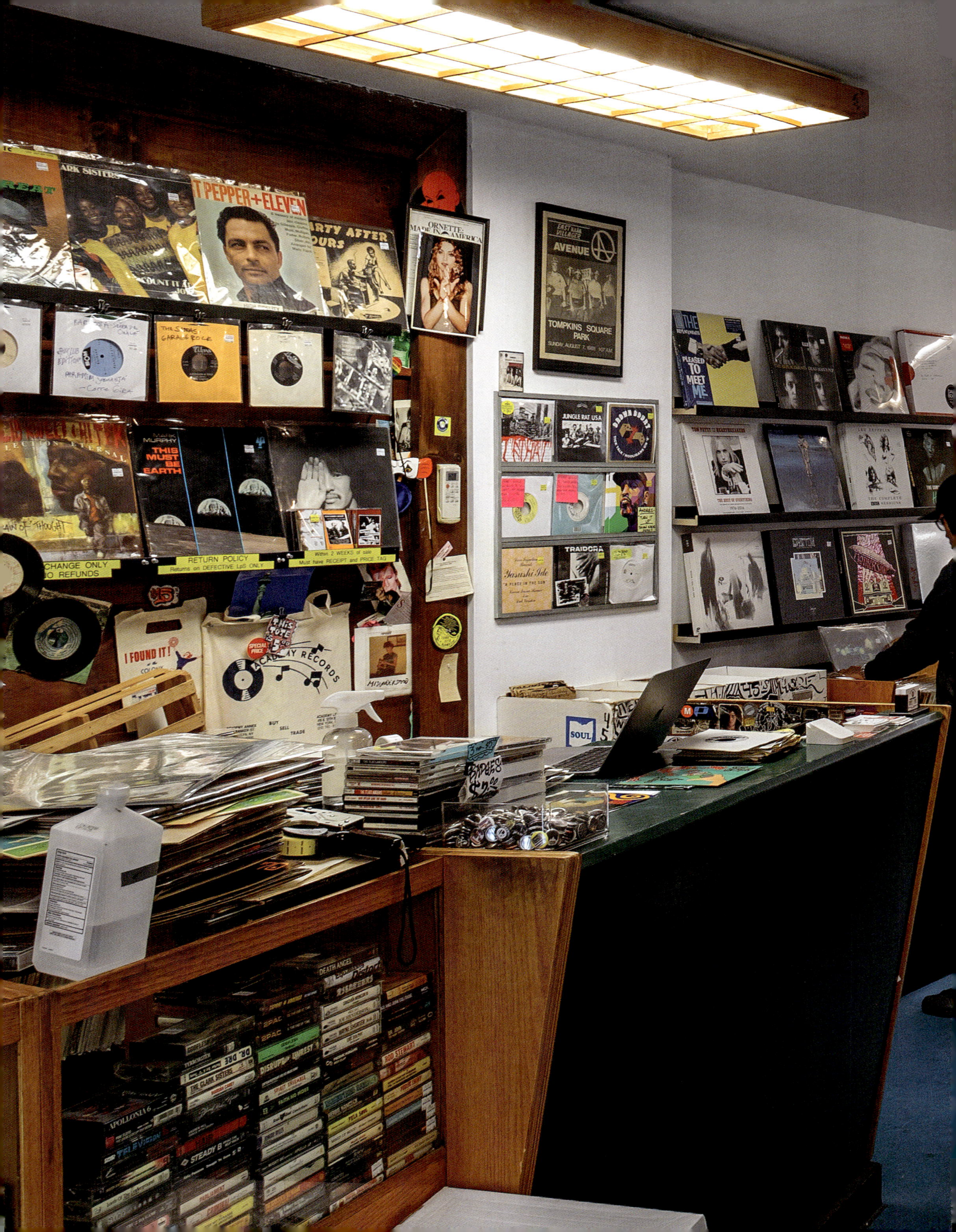

PEPPER + ELEVEN
ORNETTE:
MADE IN AMERICA
EAST VILLAGER
AVENUE
TOMPKINS SQUARE PARK
MARK MURPHY
THIS MUST BE EARTH
PLEASED TO MEET ME
JUNGLE RAT USA
TRAIDORA
Yasushi Ide
CHANGE ONLY
O REFUNDS
RETURN POLICY
Returns on DEFECTIVE LPs ONLY
Within 2 WEEKS of sale
Must have RECEIPT and PRICE TAG
I FOUND IT!
SPECIAL PRICE
BUY
SELL
TRADE
SOUL

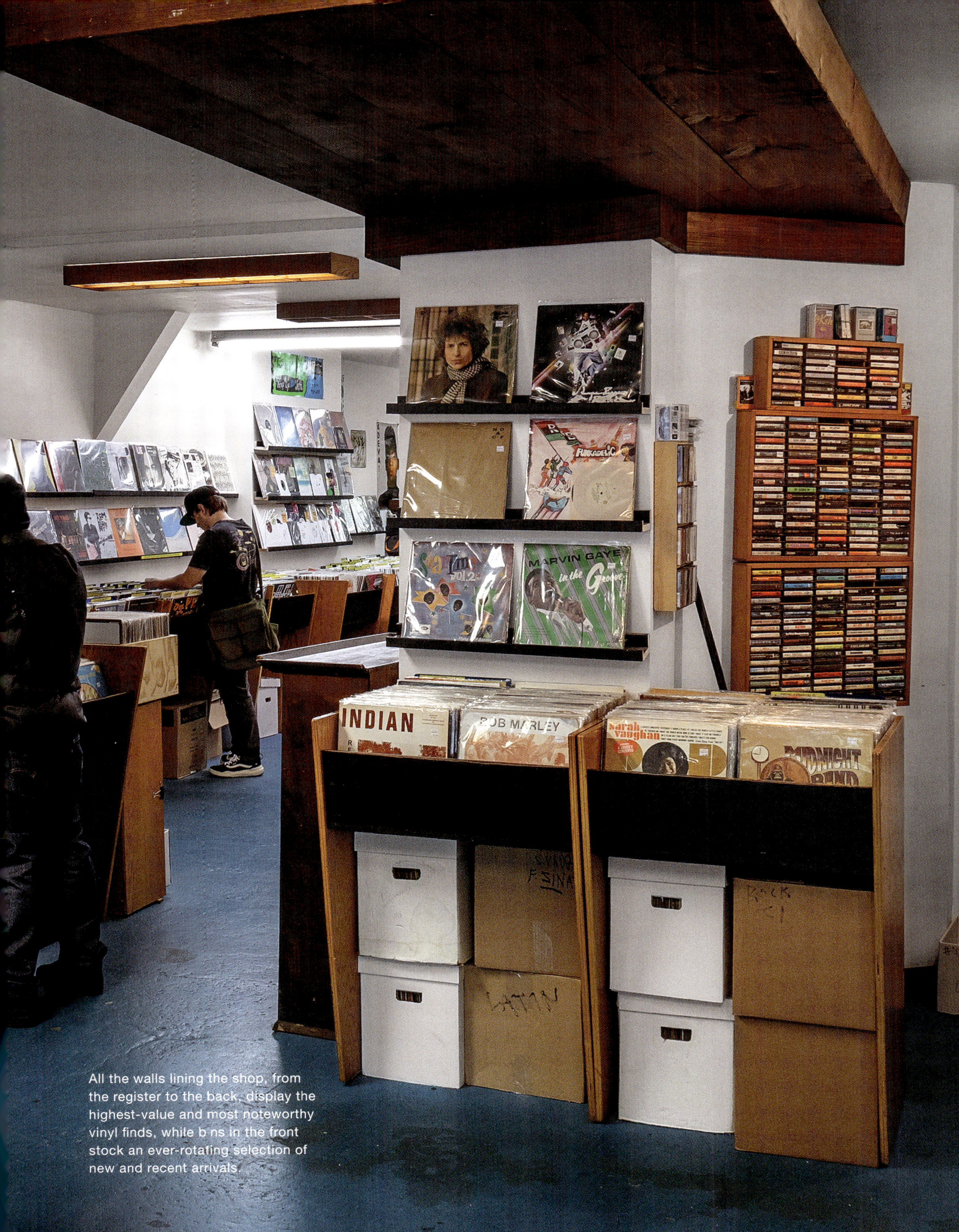

All the walls lining the shop, from the register to the back, display the highest-value and most noteworthy vinyl finds, while bins in the front stock an ever-rotating selection of new and recent arrivals.

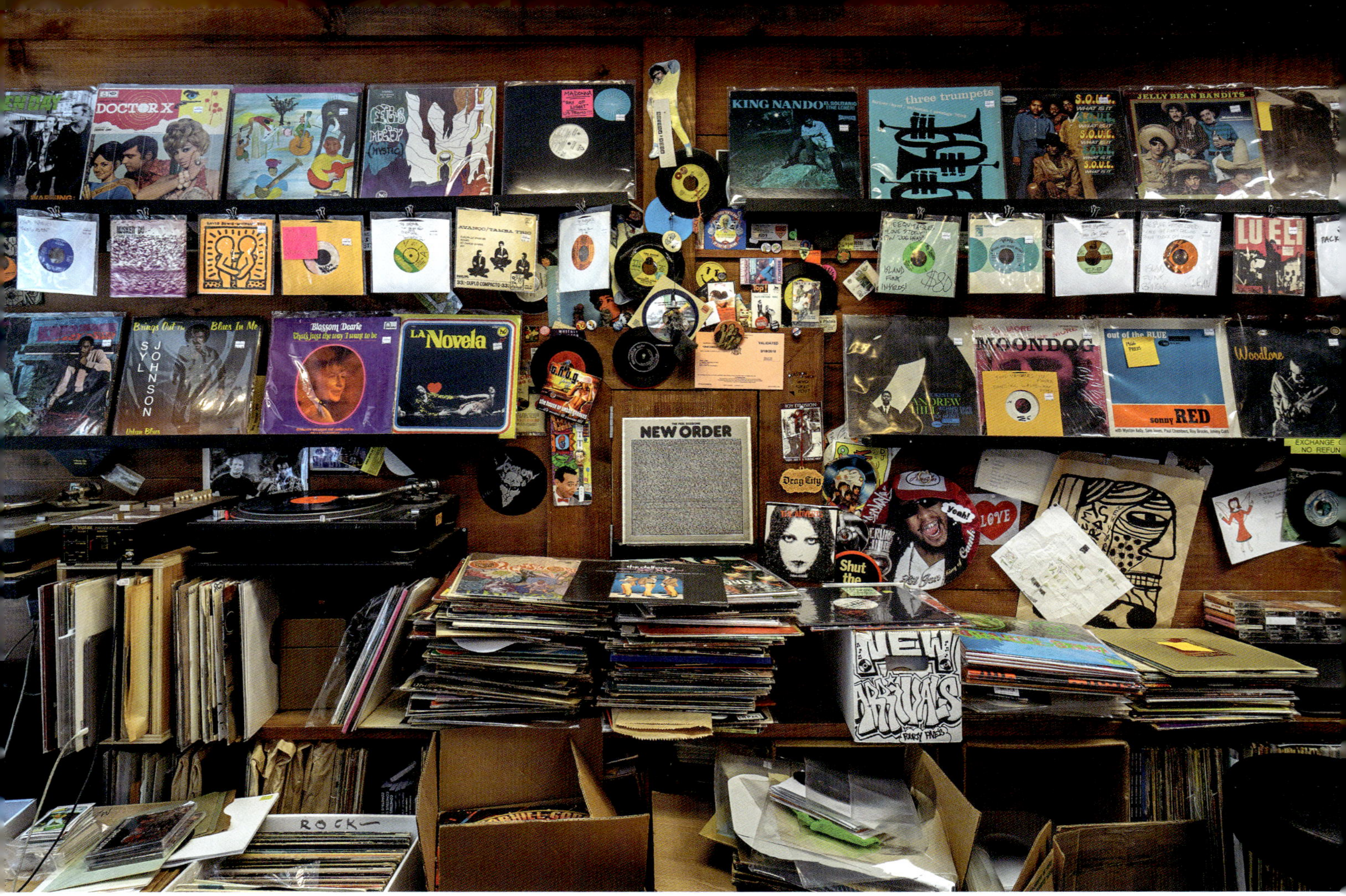

RIGHT Adam Opet, an accomplished visual artist who works at Academy Records, added his distinctive ink drawings to the boxes of 45s.

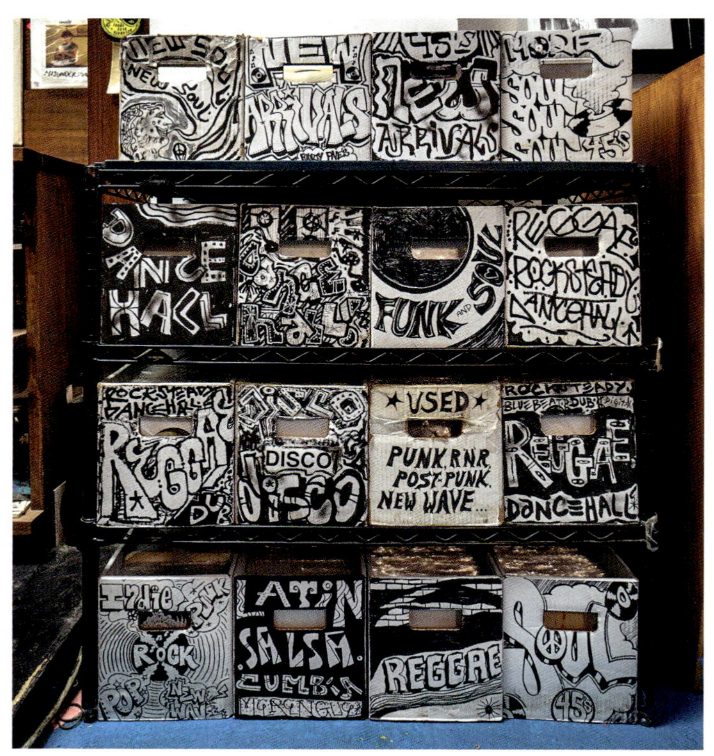

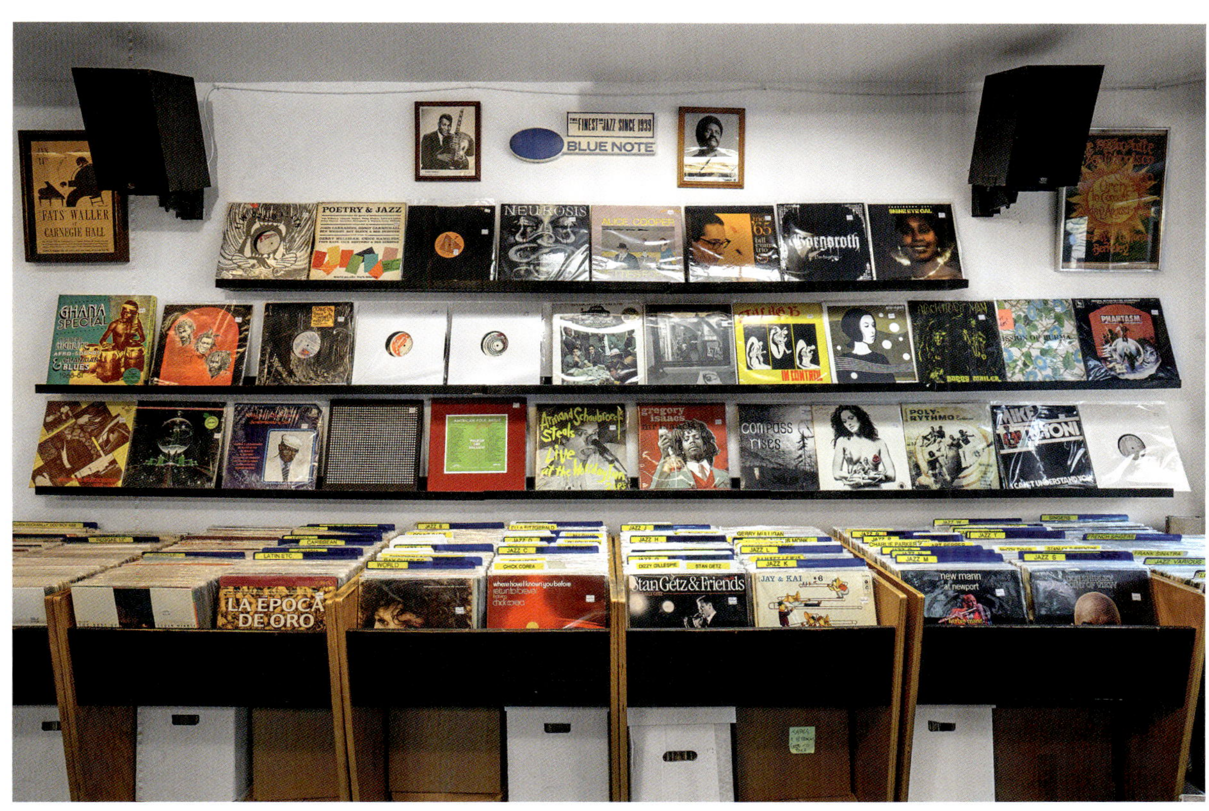
FATS WALLER
CARNEGIE HALL
THE FINEST IN JAZZ SINCE 1939
BLUE NOTE
POETRY & JAZZ
NEUROSIS
ALICE COOPER
Gorgoroth
GHANA SPECIAL
PHANTASM
IN CONTROL
compass rises
POLY-RYTHMO
LA EPOCA DE ORO
Stan Getz & Friends
JAY & KAI
new mann at newport
DIZZY GILLESPIE
STAN GETZ
CHICK COREA

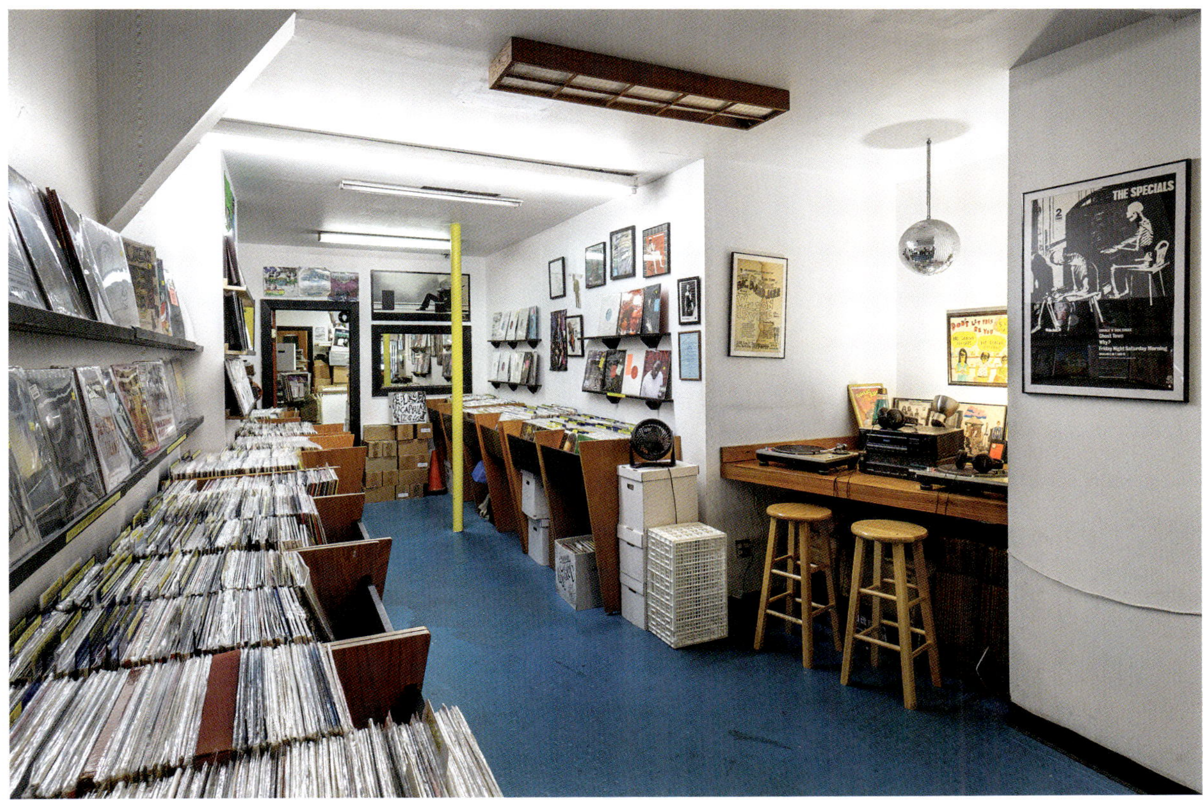
THE SPECIALS

"Vinyl records, for my generation, were like toys—we started with Fisher-Price turntables. DJing, how we do it today, started in the early '80s. But in the beginning, it was just being a child—being curious and touching a record."

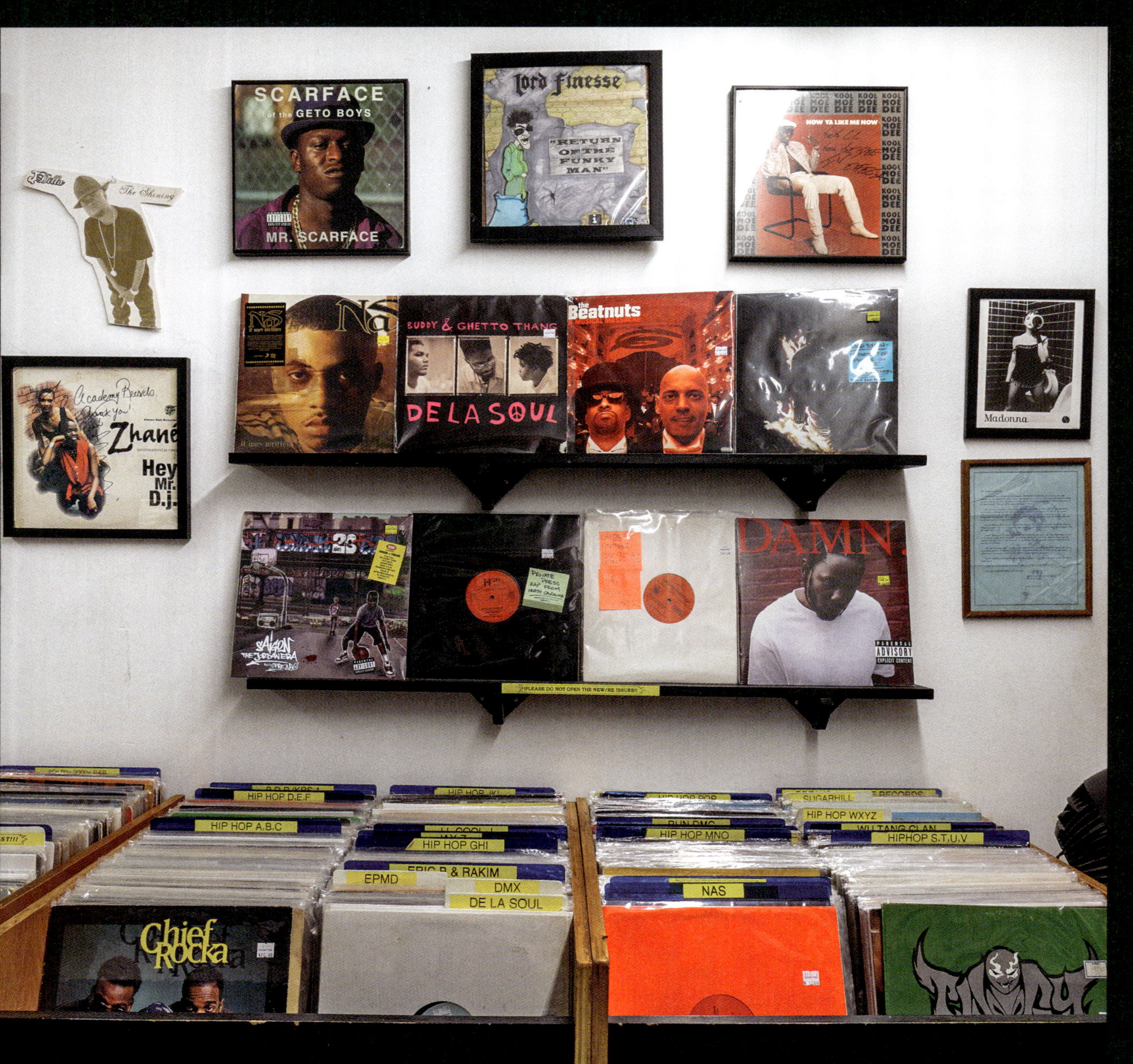

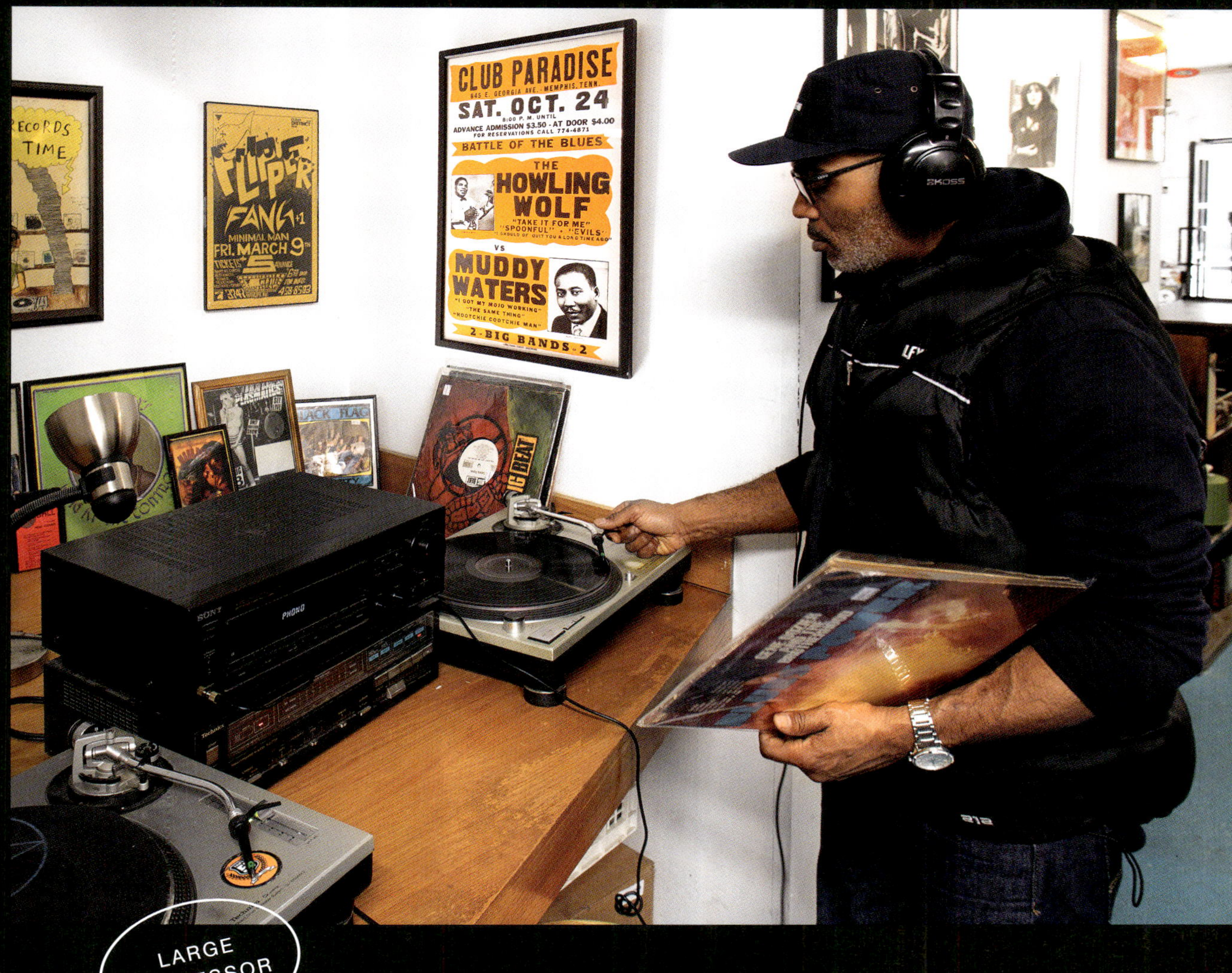

LARGE PROFESSOR

PRODUCER, DJ, AND RAPPER

Plenty of New York hip-hop veterans would make a good Academy Records tour guide—but only one of them produced three tracks on Nas's *Illmatic*. Born and raised in Flushing, Queens, William Paul Mitchell, a.k.a. Large Professor, turned a hobby of tinkering with pause tapes and a Casio SK-1 sampling keyboard into a career, producing for the likes of A Tribe Called Quest, Busta Rhymes, Mobb Deep, Big Daddy Kane, and his own group, Main Source. (When Large Professor made his first of countless beats for Eric B. and Rakim, he was still in high school.) Today, he remembers well when the sample-sourcer's haven Academy came on the scene. His first time through its doors, he arrived with an armful of records for sale.

A familiar face at vinyl conventions around the country, Large Professor has amassed a collection even he jokingly calls "crazy." But as Academy's selection began to establish a signature style, he found himself stopping in more frequently in search of something specific. When it comes to his taste development, Large Professor credits his late mentor Paul C, who engineered East Coast classics like Biz Markie's "Just A Friend" and Queen Latifah's "Ladies First," with teaching him "virtually everything" he knows about beat-making. Large Professor in turn passed this knowledge down to Nas, his own protégé. It all goes back to the motto he lives by: "Each one, teach one."

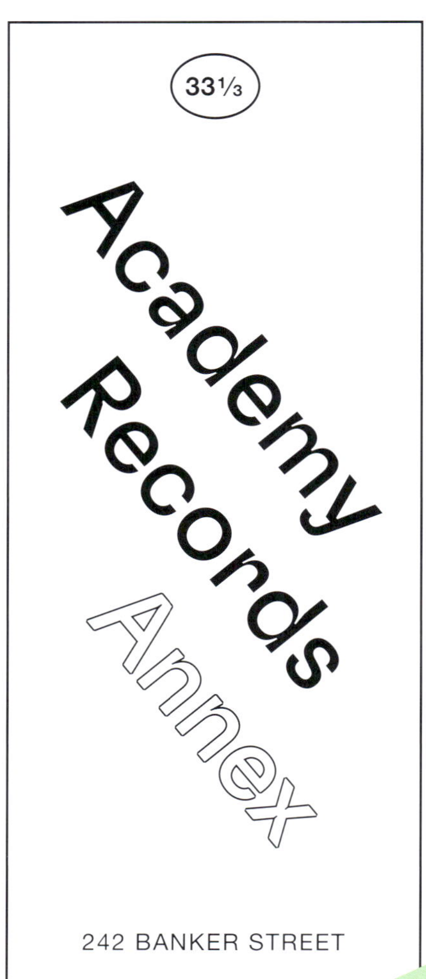

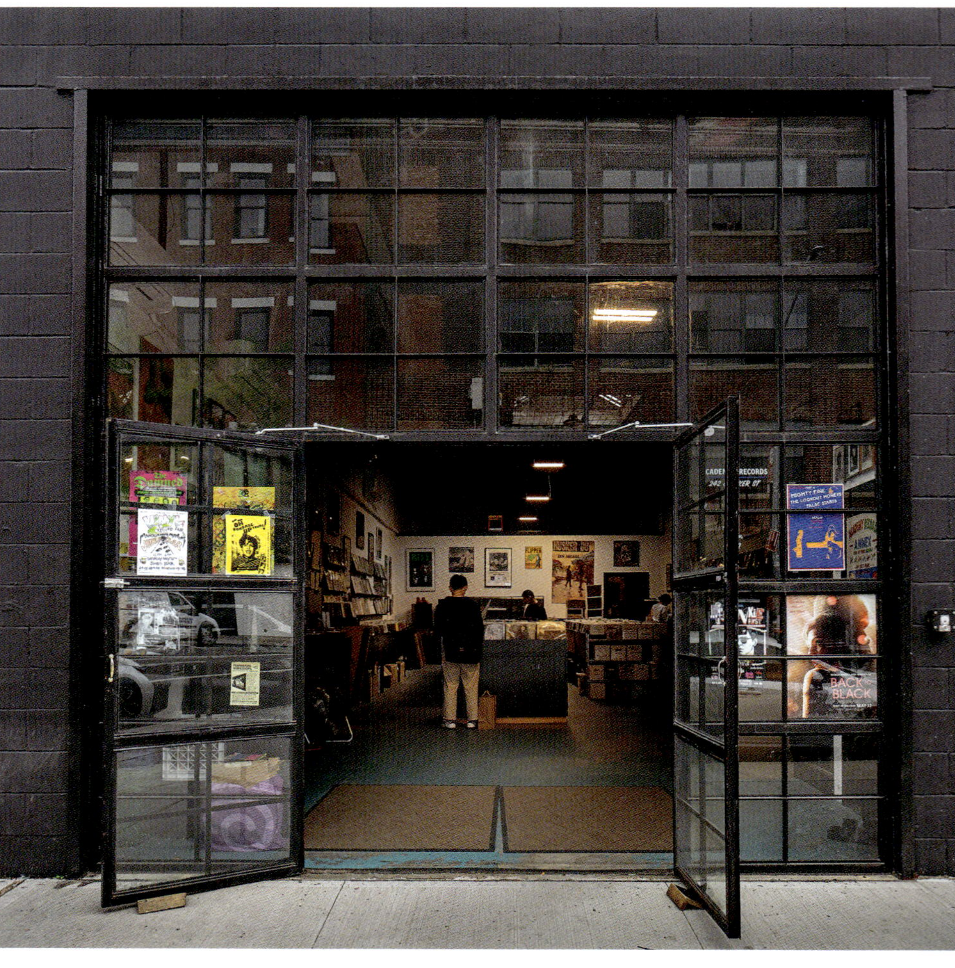

ABOVE In 2003 the business expanded to Williamsburg, Brooklyn, under the name Academy Records Annex. Ten years later, the Annex moved to Greenpoint, where it's now located in a spacious converted warehouse close to the East River.

OPPOSITE TOP The staff have thoughtfully placed handwritten descriptive notes on some of the wall titles, including "Best Disco Song Ever!!" on George Smallwood's "You Know I Love You" 7-inch record, and "Very Rare!! Early '80s Nigerian Disco/Boogie" on Livy Ekemezie's album *Friday Night*.

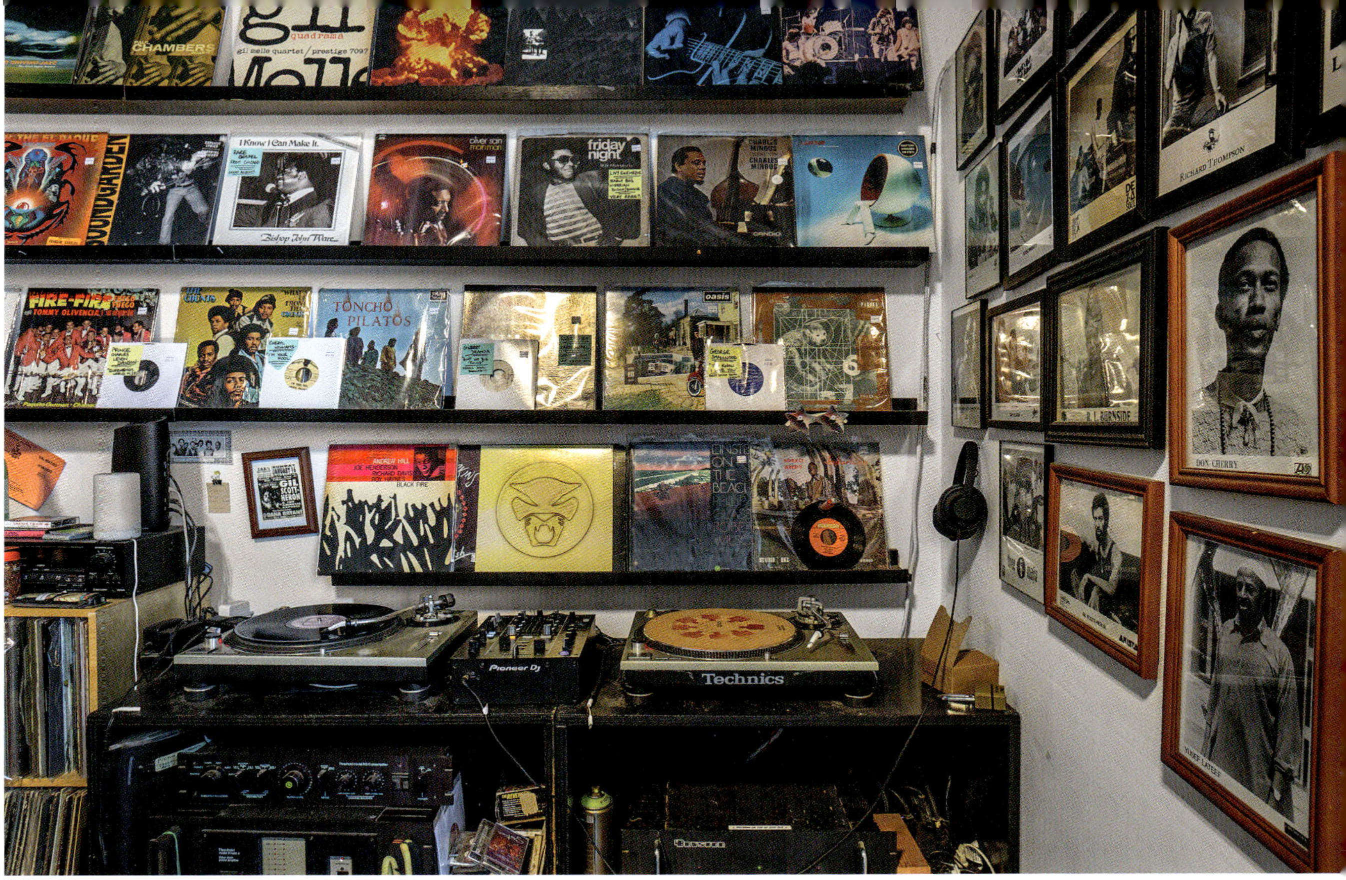

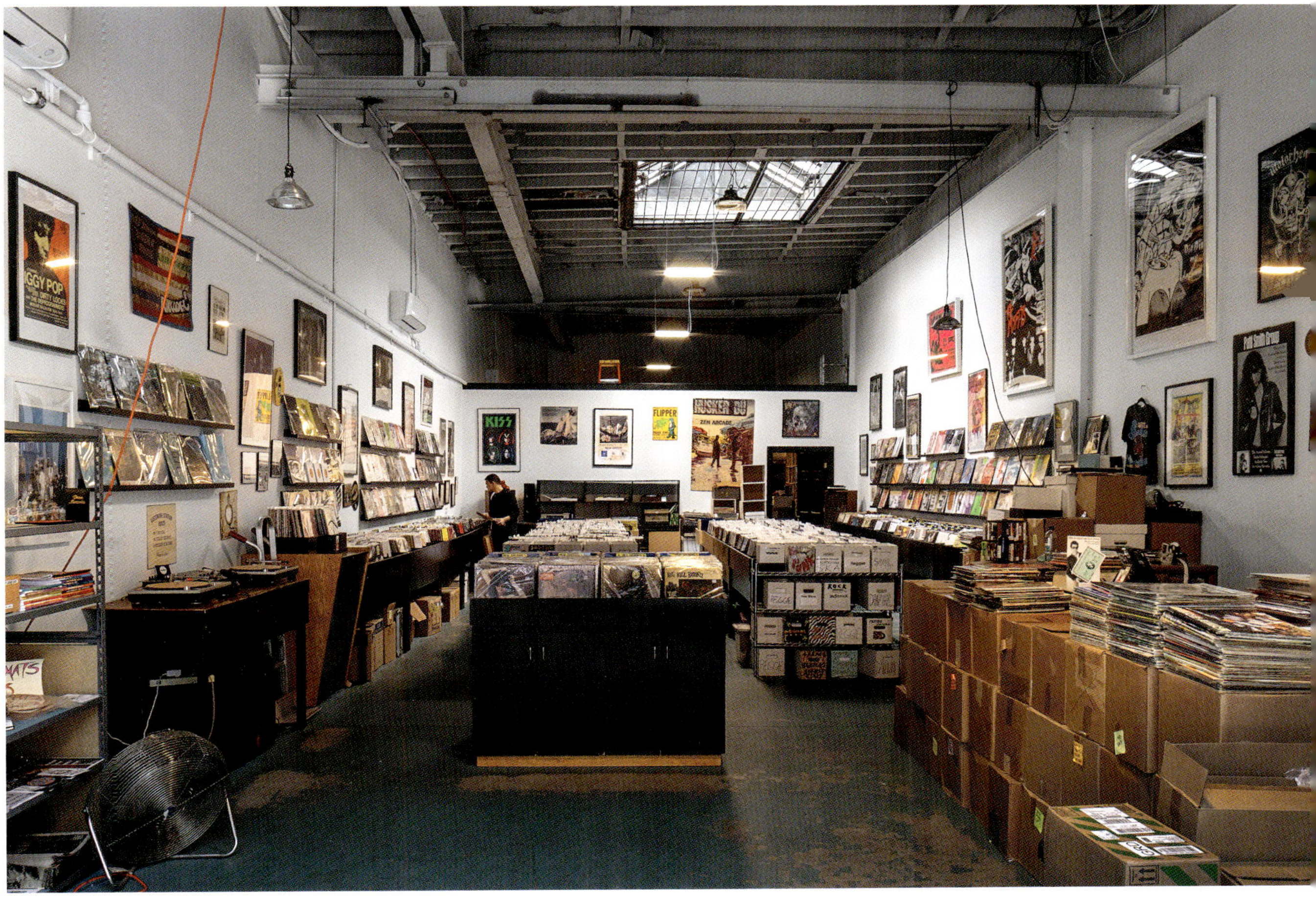

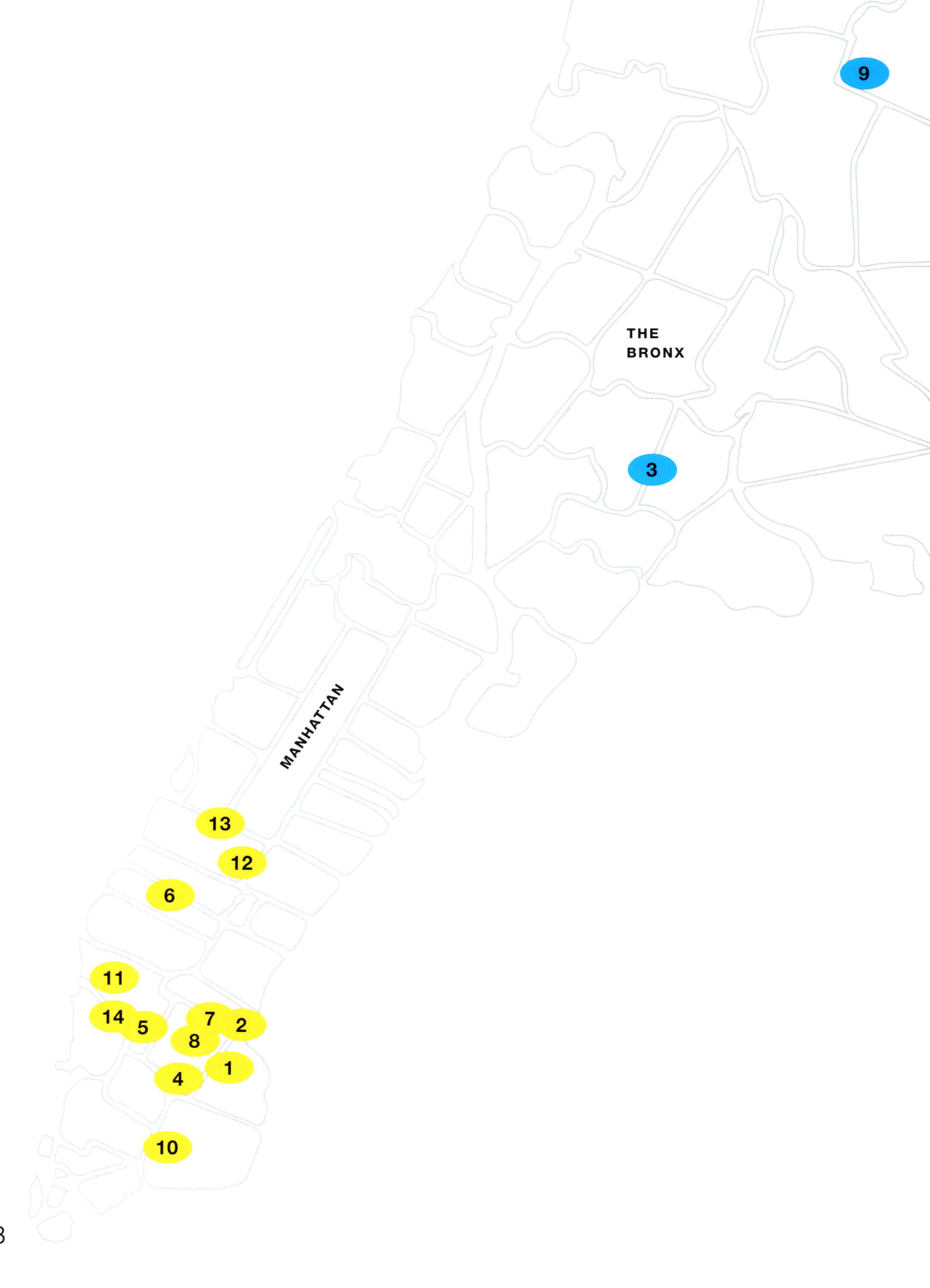
9
THE
BRONX
3
MANHATTAN
13
12
6
11
14
5
7
2
8
1
4
10

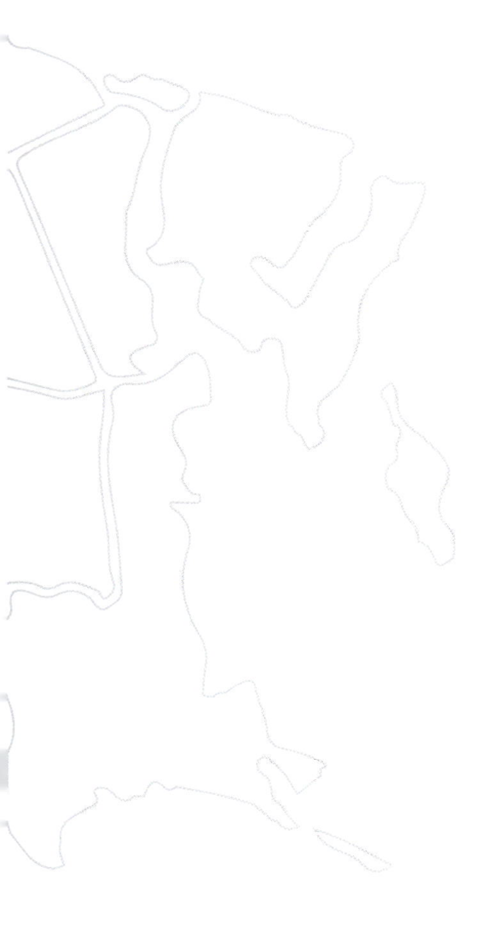

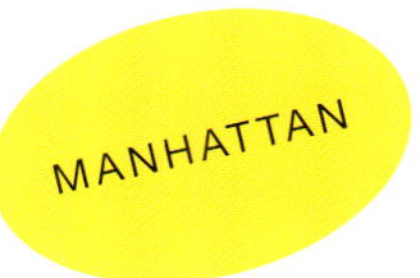

THE BRONX

1 A-1 Record Shop
2 Academy Records
3 Casa Amadeo
4 Ergot Records
5 Generation Records
6 Jazz Record Center
7 Limited to One Record Store
8 Manhattan45
9 Moodies Records
10 Paradise of Replica
11 Record Runner
12 Rough Trade
13 RPM Underground
14 Village Revival Records

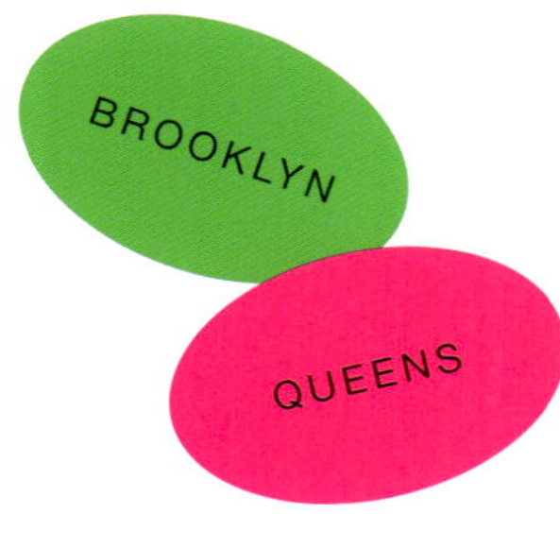

1 Academy Records Annex
2 Almost Ready Records
3 Billy's Record Salon
4 Black Gold Records
5 Black Star Vinyl
6 Blue-Sun
7 Captured Record Shop
8 Deep Cuts Record Store
9 Earwax Records
10 Face Records NYC
11 Human Head Records
12 Legacy
13 Majors Records & Video
14 Pancakes Records
15 Rebel Rouser
16 Record City
17 Record Shop
18 Second Hand Records NYC
19 Superior Elevation Records
20 VP Records

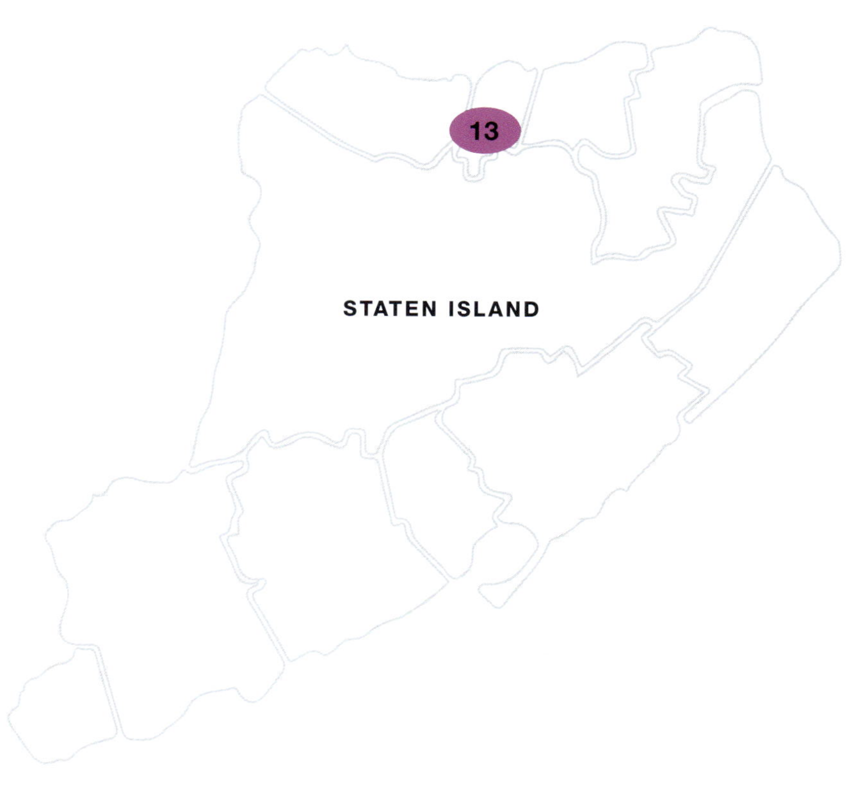

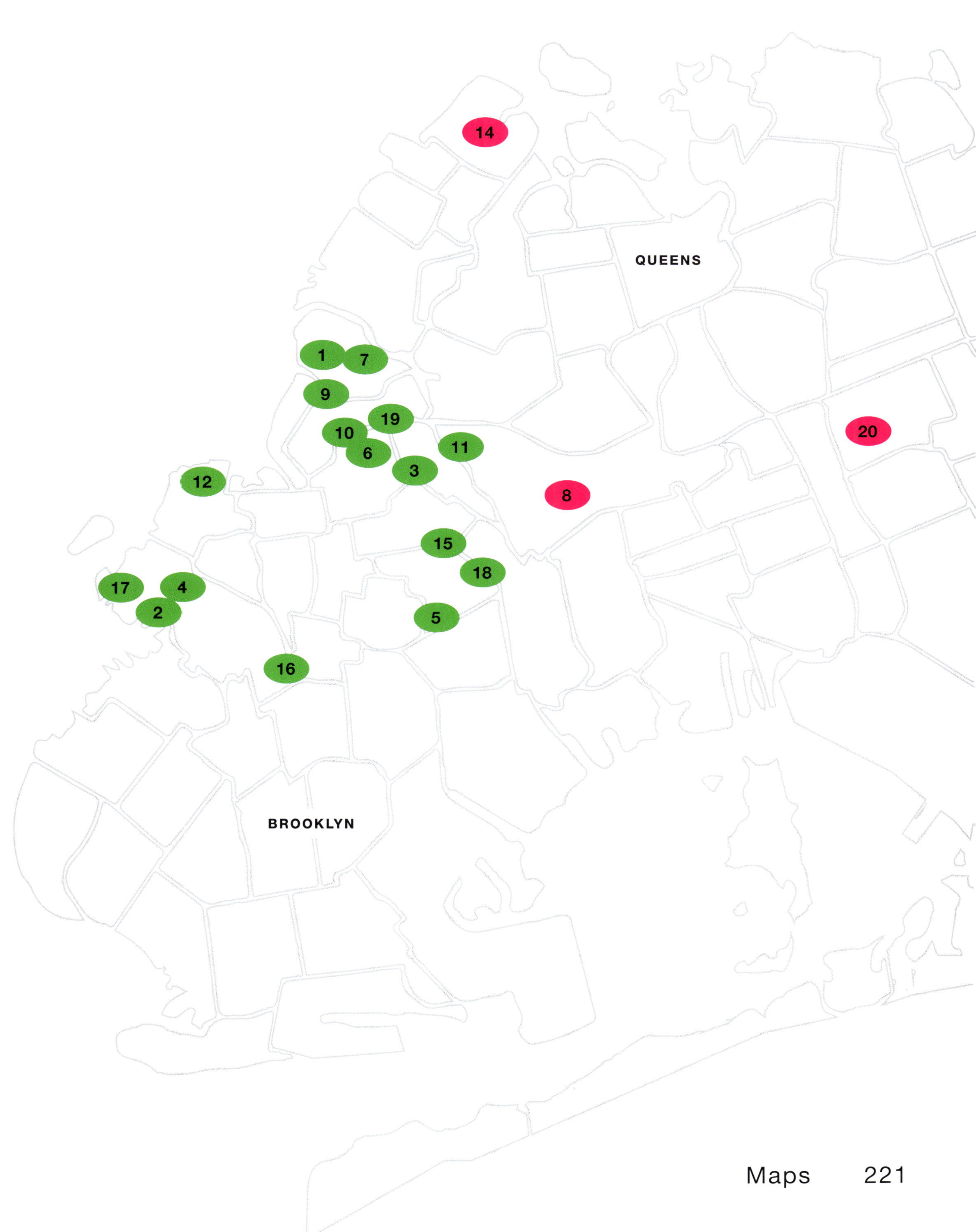
14
QUEENS
1
7
9
19
10
6
11
3
12
8
20
15
18
17
4
2
5
16
BROOKLYN

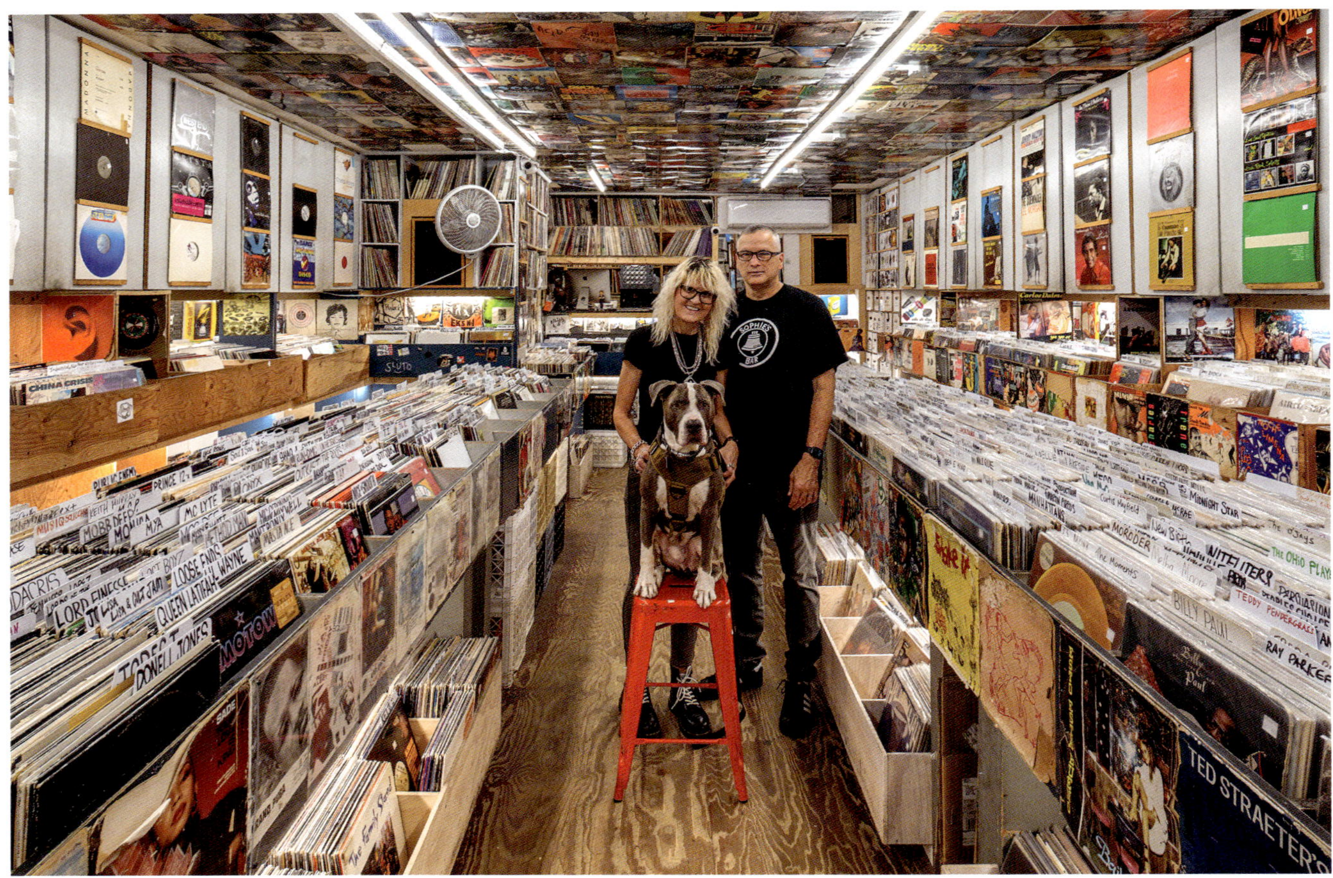

Biographies

JAMES T. & KARLA L. MURRAY are husband-and-wife architectural and interiors photographers and videographers based in New York City. Since 1997 they have focused their lens on the streetscape through portraits of store fronts and shop owners, seeking to capture the spirit, energy, and cultural diversity of individual neighborhoods through their work.

James and Karla's critically acclaimed books include *Great Bars of New York City: 30 of Manhattan's Favorite Storied Drinking Establishments*; *Store Front NYC: Photographs of the City's Independent Shops, Past and Present*; *Store Front: The Disappearing Face of New York*; *New York Nights*; *Store Front II: A History Preserved*; and *Broken Windows: Graffiti NYC*. Their work has been widely exhibited around the world, including in solo exhibitions at the Brooklyn Historical Society, Clic Gallery, the Storefront Project Gallery in New York City, and Fotogalerie im Blauen Haus in Munich, as well as group shows at the New-York Historical Society and the Museum of Neon Art in Glendale, California. Their photographs are part of the permanent collections of major institutions, including the Smithsonian Center for Folklife and Cultural Heritage in Washington, DC; the New York Public Library; and NYU Langone Medical Center.

Their photography has appeared in numerous publications including *The New York Times*, *The London Telegraph*, *The Wall Street Journal*, the *New York Post*, *New York* magazine, and *The New Yorker*. James and Karla were awarded the 2015 Regina Kellerman Award by the Greenwich Village Society for Historic Preservation (GVSHP) in recognition of their significant contribution to the quality of life in Greenwich Village, the East Village, and NoHo. From 2017 through 2020 they were awarded Creative Engagement Manhattan Arts Grants by the New York State Council on the Arts, administered by the Lower Manhattan Cultural Council. They received the prestigious Art in

OPPOSITE James, Karla, and their dog Hudson at A-1 Record Shop.

RIGHT Hattie at Ergot Records.

the Parks: UNIQLO Park Expressions Grant in 2018 for their public art installation, *Mom-and-Pops of the L.E.S.*, and in 2025 received the GANYC Apple Award for Outstanding Achievement in NYC Photography for their book *Great Bars of New York City*, from the Guides Association of New York City.

James and Karla live in the East Village of Manhattan with their rescue dog, Hudson. Their work can be viewed at jamesandkarlamurray.com and on their Instagram and YouTube accounts @jamesandkarla.

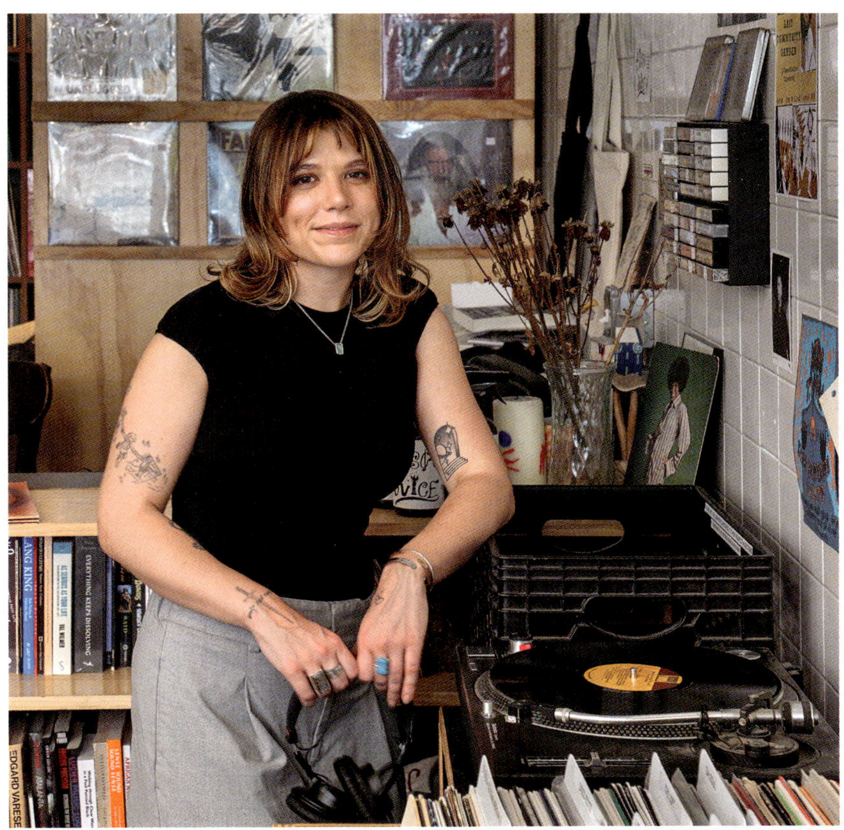

HATTIE LINDERT is a journalist and critic based in Brooklyn, New York. A former staff writer at *Pitchfork*, *The A.V. Club*, and *People* magazine, she currently serves as an editor at electronic music hub *Resident Advisor*, and as a contributing editor at independent music publication *No Bells*. She has published writing with *Rolling Stone*, *The Face*, the *Los Angeles Review of Books*, *Stereogum*, *Paste*, and more. She was born and raised in Vermont. This is her first book.

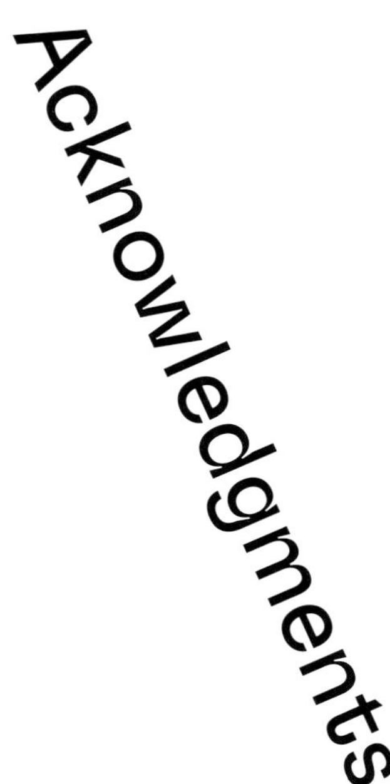

JAMES T. & KARLA L. MURRAY: This project would not have been possible without the generous support of many people. We particularly want to thank all of the business owners whose establishments appear in this book and all of the managers and employees, including Patricia "Miss Pat" Chin at VP Records, Seth "Shef" Yamasaki at A-1 Record Shop, and Adam Opet at Academy Records, who shared interesting stories and offered assistance during our shoots. We would also like to acknowledge the legendary DJs, musicians, and collectors for their enthusiastic participation and support, including Large Professor, Eli Escobar, Kristine Barilli, Ryo Sasaki, Zoe Wiggins, and Shawn Dub. Additionally, we would like to thank DJ Domewrecka, DJ Solespin, Deidre Irvine, Muriel Urquhart, and Robert Watlington, who we captured while shopping. Finally, we gratefully acknowledge our editor, Ali Gitlow, for bringing this project to life and for her continuous guidance; the wonderful team at Prestel Publishing, who have been a pleasure to work with; our production manager, Luisa Klose, for ensuring our photos shine through; our copyeditor, Adaobi Obi Tulton, for her attention to detail; our designer, Sebit Min, for her creativity and design; and our co-author, Hattie Lindert, for her impeccable storytelling.

HATTIE LINDERT: The number of people who contribute to weaving a city-wide epic like this one is far too many to thank on one page. To every shop owner, DJ, musician, collector, and audiophile who spoke with us along the way: thank you for helping to illustrate a big, beautiful picture. Thank you to Ali Gitlow, Adaobi Obi Tulton, and Sebit Min for treating this text with a thorough dose of TLC. And an enormous thanks to James and Karla Murray, two true originals with more Empire City knowledge between them than the New York Public Library itself. To a humbling and incomplete list of people, past and present, who have taken time out of their lives to nurture my writing and demolish my run-on sentences. This includes but is not limited to Matthew Strauss, Evan Minsker, Drew Gillis, Mary Kate Carr, Kieran Press-Reynolds, Christian Moro, Anna Gaca, Cat Zhang, Jeremy Larson, Mano Sundaresan, Kylie Cheung, Isabelia Herrera, Rawiya Kameir, Aileen Gallagher, Philip Sherburne, Megan Buerger, Tyler Grisham, Paul Thompson, Kiana Mickles, Ryan Dombal, Arielle Gordon, Carlos Hawthorn, Rachel Grace Almeida, Gabriel Szatan. Thank you to mom and dad for the unending (and sometimes unforgiving) encouragement. To Uncle Bill, for introducing me to New York, and to Caroline for making it home. And to Matthew Ritchie—thanks for helping me fix my turntable.

Editorial direction:
ALI GITLOW

Copyediting and proofreading:
ADAOBI OBI TULTON

Design and typesetting:
SEBIT MIN

Production:
LUISA KLOSE

Separations:
Reproline Mediateam, Munich

Printing and binding:
DZS Grafik, d.o.o., Ljubljana

Penguin Random House Verlagsgruppe
FSC® N001967

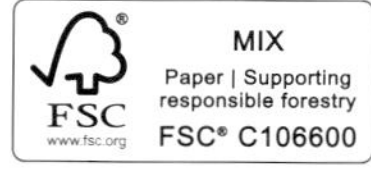

Printed in Slovenia
ISBN 978-3-7913-9353-7
www.prestel.com

Front cover image: the interior of A-1 Record Shop (see p. 8).

A Library of Congress Control Number is available.

A CIP catalogue record for this book is available from the British Library.